Lecture Notes in Artificial Intelligence   8387

Subseries of Lecture Notes in Computer Science

More information about this series at http://www.springer.com/series/1244

Zygmunt Vetulani · Joseph Mariani (Eds.)

Human Language Technology Challenges for Computer Science and Linguistics

5th Language and Technology
Conference, LTC 2011
Poznań, Poland, November 25–27, 2011
Revised Selected Papers

 Springer

Editors
Zygmunt Vetulani
Adam Mickiewicz University
Poznań
Poland

Joseph Mariani
IMMI-CNRS
Orsay
France

ISSN 0302-9743
ISBN 978-3-319-08957-7
DOI 10.1007/978-3-319-08958-4

ISSN 1611-3349 (electronic)
ISBN 978-3-319-08958-4 (eBook)

Library of Congress Control Number: 2014945215

LNCS Sublibrary: SL7 – Artificial Intelligence

Springer Cham Heidelberg New York Dordrecht London

Printed on acid-free paper

Springer is part of Springer Science+Business Media (www.springer.com)

Preface

In the technologically advanced world, the Information Society Age has become reality. As we have observed on other occasions, this results from the transformation of the human technological environment of the twenties century into one that is not only rich in information but also an interactive environment. The growing role of language technologies, as predicted by Antonio Zampolli as early as the 1960s, is clear to those living in the Information Society Age, at least to those who can say "…way back then, when there was no Internet…"[1]. This transformation is a product (or rather, a by-product) of long-term political and economic globalization.

Today's globalization process is not the first in the history of humankind. Ancient empires and the Christian civilization that succeeded the Roman Empire serve well as earlier examples. In both cases, there was extensive exchange of ideas and codification of social norms as written laws and regulations. There was general acceptance of Latin as a lingua franca in those times. For many centuries, especially during the Middle Ages, Latin became the medium of communication for intellectual elites in different countries. This contributed to rapid technological development and to a new social stratification based on access to accumulated knowledge. Social and political revolutions between the eighteenth and twentieth centuries brought new ideas of liberty, equality, fraternity, and solidarity into play. These ideas sought general acceptance through a complex and often turbulent process that endures to this day. Nowadays, English has taken the place of Latin to facilitate the cross-border exchange of ideas and knowledge, but expectations have meanwhile increased: it is now commonly accepted in most countries that information and cultural values should be a part of a common heritage, shared and freely accessible to every human being. An ambitious programme of this kind can only be achieved by the use of appropriate technologies.

Language technologies, whose development is expected to speed up the process and to make the information circuit even more efficient and human-friendly, are in the mainstream of these global phenomena. For the same reasons as "ancient" global technologies (such as transport infrastructure, telecommunications, or classic media), language technologies need to be widely accessible, global, robust, and complete.[2] These requirements create new challenges. One challenging task is to fill the gaps in existing language resources and technologies. Gaps exist for most (if not all) languages, including English, because of variable technological development resulting from local political and economic constraints. From the first days of the LTC conferences, the organizers and the Program Committee have paid special attention to

---

[1] Such a phrase was recently pronounced by one of Zygmunt Vetulani's students (20 years old) during a class on Human-Computer Communication.

[2] The META-Share initiative of 2011 redefined the requirements with respect to language technologies and resources in terms of *openness, distribution, interoperability,* and *security* (cf. http://www.meta-net.eu, access Nov. 12, 2011).

ensuring that the message has been communicated to the LTC participants, and several authors are in fact contributing to the discussion on these issues.

Reducing these gaps is a major challenge. In order to address this topic, a specific workshop on less-resourced languages was organized for the second time at the conference. This time, it was entitled "Less-Resourced Languages: Addressing the Gaps in Language Resources and Technologies", and was organized by Khalid Choukri, Joseph Mariani, and Zygmunt Vetulani, with the support of ELRA, FLaReNet, and META-NET. Closing existing gaps in language resources (LR) and technologies (LT) is a challenging task not only for less-resourced languages (LRL) but also for technologically more advanced ones. However, the needs of less-resourced languages are worth considering specifically in order to reduce imbalances between languages. The European Commission supports a large number of initiatives whose objectives include producing inventories and facilitating the sharing of language technologies and resources, including projects conducted within FlaReNet, ELRA, META-NET, CESAR, METANET4U, or META-NORD such as LRE Map, Program Surveys, Language Matrices, Language Gaps, Language White Papers, and META-SHARE infrastructure. These are now available and contribute to better understanding the current landscape and devising possible solutions for each individual language and technology, including availability, quality, maturity, sustainability, and economic context. Various approaches have been proposed to address this challenge, either as monolingual processing addressing Basque, Luxemburgish, Quechua, or the Magahi Indian language, as bilingual processing for the Chinese–Japanese and Basque–Irish language pairs, and through multilingual processing, with specific focus on the 22 official Indian languages, as well as many other languages (French, English, Spanish, Vietnamese, Khmer, Pinyin Chinese, Ga, and Kistaninya). A great deal of effort is nowadays devoted to the open sharing of data, including sharing the methodology of LR creation and the collaborative definition of metadata and data formats. The cross-language portability of models, technologies, methodologies, and approaches is an important dimension to take into account at the design stage. Adopting a generic multilingual approach should therefore be encouraged. Actions should also be taken in the short term, as the gaps for less-resourced language may even get wider. A coherent action plan should be developed, based on several key factors: an open source approach, extensive standardization, the reuse of language foundations, tools and applications, and incremental design and development.

This volume contains the revised and in many cases substantially extended versions of 44 selected papers presented at the 5th Language and Technology Conference. This selection was made from the 111 high-quality contributions written by 253 authors accepted for presentation at the conference by an international jury using blind reviews. These evaluations were in general taken into account in the selection process for this volume, although there was some subjective selection. In a small number of cases, interesting papers presenting partial or preliminary results of ongoing research and development were not considered appropriate for publication in this volume, and it is hoped that more complete results will be available soon.

The selection of revised papers illustrates well the complexity and diversity of the field of Human Language Technologies. The papers collected in this volume report on many man-years of hard work by 119 authors (and their teams) representing research institutions from 22 countries[3]: Australia, Bulgaria, Croatia, the Czech Republic, France, Germany, Hungary, India, Iran, Ireland, Italy, Japan, Malta, Nigeria, Norway, Poland, Serbia, Slovakia, Spain, Sweden, Switzerland, and the United Kingdom[4].

The papers have been grouped into nine thematic chapters. Clustering the articles was a difficult task as in most cases the contributions addressed more than one thematic area, so our decisions should be considered as an approximation. In particular, the allocation of papers to chapters may not correspond to their allocation to LTC thematic sessions or to the authors' preferences. The nine chapters are:

1. Speech (3)
2. Parsing (3)
3. Computational Semantics (6)
4. Text Analysis (8)
5. Text Annotation (4)
6. Language Resources: General Issues (2)
7. Language Resources: Ontologies and Wordnets (7)
8. Machine Translation (4)
9. Problems Concerning Less Resourced Languages (7)

The ordering of the first four chapters follows the natural order that humans use to understand NL-messages: speech, morphology, syntax and semantics, text analysis. The next chapter focuses on text annotation and the following two on resources. Then comes the chapter on machine translation (MT), historically the first well-defined area of language engineering directly addressing applications of general interest. We close the volume with a large chapter (eight papers) that explicitly address the particular problems of less-resourced languages, traditionally an area of key interest at the Language and Technology conferences. We do not apply any specific ordering of contributions within chapters. Papers are presented in alphabetical order by the first author's family name.

The first chapter, Speech, contains three contributions. The first presents an implementation of two text-to-speech (TTS) systems for Ibibio, a language used in southeastern Nigeria, using a statistical-parametric approach (Ekpenyong, Udoh, Udosen, Urua)[5]. The next paper describes the design, development and evaluation of the Slovak dictation system for the APD judicial domain (Rusko, Juhár, Trnka, Staš, Darjaa, Hládek, Sabo, Pleva, Ritomský, Lojka). It is followed by a paper offering a further contribution to the intonational modelling of backchannels in Italian, useful for improving naturalness in voice-based dialogue systems for this language (Savino).

Three contributions appear in the Parsing chapter. We open with a presentation of a technique of combining multiple data-driven dependency parsers for parsing Arabic

---

[3] Against 253 authors from 35 countries participating in the LTC 2011.

[4] The language coverage is larger than may be inferred from the list of 22 countries. For example, languages such as Luxembourgish or Sanskrit do not correspond to the affiliations of the authors of some of the papers.

[5] Moses Ekpenyong (University of Uyo, Nigeria) won a Best Student Paper LTC Award

(Alabbas, Ramsay). The next article presents a parsing algorithm to combine coordinated syntactic structures partially parsed using a coordination-free grammar (Dufour-Lussier, Guillaume, Perrier). In the last contribution of the chapter, an automaton-based lexical disambiguation process for lexicalized tree-adjoining grammar (Gardent, Parmentier, Perrier, Schmitz) is presented.

Various issues of Computational Semantics are of primary interest in the next chapter, which includes six contributions. It opens with a contribution to the automatic resolution of lexical anaphors in Sanskrit, the reference language for the Indo-Aryan family, with the help of POS tagging (Gopal, Jha). The second paper presents a multi-pass graph labeling approach for unsupervised co-reference resolution solved by relaxation labeling (Moosavi, Ghassem-Sani). In the third paper, the author presents the construction of the set of formal spatio-temporal relations expressed in the XCDC model that are conceptualized in a natural language (Osiński). Sentiment analysis is the focus of the fourth paper, where the authors show how a simple technique can improve classification by normalizing term weights in the basic bag-of-words method (Pak, Paroubek, Fraisse, Francopoulo). The next paper describes work on textually recording non-linear elements of Polish Sign Language utterances (Romaniuk, Suszczańska, Szmal). The last article of this chapter presents a method for resolving certain semantic ambiguities by means of a constraint calculus (RCC-5) and an algorithm for spatial reasoning (Walas, Jassem).

Eight papers appear in the Text Analysis chapter, opening with a paper on a complex system of natural language processing that performs extraction of basic facts as result of morphological, syntactic and semantic analysis (Baisa, Kovář). The second paper deals with text normalization applied to a historical dialect of German (Early New High German between 1350 and 1650) by mapping historical word forms to modern ones (Bollmann, Petran, Dipper). A rule-based method to capture the tense, aspect, and mood (TAM) features of Hindi verb groups was investigated by the authors of the third paper (Choudhary, Pandey, Jha). The next paper presents research on reference resolution and personal name recognition in German Alpine texts (Ebling, Sennrich, Klaper). The fifth paper is a contribution to supervised machine learning techniques applied to topic tracking problems (Fukumoto, Suzuki, Yamamoto). The next paper will be of interest to those concerned with the recognition of the textual extent of temporal expressions (Mazur, Dale). The seventh paper presents results on applying text mining techniques to named entity recognition (Nouvel, Antoine, Friburger). The last contribution is about the identification of lexical bundles in school textbooks (Ribeck, Borin).

Four papers form the Text Annotation chapter. The first presents a framework for dialogue act annotation performed semi-automatically by using statistical models trained on previously annotated dialogues (Ghigi, Martinez-Hinarejos, Benedi). In the second, the authors propose a method to calculate confidence measures for an automatic dialogue annotation model (tested on a task-oriented human–computer corpus of railway information; Martinez-Hinarejos, Tamarit, Benedi). The third contribution presents a version of the morphosyntactically annotated Serbian translation of Orwell's *1984* and the resources used for annotation (Krstev, Vitas, Trtovac). The last paper of the chapter reports on video analysis algorithms used for the annotation of video recordings in language diversity preservation, considered an important part of the cultural heritage of humanity (Lenkiewicz, Drude, Lenkiewicz, Gerbe, Manseri, Schreer, Schwenninger, Bardeli).

The chapter entitled "Language Resources: General Issues" contains two articles. The first is a position paper about crowdsourced microworking systems in frequent use for the collection and processing of language resources (Fort, Adda, Sagot, Mariani, Couillault). The second paper discusses the relationship between language resources conceived from a local perspective and a shared framework conceived from a global perspective that supplies such resources for local re-use or enhancement (Rosner, Attard, Thompson, Gatt, Ananiadou).

The next chapter entitled "Language Resources: Ontologies and Wordnets" contains seven contributions. The purpose of the first paper is to show how to add sense descriptions to GermaNet from Wiktionary automatically (Henrich, Hinrichs, Vodolazova). The second article describes a data manipulation language designed for WordNet-like lexical databases (Kubis)[6]. The third is on transforming a subject heading language used in Polish library catalogues (KABA) into a fully machine-readable thesaurus (Mazurek, Sielski, Walkowska, Werla). The fourth contribution is about enhancing the functionality of tagging systems in the field of history and culture by introducing WordNet-like ontologies (Marciniak). The author of the next paper addresses issues connected with natural language based ontologies and proposes an ontology infrastructure (IMAGACT) as a way to fill the current gap in action ontologies (Moneglia). The next is a presentation of an automatic, language-independent approach to extending an existing wordnet by recycling freely available bilingual resources (Sagot, Fišer). The closing article of this chapter presents recent advances in the long-term project "PolNet – Polish WordNet" since the first public release of PolNet 1.0 presented at LTC 2011 (Vetulani).

The next chapter of four papers contribute directly to Machine Translation. In the first one the authors describe an approach to improve the performance of sampling-based multilingual alignment on translation tasks by investigating the distribution of n-grams in the translation tables (Luo, Lardilleux, Lepage). The second proposes a basic research for example-based machine translation consisting in a study of analogies between chunks of text in 11 European languages (Takeya, Lepage). The third paper presents a comparative study of Corpus-Based MT paradigms: statistical (SMT), example-based (EBMT), and a hybrid (EBMT-SMT) one for the German–Romanian language pair (Gavrila, Elita). In the last paper of the chapter the authors demonstrate that the style of the training corpus may influence the quality of the translation output in statistical machine translation systems (Gavrila, Vertan).

Finally, the volume ends with seven papers classified as contributions to problems specifically addressing less-resourced languages. The first contribution of the LRL chapter is concerned with the analysis of observations collected in the Language White Papers of the CESAR project. The objective of this study is to fix gaps in Language resources, tools and services for the six languages included in the project, i.e., Bulgarian, Croatian, Hungarian, Polish, Serbian, and Slovak (Tadić, Váradi, Garabík, Koeva, Ogrodniczuk, Vitas). The next two papers each address a particular

---

[6] Marek Kubis (Adam Mickiewicz University, Poland) won a Best Student Paper LTC Award.

language: Luxembourgish and Magahi. In the first one, the first LVASR (large vocabulary automatic speech recognition) system for Luxembourgish is presented (Adda-Decker, Lamel, Adda, Lavergne). The second describes the first attempt to develop an annotated corpus of Magahi, an Indo-Aryan language spoken by 14 million people, but until now without language resources and with few written texts (Kumar, Lahiri, Alok). A special case of bilingual processing is the focus of the next paper, where adapting to Irish a multi-choice quiz generation system originally developed for Basque and English is discussed from the LRL's point of view (Maritxalar, Ui Donnchadha, Foster, Ward). Finally, the last three papers are about issues pertaining to several languages of this group. The first presents a generic approach to text normalization, important for building multipurpose multilingual text corpora involving LRLs (Bigi). The second paper describes parallel corpora created simultaneously in 12 major Indian languages including English (Choudhary, Jha)[7]. The last paper in the volume presents a strategy for the incremental construction of deep parsing grammars on the basis of interlinear glossed text data, available for languages with little or no digital resources (Hellan, Beermann).

February 2014   Zygmunt Vetulani
                                                              Joseph Mariani

---

[7] Narayan Choudhary (Javaharlal Nehru University, India) won a Best Student Paper LTC Award.

Organization

Organizing Committee

Zygmunt Vetulani (Conference Chair)	Adam Mickiewicz University, Poznań, Poland
Wojciech Czarnecki	Adam Mickiewicz University, Poznań, Poland
Marek Kubis (Secretary)	Adam Mickiewicz University, Poznań, Poland
Jacek Marciniak	Adam Mickiewicz University, Poznań, Poland
Tomasz Obrębski	Adam Mickiewicz University, Poznań, Poland
Jędrzej Osiński	Adam Mickiewicz University, Poznań, Poland
Grzegorz Taberski	Adam Mickiewicz University, Poznań, Poland

LTC Program Committee

Victoria Arranz
Nuria Bel
Janusz S. Bień
Krzysztof Bogacki
Christian Boitet
Leonard Bolc
Lynne Bowker
Gerhard Budin
Nicoletta Calzolari
Nick Campbell
Julie Carson-Berndsen
Khalid Choukri
Adam Dąbrowski
Elżbieta Dura
Katarzyna Dziubalska-Kołaczyk
Tomaz Erjavec
Cedrick Fairon
Christiane Fellbaum
Maria Gavrilidou
Dafydd Gibbon
Marko Grobelnik
Franz Guenthner
Jan Hajic

Eva Hajičová
Roland Hausser
Steven Krauwer
Eric Laporte
Yves Lepage
Gerard Ligozat
Natalia Loukachevitch
Bente Maegaard
Bernardo Magnini
Alfred Majewicz
Joseph Mariani
Jacek Martinek
Gayrat Matlatipov
Keith J. Miller
Asunción Moreno
Jan Odijk
Nicholas Ostler
Karel Pala
Pavel S. Pankov
Patrick Paroubek
Stelios Piperidis
Emil Pływaczewski
Gabor Proszeky
Adam Przepiórkowski

Reinhard Rapp
Mohsen Rashwan
Mike Rosner
Justus Roux
Vasile Rus
Rafał Rzepka
Kepa Sarasola Gabiola
Frédérique Ségond
Zhongzhi Shi
Hanna Szafrańska
Ryszard Tadeusiewicz
Marko Tadić
Dan Tufiş
Hans Uszkoreit
Tamás Váradi
Cristina Vertan
Zygmunt Vetulani (Chair)
Piek Vossen
Tom Wachtel
Jan Węglarz
Mariusz Ziółko
Richard Zuber

LRL Workshop Program Committee

Co-chairs: Khalid Choukri, Joseph Mariani, Zygmunt Vetulani

Martine Adda-Decker

Nuria Bel

Gerhard Budin

Nicoletta Calzolari

Chris Cieri

Daffyd Gibbon

Shuichi Itahashi

Girish Nath Jha

Alfred Majewicz

Asunción Moreno

Jan Odijk

Stellios Piperidis

Gabor Proszeky

Mohsen Rashwan

Justus C. Roux

Kepa Sarasola Gabiola

Virach Sornlertlamvanich

Marko Tadić

Chiu-yu Tseng

Dan Tufiş

Invited Reviewers

Gilles Adda

Izaskun Aldezabal

Iñaki Alegria

Xabier Artola-Zubillaga

Stéphanie Audrit

Noémi Boubel

Krzysztof Ciesielski

Eleanor Clark

Pawel Dybala

Tomaž Erjavec

Francesca Frontini

Radovan Garabík

Marek Grác

Elzbieta Hajnicz

Olivier Hamon

Milos Jakubicek

Maciej Karpinski

Marek Kubis

Penny Labropoulou

Piroska Lendvai

Robert Lew

Khabibulla Madatov

Jacek Marciniak

Malgorzata Marciniak

Márton Miháltz

Agnieszka Mykowiecka

Zuzana Nevěřilová

Tomasz Obrębski

Maciej Ogrodniczuk

Csaba Oravecz

Jędrzej Osinski

Alexander Panchenko

Jungyeul Park

Piotr Pęzik

Dawid Pietrala

Michal Ptaszynski

Sophie Roekhaut

Irene Russo

Bálint Sass

Aleksander Wawer

Stephanie Weiser

Marcin Woliński

The reviewing process was effected by the members of Program Committees and invited reviewers recommended by Program Committee members.

Contents

Language Resources: General Issues

Language Resources: Ontologies and Wordnets

Machine Translation

Problems Concerning Less Resourced Languages

Speech

Improved Syllable-Based Text to Speech Synthesis for Tone Language Systems

Moses Ekpenyong[1]([✉]), EmemObong Udoh[2], Escor Udosen[3],
and Eno-Abasi Urua[2]

[1] Department of Computer Science, University of Uyo, Uyo, Nigeria
mosesekpenyong@uniuyo.edu.ng, mosesekpenyong@gmail.com
[2] Department of Linguistics and Nigerian Languages, University of Uyo, Uyo, Nigeria
{ememobongudoh,eno-abasiurua}@uniuyo.edu.ng, ememobongudoh@gmail.com
[3] Department of Linguistics and Communication Studies, University of Calabar,
Calabar, Nigeria
escorudosen@gmail.com

Abstract. In this contribution, we document the series of progress towards attaining a generic and replicable system that is applicable not only to Nigerian languages but also other African languages. The current system implements a state-of-the-art approach called the Hidden Markov Model (HMM) approach and aims at a hybridised version which front end components would serve other NLP tasks, as well as future research and developments. We continue to tackle the language specific problems and the 'unity of purpose' phenomenon for tone language systems and improve on the speech quality as an extension of our LTC'2011 paper. Specifically, we address issues bordering on tone modelling using syllables as basic synthesis units, with an 'eye ball' assessment of the synthesised speech quality. The results of this research offer hope for further improvements, and we envisage an unsupervised system to minimise the labour intensive aspects of the current design. Also, with the active collaboration network established in the course of this research, we are certain that a more robust system that would serve a wide variety of applications will evolve.

Keywords: FST · HMM · NLP · Speech synthesis · Tone modelling

1 Introduction

The application of HMMs dates back to the late 1960s and early 1970s. HMMs are statistical models used for representing various types of sequential data and were first applied to speech synthesis in 1995 [1]. Hidden Markov modelling has grown in popularity and has recently been used with great effectiveness in the field of speech technologies [2–7]. It is a statistical parametric approach, and learns the model from data. The model is parametric because speech is described using parameters rather than stored exemplars. It is statistical because these parameters are described using statistic concepts such as the means and variances

© Springer International Publishing Switzerland 2014
Z. Vetulani and J. Mariani (Eds.): LTC 2011, LNAI 8387, pp. 3–15, 2014.
DOI: 10.1007/978-3-319-08958-4_1

of probability density functions, which capture the distribution of parameter values observed in the training data [8].

HMM-based text-to-speech (TTS) is structured into two stages, namely training and synthesis [9]. The training stage adopts a similar procedure to speech recognition systems, except that the spectrum - mel-cepstral coefficients [10] and their dynamic features, and excitation - logarithmic fundamental frequencies ($logF0$) and its dynamic features, are extracted from a speech database and modelled by context-dependent HMMs that incorporate phonetic, linguistic and prosodic contexts. The excitation parameters are further modelled using multi-space probability distributions (MSPDs) [11] to ensure the accuracy of variable dimensional parameter sequence such as logF0 with unvoiced regions. The synthesis stage accepts the phone context sequence generated from text analysis, concatenates the corresponding HMM sequence, and generates the F0s and spectral parameters. These speech parameters are finally transformed into a waveform using synthesis filters [12].

The current synthesis technique adopted in this paper combines rule-based and statistical methods for developing the language model and corpus mark-up model. It offers a state-of-the-art solution for developing adaptable and replicable systems that address several levels of infrastructural and linguistic application issues, as well as a methodology for implementing and evaluating the system and its components. we implement this approach for Ibibio and improve on a syllable HMM-based prototype [13]. The proposed approach is well known for its flexibility in modifying and adapting voice patterns/characteristics, speaking styles and emotions, thus, presenting a more dynamic structure which outsmarts most unit-selection systems.

2   The Ibibio Language

Ibibio is a Lower Cross tone language spoken by approximately four million (4,000,000) speakers in the South-east coastal region of Nigeria [14]. Though the language has received some form of attention in the area of syntax and morphology [15–17], not much is done towards building computational resources for the language. The language has a complex morphology and couple with its interaction with the tone structure makes prediction very difficult. In this section, we discuss the phrase structure and morphology of Ibibio. The essence of this discussion is to enhance readers' understanding of the principles employed in generating Heterogeneous Relation Graphs (HRGs) - a major component of our front end, used in word, syllable and phrase properties extraction of speech utterance(s).

2.1   Ibibio Phrase Structure

Phrase structure rules are used to define the grammar of a language. They generate the deep structures of a sentence and constitute re-write rules employing symbols for its operations. We propose a phrase structure grammar that extends

S	$\rightarrow < NP >< VP >$
NP	$\rightarrow < N >< DET > \mid < QUANT >< N >< DET >$
VP	$\rightarrow < AUX >< COP\mid V > \mid < AUX >< V >< NP > \mid$ $< AUX >< V > \mid < AUX >< PRED >$
DET	$\rightarrow < ART\mid DEM >$
AUX	$\rightarrow < CONC >< MOD > \mid < CONC >< TENSE >$ $\mid < CONC >< ASP > \mid < CONC >< MOD >$ $< TENSE > \mid < CONC >< TENSE >< ASP >$
TENSE	$\rightarrow < PAST\mid PRESENT\mid FUTURE >$
ASP	$\rightarrow < INCEPT\mid HABIT\mid COMPL >$
PRED	$\rightarrow$ NP

Fig. 1. Essien's (1990) Ibibio phrase structure

Essien's [14] phrase structure grammar (PSG) for simple, positive Ibibio sentences (see Fig. 1.).

In our proposal, we also consider inflection which is important in the language's morphology. An Ibibio sentence can now be viewed as a field with three subsets (i.e., $S \rightarrow < NP >< INFL >< VP\mid VP' >$). The initial symbol (S) exists, and generates more strings of symbols called productions. Using rewrite rules, we construct an extended phrase structure grammar (PSG) for Ibibio as shown in Fig. 2.

S	$\rightarrow < NP >< INFL >< VP\mid VP' >$
NP	$\rightarrow < QUANT >< N* > \mid < QUANT >< N >< PRO >$ $\mid < QUANT >< PRO > \mid < ADJ.P >< N* >$ $\mid < N > \mid < N >< PRO > \mid < N >< PRO >< AJN >$ $\mid < N >< AJN > \mid < PRO > \mid < DET >< N >$ $\mid < PP >< N >$
INFL	$\rightarrow < AGR >< TENSE > \mid < AGR >< MOD >$ $\mid < AGR >< ASP >$
VP	$\rightarrow < COP.V\mid V* > \mid < V* >< ADJ.P > \mid < V* >< NP > \mid <$ $V* >< ADV.P > \mid < V* >< COMP\_P >$
VP'	$\rightarrow < V ><$AGR-S$> \mid < V >< NP ><$AGR-S$>$
DET	$\rightarrow < ART\mid DEM >$
TENSE	$\rightarrow < PAST\mid PRESENT\mid FUTURE >$
AGR	$\rightarrow < PERS >< NUM >$
ASP	$\rightarrow < INCEPT\mid HABIT\mid COMPL >$
PP	$\rightarrow < PREP >< NP >$
AGR-S	$\rightarrow < PERS >< NUM >< TP >$
ADJ.P	$\rightarrow < ADJ >< N >$
ADV.P	$\rightarrow < ADV >< ADV >$
TP	$\rightarrow < TENSE >< NEG\_P >$
NEG_P	$\rightarrow < NEG >< VP >$
COMPL_P	$\rightarrow < COMP > S$

Fig. 2. Extended Ibibio phrase structure

The extended PSG in Fig. 2 is comprehensive and considers all possible productions of the language. The productions are properly labelled to distinguish top-level productions from lower-level transitions. Also, our grammar structure can generate both simple and complex sentences in Ibibio and has been used to implement a morpho-syntactic analyser framework for Ibibio [18]. A symbol table which defines the various notations of the PSG is given in Table 1:

Table 1. Symbol table defining the various notations of Ibibio PSG

Symbol	Definition	Symbol	Definition
S	Sentence	HABIT	Habitual
NP	Noun phrase	COMPL	Completive
INFL	Inflection	PP	Prepositional phrase
VP	Verb phrase	PREP	Preposition
COP.V	Copulative verb	AGR-S	Subject agreement
V	Verb	PERS	Person
ADV.P	Adverbial phrase	NUM	Number
COMP_P	Complement projection	TP	Tense projection
VP'	Verb phrase prime	ADJ.P	Adjectival phrase
DET	Determinant	ADJ	Adjective
TENSE	Tense	N	Noun
AGR	Agreement	ADV	Adverb
ASP	Aspect	NEG_P	Negation projection
INCEPT	Inceptive		

2.2 Ibibio Morpho-Syntactic Analysis

Example FSTs implementing the extended PSG for the Ibibio language (see Fig. 2) are given in Figs. 3, 4, 5, 6, 7, 8, 9, 10, 11, 12, 13, 14, 15 and 16. These FSTs are useful for defining the morphological rules of the language and for future research on morpho-syntactic analysis of tone language systems:

3   HMM-Based Tone Language Synthesis

3.1   Speech Database

Our current Ibibio speech database contains a total of 1,140 utterances (or sentences) representing about two hours of speech, read by a professional speaker. These utterances came from various sources ranging from written texts in Ibibio (text books, stories, news readings and formulated sentences) to transcribed documentaries. The recording instruments used for collecting the speech data

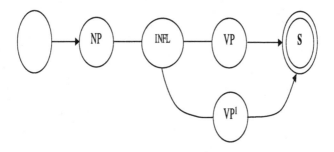

Fig. 3. FST for Ibibio sentence (S)

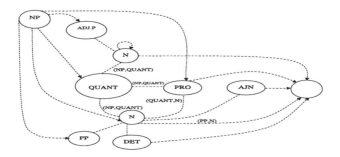

Fig. 4. FST for Ibibio Noun Phrase (NP)

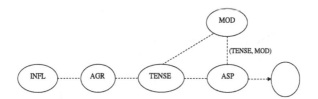

Fig. 5. FST for Ibibio Inflection (INFL)

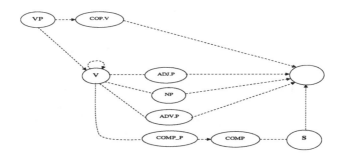

Fig. 6. FST for Ibibio Verb Phrase (VP)

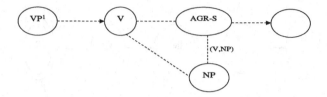

Fig. 7. FST for Ibibio Verb Phrase prime (VP′)

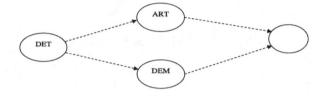

Fig. 8. FST for Ibibio Determinant (DET)

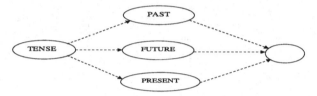

Fig. 9. FST for Ibibio Tense (TENSE)

Fig. 10. FST for Ibibio Agreement (AGR)

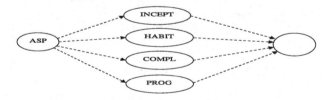

Fig. 11. FST for Ibibio Aspect (ASP)

Fig. 12. FST for Ibibio Prepositional Phrase (PP)

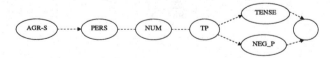

Fig. 13. FST for Ibibio Subject Agreement (AGR-S)

Fig. 14. FST for Ibibio Adjectival Phrase (ADJ.P)

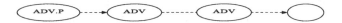

Fig. 15. FST for Ibibio Adverbial Phrase (ADV.P)

Fig. 16. FST for Ibibio Negation Projection (NEG_P)

were a portable Marantz Professional PMD660 DAT recorder and Sony F-V420 dynamic microphone. The recording was done at the Communications Arts Studio of the University of Uyo, and the speech frequency was sampled at 44.1 kHz. Though the recording sessions witnessed some challenges such as session breaks due to intermittent power availability, we were still able to keep the sessions under check.

3.2 The Front End

The initial front end design of this research is a text-to-segments framework implemented using Speect [19], a multilingual speech synthesis system that offers application programming interfaces, as well as environment for research and development of TTS systems and voices. We obtained from this implementation, the HRGs describing the linguistic structures of the language. To ensure adaptability and replicability of our synthesisers, we adopted the data-driven approach in developing the front end. Our front end modules generated the necessary linguistic information (units or labels) in HTS format automatically from input data-files. We do not rely heavily on hard-coding the linguistic details; rather the users have to specify these units for their language in a specific format. The Speect TTS software tool provided the engine for the generation of the utterance text-to-segments structure - the HRGs. This structure was then flattened to extract a syllabified representation of the input utterance. A carbon-copy of the syllabified corpus (the flattened structure) was finally created with the letters (phonemes) replaced with some defined tone symbols using an extractor (a script) with each utterance spilt to their respective label files, as demanded by HTS. Also, the HTS question file for voice training and synthesis was scripted and fashioned for easy adaptation to other tone language systems. A complete structure of the front end design components comprising the required input and output files is found in [13], while the necessary processing scripts are available in [20].

3.3 Modelling Context Features

Context-dependent labels and decision trees were introduced in this research to enable the investigation of language specific features, and questions relating to these features were asked, to build the decision tree algorithm. Figure 17 represents a context-dependent label format of [21], modified for tone language HTS synthesis:

$$P_1^\wedge P_2 - P_3 + P_{=}P_5@P_6 - P_7$$
$$/A : x\_x\_a_3/B : x - x - b_3@b_4 - B_5\&b_6 - b_7\#x - x\$x - x!x - x; x - x|b_{16}$$
$$/c_1 + c_2 + c_3$$
$$/D : d_1\_d_2/E : e_1 + e_2@e_3 + e_4@e_5 + e_6\#e_7 + e_8/F : f_1 - F_2$$
$$/G : g_1\_g_2/H : h_1 = h_2@h_3 = h_4|x/I : i_1\_i_2$$
$$/J : j_1 + j_2 - J_3/TL : t_1\_TC : t_2\_TR : t_3$$

Fig. 17. HMM-based context-dependent label format for tone language synthesis

where $P_1, P_2, ...$ are feature label statistics. For each feature label considered, a corresponding question is added to the question file. The format of the question file allows one to write regular (grep-like) expressions that determine the label(s) matching a particular context feature. Our question file generator prepares the question file automatically from an enriched label file of each utterance. The generator also sieves information from the language's phoneme inventory which describes the place and manner of articulation of the phoneme(s) in question. The full question list is then used during training to tie the model parameters. However, depending on the modelled parameters (spectral, pitch and duration) the most significant question varies, although questions regarding the specific language phonemes are dominant.

A description of the implemented linguistic features (or labels) is detailed in [20, 22]. Due to the peculiar nature of tone language synthesis and for the purpose of replication, the scripts responsible to automate the front end processes were developed from scratch.

3.4 Modelling Tone

In Fig. 18, a finite state transducer (FST) for modelling the tonetactics of Ibibio is proposed. To ensure completeness of the FST, we have captured all the possible interactions of tone in the language. The FST does the prediction of the next tone using tonal constraints formulated in [13] for Ibibio. In the figure, double circles represent acceptance states, signifying a possible end of an utterance. Broken arrows indicate syllable boundaries while thick arrows show word or phrase boundary transitions. An utterance is initiated by any of the level tones, i.e., a High (H) or Low (L) tone state. We assume in the FST that the HL and LH tones are implicit derivations of H and L transitions. Figure 18 can be

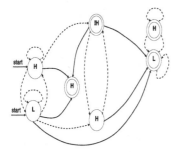

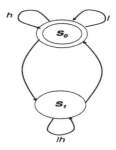

Fig. 18. Ibibio tone FST

Fig. 19. A two state representation of Fig. 20

condensed into a two state finite state machine (FSM) that shows only the basic tones (H, L and !H). The resultant FSM in Fig. 19 represents a generic structure that shells the details of Fig. 18.

Speech Parameters Extraction. The STRAIGHT [23] spectral analysis method was used to extract 55th order Mel-cepstral coefficients at a 5 ms frame-shift. For F0 estimation, we employed a procedure that votes across three different F0 trackers (instantaneous-frequency-amplitude-spectrum (IFAS), a fixed point analysis (TEMPO), and the ESPS tool *'getF0'*. Following [24], the F0s were transformed onto the Mel scale before acoustic modelling. In building the training models for Ibibio, we considered only linguistic labels relevant to tone languages, and scripted an automatic labelling of these features to a label file (for each utterance). Features not related to tone languages (e.g. stress features) were however marked 'not relevant', i.e., with an x (see Fig. 17). Additionally, we appended the tone context-dependent label features for tone prediction to this specification, e.g.: $/TL : t_1\_TC : t_2\_TR : t_3$

Our tone labelling algorithm models what happens at the syllable level. Each phone in the syllabified tone-tagged utterance file is mapped to a corresponding model (i.e., a context-dependent label) in the label file. Where a centre phoneme has no tone bearing unit as its neighbour (i.e., is a consonant), the immediate tone either to the left or right of the centre phone is used to label the model. This approach represents a new dimension to dealing with the tonetactics of Ibibio.

4   Synthesis Experiments and Results

In [13], phone and syllable HMM-based synthesis systems built from approximately twenty minutes of speech corpus were compared. We observed wide variation in power levels of some of the recorded voices and normalised these levels using a power normalisation algorithm. We also resized inconsistent F0 distributions by establishing a threshold at the centre of the plots and re-parameterized the audio files. These adjustments were iteratively done to obtain a fairly uniform spread before re-synthesis. In summary, synthesised voices with syllable

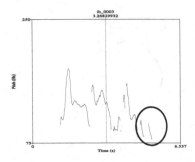

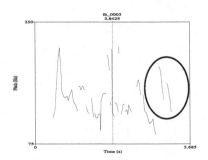

Fig. 20. Pitch contour of an original Ibibio utterance

Fig. 21. Pitch contour of synthetic speech with (only) quinphone labels

evidence outperformed those with only phone features. In the next section, we 'eye ball' the synthesised speech and validate the presence of tone as well as syllable co-ordination.

4.1   Pitch Analysis

A pitch analysis of the waveform obtained from extended synthesis experiments [20, 22], was carried out to compare the performance of an original voice - system A, with three synthesis systems: (i) system with only phonetic context (quin-phones) - system B; (ii) system with full context without tone labels - system C; (iii) system with full context and tone labels - system D, to investigate the relevance of tone evidence and the advantage of using syllables as basic synthesis units. Figure 20 shows the pitch contour plot of the recorded (original) utterance (system A). Comparing this to the contour of system B (see Fig. 21), we observed that the contour in Fig. 21 appears distorted with more broken lines (i.e., does not resemble the original speech contour in Fig. 20). This reveals poor acoustic rendering. Also, an informal listening test does not only confirm the effect of distortions and broken contours, but also a tone-deaf utterance. For instance, in both figures (Figs. 20 and 21), we have encircled the most prominent contours of the last two words to show this effect. Clearly, we observed in Fig. 21 that the quinphone labels of the synthetic speech wrongly synthesised the last two words with high tones instead of low tones. This defect is due to the lack of tone information in the models.

But, the pitch contour of a synthesised waveform of system C presented in Fig. 22 revealed a more defined speech contour. An objective listening test gave a fairly intelligible utterance that requires improvements, though the last two words were still wrongly synthesised. Figure 23 shows a fairly well-formed pitch contour resulting from the synthesis of system D. The resulting contour as can be seen, fairly mimics the contour pattern of the original recording in Fig. 21, and the voices from this implementation sound more intelligible, well syllabified and properly tone marked. We validate the above claim by extracting the F0 contours for the systems under this experiment. In Fig. 24, we observed that the original recording (system A) and synthesised voice with tone (system D) are

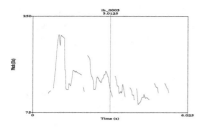

Fig. 22. Pitch contour of synthetic speech synthetic speech with full context without tone labels (system C)

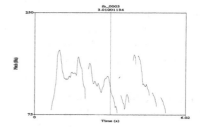

Fig. 23. Pitch contour of synthetic speech with full context and tone labels (system D)

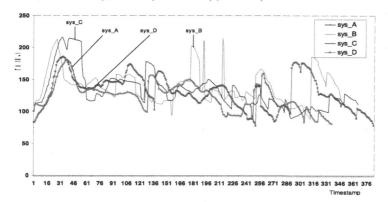

Fig. 24. F0 contours for each of four systems evaluated in the listening test. The Ibibio utterance, written in SAMPA is 'eJe amaanam aNwuNu ke mmo owo enie ntreubOk ke usVN OmmO keed keed', translation in English: S/he made it clear that people have individual limitations/challenges. Source: [20, 22].

relatively similar, therefore suggesting the importance of integrating tone and syllable information in tone language synthesis.

5   Conclusion

Modelling and synthesis of tone language systems are yet to undergo effective investigation because of the numerous problems they present [20, 25, 26]. Apart from Mandarin, a Chinese tone language, which can easily be dealt with given the evidence of well-defined phonemic structure, African languages present a knotty pattern which toughens prediction. They possess additional morphological complexity and are highly problematic. Research works in this area require a more defined methodology such as the data-driven techniques and automatic approaches. Unsupervised techniques to speech synthesis (i.e., where the synthesis system uses less linguistic evidence) will mark a major breakthrough in speech synthesis research. But from literature available to us at the moment; they are yet to be fully explored for tone language systems. This paper therefore represents a pioneering investigation that defines a supervised framework with workable and tested synthesis prototypes that will advance into an unsupervised system for African tone languages. To further improve on the speech quality, we are in the process of increasing the speech corpus database.

Acknowledgments. This research has received support from the following grants: The Local Language Speech Technology Initiative (LLSTI) Industry-University grant, the Science and Technology Education Post-Basic (STEP-B)/World Bank assisted Project grant and the Federal Government of Nigeria (FGN)/Tertiary Education Trust Fund (TETFund) Staff training grant. We also acknowledge Professor Simon King, of the Centre for Speech Technology Research (CSTR), University of Edinburgh, Scotland for accepting to host part of this research in his laboratory.

References

1. Masuko, T.: HMM-based speech synthesis and its applications. Ph.D. thesis, Tokyo, Japan (2002)
2. Yoshimura, T., Tokuda, K., Masuko, T., Kobayashi, T., and Kitamura, T.: Simultaneous modeling of spectrum, pitch and duration in HMM based speech synthesis. In: EUROSPEECH Conference (1999)
3. Zen, H., Toda, T., Nakamura, M., Tokuda, K.: Details of nitech HMM-based speech synthesis system for the Blizzard Challenge 2005. IEICE Trans. Inf. Syst. **E90–D**(1), 325–333 (2007)
4. Ling, Z.-H., Wu, Y.-J., Wang, Y.-P., Qin, L., Wang, R.H.: USTC system for Blizzard Challenge 2006: an improved HMM based speech synthesis method. In: Blizzard Challenge (2006)
5. Black, A., Zen, H., Tokuda, K.: Statistical parametric synthesis. In: ICASSP, Hawaii, pp. 1229–1232 (2007)
6. Raitio, T.: Hidden Markov model based finnish text-to-speech system utilizing glottal inverse filtering. M.Sc. thesis, Espoo, Finland (2008)
7. Guan, Y., Tian, J., Wu, Y.-J., Yamagishi, J., Nurminen, J.: A unified and automatic approach to Mandarin HTS system. In: 7th ISCA Speech Synthesis Workshop, pp. 1–5 (2010)
8. King, S.: A Tutorial on HMM Speech Synthesis (Invited Paper). In: Sadhana - Academy Proceedings in Engineering Sciences, Indian Institute of Sciences (2010)
9. Zen, H., Oura, K., Nose T., Yamagishi, J., Sako, S., Toda, T., Masuko, T., Black, A.W., Tokuda, K.: Recent development of the HMM-based speech synthesis system (HTS). In: APSIPA Annual Summit and Conference, Sapporo, Japan, pp. 121–130 (2009)
10. Fukada, T., Tokuda, K., Kobayashi, T., Imai, S.: An adaptive algorithm for mel-cepstral analysis of speech. In: ICASSP, pp. 137–140 (1992)
11. Tokuda, K., Masuko, T., Miyazaki, N., Kobayashi, T.: Hidden Markov models based on multi-space probability distribution for pitch pattern modeling. In: Acoustics, Speech, and Signal Processing, vol. 1, pp. 229–232 (1999)
12. Imai, S.: Cepstral analysis synthesis on the mel frequency scale. In: ICASSP'83, pp. 93–96 (1983)

13. Ekpenyong, M., Urua, E.-A., Udosen, E., Udoh, E.: Adaptable phone and syllable HMM-based Ibibio TTS systems. In: Vetulani, Z. (ed.) 5th Language and Technology Conference (LTC), Poznan, Poland, Fundacja Uniwersytetu im. A. Mickiewicza, pp. 355–360 (2011)
14. Essien, O.E.: A Grammar of the Ibibio Language. University Press Limited, Ibadan (1990)
15. Simmons, D.: Ibibio verb morphology. Afr. Stud. **16**(1), 1–19 (1957)
16. Urua, E.E.: Aspects of Ibibio phonology and morphology. Ph.D. thesis, Ibadan, Nigeria (1990)
17. Akinlabi, A., Urua, E.: Foot structure in Ibibio verb. J. Afr. Lang. Linguist. **23**, 119–160 (2002). Walter De Gruyter
18. Ekpenyong, M., Udoh, E.O.: Morpho-syntactic analysis framework for tone language text-to-speech systems. Comput. Inf. Sci. **5**(4), 83–101 (2012)
19. Louw, J.A.: Speect: a multilingual text-to-speech system. In: Proceedings of 19th Annual Symposium of the Pattern Recognition Association of South Africa (PRASA), Cape Town, pp. 165–168 (2008)
20. Ekpenyong, M.E.: Speech synthesis for tone language systems. Ph.D. thesis, University of Uyo, Nigeria (2013)
21. Zen, H.: An example context-dependent label format for HMM-based speech synthesis in English. https://wiki.inf.ed.ac.uk/twiki/pub/CSTR/F0parametrisation/ hts_lab_format.pdf (2006). Accessed 19 May 2011
22. Ekpenyong, M., Urua E.-A., Watts, O., King, S. and Yamagishi, J.: Statistical parametric speech synthesis for Ibibio, Speech Commun. First online: February 2013. doi:10.1016/j.specom.2013.02.003
23. Kawahara, H., Masuda-Katsuse, I., Cheveigne, A.: Restructuring speech representations using a pitch-adaptive time-frequency smoothing and an instantaneous-frequency based F0 extraction: possible role of a repetitive structure in sounds. Speech Commun. **27**(3), 187–207 (1999)
24. Yamagishi, J., Nose, T., Zen, H., Ling, Z., Toda, T., Tokuda, K., King, S., Renals, S.: Robust speaker-adaptive HMM-based text-to-speech synthesis. IEEE Trans. Audio Speech Lang. Process. **17**(6), 1208–1230 (2009)
25. Gibbon, D., Urua, E.-A., Ekpenyong, M.: Problems and solutions in African tone language text-to-speech. In: International Tutorial and Research Workshop on Multilingual Speech and Language Processing, Stellenbosch, paper 14 (2006)
26. Ekpenyong, M., Urua, E.-A., Gibbon, D.: Towards an unrestricted domain TTS system for African tone languages. Int. J. Speech Technol. **11**, 87–96 (2008)

Slovak Automatic Dictation System for Judicial Domain

Milan Rusko[1(✉)], Jozef Juhár[2], Marián Trnka[1], Ján Staš[2],
Sakhia Darjaa[1], Daniel Hládek[2], Róbert Sabo[1], Matúš Pleva[2],
Marián Ritomský[1], and Martin Lojka[2]

[1] Institute of Informatics, Slovak Academy of Sciences,
Dúbravská cesta 9, 845 07 Bratislava, Slovakia
{milan.rusko,marian.trnka,utrrsach,robert.sabo,
marian.ritomsky}@savba.sk
[2] Department of Electronics and Multimedia Communications,
Faculty of Electrical Engineering and Informatics,
Technical University of Košice, Park Komenského 13, 042 00 Košice, Slovakia
{jozef.juhar,jan.stas,daniel.hladek,matus.pleva,
martin.lojka}@tuke.sk

Abstract. This paper describes the design, development and evaluation of the Slovak dictation system for the judicial domain. The speech is recorded using a close-talk microphone and the dictation system is used for on-line or off-line automatic transcription. The system provides an automatic dictation tool in Slovak for the employees of the Ministry of Justice of the Slovak Republic and all the courts in Slovakia. The system is designed for on-line dictation and off-line transcription of legal texts recorded in acoustical conditions of typical office. Details of the technical solution are given and the evaluation of different versions of the system is presented.

Keywords: Automatic speech recognition · Slovak language · Judicial domain

1 Introduction

Dictation systems for major world languages have been available for years. The Slovak language, a Central European language spoken by a relatively small population (around 5 million), suffers from the lack of speech databases and linguistic resources, and these are the primary reasons for the absence of a dictation system until recently.

We describe the design, development and evaluation of a Slovak dictation system named APD (Automatický Prepis Diktátu – *Automatic Transcription of Dictation*) for the judicial domain.

The development of the automatic transcription systems for the judicial domain is a very challenging task from the research and development point of view. (see e.g. [1]). On the other hand there is a market demand for such technologies. Court room speech transcription is considered as one of the greatest challenges for the front-end of speech recognition and the authors with the cooperation with the Ministry of Justice of the Slovak Republic decided to divide the task into three stages.

© Springer International Publishing Switzerland 2014
Z. Vetulani and J. Mariani (Eds.): LTC 2011, LNAI 8387, pp. 16–27, 2014.
DOI: 10.1007/978-3-319-08958-4_2

The long-term goal is to use automatic speech processing technologies to make the judicial proceedings more effective and transparent. In order to fulfill this task, the whole legal process should be recorded and the speech utterances of all the participants should be captured and stored.

It was decided to build the dictation system for personal use in a quiet room environment in the first phase. The judges will use the system for the preparation of legal documents which are now dictated to an assistant. This stage is also intended to get the users accustomed to the new technology and gain experience with its use.

The second stage will deal with the on-line dictation by the judge and prosecutor during the trial in the acoustical conditions of the judgment hall. In this stage the focus will be given on indexing of the audio recordings using speech recognition and their storage and archiving.

The third phase should lead to a systematic and mandatory use of recording and transcribing the entire court hearings and develop a methodology and infrastructure for their use.

The paper is organized as follows: Sect. 2 introduces speech databases and annotation, Sect. 3 describes building of the APD system, Sect. 4 presents the evaluation of the dictation system, and Sect. 5 closes the paper with the discussion.

2 Speech Databases and Annotation

Several speech databases were used for acoustic models training and recognizer testing during the development of the APD dictation system. The APD database is gender-balanced and contains 250 hours of recordings (mostly read speech) from 250 speakers. It consists of two parts: APD1 and APD2.

APD1 contains 120 hours of reading transcripts of court decisions, recorded in sound studio conditions. In order to comply with current Slovak legislation on the protection of personal data, all names, addresses, and some numbers had to be changed.

APD2 contains 130 hours of read phonetically rich sentences, newspaper articles, internet texts and spelled items. This database was recorded in offices and conference rooms.

The recording of APD1 and APD2 was realized using a quiet PC with an EMU Tracker Pre USB 2.0 and E-MU 0404 USB 2.0 Audio Interface/Mobile Preamp. To obtain the signal from the different types of microphones (for future flexibility in creating acoustic models for various applications) the audio signal was simultaneously recorded to three channels with four sound tracks in total:

1. Close-talk channel using Sennheiser ME3 headset microphone with Sennheiser MZA 900 P In-Line preamplifier
2. Table microphone channel using Rode NT-3 microphone
3. Dictaphone channel that used PHILIPS Digital Voice Tracer LFH 860/880 dictaphone with its built in stereo microphone (occupying two audio tracks).

The recordings in the first two channels have 48 kHz sampling frequency and 16 bit resolution. They were later down-sampled to 16 kHz for training and testing.

The APD database was extended by the "Parliament" database which contains 96 hours of recordings realized in the main conference hall of the Slovak Parliament using conference "goose neck" microphones [2]. The sampling frequency was 48 kHz in 256 kbps CBR stereo AC-3 format. The recordings were later converted to 16 kHz mono PCM and resolution of 16 bit for training and testing. The database consists of annotated spontaneous and read utterances of 142 speakers and is not balanced for gender. In accordance with the gender structure of the Slovak Parliament it has 90 % male speakers and 10 % of female speakers.

The databases were annotated by our team of trained annotators (university students) using the Transcriber annotation tool [3] slightly adapted to meet our needs. The annotated databases underwent the second round of annotation focused on checking and fixing mistakes of the first round of annotation. The annotation files were automatically checked for typos using a dictionary-based algorithm and for correctness of event annotations from closed predefined set. The dictionary based algorithm used a dictionary with alternative pronunciations, and a high Viterbi score of forced alignment was taken to indicate files with bad annotation. Roughly 5-10 % of the files were identified as candidates for having bad annotation, and most of them really contained mistakes. The spelling of numbers was automatically checked and mistakes were corrected.

3   Building the APD System

The software solution for the APD system is designed to contain 3 layers (see Fig. 1). The CORE layer consists of the speech recognition system which communicates with the VIEW layer through the CONTROLLER layer. Such a modular design allowed us to experiment with more cores within the APD system.

Two cores were investigated. The first, in-house weighted finite state transducer (WFST) based speech recognizer, derived from the Juicer ASR decoder [4], and the second, the Julius speech recognizer [5, 6], was used mainly as our reference speech recognition engine.

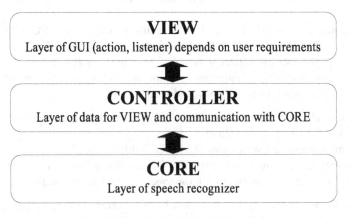

Fig. 1. The design of the APD system

3.1 Acoustic Modeling

We used a triphone mapped HMM system described in detail in [7]. Here, we briefly introduce the acoustic modeling that also has been used in the APD system.

The process of building a triphone mapped HMM system has 4 steps:

1. Training of monophones models with single Gaussian mixtures.
2. The number of mixture components in each state is incremented and the multiple GMMs are trained.
3. The output state distributions of the monophones are cloned for all triphones, triphone mapping for clustering is applied.
4. The triphone tied system is trained.

The models from Step 1 were used for the calculation of acoustic distances. The acoustic distance AD of two phonemes i and j was calculated as:

$$AD(i,j) = \sqrt{\frac{1}{V_f} \sum_{k=1}^{V_f} \frac{\left(\mu_{ik} - \mu_{jk}\right)^2}{\sigma_{ik}\sigma_{jk}}}$$

where V_f is the dimensionality of feature vector f, μ and σ are means and variances, respectively. The distance is calculated for each emitting state, resulting in i–j–1, i–j–2 and i–j–3 values for the phoneme pair (considering conventional 5 states HMM model of a phoneme, where 0th and 4th are non-emitting states).

The triphone distance TD between two triphones is defined by the following equation:

$$TD(P_a - P + P_b, P_c - P + P_d) = w_{left}AD(P_a - P_c - 3) + w_{right}AD(P_b - P_d - 1)$$

where w are context weights of the phoneme P. Then map each triphone m from the list of all possible triphones (approx. 87 k triphones), which includes unseen triphones as well, on the closest triphone $n*$ from the list of selected triphones with the same basis phoneme using metrics:

$$n^* = TriMap(m) = \arg \min_n (TD(m, n))$$

where $n \in \{n_1, \ldots, n_N\}$, selects N most frequent triphones in the training database (usually from 2000 to 3500).

This triphone map is then applied in Step 3 instead of conventional decision tree based state clustering, and retrained in Step 4.

Adaptation of Acoustic Models. For speaker adaptation we considered these adaptation methods and their combinations: MLLR, semi-tied covariance matrices, HLDA, and CMLLR. In our experiments we tried to choose a method that is able to improve recognition accuracy even if only a small-sized adaptation data is available. The second requirement was the simplicity of the adaptation process due to computational complexity.

For our experiments, the left-to-right three tied-state triphone HMM with 32 Gaussians was trained on recordings of parliamentary speech database and used for adaptation [8]. A part of Euronounce bilingual database [9] containing phonetically rich sentences in the speakers' mother tongue was used for the adaptation experiments.

Adapted models were evaluated on the continuous speech with large vocabulary (>420 k words) and the achieved results are illustrated in Table 1. As we can see from the table the highest accuracy improvement with small adaptation data (50 sentences, 5 minutes of speech or less) was achieved with Maximum Likelihood Linear Regression [10] for male as well as female speakers [11].

Due to this fact we have chosen MLLR as the most suitable adaptation method for implementation. In APD LVCSR system the supervised MLLR adaptation was implemented using the predetermined regression classes.

Table 1. Evaluation of acoustic models with 4, 8, 16, and 32 Gaussians per state adapted to a male speaker

Man speaker	Basic AM WER [%]	Semi-tied WER [%]	Semi-tied + HLDA WER [%]	MLLR WER [%]	CMLLR + MLLR WER [%]
4 mix	31.06	21.12	14.31	19.08	21.39
8 mix	25.96	24.39	13.24	14.57	16.38
16 mix	21.36	34.69	14.87	10.96	12.18
32 mix	17.89	46.53	16.41	11.12	11.50

Figure 2 illustrates how MLLR was implemented. As can be seen, we focused on mean vectors adaptation while variances of mixtures stayed the same as in the original un-adapted acoustic model. The algorithm iterated through every class with assigned adaptation vectors of every adaptation sentence.

Firstly, we have calculated the score of every mixture for the aligned state. Then we were able to calculate γ as a normalized weight for every mixture of state and matrix X as the sum of multiplications of γ, feature vector O and extended mean vector Eu for all previous mixtures. The matrix Y is calculated as a sum of multiplication of the extended mean vectors Eu_{max} of mixture with highest score b_{max} within state of HMM. In this case the γ was equal to one.

After the matrices X and Y were calculated for all classes, it was possible to calculate transformation matrix W as a multiplication of matrix X and inverted matrix Y for that particular class.

When transformation matrices are known for every class it is possible to adapt all mean vectors of the acoustic model using an appropriate transformation matrix for a given mixture.

3.2 Language Modeling

Text Corpora. The main assumption in the process of creating an effective language model (LM) for any inflective language is to collect and consistently process a large amount of text data that enter into the process of training LM.

```
for all classes(i)
    for all adaptfiles
        for all vectors
            total score=calculate score for all mix
            for all mixtures of assigned state
                γ=score[mix]/total score
                Compute X_i+=γ.O.Eu
            end
            find mixture with highest score (b_max)
                Compute Y_i+=γ.Eu_max.Eu_max
        end
    end
end
for all classes(i)
    inverse Y_i
    Compute W_i=X_i.Y_i^{-1}
end
for all classes(i)
    for all mixtures
        adaptMean=W_i.Eu
    end
end
```

Fig. 2. Pseudo code of implemented MLLR

Text corpora were created using a system that retrieves text data from various Internet pages and electronic documents that are written in Slovak [12]. Text data were then normalized by additional processing such as word tokenization, sentence segmentation, numerals transcription, abbreviations expanding, and others.

The system for text gathering also includes application of constraints such as filtering of grammatically incorrect words by spelling check, duplicity verification of text documents, and other constraints.

The text corpus containing more than 2 billion of Slovak words in 120 million sentences was split into several different domains, as we can see in Table 2 [13].

Table 2. Statistics of text corpora

Text corpus	# sentences	# tokens
Web corpus	50 694 708	748 854 697
Broadcast news	36 326 920	554 593 113
Judicial corpus	18 524 094	565 140 401
Corpus of fiction	8 039 739	101 234 475
Unspecified text	4 071 165	55 711 674
Annotations	485 800	4 434 217
Development set	1 782 333	55 163 941
Together	**119 924 759**	**2 085 132 518**

Vocabulary. The vocabulary used in modeling of the Slovak language was subsequently selected using standard methods based on the most frequent words in the text corpora mentioned above and maximum likelihood approach for the selection of specific words from the judicial domain [13]. The vocabulary was extended with specific proper nouns and geographic entities in the Slovak Republic.

We have also proposed an automatic tool for generating inflective word forms for names and surnames which are used in language modeling using word classes based on their grammatical category [14]. The final vocabulary contains 325 555 unique word forms, 22 grammatically dependent classes with 97 678 proper nouns and geographic entities and 5 tags for noise events (474 450 pronunciation variants).

Language Model. The process of building a language model for the Slovak language consists of the following steps.

First, the statistics of trigram counts from each of the domain-specific corpora are extracted. From the extracted n-gram counts the statistics of counts-of-counts are computed for estimating the set of Good-Turing discounts needed in the process of smoothing LMs. From the obtained discounts the discounting constants used in smoothing LMs by the modified Kneser-Ney algorithm are calculated.

Particular trigram domain specific LMs are created using SRILM Toolkit [15] with the vocabulary and smoothed by the modified Kneser-Ney or Witten-Bell algorithms. In the next step, the perplexity of each domain-specific LM for each sentence in the development data set from the field of judiciary is computed. Perplexity is a standard measure of quality of LM which is defined as the reciprocal value of the (geometric) average probability assigned by the LM to each word in the evaluated (development) data set.

From the obtained collection of files, the parameters (interpolation weights) for individual LMs are computed by the minimization of perplexity using an EM algorithm. The final LM adapted to the judicial domain is created as a weighted combination of individual domain-specific trigram LMs combined with linear interpolation.

Finally, the resulting model is pruned using relative entropy-based pruning in order to use it in the real-time application in domain-specific task of Slovak LVCSR [13].

3.3   User Interface

The text output of the recognizer is sent to a text post-processing module. Some of the post-processing functions are configurable though the user interface. After launching the program, the models are loaded and the text editor (Microsoft Word) is opened. The dictation program is represented by a tiny window with **start/stop, launch Word, microphone sensibility,** and **main menu** buttons (see Fig. 3 from APD 0.9 version of the system). There is also a sound level meter placed in line with the buttons.

The main menu contains **user profiles**, audio setup, program settings, off-line transcription, user dictionary, speed setup, help, and "about the program" submenus. The user profiles submenu gives an opportunity to create a new user profile (in addition to the general "**male**" and "**female**" profiles that are available with the installation). The procedure of creating a new profile consists of an automatic microphone sensitivity setup procedure and reading of 60 sentences for the acoustic

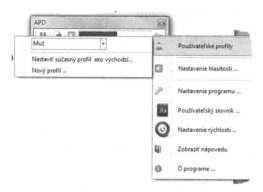

Fig. 3. APD interface screenshot

model adaptation. The new profile keeps information about the new user program and audio settings, user dictionary etc. The **audio setup** submenu opens the audio devices settings from the control panel. The **program settings** submenu makes it possible to:

- create user-defined corrections/substitutions (abbreviations, symbols, foreign words, named entities with capital letters, etc.)
- define voice commands
- insert user defined MS Word files using voice commands.

The **off-line transcription** mode makes it possible to transcribe recorded speech files into text. The **user dictionary** submenu allows the user to add and remove items in the dictionary. The words are inserted in the orthographic form and the pronunciation is generated automatically. The **speed setup** submenu allows the user to choose the best compromise between the speed of recognition and its accuracy. The **help** submenu shows the list of basic commands and some miscellaneous functions of the program.

The dictation program has a **special mode for spelling**. The characters are entered using the Slovak spelling alphabet (a set of words which are used to stand for the letters of an alphabet). The numerals, roman numerals and punctuation symbols can be inserted in this mode as well. This mode uses its own acoustic and language models. Large amount (approx. 60 k words) of Slovak proper nouns is covered by the general language model, but the user can also switch to a special mode for proper names, that have a special, enriched "name vocabulary" (approx. 140 k words) and a special language model.

4   Evaluation

We evaluated core speech recognizers of the APD systems, and the overall performance of dictation in the judicial domain.

4.1   Comparison of Core ASR Systems

The design of the system allowed us to use more speech recognition engines. The first one, the in-house speech recognition system, has been derived from the Juicer ASR system. All HTK dependencies were removed and considerable speed enhancing improvements were implemented, such as fast loading of acoustic models, and fast model (HMM state) likelihood calculation.

We implemented the highly optimized WFST library for transducer composition, which allowed us to build huge transducers considerably faster (WFST composition was 4 times faster) than with the standard AT&T FSM library. See [16, 17] for more details.

The second one, the Julius speech recognition system was used as the reference ASR system.

The comparison was performed on Parliament task (using the training set of utterances from Parliament database, and the 3 hours testing set not included in the training set.).

We can also view this comparison in light of the comparison between a conventional ASR system (Julius) and a WFST based ASR system. The dictionary used in the experiment contained about 100 k words. Table 3 shows the results.

Table 3. ASR core systems comparison

Decoder	Task	n-gram	WER [%]
Julius	Parliament 100 k	3	17.5
In-house	Parliament 100 k	3	17.2
In-house	Parliament 100 k alt. silences (sp)	3	16.4
In-house	Parliament 100 k	4	17.2

We see from the comparison that the performance of WFST-based (in-house) decoder is very similar to the conventional sophisticated decoder (Julius, forward search with bigram LM and backward speech with reversed trigram LM). We were able to achieve a performance gain with easy manipulation of the search network – WFST. Adding alternatives to every silence in the graph, null transition and sil transition to every sp transition, we observed significant improvement.

However, this improvement was accompanied by bigger transducers. Building such a transducer was a tractable problem for this smaller vocabulary (100 k words), however for real tasks with 433 k words we had in the APD system, the building and the use of such huge transducers was not possible.

4.2   Performance of the APD System

The testing set of 3.5 hours consists of recordings taken from APD2 database. It was not included in the training set. Table 4 shows the results.

Two gender profiles are available within the APD system. Each profile used gender dependent acoustic models, and Table 4 presents the results of male models.

Table 4. Evaluation of the APD dictation system

Acoustic model	WER [%]
APD1 + APD2	7.72
APD2 + Parliament	5.83
APD1 + APD2 + Parliament	5.26
Male APD1 + APD2 + Parliament	5.38
Male MPE APD1 + APD2 + Parliament	5.35

The testing set contained around 2 hours of male recordings, the subset of full testing set.

Discriminative modeling was also used. Both MMI and MPE models were trained. While on the Parliament task more than 10 % relative improvement was observed, on the APD task we got only slight improvement.

5 Conclusions

We presented the design and development of the first Slovak dictation system for the judicial domain. Using in-domain speech data (the APD speech database) and text data, good performance has been achieved.

Last year the APD system has been installed and used by 1200 persons (judges, court clerks, assistants and technicians) at different institutions belonging to the Ministry of Justice. During this period the activation module of the system registered 700 automatic preinstalled version (using special image on new computers for this purpose), 410 email activations using court IT specialist installation and 94 telephone activations by judges or other court end-users. There was a telephone and email help desk provided by the development team and a web questionnaire for end-users realized inspired by [18]. The results of the field tests are analyzed and the results will be published soon.

We can conclude that the first version of APD is already used at the organizations belonging to the Ministry of Justice of the Slovak Republic. For dissemination of the APD system a product leaflet was distributed to the courts, the end-user and IT specialist training was prepared and finally an internal circular letter from the Ministry of Justice to the courts was sent to inform the end-users about the possibility to speed up the court proceedings.

Further we plan to extend the APD system with automatic speech transcription used directly in the court rooms, and later with speech transcription of whole actions in court, similarly as described in Polish and Italian speech transcription systems for judicial domain [1]. The system will be designed to cope with factors such as distant talk microphones, cross channel effects and overlapped speech.

Acknowledgements. The research of Technical university of Kosice team presented in this paper was supported by the Ministry of Education, Science, Research and Sport of the Slovak Republic under research project VEGA 1/0386/12 (20 %) and Research and Development

Operational Program funded by the ERDF under the projects ITMS-26220220141 (40 %) & ITMS-26220220155 (40 %). The research of Slovak Academy of Sciences team presented in this paper was supported by the Ministry of Education, Science, Research and Sport of the Slovak Republic under research project VEGA 2/0202/11 (100 %).

References

1. Lööf, J., Falavigna, D., Schlüter, R., Giuliani, D., Gretter, R., Ney, H.: Evaluation of automatic transcription systems for the judicial domain. In: Proceedings of the IEEE Workshop on Spoken Language Technology, San Francisco, CA, USA, pp. 194–199 (2010)
2. Darjaa, S., Cerňak, M., Beňuš, Š., Rusko, M., Sabo, R., Trnka, M.: Rule-based triphone mapping for acoustic modeling in automatic speech recognition. In: Habernal, I., Matoušek, V. (eds.) TSD 2011. LNCS (LNAI), vol. 6836, pp. 268–275. Springer, Heidelberg (2011)
3. Barras, C., Geoffrois, E., Wu, Z., Liberman, M.: Transcriber: development and use of a tool for assisting speech corpora production. Speech Commun. Speech Annot. Corpus Tools 33(1–2), 5–22 (2001)
4. Moore, D., Dines, J., Doss, M.M., Vepa, J., Cheng, O., Hain, T.: Juicer: a weighted finite-state transducer speech decoder. In: Renals, S., Bengio, S., Fiscus, J.G. (eds.) MLMI 2006. LNCS, vol. 4299, pp. 285–296. Springer, Heidelberg (2006)
5. Lee, A., Kawahara, T., Shikano, K.: Julius – an open source real-time large vocabulary recognition engine. In: Proceedings of EUROSPEECH 2001, Aalborg, Denmark, pp. 1691–1694 (2001)
6. Lee, A., Kawahara, T.: Recent development of open-source speech recognition engine julius. In: Proceedings of the 2009 Asia-Pacific Signal and Information Processing Association, Annual Summit and Conference, APSIPA ASC 2009, Sapporo, Japan, pp. 131–137 (2009)
7. Darjaa, S., Cerňak, M., Trnka, M., Rusko, M., Sabo, R.: Effective triphone mapping for acoustic modeling in speech recognition. In: Proceedings of INTERSPEECH 2011, Florence, Italy, pp. 1717–1720 (2011)
8. Papco, M., Juhár, J.: Comparison of acoustic model adaptation methods and adaptation database selection approaches. J. Electr. Electron. Eng. 3(1), 147–150 (2010). ISSN: 1844-6035
9. Jokisch, O., Wagner, A., Sabo, R., Jackel, R., Cylwik, N., Rusko, M., Ronzhin, A., Hoffman, R.: Multilingual speech data collection for the assessment of pronunciation and prosody in a language learning system. In: Proceedings of the 13th International Conference Speech and Computer, SPECOM 2009, St. Petersburg, Russia, pp. 515–520 (2009)
10. Leggetter, C.J., Woodland, P.C.: Maximum likelihood linear regression for speaker adaptation of continuous density hidden Markov models. Comput. Speech Lang. 9(2), 171–186 (1995)
11. Papco, M., Juhár, J.: MLLR adaptation of speaker independent acoustic model to a new speaker in LVCSR. In: Proceedings of the 7th International Workshop on Digital Technologies, DT 2010, Žilina, Slovakia, pp. 1–4 (2010)
12. Hládek, D., Staš, J.: Text Mining and Processing for Corpora Creation in Slovak Language. J. Comput. Sci. Control Syst. 3(1), 65–68 (2010)

13. Juhár, J., Staš, J., Hládek, D.: Recent progress in development of language model for Slovak large vocabulary continuous speech recognition. In: New Technologies: Trends, Innovations and Research, InTech, Rijeka, Croatia, pp. 261–276 (2012)
14. Staš, J., Hládek, D., Juhár, J.: Morphologically motivated language modeling for Slovak continuous speech recognition. J. Electr. Electron. Eng. **5**(1), 233–236 (2012)
15. Stolcke, A.: SRILM – an extensible language modeling toolkit. In: Proceedings of ICSLP 2002, Denver, Colorado, USA, pp. 901–904 (2002)
16. Lojka, M., Juhár, J.: Fast construction of speech recognition network for Slovak language. J. Electr. Electron. Eng. **3**(1), 111–114 (2010)
17. Juhár, J., Lojka, M.: Fast construction of static speech recognition network with low memory requirement. In: Proceedings of the International Conference on Applied Electrical Engineering and Informatics, AEI 2011, Venice, Italy, pp. 163–166 (2011)
18. Alapetite, A., Boje Andersen, H., Hertzum, M.: Acceptance of speech recognition by physicians: a survey of expectations, experiences, and social influence. Int. J. Hum Comput Stud. **67**(1), 36–49 (2009)

The Intonation of Backchannel Tokens in Italian Collaborative Dialogues

Michelina Savino[(⊠)]

Department of Education, Psychology, Communication,
University of Bari, Bari, Italy
michelina.savino@uniba.it

Abstract. This paper offers a contribution to the intonational modelling of backchannel lexical and non-lexical tokens in Italian, which can be used for improving naturalness in voice-based dialogue systems. Results of pragmatic and intonation analysis of five Map Task dialogues show that backchannel tokens can convey the intention of giving vs taking the floor by means of a rising vs falling terminal contour. However, they also indicate that this general rule can be override when other pragmatic and/or paralinguistic meanings need to be additionally conveyed.

Keywords: Backchannels · Acknowledgement tokens · Intonation · Map Task dialogues · Conversational moves · Turn-taking

1 Introduction

One of the still persisting challenges in man-machine interaction is the possibility of developing voice-based dialogue systems which can really help reproducing the naturalness of interaction between human beings. An important aspect of human speech communication whose modelling and implementation could strongly contribute to improve naturalness is represented by the use of backchannel or acknowledgement tokens (for example, Cathcart et al. 2003; Gravano and Hirschberg 2009; Misu et al. 2011). They include lexical and non-lexical tokens (like 'yes', 'yeah', 'mm', 'uh uh', and so on) which can be generally used for signalling that the listener is attending to the speaker and prompting her/him to go on, even though the range of their possible paralinguistic meanings and pragmatic functions can be wider (understanding, agreement, appreciation, assessment, passive recipiency, incipient speakership, etc. as mainly described in Conversation Analysis works, see for example Schegloff 1982; Jefferson 1983), also depending on communicative contexts. Since most of backchannels are non-lexical tokens, a crucial role in signalling those functions is played by intonation on its own, where intonational features can be obviously language-dependent. In this respect, a number of studies have been devoted to the description of the main prosodic characteristics of acknowledgement tokens in a number of languages (see for example Caspers 2000 for Dutch, Jurafsky et al. 1998, Ward 2004, Benus et al. 2007 for American English, Ward 1998 for Japanese), for linguistic-theoretical description aims as well as for modelling purposes in man-machine interaction. As far as Italian is concerned, one previous study has been

© Springer International Publishing Switzerland 2014
Z. Vetulani and J. Mariani (Eds.): LTC 2011, LNAI 8387, pp. 28–39, 2014.
DOI: 10.1007/978-3-319-08958-4_3

attested, which consists of a preliminary investigation on duration and tonal features of a wide range of short expressions including backchannels (Cerrato and D'Imperio 2003). In all these studies, analysis was carried out on task-oriented dialogues.

Aim of this paper is to provide a further contribution for determining the role of intonation in Italian backchannels, whose modelling can be useful for improving naturalness in Italian voice-based dialogue systems. Analysis is based on task-oriented dialogues, making results comparable with those obtained for other languages. Also, in eliciting data some parameters for controlling and enhancing backchanneling have been used, and a more "context-based" approach in interpreting backchannel functions has been adopted. Moreover, in classifying backchannels tokens with respect to the turn-taking dynamics, a "non-intonation based" operational definition is proposed, which avoids circularity in the pragmatic interpretation of such tokens as implying taking vs yielding the turn during interaction.

2 Materials and Methodology

2.1 Corpus

Spoken materials analysed consist of five Bari Italian dialogues elicited with a modified version of the Map Task method (Anderson et al. 1991), each having an average duration of 10–20 min, corresponding to the spoken productions of ten speakers. In a Map Task session, pairs of participants – an Instruction Giver (henceforth IG), and an Instruction Follower (henceforth IF) – is given a map. One of the two maps has a route drawn on it, and the task consists in reproducing as accurately as possible the route on the other map by exchanging information via the verbal channel. The task is complicated by the fact that the two maps are not identical in terms of presence and position of the landmarks, thus stimulating possible misunderstanding like in natural, everyday interaction. Differently from the original Map Task methodology, in Bari Italian sessions participants were not informed in advance that the two maps were different; neither they were told that the maps were identical, even though this is was they assumed (Grice and Savino 2003). In other words, before starting the task participants assumed they initially shared the same background knowledge (how this aspect has an influence on backchannel intonation will be discussed in Sect. 3.2).

In each recording session, eye contact was always inhibited, in order to maximise the use of the verbal channel during communication, including the production of verbal backchannels. In Map Task sessions, lack of eye contact stimulates the production of verbal backchannels in order to provide dialogue partners with increased verbal feedback (Boyle et al. 1994), presumably as a compensation for the missed non-verbal feedback normally conveyed by body gestures and gaze. Because of the impossibility of seeing each other, participants need to use more verbal feedback also for regulating turn-taking as much efficiently as possible. Besides the possibility of controlling these kinds of parameters during interaction, collaborative dialogues like Map Tasks are particularly suitable for studying and modelling intonation of backchannels for human-machine interaction (especially for voice-based dialogue systems). In fact, in such interactional contexts the successfulness of information transferring is crucial for accomplish the assigned task, where the role of verbal feedback and turn-taking regulation is fundamental in making such an information exchange effective.

2.2 Pragmatic and Intonation Analysis

As a first step, a pragmatic analysis of the dialogues based on both orthographic transcripts and audio files listening was carried out. Such analysis consists of pragmatic annotation of utterances in terms of conversational moves, according to the Map Task coding scheme (Carletta et al. 1997). This scheme provides a broad category for describing backchannel phenomena, namely the ACKNOWLEDGE conversational move, defined as "[...] a verbal response that minimally shows that the speaker has heard the move to which it responds, and often demonstrates that the move was understood and accepted" (Carletta et al. 1997, p. 19).

Since we were interested in determining possibly specific intonational cues used in backchannels for regulating turn-taking during interaction, in the pragmatic analysis we included a further distinction (introduced by Jefferson 1983 and used later by Jurafsky et al. 1998) between:

- ACKNOWLEDGE tokens reflecting Passive Recipiency (henceforth PR), also called continuers, acknowledging that the other speaker still has the turn;
- ACKNOWLEDGE tokens reflecting Incipient Speakership (henceforth IS), indicating the intention of taking the floor, reflecting "[...] preparedness to shift from recipiency to speakership" (Jefferson 1983, p. 4).

Decision on whether an ACKNOWLEDGE token could be classified as an example of PR or IS was based on whether a change of speaker occurred after that token or not. Following Cathcart et al. (2003), we identified Transition Relevance Places (henceforth TRPs, defined as points for potential turn switching between conversational partners, Sacks et al. 1974) at move boundaries. When a change of speaker was observed after the ACKNOWLEDGE token/move, that token was categorised as an ACKNOWLEDGE_PR, like in the following excerpt:

IG: vai verso destra
    ('go rightwards')
    INSTRUCT
IF: sì
    ('yes')
    ACKNOWLEDGE_PR
IG: poi risali
    ('then go up again')
    INSTRUCT

When after an ACKNOWLEDGE token/move the same speaker went on speaking (i.e., no change of speaker was involved after backchanneling), that token was labelled as an ACKNOWLEDGE_IS, like in the following excerpt (bars indicate move boundaries within the same turn):

IG: devi passare sempre alla sinistra del bar
   ('you have to go through the left side of the bar')
   INSTRUCT
IF: sì || ma il bar io me lo lascio sulla sinistra?
   ('yes' || ' but the bar, shall I leave it from the left side?')
   ACKNOWLEDGE_IS || QUERY_YN
IG: sì sì sì
   ('yes yes yes')
   REPLY_YN

This operational criterion was adopted in order to avoid circularity in the pragmatic interpretation of backchannels in turn-taking, i.e. using intonation contour for classifying these tokens as reflecting PR or IS when the scope of the study is *deriving* their intonational characterisation with respect to PR and IS.

Items selected for intonation analysis are all lexical and non-lexical (monosyllabic and bisyllabic) tokens used in ACKNOWLEDGE moves, such as 'sì' (yes), 'mm', 'okay' (this English token is normally used as such by Italian speakers), 'eh', 'aha', etc., for a total amount of 463 tokens. All tokens have been intonationally analysed in terms of overall F0 shapes (fall, rise, fall-rise, etc.), basing on both perceptual judgement and F0 inspection. Pragmatic and intonation annotations have been carried out by two independent labellers (inter-labellers' agreement score > 89 %) using the Praat software tool for speech analysis (Boersma and Weenink 2001). Results discussed in this paper refer to the mostly occurring acknowledgement tokens in our Bari Italian dialogues, namely 'sì', 'mm', 'okay', 'eh' (342 tokens).

Note that these tokens are also found in the dialogues as positive replies (REPLY_Y conversational moves) to yes-no questions (QUERY_YN, CHECK and ALIGN conversational moves). An intonational characterisation of these tokens in relation to the two different pragmatic functions (acknowledgements vs positive replies) is described in Savino (2010), and preliminary results on prosodic features useful for their pragmatic disambiguation are provided in Savino and Refice (2013).

3 Results and Discussion

3.1 Backchannels and Turn-Taking

In modelling backchannels and their relation to turn-taking, it could also be useful to determine whether token type choice might be a parameter involved in such a dynamics, as suggested by Conversational Analysis (for example, Jefferson 1983). Figure 1 shows the distribution (in percentage) of the four main token types ('sì', 'mm', 'okay', 'eh') with respect to PR vs IS conveyed in backchanneling. To the extent of the statistical significance of our data, results show that in our dialogues Italian tokens 'sì' and 'mm' are mostly used for reflecting PR in backchanneling (i.e.

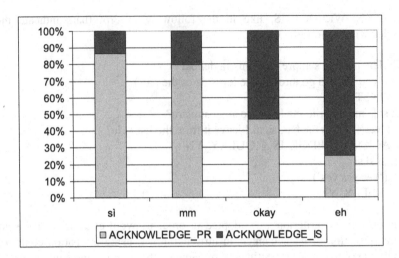

Fig. 1. Distribution of the four main token types across the two ACKNOWLEDGE modalities, i.e. ACKNOWLEDGE_PR (Passive Recipiency; current speaker does not take the turn after acknowledging) and ACKNOWLEDGE_IS (Incipient Speakership, current speaker takes the floor after acknowledging).

when speakers do not take the turn afterwards), token 'eh' is mostly correlated with IS (i.e. when speakers do take the floor after backchanneling), whereas 'okay' seems to be almost equally used in both cases. These results suggest for Italian a possibly different preference in ACKNOWLEDGE token choice in relationship to PR vs IS in comparison to English. According to Jefferson (1983), in fact, in English 'mm' is mostly used with PR, whereas 'yes'/'yeah' is mainly associated with IS. Even though more statistical data is needed to confirm this preliminary outcome, it nevertheless indicates that token choice is an important language-specific and cultural parameter to take into account when modelling backchannels, especially for human-machine interaction.

As to the intonation analysis, Fig. 2 shows the overall distribution (in percentage) of intonation contours with rising vs falling terminal contour across the two main token types, i.e. those implying PR (ACKNOWLEDGE_PR) and those reflecting IS (ACKNOWLEDGE_IS). It can be observed that tokens involving taking the floor after backchanneling are predominantly characterised by a falling terminal contour, whereas the F0 shape of tokens implying not taking the turn after backchanneling mostly ends with a rise. These results suggest a specific role of intonation in signalling turn-taking during backchanneling.

3.2   Passive Recipiency and Pragmatic Context

Results presented in Sect. 3.1 above are also compatible with the general meaning of "openness, non-conclusiveness, continuity" attributed to rising/high pitch, and the opposite meaning to the falling/low pitch, as enunciated by the frequency code theory

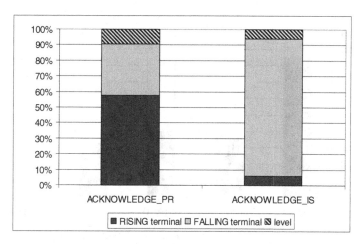

Fig. 2. Distribution of rising vs falling terminal contours across the two ACKNOWLEDGE modalities, i.e. Passive Recipiency (PR) and Incipient Speakership (IS).

(Ohala 1984). On the other hand, rising terminal backchannels functioning as continuers (i.e. involving PR) have been attested also in other languages (see refs. cited in Sect. 1). However, our statistics show that, differently from the clear-cut intonational characterisation of acknowledgement tokens implying IS, that of tokens involving PR shows some variability, since around 30 % of cases have a falling instead of a rising terminal F0 pattern. It can be hypothesised that in Italian backchannel continuers, the intonational choice could be influenced by additional pragmatic meanings "triggered" by specific pragmatic contexts. In order to verify this hypothesis, we identified these interactional pragmatic contexts as the conversational move pairs consisting of the ACKNOWLEDGE_PR token/move produced by the current speaker and the move realised by dialogue partner in his/her immediately preceding turn (when the partner's turn consisted of more than one conversational moves, only the last one was considered for the analysis). Figure 3 shows the distribution of falling vs rising terminals in ACKNOWLEDGE_PR tokens as a function of different interactional contexts, namely whether the dialogue partner's immediately preceding turn realised an INSTRUCT (giving instructions), an EXPLAIN/CLARIFY (giving explanations or clarifications), a REPLY_W (replying to a wh-question), a REPLY_ YN (giving a positive or negative answer to a yes-no question), or an ACKNOWL-EDGE move. It can be noted that the PR tokens with a terminal rise are predominantly concentrated (>80 % of cases) as following INSTRUCT moves, whereas those characterised by a falling terminal contour *always* occur as feedbacks to ACKNOWLEDGE moves, and as backchannel tokens immediately produced after EXPLAIN/CLARIFY, REPLY_W, and REPLY_YN moves in the majority of cases.

We also looked at the possible correlation between the terminal contour type of ACKNOWLEDGE_PR tokens and that of the above mentioned dialogue partners' immediately preceding moves. Such a distribution is given in Table 1, where it can be observed that PR backchannel tokens ending with a rising F0 contour are

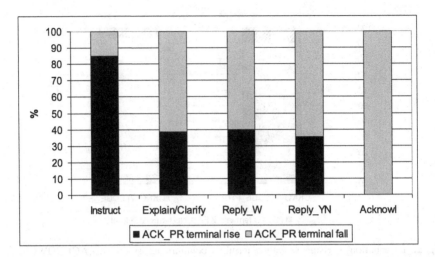

Fig. 3. Distribution of rising vs falling terminal contours in ACKNOWLEDGE_PR tokens as a function of the dialogue partner's conversational move realised in his/her turn immediately preceding the ACKNOWLEDGE_PR token.

Table 1. Distribution of rising vs falling terminal contours in ACKNOWLEDGE_PR tokens as a function of the dialogue partner's conversational move and relating terminal contour type realised in his/her turn immediately preceding the ACKNOWLEDGE_PR token.

Preceded by➔	INSTRUCT terminal rise (%)	INSTRUCT terminal fall (%)	EXPLAIN/REPLY/ ACKNOWLEDGE terminal rise (%)	EXPLAIN/REPLY/ ACKNOWLEDGE terminal fall (%)
ACKNOWLEDGE_PR terminal rise	90	0	1	9
ACKNOWLEDGE_PR terminal fall	0	37	0	63

predominantly preceded by partners' conversational moves marked by a rising terminal as well. On the other hand, PR tokens with terminal falls function mostly as feedback to dialogue partners' immediately preceding moves being also characterised by a terminal fall. These results indicate that the typical use of a rising terminal contour in backchannels with PR can be conditioned by additional pragmatic and communicative meanings to be conveyed beyond that of turn-taking disposition.

3.3   Backchannels, Common Ground and Speaker Attitude

Outcomes discussed so far on ACKNOWLEDGE_PR tokens have been focussed on the distribution of contour types as grouped into two overall categories: F0 contours ending with either a rise or a fall. In order to shed more light on the range of possible additional meanings which can be conveyed by intonation in these backchannels, an overview of specific intonation patterns encountered in the dialogues are presented and discussed. As shown in Fig. 4, for the F0 terminal rising backchannels a wide range of contours is available: rise, fall-rise, stylised rise, and high rise (note that in the figure, rise and high rise are collapsed in one category). In the dialogues, it has been observed that rise, fall-rise and stylised-rise contours are normally found in tokens signalling understanding/agreement about information (typically, instructions) being received by the dialogue partner, i.e. in backchannels following INSTRUCT moves as described in Sect. 3.2.

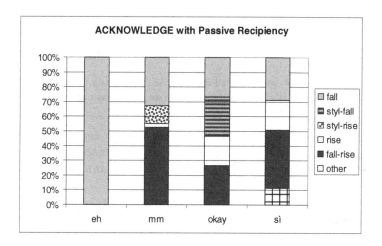

Fig. 4. Distribution of intonation contour types across the four token types as realised in ACKNOWLEDGE_PR moves.

The rising contour seems to be the "default" F0 shape for ACKNOWLEDGE_PR tokens. An example of token 'sì' with a rising contour is shown in Fig. 6(a). It has also been observed that the fall-rise and the stylised rise are used by dialogue participants when transferred information – typically via instructions about presence and/or position of landmarks – are fully compatible with features on her/his own map. In other words, they are used for confirming the current status of common background knowledge (common ground, see for example Clark and Schaefer 1989; Clark and Brennan 1991), and for conveying a consequently positive speaker's attitude. In particular, the stylised rise is only found in 'mm' tokens, and in this case they are produced as bisyllabic, as also observed in English backchannels (Ward 2004). The stylised rise is realised as a pitch step-up from the first to the second syllable, where the pitch excursion is not wide. An example of a 'mm' token with stylised rise is shown in Fig. 5(b), whereas Fig. 5(a) offers an example of 'mm' with fall-rise (in this case the token is realised as bimoraic).

A number of backchannels with a high rising pitch contour were also encountered, typically produced by IFs at/around the end of a set of instructions for completing a (sub)task. This contour type has been already described in Bari Italian for signalling pre-finality, i.e. marking the antepenultimate item in a sequence (Savino 2001, 2004).

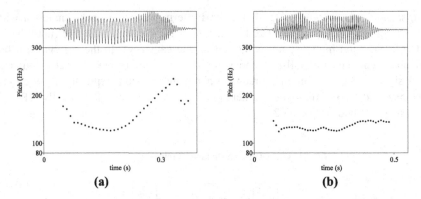

Fig. 5. ACKNOWLEDGE_PR 'mm' realised as a fall-rise (a), and as a stylised rise (b). Note that in the first case the token is realised as bimoraic, in the second as bisyllabic.

This suggests that in ACKNOWLEDGE_PR tokens, this contour conveys speaker's understanding/agreement that the end of a (sub)set of instructions for completing a (sub)task is approaching. An example of such a contour is shown in Fig. 6(b).

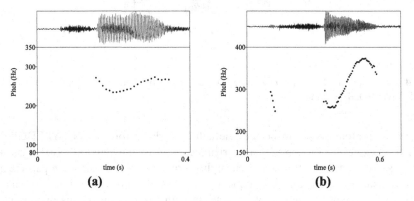

Fig. 6. ACKNOWLEDGE_PR 'sì' realised with a rise (a), and with a high rise (b). Note that in the latter case it signals that the end of a (sub)task is approaching

As to the ACKNOWLEDGE_PR tokens realised with a falling terminal, intonation analysis reports cases of fall and stylised fall melodic shapes (Fig. 4). By looking at the dialogue contexts where a falling rather than the typical rising terminal contour is encountered, we observed that fall and stylised fall F0 patterns are usually found where participants have not discovered yet that the two maps are different. Such contours are typically produced in backchannels by IFs when receiving instructions for drawing the route which are not compatible with presence and/or position of landmarks on her/his own map. Even though the use of backchannels generally implies signalling understanding and agreement, in these cases a falling contour seems to convey disagreement or disappointment about what is assumed to be the currently shared background knowledge. Therefore, a falling contour seems to signal a *negative* backchanneling, as there is a mismatch between participants' assumed common background knowledge at that moment of the interaction.

Some cases of fall and stylised fall in acknowledgement tokens with RP are also found at the last turn(s) of the dialogue. Because of their position within the dialogue, and the melodic shape typically associated the meaning of "finality, conclusiveness", these backchannels can be interpreted as signalling understanding/agreement that the task has been completed. Some other cases of such falling contours are typically found in tokens acknowledging interlocutor's preceding acknowledgment, as already shown in Sect. 3.2 above. This outcome is particularly interesting, as the occurrence of this pragmatic type of backchannels contrasts with the formal definition of these token types proposed by Ward and Tsukahara (2000). According to these authors, back-channels do not require acknowledgement by the other speaker, yet our results show that this is possible, demonstrating that backchannel strategies can largely vary, depending on individual, cultural and above all communicative context variables. Examples of a 'mm' token realised with a fall (a) and 'okay' with a stylised fall (b) are shown in Fig. 7. Note that the stylised falls are intonationally realised as an F0 step-down from the first to the second syllable, with a relatively reduced pitch excursion.

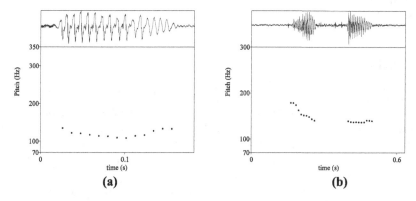

Fig. 7. ACKNOWLEDGE_PR 'mm' realised with a falling contour (a), and 'okay' with a stylised fall (b). The former is observed when the speaker finds out a mismatch in assumed shared background knowledge, the latter at the end of the whole task.

Finally, the distribution of intonation contours across the four main ACKNOWLEDGE_PR tokens (Fig. 4) shows that the token 'eh' is always realised with a falling F0 pattern. In this case, there is a specific choice not only in terms of melodic shape, but also in terms of token type for cueing information status, speaker's attitude and discourse structure while acknowledging understanding, as described above for falling terminal backchannels.

The intonational choices of ACKNOWLEDGE_PR tokens in relation to the pragmatic functions and attitudinal meanings discussed above are schematised in Table 2.

Table 2. Intonation contours and their association with pragmatic functions/paralinguistic meanings in ACKNOWLEDGE_PR tokens as observed in Bari Italian Map Task dialogues (BK = Background Knowledge).

Pragmatics	rise	high rise	fall-rise	styl-rise	fall	styl-fall
Acknowledges understanding/agreement on received info ("default")	x					
Confirms current status of assumed common BK			x	x		
Signals end of instructions set for completing a (sub)task is approaching		x				
Signals disagreement or disappointment on assumed currently shared BK					x	
Acknowledges dialogue partner's previous acknowledgement					x	x
Signals end of (set of instructions for completing) the (sub)task					x	x

4 Conclusions

Results from pragmatic and intonation analysis of Bari Italian Map Task dialogues have provided a number of intonational features for modelling backchannel or acknowledgement tokens which can be useful for improving naturalness in speech dialogue systems for Italian. They have shown that when speakers do not take the floor after backchanneling, they produced acknowledgement tokens predominantly characterised by a rising terminal intonation pattern. On the other hand, when speakers take the turn right after backchanneling, their acknowledgement tokens have a falling terminal instead. Therefore, in Italian the intention of taking the floor or not while backchanneling seems to be conveyed intonationally by a falling vs rising terminal F0 contour. However, analysis also suggests that the general "rule" of a terminal rising for signalling the intention of yielding the floor might not be applied when additional co-occurring pragmatic and/or paralinguistic meanings need to be conveyed, like for example the status of participants' assumed shared background information at that time of interaction, or the current stage of interaction with respect to the end, i.e. the accomplishment of the task.

References

Anderson, A., Bader, M., Bard, E.G., Boyle, E., Doherty, G., Garrod, S., Isard, S., Kowtko, J., MacAllister, J., Miller, J., Sotillo, C., Thompson, H., Weinert, R.: The HCRC map task corpus. Lang. Speech **34**(4), 351–366 (1991)

Benus, S., Gravano, A., Hirschberg, J.: The prosody of backchannels in American English. In: 16th International Congress of Phonetic Sciences, Saarbruecken, pp. 1065–1068 (2007)

Boersma, P., Weenink, D.: Praat, a system for doing phonetics by computer. Glot Int. **5**(9/10), 341–345 (2001)

Boyle, E., Anderson, A.H., Newlands, A.: The effects of visibility on dialogue and performance in a cooperative problem solving task. Lang. Speech **37**(1), 1–20 (1994)

Carletta, J., Isard, A., Isard, S., Kowtko, J., Doherty-Sneddon, G., Anderson, A.: The reliability of a dialogue structure coding scheme. Comput. Linguist. **23**(1), 13–32 (1997)

Caspers, J.: Melodic characteristics of backchannels in Dutch Map Task dialogues. In: International Conference of Spoken Language Processing 2000, Bejing (2000)

Cathcart, N., Carletta, J., Klein, E.: A shallow model of backchannel continuers in spoken dialogue. In: 10th Conference of the European Chapter of the ACL, vol. 1, pp. 51–58 (2003)

Cerrato, L, D'Imperio, M.: Duration and tonal characteristics of short expressions in Italian. In: 15th International Congress of Phonetic Sciences, pp. 1213–1216 (2003)

Clark, H.H., Brennan, S.E.: Grounding in communication. In: Resnick, L.B., Levine, J., Tearsely, S.D. (eds.) Perspectives on Socially Shared Cognition, pp. 127–149. American Psychological Association, Washington (1991)

Clark, H.H., Shaefer, E.F.: Contributing to discourse. Cog. Sci. **13**, 259–294 (1989)

Gravano, A., Hirschberg, J.: Backchannel-inviting cues in task-oriented dialogue. In: Interspeech 2009, pp. 1019–1022 (2009)

Grice, M., Savino, M.: Map tasks in Italian: asking questions about given, accessible and new information. Catalan J. Linguist. **2**, 153–180 (2003)

Jefferson, G.: Notes on systematic deployment of the acknowledgment tokens "yeah" and "mm hm". TILL, Tilburg University, The Netherlands (1983)

Jurafsky, D., Shriberg E., Fox, B., Curl, T.: Lexical, prosodic, and syntactic cues for dialogue acts. In: ACL/COLING Workshop on Discourse Relations and Discourse Markers, pp. 114–120 (1998)

Misu, T., Mizukami, E., Shiga, Y., Kawamoto, S., Kawai, H., Nakamura, S. (2011). Towards contruction of spoken dialogue system that evokes users' spontaneous backchannels. In: SIGDIAL 2011, Portland, pp. 259–265

Ohala, J.: An ethological perspective on common cross-language utilization of F0 of voice. Phonetica **41**, 1–16 (1984)

Sacks, H., Schegloff, E.A., Jefferson, G.: A simplest systematics for the organization of turn-taking for conversation. Language **50**(4), 696–735 (1974)

Savino, M.: Non-finality and pre-finality in Bari Italian intonation: a preliminary account. In: Eurospeech 2001, Aalborg, pp. 939–942 (2001)

Savino, M.: Intonational cues to discourse structure in a variety of Italian. In: Gilles, P., Peters, J. (eds.) Regional Variation in Intonation, pp. 145–159. Niemeyer, Tübingen (2004)

Savino, M.: Prosodic strategies for backchanneling in Italian Map Task dialogues. In: ISCA Tutorial and Research Workshop on Experimental Linguistics, Athens, pp. 157–160 (2010)

Savino, M., Refice, M.: Acknowledgement or reply? Prosodic features for disambiguating pragmatic functions of the Italian token 'sì'. In: SpeD 2013, Cluj-Napoca, pp.117–122 (2013)

Schegloff, E.: Discourse as an interactional achievement: some uses of 'hu huh' and other things that come between sentences. In: Tannen, D. (ed.) Analyzing Discourse: Text and Talk, pp. 71–93. Georgetown University Press, Washington DC (1982)

Ward, N.: The relationship between sound and meaning in Japanese backchannels grunts. In: Meeting of the Japanese Association for National Language Processing, Fukuoka, pp. 464–467 (1998)

Ward, N.: Pragmatic function of prosodic features in non-lexical utterances. In: Speech Prosody 2004, Nara, (on CD-ROM) (2004)

Ward, N., Tsukahara, W.: Prosodic features which cue back-channel responses in English and Japanese. J. Pragmat. **32**, 1177–1207 (2000)

Parsing

Improved Parsing for Arabic by Combining Diverse Dependency Parsers

Maytham Alabbas[1] and Allan Ramsay[2](✉)

[1] Department of Computer Science, College of Science,
Basrah University, Basrah, Iraq
`maytham.alabbas@gmail.com`
[2] School of Computer Science,
University of Manchester, Manchester, M13 9PL, UK
`ramsay@cs.man.ac.uk`

Abstract. Recently there has been a considerable interest in dependency parsing for many reasons. First, it works accurately for a wide range of typologically different languages. Second, it can be useful for semantics, since it can be easier to attach compositional rules directly to lexical items than to assign them to large numbers of phrase structure rules. Third, robust machine-learning based parsers are available. In this paper, we investigate two techniques for combining multiple data-driven dependency parsers for parsing Arabic, where we are faced with an exceptional level of lexical and structural ambiguity. Experimental results show that combined parsers can produce more accurate results, even for imperfectly tagged text, than each parser produces by itself for texts with the gold-standard tags.

Keywords: Dependency parsing · MSTParser · MALTParser · System combination

1 Introduction

One popular way of improving accuracy in natural language processing (NLP) tasks is by system combination. This is concerned with combining different models which perform the same task to exploit the unique advantage of each model and reduce some of the random errors. In this paper, we evaluate different techniques for combining data-driven dependency parsers for Arabic. Dependency parsing has become widely used in machine translation, question answering, relation extraction and many other NLP applications for two main reasons [1]. Firstly, it seems as though dependency parsing is more appropriate for free word order languages (e.g. Arabic and Czech) than approaches based on phrase-structure grammar where non-canonical order is dealt with in terms of 'movement'; secondly the dependency based approach lends itself to development of fast robust reasonably accurate syntactic parsers by exploiting techniques from machine learning.

© Springer International Publishing Switzerland 2014
Z. Vetulani and J. Mariani (Eds.): LTC 2011, LNAI 8387, pp. 43–54, 2014.
DOI: 10.1007/978-3-319-08958-4_4

In general, parsers make mistakes and these mistakes will increase if the input of the parsers is incorrectly tagged. These will lead to extra mistakes in the next step of any NLP system that depends on the output of such a parser. It is thus misleading to evaluate the performance of a parser by testing it on perfectly tagged text, because in any real application the text in question is likely to contain erroneous tags. The current work investigates the effectiveness of combining several data-driven parsers for complex Arabic text (imperfectly tagged and with some sentences 100+ words in length) to exploit the unique advantage of each parser and reduce some of the random mistakes. In these experiments we use the MADA tagger [2], which achieves around 96 % accuracy compared with the Penn Arabic treebank (PATB) corpus (here, we consider the PATB corpus as a gold-standard). MADA is widely regarded as producing state of the art results for Arabic, which is notoriously difficult to tag. The key problem for Arabic is that it is more ambiguous than many other languages (e.g. English) for many reasons. The first reason is that Arabic contains an exceptionally high level of lexical ambiguity. This arises from two sources: (i) Arabic is written with the short vowels, and a number of other phonetically distinctive items, omitted; and (ii) at the same time, it has very productive derivational morphology, which means that for any root there will be a number of derived forms which differ only in their short vowels; and it has complex non-concatenative inflectional morphology, which means that there are forms of the same lexeme which differ in a variety of ways. The second point here means that the omission of short vowels is much more problematic than is the case in, for instance, English, where text-messages also omits short vowels. The English sentence *'she snt me a txt msg'* is easy to interpret, despite the lack of vowels in the open-class words, because there are very few, if any, other words in English that would produce the same forms. The situation in Arabic is very different, with a single written form corresponding to 10 or more different lexemes.

It should be noted that it is the combination of lack of diacritics and productive derivational and inflectional morphology that leads to the problem. The lack of diacritics is not, by itself, an insurmountable problem.

In addition, Arabic is highly syntactically flexible [3]. It has a comparatively free word order, where sentence components can be reordered without affecting the core meaning (non-canonical word orders are usually employed to change the focus of a sentence without changing its propositional content), e.g. besides the regular sentence of verb-subject-object (VSO), Arabic allows other potential surface forms such as SVO and VOS constructions. The potential of allowing such non-canonical orders leads to considerable ambiguity.

Furthermore, Arabic is a pro-drop language. It is similar to some other languages, such as Spanish, Italian and Japanese, where subject pronouns can be omitted [4]. Again, the potential absence of a subject is not unique to Arabic, but it is worse here than in a number of other languages because Arabic verbs can typically occur either intransitively or transitively (and to complicate matters even further the active and passive forms of a verb are often indistinguishable in the written form). In such cases, it is hard to tell whether a sequence consisting of a verb and a following noun phrase (NP) is actually an intransitive use of the verb, with the NP as subject, or a transitive use with a zero subject, or indeed a passive use.

Finally, Arabic makes use of 'equational sentences', consisting of an NP and a predication (e.g. another NP or a prepositional phrase (PP)). Given that Arabic nouns typically do not carry overt case markers, it is very hard to tell whether two adjacent nouns form a complex NP, with one of the nouns serving as an adjective; or a 'construct NP', where one of them is serving as a possessive determiner; or a verbless sentence. Thus there is considerable scope for ambiguity in the analysis of Arabic sentences. They also tend to be rather long. The typical sentence length is 30–40 words, and sentences whose length exceeds 100 words are not uncommon, and this also poses a problem for traditional parsing algorithms.

Given this wide range of sources of ambiguity, it is unsurprising that parsing algorithms have difficulty with Arabic text. It therefore seemed worth investigating whether we could improve the performance of individually unreliable parsers by combining them. The starting points were MSTParser [5] and the family of parsers provided by MALTParser [6].

2   Data Resources

We used the Penn Arabic treebank (PATB) [7] Part 1 v3.0 as a resource that provides us with annotations of Arabic at different levels of structure (at the word, the phrase and the sentence levels). The PATB is annotated for part-of-speech (POS), morphological disambiguation and for syntactic structure. It also provides diacritisations, empty categories, some semantic tags and lemma choice. The PATB includes 734 stories representing 145,386 words (166,068 tokens after clitic segmentation; the number of Arabic tokens is 123,796). The sentences in the PATB are fairly long–the average sentence length is around 28 words, with some sentences containing 100+ words. This corpus contains about 5000 phrase-structure trees, whereas we want dependency trees. To convert from phrase structure trees to dependency trees we adapted the algorithm described by Xia and Palmer [8]. This algorithm uses the idea of a head percolation table as explained by Collins [9]. Xia and Palmer use the following steps to make the conversion from the phrase structure to dependency format:

1. Depending on the head percolation table, specify the head child of each node in a phrase structure;
2. Make the head of each non-head child depend on the head-child head in the dependency format.

Even the PATB corpus is not guaranteed to be 100 % accurate, since it was obtained by some mixture of automatic and manual tagging, and both of these are liable to error. It is, however, the most accurate corpus available. In the current paper we will concentrate on a coarse-grained tagset. We therefore omit inflectional markers (case, number and gender) from the PATB fine-grained tagset (306 tags) to obtain 40 tags (e.g. the fine-grained tags 'NOUN+CASE_DEF_ACC', 'NOUN+CASE_ DEF_GEN', 'NOUN+CASE_DEF_GEN+POSS_PRON_3MS', 'NOUN+CASE_DEF _NOM' grouped to 'NOUN'). For more details about the conversion technique we used here, see Alabbas and Ramsay [10].

3   Dependency Parsing

Two data-driven dependency parsers are used in our experiments. The key advantages of these parsers are that they are robust and fairly fast. They are not perfectly accurate, but they are reported as achieving the state-of-the-art results. We have chosen the following parsers:

- MALTParser [6], a parser generator for dependency parsing, which can be used to create a parser for any language by giving it a dependency treebank of this language. It is an implementation of inductive dependency parsing [11]. A lot of learning and parsing algorithms are supported by MALTParser. It supports both projective and non-projective parsing.
- MSTParser [5], a dependency parser that searches for maximum spanning trees over directed graphs. Dependency structure models are based on large-margin discriminative training methods. It also supports both projective and non-projective parsing.

Both these parsers induce a parsing model from treebank data and parse new tagged data using the induced model. The details of how these parsers work are described by their authors. What matters here is how use them in combination to improve the accuracy of parsing complex Arabic texts.

4   Combining Parsers

We are interested in evaluating the effects of combining the dependency trees that are output by multiple parsers to produce better dependency tree accuracy for Arabic. We used two techniques to achieve our goal. Firstly, we use a voting technique similar to that suggested by Zeman and Žabokrtský [12] that combines the output of independent parsers by looking at the majority suggestion from the component systems to produce the analysis with the most support. The second technique is a statistical one, which finds the most reliable parser of the correct HEAD and the most reliable parser of the correct DEPREL (dependency relation in CoNLL-X format) for each POS tag. According to the POS tag, we can decide which parser should be trusted for each token in the tree where at least two parsers disagree.

5   Experiments

As we mentioned before, the aim of the current paper is to investigate the evaluation of combining parsers for Arabic where the input is incorrectly tagged[1] and

---

[1] In any real application the tagging will have been carried out by some tagger which is not 100 % reliable. The nature of the tagging errors may affect the performance of the parser, so in order to assess the utility of a parser it should be tested on text which has been tagged by the tagger which will be used in the application, rather than on text with manually assigned or corrected tags.

some sentences are very long. Therefore, to make our experiments more realistic, the PATB corpus is retagged by using the MADA tagger, which achieved around 96 % accuracy compared with the gold-standard. MADA also uses a slightly extended version of the PATB tagset, with some extra classification of nouns. In all experiments we will concentrate on a coarse-grained tagset. We therefore omit inflectional markers (case, number and gender) from the MADA fine-grained tagset (356 tags) to obtain 57 tags. This gives us a version of the corpus, which we will refer to as the MATB corpus, which is imperfectly tagged. It is worth noting that the accuracy of the parsers on MATB is between 98 % and 99 % of their accuracy on the PATB, despite the fact that the tagger is only 96 % accurate: somehow the parsers seem to be able to compensate for the mistakes made by the tagger.

All parsers that are used in the current paper are trainable parsers. In order to establish the baseline performance of each parser and to obtain some feel for how the size of the training set affects their accuracy, we plotted accuracy against size of training set for 16 datasets starting with 250 sentences and incrementing by 250 sentences at each step up to 4000 sentences, testing with a held-out set of 1000 sentences. The average sentence length of the testing set is around 32 words, with some sentences containing 100+ words. For all the experiments described below the *label attachment score* (LA), i.e. the percentage of tokens with correct HEAD and DEPREL, is used.

In our experiments we will use MSTParser and three parsing algorithms for MALTParser: *Nivre arc-eager*, which produces projective dependency graphs (we called it MALTParser$_1$), *Stack eager*, which produces non-projective graphs (MALTParser$_2$) and *Planar eager* (MALTParser$_3$). Figure 1 shows the results when we used the isolated parsers for 16 datasets for training and the same testset (the results for MALTParser$_3$ were very similar to those for MALTParser$_1$ and MALTParser$_2$). The result with 4000 training set provides a highest accuracy for each parser.

Figure 1 shows effect of increasing the size of the training set for the three parsers, with a sharp initial improvement which is beginning to flatten out after 4000 sentences. It seems unlikely that increasing the training sets further will produce an accuracy much above 89 % for any of the parsers, though the curve for MSTParser has not leveled quite as badly as those for the two MALTParsers.

In the remaining experiments in this section, we will concentrate on the LA of the parsers when the training set is 4000 sentences. Therefore, the highest accuracy for each parser is as shown in Table 1 for MATB corpus, with the equivalent accuracy for the PATB corpus given for reference. It is worth noting that the difference the accuracy on MATB is around.

Because of the ambiguity in Arabic, parsing is difficult and the accuracy is lower than for dependency parsing of many languages. It is thus even more important to find ways of making the best possible use of the available resources. In order to see how best to combine the parsers, we used two approaches to the task.

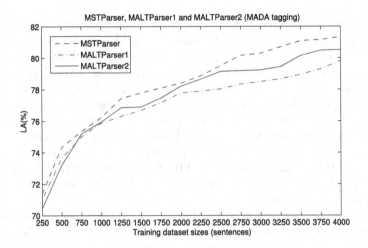

Fig. 1. LA for MSTParser, MALTParser₁ and MALTParser₂, MATB corpus.

Table 1. Highest LA for all parsers for both MATB and PATB corpora.

Parser	LA	
	MATB corpus (%)	PATB corpus (%)
MSTParser	81.3	82.8
MALTParser₁, *Nivre arc-eager*	79.8	81.3
MALTParser₂, *Stack eager*	80.5	81.1
MALTParser₃, *Planar eager*	77.3	78.8

5.1   Backoff Strategies

If you have several parsers and they all propose a particular head:daughter pair, then the only thing you can do is to accept that proposal. The key issue is what to do when they disagree, but before investigating this it is worth looking at what happens when they do agree.

We therefore looked at the precision, recall and F-score for various combinations of parsers on cases where they agreed. Table 2 shows the precision, recall and F-score for the merge of the parsers output where they agree, either pairwise or unanimously.

Unsurprisingly, the precision on the cases where they agree is considerably higher than the accuracy of any one parser in isolation. More importantly, when we combine only two parsers, we find that the combination of MSTParser with either of MALTParser₁ and MALTParser₂ gives better precision *and* higher recall than combining MALTParser₁ and MALTParser₂. This is slightly surprising: MSTParser uses a different approach, and possibly different information, from the MALTParser family, and hence when it agrees with one of the MALT-Parsers it is likely that they have arrived at the same conclusion by different routes, and hence that this conclusion has good supporting evidence. At the

Table 2. Precision, recall and F-score for agreement output for two parsers, PATB corpus.

Parsers	Precision (%)	Recall (%)	F-score
MSTParser+MALTParser$_1$	89.3	72.3	0.80
MSTParser+MALTParser$_2$	89.8	73.2	0.81
MALTParser$_1$+MALTParser$_2$	88.7	71.8	0.79
Three parsers agree	**92.3**	67.2	0.78
At least two parsers agree	89.8	**80.3**	**0.85**

same time, the fact that they use different approaches and information would seem likely to make them less likely to agree, which would tend to reduce the recall.

In general, however, a parser is required to give a complete analysis, so we have to devise a backoff strategy for cases where the parsers do not all agree. We consider two possible front-line strategies–taking the output if all three parsers agree (highest precision in Table 2) and taking the output if any pair agree (highest F-score in Table 2)–and investigate a range of backoff strategies.

These split into two groups: a set of voting strategies, similar to those suggested by Zeman and Žabokrtský [12], and an approach based on identifying which parser is best at dealing with relations involving particular kinds of words. This latter approach has proved very effective for combining POS taggers [4], and it seemed *prima facie* plausible that it would work for parsing as well.

Voting-Based Backoff. In order to improve the accuracy (not just the precision) of parsing, we applied three different voting-based experiments. In the first of these, we take the HEAD from one parser and the DEPREL from a different parser (both of these are prespecified). Table 3 shows the results obtained from applying this approach with different parsers for the two tasks, applied to each of the front-line strategies.

The results of this experiment show that it is better to start with the higher recall/lower precision (majority) front-line approach than with the high precision/low recall (unanimous) starting point. The key here is that it better to get reasonable coverage of a large number of cases before falling back on less reliable methods–relying on unanimity for the first stage leaves nearly a third of cases to be covered by the backoff strategy.

The second technique takes two prespecified parsers and accepts their output where they agree and backs off to the third parser when they do not, e.g. accept the result of MALTParser$_1$ and MALTParser$_2$ if they agree and backoff to MST-Parser if they do not (whether or not the backoff parser agrees with either of the chosen pair). The experimental results of this technique are shown in Table 4.

The results of this experiment are similar to those obtained for majority voting in Table 3, with the combination of MALTParser$_1$ and MALTParser$_2$ as

Table 3. LA using prespecified parsers for HEAD and DEPREL, unanimous and majority voting, MATB corpus.

Backoff to		LA	
HEAD	DEPREL	Backoff unless unanimous (%)	Backoff unless at least two agree (%)
MSTParser	MALTParser$_1$	78.5	**83.5**
MSTParser	MALTParser$_2$	78.7	**83.5**
MALTParser$_1$	MSTParser	77.6	**83.1**
MALTParser$_2$	MSTParser	78.2	**83.1**
MALTParser$_1$	MALTParser$_2$	77.3	**82.9**
MALTParser$_2$	MALTParser$_1$	77.4	**83.1**

Table 4. LA for third technique for combination MSTParser, MALTParser$_1$ and MALTParser$_2$ with majority voting, MATB corpus.

Agree	Backoff to	LA (%)
MSTParser+MALTParser$_1$	MALTParser$_2$	**83.1**
MSTParser+MALTParser$_2$	MALTParser$_1$	**83.0**
MALTParser$_1$+MALTParser$_2$	MSTParser	**83.7**

the front-line and MSTParser as backoff achieving 83.7 %, which is the highest LA for all experiment results in the current paper.

In the next experiments we re-apply majority voting with prespecified backoff to distinct parsers for the HEAD and the DEPREL (column two of Table 3) and the method from Table 4 to three members of the MALTParser family to check if these techniques still give positive results. The results of these experiments are shown in Tables 5 and 4 respectively.

The results of second and third techniques give better results than the highest accuracy for all MALTParsers in isolation for both MATB and PATB corpora (see Table 1), but they are all lower than the parallel experiments involving MSTParser.

Confidence-Based Backoff. In this experiment, we used a technique that depends on using the parser which is known to be most reliable for each POS tag, e.g. using MSTParser for suggesting a relation between a noun and a verb if it is the most reliable parser for relations involving nouns as HEADs. We found the most reliable parser for the correct HEAD and the correct DEPREL of each POS tag in our tagset (57 tags) where each parser agrees with the PATB corpus and then used these confidence levels to decide how much each parser should be trusted for each POS tag. All the experiments below were carried using 5-fold cross-validation over a set of 5000 sentences from the MATB corpus (we trained

Table 5. Majority voting with distinct prespecified backoffs for combinations of MALTParser$_1$, MALTParser$_2$ and MALTParser$_3$, MATB corpus.

Backoff to		LA
HEAD	DEPREL	Backoff unless at least two agree (%)
MALTParser$_1$	MALTParser$_2$	**81.1**
MALTParser$_1$	MALTParser$_3$	**81.1**
MALTParser$_2$	MALTParser$_1$	**81.5**
MALTParser$_2$	MALTParser$_3$	**81.5**
MALTParser$_3$	MALTParser$_1$	**80.9**
MALTParser$_3$	MALTParser$_2$	**80.7**

Table 6. LA for third technique for combination MALTParser$_1$, MALTParser$_2$ and MALTParser$_3$ with majority voting, MATB corpus.

Agree	Backoff to	LA (%)
MALTParser$_1$+MALTParser$_2$	MALTParser$_3$	**80.7**
MALTParser$_1$+MALTParser$_3$	MALTParser$_2$	**81.5**
MALTParser$_2$+MALTParser$_3$	MALTParser$_1$	**81.2**

Table 7. Highest LA for MSTParser, MALTParser$_1$ and MALTParser$_2$ for MATB corpus, average of 5-fold cross-validation.

Parser	LA (%)
MSTParser	80.3
MALTParser$_1$	78.5
MALTParser$_2$	79.2

the parsers on 3000 sentences and used another 1000 sentence to compute POS tags confident level while the testset still the same as previous). The highest LA for MSTParser, MALTParser$_1$ and MALTParser$_2$ is explained in Table 7.

Table 8 shows examples of which parser is most reliable for each POS tag for both HEAD and DEPREL.

As noted above, we find that, for instance, MALTParse$_1$ should be trusted when the POS tag is 'ADJ' or 'NEG_PART' for both the HEAD and the DEPREL, whereas MALTParser$_2$ should be trusted when the POS tag is 'PRON'. On the other hand, if the POS tag is 'CONJ' or 'NOUN_PROP' MSTParser should be trusted for the HEAD only, whereas MALTParser$_2$ should be trusted for the DEPREL. The results of this experiment are shown in Table 9.

This approach does outperform each of the individual parsers, and it also achieves better F-score (which here is equal to accuracy) than the simple

Table 8. Some POS tags with trusted parsers(s) for HEAD and DEPREL, MATB corpus.

POS-tag	HEAD	DEPREL
ADJ, NEG_PART	MALTParser$_1$	MALTParser$_1$
ADJ_COMP	MSTParser, MALTParser$_2$	MALTParser$_2$
CONJ, NOUN_PROP	MSTParser	MALTParser$_2$
PV	MALTParser$_2$	MSTParser
DET+NOUN_PROP	MALTParser$_2$	MALTParser$_1$
NOUN, IV	MSTParser	MSTParser
PRON	MALTParser$_2$	MALTParser$_2$
PSEUDO_VERB	MALTParser$_1$	MSTParser, MALTParser$_2$

Table 9. LA for combining parsers based on most confident parser, MATB corpus.

Technique	LA (%)
Three agree, backoff to most confident parser	78.9
At least two agree, backoff to most confident parser	**81.5**
MSTParser+MALTParser$_1$, backoff to most confident parser	79.2
MSTParser+MALTParser$_2$, backoff to most confident parser	79.5
MALTParser$_1$+MALTParser$_2$, backoff to most confident parser	80.2
Most confident parser only	77.7

majority vote with no backoff from Table 2, but it is substantially worse than the best of the voting strategies.

6   Conclusion

For the above experiments, the best results were obtained by asking a predefined pair of parsers whether they agree on the head for a given item, and backing off to the other one when they do not. This fits with Henderson and Brill [13]'s observations about a similar strategy for dependency parsing for English. It seems likely that the problem with relying on the most confident parser for each individual daughter-head relation is that this will tend to ignore the big picture, so that a collection of relations that are individually plausible, but which do not add up to a coherent overall analysis, will be picked. Within the voting based strategies, ones that involve MSTParser in the backoff strategy (lines 1–4 of Table 3, line 3 of Table 4) outperform ones in which MSTParser is part of the front-line, with one of the MALTParser family in the backoff (lines 5 and 6 of Table 3, lines 1 and 2 of Table 4), or ones which do not involve MSTParser at all (Tables 5 and 6). It seems plausible that this is because the machinery underlying MSTParser and the information it uses are quite distinct from that used within the MALTParser family. If it is part of the first line majority vote, then the fact that it has agreed with one of the MALTParser family suggests that there is strong evidence for the given proposal, so that the front-line is likely to be correct a good deal of the time. If it is part of the backoff, then it will only be called on in cases where the MALTParser family disagree, in which case the evidence for either of these is weak and something which relies on other evidence is likely to be helpful.

We intend to try using a *stacking technique* [14] by making the outputs of the data-driven parser(s) to guide another parser, here we will use a more linguistically-motivated parser. This will decrease the search space needed by the second parser and will hence enable it to arrive at its decisions, which are by definition linguistically plausible, more rapidly.

Acknowledgments. Maytham Alabbas owes his deepest gratitude to Iraqi Ministry of Higher Education and Scientific Research for financial support in his PhD study. Allan Ramsay's contribution to this work was partially supported by Qatar National Research Foundation grant NPRP 09-046-6-001.

References

1. Kübler, S., McDonald, R., Nivre, J.: Dependency Parsing. Synthesis Lectures on Human Language Technologies. Morgan & Claypool Publishers, Portland (2009)
2. Habash, N., Rambow, O., Roth, R.: MADA+TOKAN: a toolkit for Arabic tokenization, diacritization, morphological disambiguation, POS tagging, stemming and lemmatization. In: Proceedings of the 2nd International Conference on Arabic Language Resources and Tools, Cairo, Eygpt, The MEDAR Consortium, pp. 102–109 (2009)
3. Alabbas, M., Ramsay, A.: Evaluation of dependency parsers for long Arabic sentences. In: Proceeding of 2011 International Conference on Semantic Technology and Information Retrieval (STAIR'11), Putrajaya, Malaysia, IEEE, pp. 243–248 (2011)
4. Alabbas, M., Ramsay, A.: Improved POS-tagging for Arabic by combining diverse taggers. In: Iliadis, L., Maglogiannis, I., Papadopoulos, H. (eds.) Artificial Intelligence Applications and Innovations. IFIP AICT, vol. 381, pp. 107–116. Springer, Heidelberg (2012)
5. McDonald, R., Pereira, F.: Online learning of approximate dependency parsing algorithms. In: Proceedings of the 11th Conference of the European Chapter of the Association for Computational Linguistics (EACL 2006), Trento, Italy, Association for Computational Linguistics, pp. 81–88 (2006)
6. Nivre, J., Hall, J., Nilsson, J., Chanev, A., Eryigit, G., Kübler, S., Marinov, S., Marsi, E.: MaltParser: a language-independent system for data-driven dependency parsing. Nat. Lang. Eng. **13**(02), 95–135 (2007)
7. Maamouri, M., Bies, A.: Developing an Arabic treebank: methods, guidelines, procedures, and tools. In: Proceedings of the Workshop on Computational Approaches to Arabic Script-based Languages (Semitic '04), Geneva, Switzerland, Association for Computational Linguistics, pp. 2–9 (2004)

8. Xia, F., Palmer, M.: Converting dependency structures to phrase structures. In: Proceedings of the 1st International Conference on Human Language Technology Research (HLT 2001), San Diego, USA, Association for Computational Linguistics, pp. 1–5 (2001)

9. Collins, M.: Three generative, lexicalised models for statistical parsing. In: Proceedings of the 35th Annual Meeting of the Association for Computational Linguistics and 8th Conference of the European Chapter of the Association for Computational Linguistics (ACL'97), Madrid, Spain, Association for Computational Linguistics, pp. 16–23 (1997)

10. Alabbas, M., Ramsay, A.: Arabic treebank: from phrase-structure trees to dependency trees. In: META-RESEARCH Workshop on Advanced Treebanking at the 8th International Conference on Language Resources and Evaluation (LREC 2012), Istanbul, Turkey, pp. 61–68 (2012)

11. Nivre, J.: Inductive Dependency Parsing. Text, Speech and Language Technology, vol. 34. Springer, Heidelberg (2006)

12. Zeman, D., Žabokrtský, Z.: Improving parsing accuracy by combining diverse dependency parsers. In: Proceedings of the 9th International Workshop on Parsing Technology (IWPT 2005), Vancouver, British Columbia, Canada, Association for Computational Linguistics, pp. 171–178 (2005)

13. Henderson, J., Brill, E.: Exploiting diversity in natural language processing: combining parsers. In: Proceedings of the 1999 Joint SIGDAT Conference on Empirical Methods in Natural Language Processing and Very Large Corpora (EMNLP/VLC-99), Maryland, USA, Association for Computational Linguistics, pp. 187–194 (1999)

14. Nivre, J., McDonald, R.: Integrating graph-based and transition-based dependency parsers. In: Proceedings of the 46th Annual Meeting of the Association for Computational Linguistics: Human Language Technologies (ACL-08: HLT), Columbus, Ohio, USA, Association for Computational Linguistics, pp. 950–958 (2008)

Parsing Coordination Extragrammatically

Valmi Dufour-Lussier[✉], Bruno Guillaume, and Guy Perrier

LORIA (CNRS, Inria, Université de Lorraine, Nancy),
BP 239, 54506 Vandœuvre-lès-Nancy, France
{valmi.dufour,bruno.guillaume,guy.perrier}@loria.fr

Abstract. We propose to process coordination at the parsing level as a linguistic performance issue, outside the grammar, rather than as a matter of competence. We apply a specific algorithm to combine coordinated syntactic structures that were partially parsed using a coordination-less grammar, resulting in a directed acyclic parse graph in which constituent sharing appears sharply. This article presents an algorithm working within the framework of tree-adjoining grammars (although it can be adapted to other formalisms) that is able to handle many types of coordinating constructions, including left and right node raising, argument clusters, and verb gapping.

1 Introduction

Coordination is a frequent feature of natural language, yet it is extremely difficult to parse. One reason is that coordination of non-constituents is difficult to describe using the same formal tools as are used to model the "basic", coordination-free part of language.

Coordination gives rise to two linguistic phenomena, sharing of syntactic substructures and elision of constituents [8], which cannot be appropriately captured with the classical form of a tree, neither in a constituency nor in a dependency-based approach.

A first answer is to ignore the aspects violating treeness of structures. Most statistical parsing methods aim at building trees and thus choose to ignore complex structures going beyond treeness [6].

The main attempts to take complex coordinated structures into account are found in formal grammar-based approaches of parsing [1,5,7–10], using one of two ways:

- Adding specific elementary constructions to the grammar. Since coordination is highly polymorphic, the number of structures added can be important, especially in the case of lexicalized grammars.
- Modifying the parsing algorithms to take the specificity of coordination into account.

In both cases, this results in a reduction of the efficiency of parsing algorithms [11]: the ambiguity in the choice of elementary structures and bounds of conjuncts increases, and the resulting structures are more complex.

© Springer International Publishing Switzerland 2014
Z. Vetulani and J. Mariani (Eds.): LTC 2011, LNAI 8387, pp. 55–66, 2014.
DOI: 10.1007/978-3-319-08958-4_5

All these approaches have a common feature: they integrate the treatment of coordination within a unique parsing process. Turning away from a formal grammar-based approach, we propose to move the treatment of coordination outside of the general grammatical parsing process. This fits in with a linguistic idea that coordination may be beyond the scope of competence [3].

The principle is to alternate general parsing steps with coordination processing steps: choices are postponed until enough information is available to guide the coordination processing, as is the case with some existing parsers that use several "passes" [2]. This is not simply a matter of ordering parsing steps: the method is designed to produce directed acyclic graphs (DAGs), a syntactic representation richer than the one generated by the tree-based, coordination-less grammar.

The algorithm that encodes the coordination resolving steps requires the definition of notions related to DAGs. Section 2 is dedicated to this.

The general design of this alternation between general parsing steps and coordination resolving steps is described in Sect. 3.

The following sections present the specialization of the algorithm in the three cases that are considered in this article: coordination of constituents without sharing (Sect. 4), coordination with peripheral sharing (Sect. 5), and coordination with head gapping (Sect. 6).

The algorithm is not linked to a specific grammatical formalism, but we chose one to help explain it in details. We used Tree-Adjoining Grammar (TAG), a simple and well-known formalism that has two syntactic composition operations: substitution and adjunction [4]. For the sake of simplicity, we consider only two features: the grammatical category, written *cat*, and the syntactic function, written *funct*. We do not distinguish between top and bottom features.

2   Preliminary Definitions

By using DAGs instead of trees as representations for the syntactic structure of strings, many usual concepts such as root or leaf do not have an obvious sense. In this section, we define useful concepts applicable in directed acyclic graphs parsing, keeping as close as possible to the tree terminology.

We call the sink vertices **leaf nodes** and the source vertices **root nodes**. A DAG with a unique root is called a **rooted DAG** or an RDAG; it is worth noting that an RDAG is always connected. In the rest of the paper, all the graphs we consider are lists of RDAGs. In fact, trees are particular cases of RDAGs and all the algorithms presented in the paper preserve this graph property.

Nodes in parse graphs are labelled with morpho-syntactic features. According to the TAG formalism, leaf nodes are divided into **substitution nodes**, **foot nodes** and **anchor nodes**. Substitution nodes are to be merged with the root of an initial tree, foot nodes are to be used in an adjunction and anchor nodes are labelled with words of the language. A DAG is **saturated** if it has no substitution nodes and no foot node[1].

We define two partial orders in DAGs. In TAG trees, all children of a given node are totally ordered. This order is maintained through derivation and thus, in DAGs, the out-edges of a given node are totally ordered. Anchor nodes are totally ordered too (by the word order of the input sentence). This order is written $\prec$.

In a tree, if N is an ancestor of M, there is a unique path (a list of nodes such that each one is a child of the previous one) from N to M. In a DAG, there can be several paths from N to M. The most interesting paths are the leftmost and rightmost paths (written $\overleftarrow{\mathbf{path}}$ and $\overrightarrow{\mathbf{path}}$). They are defined recursively as follows:

- $\overleftarrow{\mathbf{path}}(N, N) = \overrightarrow{\mathbf{path}}(N, N) = \{N\}$;
- If N is an ancestor of M, with $N \neq M$, then at least one daughter of N is an ancestor of M. Let N_l be the leftmost child of N which is an ancestor of M. Then, define $\overleftarrow{\mathbf{path}}(N, M) = \{N\} :: \overleftarrow{\mathbf{path}}(N_l, M)$;
- If N is an ancestor of M, with $N \neq M$, then at least one daughter of N is an ancestor of M. Let N_r be the rightmost child of N which is an ancestor of M. Then, define $\overrightarrow{\mathbf{path}}(N, M) = \{N\} :: \overrightarrow{\mathbf{path}}(N_r, M)$;

Every node N of a DAG has a **yield**, denoted **yield**(N), which is the set of all its descendants that are anchor nodes.

Let $\mathcal{T}$ be a RDAG and $w_1, \ldots, w_n = \mathbf{yield}(\mathbf{root}(\mathcal{T}))$ such that $w_1 \prec w_2 \prec \ldots \prec w_n$. The **right frontier** of $\mathcal{T}$ (written $\mathcal{T}_{\searrow}$) is defined as $\overrightarrow{\mathbf{path}}(\mathbf{root}(\mathcal{T}), w_n)$. The **left frontier** of $\mathcal{T}$ is defined as $\overleftarrow{\mathbf{path}}(\mathbf{root}(\mathcal{T}), w_1)$.

In order to compare nodes to establish their suitability for coordination, we introduce the notation $N_1 \sim N2$, which stands for the fact that N_1 and N_2 have the same value for both the *cat* and the *funct* features.

3 Alternation Between Parsing and Resolving

The general idea of the algorithm is that control is successively exchanged between a *partial parser* and a *coordination resolver*. The sentence to parse is first split into segments following the punctuation and the coordination conjunctions. This does not require the bounds of the conjuncts to be determined at this step. Consider the following sentence:

(1) {*John knows Peter*}, {*whom Mary likes*} and {*Max hates*}, but {*never met him*}.

It is split into four segments delimited with curly brackets.

The parser then builds syntactic structures representing partial parses of the different segments. With the example, we obtain four syntactic structures corresponding to the four segments.

---

[1] In TAG, a node can also contain a mandatory adjunction, so a TAG tree is saturated only if all its mandatory adjunctions have been performed.

At this point, control is transferred to a selector, which picks two contiguous syntactic structures, $\mathcal{S}_{\mathcal{L}}$ and $\mathcal{S}_{\mathcal{R}}$, to be combined. The selector uses information coming from the different structures, for instance the category of their roots, but the purpose of this article is not to explain how the selector works.

If $\mathcal{S}_{\mathcal{L}}$ and $\mathcal{S}_{\mathcal{R}}$ are separated with a punctuation sign, control is then transferred to a punctuation resolver. If they are separated with a coordination conjunction, control is transferred to the coordination resolver. This article focuses on the coordination resolver only.

For instance, assume that in example (1), the selector has chosen the syntactic structures associated with *whom Mary likes* and *Nicolas hates* for $\mathcal{S}_{\mathcal{L}}$ and $\mathcal{S}_{\mathcal{R}}$. The syntactic structures $\mathcal{S}_{\mathcal{L}}$ and $\mathcal{S}_{\mathcal{R}}$ are lists of RDAGs.

Three types of sharing between conjuncts are distinguished and require a different treatment:

- In the coordination of constituents without sharing, the unique root of $\mathcal{L}$ (resp. $\mathcal{R}$) is coordinated with a node from the left frontier of $\mathcal{R}$ (resp. the right frontier of $\mathcal{L}$).
- In the coordination with peripheral sharing, the left (resp. right) frontier of $\mathcal{L}$ and the left (resp. right) frontier of $\mathcal{R}$ can share substructures (possibly introducing graphs as replacement for trees).
- In the coordination of argument clusters and coordination with verb gapping, a correspondence between the roots of two or three sub-RDAGs of $\mathcal{L}$ and the roots of two or three leftmost RDAGs of $\mathcal{S}_{\mathcal{R}}$ can be found with respect to certain conditions. A parallel structure is re-built by duplicating some parts of $\mathcal{L}$ and by combining them with the leftmost RDAGs of $\mathcal{S}_{\mathcal{R}}$.

The resolver uses a merging mechanism which combines $\mathcal{S}_{\mathcal{L}}$ and $\mathcal{S}_{\mathcal{R}}$ into a shorter list or RDAGs. In the two first cases, described in Sects. 4 and 5, the merging implies the rightmost RDAG $\mathcal{L}$ of $\mathcal{S}_{\mathcal{L}}$ and the leftmost RDAG $\mathcal{R}$ of $\mathcal{S}_{\mathcal{R}}$. In the last case, described in Sect. 6, two or three RDAGs of the same side are concerned by the merging.

4   Constituent Coordination Without Sharing

In the following, we use the notations $\mathcal{C}_{\mathcal{L}}$ and $\mathcal{C}_{\mathcal{R}}$ for the sub-RDAGs that are coordinated: the first step of the algorithm is to identify $\mathcal{C}_{\mathcal{L}}$ and $\mathcal{C}_{\mathcal{R}}$.

We assume that at least one the RDAGs $\mathcal{L}$ or $\mathcal{R}$ is saturated and represents a complete constituent. The three examples below illustrate this case. The projections of $\mathcal{L}$ and $\mathcal{R}$ on the sentence are represented between square brackets. If one of them is saturated, its projection is represented in bold.

(2) [*Max introduces the son of his friend*]$_{\mathcal{L}}$ and [**Mary**]$_{\mathcal{R}}$ *to his director.*

(3) *Today* [**the engineer**]$_{\mathcal{L}}$ and [**the boss of the company**]$_{\mathcal{R}}$ *are coming.*

(4) [**John knows that Mary likes tea**]$_{\mathcal{L}}$ but [**she hates coffee**]$_{\mathcal{R}}$.

In example (2), $\mathcal{L}$ is not saturated because we consider that the verb *intro-duces* also requires an indirect object; in examples (3) and (4), both $\mathcal{L}$ and $\mathcal{R}$ are saturated.

To combine $\mathcal{L}$ with $\mathcal{R}$, one has first to select one of them that is saturated. Say that the selected saturated RDAG is $\mathcal{R}$, hence $\mathcal{C}_\mathcal{R} = \mathcal{R}$.

Then, in the right frontier $\mathcal{L}_\searrow$ of $\mathcal{L}$, we have to find a node representing a constituent that can be coordinated with the constituent represented by $\mathbf{root}(\mathcal{R})$. We consider that two constituents can be coordinated if they have the same grammatical category and the same syntactic function[2]. This is expressed with an equivalence relation between nodes, denoted $\sim$. Let $\mathcal{H}_\mathcal{L} = \{N \in \mathcal{L}_\searrow \mid N \sim \mathbf{root}(\mathcal{R})\}$. If $\mathcal{H}_\mathcal{L} = \emptyset$, the coordination fails. If $\mathcal{H}_\mathcal{L}$ has more than one node, there is coordination scope ambiguity, which is the case for all examples above. For instance, for sentence (2):

(2-a) *Max introduces the son of [his friend]$_{\mathcal{C}_\mathcal{L}}$ and [Mary]$_{\mathcal{C}_\mathcal{R}}$ to his director.*

(2-b) *Max introduces [the son of his friend]$_{\mathcal{C}_\mathcal{L}}$ and [Mary]$_{\mathcal{C}_\mathcal{R}}$ to his director.*

We pick a node S from $\mathcal{H}_\mathcal{L}$. A new node C is created and interposed between S and its parent, and $\mathbf{root}(\mathcal{R})$ is made a right sister of S. The new node C has the same category and the same syntactic function as S and $\mathbf{root}(\mathcal{R})$.

In cases of extraction, the algorithm takes the barriers to extraction into account. Consider the following example:

(5) **John knows Peter whom Mary likes]$_\mathcal{L}$ and [Nicolas hates him]$_\mathcal{R}$.**

The algorithm succeeds by considering the parse tree of *Nicolas hates him* as the selected saturated RDAG $\mathcal{R}$. The left RDAG $\mathcal{L}$ is the parse tree of *John knows Peter whom Mary likes*. In its right frontier, three nodes are candidate to coordination with the root $N_\mathcal{R}$ of $\mathcal{R}$, if we only consider their grammatical category S: the roots $N_{\mathcal{L}_1}$, $N_{\mathcal{L}_2}$ and $N_{\mathcal{L}_3}$ of the respective RDAGs of *John knows Peter whom Mary likes*, of *whom Mary likes*, and of *Mary likes*. The nodes $N_{\mathcal{L}_2}$ and $N_{\mathcal{L}_3}$ should be rejected, and it is done, if we consider the functions of the nodes: they have the function of noun modifier whereas $N_{\mathcal{L}_1}$ does not. $N_{\mathcal{L}_1}$ is therefore the only node that is equivalent to $N_\mathcal{R}$.

5   Peripheral Sharing

In the previous section, the algorithm coordinates two independent RDAGs $\mathcal{C}_\mathcal{L}$ and $\mathcal{C}_\mathcal{R}$ by considering that the root of one is the conjunct of a node in the frontier for the other one. However, coordination often entails sharing between $\mathcal{C}_\mathcal{L}$ and $\mathcal{C}_\mathcal{R}$:

- $\mathcal{C}_\mathcal{L}$ and $\mathcal{C}_\mathcal{R}$ may have an identical syntactic context which is expressed with identical tree fragments over $\mathcal{C}_\mathcal{L}$ and $\mathcal{C}_\mathcal{R}$; when they are coordinated, the identical fragments are merged;

---

[2] We left aside the subtleties concerning the constraints in the coordination of constituents, such as coordination of unlikes.

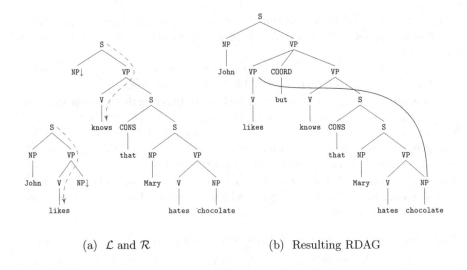

(a) $\mathcal{L}$ and $\mathcal{R}$ (b) Resulting RDAG

Fig. 1. Algorithm run on sentence *John likes but knows that Mary hates chocolate.*

– $\mathcal{C}_{\mathcal{L}}$ and $\mathcal{C}_{\mathcal{R}}$ may share sub-RDAGs representing common arguments or modifiers; sharing of sub-RDAGs is realized with common daughter nodes, which
is possible because syntactic structures are DAGs and not trees.

We call the first kind of sharing *context merging* and the second kind of sharing *argument sharing*—the latter includes the sharing of modifiers. The three
examples below illustrate these two cases of sharing. Projections of $\mathcal{C}_{\mathcal{L}}$ and $\mathcal{C}_{\mathcal{R}}$
on the sentence appear between square brackets; projections of the shared part
corresponding to argument sharing are underlined, and projections of the shared
part corresponding to context sharing are overlined.

(6) $\overline{Nicolas}$ [*often carries goods*]$_{\mathcal{C}_{\mathcal{L}}}$ and [*takes persons at the same time*
    from Paris to Lyon with his green truck]$_{\mathcal{C}_{\mathcal{R}}}$.

(7) *John knows Peter* $\overline{whom}$ [*Mary likes*]$_{\mathcal{C}_{\mathcal{L}}}$ and [*Nicolas hates*]$_{\mathcal{C}_{\mathcal{R}}}$.

(8) $\overline{John}$ [*likes*]$_{\mathcal{C}_{\mathcal{L}}}$ but [*knows that Mary hates* <u>*chocolate*</u>]$_{\mathcal{C}_{\mathcal{R}}}$.

In examples (6) and (8), $\mathcal{C}_{\mathcal{L}}$ and $\mathcal{C}_{\mathcal{R}}$ represent the syntactic structure of
two coordinated verb phrases, whereas in example (7) they represent incomplete
sentences. To take peripheral sharing into account, it is necessary to extend the
algorithm presented in Sect. 4.

5.1 The Run of the Algorithm on an Example

We first present the extension of the algorithm in an intuitive way on sentence (8). We travel along the right frontier of $\mathcal{L}$, that is S, VP, V, `likes`, and
the left frontier of $\mathcal{R}$, that is S, VP, V, `knows`, from the top to the bottom.

At each step of the travel, we denote the current position of the examined node in the right frontier of $\mathcal{L}$ with the variable $N_{\mathcal{L}}$ and the current position of the examined node in the left frontier of $\mathcal{R}$ with the variable $N_{\mathcal{R}}$. We initialise $N_{\mathcal{L}}$ and $N_{\mathcal{R}}$ with two nodes of the respective frontiers. One of the nodes must be a root, and $N_{\mathcal{L}} \sim N_{\mathcal{R}}$ must hold. In our example, we have only one possibility: $N_{\mathcal{L}}$ and $N_{\mathcal{R}}$ are the roots S of the two frontiers.

Since we aim at coordinating constituents at the lowest level in the syntactic structure, we try to merge as much as possible the subtrees rooted at $N_{\mathcal{L}}$ and $N_{\mathcal{R}}$. To examine if $N_{\mathcal{L}}$ and $N_{\mathcal{R}}$ can be merged, we have to look at their daughters. We start with their daughter nodes $D_{\mathcal{L}}$ and $D_{\mathcal{R}}$ on the frontiers. Both have the same category VP and they verify the condition $D_{\mathcal{L}} \sim D_{\mathcal{R}}$. Then, we have to look at the right sisters of $D_{\mathcal{L}}$ and the left sisters of $D_{\mathcal{R}}$. There is only a left daughter of $D_{\mathcal{R}}$, a substitution node NP. This node can be saturated by merging it with the corresponding left sister of $D_{\mathcal{L}}$. All conditions for merging $N_{\mathcal{L}}$ and $N_{\mathcal{R}}$ hold and we merge them as their daughter nodes NP.

The current values of $N_{\mathcal{L}}$ and $N_{\mathcal{R}}$ become the nodes $D_{\mathcal{L}}$ and $D_{\mathcal{R}}$. Then, we repeat the same step of computation from the new values of $N_{\mathcal{L}}$ and $N_{\mathcal{R}}$. The new values of $D_{\mathcal{L}}$ and $D_{\mathcal{R}}$ are the V daughters. The first condition for merging the new values of $N_{\mathcal{L}}$ and $N_{\mathcal{R}}$ holds but not the second one: the right sister of $D_{\mathcal{L}}$, a substitution node NP, cannot merge with a right sister node of $D_{\mathcal{R}}$. The process of merging halts and the proper coordination process starts.

The current nodes $N_{\mathcal{L}}$ and $N_{\mathcal{R}}$ represent the two constituents having to be coordinated. For this, we insert a new node C between $N_{\mathcal{L}}$, $N_{\mathcal{R}}$ and their common mother node. We add a new subtree of C between $N_{\mathcal{L}}$ and $N_{\mathcal{R}}$ with a unique daughter node, the anchor of the conjunction, *but*.

Then, the descent along the two frontiers continues. $D_{\mathcal{L}}$ has a right sister S, which is a substitution node NP. This node must be saturated, the constraints between the yields of $N_{\mathcal{L}}$ and $N_{\mathcal{R}}$ must be obeyed. They must be adjacent. As a consequence, S is saturated by merging it with a node M of the right frontier of the subtree rooted at $N_{\mathcal{R}}$. This frontier is VP, S, S, VP, NP, chocolate. Because of the constraint $S \sim M$, the only possible value for M is node NP. Note that the path from $N_{\mathcal{L}}$ to S does not have the same length and the same labeling as the path from $N_{\mathcal{R}}$ to M. The two paths nonetheless obey certain constraint, expressed as an equivalence relation between paths, which will be discussed later.

After merging S and M, the descent continues. The current values of $N_{\mathcal{L}}$ and $N_{\mathcal{R}}$ become the nodes $D_{\mathcal{L}}$ and $D_{\mathcal{R}}$. The new values of $D_{\mathcal{L}}$ and $D_{\mathcal{R}}$ are the respective anchors likes and knows. Since they have no sister node, the algorithm ends, and the resulting syntactic structure is that of Fig. 1b.

5.2   The Algorithm

As the previous example illustrates it, there are two stages in the algorithm:

- In the *context merging* stage, the two sub-RDAGs rooted at the initial values of $N_{\mathcal{L}}$ and $N_{\mathcal{R}}$ are merged as deeply as possible up to the coordinated nodes;
- These two nodes are the starting point of the *argument sharing* stage, in which substitutions and adjunctions to be realized on the right of the right frontier

of $\mathcal{L}$ are performed by sharing with realized substitutions and adjunctions on the right frontier of $\mathcal{R}$; in a symmetrical way, substitutions and adjunctions on the left of the left frontier of $\mathcal{R}$ are realized by sharing with substitutions and adjunctions on the left frontier of $\mathcal{L}$.

---

1 **choose_one** $(N_\mathcal{L}, N_\mathcal{R})$ *in* $\mathcal{L}_\searrow \times \mathcal{R}_\nearrow$ *the right frontier of* $\mathcal{L}$ *and the left frontier*
    of $\mathcal{R}$, *such that* $N_\mathcal{L} \sim N_\mathcal{R}$ *and one of them is a root*
2 | **while** *not FINISH* **do**
3 | $D_\mathcal{L} \leftarrow$ the daughter nodes of $N_\mathcal{L}$ on the right frontier;
4 | $D_\mathcal{R} \leftarrow$ the daughter nodes of $N_\mathcal{R}$ on the left frontier;
5 | **if** $D_\mathcal{L} \sim D_\mathcal{R}$ **then**
6 | $\mathcal{H}_\mathcal{L} \leftarrow$ the list of the left sister nodes of $D_\mathcal{L}$;
7 | $\mathcal{H}_\mathcal{R} \leftarrow$ the list of the left sister nodes of $D_\mathcal{R}$;
8 | **if** $\mathcal{H}_\mathcal{L}$ *and* $\mathcal{H}_\mathcal{R}$ *have the same length* n **then**
9 | **for** $1 \leq k \leq n$ **do**
10 | **if** *the subtrees rooted at* $\mathcal{H}_\mathcal{L}[k]$ *and* $\mathcal{H}_\mathcal{R}[k]$ *can be merged*
          then
11 | merge them
12 | **else**
13 | FINISH $\leftarrow$ True; BREAK
14 | **end**
15 | **end**
16 | **else**
17 | FINISH $\leftarrow$ True
18 | **end**
19 | **else**
20 | FINISH $\leftarrow$ True
21 | **end**
22 | **if** *not FINISH and* $D_\mathcal{L}$ *and* $D_\mathcal{R}$ *and not anchors* **then**
23 | $N_\mathcal{L} \leftarrow D_\mathcal{L}$; $N_\mathcal{R} \leftarrow D_\mathcal{R}$
24 | **end**
25 | **end**
26 | Insert a new node C between $N_\mathcal{L}$ and $N_\mathcal{R}$ and their eventual common
    mother node
27 **end**

Algorithm 1. Left context merging

The first stage is presented in Algorithm 1. To simplify the presentation, only left merging, as in the example, is considered.

The second stage of the algorithm for argument sharing is shown in details in Algorithm 2. Again, only right argument sharing is considered. It starts at the end of the first stage with $N_{\mathcal{L}_0}$ and $N_{\mathcal{R}_0}$ being the roots of the two coordinated structures $\mathcal{C}_\mathcal{L}$ and $\mathcal{C}_\mathcal{R}$. From $N_{\mathcal{L}_0}$, we go down along the right frontier of $\mathcal{C}_\mathcal{L}$ until we find a node which has substitution leaves as daughter nodes at the right of the daughter node on the frontier, or where a right adjunction is allowed. The current position along this frontier is represented with the variable $N_\mathcal{L}$. To simplify the presentation of the algorithm, we assume that $N_\mathcal{L}$ has one daughter at most that is on the right of the frontier.

In parallel, from $N_{\mathcal{R}_0}$, we go down along the right frontier of $\mathcal{C}_\mathcal{R}$ to find a node $M_\mathcal{R}$ that shares a sub-RDAG with $N_\mathcal{L}$. The current position from which we look for $M_\mathcal{R}$ is represented with the variable $N_\mathcal{R}$.

Here is how the algorithm deals with substitution and adjunction sharing:

Substitution sharing. When $N_\mathcal{L}$ has a rightmost daughter which is a substitution leaf $N_r^\downarrow$, we search top-down for the first node $M_\mathcal{R}$ in the right frontier of the sub-RDAG rooted at $N_\mathcal{R}$ that has a rightmost daughter M_r able to fill the substitution leaf $N_r^\downarrow$. The paths from $N_\mathcal{L}$ to $N_r^\downarrow$ and from $N_\mathcal{R}$ to M_r must be equivalent in a sense that will be specified shortly. Nodes M_r and $N_r^\downarrow$ are merged.

Adjunction sharing. When $N_\mathcal{L}$ allows for an adjunction, the only possible adjunction is a right adjunction[3] we search top-down for the first node $M_\mathcal{R}$ in the right frontier of the sub-RDAG rooted at $N_\mathcal{R}$ that results from a right adjunction and that can share this adjunction with $N_\mathcal{L}$. To perform it, an equivalence condition on paths in the same sense as for substitution must be verified. If we find such a node $M_\mathcal{R}$, then we have to decide (line 5 of the algorithm) whether to share the adjunction (lines 6 to 9) or not.

Our presentation of the algorithm makes it non-deterministic: a choice is made among the possible conjuncts in stage 1, and choices are made as well between possible substitutions and adjunctions in stage 2. A deterministic formulation of the algorithm would simply need to enumerate the list of solutions.

Graph modifications the algorithm can use for substitution and for adjunction sharing are shown in Fig. 2. The top and bottom parts of the figures describe the graph before and after the modifications; grey nodes identify $N_\mathcal{L}$ and $N_\mathcal{R}$ in the top part, and the next iteration's starting point in the bottom part.

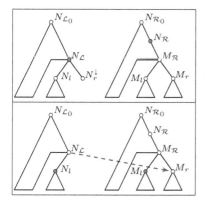 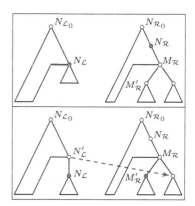

Fig. 2. Substitution sharing (on the left) and adjunction sharing (on the right)

---

[3] A right adjunction comes from a right auxiliary tree, that is a tree where the foot node is the leftmost leaf.

1 Initialise $N_{\mathcal{L}}$ and $N_{\mathcal{R}}$ with the roots $N_{\mathcal{L}_0}$ and $N_{\mathcal{R}_0}$ of the structures being
  coordinated after the stage of context merging;

2 **while** *not FINISH* **do**

3   **if** *some adjunction is allowed at $N_{\mathcal{L}}$* **then**

4   **choose_one** $M_{\mathcal{R}}$ *in* $N_{\mathcal{R}\searrow}$ *such that* $\overrightarrow{\mathbf{path}}(N_{\mathcal{L}_0}, N_{\mathcal{L}}) \approx \overrightarrow{\mathbf{path}}(N_{\mathcal{R}_0}, M_{\mathcal{R}})$
        and $M_{\mathcal{R}}$ is the root of a right auxiliary tree

5   **choose**

6   (see adjunction sharing, Fig. 2);

7   Insert a node $N'_{\mathcal{L}}$ between $N_{\mathcal{L}}$ and its mother node with the
                same category;

8   Add all daughters of $M_{\mathcal{R}}$ on the right of its foot node $M'_{\mathcal{R}}$ as
                right daughters of $N'_{\mathcal{L}}$;

9                 $N_{\mathcal{R}} \leftarrow M'_{\mathcal{R}}$

10   **or** Do nothing

11   **end**

12   **else if** *$N_{\mathcal{L}}$ has a rightmost daughter which is a substitution node N_r* **then**

13   (see substitution sharing, Fig. 2);

14   **choose_one** $M_{\mathcal{R}}$ *in* $N_{\mathcal{R}\searrow}$ *such that* $\overrightarrow{\mathbf{path}}(N_{\mathcal{L}_0}, N_{\mathcal{L}}) \approx \overrightarrow{\mathbf{path}}(N_{\mathcal{R}_0}, M_{\mathcal{R}})$
        and $M_{\mathcal{R}}$ has a rightmost daughter $M_r \sim N_i$

15             $N_{\mathcal{L}} \leftarrow N_l$ where N_l is the immediate left sister of N_r;

16             $N_{\mathcal{R}} \leftarrow M_l$ where M_l is the immediate left sister of M_r;

17   Merge M_r and N_r

18   **end**

19   **else** neither adjunction sharing nor substitution sharing

20   **if** *$N_{\mathcal{L}}$ is a leaf* **then**

21   FINISH

22   **else**

23             $N_{\mathcal{L}} \leftarrow$ the rightmost daughter of $N_{\mathcal{L}}$

24   **end**

25

26 **end**

Algorithm 2. Right argument sharing

We now define the equivalence relation between paths $\approx$. It depends on the language and on the choice of the representation of syntactic trees. There is no room to define the relation exhaustively for a given language and choice of syntactic representation here, but we can sketch it. In our settings, it is the smallest equivalence relation such that: *a*) if $N \sim M$ then $\{N\} \approx \{M\}$, *b*) $p \approx p.(\mathrm{S}, \mathrm{obj}).(\mathrm{VP}, \mathrm{head})$, and *c*) $p.(X, \mathit{funct}) \approx p.(X, \mathit{funct}).(X, \mathit{funct})$. The condition *b* is meant to go through object clauses, whereas *c* is meant to go through constituents with adjoined modifiers, such as in sentence (8).

6 Verb Gapping and Argument Clusters

Verb gapping is a grammatical construction in which two clauses are coordinated and the verb of the second clause is replaced with a gap. This means that the verb of the first conjunct is picked up again as the verb of the second conjunct.

Argument clusters is another grammatical construction in which the second conjunct is a cluster of constituents, which are all arguments of the same predicate which is absent from this conjunct. It is a resumption of the predicate that is the head of the first conjunct.

Sentences (9) and (10) illustrate verb gapping and argument cluster. The projections of the left and right RDAGs are between square brackets. The part of the left segment that is replaced with a gap in the right segment is in a box.

(9) [*John* $\boxed{buys}$ *a car*] *and* [*Maria*] [*a shower*].

(10) [$\boxed{Nicolas\ carries\ goods}$ *from Paris to Lyon*] *and* [*from Lyon*] [*to Nancy*].

Verb gapping and argument clusters are processed with a common algorithm because, in both situations, the head of the syntactic structure of the second conjunct is lacking and one has to reuse the head of the first conjunct to build this syntactic structure.

The input of the algorithm is a RDAG $\mathcal{L}$ representing the syntactic structure of the parsed phrase on the left of the conjunction and a list of RDAGs $\mathcal{R}_1, \ldots, \mathcal{R}_n$ representing the partial parse of the phrase on the right, ordered with respect to the linear order of the sentence. The first step of the algorithm is to establish a bijection between $\mathbf{root}(\mathcal{R}_1), \ldots, \mathbf{root}(\mathcal{R}_p)$ of the p first RDAGs from the n right RDAGs and p nodes $N_1, \ldots, N_p$ from $\mathcal{L}$, verifying the following properties:

- For any i such that $1 \leq i \leq p$, $N_i \sim \mathbf{root}(\mathcal{R}_i)$;
- The projections on the sentence of $N_1, \ldots, N_p$ constitutes two continuous segments[4] immediately on the left of the conjunction, separated by a word w.

The second step is to select a node N that dominates $N_1, \ldots, N_p$ in $\mathcal{L}$, and whose head is w. This node is necessarily a node from the right frontier of $\mathcal{L}$ and it represents the left conjunct. The third step is to duplicate the sub-RDAG $\mathcal{T}$ rooted at N with $N_1, \ldots, N_p$ and w as leaves. In the clone $\mathcal{T}'$, the leaves $N_1, \ldots, N_p$ are replaced with $\mathbf{root}(\mathcal{R}_1), \ldots, \mathbf{root}(\mathcal{R}_p)$ but w is shared with $\mathcal{T}$. Finally, $\mathcal{T}$ and $\mathcal{T}'$ are coordinated as in Sect. 4.

7   Results

The algorithm was simulated on the 14 sentences from section 0 of the Penn Treebank that contain either peripheral sharing or gapping. The algorithm returned at least a parse for all sentences but two, which both involved coordination of unlikes, which our algorithm cannot handle. An average of 1.3 parses was returned per sentence. The parse from the Penn Treebank was always among the returned parses, and all but three parses arguably described genuine ambiguity in the scope of coordination[5].

---

[4] The first one can be empty.

[5] Detailed results: http://wikilligramme.loria.fr/doku.php?id=ecp:ecp

8 Conclusion

In this article we presented an algorithm that allows for parsing of coordination outside the scope of grammar. This algorithm is able to interact with any parser using a coordination-less grammar, thus returning incomplete parses, and reconstruct a complete parse graph from the fragments returned by the parser. While we used TAGs to aid with the presentation and evaluation, we believe this algorithm could be applied to other formalisms with little adaptation.

A first evaluation shows that the algorithm deals appropriately with most types of coordination, including right node raising and gapping. Unsurprisingly, the only cases where it failed to parse coordination were with coordination of unlikes. The algorithm adds little ambiguity, and most of it is justified as genuine coordination scope ambiguity.

Future works will involve a more full-fledged evaluation within different grammatical frameworks, with special respect for the effect of different equivalence relations between nodes of two graphs.

References

1. Beavers, J., Sag, I.: Coordinate ellipsis and apparent non-constituent coordination. In: 11th International Conference on HPSG (2004)
2. Bourigault, D.: Un analyseur syntaxique opérationnel: SYNTEX. Habilitation thesis, Université Toulouse-Le Mirail (2007)
3. Frank, R.: Coordinating parsing and grammar. GLOT Int'l 1(4), 4–8 (1995)
4. Joshi, A., Schabes, Y.: Tree-Adjoining Grammars. Handbook of Formal Languages, pp. 69–123. Springer, New York (1997)
5. Kaplan, R., Maxwell, J.: Constituent coordination in lexical-functional grammar. In: Proceedings of the 12th Conference on Computational Linguistics, pp. 303–305 (1988)
6. Kübler, S., McDonald, R., Nivre, J.: Dependency Parsing. Morgan and Claypool, San Francisco (2009)
7. Le Roux, J., Perrier, G.: La coordination dans les grammaires d'interaction. TAL 47(3), 89–113 (2006)
8. Mouret, F.: Grammaire des constructions coordonnées. Coordinations simples et coordinations à redoublement en français contemporain. Ph.D. thesis, Université Paris 7 (2007)
9. Sarkar, A., Joshi, A.: Coordination in tree adjoining grammars: formalization and implementation. In: 16th Conference on Computational Linguistics, pp. 610–615. ACL (1996)
10. Steedman, M.: Dependency and coordination in the grammar of Dutch and English. Language 61(3), 523–568 (1985)
11. White, M.: Efficient realization of coordinate structures in combinatory categorial grammar (2004)

Lexical Disambiguation in LTAG Using Left Context

Claire Gardent[1], Yannick Parmentier[2], Guy Perrier[3(✉)],
and Sylvain Schmitz[4]

[1] CNRS, LORIA, Nancy, France
[2] Université d'Orléans, ENSI de Bourges, LIFO, Orléans, France
[3] Université de Lorraine, LORIA, Nancy, France
`guy.perrier@loria.fr`
[4] ENS Cachan, LSV, Cachan, France

Abstract. In this paper, we present an optimization for parsing with Lexicalized Tree-Adjoining Grammar which takes inspiration from previous work on polarity based grammar abstraction (Bonfante et al. [3]). We illustrate the impact of this optimization on two benchmarks and we relate our approach to the more general optimization framework proposed for Interaction Grammars by Bonfante et al. [2] and Morey [11].

Keywords: Parsing · Lexical disambiguation · Lexicalized tree adjoining grammar · Supertagging

1 Introduction

When parsing with a lexicalized grammatical formalism such as *lexicalized tree adjoining grammars* (LTAG), a first step (called *lexical selection*) consists in retrieving, for each word of the sentence to parse, the associated grammatical structures (here the elementary LTAG trees).

As shown by Bangalore and Joshi [1], in large lexicalized grammars, lexical selection usually yields an intractable search space. This is because each given word may be associated with hundreds of grammatical structures resulting in an exponential number of sequences of structures to be explored (namely, the cartesian product of the sets of lexical entries of each word of the sentence to parse). In practice however, very few of these sequences can yield a complete parse.

In this paper, we adapt an optimization technique proposed by Bonfante et al. [3] for interaction grammars [13] to prune the initial search space to LTAG and we illustrate the impact of this optimization on two benchmarks. We also relate our approach to a more general optimization technique proposed by Bonfante et al. [2] and Morey [11].

The paper is structured as follows. In Sect. 2, we summarize related work. Section 3 gives a brief introduction to LTAG. In Sects. 4 and 5, we present the

© Springer International Publishing Switzerland 2014
Z. Vetulani and J. Mariani (Eds.): LTC 2011, LNAI 8387, pp. 67–79, 2014.
DOI: 10.1007/978-3-319-08958-4_6

optimization proposed and we illustrate its impact on two small benchmarks. In Sect. 6, we relate our approach to the more general approach of *companions* introduced in [2, 11]. Section 7 concludes.

2   Related Work

Drawing inspiration from part-of-speech tagging techniques, Bangalore and Joshi [1] use n-grams and probabilities to compute the set of most probable grammatical structures given an LTAG and an input string. This probability-based lexical selection is called *supertagging*. A major drawback of this approach is that it heavily relies on the training corpus used for assigning lexical probabilities. Supertagging may thus ignore valid structures (i.e. structures that are in fact needed to parse the input sentence), which in turn can degrade parsing accuracy.

To prevent lexical selection from ignoring valid structures, Boullier [5] proposed to compute an abstract grammar from the input one, and to use this abstract grammar to parse the input sentence. For each set of abstract structures that succeed in parsing the input sentence, one then selects the corresponding original structures and parse with the original grammar. This technique improves parsing efficiency only if parsing with the abstract grammar is significantly less complex than parsing with the input grammar. In his experiments, Boullier abstracted a context-free grammar (CFG) from an LTAG: the most common parsing algorithms for LTAGs have a polynomial time complexity in $O(n^6)$, n being the length of the input sentence, while those for CFGs have a complexity in $O(n^3)$. The main drawback of this approach is that one needs to first parse with the abstract grammar, which may still be quite time-consuming.

Following Boullier, Bonfante et al. [3] proposed a non-probabilistic lexical selection algorithm which uses a *polarity-based abstraction*, an abstraction inspired by interaction grammar [13]. In this formalism, grammatical structures are tree descriptions where nodes are labeled with polarized feature-structures and parsing corresponds to computing syntactic tree models where polarities are neutralized. Bonfante et al. thus aimed at reducing the initial search space by applying a preliminary filter based on the polarity constraints. In their approach, each input grammatical structure is associated with a set of polarities. Valid lexical selection sequences are then those sequences whose total polarity set is neutral (we will elaborate on this in Sect. 4).

Perrier [14] proposes a finer abstraction in which the position of the polarities with respect to the anchor of the elementary structures of the grammar is taken into account. On this basis, he proposes a disambiguation algorithm which takes into account the linear order of the words in the sentence.

As discussed in Sect. 6, our work takes inspiration from [3, 14] and proposes an algorithm that is similar to that proposed in [14] though less costly in terms of space.

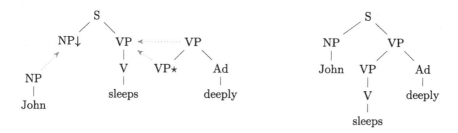

Fig. 1. Tree rewriting in an LTAG.

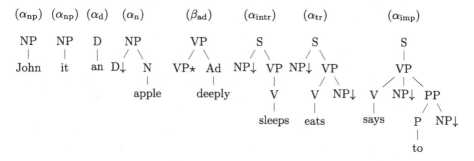

Fig. 2. A toy LTAG for English.

3 Lexicalized Tree-Adjoining Grammars

A tree-adjoining grammar [8] is a tree rewriting system, where elementary trees can be rewritten using one of the two following operations: *substitution* and *adjunction*. Substitution consists in replacing a leaf node (marked with '↓') of an elementary or derived tree with an elementary tree whose root is labeled with the same syntactic category as this leaf node. Adjunction consists in replacing an internal node of an elementary or derived tree with an elementary tree having both a root node and a distinguished leaf node (marked with '⋆', and called the *foot* node) labeled with the same category as this internal node.

Furthermore, in a *lexicalized* TAG, every elementary tree is associated with at least one lexical item called its *anchor*. If a tree is associated with several lexical items, there is one anchor, and several *co-anchors*. Figure 1 shows on the left the substitution (resp. adjunction) of a tree anchored by 'John' (resp. 'deeply') into a tree anchored by 'sleeps', the two operations resulting in the *derived* tree displayed on the right. Figure 2 shows a toy LTAG that will be used throughout to illustrate the workings of the algorithms.

4 Lexical Disambiguation

Following Bonfante et al. [3,4], our approach for lexical disambiguation uses a polarity-based abstraction over the input grammar. We first explain how this abstraction is built by Bonfante et al. [3]. We then show how it can be applied to LTAG. Finally we show how this first filtering algorithm can be extended to improve disambiguation performance by taking word order information into account.

4.1 Polarity-Based Lexical Disambiguation

Bonfante et al. [3] define a framework for lexical disambiguation which involves the following three-steps:

Polarization: First, the input grammar is polarized. That is, each grammatical structure g is associated with a set of polarities S_g where a *polarity* is a tuple (f, v, p) with f is a feature, v a value, and p a (possibly negative) integer. The sets of possible features and feature values are assumed to be finite. Since the grammar is lexicalized, we can associate each word w of the lexicon with its corresponding multiset of polarities M (recall that a word can anchor several grammatical structures, each associated with a possibly non-unique set of polarities).

Neutralization: Second, an abstract lexical selection is operated using the previously computed polarized grammar. This amounts to first computing the cartesian product P of the multisets associated with the words $w_1 \cdots w_n$ of the input sentence: $P = M_1 \times \cdots \times M_n$. Then, a binary rewriting rule, called the *neutralization* rule, is applied on the elements $E = (S_1, \ldots, S_n)$ of this product P as follows: Let (S, S') be a couple of polarity sets in E, these are replaced with a set $S + S'$ such that:
  – if a feature f with value v is present in both S and S' as (f, v, p) and (f, v, p') respectively, then the polarity $(f, v, p + p')$ is added to $S + S'$.
  – any other polarity (f, v, p) in $S \cup S'$ is copied into $S + S'$.
  This rewriting goes on (in an arbitrary order) until all elements of E have been consumed, thus producing one polarity set per element E in P.

Filtering: In the end, an element E of P is called *well-formed* if, after neutralization, it consists of exactly one polarity $(cat, S, +1)$ (where S is the category of sentences), an arbitrary number of polarities of the form $(f, v, 0)$ and nothing else. Filtering only keeps the well-formed elements in P. For each such element, the associated grammatical structures in the input grammar are lexically selected.

A crucial point of this approach lies in the definition of polarization. It ought to include enough information to distinguish between useful grammatical structures in the context of the sentence to parse, and useless ones. Yet it should not lead to a complex, time-consuming abstraction: applying neutralization to polarized structures should remain fast.

4.2 Application to LTAG

We now show how this lexical disambiguation process can be applied to LTAG.

The polarization step consists in associating each tree t of the input LTAG with a set of polarities. For LTAG, we define our polarities to be of the form (cat, x, p), where x is a syntactic category labeling a tree node and $p = 1 - n$ with n the number of substitution or foot nodes labeled with x if x is the category of the root and $p = n$ otherwise.

For instance, the tree schemas used in Fig. 1 are polarized as follows:

$$polarities(\alpha_{np}) = \{(cat, NP, +1)\} \,,$$
$$polarities(\alpha_{intr}) = \{(cat, S, +1), (cat, NP, -1)\} \,,$$
$$polarities(\beta_{ad}) = \{(cat, VP, 0)\} \,.$$

To take co-anchors into account, we change co-anchors in the grammar to substitution leaves and we add corresponding single node trees to match these new requirements.

The neutralization step first constructs the cartesian product of the set of polarities according to the sentence to parse. In the case of Fig. 1 ('John sleeps deeply'), this set contains a single element:

$$P = \big\{\{(cat, NP, +1)\}, \{(cat, S, +1), (cat, NP, -1)\}, \{(cat, VP, 0)\}\big\} \,.$$

Next, neutralization sums the polarities for compatible (f, v) pairs for each element E of P. In our toy example, neutralization yields the following set of polarities for the single element of P:

$$neutralization(E) = \{(cat, S, +1), (cat, NP, 0), (cat, VP, 0)\} \,.$$

The filtering step keeps the well-formed elements of P. In our case, there is only one element in P and it is well-formed.

Note that lexical selection based on polarization as presented here does not rely on any particular word order. One can compute the well-formed elements of P following or not the word order defined by the input sentence.

4.3   Automata Representation

Using an automaton to represent the results of lexical selection is necessary in order to deal with the large number of resulting sequences of structures, and can be seamlessly integrated in the parsing process with the same $O(|G| \cdot n^6)$ time complexity, now with n being the number of states [9]. Hence we assume lexical selection to yield an automaton, which can later be processed by the parsing algorithm. The various lexical disambiguation algorithms strive to eliminate spurious paths from this automaton, i.e. combinations of grammatical structures that cannot yield a valid parse. In the case of polarity filtering, this *polarity automaton* tags each state with the sum of the polarities associated with the structures labeling the path from the initial state to that state. For instance,

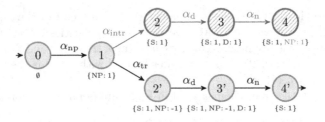

Fig. 3. A polarity automaton for the sentence 'John eats an apple' (Color figure online).

the sentence 'John eats an apple' yields the polarized automaton shown in Fig. 3 (where we only display the non-zero polarities).

Thus the final states of the polarity automaton indicate the (common) neutralization result for all the paths that lead into them, and the filtering step can be implemented by only keeping the paths that lead to a well-formed final state. For instance in Fig. 3, the top branch (in red) is discarded by the filtering step because state 4 is not a well formed final state.

4.4   Lexical Disambiguation Using Word Order

As mentioned earlier, the polarity-based lexical selection introduced in Sect. 4.1 does not take word order into account. In order to enhance lexical disambiguation, we propose to use *left context* information by extending the algorithm presented in Sect. 4.2 as follows.

The polarization of the input grammar is extended to produce *pairs* of sets of polarities. The first element in this pair is the classical polarity set, and the second element is a polarization related to the left context, that only takes (a) the root node and (b) the substitution nodes situated to the left of the anchor into account. For instance, the two trees for the word 'eats' and the imperative tree for 'say' are associated with the following polarity sets:

$$polarities(\alpha_{tr}) = \big(\{(cat, S, +1), (cat, NP, -2)\}, \{(cat, S, +1), (cat, NP, -1)\}\big),$$

$$polarities(\alpha_{intr}) = \big(\{(cat, S, +1), (cat, NP, -1)\}, \{(cat, S, +1), (cat, NP, -1)\}\big).$$

$$polarities(\alpha_{imp}) = \big(\{(cat, S, +1), (cat, NP, -2), (cat, to, -1)\}, \{(cat, S, +1)\}\big)$$

Neutralization is then applied to the two components of the pair. Let (a_1, b_1) and (a_2, b_2) be two such pairs:

$$(a_1, b_1) + (a_2, b_2) = (a_1 + a_2, b_1 + b_2).$$

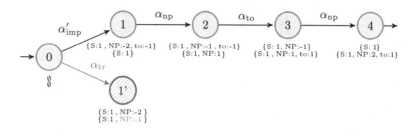

Fig. 4. Lexical selection using left context for 'Say it to John.'

Filtering still enforces the result of neutralization to be well-formed on the first coordinate, but additionally constrains the successive neutralization results to only contain non-negative polarities in the second coordinate: during each neutralization step, $b_1 + b_2$ is constrained to only contain polarities of the form (f, v, i) where $i \geq 0$. Intuitively, this constraint excludes sequences where a requirement on the left of the current token has not been fulfilled.

Automata Representation. Let us now see how this extension impacts the automaton-based implementation of lexical selection. Because the automaton construction already relied on the input sentence order, the extension is easily implemented by decorating the states with pairs of polarity sets. The non-negativity constraint on the second component (which accounts for the left context polarities) is checked on-the-fly: as soon as a state has a negative polarity in the second component, the construction of its successors aborts.

Consider the sentence 'Say it to John' and the grammar of Fig. 2.[1] The resulting automaton is shown in Fig. 4. We notice that only the imperative tree schema α_{imp} for 'say' prevents the left context abstraction from having negative polarities; the construction for the transitive tree schema α_{tr} (e.g., 'John said it') aborts immediately. This is a vast improvement over the basic polarity automaton, which requires building a full automaton before filtering can take place and select well-formed final states.

5   Implementation and Evaluation

In order to evaluate the benefits brought by left context, we have implemented polarity-based lexical selection using left context within the TuLiPA parser [12].[2] TuLiPA is an open source parser for mildly context-sensitive formalisms which supports LTAG and already includes the automaton-based lexical selection of

---

[1] Recall that the grammar is modified so that co-anchors are represented as substitution nodes and additional single node trees are added to match these nodes. This explains why the α_{imp} tree schema carries a *to* polarity feature.

[2] See http://sourcesup.renater.fr/tulipa

Table 1. Polarity-based lexical disambiguation.

Sentence	Sequences		States	
	Initial	Polarity	Polarity	Context
'Jean aime Marie'	12	2	26	4
(*John loves Mary*)				
'Marie dort'	3	1	5	3
(*Mary sleeps*)				
'Jean qui dort aime Marie'	36	8	78	7
(*John who sleeps loves Mary*)				
'Marie est appelée par Jean'	6	1	21	9
(*Mary is called by John*)				
'Jean qui dort est aimé par Marie'	18	4	63	13
(*John who sleeps is loved by Mary*)				

Bonfante et al. [3] presented in Sect. 4. This makes it easier to compare the two approaches.

To exhibit the benefits of left-context disambiguation, we used two types of resources, a toy LTAG and a large one. These are described below. The question of which metrics to use to evaluate the gain of polarity filtering is not trivial. We chose to compare the sizes of automata when using left context or not. Another interesting metrics would be total parsing times, even if the additional cost of automaton-based filtering is expected to be negligible compared with the cost of parsing with highly ambiguous grammars. Due to time and space restrictions, this is left for future work.

5.1   Qualitative Study

In a first experiment, we performed polarity-based lexical selection using a toy LTAG made of 12 tree schemas (intransitive verb with clitic/canonical/extracted subject, active transitive verb with clitic/canonical/extracted subject, passive transitive verb with clitic/canonical/extracted subject, proper nouns, clitics and auxiliaries), 9 lemmas, and 30 morphological entries. There is no part-of-speech tagging ambiguity in our toy lexicon, i.e. lexical ambiguity here is purely grammatical. The results are given in Table 1.

In Table 1, the first two figures provide the lexical ambiguity of the sentence before and after polarity-based filtering. In these toy examples, the remaining lexical ambiguity is the same whether we only use polarities or also consider left context information. The last two figures give the number of states in the automata representations after polarity filtering and polarity and left context filtering, respectively. One can notice that using left context significantly reduces the size of the automaton, even with a small grammar and short sentences.

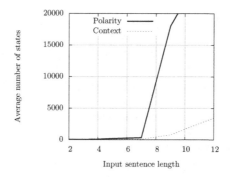

Fig. 5. Distribution of polarity automata sizes on the TSNLP.

5.2 Quantitative Study

In a second experiment, we used the French LTAG of Crabbé [6]. This grammar is compiled from a metagrammar developed in the XMG language [7].[3] It contains 6,080 tree schemas, and focuses on verbal, adjectival and nominal predicatives.

We used this grammar to evaluate polarity-based lexical disambiguation on a subset of the Test Suite for Natural Language Processing [10]. This subset contains 90 sentences whose length ranges from 2 to 12 words. Figure 5 displays the average number of states of the automaton (y-axis) depending on the length of the input sentence (x-axis). One can notice the combinatorial explosion of the size of the 'Polarity' automata of Bonfante et al. [3] compared to the 'Context' automata, when considering sentences with more than seven words.

As suggested by Fig. 5, for polarity filtering to stay computationally tractable when parsing real data, optimizations are needed. From these first experiments, using information about left context seems to be adequate in practice. This still needs to be confirmed with other evaluation resources and metrics.

6 Generalization to Companions

We now show that the optimization we proposed for LTAG is a special case of the more general optimization framework developed in [2,11].

6.1 The Notion of a Companion

In a polarized grammar, each grammatical structure is associated with a polarity and saturation rules define valid polarity combinations. For instance in LTAG, two trees may only combine if their polarity sets contains a positive and a negative triple for the same category e.g., $\{cat, \text{NP}, +1\}$ and $\{cat, \text{NP}, -1\}$). Given a polarized grammar, Bonfante et al. [3] defines *companions* as follows.

---

[3] Crabbé's metagrammar is available from https://sourcesup.renater.fr/scm/viewvc.php/trunk/METAGRAMMARS/FrenchTAG/?root=xmg and its French documentation from http://www.linguist.univ-paris-diderot.fr/~bcrabbe/frenchgrammar/.

Definition 6.1. *Let G be a polarized grammar. Given two grammatical structures G_1 and G_2 in G with polarities p_1 and p_2 respectively, p_2 is a companion of p_1 iff G_1 and G_2 can be combined by the grammar rules of G and p_1, p_2 is a valid polarity combination according to the saturation rules defined by G.*

Although the definition was initially designed for interaction grammars, it straightforwardly extends to the polarized version of LTAG described in Subsect. 4.2. Thus for instance, given the elementary trees of Fig. 1, the polarity $\{cat, NP, -1\}$ triggered by the substitution node of α_{intr} is a companion of the positive polarity $\{cat, NP, +1\}$ associated with the root node of α_{np}. More generally, the companions of a polarity in LTAG can be defined as follows. Given an initial tree whose root node has category C, the companions of the polarity of this root node are the polarities of all substitution nodes with category C. To account for word order and encode a filtering exploiting left context information as proposed in Subsect. 4.4, companions are furthermore divided into left- and right-companions. A left companion is a polarity associated with a substitution node occurring to the right of the anchor of the tree containing that substitution node. Conversely, a right companion is associated with a substitution node occurring to the left of the anchor of the tree containing that substitution node.

6.2   Using Companions for LTAG Filtering

Morey [11] presents a general framework for filtering the initial search space when parsing with polarized grammars and in particular with interaction grammars. In particular, he defines the ICP algorithm which is based on the *Integer Companionship Principle* (ICP) and applies to systems with *linear polarities*. A polarity system is said to be linear if its non saturated polarities are grouped by pairs such that the only possible combination for a non saturated polarity is with its paired polarity. Thus the system of polarities for LTAG is linear: it has two non saturated polarities + and −. Furthermore, one positive polarity combines with exactly one negative polarity and conversely.

The ICP for interaction grammars is informally as follows:

> *For every path of the automaton, every polarity of a grammatical structure on this path must find a companion on the same path, and every possible companion on the path must be the companion of one polarity at most on the path, otherwise the path can be removed.*

The ICP algorithm starts from some input automaton of lexical selections and builds, from this initial automaton, an automaton which validates the constraints enforced by the ICP. At each step of the automaton construction process, polarity information is updated and a constraint (called RC or *right-companion constraint*) is applied to filter paths which violate this constraint. We now explain each of these points.

Each state q in the ICP automaton is associated with a record r that summarizes the state of saturation for the polarities of each polarized category or co-anchor C present in the initial automaton. More specifically, for each category C, r records a triple $(root, sat, sub)$:

- *root* is the number of root nodes with category C whose polarity is not saturated
- *sat* is the number of root nodes with category C whose polarity has been saturated with substitution nodes placed occurring to the right of their anchor (i.e. with left companions)
- *lc* is the number of left companions associated with nodes of category C which have not yet been saturated.

For instance, the record associated with a state occurring after a single transition from the initial state labeled with the tree schema α_{imp} would be $\{$S: $(1, 0, 0)$, NP: $(0, 0, 2)$, to: $(0, 0, 1)\}$. This says that the tree schema α_{imp} introduces an unsaturated root node with category 'S', two left companions of category 'NP' and one of category 'to' (i.e. three unsaturated substitution sites occurring to the right of their anchor).

Note that information about right companions (i.e. unsaturated substitution sites occurring to the left of their anchor) is not recorded. This is because right companions must be saturated immediately and thus need not be passed on through the automaton. As we shall see below the information is used by the RC-constraint however thereby filtering out paths violating this constraint.

Two constraints ensure the elimination of sequences of grammatical items which cannot possibly lead to a valid parse.

The first constraint, the *right-companion constraint* requires that all states must be such that the sum *root* + *sat* of saturated and unsaturated root nodes with category C is bigger or equal to the number *rc* of right companions of category C. This effectively enforces the left context constraint discussed in Sect. 4 in that it requires that for any substitution node occurring to the left of the anchor there is a corresponding root node of the same category. This root node may be unsaturated (it has not been substituted in) or saturated (it has already been combined with a left companion, i.e. a substitution site occurring to the right of its anchor). In each case, it can be used to satisfy the right companion requirement and the polarity information is updated accordingly, i.e. either *root* or *sat* is decremented, and *lc* is possibly incremented.

Thus for instance, given the sentence 'Say it to John', selecting the transitive tree schema α_{tr} for 'say' would result in a state tagged with $\{$S: $(1, 0, 0)$, NP: $(0, 0, 1)\}$ where the number of saturated and unsaturated roots of category 'NP' (0) is smaller than the number of right companions (1). Since the RC-constraint is violated this state is not created and the path aborts. As a result, all combinations of α_{tr} with the tree schemas selected by 'it', 'to' and 'John' will be ignored during parsing.

The second constraint, the *valid path constraint*, states that in the final state of a valid path (i.e. a path that will be considered for parsing), the *lc* value is null for all categories (all substitution nodes occurring to the right of the anchor of their containing tree have been filled), the *root* value is 1 for the S category and null for all other categories (all root nodes have been substituted in a substitution site). Since the RC-constraint ensures that all right companions have been saturated, this additional constraint ensures that the ICP principle is respected, i.e. that each every polarity on a path of the automaton has a companion on the same path, and further that each companion on a path is the companion of exactly one polarity on this path.

In sum, we have informally shown that the ICP algorithm integrates the Left-Context constraint. A formal proof is outstanding. An other open issue concerns the relative efficiency of the two algorithms (ICP and Left-Context Polarity filtering). The state information carried by the states of the ICP is richer than that of the Left-Context algorithm, thereby inducing a larger number of states when building the automaton. To assess the impact of this difference on effective running times, an empirical comparison would be needed.

7 Conclusion

In this paper, we presented a polarity based lexical disambiguation technique for LTAG and showed that it significantly reduces the size of the automata from which parsing proceeds. We also related out proposal to the general framework for polarity based lexical selection disambiguation presented by Bonfate et al. [3], Perrier [14], and Morey [11]. Future work includes a formal proof of the relation between these approaches and a large scale empirical evaluation of the impact of the proposed filtering technique on parsing efficiency. Another interesting question concerns the definition of polarization. Here we restricted polarities to syntactic categories. It would be interesting to investigate how the approach extends to the rich set of feature values usually present in large scale LTAG.

References

1. Bangalore, S., Joshi, A.: Supertagging: an approach to almost parsing. Comput. Linguist. **25**(2), 237–265 (1999)
2. Bonfante, G., Guillaume, B., Morey, M.: Dependency constraints for lexical disambiguation. In: IWPT 2009, pp. 242–253 (2009)
3. Bonfante, G., Guillaume, B., Perrier, G.: Polarization and abstraction of grammatical formalisms as methods for lexical disambiguation. In: COLING 2004, pp. 303–309 (2004)
4. Bonfante, G., Le Roux, J., Perrier, G.: Lexical disambiguation with polarities and automata. In: Ibarra, O.H., Yen, H.-C. (eds.) CIAA 2006. LNCS, vol. 4094, pp. 283–284. Springer, Heidelberg (2006)
5. Boullier, P.: Supertagging: a non-statistical parsing-based approach. In: IWPT 2003, pp. 55–66 (2003)
6. Crabbé, B.: Représentation informatique de grammaires fortement lexicalisées: application à la grammaire d'arbres adjoints. Ph.D. thesis, Université Nancy 2 (2005)
7. Duchier, D., Le Roux, J., Parmentier, Y.: The metagrammar compiler: An NLP application with a multi-paradigm architecture. In: Van Roy, P. (ed.) MOZ 2004. LNCS, vol. 3389, pp. 175–187. Springer, Heidelberg (2005)
8. Joshi, A., Schabes, Y.: Tree-Adjoining Grammar. Handbook of Formal Languages, pp. 69–123. Springer, Berlin (1997)
9. Lang, B.: Recognition can be harder than parsing. Comput. Intell. **10**, 486–494 (1994)

10. Lehmann, S., Oepen, S., Regnier-Prost, S., Netter, K., Lux, V., Klein, J., Falkeda, K., Fouvry, F., Estival, D., Dauphin, E., Compagnion, H., Baur, J., Balkan, L., Arnold, D.: TSNLP - Test suites for natural language processing. In: COLING 1996, pp. 711–716 (1996)
11. Morey, M.: Étiquetage grammatical symbolique et interface syntaxe-sémantique des formalismes grammaticaux lexicalisés polarisés. Ph.D. thesis, Université de Lorraine (2011)
12. Parmentier, Y., Kallmeyer, K., Lichte, T., Maier, W., Dellert, J.: A syntax-semantics parsing environment for mildly context-sensitive formalisms. In: TAG+9, pp. 121–128 (2008)
13. Perrier, G.: Interaction grammars. In: COLING 2000, pp. 600–606 (2000)
14. Perrier, G.: Désambiguisation lexicale à l'aide d'automates de polarités. Technical report INRIA (2008). http://hal.archives-ouvertes.fr/inria-00278443

Computational Semantics

Computational Geometry

Resolving Anaphors in Sanskrit

Madhav Gopal[1]([⊠]) and Girish Nath Jha[2]

[1] Centre for Linguistics, SLL & CS,
Jawaharlal Nehru University, New Delhi, India
mgopalt@gmail.com
[2] Special Centre for Sanskrit Studies, Jawaharlal Nehru University,
New Delhi, India
girishjha@gmail.com

Abstract. This paper is based on the M.Phil. dissertation of the first author. It talks about the automatic resolution of lexical anaphors in Sanskrit with the help of POS tagged data. The present approach exploits the grammatical features of Sanskrit language in determining the antecedents of anaphors and cataphors. A system called SARS has been developed and implemented. The input to the system is the POS tagged Sanskrit text in which various morphological features are attached to the words. The system is currently handling intra-sentential anaphors/cataphors and giving encouraging results.

Keywords: Anaphora resolution · Sanskrit · Pañcatantra · Reflexives · Reciprocals · Anaphors and cataphors · POS tagging

1 Introduction

Anaphora resolution has proven to be a formidable task for computers to perform. It plays a significant role in most of the NLP applications such as machine translation (MT), text summarization, question answering systems, information extractions etc. It is a very wide topic in NLP and generally, it includes lexical anaphors, third person pronouns, and other anaphoric items. In Sanskrit anaphor resolution is in initial state and has received very little computational research. Until now, only a few works (Jha et al. 2008, 2009, 2011) are available on this topic.

The present work is a small effort to help Sanskrit make translatable mechanically in other human languages so that it could be reachable to maximum number of people of the world sharing knowledge stored in it. Anaphora resolution systems are of crucial importance for correct translation. When translating into languages which mark the gender of pronoun, for example, it is essential to resolve the anaphoric relation in source language. In translation, the reference to a discourse entity encoded by a source language anaphor by the speaker (or writer) has not only to be identified by the hearer (translator or translation system) but also re-encoded in a co-referential/co-specificational expression of the target language. So, to do these things efficiently we need an anaphora resolution system for Sanskrit.

© Springer International Publishing Switzerland 2014
Z. Vetulani and J. Mariani (Eds.): LTC 2011, LNAI 8387, pp. 83–92, 2014.
DOI: 10.1007/978-3-319-08958-4_7

2   Early Works on Sanskrit Anaphora Resolution

Jha et al. (2008, 2009, 2011) have done a wider case study of anaphors in Sanskrit scanning the language from the epics to *śivarājavijayam*. They have discussed about the concept of anaphora and anaphora resolution techniques in Indian intellectual tradition including Vyākaraṇa, Nyāya, and Mīmāmsā. The papers have focused on pronominal anaphors and proposed a workable solution in terms of an algorithm. A Sanskrit Analysis System (SAS) containing several modules has also been developed that will supposedly assist the resolution. We have modified their generalisations and have presented the algorithm based on our study of the language in the text of Pañcatantra (PT). Thus, we have deviated from their proposal for reflexives and reciprocals.

Pralayankar and Devi (2010) also have presented an algorithm, which reportedly identifies different types of pronominals and their antecedents in Sanskrit. The computational grammar implemented there "uses very familiar concepts such as clause, subject, object etc., which are identified with the help of morphological information and concepts such as precede and follow". The method adopted for resolving the anaphors is by exploiting the morphological richness of the language. The system is reportedly giving encouraging results. This work is also not flawless. In their algorithms they have ignored the fact that Sanskrit reflexives are impersonal, i.e. they do not encode person feature and also that Sanskrit reflexives do not agree in gender with their antecedents. The algorithm does not consider reciprocals and cataphoric usage of reflexives and reciprocals. The paper does not define the term 'possessive' used in the algorithm.

3   Lexical Anaphors in Sanskrit

Sanskrit has a great number of lexical anaphors like other vocabulary items. It has only the nominal form of the anaphors: reflexives and reciprocals. The reflexive pronouns, like any nominal, inflect for case (barring *svayam*). The possessive reflexives, which could be more appropriately named as 'reflexive possessive adjectives', even inflect for number and gender also. The reciprocals are largely stagnant forms and do not inflect for any grammatical feature. However, very rarely casal inflections of some reciprocals are also available in Sanskrit texts. The reflexives and reciprocals are also used in compound constructions[1].

3.1   Reflexives

Sanskrit reflexives do not encode person feature; they are impersonal. The reflexive pronouns found in the PT could be classified in three categories:

---

[1] Our study of lexical anaphors described here is based on our study of the *Pañcatantra*. The examples are taken from different sections of this text and in transliteration we have followed IAST.

3.1.1 Proper Reflexives

In the text we have found *ātman* as the only proper reflexive pronoun. Like personal pronouns, it takes case suffixes, but it is invariant for gender and person features. In contrast to personal pronouns, referent *number* is not a coded feature of the reflexive *ātman*. However, its genitive forms behave like possessive reflexives and agree with the number of the antecedent, but unlike other possessive reflexives, they do not vary for gender agreement with the possessed item.

(1)   *tataḥ* ***aham***   *pūrvam eva*   ***ātmāna-m***
       then   1sg.nom before   emph self-acc
       aratna-m   *samarpya*
       jewellery_less-acc   surrender.grn
       etān   *muñcāmi.*
       these.m.3pl.acc   release.1sg.prs
       'Then, I being without any jewellary, hereby, dedicate myself and get these people released.' <caurabrāhmṇa-kathā, mitrabheda>

3.1.2 Possessive Reflexives

sva, svīya, svaka, svakīya, ātmīya, and *nija* are possessive reflexives and are inflected for case, number and gender features. All of these possessive reflexives are semantically identical and mutually interchangeable. They are used more like an adjective and generally precede the modified element.

(2)   *tvām*   *dṛṣ-ṭvā dūrataḥ api*
       2sg.acc see-grn distantly emph
       caura-siṃha-ḥ   *praviṣ-ṭaḥ* ***svam***
       thief-lion-sg.nom enter-pspl self.m.sg.acc   *durgam.*
       fort.sg.acc
       'Seeing you distantly, the thief lion entered in his fort.' <siṃha-śaśaka-kathā, mitrabheda>

3.1.3 Intensive Reflexives

The intensive reflexive pronouns *svayam* and *svayameva* are morphologically invariant and refer to the subject of the sentence. Intensive reflexives are like emphatic markers, and that is why they are called emphatic reflexives as well. The reflexive *svayam-eva* is semantically more emphatic; *eva* itself is an emphatic in the language. Otherwise *svayam* and *svayam-eva* are the same. Both of them do not occupy an argument position in a sentence. Referent number is not a coded feature of these. This type of reflexive too is used in compounds.

(3)   *bhṛty-aiḥ*   *vinā*   ***svayam*** *rājā*
       servant.pl.ins without self   king
       loka-anugraha-kāribhiḥ
       people-welfare-doer.pl.ins
       mayūkh-aiḥ iva dīptāṃśuḥ   *tejasvī   api*
       ray-pl.ins   like sun   brilliant emph

na   śobha-te
not suit-3sg.prs.pass
'As without rays the brilliant sun does not look beautiful, so is a king
himself without servants who serve people.' <kīlotpāṭi-vānarakathā,
mitrabheda >

3.2 Reciprocals

Reciprocal pronouns do not inflect for case, gender, number, or person; however, there
is one instance of *parasparam* in the PT that has been used in genitive singular. All the
reciprocals always need either a plural antecedent or a dual one for their interpretation.
The reciprocals used in the PT include *anyōnyam, parasparam, itaretaram,* and *mitʰaḥ.*

(4)   *tau   ca **parasparam***
       3du.m.nom and rec
       mantra-yataḥ
       advise-3du.prs
       'And they (two) advise each other.' <prastāvanā-kathā, mitrabheda >

(5)   *yathā chāyā-tap-au   nityam*
       as   shadow-sun-du always
       *su-sambaddh-au   **parasparam***
       well-affiliated-du.m   rec
       evam   karma   ca kartā   ca
       same_way act.nom and doer.nom and
       *saṃ-śliṣṭ-au   **itaretaram***
       well-stick.pspl-du rec
       'As shadow and sun are always well   connected to each other, so are
       the act and doer to each other.' <mandabhāgyasomi- laka-kathā,
       mitrasamprāptikam>

(6)   *tataḥ   ca niśīth-e   yāvat*
       afterwards and midnight.loc rel
       paśya-ti   tāvat tau   eva
       see-3sg.prs then 3du.dst.m.nom only
       *dvau puruṣ-au   **mithaḥ** mantra-yataḥ.*
       two   man-du.nom rec   advise-3du.prs
       'And afterwards, when in the midnight he   sees, those two men advise each
       other.' <vṛṣabhānugaśṛgāla-kathā, mtsp>

3.3 Cataphoric Expressions

Expressions are cataphoric when they (pronoun etc.) precede the linguistic expression
necessary for their interpretation in the given discourse. In PT this kind of expressions
has been sparsely used. Some of such usages are illustrated through the following
sentences:

(7)   *tat   śru-tva   ga-ta-āyuṣa-m   iva*
       that   listen-grn   go-pspl-age-acc   as
       ātmān-am   manyamānaḥ   sañjīvaka-ḥ

       self-acc   assuming   Sanjeevaka-nom
       param   viṣāda-m   agamat.
       great   sadness-acc   go.3sg.pst
       'After listening that, Sanjeevaka believing   himself as dead, got to great
       sadness.' <śṛgāladundubhi-kathā, mitrabheda >

(8)   *tataḥ   svami-prasāda-rahit-au   kṣut-*
       then   master-mercy-less-du.nom   hunger-
       kṣāma-kaṇṭh-au   parasparam
       weak-throat-du.nom   rec
       karaṭaka-damanak-au   mantra-yete.
       Karaṭaka-Damanaka-du.nom   advise-3du.prs
       'Then, deprived of the mercy of their master, Karaṭaka and Damanaka advise
       each other.' <dantilagorambhayoḥ kathā, mitrabheda>

4   The Sanskrit Anaphora Resolution System (SARS)

The system developed is called Sanskrit Anaphora Resolution System (SARS). As input
it takes POS tagged data of Sanskrit. It goes through five processes before it gets the final
result. The input is pasted in the text area of the system which is there in the homepage of
SARS, and then is sent for processing and resolution. The pre-processor of the system
replaces the double *daṇḍas* (full stop marker in Sanskrit) with single *daṇḍas* (the double
daṇḍas are used in the text at the end of a verse). Afterwards, the data is tokenized in
single sentences delimited by a single *daṇḍa*. After sentence tokenization each word is
tokenized. The system considers a single tokenised sentence at a time for resolving the
anaphors. In each tokenized sentence the system first checks whether a reflexive or
reciprocal is available in the sentence in question. If they are not there then it leaves that
sentence and considers next sentence for the same. And if they are there, it searches for
its antecedents as per our rules (see the algorithm) and resolves it. After resolving the
anaphor in a sentence it moves on to the next sentence and operates likewise till the end
of the input text. The candidates for being the antecedents of reflexives (PRF) and
reciprocals (PRC) are common nouns (NC), proper nouns (NP), personal pronouns
(PPR) and relative pronouns (PRL) as per our generalisations in the PT. All these
categories are simply identified on the basis of their morphosyntactic tags. Thus POS
tagging information is very crucial for anaphora resolution in this system.

4.1   Methods and Techniques Used

SARS is planned to develop in web architecture. The system tools are Java based. Front
end is done in Java Server Pages (JSP) running on the web server called Apache
Tomcat. The programming has been done in the Java environment. The system takes
the input in text area, and then sends it for tokenisation and other steps described
earlier.

4.2   The POS Tagging of the text

To conduct this research we have taken the text of PT which was POS tagged by the authors with Indic Language POS Tagset (IL-POST) developed by Microsoft Research India. The corpus was subsequently published by the LDC (http://www.ldc.upenn.edu/Catalog/CatalogEntry.jsp?catalogId=LDC2011T04). The IL-POST is a standard framework for tagging major Indian languages. This is a hierarchical tagset, based on guidelines similar to EAGLES. This tagset encodes information at three levels - Categories, Types, and Attributes. It is supposed to provide cross-linguistic compatibility, reusability, and interchange-ability. The tags used are extremely fine-grained, and incorporate a great deal of information about case, gender, number and so on. The IL-POST is able to accommodate all desired linguistic features of Sanskrit and the tagged corpus remains compatible with other languages tagged by a brethren tagset (Jha et al. 2009, 2011).

4.3   The SARS Algorithm

Currently the system considers only lexical anaphors (reflexives and reciprocals) and it identifies intrasentential antecedents of these anaphors in the input text. The algorithm is based on our study of lexical anaphors in the PT and it may work for the other similar texts as well.

4.3.1   Algorithm for Reflexive Anaphora

1. Tokenize each sentence (S) of the input text.
2. Pick up the S in which PRF tag occurs.
3. Check whether the S has NP, NC, PPR, or PRL.
4. Consider all the NP, NC, PPR, and PRL in the S that precede the PRF.
5. Check whether NP, NC, PPR, or PRL has/have .nom tag.
6. If one of the NP, NC, PPR, or PRL has .nom tag, then that word is identified as the antecedent of the PRF.
7. If more than one of these have .nom tag then the nearest to PRF would be its antecedent.
8. If the conditions 6 or 7 are not met then the NP, NC, PPR, or PRL having .ins tag would be considered the antecedent of the PRF.

4.3.2   Algorithm for Reflexive Cataphora

9. If the S does not have any preceding NP, NC, PPR, or PRL with.nom tag then consider the following NP, NC, PPR, or PRL containing.nom tag.
10. If one of the following NP, NC, PPR, or PRL has .nom tag, then that word is identified as the antecedent.

11. If more than one of these have.nom tag, then the nearest to the PRF would be its antecedent.
12. If the conditions 9 or 10 are not met then the NP, NC, PPR, or PRL having.ins tag would be considered the antecedent of the PRF.

4.3.3 Algorithm for Reciprocal Anaphora

1. Tokenize each sentence (S) of the input text.
2. Pick up the S in which the PRC tag occurs.
3. Check whether the S has NP, NC, PPR, or PRL.
4. Consider all the NP, NC, PPR, and PRL in the S that precede the PRC.
5. Check whether NP, NC, PPR, or PRL has/have .du.nom or .pl.nom tag.
6. If one of the NP, NC, PPR, or PRL has .du.nom or .pl.nom tag, then that word is identified as the antecedent of the PRC.
7. If more than one of these have .du.nom or .pl.nom tag then the nearest to the PRC would be its antecedent.
8. If all of them are containing .sg.nom tag then all of them would be antecedents of the PRC.
9. If the conditions 6, 7 or 8 are not met then the NP, NC, PPR, or PRL having .du.ins or. pl.ins tag would be considered the antecedent of the PRC.

4.3.4 Algorithm for Reciprocal Cataphora

10. If the S does not have any preceding NP, NC, PPR, or PRL then consider the following NP, NC, PPR, or PRL containing .du.nom or .pl.nom tag.
11. If one of the following NP, NC, PPR, or PRL has .du.nom or .pl.nom tag, then that word is identified as the antecedent of the PRC.
12. If more than one of the following NP, NC, PPR, or PRL have .du.nom or .pl.nom tag, then the nearest to the PRF would be its antecedent.
13. If all of the following NP, NC, PPR, or PRL have .sg.nom tag, then all of them would be collectively identified as the antecedent of the PRC.
14. If the conditions 11, 12 or 13 are not met then the NP, NC, PPR, or PRL having .du.ins or. pl.ins tag would be considered the antecedent of the PRC.

5 Testing of SARS

SARS has been tested on 3659 sentences from the POS tagged text of PT. These sentences are of various types that have been given to SARS for anaphora resolution. Before entering the data into the program for resolution we have noted the number of anaphor occurrences in the input text. In the input data 90 PRF (reflexives) and 25 PRC (reciprocals) were found (total 115 anaphor occurrences). Later on the number of anaphor antecedent pairs resolved by the system is noted. The intersentential and zero pronoun cases which remained unresolved have also been noted; such cases were 25 for reflexives and 1 for reciprocal has been found in such use. All these readings have been taken manually. The number of correctly and incorrectly found anaphor antecedent pairs is noted. Table 1 presents the summary of results we have obtained after testing SARS:

Table 1. Evaluation results of Sanskrit anaphors

Anaphors	Total	Correct	Wrong	Unresolved
Reflexives	90	50	15	25
Reciprocals	25	20	4	1
Total	115	70	19	26

5.1   Result Analysis and Limitation

Currently this system is giving results for intrasentential lexical anaphors. The results are encouraging. There were 89 intrasentential lexical anaphors and cataphors in the input text and out of which 70 were correctly resolved. However, an improvement is needed for better results. The system is not able to handle intersentential anaphors at present state. Also, if a sentence has both a reflexive and a reciprocal, it picks up one of them and gives the result. The cases of reflexive compounding and reciprocal compounding are not handled. We are reporting an ongoing work; in future, hopefully, we shall be reporting better results.

5.2   Limitations of the System

The system is able to identify only intrasentential lexical anaphors. There are a lot more anaphoric usages in the language that, yet, need to be handled automatically in order to facilitate the language processing tasks. The intersentential cases of reflexives and reciprocals are yet to be resolved. The system does not recognise clause boundaries and does not work for complex sentences validly. The compounding of all kinds of pronouns is a new type of problem in anaphora resolution research in Sanskrit. Such structures increase the load of the machine and reduce the efficiency of the system. The present system does not take care of compound reflexives and compound reciprocals. To resolve them it will require a separate module called compound processor. Also, the system does not consider pro drop, that is, zero pronoun cases.

6   Conclusion and Further Research

The applications of anaphora resolution are enormous. SARS program can prove to be a very useful tool for machine translation systems. If the anaphors and their antecedents are known to machine, the machine can take care of them when they are being translated in typologically different languages as there might be some issues of agreements. To fit to these agreements such resolution is unavoidable. As the system developed is highly scalable, it can be used for other Sanskrit texts with the same performance.

This is a small research on designing an anaphor resolution system for Sanskrit. The input to the system is POS tagged Sanskrit data. The linguistic analysis of the data for machine is based on the tagging information only. As the system is currently handling only intrasentential anaphors, it would have to be enhanced to cover wider areas of coreference resolution like intersentential anaphor handling and also to resolve third person pronouns which are often anaphoric. With the help of verbal inflections the cases of zero pronouns can also be handled, as the Sanskrit verb encodes information about its subject also. The use of anaphoric adjectives is a predominant feature of Sanskrit and their resolution is also warranted. To what extent morphological features will solve the problem and how the rest problems would be solved – are some of the relevant questions which require rigorous research in order to resolve satisfactorily.

To use this system professionally for other Sanskrit texts as well we would need the following additions:

- adding a sandhi processing module
- adding lexical resources
- adding compound processing module
- adding a comprehensive POS tagger

For the smooth running of the system the issues of sandhi splitting, compound processing, and punctuation marking need to be taken care of efficiently. In comparison to other Indian languages Sanskrit texts are a bit complex and therefore their pre-processing has to be done rigorously.

References

Gopal, M., Mishra, D., Singh, D.P.: Evaluating tagsets for Sanskrit. In: Jha, G.N. (ed.) Sanskrit Computational Linguistics. LNCS, vol. 6465, pp. 150–161. Springer, Heidelberg (2010)

Gopal, M.: Anaphor Resolution in the Sanskrit Text Panchatantra: A Rule Based Approach to Resolve Lexical Anaphors in Sanskrit. LAP LAMBERT Academic Publishing, Verlag, Paperback (2012)

Hobbs, J.: Resolving pronoun references. Lingua **44**, 311–338 (1978)

Jha, G.N., et al.: Anaphors in Sanskrit. In: Johansson, C. (ed.) Proceedings of the Second Workshop on Anaphora Resolution (WAR-II), NEALT Proceedings Series vol. 2. pp. 11–25. Tartu University Library, NEALT, Estonia (2008)

Jha, G.N., Sobha, L., Mishra, D.: Discourse anaphor and resolution techniques in Sanskrit. In: Sobha L., Branco, A., Mitkov, R. (eds.) Proceedings of the 7th Discourse Anaphora and Anaphora Resolution Colloquium (DAARC 2009), pp. 135–150. AU-KBC Research Centre, Chennai (2009)

Jha, G.N., Gopal, M., Mishra, D.: Annotating Sanskrit corpus: adapting IL-POSTS. In: Vetulani, Z. (ed.) LTC 2009. LNCS (LNAI), vol. 6562, pp. 371–379. Springer, Heidelberg (2011)

Lappin, S., Leass, H.J.: An algorithm for pronominal anaphora resolution. Comput. Linguist. **20** (4), 535–561 (1994)

Pralayankar, P., Devi, S.L.: Anaphora resolution algorithm for Sanskrit. In: Jha, G.N. (ed.) Sanskrit Computational Linguistics. LNCS, vol. 6465, pp. 209–217. Springer, Heidelberg (2010)

Unsupervised Coreference Resolution Using a Graph Labeling Approach

Nafise Sadat Moosavi$^{(\boxtimes)}$ and GholamReza GhassemSani

Sharif University of Technology, Tehran, Iran
n_moosavi@ce.sharif.edu, sani@sharif.edu

Abstract. In this paper, we present a new unsupervised coreference resolution method, that models coreference resolution as a graph labeling problem. The proposed approach uses an incremental graph development method that hierarchically deploys coreference features from higher precision to lower ones. Then, a relaxation labeling method is used for solving the graph labeling problem.

Keywords: Unsupervised coreference resolution · Graph labeling · Relaxation labeling · Hierarchical graph development

1 Introduction

Coreferences are relations that hold between expressions which refer to the same entities. Expressions are often called mentions of entities. A coreference is a reflexive, symmetric, and transitive equivalence relation. The reflexive and transitive closure over coreference relations generates equivalence classes of mentions, which are called coreference chains.

Coreference resolution is equivalent to the set partitioning problem in which the search space is the set of all mutually disjoint subsets of mentions. From a language engineering perspective, the accurate identification of the entities that are referred to is an important challenge. Numerous natural language processing (NLP) tasks such as information extraction, question answering, automatic summarization, machine translation, and natural language generation can benefit from availability of a coreference resolution system.

By using coreference information, we can construct a graph G in which each mention is a vertex, and each coreference relation forms an edge between corresponding vertices. In this way, coreference resolution can be formulated as a graph labeling problem: all vertices with the same label are considered to be in a same coreference chain.

Several earlier works modeled coreference resolution as a graph labeling or graph partitioning problem [1–5]. In this paper, we present a new unsupervised coreference resolution system, which also casts coreference resolution as a graph labeling problem. It employs relaxation labeling method for labeling assignment.

© Springer International Publishing Switzerland 2014
Z. Vetulani and J. Mariani (Eds.): LTC 2011, LNAI 8387, pp. 93–103, 2014.
DOI: 10.1007/978-3-319-08958-4_8

The presented system has been inspired by the success of two successful coreference systems [4,6]. However, our system deploys a new hierarchical graph construction method for developing the adjacency graph.

The hierarchical graph construction method helps the labeling algorithm to just consider the most reliable set of neighbors when it tries to label mentions at each pass of the algorithm.

2   Related Work

Recently, the accessibility of annotated coreference data (MUC conferences and ACE evaluations) has brought up the deployment of a wide variety of supervised machine learning approaches for the problem of coreference resolution [7]. The focus of statistical approaches to coreference resolution has been moved from attainment of simple pairwise models (which determine whether two mentions are referring to the same entity [8,9]) to the use of rich linguistic features [10,11], and utilization of advanced learning techniques [12].

Some recent works on coreference resolution have shown that a rich feature set that can model lexical, syntactic, semantic, and discourse aspects of mentions is essential for the success of the coreference task [13–15]. When these rich features are combined with the complexity of coreference models, supervised approaches will be more dependent on annotated data and less appropriate for languages with insufficient or no annotated data.

Because of the increasing importance of multilingual processing in NLP community, developing unsupervised or semi-supervised methods for automatic processing of languages with limited resource has become more essential.

Unsupervised learning methods totally eliminate the need to annotated data, and remarkably, recent unsupervised coreference resolution methods compete with their supervised counterparts [6,7,14–16].

Motivated in part by such observations, in this paper, we present a new unsupervised model for coreference resolution. We model unsupervised coreference resolution as a graph labeling problem which is solved by a relaxation labeling algorithm. The proposed method has been inspired by the success of two earlier coreference systems [17,18], and it benefits from some advantages of both approaches. Sapena et al. [17] can be considered as a supervised counterpart of our approach, and Raghunathan et al. [18] is a rule-based system that deploys coreference features in a sieve architecture. The sieve architecture allows more precise features to be considered before low precision features in coreference decisions. Therefore, the decisions made based on more precise features will not be affected by lower precision ones.

3   Coreference Resolution as Graph Labeling

The input of a coreference resolution system includes a document consisting of a set of mentions. Mentions are typically a number of noun phrases that are headed by some pronominal or nominal terminals. An intra-document coreference resolution system partitions such mentions based on their underlying referent entities. Using relations between document's mentions, we can construct an undirected graph in which each mention is represented as a vertex, and each edge corresponds to a coreference relation between two mentions. In other words, assigning mentions to entities can be formulated as a graph labeling problem [4]. As we consider graphs whose vertices represent mentions, here, vertices and mentions are used interchangeably.

It is desired to model the mutual influence between neighboring mentions for simultaneously estimating labels of all mentions in a document. Theoretically, such a model can cover long-range influences between transitively related mentions. Such influences decrease as the distance of two mentions increases. However, for tractability purpose, one should focus on the strongest dependencies between neighbors. Such a model, which is called first-order Markov random Fields [19], cannot be solved in a closed analytic form and is therefore addressed by an iterative technique called relaxation labeling [20].

Relaxation labeling is an iterative optimization process which efficiently solves the problem of assigning a set of labels to a set of variables, while satisfying a set of constraints. Relaxation labeling aims at a label assignment that satisfies as many constraints as possible. In other words, it uses contextual information, which is expressed as a number of constraint functions, for reducing local ambiguities in graph labeling.

One significant feature of relaxation labeling is its ability to deal with any kind of constraints. The algorithm is independent of the complexity of defined constraints (i.e., complexity of modeled application), and it can be improved by using any available constraints. Thus, complex constraints can be used without the need to change the algorithm. Relaxation labeling is applied to various NLP tasks such as POS tagging [21], shallow parsing [22], and supervised coreference resolution [4].

4   System Description

As discussed before, we cast coreference resolution as a graph labeling problem. This was at first inspired by the successful results of [17], which benefits from combining group classification and chain formation methods in a same step. Combination of group classification and chain formation methods in a global method ensures the consistency of solutions [17].

The domain knowledge (i.e., coreference relations) is combined with the model through coefficients of a compatibility matrix. Since the compatibility matrix is a key element of weighted label assignments, the choice of these coefficients is crucial for the success of the algorithm.

These coefficients can be set manually based on the problem specification, or alternatively, they can be learned from a training set. For instance, Sapena et al. [17] uses a decision tree for learning compatibility coefficients. For our method to be unsupervised and therefore independent from any training data, compatibility coefficients should be determined in an unsupervised manner. One possible solution for computing compatibility coefficients is to use Wagstaff and Cardie's approach [23] for deriving incompatibility functions from linguistic features. However, using their method will bring up the concern of setting different heuristic and experimental parameters for weights of compatibility functions [23].

We adopt the idea of sieve architecture presented in [18] for this purpose. The proposed system of Raghunathan et al. [18] is based on the fact that a small number of high precision features is often overwhelmed by a larger number of low precision ones. Thus, Raghunathan et al. [18] proposed a multi-pass system in which higher precision features are deployed at earlier stages of coreference decisions.

We deploy this multi-pass idea in our coreference resolution System. Therefore, our system is a layered system in which each layer is constructed based on different coreference knowledge, and feeds its output forward to the next layer. The layers are organized in a way that highest precision feature is used at the first layer, and successive layers deploy features with decreasing precisions.

The layered architecture is deployed in the graph construction phase; graph is developed incrementally based on different features at each pass, and then the relaxation labeling algorithm is applied to the current partially constructed graph. Therefore, the algorithm will just consider more certain neighborhood relations (i.e., the neighborhood relations that contain higher precision features); unattached vertices will be labeled later at subsequent passes. After determination of weighted label assignments in each partially constructed graph, some of the assignments are determined as being confident enough. These assignments will not change at later passes and therefore will not be affected by weaker features.

4.1 Relaxation Labeling

Suppose that Λ is the set of possible labels for a set of variables V; $V = \{v_1, \ldots, v_n\}$ is a set of vertices which, in our modeling, corresponds to the document's mentions, and $R = \{r_{ij}\}$ is a compatibility matrix that defines relations between variables (i.e., adjacency matrix in our problem). Each coefficient r_{ij} corresponds to a constraint regarding to v_i and v_j. A higher value for r_{ij} indicates a higher possibility for v_i and v_j to have the same label.

Relaxation labeling starts by assigning initial labels to all variables. It then iteratively modifies label assignments in a manner that the labeling satisfies as many constraints as possible, where constraints are defined by the compatibility matrix. Information of the compatibility matrix and the current label assignment are used for parallel update of labels. In other words, each variable $v_i \in V$ gets an initial probability vector $\bar{p}_i{}^0$, which has one element for each possible label of v_i. $p_i^{(t)}(\lambda)$ is an element of $\bar{p}_i{}^{(t)}$, which corresponds to the probability of assigning label λ to variable v_i at the tth iteration. The whole set of $\bar{p} = \{\bar{p}_1, \ldots, \bar{p}_n\}$ is denominated as weighted label assignments.

A support function is defined for each possible label λ of each variable v_i. The compatibility of the current label assignments of neighbors of v_i, and hypothesis "λ is the label of v_i", is measured by this support function. The support function is defined as follows:

$$S_i^{(t)}(\lambda; \bar{p}) = \sum_{j \in neighbors(v_i)} r_{ij} \times p_j^{(t)}(\lambda) \tag{1}$$

Clearly, the higher value of the support function indicates that it is more probable to label v_i with λ. The support function is then used for updating label assignments:

$$p_i^{(t+1)}(\lambda) = \frac{p_i^{(t)}(\lambda) \times (-m + s_i^{(t)}(\lambda, \bar{p}^{(t)}))}{\sum_{\sigma \in \Lambda} p_i^{(t)}(\sigma) \times (-m + s_i^{(t)}(\sigma, \bar{p}^{(t)}))}, \tag{2}$$

where $m = min(\bar{s}_i^{(t)})$.

We use a negative value for r_{ij} when v_i and v_j are incompatible in terms of coreference features (e.g., their gender features are incompatible). Therefore, s_i can have negative values. m is added for negative support values, and the denominator is for normalizing the result, so that $p_i^{(t+1)}(\lambda)$ will remain a probability.

The process of calculating $p_i^{(t+1)}(\lambda)$ continues until the algorithm converges to stable values for p, or it reaches a predefined maximum number of iterations. Relaxation labeling complexity is linear in proportion to the number of variables (i.e., number of mentions in a document).

4.2   Hierarchical Graph Development

In each pass of our hierarchical graph development algorithm, the system processes all mentions of a document. Supposing the algorithm is in pass j, containing feature set $F_j = \{f_1^j, \ldots, f_m^j\}$, where m is the number of features enclosed in pass j. For each mention m_i, the adjacency graph development process will be performed as follows:

Every mention m_k located before m_i is considered as a candidate for graph development. If both m_k and m_i share one of features $\{f_1^j, \ldots, f_m^j\}$, the vertices v_k and v_i corresponding to m_k and m_i, will be attached by a new edge (only if they were unattached before). There is two possible values for edge weights (i.e., r_{ij}): +1 and −1. A weight of +1 represents a preference, and a weight of −1 represents a restriction. The partially constructed graph of each pass contains only the vertices that have at least one edge to some other vertices.

The features that are used at each pass of the system and their corresponding weights are listed in Table 1. It is notable that the first 6 passes mostly consider non-pronoun mentions and the last pass is only for pronouns. A detailed description of the used features can be found in [6, 13, 14].

4.3   Initialization and Post-processing of Each Pass

We use the same approach as [17] for initializing weighted label assignments. The first non-pronoun mention has no previous mention to be referred to, and it will be considered as the beginning of a new entity. The label assignment of this mention is marked as a first confident assignment in our model. The final label assignments of each pass are considered as the initial label assignments of the next pass. Indeed, if a vertex has a positive neighbor (i.e., a neighbor with a positive weight) with a confident label assignment, it's weighted label assignment will also be marked as a confident assignment at the end of the current pass, and therefore, it would not be changed at later passes.

5   Experiments

5.1   Data

In this work, the following data sets are used for the evaluation purpose.

– ACE2004-NWIRE: the newswire part of ACE 2004. It consists of 128 documents and 11413 mentions.

Table 1. The feature sets of each pass of the system and their corresponding weights.

Pass	Weight	Feature
1	+1	Exact match
2	+1	Appositive
		Role appositive
		Alias
		Demonym
		Relative Pronoun
	−1	Gender mismatch
		Number mismatch
		Entity type mismatch
3	+1	Head match + same non-stop words + compatible modifiers
4	+1	Head match + same non-stop words
		Head match + compatible modifiers
5	+1	Head match
6	+1	Substring
7	+1	Gender match
		Number match
		Entity type match
		Animacy match
		Both speak

- ACE2004-ROTH-DEV: A development set of ACE 2004, which is first utilized in [13]. It consists of 68 documents and 4536 mentions.
- ACE2004-CULOTTA-TEST: A test split of ACE 2004, which is first utilized in [24]. It consists of 107 documents and 5469 mentions.

5.2 Results

The experimental results of our approach are presented in Table 2. Since most of existing evaluations on ACE data sets are based on gold mentions, we also use gold mention boundaries for our experiments. In order to measure the impact of hierarchical graph development, we also present results of a single pass flat variant of our system. This variant constructs the adjacency graph in a single step and uses all features of the multi-pass system in just one step. In this version, edge weights are computed as follow:

$$w_{ij} = \min(1, \sum_{f \in F} \delta_k f_k(m_i, m_j)), \tag{3}$$

where δ_k is a fix weight considered for each feature f_k. Since the first three passes of the multi-pass system contain higher precision features, δ_k is set to $+1$ for such features (δ_k is set to -1 for the features of pass 2 that add a negative edge). δ_k is set to 0.25 for other features. The preprocessing pipelines of both variants of the proposed system are the same as that of [13].

As it is shown, the results of the multi-pass system are considerably higher than that of the single pass variant. However, we still need some further work to reach the performance of more successful unsupervised coreference systems (e.g., [6,14]).

Table 2. Experimental results on ACE 2004 data sets.

System	MUC			B^3		
	R	P	F1	R	P	F1
ACE2004-NWIRE						
Single-pass	53.0	72.1	61.1	41.0	70.2	51.8
Multi-pass	69.1	67.2	68.1	72.6	69.4	71.0
ACE2004-ROTH-DEV						
Single-pass	52.8	76.8	62.6	39.0	78.7	52.2
Multi-pass	69.1	67.1	68.1	73.2	71.6	72.4
ACE2004-CULOTTA-TEST						
Single-pass	52.5	73.5	61.3	41.5	72.6	52.8
Multi-pass	63.5	60.7	62.1	70.4	69.0	69.7

Table 3. Pairwise errors made by our system on the ACE2004-NWIRE data set. Each cell indicates error rate made on the specified configuration.

		Antecedent type		
		Proper	Nominal	Total
Anaphora type	Proper	241/1140	53/171	249/1311
	Nominal	56/257	493/921	549/1178
	Pronoun	286/566	285/451	553/1017

5.3   Error Analysis

Table 3 shows the number of pairwise errors made by the proposed multi-pass system on ACE2004-NWIRE. As it is shown, most errors are made on the nominal anaphora with nominal antecedents. There are several reasons causing a rather high rate for this type of errors. Typically, such errors are caused by wrong head match assumptions, and missing semantic and syntactic compatibility information of the two nominal mentions. Lee et al. [6] uses the first mention of each cluster at most passes; the first mention of each cluster is often more representative than other mentions of that cluster. This can reduce errors such as those made by wrong head match assumptions. Using additional linguistic knowledge such as parse trees, binding theory, salience hierarchy, richer semantic knowledge, and cluster-wise feature sets can further decrease coreference decision errors.

6   Post Conference Section

In this section, we propose an alternative approach for the hierarchical graph development. The main purpose of the hierarchical graph development is the appropriate selection of neighbors in Eq. 1. Graph is at first constructed based on more precise features. Therefore, at each pass of the algorithm, the *neighbors* function just returns more important neighbors of each mention, and the label assignments will be determined based on the label assignments of those neighbors.

As an alternative way for this hierarchical graph development method, we can use a different *neighbors* function in Eq. 1, which provides the same benefit for the labeling algorithm.

Suppose that $F = \{F_1, \ldots, F_m\}$ is a set of feature sets in which each F_i contains one or more binary coreference features, and all F_is are ordered based on their precisions. This ordering can be done manually based on some linguistic knowledge [6], or it can be done based on an automatic feature ordering method. Given F, we can define the *neighbors* function as follows:

$$neighbors(v_i) = \{v_j | \exists_{f_l \in F_k} f_l(v_i, v_j) = true\} \qquad (4)$$

where k is the first index for which there exist a $f_l \in F_k$ with a *true* value for v_i and at least one other vertex. In this way, less precise features will just be considered in the absence of more precise features.

Using this new *neighbors* function, all mention can be labeled simultaneously in just one pass, while the labeling algorithm considers more precise neighbors of each mention for determining label assignments. In this way, the resolution process will be less time consuming while it still benefits from the hierarchical use of coreference features.

7   Conclusions

In this paper, we examine and evaluate the applicability of relaxation labeling in unsupervised coreference resolution, which has been inspired by the earlier work of [17], where relaxation labeling technique is used for supervised coreference resolution.

In comparison to [17], our model is totally unsupervised (i.e., it does not need any labeled data for determining edge weights), and it uses a hierarchical graph development algorithm. This hierarchical graph construction method prevents the small numbers of high precision features to be overwhelmed by a larger number low precision ones. In the hierarchical graph construction, instead of considering the whole set of neighbors, the labeling algorithm just considers the most reliable set of neighbors for labeling a mention at each pass.

We also present a new *neighbors* function as an alternative way to the hierarchical graph development method that provides the same benefits, while being less time consuming.

Although the presented system underperforms the state-of-the-art systems, it shows promising results and can be further improved in several ways. A natural way to extend the model is to incorporate more linguistic knowledge sources, such as those used in [6,14].

References

1. McCallum, A., Wellner, B.: Toward conditional models of identity uncertainty with application to proper noun coreference. In: Proceedings of the IJCAI-03 Workshop on Information Integration on the Web, Acapulco, Mexico, 9–10 August 2003, pp. 79–86 (2003)
2. Lang, J., Qin, B., Liu, T., Li, S.: Unsupervised coreference resolution with hypergraph partitioning. Comput. Inf. Sci. **2**, 55–63 (2009)
3. Cai, J., Mújdricza-Maydt, É., Strube, M.: Unrestricted coreference resolution via global hypergraph partitioning. In: Proceedings of the Shared Task of the 15th Conference on Computational Natural Language Learning, Portland, Oregon, 23–24 June 2011, pp. 56–60 (2011)
4. Sapena, E., Padró, L., Turmo, J.: RelaxCor participation in CoNLL shared task on coreference resolution. In: Proceedings of the Shared Task of the 15th Conference on Computational Natural Language Learning, Portland, Oregon, 23–24 June 2011, pp. 35–39 (2011)

5. Martschat, S., Cai, J., Broscheit, S., Mújdricza-Maydt, É., Strube, M.: A multi-graph model for coreference resolution. In: Proceedings of the Shared Task of the 16th Conference on Computational Natural Language Learning, Jeju Island, Korea, 12–14 July 2012, pp. 100–106 (2012)
6. Lee, H., Chang, A., Peirsman, Y., Chambers, N., Surdeanu, M., Jurafsky, D.: Deterministic coreference resolution based on entity-centric, precision-ranked rules. Computat. Linguist. **39**, 885–916 (2013)
7. Ng, V.: Supervised noun phrase coreference research: the first fifteen years. In: Proceedings of the 48th Annual Meeting of the Association for Computational Linguistics, Uppsala, Sweden, 11–16 July 2010, pp. 1396–1411 (2010)
8. Soon, W.M., Ng, H.T., Lim, D.C.Y.: A machine learning approach to coreference resolution of noun phrases. Comput. Linguist. **27**(4), 521–544 (2001)
9. Yang, X., Zhou, G., Su, J., Tan, C.L.: Coreference resolution using competition learning approach. In: Proceedings of the 41st Annual Meeting of the Association for Computational Linguistics, Sapporo, Japan, 7–12 July 2003, pp. 176–183 (2003)
10. Ji, H., Westbrook, D., Grishman, R.: Using semantic relations to refine coreference decisions. In: Proceedings of the Human Language Technology Conference and the 2005 Conference on Empirical Methods in Natural Language Processing, Vancouver, B.C., Canada, 6–8 October 2005 pp. 17–24 (2005)
11. Ponzetto, S.P., Strube, M.: Semantic role labeling for coreference resolution. In: Companion Volume to the Proceedings of the 11th Conference of the European Chapter of the Association for Computational Linguistics, Trento, Italy, 3–7 April 2006, pp. 143–146 (2006)
12. Denis, P., Baldridge, J.: Specialized models and ranking for coreference resolution. In: Proceedings of the 2008 Conference on Empirical Methods in Natural Language Processing, Waikiki, Honolulu, Hawaii, 25–27 October 2008, pp. 660–669 (2008)
13. Bengtson, E., Roth, D.: Understanding the value of features for coreference resolution. In: Proceedings of the 2008 Conference on Empirical Methods in Natural Language Processing, Waikiki, Honolulu, Hawaii, 25–27 October 2008, pp. 294–303 (2008)
14. Haghighi, A., Klein, D.: Simple coreference resolution with rich syntactic and semantic features. In: Proceedings of the 2009 Conference on Empirical Methods in Natural Language Processing, Singapore, 6–7 August 2009, pp. 1152–1161 (2009)
15. Haghighi, A., Klein, D.: Coreference resolution in a modular, entity centered model. In: Proceedings of Human Language Technologies 2010: The Conference of the North American Chapter of the Association for Computational Linguistics, Los Angeles, Cal., 2–4 June 2010, pp. 385–393 (2010)
16. Martschat, S.: Multigraph clustering for unsupervised coreference resolution. In: Proceedings of the Student Research Workshop at the 51st Annual Meeting of the Association for Computational Linguistics, Sofia, Bulgaria, 5–7 August 2013 (2013, to appear)
17. Sapena, E., Padró, L., Turmo, J.: A global relaxation labeling approach to coreference resolution. In: Proceedings of Coling 2010: Poster Volume, Beijing, China, 23–27 August 2010, pp. 1086–1094 (2010)
18. Raghunathan, K., Lee, H., Rangarajan, S., Chambers, N., Surdeanu, M., Jurafsky, D., Manning, C.: A multi-pass sieve for coreference resolution. In: Proceedings of the 2010 Conference on Empirical Methods in Natural Language Processing, Cambridge, Massachusetts, 9–11 October 2010, pp. 492–501 (2010)
19. Pelkowitz, L.: A continuous relaxation labeling algorithm for markov random fields. IEEE Trans. Syst. Man Cybern. **20**, 709–715 (1990)

20. Hummel, R., Zucker, S.W.: On the foundations of relaxation labeling processes. IEEE Trans. Pattern Anal. Mach. Intell. **5**, 267–287 (1983)
21. Marquez, L., Padro, L.: A flexible pos tagger using an automatically acquired language model. In: Proceedings of the Eighth Conference on European Chapter of the Association for Computational Linguistics, pp. 238–245 (1997)
22. Voutilainen, A., Padro, L.: Developing a hybrid NP parser. In: Proceedings of the Fifth Conference on Applied Natural Language Processing, pp. 80–87 (1997)
23. Cardie, C., Wagstaff, K.: Noun phrase coreference as clustering. In: Proceedings of the 1999 SIGDAT Conference on Empirical Methods in Natural Language Processing and Very Large Corpora, College Park, Maryland, 21–22 June 1999, pp. 82–89 (1999)
24. Culotta, A., Wick, M., McCallum, A.: First-order probabilistic models for coreference resolution. In: Proceedings of Human Language Technologies 2007: The Conference of the North American Chapter of the Association for Computational Linguistics, Rochester, New York, 22–27 April 2007, pp. 81–88 (2007)

The XCDC Relations
as a Spatio-Temporal Ontology

Jędrzej Osiński[(✉)]

Faculty of Mathematics and Computer Science,
Adam Mickiewicz University, Poznań, Poland
josinski@amu.edu.pl

Abstract. Qualitative techniques are important in artificial intelligence. The extended CDC (XCDC) formalism can be successfully used for representation and reasoning about the spatio-temporal aspects of complex events. The model was implemented and tested in the POLINT-112-SMS system providing assistance to the security staff during a large-scale event involving a large number of participants. In this paper we present the process of the construction of the set of spatio-temporal relations expressed in the XCDC model which are conceptualized in a natural language. We also discuss the properties of this collection and show how these relations can be simply combined and partially ordered to get an ontology-like structure.

Keywords: Natural language processing · XCDC · Qualitative knowledge

1 Introduction to the XCDC Model

Qualitative techniques, which make abstraction from quantitative knowledge, are important in artificial intelligence and widely applied in the systems with a natural language input. They can be successfully used for spatial reasoning including describing spatial relations between objects, computing positions or for assessing similarity between spatial scenes. One of the most popular formalism is the Cardinal Direction Calculus (CDC) first presented in [1]. The key idea of that formalism is based on dividing the plane around the reference object (i.e. the object from which the direction relation is determined) into nine regions named after the geographical directions: NW, N, NE, W, O (central region meaning the same location), E, SW, S and SE. These areas, called direction tiles, are closed, unbounded (except for O), their interiors are pairwise disjoint and their union is the whole plane. Directions between the reference object A and target object B are represented in a 3 times 3 direction-relation matrix denoted by dir(A, B) which we define as follows:

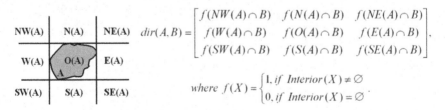

$$dir(A,B) = \begin{bmatrix} f(NW(A)\cap B) & f(N(A)\cap B) & f(NE(A)\cap B) \\ f(W(A)\cap B) & f(O(A)\cap B) & f(E(A)\cap B) \\ f(SW(A)\cap B) & f(S(A)\cap B) & f(SE(A)\cap B) \end{bmatrix},$$

$$\text{where } f(X) = \begin{cases} 1, \text{if } Interior(X) \neq \varnothing \\ 0, \text{if } Interior(X) = \varnothing \end{cases}.$$

© Springer International Publishing Switzerland 2014
Z. Vetulani and J. Mariani (Eds.): LTC 2011, LNAI 8387, pp. 104–115, 2014.
DOI: 10.1007/978-3-319-08958-4_9

There is also an equivalent notation (after [9]) which we will use further in this paper for better clarity of complex formulas: cardinal direction between a reference and a target object is an expression $R_1:...:R_k$ where

1. $1 \leq k \leq 9$,
2. $R_1,...,R_k$ included in {NW, N, NE, W, O, E, SW, S, SE},
3. Ri $\neq$ Rj for every i, j such that $1 \leq i, j \leq k$ and i $\neq$ j.

For practical reason we also define Udir symbol which concerns the sum of all 9 basic relations, i.e.

Udir := NW:N:NE:W:O:E:SW:S:SE.

Now we can define the XCDC (eXtended CDC) formalism originally introduced in [7] which is based on two modifications. Firstly, we describe the spatial relation between objects A and B from two independent perspectives using the pair (instead of one) of direction-relation matrices in which the reference and target object exchange their roles, i.e. we create the structure [dir(A, B), dir(B, A)]. The second stage of the extension is based on using 3D to illustrate static elements of space and dynamic events. We consider an object as a combination of both a temporal span (a time interval, one dimension) and a spatial extension (space region) expressed in two dimensions (as we make abstraction from the actual vertical dimension of these objects) – see Fig. 1a. To distinguish a geographic direction from the element of a matrix, we add the symbol * to the former (i.e., N* denotes the geographic north direction, while N describes a direction-relation matrix). With a 3D representation we can describe situations using three main projections (see Fig. 1b.): on the N*-E* plane, on the T-N* plane and on the T-E* plane. Finally we define the relation between two spatio-temporal objects A and B as follows:

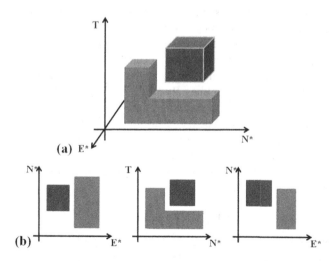

Fig. 1. The spatio-temporal relation between objects (a) and the corresponding projections (b).

$$TS(A,B) = [dir_{N^*-E^*}(A,B), dir_{N^*-E^*}(B,A), dir_{T-N^*}(A,B),$$
$$dir_{T-N^*}(B,A), dir_{T-E^*}(A,B), dir_{T-E^*}(B,A)],$$

where $dir_{X-Y}(A, B)$ denotes a direction-relation matrix for the projection on the X-Y plane. The applications of the XCDC formalism were discussed in [4, 5].

In the next sections we will show how the natural language sentences describing spatio-temporal relations can constitutes a hierarchical, treelike structure of XCDC expressions.

2 Research Methodology

The aim of the research was to define the set of XCDC relations conceptualized in a natural language which could be recognized as a complete and useful collection in many applications. The source of difficulties is the fact that the XCDC formalism provides 26*9 possible combinations most of which has no spatio-temporal interpretation (are incorrect) and many of the remaining has no corresponding simple natural language sentence. Also there are many synonyms in describing spatial and temporal situations. Moreover some expressions (e.g. *in the north-west of*) are the special cases of more general sentences (e.g. *inside*) so the hierarchy has to be discussed too. The overall analysis was based on the three main components described below.

2.1 Corpus Analysis

POLINT-112-SMS system (see [10–12]) is intended to support information management and decision making in emergency situations. The system interprets short messages in the form of SMS texts and processes information provided by the human user. POLINT-112-SMS has the status of a working prototype and was tested in a controlled environment (where actors presented different possible soccer supporters behaviors; two experiments at Warta stadium located in Poznań) as well as during the real soccer match (at Olimpia stadium). In the both cases the human users were police experts who had received no guidelines about the language of the SMS texts or the messages frequency. They were asked to inform the system about any facts important from the security point of view. Each user decided himself which events (but also people, places and objects) should be described and at what level of details. During the analysis of the collected corpus we have selected the group of spatio-temporal relation which could be potentially sufficient in a similar application. The overall results are presented in Table 1:

Table 1. Corpus analysis

Experiment	Users	TS-MN	TS-RN	TS-SU
Warta 1	9	210	94.8 %	82.9 %
Warta 2	12	151	92.7 %	73.5 %
Olimpia	7	152	91.4 %	65.1 %

- the total number of spatio-temporal phrases interpreted by the system (TS-MN),
- the percentage of the spatio-temporal phrases that can be represented by the chosen language relations (TS-RN),
- the percentage of the phrases describing spatio-temporal relations, which were parsed and successfully interpreted (TS-SU).

The relatively low value of TS-SU is due to the nonstandard syntactic phenomena common in the SMS messages, which were not covered by the parser. It is also worth mentioning that taking together all 3 experiments more than 52 % messages sent by users contained spatio-temporal information. That shows the importance of this kind of analysis and potential benefits from the research output.

2.2   Comparison with Other Formalisms

After the analysis of the corpus we assessed the potential collection of XCDC relation with reference to the representational capabilities of the widely used models for spatio-temporal reasoning. In particular even if a potential language relation was not identified in the corpus it was accepted as long as its equivalent appears in a classic models and can be represented in the XCDC formalism. Finally, the set of relations represents the properties of the following models:

- CDC (Cardinal Direction Calculus relations),
- Hernández'es model (relative relations composed with a relative distance; [2]),
- ICD-5 and ICD-9 (Internal Cardinal Direction relations) introduced in [6],
- RCC-5 (Region Connection Calculus; topological relations) as presented in [3].

The comparative analysis of the XCDC and classic models has been recently discussed in [8]. The methods of the conversion of the basic relations expressed in the previous models to the structures of the XCDC formalism were also introduced in that paper.

2.3   Questionnaire Research

The questionnaire research was performed via Internet using free web platform eBadania.pl. The aim of the experiment was to collect the information about the language habits and the self-assessment of the perceptual abilities of potential users of application implementing the XCDC formalism. A total number of 1047 participants filled in the online questionnaire. They were asked about the frequency of using different classes of spatial sentences in an everyday life on a scale of 1 (*never*) to 5 (*very often*). The most popular were relative external direction relations (e.g. *in front of*) – 60 % judged for 5, 25.8 % - for 4, while absolute external relations (as described in Sect. 3): 4.3 % - for 5, 11.8 % - for 4, 20.3 % - for 3. The directions based on clock position (e.g. *on your six*) are the least popular – 45,8 % judged them to 1. Some of the questions were also concerning the way of recognizing geographical directions and the self-confidence in doing it correctly. E.g. the participants were asked whether they can indicate the real north direction at the moment of filling in the questionnaire. Only less than 5 % answered they are not able to do it. This particular result shows that although the geographical directions are not very popular in everyday usage they are a very good basis for a spatio-temporal ontology applicable in advanced systems.

3 Language Relations

The result of the research described above is the set of relations conceptualized by speakers and reflected directly in various natural languages (as e.g., English, Polish, etc.). We will list them now however omitting relative relations (e.g. in front of, in the left part of) which can be easily converted into absolute relations. It is enough to define the orientation of the system of coordinates and the object located in its center. We attribute symbolic names to the relations and divide them into the categories which describe their relationship with the reference object (internal/external).

(external direction relations which refer to the 8 basic geographical directions; describe the mutual spatial configuration of two disconnected objects)

- r_nw (e.g. *B is to the north west of A*),
- r_n (e.g. *B is to the north of A*),
- r_ne (e.g. *B is to the north-east of A*),
- r_w (e.g. *B is to the west of A*),
- r_e (e.g. *B is to the east of A*),
- r_sw (e.g. *B is to the south-west of A*),
- r_s (e.g. *B is to the south of A*),
- r_se (e.g. *B is to the south-east of A*),

(internal direction relations which describe a situation where a target object is located inside a reference one)

- r_in_nw (e.g. *B is in the north-west of A*),
- r_in_n (e.g. *B in the north of A*),
- r_in_ne (e.g. *B in the north-east of A*),
- r_in_w (e.g. *B in the west of A*),
- r_in_e (e.g. *B is in the east of A*),
- r_in_sw (e.g. *B is to the south-west of A*),
- r_in_s (e.g. *B is to south of A*),
- r_in_se (e.g. *B is in the south-east of A*),

(topological relations that make abstraction from the cardinal direction; we use them in an everyday language when the cardinal direction is unknown or the particular relationship concerns all the directions)

- r_in (e.g. *B is inside A*),
- r_out (e.g. *B is outside of A*),
- r_surrounded (e.g. *B is surrounded by A*),
- r_somewhere (e.g. *B is somewhere in the region of A*),

(temporal relations)

- r_before (e.g. *B is before A*),
- r_after (e.g. *B is after A*),
- r_sametime (e.g. *B is at the same time as A*),
- r_during (e.g. *B is during A*),
- r_sometime (e.g. *B is sometime around A*).

of the above relations we assign the XCDC structure TS(A, B) as shown in Tables 2 and 3. The structure describes spatio-temporal relations in the three projections discussed in the first section of this paper. As an example, let us analyze the structures which refer to the relations: r_n and r_after (matrix notations were presented at Fig. 2). First two matrices of the r_n relation describe only the spatial aspect: they inform that B is to the north (geographical) of A (first matrix) and A can cover maximum three tiles around B depending on its actual size (second matrix). The lack of the information about the size of the objects also implies the three 1's in the last four matrices of the r_after relation. In the system, which is intended to support public security (like POLINT-112-SMS), it is better to get too many possible positions rather than have one of them missing (which could cause a dangerous situation, e.g. if we ask for the localization of an armed person). That is why in the definition of r_after first two matrices have only 1's: the spatial information cannot be calculated. Similarly, r_n has no information about the temporal relation (three 1's in the projection on the T-N* plane). On the other hand in the projection on the T-E* plane object B is inside A (what generates 1's only in the middle column), however we do not know the temporal relation (so there are three 1's). The last matrix in the structure of r_n has all 1's because we cannot specify the temporal relation between A and B as well as the size of the object A (e.g. which tiles around object B it covers). It is important to highlight that all the relations independently from their actual type describe a spatio-temporal relationship. For example, also r_n contains the facts about a temporal aspect although they are too general to be successfully used (are equivalent to r_sometime).

4 Properties

For the further discussion we first define few symbols and operations.

Def.: Let DIR be a set of all the 3×3 binary relations, e.g. $DIR = 2^R$ where $R = \{NW, N, NE, W, O, E, SW, S, SE\}$.

Def.: Let A in DIR. Then A_R where $R = \{NW, N, NE, W, O, E, SW, S, SE\}$ is the value (0 or 1) of an element in matrix A which corresponds to a tile in the classic CDC definition.

Let $\lor$ be a symbol of logical alternative and $\land$ – logical conjunction.

Def.: Let A, B, C DIR. Then +dir: DIR2 → DIR is a binary operation such that $C = A +_{dir} B$ if and only if $C_R = A_R \lor B_R$ for every $R = \{NW, N, NE, W, O, E, SW, S, SE\}$.

Table 2. The spatial relations in the XCDC model.

Relation	dirN*-E*(A, B)	dirN*-E*(B, A)	dirT-N*(A, B)	dirT-N*(B, A)	dirT-E*(A, B)	dirT-E*(A, B)
Undef.	Udir	Udir	Udir	Udir	Udir	Udir
r_nw	NW	SE	NE:E:SE	NW:W:SW	NW:W:SW	NE:E:SE
r_n	N	SW:S:SE	NE:E:SE	NW:W:SW	N:O:S	Udir
r_ne	NE	SW	NE:E:SE	NW:W:SW	NE:E:SE	NW:W:SW
r_w	W	NE:E:SE	N:O:S	Udir	NW:W:SW	NE:E:SE
r_e	E	NW:W:SW	N:O:S	Udir	NE:E:SE	NW:W:SW
r_sw	SW	NE	NW:W:SW	NE:E:SE	NW:W:SW	NE:E:SE
r_s	S	NW:N:NE	NW:W:SW	NE:E:SE	N:O:S	Udir
r_se	SE	NW	NW:W:SW	NE:E:SE	NE:E:SE	NW:W:SW
r_in_nw	O	O:E:S:SE	N:O:S	NW:N:W:O:SW:S	N:O:S	N:NE:O:E:S:SE
r_in_n	O	O:S	N:O:S	NW:N:W:O:SW:S	N:O:S	N:O:S
r_in_ne	O	W:O:SW:S	N:O:S	NW:N:W:O:SW:S	N:O:S	NW:N:W:O:SW:S
r_in_w	O	O:E	N:O:S	N:O:S	N:O:S	N:NE:O:E:S:SE
r_in_e	O	W:O	N:O:S	N:O:S	N:O:S	NW:N:W:O:SW:S
r_in_sw	O	N:NE:O:E	N:O:S	N:NE:O:E:S:SE	N:O:S	NW:N:W:O:SW:S
r_in_s	O	N:O	N:O:S	N:NE:O:E:S:SE	N:O:S	N:O:S
r_in_se	O	NW:N:W:O	N:O:S	N:NE:O:E:S:SE	N:O:S	NW:N:W:O:SW:S
r_in	O	Udir	N:O:S	Udir	N:O:S	Udir
r_out	Udir \ O	Udir \ O	Udir	Udir	Udir	Udir
r_surrounded	O	Udir \ O	N:O:S	Udir	N:O:S	Udir
r_somewhere	Udir	Udir	Udir	Udir	Udir	Udir

Table 3. The temporal relations in the XCDC model.

Relation	$dirN^*$-$E^*(A, B)$	$dirN^*$-$E^*(B, A)$	$dirT$-$N^*(A, B)$	$dirT$-$N^*(B, A)$	$dirT$-$E^*(A, B)$	$dirT$-$E^*(A, B)$
Undef.	U_{dir}	U_{dir}	U_{dir}	U_{dir}	U_{dir}	U_{dir}
r_before	U_{dir}	U_{dir}	SW:S:SE	NW:N:NE	SW:S:SE	NW:N:NE
r_after	U_{dir}	U_{dir}	NW:N:NE	SW:S:SE	NW:N:NE	SW:S:SE
r_sametime	U_{dir}	U_{dir}	W:O:E	W:O:E	W:O:E	W:O:E
r_during	U_{dir}	U_{dir}	W:O:E	U_{dir}	W:O:E	U_{dir}
r_sometime	U_{dir}	U_{dir}	U_{dir}	U_{dir}	U_{dir}	U_{dir}

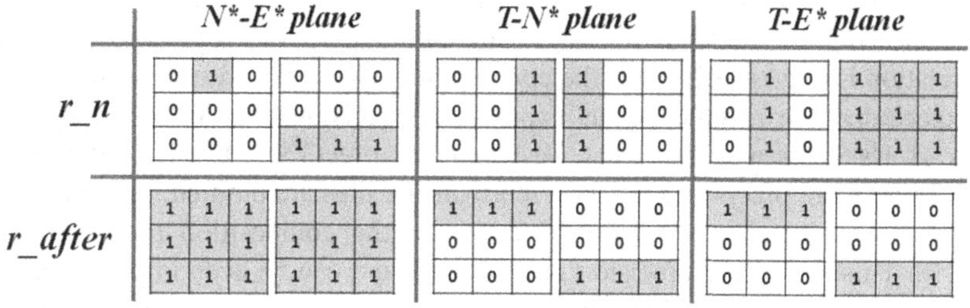

Fig. 2. The XCDC structures for language relations: r_n and r_after

Def.: Let A, B, C DIR. Then ·dir: DIR2 → DIR is a binary operation such that C = A $\cdot_{dir}$ B if and only if $C_R = A_R \wedge B_R$ for every R = {NW, N, NE, W, O, E, SW, S, SE}.

Def.: Let DIR_{TS} denotes the set of all the structures of the XCDC formalism, e.g. $DIR_{TS} := \{[M_1, M_2, M_3, M_4, M_5, M_6]: M_i \ DIR, 1 \le i \le 6\}$.

Def.: Let $+_{TS}: DIR^2 \to DIR$ be a binary operation that is defined as follows:

$[M_1, M_2, M_3, M_4, M_5, M_6] +_{TS} [M'_1, M'_2, M'_3, M'_4, M'_5, M'_6] :=$
$[M_1 +_{dir} M'_1, M_2 +_{dir} M'_2, M_3 +_{dir} M'_3,$
$M_4 +_{dir} M'_4, M_5 +_{dir} M'_5, M_6 +_{dir} M'_6],$

where M_i, M_i' in DIR for $1 \le i \le 6$.

Def.: Let $\cdot_{TS}: DIR^2 \to DIR$ be a binary operation that is defined as follows:

$[M_1, M_2, M_3, M_4, M_5, M_6] \cdot_{TS} [M'_1, M'_2, M'_3, M'_4, M'_5, M'_6] :=$
$[M_1 \cdot_{dir} M'_1, M_2 \cdot_{dir} M'_2, M_3 \cdot_{dir} M'_3,$
$M_4 \cdot_{dir} M'_4, M_5 \cdot_{dir} M'_5, M_6 \cdot_{dir} M'_6],$

where M_i, M_i' in DIR for $1 \le i \le 6$.

To sum up there are two operators $+_{dir}$, $\cdot_{dir}$ for calculation on direction-relation matrices and two operators $+_{TS}$, $\cdot_{TS}$ which arguments are XCDC structures.

In the previous section we have discussed the example of r_n and r_after relations conceptualized in a natural language. Although they describe different aspects (spatial and temporal) of the given environment, they can be easily composed e.g. in the situation when a user sends to a system a complex message like the following:

The fight has began after the meeting and to the north of the position where the meeting took place. First we identify the language relations hidden in the message, then we calculate the composition of the corresponding XCDC structures. As a result we get a single structure describing the spatio-temporal relationship between the two objects – fight and meeting:

r_after $\cdot_{TS}$ r_n = [N $+_{dir}$ U_{dir}, SW:S:SE $+_{dir}$ U_{dir}, NE:E:SE $+_{dir}$ NW:N:NE, NW:W:SW $+_{dir}$ SW:S:SE, N:O:S $+_{dir}$ NW:N:NE, U_{dir} $+_{dir}$ SW:S:SE] =

= [N, SW:S:SE, NE, SW, N, SW:S:SE].

The composition provides memory saving (expressed in the number of TS structures stored in a database) what also implies faster search. It is also important to notice (following the guidance from [2]) that although the discriminating power of a single relation is intentionally low, the combination of several structures can even lead to unexpectedly fine results. Let us express the precision of a TS structure by the number of 1's in its matrices what we denote by prec(TS). Of course the less the number is the more precise it the fact – more unsure tiles are omitted. In our example, prec(r_after) = 30 and prec(r_n) = 22, however the composition prec(r_after $\cdot$TS ι_n) = 10. This increasing precision is significant and can be even improved as soon as the user of a system provides some additional information about the spatio-temporal relation between the analyzed objects.

While analyzing the introduced set of spatio-temporal relations conceptualized in a natural language we can notice that some of their properties are in accordance with intuitive features of the real world. This similarity not only allows for a natural usage of the XCDC model but also protects from an accidental breaking the constraints connected with the quality of an environment. In particular the sum of all the external direction relations covers all the tiles of r_out structure (if a given object B is located in a specific direction with respect to the reference object A, then surely the B is outside the minimal bounding box O(A)), e.g.

r_nw $+_{dir}$ r_n $+_{dir}$ r_ne $+_{dir}$ ... $+_{dir}$ r_s $+_{dir}$ r_se = r_out.
Similarly, summing up all the internal direction relations we get the r_in structure:
r_in_nw $+_{dir}$ r_in_n $+_{dir}$ ... $+_{dir}$ r_in_se = r_in.
Finally, the set of temporal relations equals r_sometime:
r_before $+_{dir}$ r_after $+_{dir}$ r_during $+_{dir}$ r_sametime =
= r_sometime.

These equations allows to conclude from an incomplete or imprecise knowledge. For example, if a user cannot specify the position of a particular person in a given sector around the playing pitch (in the soccer match context) in the language of the internal direction relations, he/she can inform a system that The person is inside the sector. The XCDC formalism allows to process such a data although the fact could be expressed more precisely. It is possible to compose the XCDC structures of different type and the level of precision.

Def.: Let R, Q in DIR, where R = R_1: ... :R_k, Q = Q_1: ... :Q_n and R_1,..., R_k, Q_1,..., Q_n in {NW, N, NE, W, O, E, SW, S, SE} for $1 \leq k, n \leq 9$. Then R is included in Q, what we denote by R $\leq_{dir}$ Q, if and only if {R1,..., Rk} in {Q1,..., Qn}.

Def.: Let A, B in DIR$_{TS}$ where A = [A_1,..., A_6], B = [B_1,..., B_6] and A_i, B_i in DIR for $1 \leq i \leq 6$. Then A $\leq_{REL}$ B if and only if $A_i \leq_{dir} B_i$ for all $1 \leq i \leq 6$.

Theorem: The set of XCDC structures together with the binary relation $\leq_{REL}$ is a partial order.

Proof: We will check the definitional properties of a partial order for any A, B, C in DIR$_{TS}$ where A = [A_1,..., A_6], B = [B_1,..., B_6], C = [C_1,..., C_6] and A_i, B_i, C_i in DIR for $1 \leq i \leq 6$:

(Reflexivity) A $\leq$REL A what is true because for every $1 \leq i \leq 6$ we have $A_i \leq_{dir} A_i$.

(Antisymmetry) Let A $\leq_{REL}$ B and B $\leq_{REL}$ A. Let $A_i = A_{i1}$: ... :A_{ik}, $B_i = B_{i1}$: ... :B_{in} where A_{i1},..., A_{ik}, B_{i1},..., B_{in} in {NW, N, NE, W, O, E, SW, S, SE} for $1 \leq k, n \leq 9$. Then {A_{i1},..., A_{ik}} in {B_{i1},..., B_{in}} in {Ai1,..., Aik} so A= B.

(Transitivity) Let A $\leq_{REL}$ B and B $\leq_{REL}$ C. Let A $\leq_{REL}$ B and B $\leq_{REL}$ C. Let $A_i = A_{i1}$: ... :A_{ik}, $B_i = B_{i1}$: ... :B_{in}, $C_i = C_{i1}$: ... :C_{im} where A_{i1},..., A_{ik}, B_{i1},..., B_{in}, C_{i1},..., C_{im} in {NW, N, NE, W, O, E, SW, S, SE} for $1 \leq k, n, m \leq 9$. Then {A_{i1},..., A_{ik}} in {B_{i1},..., B_{in}} and {B_{i1},..., B_{in}} in {C_{i1},..., C_{im}} so {A_{i1},..., A_{ik}} in {C_{i1},..., C_{im}}. Finally we get A $\leq_{REL}$ C.

Q.E.D.

The ordered structure of the introduced spatio-temporal relations conceptualized in a natural language was presented at Fig. 3. This hierarchical structure can be treated as an ontology of the spatio-temporal concepts. In particular, if for two language relations R1 and R2 there is a dependency R1 $\leq$REL R2 then the structure R1 is more precise than R1. We can also say that R1 is a special case (or hyponym) of R2.

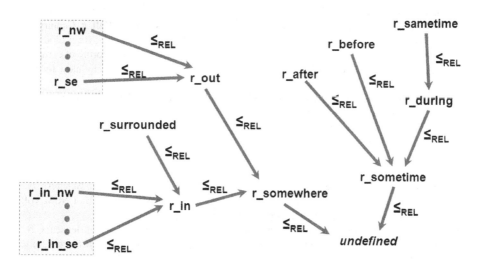

Fig. 3. The hierarchy of the spatio-temporal relations.

5 Conclusion

We have presented the construction of the set of the XCDC spatio-temporal relations which are conceptualized in a natural language. We have also shown their basic properties and the possible usage of this collection as an ontology of the spatio-temporal concepts. All this makes the above results an interesting basis for further analysis and practical applications. As discussed before this idea was already implemented in POLINT-112-SMS system. However, what is worth highlighting, the introduced set of relations is independent from a language (of a potential user) and free from any context limitations. It is general enough to be applied in many systems. of R2.

Acknowledgement. I declare that during the time of LTC 2011 I was a scholarship holder within the project "Scholarship support for PH.D. students specializing in majors strategic for Wielkopolska's development", Sub-measure 8.2.2 Human Capital Operational Programme, co-financed by European Union under the European Social Fund.

References

1. Goyal, R.K., Egenhofer, M.J.: Cardinal directions between extended spatial objects. IEEE Transactions on Knowledge and Data Engineering (2001)
2. Hernández, D. (ed.): Qualitative Representation of Spatial Knowledge. LNCS, vol. 804. Springer, Heidelberg (1994)
3. Jonsson, P., Drakengren, T.: A complete classification of tractability in RCC-5, Research notes. J. Artif. Intell. Res. **6**, 211–221 (1997). AI Access Foundation and Morgan Kaufmann Publishers
4. Ligozat, G., Vetulani, Z.: Reasoning about events: the spatio-temporal XRCD calculus. In: Hlaváčková, D., Horák, A., Osolsobě, K., Rychlý, P. (eds.) After Half a Century of Slavonic Natural Language Processing, pp. 231–245. Masaryk University, Brno (2009)
5. Ligozat, G., Vetulani, Z., Osiński, J.: Spatiotemporal aspects of the monitoring of complex events for public security purposes. Spat. Cogn. Comput.: (An Interdisciplinary Journal **11**(1), 103–128 (2011). Taylor & Francis Group
6. Liu, Y., Wang, X., Jin, X., Wu, L.: On internal cardinal direction relations. In: Cohn, A.G., Mark, D.M. (eds.) COSIT 2005. LNCS, vol. 3693, pp. 283–299. Springer, Heidelberg (2005)
7. Osiński, J.: Extending the cardinal direction calculus to a temporal dimension. In: Proceedings of FLAIRS 2009, Sanibel Island, USA (2009)
8. Osinski, J.: Extended CDC vs other formalisms – the comparative analysis of the models for spatio-temporal reasoning. In: Rutkowski, L., Korytkowski, M., Scherer, R., Tadeusiewicz, R., Zadeh, L.A., Zurada, J.M. (eds.) ICAISC 2012, Part II. LNCS, vol. 7268, pp. 679–687. Springer, Heidelberg (2012)
9. Skiadopoulos, S., Koubarakis, M.: Composing cardinal direction relations. In: Jensen, C.S., Schneider, M., Seeger, Bernhard, Tsotras, Vassilis J. (eds.) SSTD 2001. LNCS, vol. 2121, pp. 299–317. Springer, Heidelberg (2001)
10. Vetulani, Z., Marciniak, J.: Natural language based communication between human users and the emergency center: POLINT-112-SMS. In: Vetulani, Z. (ed.) LTC 2009. LNCS, vol. 6562, pp. 303–314. Springer, Heidelberg (2011)

11. Vetulani, Z., Marciniak, J., Obrebski, T., Kubis, M., Osinski, J., Walkowska, J., Kubacki, P., Witalewski, K.: POLINT-112-SMS: Beta prototype. In: Vetulani, Z. (ed.) Proceedings of the 4th Language & Technology Conference, Poznan, Poland, 6–8 November 2009, pp. 160–164. Wyd. Poznanskie, Poznan (2009)

12. Vetulani, Z., Marciniak, J., Obrebski, T., Vetulani, G., Dabrowski, A., Kubis, M., Osiński, J., Walkowska, J., Kubacki, P., Witalewski, K.: Zasoby językowe i technologie przetwarzania tekstu. POLINT-112-SMS jako przykład aplikacji z zakresu bezpieczeństwa publicznego. (Language resources and text processing Technologies. POLINT-112-SMS as example of public security application with language competence) (in Polish), Wyd. UAM, Poznań (2010)

Normalization of Term Weighting Scheme
for Sentiment Analysis

Alexander Pak[1], Patrick Paroubek[1]([✉]), Amel Fraisse[1], and Gil Francopoulo[2]

[1] LIMSI-CNRS, Université Paris-Sud, 133, 91403 Orsay Cedex, France
irokez@gmail.com, {pap,fraisse}@limsi.fr
[2] TAGMATICA, 126 rue de Picpus, 75012 Paris, France
gil.francopoulo@tagmatica.com

Abstract. N-gram models with a binary (or tf-idf) weighting scheme
and SVM classifiers are commonly used together as a baseline approach
in lots of research studies on sentiment analysis and opinion mining.
Other advanced methods are used on top of this model to improve the
classification accuracy, such as generation of additional features or using
supplementary linguistic resources. In this paper, we show how a simple
technique can improve both the overall classification accuracy and the
classification of minor reviews by normalizing the terms weights in the
basic bag-of-words method. Any other term selection scheme may also
benefit from this improved weighting scheme, if it is based on the n-gram
model. We have tested our approach on the movie review and the product
review datasets in English and show that our normalization technique
enhances the classification accuracy of the traditional weighting schemes.
The question whether we would observe similar performance increases
for other language families is still to be investigated, but our weighting
scheme can easily address any other language, since it does not use any
language specific resource apart from a training corpus.

1 Introduction

The increase of the interest in sentiment analysis is usually associated with
the appearance of web-blogs and social networks, where users post and share
information about their likes/dislikes, preferences, and lifestyle. Many websites
provide an opportunity for users to leave their opinion on a given object or a
topic. For example, the users of IMDb[1] website can write a review on a movie
they have watched and rate it on 5-star scale. As a result, given a large number of reviews and rating scores, the IMDb reflects general opinions of Internet
users on movies. Many other movie-related resources, such as cinema schedule
websites, use the information from the IMDb to provide information about the
movies including the average rating. Thus, the users who write reviews on IMDb

---

After his PhD. at LIMSI-CNRS in 2012, Alexander Pak has joined Google in Zürich
(alexpak@google.com)

[1] The Internet Movie Database: http://imdb.com.

© Springer International Publishing Switzerland 2014
Z. Vetulani and J. Mariani (Eds.): LTC 2011, LNAI 8387, pp. 116–128, 2014.
DOI: 10.1007/978-3-319-08958-4_10

influence the choice of other users, who will have a tendency to select movies with higher ratings.

Another example is social networks. It is popular among users of Twitter[2] or Facebook[3] to post messages that are visible to their friends, with an opinion on different consumer goods, such as electronic products and gadgets. The companies who produce or sell those products are interested in monitoring the current trend and analyzing people's interest. Such information can influence their marketing strategy or bring changes in the product design to meet the customers' needs.

Therefore, there is a growing need for algorithms and methods to automatically collect and process opinionated texts. Such methods are expected to classify the texts by their polarity (positive or negative), estimate the sentiments expressed and determine the opinion target and holder, where the target is the object or a subject of the opinion statement and the holder is usually the author of the text (but not limited to).

One of the basic tasks of sentiment analysis is classification of text polarity. Given a text, the system should determine whether its overall sentiment is negative or positive (or none, i.e. neutral). The general approach is to represent the text as a bag-of-words (or ngrams) with a binary weighting scheme, and use SVM for classification. Such a simple approach yields good results when provided with sufficient training data. Reference [1] reported 82.7 % accuracy on the movie review dataset. In their following work [2], the authors could improve the classification accuracy by adding a subjectivity detector to a preprocessing step, before the polarity classification, to remove objective sentences.

In this paper, we propose a simple technique for tuning the weighting scheme that improves the classification accuracy. Our technique is based on the normalization of term weights by their average term frequency across the document collection. The motivation behind this procedure is based on an observation that terms expressing an author's attitude to the described topic are unique in a document. While other terms that are not important for the classification decision are more frequent. Thus, if we divide a term's weight by its average term frequency, we prune low important words (such as articles, personal and possessive pronouns, etc.) and give more weight to unique keywords in a text. It turns out that review authors express their opinion trying to use a rich vocabulary and therefore words related to a sentiment would occur rarely in a text.

Another issue which can also be addressed by our normalization procedure is the lowering of the weights associated to the Named Entities (NE) which are strongly related to an opinion target (e.g. the name of actors, cast and producers in case of movie review dataset).

While these terms are very important for the overall classification accuracy, they are a source of bias for minor reviews. For example, if a dataset contains 10 positive reviews about the movie "Avatar", then it is very likely that the keywords "Avatar", "James Cameron" (the movie director), "Sam Worthington",

---

[2] http://twitter.com
[3] http://facebook.com

and "Zoe Saldana" (the movie cast) would cause any other review containing these keywords to be considered as a positive too. As a result, if a dataset contains an 11th negative review about "Avatar", it would be probably misclassified as positive.

Thus we can lower the importance of NEs by normalizing theirs weights with the average term frequency across the corresponding Opinion Entity Document Set (OEDS)[4].

In the next section, we give a brief overview of prior works in sentiment analysis and research on improving polarity classification accuracy. In Sect. 3, we describe our normalization technique. Section 4 presents the data we have used for the validation. We provide details about our experimental setup and results in Sect. 5. Section 6 holds a description of our normalization technique for NE features to improve the polarity classification of minor reviews. In Sect. 7, we report on experiments with a second normalization technique for minor reviews. Finally, we conclude on our work in Sect. 8.

2 Related Work

An early work by [1] on polarity classification using bag-of-words model and machine learning reported 82.7 % accuracy. The authors found that using unigram features with binary weights yielded the highest accuracy.

In a follow up work, [2] augmented the classification framework with an additional preprocessing step, during which the sentences are first being classified as subjective or objective. The authors translated subjectivity classification into a graph-partitioning problem and used the min-cut max-flow theorem to solve it. Finally, the sentences labeled as "subjective" are extracted and passed to a general polarity classifier (bag-of-words model with SVM). The reported statistically significant improvement of the classification accuracy was from 82.8 % to 86.4 %.

Reference [3] used appraisal theory to produce additional features to be used in the classification. The authors built a taxonomy of appraisal and used it to identify appraisal groups within a text, such as "extremely boring" or "not that very good". For each appraisal group, a frame with 5 slots is filled up. The slots identifiers are: Attitude, Orientation, Force, Focus, and Polarity. Combinations of the first 3 of these slots were used to generate a feature vector. When backed up with a bag-of-words based classifier, the proposed method yielded 90.2 % accuracy, and 78.3 % standalone.

Reference [4] focused on a problem of the bag-of-word model, the information loss when representing a text by a non-related terms, thus losing the information contained in word order and syntactic relations between words in a sentence. To solve this problem, the authors proposed new features: word subsequences and dependency subtrees. Word subsequences were defined as a sequence of words

---

[4] The set of documents expressing opinions about the same opinion target (the same subject), for example, all reviews about the AVATAR movie represent an Opinion Entity Document Set.

obtained from a sentence by removing zero or more words. Dependency subtrees were obtained by extracting a part of a dependency tree, a sentence representation where nodes represent words and edges represent syntactic relations between words. Efficient mining algorithms were then used to find frequent subsequences and subtrees in the dataset. The combination of the proposed features with traditional n-gram features yielded 92.9 % classification accuracy on the movie dataset.

Reference [5] took a different approach to increase the accuracy of sentiment classification. Instead of adding supplementary features or text preprocessing steps, they focused on the words weighting scheme. The authors presented delta tf-idf weight function which computes the difference of a word's tf-idf score in a positive and a negative training sets. They claimed that the proposed technique boosts the importance of words unevenly distributed between the positive and the negative classes, thus these words should contribute more in the classification. Evaluation experiments on three different datasets showed statistically significant improvement of the classification accuracy. They achieved 88.1 % accuracy on the movie dataset.

Reference [6] performed a thorough study on different weighting schemes and the impact on the sentiment analysis systems' performance. In their study, the authors have tested different variations of the classic tf-idf scheme on three datasets: movie reviews, product reviews, and blog dataset. The best results were yielded by a variation of smoothed delta tf-idf. In the experimental setup of leave-one-out cross validation, the polarity classification accuracy on the movie and the product review datasets was 95–96 % depending on the scoring function variant used.

3   Proposed Method

3.1   Weighting Schemes

We will now give the formula describing our normalization function and present the rationale behind it.

Given a text T as a set of terms:

$$T = \{t_1, t_2, \ldots, t_k\} \tag{1}$$

we define a feature vector of T as

$$\mathrm{tf}^{\mathrm{w}} = \{w(t_1), w(t_2), \ldots, w(t_k)\} \tag{2}$$

where $w(t_i)$ is a weight function of a term t_i (Table 1). We define a normalized feature vector as

$$\mathrm{tf}^{\mathrm{w}}_{\mathrm{n}} = \{\frac{w(t_1)}{n(t_1)}, \frac{w(t_2)}{n(t_2)}, \ldots, \frac{w(t_k)}{n(t_k)}\} \tag{3}$$

where $n(t_i)$ is a normalization factor of a term t_i (Table 2).

Table 1. A list of term weight functions

Notation	Equation
binary (bin)	1 (if $t_i \in T$, 0 otherwise)
term frequency (tf)	$\mathrm{tf}(t_i)$
inverse document frequency (idf)	$\log \frac{D}{\mathrm{df}(t_i)+1}$
term frequency inverse document frequency (tf-idf)	$\mathrm{tf}(t_i) \cdot \log \frac{D}{\mathrm{df}(t_i)}$
delta inverse document frequency (Δidf)	$\log \frac{D_n \cdot \mathrm{df_p}(t_i)+1}{D_p \cdot \mathrm{df_n}(t_i)+1}$
delta term frequency inverse document frequency (Δtf-idf)	$\mathrm{tf}(t_i) \cdot \log \frac{D_n \cdot \mathrm{df_p}(t_i)+1}{D_p \cdot \mathrm{df_n}(t_i)+1}$

Table 2. A list of normalization factors

Notation	Equation
none (1)	1
average term frequency (avgtf)	$\mathrm{avg.tf}(t_i)$
square of average term frequency (avgtf2)	$\mathrm{avg.tf}^2(t_i)$

In this research, we test the following list of weight functions:

Our proposed normalization function is based on a term's average frequency:

$$\mathrm{avg.tf}(t_i) = \frac{\sum_{\forall T, t_i \in T} \mathrm{tf}(t_i)}{|\forall T, t_i \in T|} \tag{4}$$

Thus, we compare the following list of normalization factors:

For example, a traditional binary weighting scheme [1] with our notation would look as follows:

$$\mathrm{tf}_1^{\mathrm{bin}} = \{\mathrm{bin}(t_1), \mathrm{bin}(t_2), \ldots, \mathrm{bin}(t_k)\} \tag{5}$$

With our proposed normalization factor:

$$\mathrm{tf}_{\mathrm{avgtf}}^{\mathrm{bin}} = \{\frac{\mathrm{bin}(t_1)}{\mathrm{avgtf}(t_1)}, \ldots, \frac{\mathrm{bin}(t_k)}{\mathrm{avgtf}(t_k)}\} \tag{6}$$

Delta tf-idf [5] with normalization factor of square avg.tf:

$$\mathrm{tf}_{\mathrm{avgtf2}}^{\Delta\mathrm{tf}-\mathrm{idf}} = \{\frac{\Delta\mathrm{tf}-\mathrm{idf}(t_1)}{\mathrm{avgtf}^2(t_1)}, \ldots, \frac{\Delta\mathrm{tf}-\mathrm{idf}(t_k)}{\mathrm{avgtf}^2(t_k)}\} \tag{7}$$

Our normalization function is based on an observation that review authors tend to use rich vocabulary when expressing their attitude towards a movie or a product. Thus, the terms related to the sentiment expression (such as "outstanding") have average term frequency close or equal to 1. While other non-subjective

Table 3. Top-20 unigrams ordered by Δtf-idf (on the left) and normalized Δtf-idf (on the right) from the movie dataset. Unigrams related to movie or person names are highlighted bold.

Word	Avg.tf	Word	Avg.tf
ideals	1.33	conveys	1.08
frances	1.36	detract	1.09
comforts	1.00	criticized	1.00
supports	1.00	notoriety	1.00
ideology	1.20	ideal	1.33
gattaca	4.20	outstanding	1.06
outstanding	1.06	weaknesses	1.27
criticized	1.00	ideology	1.20
elmore	1.33	brisk	1.00
hawthorne	1.22	avoids	1.00
downside	1.00	judges	1.00
lebowski	6.88	slip	1.00
cunning	1.25	**frances**	1.36
gripping	1.06	**hawthorne**	1.22
judges	1.00	astounding	1.00
gretchen	1.38	scholars	1.00
unravel	1.00	discussion	1.00
burbank	2.00	hers	1.00
linney	1.38	abstract	1.00
niccol	2.38	obstacle	1.13

terms have higher average term frequency. Those include movie names, actors, brands and product parts as they are mentioned several times within texts.

The proposed delta tf-idf is supposed to target the same problem, filtering out general terms and favor the terms that are distributed unevenly in polarity sets. However, it creates a bias when a movie or a product name appears more often in positive (or negative) reviews.

We illustrate this example in Table 3, where a top-20 unigrams are shown with the number of positive and negative reviews they appear in and an average term frequency. In the left part of the table, we show unigrams ordered by delta tf-idf and in the right part ordered by delta tf-idf normalized by average frequency. As we can see, in the left part there are more unigrams related to a movie name or a person name (actors or movie-makers). For example, a movie name "gattaca" has a high rank according to delta tf-idf, because it has 19 positive reviews and no negative ones. The average term frequency of the term "gattaca" is 4.2, thus we can lower the importance of this term by normalizing its weight with the average term frequency (avg.tf).

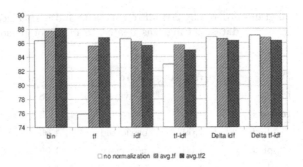

Fig. 1. Reported accuracy (in %) on the movie review dataset for document polarity classification across different weighting schemes and normalization factors.

4   Experimental Setup

To test our approach, we used two different datasets. The first is the movie review dataset[5], that has been first used in [1] and then in other research on sentiment analysis. The reviews are divided into a positive and a negative sets, each containing 1000 documents.

The second dataset consists of product reviews[6] from Amazon and was first used in [7]. The dataset is divided into 4 categories of products: books, DVDs, electronics, kitchen&housewares. Each category contains 1000 positive and 1000 negative reviews. This dataset is considered multi-domain as the contained documents are about various topics, as compared to the movie dataset which covers only the domain of movies.

We used an open source implementation of SVM classifier from the LIB-LINEAR package [8] with default parameters and linear kernel. Each of the two datasets was evaluated separately using 10-fold cross validation. For our main evaluation criteria, we measured the average polarity classification accuracy (Fig. 1).

5   Results

The results of the reported accuracy on the movie reviews and the product reviews datasets, for document polarity classification, are presented in Tables 4 and 5.

First, we observe the same results as [1] reported on the movie review dataset: binary features outperform term frequency and tf-idf. We also observe the advantage of the delta tf-idf weighting scheme. Without any normalization, delta tf-idf yields the highest accuracy on the movie review dataset: 87.5 %.

---

[5] http://www.cs.cornell.edu/people/pabo/movie-review-data/

[6] http://www.cs.jhu.edu/~mdredze/datasets/sentiment/

Table 4. Reported accuracy on the movie review dataset for document polarity classification. The maximum accuracy is highlighted with a bold font.

Weight func.	Normalization		
	none	avg.tf	avg.tf2
bin	86.40	**87.75**	**88.15**
tf	75.90	85.60	86.80
idf	86.65	86.20	85.65
tf-idf	83.00	85.70	85.00
Δidf	86.85	86.60	86.35
Δtf-idf	**87.05**	86.75	86.35

Table 5. Reported accuracy on the product review dataset for document polarity classification. The maximum accuracy is highlighted with a bold font.

Weight func.	Normalization		
	none	avg.tf	avg.tf2
bin	78.77	79.36	79.71
tf	77.37	79.50	80.05
idf	79.06	79.02	79.10
tf-idf	78.66	79.00	78.76
Δidf	80.43	**80.76**	**80.83**
Δtf-idf	**80.69**	80.62	80.69

We further observe that our normalization technique improves the performance of binary (bin), term frequency (tf) and tf-idf weighting schemes. The accuracy of the tf scheme improves drastically, from 75.9 % to 86.80 % with avg.tf2 normalization. The bin scheme with the normalization yields the best results on the movie review dataset: 88.15 %. The accuracy of idf, Δidf and Δtf-idf schemes with the normalization decreases slightly.

The general observation from the product review evaluation is that cross-domain sentiment analysis is a more difficult task, as we can see in the results. The average performance of all the approaches are around 79–80 % as compare to 85–87 % on movie reviews. Similar results are obtained as in the movie review evaluation: Δtf-idf outperforms binary scheme, which in its turn outperforms term frequency and yields slightly better results than tf-idf. The normalization boosts the performance of the tf scheme, from 77.37 % to 80.05 %, such that it even outperforms the binary (79.71 %) and tf-idf schemes (79 %) with and without the normalization. The best result 80.83 % is yielded by the normalized Δidf which is slightly better than its version not normalized.

6   Named Entity Weighting for Improving Minor Opinion Polarity Classification

Most of the opinion mining models consider three elements, the opinion expression, the source and the target [9]. We are here interested by the opinion target. It is often referred to by means of Named Entities (person, product organization name, or location) in conjunction with the occurrence of a set of associated Named Entities, like for instance the cast or the film director, when the target is a movie.

In the classical approach used for opinion mining and polarity analysis, i.e. supervised machine learning with n-gram features [10], the system is often biased towards the majority opinion expressed in the training data. In particular, the NE n-grams used to refer to the opinion target are identified by the system as clues for the majority opinion, exactly in the same way as the specific vocabulary for expressing this opinion.

For instance, if we consider a film that has been a success like *AVATAR*, it is not only the mention of its title that would trigger a positive review classification, but also the presence of the name of the film director *James Cameron*, and this even for rarely occurring negative reviews.

Furthermore, NEs are not part of the general vocabulary used to express opinions and sentiments. In our mind an opinion mining system should be able to distinguish between the clues given by the explicit expression of opinion, and the clues associated to contextual features like NEs. The latter could be used in a second stage decision process for choosing the final opinion class. The advantage would be for the system first to be able to properly classify minority opinions and second to provide a justification about its classification decision in terms of either the language used in the opinion expression or the presence of contextual features, like particular NEs. To this end, we propose a second normalization weighting schemes to lower the weights of NEs. Hereafter, if a term (t_i) is recognized as a Named Entity, we compute its weight using a normalization function based on an intra opinion entity term's average frequency[7]:

$$\text{intra.oe.avg.tf}(t_i)^{NE} = \frac{\sum_{\forall D_{oe}, t_i \in D_{oe}} \text{tf}(t_i)}{|\forall D_{oe}, t_i \in D_{oe}|} \tag{8}$$

Where D_{oe} is an element of the Opinion Entity Document Set for an Opinion Entity OE. As each D_{oe} is associated to a single OE entity and as review authors use NEs to describe an OE, the average term frequency of a NE across its corresponding D_{oe} is higher than the one computed over the whole corpus (Table 6).

---

[7] Computed over the Opinion Entity Document Set, i.e. the set of documents expressing opinions about the same opinion target, for example, all reviews about the AVATAR movie.

Table 6. Example of movie reviews extracted from the Imdb dataset. Terms NEs are highlighted bold.

Entity	Reviews
AVATAR	More of the **James Cameron** genius.
	Kudos to **Cameron**, **Avatar** is one of the (if not The) movie of the year.
	James Cameron's **Avatar** is the most entertaining and enthralling cinematic experiences of my life.
Star Wars	**George Lucas** enjoys an almost god-like status among sci-fi/fantasy fans worldwide.
	Not to mention **John Williams'** wonderful score, without of it, the movie wouldn't have been this great it's a perfect mix, that's what it is!

Table 7. Characteristics of preprocessed movie review dataset.

Initial number of reviews		Training and test sets sizes	
pos	neg	train	test
25000	25000	3680	1580

7 Experiments

7.1 Data

For our purpose, we have split into training and test set the Large Movie Review Dataset [11] used for our experiments in a special way. The 50,000 texts have been spread evenly between an equal proportions of negative and positive opinions in both the training set and the test set, following the procedure first proposed in [10]. For each movie, the number of reviews has been fixed both for training and testing. We took 3 documents of each movie for test and 7 for training. Characteristics of both datasets are presented in Table 7. These numbers were chosen heuristically in order to maximize the total number of reviews.

To separate a dataset into training and test sets, first, we group all the reviews by their entity (movie) identified by a unique ID in the dataset. Next, we select groups that have enough numbers of positive and negative reviews. From the selected groups, from each entity we select all the reviews of a dominant polarity in this group and move them to the training set. The remaining reviews from each group are moved to the test set. We call this dataset "minor biased", because the test set contains reviews with minor polarities. We expect traditional settings for polarity classifiers to yield worse results on this dataset due to the bias in reviews for each product. To prove that the drop of performance is caused effectively by the biased features, we construct a dataset composed of the same reviews but reorganized, such that the reviews in the test set for each entity have the same polarity as the dominant polarity in the training set for each entity. We call

Table 8. Classification accuracy obtained using different normalization schemes on movie reviews.

	unb.	Δ	minb.	Δ	majb.	Δ
Bigrams + binary						
no	79.6		71.9		83.5	
avg.tf	79.7	+0.1	72.8	+0.9	84.0	+0.5
avg.tf.intra.oe.avg.tf	**81.5**	**+1.9**	**76.3**	**+4.4**	84.2	+0.7
Bigrams + Delta tf-idf						
no	83.0		69.9		87.6	
avg.tf	82.9	−0.1	76.0	+6.0	86.1	−1.5
avg.tf.intra.oe.avg.tf	**84.2**	**+1.2**	**78.3**	**+8.5**	85.8	−1.8

this dataset "major biased", because the test set contains reviews with major polarities. Finally, we compose the "unbiased" dataset, by separating reviews such that entities in the test set have no reviews in the training set. Named Entities were tagged with TAGMATICA, which is an industrial strength Named Entity tagger [12].

7.2   Results

First, we prove the negative effect of entity specific features on classification accuracy of minor reviews. We ran experiments on 3 variants of the datasets: unbiased (unb), minor biased (minb), major biased (majb). We have used bigrams (bi) with binary (bin) and Delta tf-idf weights. Results on classification accuracy across the datasets and features are presented in Table 8. Notice that we cannot directly compare accuracy values across different variants of datasets, as they are composed of different test data. However, we assume that our datasets are homogeneous and results obtained with different dataset variants reflect the complexity of the classification task.

Impact of OE specific terms and NEs. Looking at Table 8, we see that Opinion-Entity-specific and Named Entities features cause performance drop on the minor biased set as compared to the unbiased set (unb vs. minb). We also observe a boost in performance on the major biased dataset in spite of a smaller training size (unb vs. majb). This shows that our classifier learns to associate OE-specific terms and NE features with the opinion entity major polarity, instead of learning the affective language model of opinion expression. Results are similar across different datasets, variants of datasets, and features. Delta tf-idf while improving overall accuracy, causes misclassification of minor review because it gives more importance to opinion entity-specific and Named Entities features. We can observe this by comparing the results of using Delta tf-idf on the minor biased set with the unbiased and major biased datasets.

Next, we have evaluated the effect of the proposed normalization schemes on classification accuracy. As we observe from the previous experiments, normalizing

NE weights with the *intra.oe.avg.tf*() increases the performance, see the highlighted locations in Table 8.

8   Conclusion

We have proposed two techniques to tune the weighting scheme of a general polarity classifier. The first technique is generic and based on a normalization of a term's weight by its average term frequency. The proposed normalization method increases the importance of terms that are rare in a document. Thereby decreasing weights of frequent terms and therefore reducing a bias when an object has more positive (or negative) reviews. The second technique lowers the importance of Named Entities about opinion targets, by normalizing their weights in the feature vector representations used by classical n-gram. For the first technique, the experimental evaluations was performed on two datasets of different size, topic and homogeneity: movie and product review dataset. Both evaluations showed that the proposed normalization method increases the performance of binary, term frequency, and tf-idf weighting schemes. The performance of the term frequency is increased significantly (from 75.9 % to 86.80 % on the movie review dataset and from 77.37 % to 80.05 % on the product reviews). The normalized binary scheme yielded the highest observed classification accuracy (88.15 %) on the movie review dataset. The normalization of Δtf-idf scheme improves slightly its performance on the product review dataset, however our scheme can be used when Δtf-idf is not available. For example, when there is no data split in two sets, or when there are more sets than two (i.e. more sentiment classes: positive, negative, neutral). In this case, a binary weighting scheme with the proposed normalization method should be used.

For the second technique, although the performance improvement is not as important for bigram models (+1.5 %) with unbiased training datasets, it is nevertheless positive which proves that our NE weighting scheme performs as well as classical methods. But the evaluation experiments performed on especially organized versions of standard datasets showed large improvement in classification accuracy of minor reviews (+8.5 %), which proves that our NE weighting scheme impacts positively the classification accuracy of minor reviews, essential for weak signals detection and early opinion trend reversal detection.

References

1. Pang, B., Lee, L., Vaithyanathan, S.: Thumbs up?: sentiment classification using machine learning techniques. In: Proceedings of the ACL-02 Conference on Empirical Methods in Natural Language Processing, EMNLP '02, pp. 79–86. Association for Computational Linguistics, Morristown (2002)
2. Pang, B., Lee, L.: A sentimental education: sentiment analysis using subjectivity summarization based on minimum cuts. In: Proceedings of the 42nd Annual Meeting on Association for Computational Linguistics, ACL '04. Association for Computational Linguistics, Stroudsburg (2004)

3. Whitelaw, C., Garg, N., Argamon, S.: Using appraisal groups for sentiment analysis. In: Proceedings of the 14th ACM International Conference on Information and Knowledge Management, CIKM '05, pp. 625–631. ACM, New York (2005)
4. Matsumoto, S., Takamura, H., Okumura, M.: Sentiment classification using word sub-sequences and dependency sub-trees. In: Pacific-Asia Conference on Knowledge Discovery and Data Mining, pp. 301–311 (2005)
5. Martineau, J., Finin, T.: Delta TFIDF: an improved feature space for sentiment analysis. In: Proceedings of the Third AAAI Internatonal Conference on Weblogs and Social Media. AAAI Press, San Jose (2009)
6. Paltoglou, G., Thelwall, M.: A study of information retrieval weighting schemes for sentiment analysis. In: Proceedings of the 48th Annual Meeting of the Association for Computational Linguistics, ACL '10, pp. 1386–1395. Association for Computational Linguistics, Morristown (2010)
7. Blitzer, J., Dredze, M., Pereira, F.: Biographies, bollywood, boom-boxes and blenders: domain adaptation for sentiment classification. In: Proceedings of the 45th Annual Meeting of the Association of Computational Linguistics, pp. 440–447. Association for Computational Linguistics, Prague (2007)
8. Fan, R.E., Chang, K.W., Hsieh, C.J., Wang, X.R., Lin, C.J.: Liblinear: a library for large linear classification. J. Mach. Learn. Res. **9**, 1871–1874 (2008)
9. Parouhek, P., Pak, A., Mostefa, D.: Annotations for opinion mining evaluation in the industrial context of the doxa project. In: Proceedings of the 7th International Conference on Language Resources and Evaluation (LREC). ELDA, Valetta (2010)
10. Pak, A.: Automatic, Adaptive, and Applicative Sentiment Analysis. Ph.D. thesis, Thèse de l'École Doctorale d'Informatique de l'Université Paris-Sud, Orsay, June 2012
11. Maas, A.L., Daly, R.E., Pham, P.T., Huang, D., Ng, A.Y., Potts, C.: Learning word vectors for sentiment analysis. In: Proceedings of the 49th Annual Meeting of the ACL, pp. 142–150. ACL, Portland (2011)
12. Francopoulo, G., Demay, F.: A deep ontology for named entities. In: Proceedings of the International Conference on Computational Semantics, Interoperable Semantic Annotation Workshop, ACL (2011)

Thel, a Language for Utterance Generation in the Thetos System

Julia Romaniuk[1], Nina Suszczańska[2], and Przemysław Szmal[2(✉)]

[1] Institute of Ukrainian Language NAS of Ukraine,
Grushevskogo 4, Kyiv 01001, Ukraine
ju.romaniuk@gmail.com
[2] Institute of Informatics, Silesian University of Technology,
ul. Akademicka 16, 44-100 Gliwice, Poland
n.w.suszczanski@gmail.com, przemyslaw.szmal@polsl.pl

Abstract. We describe first attempts to textually record non-linear elements of Polish Sign Language utterances. The effects of those experiments will be applied in the *Thetos* translator. We use the *Thel* language to textually express signed utterances. Currently our attention is focused on methods used in the PSL for manifesting emotions as well as on pauses done while signing. To detect non-linear elements we examine a predicate-argument (semantic) representation of the input utterance, and analyze syntactic relations existing between elements of input syntactic groups. This process engages specific rules that refer to features of syntactic groups and relations. We have identified a number of partial rules and found a method for building respective fragments of the output utterance. In the paper we show some of them. Additionally, we describe solutions used in the *Thel* words dictionary for mapping spoken language vocabulary to its sign language counterpart, which is definitely poorer.

Keywords: Polish Sign Language · *Thetos* system · *Polin* · *Thel* language

Introduction

Translation in the *Thetos* system, our translator of Polish texts into a sequence of sign language sentences (see, for example, [14,15], http://thetos.polsl.pl), proceeds in compliance with the classical scheme: *analysis of the input language utterance → generation of the target language utterance*. The input language is written Polish in electronic form, the target one is the Polish Sign Language (PSL).

The analysis is performed by the linguistic module of *Thetos* according to the structural linguistics rules with the scheme: *morphological analysis → syntactic analysis → semantic analysis*. Generation of the target language utterance is divided into two stages. First, sentences in a formal intermediate language are generated, then these sentences are interpreted in the token-by-token mode

© Springer International Publishing Switzerland 2014
Z. Vetulani and J. Mariani (Eds.): LTC 2011, LNAI 8387, pp. 129–140, 2014.
DOI: 10.1007/978-3-319-08958-4_11

by the animation module, which in the end produces avatar's movements. *Thel* (*Thetos* expression language) is just intermediate language of our translation system; it is a formal language for symbolic transcript of sign language utterances.

Symbolic transcript in *Thel* is the final result given by *Polin*, the module for PSL utterance linearization. *Polin* is the last link in the Polish text processing chain. *Polin's* input data are produced by *Polsem*, semantic analyzer, whose work is in turn preceded by deep parsing of sentences [8,9,12]. Syntax analyzer extracts groups of tokens in the sentence, assigns morpho-syntactic interpretations to them, discovers syntactic roles that selected groups play in the sentence. Semantic analyzer determines predicate-argument structure on the set of groups, in that – the relations PREDICATE, ACTOR, OBJECT, INSTRUMENT and OTHER, which play an important role in the transmission of content in the language of the Deaf. The semantic relations – among other things – determine the characteristics of groups that express some action, for example, for the motion action – the direction, the starting and the end point.

The linearization process can be imagined as a set of post-semantic transformations of the set of semantic representations of the input text. A set of transformation operations depends on the context, i.e. the semantic structure of the sentence. Transformations are carried out at the PSL semantics and syntax as well as on the morphological level. It is obvious that for the semantic structure usually more than one surface structure in PSL can be generated, and thus the need for determination of the equivalence of sentences. Also obvious is the fact that the only criterion for the equivalence of two statements is that in them the same content is transferred. Therefore, a restriction is imposed on the conversion operations: neither of them on no level may change the original content. The ultimate goal of linearization is to provide the content in the form of linear sequence of symbols (tokens) that encode the manual and non-manual PSL signs.

The need for linearization is due to several reasons. Let us mention just a few. First, the content of utterance in PSL is conveyed not only by manual signs. A great part of it are non-manual signs that cannot be directly expressed in words; we had to look for other means for transmitting them. Second, PSL as any other language, contains elements of frugality, which are reflected in the surface structure of the utterance, hence the need for eliding elements of the original sentence, and the elision process is not trivial. Another reason is the order of utterance in PSL, which is a positional language. Changing the word order requires appropriate transformations, in particular it concerns the transformation of passive voice sentences. Non-trivial are also processes of generating counterparts for complex sentences, utterances with negation, and even token-assemblies or combinations.

In *Thetos*, signs that represent gestures are transmitted via tokens retrieved from a dictionary or generated procedurally; non-manual part of the utterance is transmitted by means of animation control tokens. This symbolic record of the utterance is convenient for further automated processing, which in our case is animation. The reader can check out linearization results by running the service

Thetos on the website http://las.aei.polsl.pl/las2/ where a set of free services of our Linguistic Analysis Server *LAS* is available [3].

Until recently, the research has been focused on the problems of expressing the content of Polish sentences in the Linguistic-Sign System (LSS), or more precisely, its laboratory variation. Currently, research team's attention is focused on expressing the content in the PSL. Research description given below is neither a description of the current version of the form of *Thel* utterances, nor a complete description of the *Thel* grammar. We offer to the reader a description of a laboratory exploration, which, over time, after thorough testing, should become an integral part of the *Thetos* system.

It is known that PSL is a spatial language. Consequently, a language that is used for the formal transfer of content must contain elements enabling a linear description of a non-linear utterance. The first attempts to introduce such a notation appeared in [16]. Our work is largely based on the results of studies in the field of sign linguistics published in this monograph and other papers, as e.g. [5,17]. In *Thel* we decided to organize the notation of utterance differently than it is done in that set of publications. The used there organization addressed to the human reader proved to be inconvenient to continue electronic processing in *Thetos* and therefore was transformed. The difference consists among other things in introducing a control character BEFORE and not AFTER the structure, which refers to it. Positioning control characters this way is associated with a natural run of interpretation by the animation module: facial expression first and then the gesture, to which this facial expression refers (for example, *smiling + child*, and not *child*, then *smile*).

In PSL meaning of a sign (gesture) is often reinforced by facial expressions or body movements. It is *Polin's* task to extract linguistic phenomena that convey non-verbal signs, and to record them in a linear form in *Thel*. Currently we make attempts to partially solve this very complex and difficult problem. Our research is based on the fact that rich resources of the natural language (in our case – the Polish written language) allow transmission of nonverbal elements. According to our observations, this goal is served by details of syntactic structure, relations between components of groups of tokens, order of groups in the sentence in relation to the predicate group, etc. The beginnings of works in this direction are described in the following sections.

1   The *Thel* Language – General Information

Usually a model of language contains an alphabet and a grammar. The alphabet V_T of the *Thel* language consists of two alphabets:

$$V_T = V_P + V_{St}.$$

V_P is the alphabet of dictionary gestures and as such it contains lexemes and some word forms of the Polish language. V_{St} contains in turn avatar behavior control characters.

The V_{St} alphabet consists of the following sets:

- V_S, separator set,
- V_E, set of characters that represent emotional load,
- V_M, manipulation character set.

The formal shape of these sets-alphabets is given below.

The elements of the V_S set fulfill two functions: they separate lexical units in the text and define the duration of pause between respective gestures.

$$V_S = \{SP, EP/EG, ES\},$$

where SP – space or horizontal tabulation mark, EP/EG – end-of-phrase (end-of-group) mark, comma, ES – end-of-sentence. ES can be expressed in the text by a dot, a question or an exclamation mark, a comma dividing the compound sentence, etc. The pause symbols are inserted while parsing the input text. The SP pause is very short, the ES pause lasts the longest.

The V_E alphabet now includes characters (currently 8) that correspond to the types of emotional manifestations or ratings (otherwise: characteristics), which belong to the given entry and which can be processed by the *Polin* processor:

$$V_E = \{\hat{}, |, \sim, =,), (, !, ?\},$$

where individual characters are a symbolic record of names of emotions, which within animation should be mirrored in avatar's facial expression. The emotional types in question are the following:

^	thanksgiving (owe),
|	request (ask),
~	apology (apologetically),
=	neutral (familial),
)	positive load (doggy),
(	negative load (war),
!	very expressive load (o!),
?	question (enquiringly).

The V_M set is currently composed of the characters '#' and '_' :

$$V_M = \{\#, \text{-}\}.$$

The '#' character precedes a number, with which it is used to distinguish the meanings of words having the same spelling, for example, pokój#1 (room) and pokój#2 (peace). In turn, the character '_' is used to connect two words: in PSL and LSS some clusters of words are represented by a single sign, for example *nie_masz* (*you_don't_have*), *nie_mieć* (*not_to_have*), etc.

It should be noticed that V_P is the basic signs alphabet, while the remaining alphabets: V_S, V_E, and V_M contain characters for animation control. All collections are open and can be supplemented by authorized persons.

The *Thel* grammar now contains a dozen or so rules; it is open and will be developed with the development of algorithms for non-linear elements translation.

2   The Problem of Vocabulary in *Polin*

The V_P alphabet contains elements of different types. First of all it is the dictionary of equivalents of PSL gestures that belongs to it. Among other V_P elements, especially noteworthy are compound signs, so called bi-signs [7], for example, *apteka(pharmacy)* ≡ *lekarstwo sklep (drug store)*, *brudas(sloven)* ≡ *brudny czowiek (dirty man)*, etc. [13]. Another type are token groups that represent a single sign, the meaning of which is not the sum of the meanings of the components: *nie_mieć (not_to_have)*, *nie_ma (has_not)*, *dowód_osobisty (identity_card)*, etc. As stated above, successive tokens are linked with a '_' mark.

Thel utterance linearization starts with building its dictionary part on the basis of the predicate-argument structure of the sentence and its syntactic representation. The words for the utterance are retrieved from the *Morf* database of *Polmorph* morphological analyzer [4]. The difference in dictionary resources of *Morf* and V_P is vast: currently the *Morf* dictionary contains 90,000 entries, and V_P – 1500. The problem of missing words in the PSL is now partially solved in the process of animation: the words are replaced by synonymous gestures, and in their absence they are spelled. Increasing V_P vocabulary cannot fully solve this problem: the set of described sign language gestures has a bit more than 6,000 items.

In the current version of *Polin* the compound sign problem has been solved by the introduction of two dictionaries. Each entry in the first one is a sequence of words to be connected with an underscore '_', for example:

> aparat_fotograficzny *(camera)*
> aparat_słuchowy *(hearing aid)*
> bez_smaku *(tasteless)*
> dowód_osobisty *(identity card)*
> bać_się *(to fear)*
> hak_holowniczy *(tow hook)*
> karetka_pogotowia *(ambulance)*
> kaseta_wideo *(videocasette)*

The second dictionary contains words to be replaced with another symbol, for example:

> apteczka turystyczna ⇒ apteka
> *(tourist medkit)*   *(pharmacy)*
> atmosfera Ziemi ⇒ atmosfera
> *(Earth's atmosphere)*   *(atmosphere)*
> całować się ⇒ całowanie
> *(to kiss each other)*   *(kissing)*
> dostosować się ⇒ przyzwyczaić
> *(to conform)*   *(to accustom)*
> elektroniczna poczta ⇒ e-mail
> *(electronic mail)*
> klatka schodowa ⇒ schody
> *(stair-case)*   *(stairs)*

koło podbiegunowe ⇒ biegun
(A[nta]rtic Circle, litt. sub-pole circle)   (pole)
opalać się ⇒ opalenizna
(to sunbathe/to tan)   (tan)

The source on which these two dictionaries have been drawn is *The PSL Travel Dictionary* [19], compiled from several PSL dictionaries. Using our new dictionaries during linearization, on one hand allows to reduce differences between V_P and *Morph*, on the other – makes the result of translation closer to the PSL form. For example, you can see a difference in the translation of sentences *Idę się opalać.* (*I'm going to sunbathe.*) and *Ona opaliła się.* (*She became tanned.*) obtained without and with dictionaries:

Text	LSS	PSL
Idę się opalać.	JA IŚĆ SIĘ OPALAĆ.	JA IŚĆ OPALENIZNA.
(I'm going to sunbathe/ to tan.)	*(I to_go to_sunbathe/ to_tan.)*	*(I to_go tan.)*
Ona opaliła się.	ONA OPALIĆ SIĘ.	ONA OPALENIZNA.
(She became tanned.)	*(she to_tan.)*	*(she tan.)*

3   *Thel* Grammar Basics

Thel grammar, as well as input syntax grammar, is based on SGS, the Syntactic Groups System formalism [2] and is very similar to SGGP, the Syntax Groups Grammar for Polish [11,12] . Just as SGGP, it operates syntactic groups mechanism rather than single words. The difference consists, inter alia, in the component order in the group, including the sentence group, and in using animation control characters.

The structure of sentences in *Thel* is compliant with the schema SVO or SVOI [13]. In the end of the sentence one or two adverbial groups may occur. As mentioned, the text in *Thel* is generated by the *Polin* processor, whose input data is a collection of predicate-argument structures of single sentences of the text being analyzed; the collection is the result of work of the semantic analyzer *Polsem*. The list of semantic roles for syntactic groups in *Thel* is the same as in Polish [9]. And so, the structure of sentence in *Thel* looks like this:

ACTOR ACTION + REFERENTIAL ARGUMENTS +
ATTRIBUTE ARGUMENTS.

Each component of the sentence is replaced by tokens – the components of a respective syntactic group found while parsing the sentence in Polish. Then the sentence in *Thel* is linearized. Linearization is carried out as follows: The pattern that annotates the group structure is analyzed and in accordance with the resulting information lexemes are printed: first those of the base group BG, then of BG's attributes, then – lexemes of the groups that are basic for the groups associated with BG, then of the attributes of those lower level basic groups, etc. With this, the result is analyzed and adjusted in accordance with the PSL (or LSS) grammar: some words in LSS and PSL are not one form, but two or more, for example *dziecko* and *dzieci* (*child/children*), *mieć* and *masz* (*to_have/you_have*); several other examples we give above while writing about clusters of words.

Correction of the utterance sometimes encounters problems that are difficult to resolve. For example, it is not clear for the Authors how to use the word *być* (*to_be*) in the future tense: whether the form *będzie* (*will_be*) everywhere, or there are exceptions.

PSL is a powerful language; a huge role in it is played by the possibility of parallel transmission of content, among other things by means of complex signs representing semantic-syntactic structures. We consider two possibilities of PSL formalization: dictionary-based and procedural. In the dictionary-based approach one needs to gather all the language constructs in a dictionary, along with a detailed description of the manual and non-manual part. In the procedural approach the central role plays finding in the written language constructions, which may be helpful in interpreting the text onto *Thel* language elements, and writing a program to process such structures.

Both approaches have their pros and cons. The dictionary approach must take into consideration the size of the complex gestures dictionary, as well as difficulty to construct such a dictionary and the time complexity of browsing it. Great help in the preparation of such a dictionary could be a sign language corpus [1,10]. The procedural approach reduces the time of building the dictionary and simplifies the process of its management, but the translation may not be as precise as by the lexical approach, where the level of avatar's signing can be brought to perfection.

In [6] the following list of non-manual element types was given:

- face mime, which concerns the parts of face:
  eye-bows, eyes, mouth; face expression,
- direction of looking,
- sight contact,
- head movement (nodding involved),
- torso movement (leaning to the front involved),
- rotations,
- pauses,
- accelerating and slowing down,
- articulation lengthening and shortening,
- sound articulation.

Theoretically, for all non-manual elements their counterparts in the *Thel* language and – in consequence – also in the signed message should be found.

Unfortunately, the knowledge we at present have doesn't allow us to accomplish as ambitious undertaking as that. We have focused at selected elements from the list mentioned above. First attempts at putting into effect concern the face mime, connected with mouth and facial expression for selected names of emotion; first experiments in emotional states transmission were described in [9]. The next non-manual element under research are pauses.

A part of *Thel* rules we consider now, connected with introduction of control characters, has been given in dictionaries. For example, in the emotional load dictionary to each entry a control character is assigned. Lack of character before a word in a *Thel* utterance means a neutral load. To express emotion intensity (i.e. intensity of mime) the control character should be repeated; this is also a dictionary rule.

There also exist non-dictionary rules that generate characters to control the face mime and body movements. These rules are "fired" or not what is directly dependent of the results of semantic and syntactic analysis of the sentence being translated. For example, interpretation of the group *mały wiejski domek* (*little rural house = cottage*) is transmitted by the token sequence *mały_domek wiejski_domek* (*little_house rural_house*). Base for this is attributive relation between *mały* and *domek* and conformance relation between *mały* and *wiejski*. Syntactic relation interpretation rules are discussed in the next section.

Another very simple example is transmission of a question or an „exclamation", when a sentence in Polish is terminated with '?' or '!'. One of syntactic analysis results is to assign to the sentence its syntactic-semantic interpretations. To the syntactic-semantic features of the sentence it belongs its classification as affirmative, interrogative, or imperative. This feature is generated on the basis of sentence structure analysis or the character that terminates the sentence.

Notation of utterance in *Thel* is different from the notation used in sign linguistics. If traits of the sentence are those of an interrogative one, then before writing its translation into *Thel* the control character '?' is put, which in the given context is an interrogation operator; its scope extends over the fragment of the sentence to the first respective pause. The operator needs appropriate facial expression animation, i.e.: wide eyes and raised eyebrows, and before the pause – body tilting toward the interlocutor. If the sentence is an exclamatory one then before its record in *Thel* the exclamation mark '!' is put. As previously, the scope of the '!' operator ends when the first respective pause is met. These two simple rules have one non-simple nuance – before applying them we need to classify pauses in *Thel* and to define rules how to detect in the utterance the place they should be situated. There remains an open question: to what kind of pause the abovementioned operators work.

Another example is the predicate-argument structure interpretation in case when ACTOR and OBJECT are positioned in the signing space. Sentence partition into predicate and its arguments, and definition of semantic relations between them allow to identify some non-manual elements. It is possible, for example, to mark off the direction of signing: the movement proceeds from ACTOR to OBJECT.

Rules for syntactic relations interpretation look a bit more complicated.

4   Syntactic Relation Interpretation Rules

The need for syntactic relation interpretation is a consequence of the fact that it's indispensable to express in the output utterance the features of semantic elements of the sentence. For example, if ACTOR or OBJECT are noun groups then their detailed features are hidden in inter-element relations, and not in the verbal part only. For selected groups and selected relations we have succeeded to separate several rules, which allow for non-manual signs generation.

Example 1. Let's consider a noun group, among components of which there occurs a relation of #attr(arg1,arg2) type, where arg2 is the word being characterized – the main gesture, and arg1 is the word that characterizes it. The component arg1 may be interpreted as a non-manual operator that modifies the meaning of arg2 and as such it is transmitted by means of face mime and body movements. In *Thel* such construction may be transformed into the form of a single sign: the gesture ARG1_ARG2, where underscore '_' is the control character used to join the tokens that represent compound sign parts.

Similar linguistic constructions may be denoted differently (see e.g. [6]), as a two-sign sequence ARG2 ARG1. This denotation format can also be obtained by means of interpretation of the relation #attr(arg1,arg2). Let's return to the noun group example given in the preceding section. The group is: *mały wiejski domek* (*little rural house*). Between its components there exist relations #conf(**mały**,wiejski) #attr(wiejski,domek). The conformance relation is transformed: #conf(**mały** , #attr(wiejski,domek)) ⇒ #attr(**mały**,domek) . Thereafter, the syntactic relations representation takes the form:

#attr(**mały**,domek) #attr(wiejski,domek).

The relation #attr is interpreted into the *Thel* language, and output signs may have one of the forms given below[1]:

DOMEK MAŁY DOMEK WIEJSKI   (1)

DOMEK MAŁY WIEJSKI   (1')

MAŁY_DOMEK WIEJSKI_DOMEK   (1")

□

In the case given above it is not definitely clear for us whether reception of linguistic constructions this kind is identical or to some extent close. Our doubts stem from the analysis of the manual and non-manual movements description in [16], p. 84. From that description it follows that the meaning of arg1 is in a nontrivial way transferred into the manual part of the total sign. There is an example there: *potężne_drzewo* (*powerful_tree*), where to the manual part,

---

[1] Current form of interpretation is: = MAŁY = WIEJSKI DOMEK. (= *little* = *rural house*.), where the character '=' means a neutral face expression. However after first experiments we tend to give using the character '=' up because it brings nothing in animation whereas it may augment the pause between words, what is an undesired effect.

which is the gesture DRZEWO (*tree*), one adds elbow movement from the gesture POTĘŻNY (*powerful*). However, there is a concern that the construction DRZEWO POTĘŻNY (*tree powerful*) will be signed a bit differently. From here the problem ensues how to define the preferred form for transmitting compound signs generated in a procedural way.

Example 2. The relation #mod(arg1,arg2), which appears in the noun group, may be interpreted in *Thel* as ARG1_ARG2 or as ARG2 ARG1. For instance, interpretation in *Thel* of the group *bardzo mały wiejski dom* (*very little rural house*) may have one of the following forms:

DOM MAŁY BARDZO DOM WIEJSKI	(2)
DOM BARDZO_MAŁY WIEJSKI	(2')
MAŁY_DOMEK WIEJSKI_DOMEK BARDZO_MAŁY	(2")
BARDZO_MAŁY_DOMEK WIEJSKI_DOMEK	(2"')

□

Example 3. The same as it is in case of noun groups in example 2, the relation #mod is interpreted in case of adverb or verb groups[2].

For instance, interpretation of the adverb group *bardzo gorąco* (*very hot*) with the relation #mod(bardzo,gorąco) has the form BARDZO_GORĄCO. Interpretation of the verb group *bardzo chciał* (*he/she/it wanted very much*) with the relation #mod(bardzo,chcieć) (#mod(*very_much, to_want*)) has the form BARDZO_CHCIEĆ. This compound sign is demonstrated by the manual sign CHCIEĆ (*to want*) with its non-manual modification by BARDZO (*very/very much*). In this case however, likewise in example 1, there remains an open question, what part of the gesture BARDZO meaning is transferred into the totality of the compound sign.   □

Example 4. Verb group grammar allows for grouping the construction verb + *się* (verb + *one's*), also in the case, where *się* does not appear in direct neighborhood of the verb. This fact helps in interpreting this kind of group as a single compound sign: UBIERAĆ_SIĘ (*to_get_dressed*) and the like.   □

Example 5. If in a verb group there occurs the relation #not(arg1,arg2), the preferred interpretation of this group in *Thel* has the form ARG1_ARG2. By this, ARG2 can have the structure described in example 4. For instance, NIE_UBIERAĆ _SIĘ (*to_not_get_dressed*).   □

Example 6. Adverb and attribute groups with *nie*: *nie_bardzo* (*not_very_much*), *nie_ładny* (*not_nice*) and the like are interpreted the same way as described in example 5.   □

Rules for interpreting into *Thel* relations that occur in the SGGP grammar are in a working out stage.

---

[2] Let's remind that the verb group structure in the SGGP grammar is different than it is established in the traditional linguistics. For example, object can never be a verb group component.

5 Conclusions

PSL is a highly semantic language for content transmission. For correct automatic translation of written text into PSL an indispensable thing is electronic understanding of this text and its adequate transmission into a formal language, what at present does not seem to be possible to a full extent. Research in text understanding [18], however, allows the Authors to expect at least a partial solution of this problem. The *Thel* language should fulfill the following criteria: it should be a language for formal representation of PSL utterances, it should reflect the content of the text being translated, and it should be convenient for further electronic processing by the animation module.

Control characters that convey information concerned with non-manual elements of signed utterance being generated are an important element of *Thel*. We have started to establish ways for transmission of information, which is concerned with selected types of non-manual elements. First of all we have taken up avatar's face expression control as well as establishing the localization of pauses in articulation. We have started elaboration of rules that define what control characters and in which points of *Thel* utterances should be inserted. A part of these rules refers to the semantic layer of the utterance and concerns time-spatial relations contained in the utterance. Other rules are related to syntactic relations in selected syntactic groups types. We have also tentatively attacked problems of vocabulary connected with its poverty, with ambiguous and compound words.

It has to be noticed that supplementing *Thel* utterances with control characters is a new element in the *Polin* processor, which is now in-depth tested. The Authors think the development of the *Thel* language through introduction of new control characters to be the first step towards content transmission in the PSL.

References

1. Fabisiak, S.: Sign languages and corpus-based linguistics. Język Polski XC 4–5, 338–345 (2010). (in Polish)
2. Gladky, A.V.: Natural Language Syntactic Structures in Automated Communication Systems. Nauka, Moskva (1975). (in Russian)
3. Kulików, S.: Implementation of the linguistic analysis server for THETOS, the text into sign language translation system. Stud. Inform. **24**(3(55)), 171–178 (2003). (in Polish)
4. Lubiński, M., Suszczańska, N.: POLMORPH, polish language morphological analysis tool. In: Proceedings of the 19th IASTED International Conference APPLIED INFORMATICS - AI'2001, Innsbruck, Austria pp. 84–89 (2001)
5. Marcinkowska, A.: Metaphors and metonims as a denotation process in Polish Sign Language. M.Sc.Thesis under the direction of M. Świdziński, Division of Computer Linguistics, Polish Language Institute. Warszawa (2009). (in Polish)
6. Mikulska, D.: Non-manual elements in polish sign language. In: Świdziński, M., Gałkowski, T. (eds.) Studies on Lingual Competence and Communication of the Deaf, pp. 79–97. Zakład Graficzny UW, Warszawa (2003). (in Polish)

7. Mrozik, M.: Wstępne uwagi o morfologii polskiego języka migowego (PJM). In: Świdziński, M., Gałkowski, T. (eds.) Studies on Lingual Competence and Communication of the Deaf, pp. 59–77. Zakład Graficzny UW, Warszawa (2003). (in Polish)

8. Romaniuk, J., Suszczańska, N., Szmal, P.: An attempt to automatically translate into the sign language emotionally colored textual utterances. Speech Lang. Technol. **12/13**, 85–96 (2009/2010)

9. Romaniuk, J., Suszczańska, N., Szmal, P.: Semantic analyzer in the Thetos-3 system. In: Vetulani, Z. (ed.) LTC 2009. LNCS (LNAI), vol. 6562, pp. 234–244. Springer, Heidelberg (2011)

10. Rutkowski, P., Łacheta, J., Marganiec, B.: The Polish Sign Language (PJM) corpus project. In: SIGN 6 – 6th International Conference of Sign Language Users. Calangute, Goa, India (2013)

11. Suszczańska, N.: SG-grammar of Polish Syntax. In: Conference Speech Analysis, Synthesis and Recognition in Technology, Linguistics and Medicine, pp. 113–117, Kraków (2005). (in Polish)

12. Suszczańska, N., Szmal, P., Simiński, K.: The deep Parser for Polish. In: Vetulani, Z., Uszkoreit, H. (eds.) LTC 2007. LNCS (LNAI), vol. 5603, pp. 205–217. Springer, Heidelberg (2009)

13. Szczepankowski, B.: The Hearingless - Deaf - Deaf-mute. Chance equalization. Warszawa (1999). (in Polish)

14. Szmal, P., et al.: Translation of Polish texts into the sign language. Research project no. 8 T11C 007 17 final report. Silesian University of Technology, Gliwice (2001). (in Polish)

15. Szmal, P., et al.: Aiding hearing impaired people with a computer generation of the sign language. Research project no. 4 T11C 024 24 final report. Silesian University of Technology, Gliwice (2005). (in Polish)

16. Świdziński, M., Gałkowski, T. (eds.): Studies on Lingual Competence and Communication of the Deaf. Zakład Graficzny UW, Warszawa (2003). (in Polish)

17. Twardowska, E. (ed.): State of research on the Polish Sign Language. PZG Łódź (2008). (in Polish)

18. Vetulani, Z.: Man-machine communication. In: Computer Modeling of Linguistic Competence. Exit, Warszawa (2004). (in Polish)

19. Zajadacz, A.: The PSL Travel Dictionary. Verification in PSL: Kowalska, M., Kowalski, S., UAM internal report, Poznań (2010). (in Polish)

An Algorithm for Inconsistency Management in Spatial Knowledge Integration

Marcin Walas[(✉)] and Krzysztof Jassem

Information Systems Laboratory, Faculty of Mathematics and Computer Science,
Adam Mickiewicz University, 87 Umultowska Street, Poznań, Poland
{mwalas,jassem}@amu.edu.pl

Abstract. In the process of knowledge acquisition it is often necessary to solve the problem of ambiguous entities. The problem occurs when the same names refer to different entities in the knowledge database. We propose a method for resolving some of the ambiguities by means of the constraint calculus, namely RCC-5. We discuss the properties of our algorithm. Then we show that the algorithm can be extended to handle other types of relations. By applying a disambiguation algorithm in the process of knowledge acquisition we are able to increase the quality of the knowledge database acquired from the variety of data resources. The database is used in the prototype of our QA system, Hipisek [11].

Keywords: Knowledge acquisition · Spatial reasoning · Constraint calculus · Question answering

1 Introduction

Question Answering (QA) is a task of finding an answer to a question posed in the natural language. Answering a question related to a spatial entity requires a spatial knowledge database. Spatial knowledge may be represented either quantitatively or qualitatively. The former way (e.g. by using absolute geographical coordinates) is certainly useful in most engineering applications. However, for the sake of QA, the qualitative representation — storing relationships between spatial entities — is by far more useful, as this is how spatial information is represented in natural language [7].

There exists several comprehensive knowledge databases with spatial knowledge (both quantitative and qualitative), the best known of which are: Geonames[1] — a comprehensive geographical database and DBPedia[2], which is a structured information database extracted from Wikipedia articles [2]. Although available resources are extensive, they lack information required by a Polish language QA system such as: Polish geographical names, the Polish administrative division or names of specific Polish places (e.g. buildings, touristic attractions).

---

[1] www.geonames.org

[2] www.dbpedia.org

© Springer International Publishing Switzerland 2014
Z. Vetulani and J. Mariani (Eds.): LTC 2011, LNAI 8387, pp. 141–152, 2014.
DOI: 10.1007/978-3-319-08958-4_12

Our goal is to acquire a comprehensive spatial knowledge database for the purposes of a Polish language QA system. We aim to integrate various spatial knowledge data sources, such as Geographical Information Systems (GIS), structured data sources (e.g. the administrative division database) and semi-structured sources, from which we can extract qualitative spatial information (Wikipedia articles, touristic information web services).

Integration of various data resources is a common method used in the knowledge acquisition process. The Geonames project has incorporated several data resources and applied a wiki mechanism, which allows the users' community to correct mistakes and add new features. The DBPedia project is focused on data extraction from Wikipedia articles.

One of the main problems in the process of data integration is disambiguation of different entities sharing the same name. For example, the name *Drawa* may refer to a Polish river (an inflow of the river *Noteć*) or it may refer to a river in the Central Europe (an inflow of the river *Danube*). During the process of knowledge integration it has to be determined which is the actual entity that the name refers to.

As a solution to this problem we propose the methodology of spatial reasoning. We use Region Connection Calculus (RCC) as a general method for disambiguation. RCC is a family of calculi with the topological approach to spatial representation and reasoning. For our purposes we choose RCC-5, which allows for five relations between regions. The idea is as follows: if a new fact appears in the knowledge database (e.g. *Drawa* is located in *Poland*), then a spatial entity existing in the database (e.g. entity corresponding to the river *Drawa*, an inflow of the river *Noteć*) may be assigned to the subject or the object of the fact only if that does not lead to an inconsistency in RCC-5.

The paper is organized as follows: first we briefly describe the family of calculi (called RCC) and its recent applications in similar tasks. Next, we describe the representation of our knowledge database and the process of converting spatial facts into RCC-5 relations. We describe the algorithm for incorporating facts from various data sources into our knowledge database in accordance to the facts already stored in the database. Then we propose a way to represent imprecise information. Finally, we present the results of the evaluation and formulate conclusions.

2   Region Connection Calculus

2.1   RCC-5 Relations

RCC is a topological approach to qualitative spatial representation based on a primitive relation of connection between regions [5]. Relationships are defined by means of the $C(a, b)$ relation (*connection relation*) which holds iff regions a and b share the common point. On the basis of the C relation five basic relations for RCC-5 are defined, namely: DR (*discrete*), EQ (*equal*), PP (*proper part*), PPI (*proper part inversed*) and PO (*partial overlap*) [1]. Figure 1 illustrates the RCC-5 basic relations.

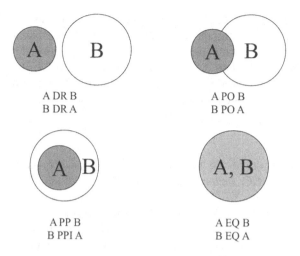

A DR B
B DR A

A PO B
B PO A

A PP B
B PPI A

A EQ B
B EQ A

Fig. 1. The set of five RCC-5 basic relations

Any subset of the basic relation set forms a relation in RCC-5. Thus RCC-5 contains 2^5 relations. *Universal relation* (denoted $\top$) is the set of all basic relations, *empty relation* (denoted $\bot$) is the empty set of basic relations. The following operations can be defined for the RCC-5 relations set: union $(R \cup S)$, intersection $(R \cap S)$, inversion (R') and composition $(R \circ S)$ [8].

RCC-5 relations are closed under composition and form a relation algebra [8]. In order to effectively calculate composition, a special table (called a composition table) should be designed.

2.2 Consistency in RCC-5

Using RCC-5 we can represent knowledge on entity relations in the form of constraints. A constraint network is formed from a set of variables V over the domain D and a set of constraints Θ on the variables of V. A network is *consistent* if it has a solution which is an assignment of values of D to the variables of V in a way that all constraints are satisfied [8]. It is proven that the consistency problem is NP-complete for RCC-5 [6].

A *path-consistency* serves as a common approximation of the constraint satisfaction problem. A given constraint network is path-consistent iff for any consistent instantiation of any two variables there exists an instantiation of any third variable s.t. all three variables taken altogether are consistent. To enforce path-consistency, the following operation is used for two variables i and j [8]:

$$\forall_k R_{ij} \Leftarrow R_{ij} \cap (R_{ik} \circ R_{kj})$$

The operation is used until a fixed point is reached. The resulting network is equivalent to the initial network (both share the same set of solutions).

If an empty set is present in the resulting network, then the initial network is not consistent. Otherwise the resulting network is path-consistent [8].

In the general case path-consistency does not imply consistency. Renz and Nebel in [6] define a subclass of RCC-5 relation set (called $\hat{H}_5$) in which path-consistency decides consistency. The $\hat{H}_5$ class contains 28 out of 32 RCC-5 relations, and includes all basic relations and the universal relation.

2.3   RCC-8

RCC-8 is an extension of the RCC-5, which consists of eight basic relations: DC (*disconnected*), EC (*externally connected*), PO (*partially overlap*), TPP (*tangential proper part*), $NTPP$ (*non tangential proper part*), EQ (*equal*), $TPPI$ and $NTPPI$ (inverse of TPP and $NTPP$ respectively).

The consistency problem is proven to be NP-complete in the RCC-8 [6]. Therefore path-consistency method is used to solve RCC-8 consistency problem.

2.4   Applications

Constraints calculi are used in the human-computer interaction systems and systems that use semantic knowledge. Vetulani et al. in [10] describe the XCDC calculus (which is based on spatio-temporal relations) applied in the module of dialogue analysis. Stocker and Sirin in [9] apply the RCC-8 calculus to support qualitative spatial reasoning in a query answering engine. Hogenboom et al. in [4] use RCC-8 to represent spatial knowledge in the Semantic Web (in OWL).

In our approach the reasoning itself is not a main issue. We use spatial reasoning only as one of the criteria to decide which entities should be assigned to processed facts. This helps us disambiguate entities bearing the same name and increase quality of the knowledge database without costly human work.

In our knowledge acquisition system we focus mainly on two relations between spatial entities: *A is located in B* and *A overlaps* with *B*. Therefore we decided to choose RCC-5, whose relations set corresponds to those maintained in our system. However, our algorithms can be easily adapted to use within other constraint calculi. As an example we describe application of the RCC-8 calculus in order to handle imprecise information.

3   Facts in the Database

In our knowledge database we store entities and facts. An *entity* is a notion for an individual object in the real world. One entity may have different names in different languages. One entity belongs to exactly one type. Entity types form a taxonomy. For example the city of *Warsaw* (a capital of Poland) with three possible names: *Warszawa* (Polish), *Warszawka* (Polish, informal) and *Warsaw* (English) forms one entity of the type *city* in our database.

A *fact* is a triple: subject entity, predicate name and object entity. A fact is the only way of knowledge representation in our database. Predicate name is a name of the relation that holds between subject and object. Predicates are typed to form a taxonomy. An example of the fact that Warsaw is located in Poland is a triple: (city Warsaw, *is located in*, country Poland).

Our entities taxonomy includes 80 entity types, among which 45 are spatial entity types. The taxonomy is based on Geonames feature codes and on the general ontology of entities used in the Polint-112-SMS project described in [10]. Entity types are organized in a hierarchical way. The relation types taxonomy includes 15 relations among which 4 are qualitative spatial relations.

The creation of a constraint network from the set of facts is done by conversion of each fact subject and object to network node and transformation of the fact relation type to the corresponding calculus relation. We define, that a fact is **calculus transformable**, if the fact relation type is semantically equivalent to a calculus relation. The following transformations are set:

- *is located in* $\rightarrow PP$
- *overlaps* $\rightarrow PO$
- *is partially located in* $\rightarrow \{PP, PO\}$

We assume that the universal relation holds between entities for which no information is available. Following Gabrielli [3] we assume that spatial entities are approximated by regions in Euclidean topological space.

Some of the relations can be inferred from the world knowledge, thus we do not store them in the database. For example, we do not keep the fact that the continent of Europe is discrete with South America. Instead, we store the rules for indirect semantic relation. This includes granularity issues, like deciding that some of the entities may be considered point-like (e.g. one building can not be inside another building). Indirect semantic relations use only DR relation.

Linking entities with indirect semantic relations is executed using handcrafted rules. Exemplary rules are:

1. If subject and object entities are of the *building* type or any of its subtype, then they are discrete (DR),
2. If subject and object entities are of the same leaf type (have no subtypes in the taxonomy) then they are discrete (DR).

We use the following procedure to create a constraint network for a given calculus:

Create constraint network from the set of facts F

```
procedure CreateNetwork(F)
input:
 set of facts F
 temporary set of facts T := F
begin:
1. repeat
2.1. changed := false
2.2. for each fact f from T:
```

```
2.2.1. if f is calculus transformable then
2.2.1.1. transform f into a calculus relation e
2.2.1.2. add e to N; if new entity is added to N
          then set changed := true
2.2.1.3. search in the knowledge database
          for calculus transformable facts with
          identical subject as the subject or object of f;
          add them to T
2.3. for each pair of entities from N which are not related
     link them with indirect semantic relations.
2.4. set F := T and clear T.
3. until changed
4. return N
```

Potentially, the network that we create may contain a large number of entities. In fact we use only small local paths inside the network. This is due to the fact, that we expand our network only in "one direction" (see point 2.2.1.3. of the CreateNetwork procedure) and that we actually store facts in "one direction" (e.g. we store the fact that A is located in B, but not the fact that B contains A).

4   Adding Facts to the Database

In this section we describe the implementation of RCC-5 in the process of developing the spatial knowledge. We develop our knowledge database by integrating various data resources. A sketch of the algorithm for adding a fact to the database is given below:

Adds a fact to the knowledge database

```
procedure ProcessFact(f)
input:
 processed fact f (subject, predicate_name, object)
begin:
1. search the database for entities that are
   either candidate subjects or candidate objects.
2. select the best pair (s, o) of candidate entities.
3. if the corresponding constraint network is path-consistent,
   then assign the pair (s, o) to f.
4. otherwise go back to (2).
5. if no appropriate pair (s, o) has been found,
   try one of the following:
5.1. introduce a new entity for
     either subject or object of f
5.2. otherwise, introduce new entities for
     both subject and object of f
```

Candidate entities are those, whose names are consistent with the names occurring in the fact (e.g. the names have at least one word in common) and are of the consistent type (the types are equal or one is a predecessor of the other in the taxonomy).

To check consistency of the network for a given assignment of entities (s, o) to f, we use the procedure CheckConsistency:

Checks path-consistency for a new fact

```
procedure CheckConsistency(f, s, o)
input:
 processed fact f,
 candidate pair of attachments for subject and object (s, o)
begin:
1. create the constraint network assuming that s and o
   are assigned to f: use the CreateNetwork procedure.
2. use path-consistency method on the constraint network
3. if the resulting network path-consistent then succeed;
   otherwise, fail (<s, o> assignment to f is inconsistent
   with the knowledge database).
```

Consider the following example: a new fact *Drawa (type: river) overlaps Croatia (type: country)* is being processed. Assume that the database contains:

– the fact: Drawa (river, id:1) *is located in* Poland (country, id:2),
– the entity: Croatia (country, id:3).

In the first step the candidates are searched for in the knowledge database. The results are: one-element set {Drawa (river, id:1)} for the subject and one-element set {Croatia (country, id: 3)} for the object. The following candidate entities may be assigned to the names Drawa and Croatia occurring in the new fact:

1. Assign entity (id: 1) to *Drawa* and entity (id: 3) to *Croatia*
2. Assign entity (id: 1) to *Drawa* and introduce a new entity for *Croatia*
3. Introduce a new entity for *Drawa* and assign entity (id: 3) to *Croatia*
4. Introduce new entities for both *Drawa* and *Croatia*

The algorithm starts with checking the first possibility. An initial constraint network is created (see Fig. 2). Then, the final network is constructed (see Fig. 3). The network is verified for consistency and the result is negative (as we assume that two countries: Croatia and Poland should be discrete).

Introducing a new country entity for Croatia and assigning id: 1 to Drawa (possibility 2.) also leads to the same inconsistency (two countries should be discrete).

Finally, assigning a new entity to Drawa (possibility 3.) does not lead to inconsistency: there exist a river entity named Drawa that overlaps with Poland and a new river entity Drawa that overlaps with Croatia.

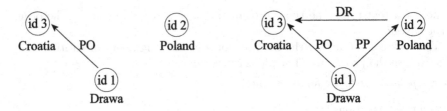

Fig. 2. Initial RCC-5 constraint network   **Fig. 3.** Final RCC-5 constraint network

4.1   Analysis of the Algorithm

In this section we show that the path-consistency method used in the *Check-Consistency* procedure decides consistency.

Algorithm attribute 1. *For any pair of nodes v and w of the constrain network N created by the function CreateNetwork (v, w) the constraint is one of:*

1. *the universal relation,*
2. *the relation created via transformation of the predicate into a RCC-5 relation,*
3. *the relation created via indirect semantic rules.*

Corollary 1. *A constraint network N used in the procedure* ProcessFact *uses only relations from the $\hat{H}_5$ relation set.*

As was said in Sect. 2.2 Renz and Nebel shown that in the $\hat{H}_5$ path-consistency decides consistency, which leads to the final corollary:

Corollary 2. *The CheckConsistency algorithm decides the consistency of the network.*

5   Algorithm Extension

We have observed that some of the knowledge sources processed by our knowledge acquisition system provide additional quantitative information (e.g. population, surface or elevation). We decided to use such kind of information in the process of disambiguation.

Our first approach was to compare the corresponding values and check if they are equal to those already stored in the database. This approach was not effective because most of the sources contain information, which values differ to some extent. For example the city of *Boston* (USA) has the population of 625,087 (according to Wikipedia) or 594,034 (according to MongoBay[3]).

In the extended algorithm we introduce the *approximate* relation, which allows to compare values with a certain tolerance level. Our goal is to model this relation in the RCC.

---

[3] http://world.mongabay.com/polish/population/pl.html

5.1   Q3 Set of Relations

We define the following relations:[4]

- $equal(x, y) \Leftrightarrow |x - y| = 0$,
- $aprox(x, y) \Leftrightarrow |x - y| > 0 \wedge |x - y| < \epsilon$,
- $notequal(x, y) \Leftrightarrow |x - y| \geq \epsilon$.

We define the C relation as follows:

$$\forall_{x,y \in \mathbb{R}} C(x, y) \Leftrightarrow |x - y| < \epsilon$$

Then, the following holds (see [12]):[5]

$$\forall_{x,y \in \mathbb{R}} DC(x, y) \Leftrightarrow notequal(x, y)$$

$$\forall_{x,y \in \mathbb{R}} EQ(x, y) \Leftrightarrow equal(x, y)$$

$$\forall_{x,y \in \mathbb{R}} ONE'(x, y) \Leftrightarrow aprox(x, y)$$

This allows us to use RCC-8 as a model for our *approximate* comparison.

5.2   Application to the Disambiguation Algorithm

In order to handle "approximacy" the disambiguation algorithm is modified as follows:

- we allow to add multiple facts at one time (all considering one subject),
- we define calculus transformable relations: *equal* and *approximate*, which are modeled in RCC-8 by EQ and EQ, ONE' respectively,[6]
- we define indirect semantic rules for the value entities with respect to the C relation defined in Sect. 5.1.

We take the following assumptions about quantitative information:

- all values in the knowledge database are in the *equal* relation,
- values introduced by a new source are considered as *approximate*,
- each entity can have at most **one** value of each type.[7]

Reasoning is carried out using path-consistency algorithm. Remark that we do not need to apply extensive modifications to our disambiguation algorithm. We only need to specify the calculus transformable relations and indirect semantic rules.

Consider the following example: the following set of facts is being processed:

---

[4] The parameter ϵ is used to set a level of tolerance when comparing two values.

[5] ONE' is the short form of: $\{EC, PO, TPP, NTPP, TPPI, NTPPI\}$. The name refers to the RCC3 relation ONE.

[6] Remark that the precise meaning of *approximate* relation is: *approximate or equal*.

[7] Hence if the source contains value for the quantitative relation, which is already stored in the knowledge database, the new value is used only for disambiguation.

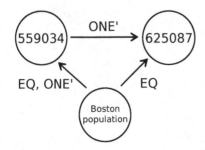 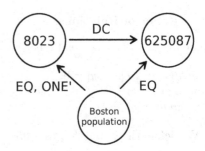

Fig. 4. Constraint network created when the name Boston refers to one city (the difference of population is in the degree of tolerance)

Fig. 5. Constraint network created when the name Boston corresponds to different cities (the population difference is too high)

```
Boston [city], is located in, USA [country]
Boston [city], population, 559,034 [value]
```

Assume that the following facts are stored in the knowledge database:

```
Boston [city] id:1, is located in, USA [country] id:2
Boston [city] id:1, population, 625,087 [value]
```

Remark that the entity *Boston* stored in the database is likely to be equal the new entity introduced by the processed fact. This is confirmed by the disambiguation algorithm, which in the first try assigns new fact entity *Boston*, to the entity with id 1. The corresponding quantitative knowledge constraint network is consistent (see Fig. 4), but no new facts are stored in the database (we do not store more than one *population* fact). Remark that if we do not allow for the *approximate* comparison we would end up with a new *Boston* entity (since it would be inconsistent with the fact stored in the database).

Now assume that we process the following fact set:

```
Boston [city], is located in, USA [country]
Boston [city], population, 8,023 [value]
```

In this case the new entity *Boston* and the entity *Boston* stored in the knowledge database are different cities. Remark that spatial relations are not sufficient to distinguish those cities (because both are located in the USA). However, using quantitative information, we end with the inconsistent constraint network (see Fig. 5). This way we identified that in this case the name *Boston* refers to a different city.

6   Results and Evaluation

We applied the above algorithms to our knowledge acquisition system HipiS-wot. We processed 9 resources which are: an administrative division database

Table 1. Comparison of the number of acquired entities in the baseline version of HipiSwot and the final version

	Baseline version	Final version
Total number of entities	232,710	261,063
Number of spatial entities	111,891	147,085
Total number of facts	307,668	298,002
Number of qualitative spatial relation facts	191,715	186,829

(TERYT), Geonames project, data extracted automatically from Wikipedia categories and web services with touristic or geospatial information.

We compared the baseline version (without the disambiguation mechanism applied) with the final version. Both versions of the system integrated the same set of data sources into the knowledge database. Using the baseline version of the system we obtained 111,891 spatial entities and 191,715 facts concerning qualitative spatial relationships. Using the final version we obtained respectively 147,085 spatial entities and 186,829 facts. A significant increase in the number of spatial entities is due to the introduction of new entities when inconsistency with the knowledge database was identified. A little decrease in the number of facts obtained is due to applying a discarding mechanism for some data resources (some resources with lesser quality were blocked from introducing new facts). Table 1 shows the results for both versions.

In the consistency check experiment we computed the number of inconsistencies occurring in the baseline version. For each spatial entity in the knowledge database we created the constraint network for all facts attached to the entity. We checked if the network was path-consistent. If not, we marked entity as inconsistent. We identified that out of 111,891 spatial entities about 21.6 % (24,170 entities) were inconsistent. All these inconsistencies were removed in the final version, due to the implementation of RCC.

7   Conclusions

In this paper we proposed an implementation of RCC to disambiguate entities in the process of knowledge acquisition. We described an algorithm that allows for discarding ambiguities, which are not path-consistent with the already acquired knowledge. We created an initial version of a knowledge database for a Polish QA system by integrating various data resources. We evaluated our results by comparing them to an earlier version of the data set.

Our algorithms are calculus-independent and may be adopted to any constraint calculus. One needs only to define the rules for transformation of the fact relation types stored in the knowledge database and the rules for indirect semantic relations between entity types for the chosen calculus.

References

1. Bennett, B.: Spatial reasoning with propositional logics. In: Doyle, J., Sandewall, E., Torasso, P. (eds.) Proceedings of the 4th International Conference on Principles on Knowledge Representation and Reasoning (KR-94), pp. 165–176. Morgan Kaufmann. Bonn (1994)
2. Bizer, C., Lehmann, J., Kobilarov, G., Auer, S., Becker, C., Cyganiak, R., Hellmann, S.: DBpedia – a crystallization point for the web of data. J. Web Semant.: Sci. Serv. Agents World Wide Web **7**, 154–165 (2009)
3. Gabrielli, N.: Investigation of the tradeoff between expressiveness and complexity in description logics with spatial operators. Ph.D. thesis, Universita degli Studi di Verona, Dipartimento di Informatica (2009)
4. Hogenboom, F., Borgman, B., Frasincar, F., Kaymak, U.: Spatial knowledge representation on the semantic web. In: ICSC '10 Proceedings of the 2010 IEEE Fourth International Conference on Semantic Computing. IEEE Computer Society, Washington, DC (2010)
5. Randell, D.A., Cui, Z., Cohn, A.G.: A spatial logic based on regions and connection. In: Nebel, B., Swartout, W., Rich, C. (eds.) Principles of Knowledge Representation and Reasoning: Proceedings of the 3rd International Conference, pp. 165–176. Morgan Kaufmann, San Francisco (1992)
6. Renz, J., Nebel, B.: On the complexity of qualitative spatial reasoning: a maximal tractable fragment of the region connection calculus. In: IJCAI, pp. 522–527 (1997)
7. Renz, J., Rauh, R., Knauff, M.: Towards cognitive adequacy of topological spatial relations. In: Habel, C., Brauer, W., Freksa, C., Wender, K.F. (eds.) Spatial Cognition 2000. LNCS (LNAI), vol. 1849, pp. 184–197. Springer, Heidelberg (2000)
8. Renz, J. (ed.): Qualitative Spatial Reasoning with Topological Information. LNCS (LNAI), vol. 2293. Springer, Heidelberg (2002)
9. Stocker, M., Sirin, E.: PelletSpatial: a hybrid RCC-8 and RDF/OWL reasoning and query engine. In: Proceedings of the 5th International Workshop on OWL: Experiences and Directions (OWLED 2009) Chantilly, VA, USA (2009)
10. Vetulani, Z., Marciniak, J., Obrebski, T., Vetulani, G., Dabrowski, A., Kubis, M., Osiński, J., Walkowska, J., Kubacki, P., Witalewski, K.: Language resources and text processing technologies. The POLINT-112-SMS system as example of application of Human Language Technology in the public security area. Adam Mickiewicz University Press, Poznań (2010)
11. Walas, M.: How to answer yes/no spatial questions using qualitative reasoning? In: Gelbukh, A. (ed.) CICLing 2012, Part II. LNCS, vol. 7182, pp. 330–341. Springer, Heidelberg (2012)
12. Walas, M.: Spatial-temporal reasoning in the question answering system. Ph.D. thesis. Adam Mickiewicz University (2013)

Text Analysis

Information Extraction for Czech Based on Syntactic Analysis

Vít Baisa[(✉)] and Vojtěch Kovář

Masaryk University, Botanická 68a, 602 00 Brno, Czech Republic
{xbaisa,xkovar3}@fi.muni.cz

Abstract. We present a complex pipeline of natural language processing tools for Czech that performs extraction of basic facts presented in a text. The input for the tool is a plain text, the output contains verb and noun phrases with basic semantic classification. Automatic syntactic analysis of Czech plays a crucial role in the pipeline. In this paper, we describe the particular tools used in the system, then we give an example of its usage and conclude with a basic evaluation of the overall system accuracy.

1 Introduction

The term *information extraction* has been recently used in two main meanings. One of them is searching for documents relevant to a query in a large collection of documents. The other meaning is extracting simple facts from a text that can be further used e.g. for highlighting or indexing. In this paper, we will use the latter meaning of the term.

Current approaches to information extraction focus rather on restricted domains and are specialized in finding a particular type of information, e.g. named entities [1,2], relations between them [3] or protein interaction [4]. However, a generalized approach with high accuracy does not seem to be achievable at the moment.

In this article we describe a system designed as a pipeline of several language tools (including morphological tagging and disambiguation, syntactic analysis and semantic classification) used for extracting general information from a text, as opposed to the particular information extraction mentioned above. Currently, the tool gives a structured information about the facts found in the sentence and the result serves as an aid for further manual processing of extracted information. Its usage is not limited to any particular text type as the language tools used in the pipeline are robust enough to cover general language.

In the following chapters we introduce the particular language tools used in the system. Then we show an example of its usage and give a basic evaluation of the overall system accuracy.

2 System Overview

The system reads a text file with one sentence per line. In the first step we tokenize each sentence (one token per a line) according to spaces and a set of

© Springer International Publishing Switzerland 2014
Z. Vetulani and J. Mariani (Eds.): LTC 2011, LNAI 8387, pp. 155–165, 2014.
DOI: 10.1007/978-3-319-08958-4_13

punctuation. As a result we get a word-per-line format that is sometimes called *vertical* or *vertical text*.

This vertical file is then analysed by morphological analyser *Ajka* [5]. High amount of various morphological tags per token needs to be pruned – therefore we use morphological disambiguator *Desamb* [6].

Syntactic analysis, the main part of the system, follows: it identifies sentence constituents: noun, verb, prepositional and adjective phrases. We use the *SET* parser [7] with slightly modified output structure. The result of this step is a list of phrases together with the morphological information (lemmas and tags).

Simple rules in the next step classifies noun and pronoun phrases according to cases. Prepositional phrases are treated in a more complex way using hypernymic structure of *Czech WordNet* [8]. Thanks to the information from WordNet, we are able to classify the prepositional phrases as *manner*, *place*, *time* and more fine-grained classes, see below.

Resulting classification is clearly arranged in form of a table which is easily readable and suitable for further processing.

3   Morphological Analysis and Disambiguation

The very first step is tokenization based on simple splitting words by spaces and punctuation. Tokenization step outputs a text in vertical format (with word forms only) which serves as input for the next step, morphological analysis.

Due to rich morphology of Czech there are thousands of possible morphological tags. We used the attributive tagset built into the morphological analyser *Ajka* [5] where each tag encodes all relevant morphological information about a word-form: a part of speech (k), case (c), gender (g), numerus (n) etc.[1] The *Ajka* algorithm itself is based on matching the input words to a system of predefined model words that define the declension paradigm.

Some word-forms are heavily ambiguous – they may correspond to many tags as in example on Table 1. The example sentence *Pravidelné krmení je pro správný růst důležité (Regular feeding is important for a proper growth)* contains very high percentage of ambiguous words which is no exception in the Czech language. Note that even some of possible morphological tags were omitted in the example for the sake of brevity.

Once morphological analysis is done, the result must obviously be disambiguated for further syntactical analysis. For this purpose we use morphological disambiguator *Desamb* which is described more in detail in [6]. It uses combination of manually prepared and statistically learned disambiguational rules. For learning the statistics, the manually disambiguated DESAM corpus [9] was used. Apart from morphological disambiguation, the *Desamb* tool can also be used for detecting sentence boundaries.

An example result of such disambiguation can be seen on Table 1 in the third column. The fourth column contains linguistic interpretations of the morphological tags.

---

[1] For a full reference, see http://nlp.fi.muni.cz/projects/ajka/.

Table 1. Morphological analysis and disambiguation of a sample sentence.

word	all possible tags	disambiguat.	interpretat.
Pravidelné Regular	k2eAgMnPc4d1, k2eAgInPc1d1, k2eAgInPc4d1, k2eAgInPc5d1, k2eAgFnSc2d1, k2eAgFnSc3d1, k2eAgFnSc6d1, k2eAgFnPc1d1, k2eAgFnPc4d1, k2eAgFnPc5d1, k2eAgNnSc1d1, k2eAgNnSc4d1, k2eAgNnSc5d1, ... (5 tags omitted)	k2eAgNnSc1d1	adjective, singular, nominative case, neuter
krmení feeding	k2eAgMnPc1d1, k2eAgMnPc5d1, k1gNnSc1, k1gNnSc4, k1gNnSc5, k1gNnSc6, k1gNnSc3, k1gNnSc2, k1gNnPc2, k1gNnPc1, k1gNnPc4, k1gNnPc5	k1gNnSc1	noun, neuter, singular, nominative case
je is	k5eAaImIp3nS, k3p3gMnPc4, k3p3gInPc4, k3p3gNnSc4, k3p3gNnPc4, k3p3gFnPc4, k0	k5eAaImIp3nS	verb, third person, singular, present tense
pro for	k7c4	k7c4	preposition, accusative case
správný proper	k2eAgMnSc1d1, k2cAgMnSc5d1, k2eAgInSc1d1, k2eAgInSc4d1, k2eAgInSc5d1, ... (18 tags omitted)	k2eAgInSc4d1	adjective, accusative case, singular, masculinum inanimate
růst growth	k5eAaImF, k1gInSc1, k1gInSc4	k1gInSc4	noun, accusative case, singular, masculinum inanimate
důležité important	k2eAgMnPc4d1, k2eAgInPc1d1, k2eAgInPc4d1, k2eAgInPc5d1, k2eAgFnSc2d1, k2eAgFnSc3d1, k2eAgFnSc6d1, k2eAgFnPc1d1, k2eAgFnPc4d1, k2eAgFnPc5d1, k2eAgNnSc1d1, k2eAgNnSc4d1, k2eAgNnSc5d1, ... (5 tags omitted)	k2eAgNnSc1d1	adjective, nominative case, singular, neuter

4   Syntactic Analysis

The result of morphological analysis and disambiguation is then used as the input to the syntactic analyser SET [7]. This rule-based analyser based on the pattern matching principle offers a number of possible outputs, including dependency and phrasal trees, phrase extraction and others.[2]

The SET algorithm searches for all possible matches of the set of manually written rules. In the second phase, the best matches are selected to draw a syntactic tree. Only one tree is produced for each sentence.

Other output formats are produced by tree-traversing algorithms. For example, to output noun phrases the system searches the tree depth-first and if it finds a noun as a head of the phrase, it prints the corresponding sub-tree. Only the biggest subtrees (that represent the so-called maximal phrases) are output.

For our purposes the output in the form of noun, adjective, adverbial, prepositional and verb phrases seemed to be optimal. Using this output, we obtained a kind of predicate-argument structure where the verb phrase stands for the predicate and other phrases for its arguments.

For an example of the SET output, see Fig. 1.

5   Classification of Phrases

The final part of the pipeline consists of a classification of noun and prepositional phrases found by the syntactic analysis. To do this, we needed to create a set of labels for the information carried by particular phrases. They needed to be informative enough to be able to gain useful information from them; especially, they should represent some pieces of the information in the text that can be asked by a wh-question. On the other hand we wanted to design them to be not hard to detect so that the output is not distorted by a huge number of bad results.

In the current version of the system, the list of the labels on the boundary of syntax and semantics is in Table 2.

For classification of the noun phrases according to the classes described above we use a two-level rule-based system (as no annotated data in this format are currently available for Czech) with exploitation of the data available in the Czech WordNet [8].

5.1   Non-prepositional Phrases

At the first level, noun and adjective phrases obtained by the syntactic analysis are classified according to cases of phrase's headword.

In the current version of the system, straightforward rules are used: nominative case is always treated as SUBJECT. Genitive and dative cases are assigned for indirect object (INOBJ) and accusative case for direct object (DIROBJ)

---

[2] For a full reference, see http://nlp.fi.muni.cz/projects/set.

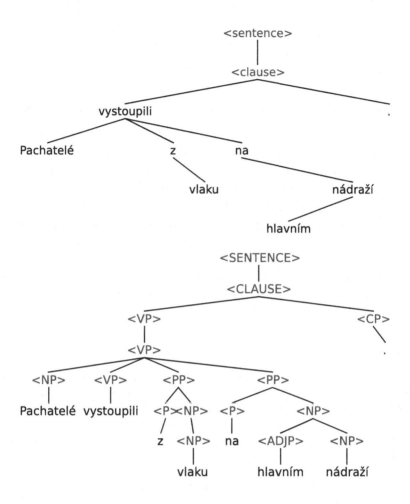

```
<s>Pachatelé vystoupili z vlaku na hlavním nádraží .
<clause>Pachatelé vystoupili z vlaku na hlavním nádraží
<vp> (): vystoupili
<phr> (k1c1gMnP): Pachatelé
<phr> (k7c2): z vlaku
<phr> (k7c6): na hlavním nádraží
</s>
```

Fig. 1. Example of the SET output: hybrid tree (on the left), constituent tree and phrasal output for sentence *Pachatelé vystoupili z vlaku na hlavním nádraží.* (*Perpetrators got off the train at the main station.*) Recognised phrases are (in the same order as in the example above): <vp> *got off*, <phr> *Perpetrators*, <phr> *the train*, <phr> *at the main station*.

Table 2. List of the labels used in the current version of the system.

SUBJECT	Answers to question *who* or *what*
VP	the Verb phrase representing the core of a clause; a predicate
INOBJ	Indirect object
DIROBJ	Direct object
MANNER	Prepositional phrase expressing manner that can be divided into subclasses WHY and HOW
TIME	a Time expression that can be further specified as SINCE-WHEN, TILL-WHEN or WHEN
LOC	Prepositional phrase expressing location that can be further divided into WHERE, FROM-WHERE, WHICHWAY and DIRECTION
ADDR	That corresponds to a phrase in vocative case; an addressee
INSTR	That corresponds to a phrase in instrumental case; an instrument

according to their functions in Czech. Vocative case corresponds with ADDR locative case is strictly prepositional in Czech and instrumental case is labeled with INSTR.

5.2 Prepositional Phrases

Classification of prepositional phrases is more complex as it can not be done simply by exploiting morphosyntactic features. For example, we can have *do Prahy* (to Prague) and *do hodiny* (within one hour), both having the same preposition and case but completely different meaning: the first one expresses location (covered by our LOC or more precisely DIRECTION), the other one is a time expression (covered by our TIME or more precisely TILL-WHEN). Clearly we needed to use some semantic information here.

Apart from the preposition itself and its case, we used the hyper-hyponymic hierarchy in the Czech WordNet together with heuristic rules for determining proper label – *time, location, manner* and their variants.

The classification algorithm then firstly prunes the space of the possible classifications based on the preposition and the case. There has been some investigation in classification of prepositions [10] but we decided to classify prepositions manually: this step is performed using rules transcribed from the Czech grammar handbook [11].

Then the algorithm searches WordNet hypernyms for all nouns in the phrase. If any of the pre-specified set of hypernyms is found, we are able to determine the phrase classification using a mapping of these hypernyms to the semantic classes. A sample of assigning WordNet hypernyms to our semantic classes can be found in Table 3.

Table 3. Example of assigning WordNet hypernyms to semantic classes.

Class	Example of hypernym
Time	Period, time, moment, dish, phenomenon, event
Location	Region, entity, group, state, continent
Manner	Organisation, quality, relationship

6 Examples and Application

In Table 4 there are some sample sentences together with extracted facts. As the motivation for development such kind of system was purely practical, in the very near future it will be employed as an aid for people analysing the text, in the form of highlighting, and as an intermediate step for text summarization.

Table 4. Examples of the output of the system.

Ministr vnitra Radek John včera v Praze schválil dlouho očekávaný zákon.					
SUBJECT	**VP**	**WHEN**	**DIROBJ**		**WHERE**
Ministr vnitra Radek John	schválil	včera	dlouho očekávaný zákon		v Praze
Minister of Inferior Radek John	has approved	yesterday	long awaited law		in Prague

Pachatelé z vlaku vystoupili až na hlavním nádraží.				
SUBJECT	**VP**	**FROM-WHERE**	**DIROBJ**	**WHERE**
Pachatelé	vystoupili	z vlaku		na hlavním nádraží
Perpetrators	got off	the train		at the main station

Při demonstracích byli zadrženi představitelé neonacistických spolků.			
SUBJECT	**VP**	**DIROBJ**	**WHERE**
představitelé neonacistických spolků	byli zadrženi		při demonstracích
neo-Nazi leagues representatives	were arrested		during demonstrations

Na semináři japonského šermu ve Valticích zemřel muž z Německa.			
SUBJECT	**VP**	**FROM**	**WHERE**
muž	zemřel	z Německa	na semináři japonského šermu ve Valticích
a man	died	from Germany	on japanese fencing seminar in Valtice

Particularly, it will help the Czech police collaborators in the task of monitoring potentially dangerous internet discussion groups.

A web interface[3] of the tool was created for demonstration and for the purpose of its proper testing by real users. The interface allows users to input one sentence, a URL or an arbitrary text and performs the analysis, as described

---

[3] http://nlp.fi.muni.cz/projekty/set/efa/wwwefa.cgi/first_page

above. The output can be displayed in form of tables, XML or interactive high-lighting mode similar to the GATE interface [12]. Screenshots of the interface are shown in Figs. 2, 3 and 4.

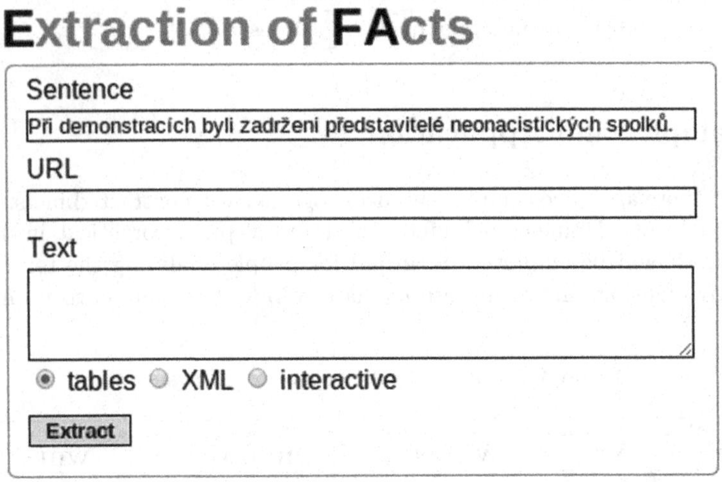

Extraction of FActs

Sentence

Při demonstracích byli zadrženi představitelé neonacistických spolků.

URL

Text

○ tables ○ XML ○ interactive

Extract

Fig. 2. Input form of the web interface for Extraction of FActs

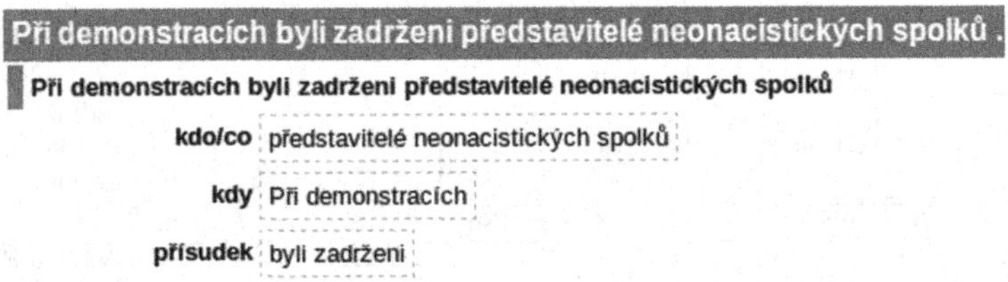

Při demonstracích byli zadrženi představitelé neonacistických spolků .

Při demonstracích byli zadrženi představitelé neonacistických spolků

kdo/co	představitelé neonacistických spolků
kdy	Při demonstracích
přísudek	byli zadrženi

Fig. 3. Output in form of a table.

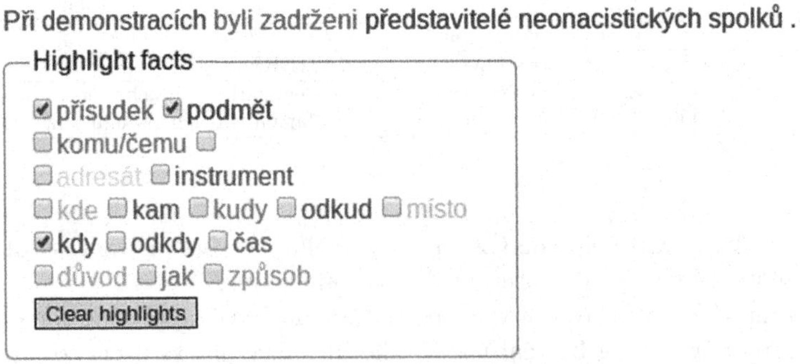

Při demonstracích byli zadrženi představitelé neonacistických spolků .

Highlight facts

☑ přísudek ☑ podmět
☐ komu/čemu ☐
☐ adresát ☐ instrument
☐ kde ☐ kam ☐ kudy ☐ odkud ☐ místo
☑ kdy ☐ odkdy ☐ čas
☐ důvod ☐ jak ☐ způsob
Clear highlights

Fig. 4. Interactive output with highlighting facts according to their classification.

6.1   On Parsing Evaluation

In a more theoretical context, this work can contribute to the discussion related to the parsing evaluation problem [13], [14]. Most of the currently used parsing evaluation techniques are based on tree similarity metrics [15], [16] which is problematic with respect to the impact on usage of natural language parsers in real-world applications.

Miyao et al. [13] proposed another procedure of comparing results of various parsers based on measuring their contribution to a practically motivated task. We are strongly convinced that this is the right way in evaluating the quality of the parsers and that searching for more such evaluation applications (as an analogy to benchmark sets) is needed.

Above we have presented a system that exploits the results of the syntactic analysis and that may be adapted to different parsers. The task of the pipeline is well-defined and practically motivated. Furthermore, as opposed to the syntactic trees, the result of the analysis is very close to the information human beings are able to extract from the text. Therefore, judging correctness of the output would be simple and efficient.

7   Evaluation

The tools for tokenization, morphological analysis and disambiguation were not evaluated within the scope of this paper. Their evaluation can be found in [6,17].

Basic evaluation of phrase extraction and phrase evaluation was carried out manually on 50 randomly selected sentences from the internet news groups as bigger gold standard data for this task are unfortunately not available for the Czech language.

For the preliminary results performed on the small testing set see Table 5. We can see that the accuracy in phrase detection (F-1 measure in this case) is around 90 % and the accuracy of the classification (percentage of correctly classified phrases among the correctly detected phrases) reaches nearly 80 %. The overall accuracy of the pipeline is then around 70 % which can be interpreted as we get about 70 % of the text correctly identified and classified.

This is certainly not enough for tasks like automatic reasoning or precise question answering however it can be fairly useful in helping people read the texts faster, creating approximate summarizations or indexing based on the extracted information that could make searching the texts more efficient.

Table 5. Evaluation

Metric	Accuracy
Phrases detected properly	87.7 %
Phrases classified properly	79.7 %
Overall accuracy	**69.9 %**

8   Future Work

Since the system is designed as a pipeline, it is obvious that performance critically depends on performance of each component. In this respect we need to focus on all of these components in our future work.

For the first step – tokenization – we plan to improve the algorithm for finding boundaries of sentences (e.g. punctuation inside parentheses).

As for morphological analysis and disambiguation there is a room for developing better rules for the *Desamb* system or alternatively to skip this step completely and run the syntactic analysis on ambiguous input which is possible but currently performs worse than analysis with unambiguous input.

Phrase extraction should be enhanced with named entity recognition and improving maximal phrases detection namely in case of PP-attachment.

We also plan to refine the phrase classification with introducing more complex rules and semantic roles contained in the verb valency lexicon Verbalex [18].

The performance for the particular task of the Czech police can be also significantly improved by adapting the tools in the pipeline to the language of internet discussion groups that is slightly different from the general language, on all levels of description. This was not done in the first version of the system and the results may have been affected by this fact. As all of the tools in the pipeline are rule-based (so there is no need for text-type-specific annotated corpora) and their development was aimed at transparency, simplicity and scalability, it should be straightforward to adapt them to the special type of text and improve the overall accuracy of the system.

Also, as one of the future aims, we plan to adapt the task described in this paper to the needs of parsing evaluation. However, this will need more work, especially creating appropriate annotated data and adapting the pipeline to various parsers.

Acknowledgements. This work has been partly supported by the Ministry of the Interior of Czech Republic within the project VF20102014003 and by the Czech Science Foundation under the projects P401/10/0792 and 407/07/0679.

We would like to thank to all our colleagues which participated on developing used tools and data sources.

References

1. Etzioni, O., Cafarella, M., Downey, D., Popescu, A., Shaked, T., Soderland, S., Weld, D., Yates, A.: Unsupervised named-entity extraction from the web: an experimental study. Artif. Intell. **165**(1), 91–134 (2005)
2. Uchimoto, K., Ma, Q., Murata, M., Ozaku, H., Isahara, H.: Named entity extraction based on a maximum entropy model and transformation rules. In: Proceedings of the 38th Annual Meeting on Association for Computational Linguistics, Association for Computational Linguistics, pp. 326–335 (2000)
3. Hasegawa, T., Sekine, S., Grishman, R.: Discovering relations among named entities from large corpora. In: Proceedings of the 42nd Annual Meeting on Association for Computational Linguistics, Association for Computational Linguistics (2004)

4. Abul Seoud, R.A., Youssef, A.B., Kadah, Y.M.: Extraction of protein interaction information from unstructured text using a link grammar parser. In: 2007 International Conference on Computer Engineering and Systems ICCES '07, Cairo, pp. 70–75 (2007)

5. Rychlý, P., Šmerk, P., Pala, K., Sedláček, R.: Morphological analyzer Ajka. Masaryk University, Technical report (2008)

6. Šmerk, P.: Unsupervised learning of rules for morphological disambiguation. In: Sojka, P., Kopeček, I., Pala, K. (eds.) TSD 2004. LNCS (LNAI), vol. 3206, pp. 211–216. Springer, Heidelberg (2004)

7. Kovář, V., Horák, A., Jakubíček, M.: Syntactic analysis as pattern matching: the SET parsing system. In: Proceedings of 4th Language and Technology Conference, Poznań, Poland, Wydawnictwo Poznańskie, pp. 978–983 (2009)

8. Pala, K., Smrž, P.: Building Czech WordNet. Rom. J. Inf. Sci. Technol. 7(1–2), 79–88 (2004)

9. Pala, K., Rychlý, P., Smrž, P.: DESAM – annotated corpus for Czech. In: Jeffery, K. (ed.) SOFSEM 1997. LNCS, vol. 1338, pp. 523–530. Springer, Heidelberg (1997)

10. O'Hara, T., Wiebe, J.: Preposition semantic classification via penn treebank and framenet. In: Proceedings of the 7th Conference on Natural Language Learning at HLT-NAACL 2003-Vol. 4, Association for Computational Linguistics, pp. 79–86 (2003)

11. Karlík, P., Grepl, M., Nekula, M., Rusínová, Z.: Příruční mluvnice češtiny. Lidové noviny (1995)

12. Cunningham, H.: Gate: an architecture for development of robust hlt applications. In: Proceedings of the 40th Annual Meeting of the Association for Computational Linguistics (ACL), pp. 168–175 (2002)

13. Miyao, Y., Sagae, K., Sætre, R., Matsuzaki, T., Tsujii, J.: Evaluating contributions of natural language parsers to protein-protein interaction extraction. Bioinformatics 25(3), 394 (2000)

14. Jakubíček, M., Kovář, V., Grác, M.: Through low-cost annotation to reliable parsing evaluation. In: PACLIC 24 Proceedings of the 24th Pacific Asia Conference on Language, Information and Computation, Sendai, Japan, Tohoku University, pp. 555–562 (2010)

15. Harrison, P., Abney, S., Black, E., Flickinger, D., Gdaniec, C., Grishman, R., Hindle, D., Ingria, R., Marcus, M., Santorini, B., Strzalkowski, T.: Evaluating syntax performance of parser/grammars of English. In: Natural Language Processing Systems Evaluation Workshop: Final Technical report RL-TR-91-362, Griffiss Air Force Base, NY, Rome Laboratory, pp. 71–77 (1991)

16. Sampson, G.: A proposal for improving the measurement of parse accuracy. Int. J. Corpus Linguist. 5(01), 53–68 (2000)

17. Sedláček, R., Smrž, P.: A new Czech morphological analyser ajka. In: Matoušek, V., Mautner, P., Mouček, C., Taušer, K. (eds.) TSD 2001. LNCS (LNAI), vol. 2166, pp. 100–107. Springer, Heidelberg (2001)

18. Hlaváčková, D., Horák, A.: Verbalex - new comprehensive lexicon of verb valencies for Czech. In: Proceedings of the Slovko Conference, Bratislava, Slovakia, VEDA (2005).

Applying Rule-Based Normalization to Different Types of Historical Texts—An Evaluation

Marcel Bollmann, Florian Petran, and Stefanie Dipper[⊠]

Department of Linguistics, Ruhr-Universität Bochum, 44780 Bochum, Germany
{bollmann,petran,dipper}@linguistics.rub.de

Abstract. This paper deals with normalization of language data from Early New High German. We describe an unsupervised, rule-based approach which maps historical wordforms to modern wordforms. Rules are specified in the form of context-aware rewrite rules that apply to sequences of characters. They are derived from two aligned versions of the Luther bible and weighted according to their frequency. Applying the normalization rules to texts by Luther results in 91 % exact matches, clearly outperforming the baseline (65 %). Matches can be improved to 93 % by combining the approach with a word substitution list. If applied to more diverse language data from roughly the same period, performance goes down to 43 % exact matches (baseline: 35 %), and to 46 % using the combined method. The results show that rules derived from a highly different type of text can support normalization to a certain extent.

Keywords: Historical language data · Spelling normalization · Rewrite rules

1 Introduction

Historical language data differs from modern data in that there are no agreed-upon, standardized writing conventions. Instead, characters and symbols used by the writer of some manuscript in parts reflect impacts as different as spatial constraints or dialect influences. This often leads to inconsistent spellings, even within one text written up by one writer.[1,2]

The ultimate goal of our research is an automatic mapping from wordforms from Early New High German (ENHG, 14th–16th centuries) to the corresponding modern wordforms from New High German (NHG). Enriching the data with modern wordform annotations facilitates further processing, e.g. by POS taggers, and simplifies wordform queries by other users working with the data.

---

[1] This is a revised and extended version of [1], evaluated on a larger test corpus than the original paper. The research reported here was financed by Deutsche Forschungsgemeinschaft (DFG), Grant DI 1558/4-1.

[2] Some of these characteristics in fact show up again in specific uses of modern language, such as contributions in chat rooms.

© Springer International Publishing Switzerland 2014
Z. Vetulani and J. Mariani (Eds.): LTC 2011, LNAI 8387, pp. 166–177, 2014.
DOI: 10.1007/978-3-319-08958-4_14

The approach we pursue, first described in [2], is to derive character replacement rules from a parallel corpus we built from two freely available texts: Luther's bible translation in the original ENHG version, and in a modernized NHG version. The idea is to exploit these resources to derive normalization rules that subsequently can be applied to historical texts which do not have modernized editions. Compared to a simple wordlist substitution approach, the rule-based method is able to capture generalizations and, consequently, to produce correct normalizations even for a number of wordforms which were not seen during training.

In our evaluation, we compare performance of the rule-based approach, a wordlist substitution method, and a combination of both. We apply those methods (i) to texts by Luther, and (ii) to further religious texts (which are less similar to NHG than Luther's texts). It turns out that the wordlist substitution method works surprisingly well, while a combined approach produces the best results. For closely-related texts, the rule-based approach outperforms the wordlist approach.

The paper is organized as follows. In Sect. 2, we introduce our data. Section 3 addresses the way we derive rewrite rules from the data, while Sect. 4 deals with the application of the rules to generate modern wordforms. Section 5 presents the comparative evaluation, Sect. 6 discusses related work and recent developments, and Sect. 7 presents a conclusion.

2 Corpora

2.1 Luther Bible

In our approach, replacement rules are derived from a word-aligned parallel corpus. A source that provides parallel texts in many languages, including historical ones, is the bible. We retrieved two editions of the bible translated by Martin Luther from the web[3]: the original ENHG version of the 1545 bible (which has been enriched with modern punctuation), as well as a revised NHG version of it, which uses modern spelling and replaces extinct words by modern ones

We aligned the editions on the basis of verses, sentences, and words, using the Gargantua toolkit [3] and the GIZA++ toolkit [4]. To minimize noise in our system's input, alignment pairs with a length difference of more than five characters were excluded from further processing. Since the two languages are highly similar – around 65 % of the pairs align identical wordforms – a length difference of that magnitude rarely leads to meaningful alignments.

To assess the quality of the resulting word pairs, a small sample of 1,000 pairs of aligned non-identical wordforms was manually inspected by a student assistant. Three types of mappings can be distinguished: The large majority (61 %) consists of correct, obvious mappings (such as *vnd* – *und* 'and'). 30 % are word pairs that differ with respect to inflection or affixing (e.g. *truncken* –

---

[3] http://www.sermon-online.de

trunkenen 'drunken', *oben – obenan* 'on top'). The remaining pairs consist of historically unrelated words.

For deriving replacement rules, obvious mappings are the perfect input. The second type of mappings is still useful, to a certain extent: correct rules can be derived from the roots of the words; mapping of differing inflection and affixes, however, should probably not be learned. The last type represents less useful input for our learning approach.

The resulting corpus consists of 550,000 aligned pairs of words or phrases. We randomly split it up into sub-corpora for training (40 %), evaluation, development, and a subset for future evaluations (20 % each). The Luther bible serves as the sole source for deriving replacement rules, both for the evaluation on Luther itself and on the Anselm corpus. Evaluation results from applying the rules are presented in Sect. 5.

2.2 Anselm Corpus

In addition to Luther's texts, we evaluate the rules on other texts which show considerably more variation than Luther's bible. The data consists of different manuscripts of the text "Interrogatio Sancti Anselmi de Passione Domini" ('Questions by Saint Anselm about the Lord's Passion').[4] The text contains a collection of questions posed by Saint Anselm of Canterbury and answered by Saint Mary. In the 14th–16th centuries, this text has been written up in various German dialects (from Upper, Central, and Low German), and transformed into long and short prose and lyric versions. In total, there are more than 50 manuscripts and prints, which makes the text an exceptionally broadly-documented resource.

These manuscripts are difficult to use for deriving normalization rules, since they are rather short (about 8,000 tokens on average for the entire Anselm corpus), and also there is no modernized version available. While we experimented on semi-automatic normalization with small amounts of manually annotated training data later [5], the study reported here concerns the use of large amounts of training data from available sources. We therefore decided to try to apply the rules derived from the Luther bible to the Anselm corpus and evaluate their performance on a set of manually normalized (i.e. modernized) data. We selected four manuscripts from different major dialectal regions to capture a broad range of graphematic variation: Alemannic (ALEM), Bavarian (BAV), West Central German (WCG), and East Central German (ECG). With an average length of 6,200, they are slightly smaller than the Anselm average, but since they are carefully annotated with gold standard normalizations, they make a good sample set. The normalizations were independently done by two student assistants and manually revised by a historical linguist. For a detailed discussion of the treatment of special writing conventions, refer to [5].

---

[4] http://www.linguistics.rub.de/anselm/

ENHG:	do min	kint	hatt	geffen	das Iung	mafz mit	finen	Iungren
NHG:	da mein	kind	hatte	gegessen	das junge	mahl mit	seinen	jüngern
	as my	child	had	eaten	the young	meal with	his	disciples

Fig. 1. Passage from the ALEM text and a word-by-word normalization (NHG)

Differences between the dialects most prominently concern wordforms (e.g. *chind – kínt – kynt* 'child', *geezzen – gefzen – geffen* 'eaten') as well as word order. Figure 1 shows the normalization of an exemplary passage from the ALEM text.

3 Normalization Rules

We use a modified algorithm for computing Levenshtein distance which not only calculates the numerical edit distance, but also outputs the respective edit operations (substitution, insertion, and deletion of single characters) that map the strings to each other. Moreover, the record of edit operations was enriched with information about the immediate context of the edited character. Ex. (1) shows two sample edit operations, using the notation of phonological rewrite rules.

(1)   a. $\varepsilon \rightarrow$ h / j _ r
        ('h' is inserted between 'j' and 'r')
      b. v $\rightarrow$ u / # _ n
        ('v' is replaced by 'u' between the left word boundary ('#') and 'n')

Determining the context for these edit operations is not straightforward, because applying one rule can change the context for other rules. Since the Levenshtein implementation applies the rules from left to right, we use the (new) target word for the left context and the (unaltered) source word for the right context.

Identity Rules. In addition to canonical replacement rules, our rule induction algorithm also produces identity rules, i.e. rewrite rules that map a character to itself. Identity rules reflect the fact that words can remain unaltered when mapped to their modernized forms, and many words are modified by few characters only. Identity rules and actual rewrite rules are intended to compete with each other during the process of rewriting: whenever multiple rules are applicable at the same position within a word, the rule that is ranked higher (according to a ranking system described below) is applied. If an identity rule is ranked higher than a non-identity rule, this results in the character in question not being modified.

Sequence-Based Rules. In a second step, we merge non-identity rules, resulting in replacement rules that operate on *sequences* of characters. Whenever a series of edits occurs at the same target or source position, we assume that this is actually an insertion or deletion of a *sequence* of characters, such as an affix. Whenever edits occur at adjacent positions, we assume that it is a substitution of a character sequence by another. By merging substitutions with adjacent deletions/additions, we account for character sequences of variable length on each side of the rule.[5] As an example, see Ex. (2), mapping *jrem* to *ihrem* 'their' ('s' is for substitution, '=' means identity mapping).

(2)

Input	*j*	*r*	*e*	*m*
Operations	s	=	=	=
Output	*ih*	*r*	*e*	*m*

Epsilon Identity Rules. In the system developed so far, insertion rules are difficult to handle. In generating modern wordforms by means of the rewrite rules (see Sect. 4), they tend to apply in an uncontrollable way, garbling the words in the process. This is due to the fact that the conditions for the application of insertion rules are less specific: while substitutions and deletions require the left hand side (LHS) of the rule *and* the context to match in the source word, insertions are constrained by their two context characters only, since the LHS of the rule is empty. At word boundaries, the problem gets even worse, since only one context side is specified here. Furthermore, substitution and deletion rules compete against the identity rules for their LHS, which restricts their application—but no similar competitor exists so far to curb the application of insertion rules. We therefore introduced the concept of epsilon identity rules:

(3) $$\varepsilon \to \varepsilon/ \; \mathbf{e} \; \_ \; \mathbf{n}$$

These rules are taken to mean that no insertion should be performed in the respective context. Just as the identity rules described above compete with actual rewrite rules, epsilon identity rules compete with actual insertion rules to determine whether or not an insertion should take place. That way, they restrict the actual insertion of characters. Derivation of these rules is relatively straight-forward: after all replacement rules for an alignment pair have been generated, an epsilon identity rule is created for each position where no insertion has taken place.

Ranking of the Rules. Applying the rule induction algorithm to the development corpus yielded about 1.1 million rule instances (training corpus: 2.2 million) of about 6,500 different types (training: 7,902). These were sorted and ranked according to their frequency. Table 1 lists sample instances of rules. Not surprisingly, none of the top-ranked rules actually modifies the input word. Rank 6 is taken by the first rule that maps some real character rather than ε to itself (identity rules, '='). Rank 20 features the most frequently-seen substitution rule ('s'),

---

[5] Identity rules are excluded from the merging process. Otherwise, merging would result in mappings of entire words instead of character sequences, basically identical to a word substitution list.

Table 1. Sample rankings and rules

	Rank	Freq.	Rule
=	1	24,867	$\varepsilon \rightarrow \varepsilon$ / n _ #
=	2	18,213	$\varepsilon \rightarrow \varepsilon$ / e _ r
=	3	18,200	$\varepsilon \rightarrow \varepsilon$ / e _ n
=	4	17,772	$\varepsilon \rightarrow \varepsilon$ / # _ d
=	5	14,871	$\varepsilon \rightarrow \varepsilon$ / r _ #
=	6	14,853	n $\rightarrow$ n / e _ #
s	20	8,448	v $\rightarrow$ u / # _ n
–	176	1,288	f $\rightarrow \varepsilon$ / u _ f
+	239	932	$\varepsilon \rightarrow$ l / o _ l
	156	1,443	j $\rightarrow$ ih / # _ r
	272	796	j $\rightarrow$ ih / # _ n
	329	601	j $\rightarrow$ ih / # _ m
	605	263	$\varepsilon \rightarrow$ _ d / t _ u
	879	142	ss $\rightarrow$ ß / o _ e

Table 2. Example mappings from the Luther bible and the Anselm texts

	Original		Auto
	Old	Modernized	
Bible	jrem	ihrem	✓
	vmbher	umher	✓
	soltu	sollst du	✓
	gemachen	gemächern	†gemächer
Anselm	etleich	etliche	✓
	gessen	gegessen	✓
	vnse	unsere	†unser
	vrouwe	frau	*vrouwe
	zitt	zeit	*zittern
Both	vnd	und	✓

rank 176 the first deletion ('–'), rank 239 the first insertion rule ('+'). The bottom part of the table lists frequent sequence-based rules. The rule ranked 605th shows that the algorithm can also produce 1:N mappings, i.e. rules which map one input word to several output words. It inserts a whitespace followed by 'd' in a certain context, which applies in mappings such as *soltu – sollst du* 'should you', where *soltu* represents a contraction of verb and pronoun.

4   Generating Normalized Wordforms

Automatically normalizing ENHG texts is done on a word-by-word basis, i.e. the input of the normalizing process is always a single word form. Words are processed from left to right; for each position within a word, applicable edit rules are determined. As with the rule extraction process, the left context is matched against the output already generated up to that point, while the right context is always matched against the input word. If a rule is applied, its right-hand side is appended to the output string, and the next character from the input word is processed. The process continues until the end of the word has been reached.

Rules with sequences of characters on the left-hand side (LHS) are applicable at the position of their first LHS character. In that case, if the rule is applied, processing continues with the next character that is not part of the LHS. If there is no applicable rule for a given position in a word, the character at that position is left unchanged and processing continues with the next character.

Epsilon Rules. Epsilon rules, as explained in Sect. 3, signify whether or not an insertion between two characters should be performed. In order for this to work, only one epsilon rule can be applied between any two given characters, or otherwise multiple—possibly infinite—insertions could take place. This is achieved by treating epsilon like an ordinary letter with regard to the LHS of rules, and preprocessing words so that exactly one epsilon is placed between each character and at word boundaries. For example, the input word *jrem* 'their' is converted internally to the following form:

(4) $$\# \, \varepsilon \, j \, \varepsilon \, r \, \varepsilon \, e \, \varepsilon \, m \, \varepsilon \, \#$$

Now, whenever an epsilon rule is applied, the read/write head moves to the next character, so that no other epsilon rule can be applied at the same time in the same position. Note that this does not generally prevent the insertion of multiple characters, as those are merged into sequences during rule extraction. Of course, epsilon characters have to be ignored for all purposes except for the LHS of replacement rules; in particular, they do never contribute to rule contexts or prevent the recognition of character sequences.

Selecting an Output Variant. For each character and its context within a word, there will usually be a number of applicable rules to choose from. Therefore, several output variants can usually be generated from one input word. As our aim is to generate exactly one (modernized) form for each input word, a decision has to be made about which variant to choose. To this end, each generated variant is assigned a probability score. The probability of a replacement rule is defined as its frequency divided by the sum of all rule frequencies. Word probability is calculated from the probabilities of the rules that were used to generate it; for this, we use the weighted harmonic mean, with the length of the LHS as weights. If the LHS contains a sequence, length is counted including additional epsilons between each character. This way, all variants generated from the same input word have the same total weight, regardless of whether sequence-based rules were used or not.

Additionally, to block the generation of nonsense words, all generated variants are checked against a dictionary. From all variants that are covered by the dictionary, the one with the highest probability score is then selected as the output form. If no variant can be generated in this way, the input word is left unchanged. In the evaluation presented below, we used all wordforms from the modernized Luther bible as our dictionary. This skews the results slightly in our favor when normalizing the 1545 bible text. Using a dictionary with wordforms from current newspaper texts, however, turned out problematic, since abbreviations, typos, etc., result in too many false positives with the dictionary lookup, and the vocabulary of newspaper texts differs considerably from religious texts.

Table 2 lists sample mappings from both the Luther and the Anselm corpus. '√' marks correctly generated wordforms, '*' marks incorrect ones. Wordforms marked '†' are useful normalizations with wrong inflection, currently counted as incorrect.[6]

Wordlist Substitution. An alternative approach to normalization is the idea of using bilingual wordlists. In order to compare the rule-based method to a pure

---

[6] Note that we ignore capitalization for the time being.

Table 3. Identical tokens before (= "Original") and after normalization

		Tokens	Original	Normalization		
				Rules	Wordlist	Both
Luther	All	109,972	64.71 %	91.00 %	91.98 %	92.93 %
	Unknowns	2,911	40.88 %	76.88 %	40.88 %	76.88 %
Anselm	ALEM	8,201	39.06 %	48.81 %	49.02 %	51.35 %
	BAV	4,630	47.00 %	57.84 %	59.46 %	60.74 %
	WCG	7,409	33.84 %	41.64 %	43.53 %	44.28 %
	ECG	4,705	23.80 %	32.88 %	30.07 %	35.24 %
	Harmonic mean	–	35.42 %	42.55 %	42.58 %	45.68 %

wordlist-based approach, we created a wordlist from the Luther training corpus. The wordlist maps each historical wordform to the modern wordform that it is most often aligned with. Using this method, normalized wordforms are generated by substituting an old wordform with its modern counterpart as specified in the wordlist. If a word is not in the list, it is left unchanged.

Finally, we also tried a combination of both approaches. Here, the wordlist substitution is always tried first, with the rule-based method being applied only if the historical wordform is not found in the wordlist.

5 Evaluation

For evaluation, we generated normalized forms of all historical wordforms and compared them to their modernized counterparts. For each text, there is a number of words which do not differ at all between old and modernized versions (column "Original" in Table 3). This is the baseline for our evaluation; any normalizing process that results in less than that number of matches has done more harm than good, and it would be better to leave all words unchanged. Full evaluation results are shown in Table 3.

5.1 Luther Bible

Before normalization, the ratio of identical tokens in the historical and the modernized text of the Luther bible is 64.71 %, i.e., only a third of all wordforms even differ at all. Table 3 shows that our method increases that match ratio to 91.00 %, which is a significant increase from the baseline. Our normalization approach is not only successful in changing historical forms to modern ones, but also in correctly leaving most of the word forms (about 99 %) unchanged that do not need to be changed, as a separate evaluation showed (cf. [2]). The pure wordlist substitution method achieves 91.98 %, which is slightly—but significantly ($p < 0.005$)—better.

In order to evaluate the overlap between both methods, and to better assess the bias of using the same type of text for rule training, rule application, and deriving the dictionary, a separate evaluation was done on word pairs that were not seen during training ('Unknowns'). The wordlist-based approach cannot normalize any of those wordforms, as they have not been previously learned. The rule-based method, on the other hand, still achieves a considerable increase in matching pairs. Consequently, combining both methods yields the best results (92.93 %) for the Luther text.

5.2 Anselm Corpus

The ratio of identical tokens before normalization (= the baseline) in the Anselm texts is only 35.42 % on average. This is an indicator that these texts differ significantly more from New High German than Luther's bible, at least in spelling. Consequently, the mean match ratio after normalization is also considerably lower (42.55 %). While this is far from optimal, the increase is still notable, and both methods outperform the baseline for every text. Judging from the normalized wordforms, at least some of the normalization rules learned from the Luther bible can be successfully applied to Anselm texts. This becomes apparent from non-trivial word pairs such as *liff* – *lief* 'ran', which are correctly normalized even though they do not appear in the training corpus, so the wordlist does not cover them.

In all texts except ECG, the wordlist approach performs better than the rule-based approach, by a rather small margin (between 0.21–1.89 percentage points). The harmonic means of the ratios of correct (i.e. identical) tokens show only negligible difference between the rule-based and the wordlist approach. The combination of both methods, again, yields the best results, outperforming the individual methods by 0.75–5.17 percentage points. This indicates that the approaches complement each other to a certain extent, i.e. one sometimes succeeds where the other fails.

ECG is the only text where the rule-based approach outperforms the wordlist approach. From the four Anselm manuscripts, this text seems most dissimilar to the Luther text. Table 4 shows the number of tokens for which not a single normalized variant can be generated because there were one or more contexts

Table 4. Number of tokens with character sequences for which no applicable rule has been learned

	Tokens	Tokens	w/o rule
ALEM	8,201	2,108	25.70 %
BAV	4,630	723	15.62 %
WCG	7,409	2,735	36.91 %
ECG	4,705	2,174	46.21 %
Harmonic mean	–	–	25.61 %

with no applicable edit or identity rule. In such a case, the generation process stops and outputs the original form. This means the respective token contains at least one character trigram that was not seen in the training data. For ECG, this concerns almost half of all its tokens (46.21 %).

By comparison of Tables 3 and 4, we observe a strong correlation between the amount of applicable rules from training data and overall accuracy. BAV and ALEM, the texts with the highest accuracy after normalization, have the lowest amounts of unseen contexts. ECG, the text with the lowest accuracy, has the highest amount. These findings indicate that close relatedness of training and evaluation data is more important than large amounts of training data (this is also confirmed by [5]).

Note that we currently only count identical tokens as correct normalization. Some words produce sensible normalizations, but do not match their aligned form because of a difference in inflection: *vnse* 'our' is normalized to the masculine/neutral form *unser*, but aligned with the feminine form *unsere*.

Another difference concerns tokenization. As shown in Sect. 2, the rewrite rules for Luther include modernization of tokenization by inserting of spaces. The Anselm texts on the other hand have already been modernized with regard to token boundaries before the manual normalization takes place. This means that the rule-based approach sometimes incorrectly introduces token boundaries, e.g. modernizing *allerlibste* 'dearest' to *aller liebste*. In these cases, the normalization is still useful, but does not count as a match in our evaluation, thereby downgrading the results.

However, in many other cases, the source words contain spelling characteristics which do not occur in the bible text and therefore could not be learned. A typical example would be *vrouwe*, which should normalize to *frau* 'woman'. The spelling *v* for *f* occurs quite frequently in the ECG text, but only very rarely in the Luther bible: the appropriate rule (5) was learned exactly once from the training corpus.

(5)   v → f / # _ r

Similarly, there are no rules which would transform *ou* into *au*, as this spelling does not occur at all in Luther. Again, this spelling is a characteristic feature of the ECG text, which could be one of the reasons why this text performs worst in our evaluation. Note, however, that ECG shows the strongest synergy between the rule-based and the wordlist approaches.

6   Related Work and Recent Developments

Research in NLP for historical texts is very active, and spelling normalization as described in our paper is still state-of-the-art for the processing of this type of data [6].

Since the original publication of our paper, we expanded upon the idea of combining normalization methods by creating the Norma tool [7], which implements wordlists, rule-based normalization, and a third method based on a modified Levenshtein distance. More importantly, though, we moved away from using only the Luther bible as training data for our normalization methods, and use small fragments of in-domain training data instead, which leads to a dramatic improvement in performance. We also started to investigate the usefulness of normalization for part-of-speech tagging [8].

Another tool for spelling normalization is VARD [9], which implements its own normalization algorithms specifically targeted at Early Modern English, and offers an interface for editing and correcting the automatically normalized wordforms. While it can theoretically be adapted to other languages, we found it to perform worse than our Norma tool in a later experiment [7].

Rule-based normalization techniques similar, albeit not identical, to ours have been used for historical Dutch [10] and Swedish [11]. A project working on texts from Old Spanish [12] uses edit transducers to model the underlying rewrite rules. Work by Jurish [13] on historical German from 1780–1880 is still notable for including token context in the normalization process, contrary to most other approaches which only operate on wordform types. A different, yet promising recent approach is the application of statistical machine translation techniques on a character level [14,15].

7   Conclusion

We showed that using only unsupervised learning, a minimum of knowledge engineering, and freely available resources, it is possible to map historical wordforms to their modern counterparts with a high success rate. With Luther's bible, the rule-based method performs far better than the baseline, and a combination of this method and the wordlist-based method was shown to produce significantly better results than one method alone.

Applying the rule-based method to a different type of text results in rather low performance, although the result is still significantly better than the baseline. It turns out that substantial variations in spelling, as they occur in the Anselm texts, are problematic for the rule-based approach, as it cannot normalize character-context sequences that have not been previously learned. However, the combination of wordlists and rules shows that the coverage of both methods is not the same, and including rule-based normalization is still useful.

The Anselm data seems to suggest that abstracting the rules from their specific contexts could be beneficial in some cases, e.g., to cover common substitutions like *tz* by *z* or *u* by *v*, which are common variants in ENHG. This way, the rules derived from the Luther bible could be generalized and would apply to a wider range of character-context sequences. In later work [7], we included a distance-based normalization approach that tries to address this issue.

Furthermore, our later research [7] showed that using small amounts of in-domain training data (as opposed to only using the Luther bible for training) improves performance dramatically. Also, normalization using a combination of methods always performed better with the rule-based method than without it. Therefore, even though the initial scores reported here are rather low, the rule-based normalization approach continues to be an important part of our normalization method.

References

1. Bollmann, M., Petran, F., Dipper, S.: Applying rule-based normalization to different types of historical texts. An evaluation. In: Proceedings of the 5th Language & Technology Conference: Human Language Technologies as a Challenge for Computer Science and Linguistics, Poznan, Poland (2011)
2. Bollmann, M., Petran, F., Dipper, S.: Rule-based normalization of historical texts. In: Proceedings of the International Workshop on Language Technologies for Digital Humanities and Cultural Heritage, Hissar, Bulgaria, pp. 34–42 (2011)
3. Braune, F., Fraser, A.: Improved unsupervised sentence alignment for symmetrical and asymmetrical parallel corpora. In: Proceedings of the 23rd International Conference on Computational Linguistics (COLING), Poster Volume, Beijing, China, pp. 81–89 (2010)
4. Och, F.J., Ney, H.: A systematic comparison of various statistical alignment models. Comput. Linguist. **29**(1), 19–51 (2003)
5. Bollmann, M., Dipper, S., Krasselt, J., Petran, F.: Manual and semi-automatic normalization of historical spelling. Case studies from Early New High German. In: Proceedings of the First International Workshop on Language Technology for Historical Text(s), Vienna, Austria (2012)
6. Piotrowski, M.: Natural Language Processing for Historical Texts. Synthesis Lectures on Human Language Technologies, vol. 17. Morgan & Claypool, San Rafael (2012)
7. Bollmann, M.: (Semi-)automatic normalization of historical texts using distance measures and the Norma tool. In: Proceedings of the Second Workshop on Annotation of Corpora for Research in the Humanities (ACRH-2), Lisbon, Portugal (2012)
8. Bollmann, M.: POS tagging for historical texts with sparse training data. In: Proceedings of the 7th Linguistic Annotation Workshop and Interoperability in Discourse, Sofia, Bulgaria, pp. 11–18 (2013)
9. Baron, A., Rayson, P., Archer, D.: Automatic standardization of spelling for historical text mining. In: Proceedings of Digital Humanities 2009, Maryland, USA (2009)
10. van Halteren, H., Rem, M.: Dealing with orthographic variation in a tagger-lemmatizer for fourteenth century Dutch charters. Lang. Resour. Eval. **47**(4), 1233–1259 (2013)
11. Adesam, Y., Ahlberg, M., Bouma, G.: *bokstaffua, bokstaffwa, bokstafwa, bokstaua, bokstawa*... Towards lexical link-up for a corpus of Old Swedish. In: Proceedings of KONVENS 2012 (LThist 2012 Workshop), Vienna, Austria, pp. 365–369 (2012)
12. Porta, J., Sancho, J.L., Gómez, J.: Edit transducers for spelling variation in Old Spanish. In: Proceedings of the NODALIDA Workshop on Computational Historical Linguistics, Oslo, Norway (2013)
13. Jurish, B.: More than words: using token context to improve canonicalization of historical German. J. Lang. Technol. Comput. Linguist. **25**(1), 23–39 (2010)
14. Pettersson, E., Megyesi, B., Tiedemann, J.: An SMT approach to automatic annotation of historical text. In: Proceedings of the NODALIDA Workshop on Computational Historical Linguistics, Oslo, Norway (2013)
15. Scherrer, Y., Erjavec, T.: Modernizing historical Slovene words with character-based SMT. In: Proceedings of the 4th Biennial Workshop on Balto-Slavic Natural Language Processing (2013)

A Rule Based Method for the Identification of TAM Features in a PoS Tagged Corpus

Narayan Choudhary[✉], Pramod Pandey, and Girish Nath Jha

Jawaharlal Nehru University, New Delhi, India
{choudharynarayan,girishjha}@gmail.com,
pkspandey@yahoo.com

Abstract. For a task of natural language understanding, the identification of tense, aspect and mood (TAM) features in a given text is of importance in itself. A closer look at the verb groups in a sentence can give the exact combination of the TAM features the verb group carries. While the verb group consisting of one word could be easily interpreted for the TAM features, the TAM features of the verb groups consisting of more than one word (as witnessed in many languages) can be identified exactly through a rule based method. In this paper we present a rule based method to capture the TAM features denoted by verb groups in Hindi.

Keywords: Verb group identification · TAM identification · Tense · Aspect · Mood · Identification · Hindi · Indo-Aryan · Dravidian · Languages · Chunking · Local word grouping

1 Introduction

The exact information about the tense, aspect and mood (TAM) features can be helpful in many tasks of natural language processing (NLP) including machine translation. The statistical methods of machine translations always rely on a huge data to derive the TAM features encoded in the source language. We present here a rule based method to deduce the TAM features plus a few other information about the structure of the verb groups. The method presented here first looks for the specific patterns of the verb groups in the source language (Hindi is tested here) and then we draw templates for the participants of the verb groups and give them a label (tag) that encodes the TAM features plus any other verb group specific features.

2 Prerequisite Resources

The only prerequisite resource we need is a parts-of-speech (PoS) annotated text as the input. This PoS annotated text should have information about the category of the verb and any other TAM related inflectional marks that the verbal word may contain. We follow the Indian Languages – Parts of Speech Tagset (IL-PoST) annotation framework as described in [1]. We use as test data the Linguistic Data Consortium (LDC) corpus containing above 4800 sentences (above 98 thousand words) prepared in this framework [2]. We have also made some modifications in this annotation framework to accommodate more of the TAM markers present morphologically.

© Springer International Publishing Switzerland 2014
Z. Vetulani and J. Mariani (Eds.): LTC 2011, LNAI 8387, pp. 178–188, 2014.
DOI: 10.1007/978-3-319-08958-4_15

3   Verb Groups

By verb groups (VGs) here we mean the word constituents that have a verbal intent in the sentence. In the PoS annotation it must have a verbal mark, either main verb (VM) or auxiliary verb (VAUX). It consists of the serial verb constructions [3] also as witnessed in many languages. A verb group consists of at least one main verb and can optionally include n-number of auxiliary verbs. There cannot be a verb group consisting only of auxiliary verb(s).

4   TAM Identification

Tense, aspect and mood can be identified with a study of the verb groups of the language concerned. Generally, a descriptive grammar of the language contains all the information about the tenses, aspects and moods that the language can express through the verb groups. While the verb morphology may contain in itself the TAM features, much of the TAM features are expressed periphrastically, through the use of what is commonly called the auxiliary verbs. These auxiliary verbs in any language are limited to some exhaustively countable number of words and they denote some specific tense, aspect or mood features, separately or combined, that cannot be expressed only through morphology.

4.1   TAM Identified Through Verb Morphology

The verb morphology of any language may contain inflections for many features besides the TAM and finiteness features that are specific to verbs. For example, a verb may also inflect in agreement with the gender, number and person (GNP) and other features such as honorificity.

In Hindi, a verb root can inflect to generate 25 morphological forms. Not all of these forms encode unique TAM features. However, these 25 forms can be grouped

Table 1. TAM and finiteness features expressed through verb morphology

TAM and finiteness features	No. of forms	Co-occurring form
Imperative/verb root	1	
Infinitive	3	
Imperfect	4	
Perfect	4	Optative
Future	9	
Optative (1sg)	1	
Imperative/optative 2sg pl. honorific	1	
Imperative	2	

into a number of unique TAM and finiteness features they denote. These TAM and the finiteness features are the ones used in identifying the actual TAM features of the verb groups. Thus the following table shows the different TAM features that can be expressed through the verb morphology of Hindi.

As seen in the table above, some TAM and finiteness features are expressed by more than one form. This is because they are inflectionally marked for GNP and have a different form but denote the same TAM feature. There is also one form that is ambiguous: the perfect feature having 4 GNP forms. One of these four perfect forms (plural honorific) can also be used in the optative mood.

We identify these features through the PoS annotation. The IL-PoST framework provides for a hierarchical structure of the PoS features. This ensures that we have all of these morphological features marked at the PoS level.

4.2 TAM Identified Periphrastically

As we can see in Table 1 above, not all the tenses, aspects and moods are covered through the verb morphology. In this section we present the tenses, aspects and moods marked periphrastically.

4.2.1 Tenses Marked Periphrastically

In Hindi only future tense is marked morphologically. Present and past tenses are marked periphrastically (except for the perfect form which is commonly understood as the past marker in Hindi). The copular verb /ho/'be' is the only verb which has all the three tense forms- present, past and future. All the other verbs lack the past and present forms at the morphological level. So, when the present and past tenses are to be expressed for the verbs other than 'be', the past and present forms of this copular verb is used. This is just one type of periphrastically formed verb group we find. There are several other TAM features that are marked periphrastically.

4.2.2 Aspects Marked Periphrastically

For the aspects, Hindi has only two aspects that are marked morphologically- perfect and imperfect. For all the other aspects auxiliary verbs are used. These auxiliary verbs are actually the verbs with a lexical meaning of their own. But when they are used as auxiliary verbs, they lose their lexical meaning and give the sense of a different aspect.

The most important among the periphrastically marked aspects is the progressive aspect marker. This aspect is marked with a lexical verb, meaning "live" or "remain" or "stay". The verb form in Hindi is perfective form of the verb /rəh/. When it is used as a progressive aspect marker it loses its lexical meaning.

There are also other aspects that are marked periphrastically. Yamuna Kachru [4] notes four other aspects, namely inceptive, continuative, durative and frequentative. Kachru [4] notes that "these are not as general in distribution as imperfect, perfect and progressive." That is, they have some restrictions and cannot occur as freely as the progressive aspect. There are also some other aspects that share a boundary with the modal category. These are what Kachru [4] describes as the presumptive, contingent and past contingent.

However, we find some more of the aspects that can be witnessed in the real world data. Two aspects can get bounded together to denote a new aspect. For example, in the cases when an aspect marking lexical verb is also inflected for the morphological aspect, it can denote two aspects together. For example in the sentence below:

vəh	kɪtab	pəɽʰne	ləg-ta	tʰa
he	book	read.INF	apply-IMPF.MSG	be.PST.MSG

He used to start reading the book.

The auxiliary verb /ləg/is the inceptive marker verb while it is in the imperfective form. And thus two aspects (inceptive and imperfective) are marked simultaneously.

Table 2 below shows a summary of all the different aspects that can be identified in Hindi.

Table 2. Summary of aspects marked in Hindi

Sl. no.	Aspect name	Label/tag
1	Perfect	pft
2	Null	0
3	Continuative	cnt
4	Durative	dur
5	Imperfect	impf
6	Imperfect continuative	impf_cnt
7	Imperfect durative	impf_dur
8	Imperfect frequentative	impf_frq
9	Imperfect inceptive	impf_ince
10	Imperfect perfective	impf_pft
11	Imperfect-perfect-continuative	impf_pft_cnt
12	Perfect continuative	pft_cnt
13	Perfect durative	pft_dur
14	Perfect frequentative	pft_frq
15	Perfect-imperfect-continuative	pft_impf_cnt
16	Perfect inceptive	pft_ince
17	Progressive	prog
18	Progressive Durative	prog_dur
19	Simple	sim
20	Simple Inceptive	sim_ince

4.2.3   Moods Marked Periphrastically

Like the aspects, there are only two moods that are marked morphologically- imperative and optative. Other moods are marked periphrastically through the help of auxiliary verbs. The declarative is the default mood marker. All the moods that can be marked in Hindi verb groups are summarized in the table below (Table 3).

Table 3. Summary of moods marked in Hindi

Mood names	Label/tag
Imperative	imp
Optative	opt
Abilitative	abil
Declarative	dcl
Permissive imperative	perm_imp
Permissive optative	perm_opt
Counterfactual	cfct
Desiderative/suggestive	sugg
Permissive desiderative	perm_sugg
Optative probabilitative	opt_prob

5 Drawing Verb Group Templates

Based on the morphological features and the VM or VAUX functionality of verbs, a general template can be drawn to capture the verb groups and then assign a label to them based on the grammatical features they carry. A verb group contains at least TAM features. It may additionally contain other features such as passive voice construction and compound verb structure. This is true for all the Indo-Aryan and Dravidian languages and may be true for many other languages.

A study of different types of verb group structures in Hindi can be brought down to an abstract level of templates. We did such a study, basing ourselves on the verbal paradigms as shown in various linguistic literatures on the language [4, 5] among others).

5.1 Structure of Verb Groups in Hindi

In Hindi (and in all the major Indian languages), a verb group may constitute of one or more verbs. As per the definition provided above in §3, a verb group in Hindi may constitute of just one word and can have at most five words in it. The example sentences i-v illustrate this.

- One-word VG:-

    vəh   gəya
    he   go.PFT.MSG
    He went.

- Two-word VG:-

    vəh   ja-ta   hɛ
    he   go.IMPF.MSG   be.PRS.SG
    He goes.

– Three-Word VG:-

vəh	gʰər	ja	rəha	hɛ
he	home	go.VR	live-PFT.MSG	be.PRS.SG

He is going home.

– Four-Word VG:-

vəh	kɪtab	pəɽʰ-ta	ja	rəha	tʰa
he	book	read-IMPF.MSG	go.VR	live-PFT.MSG	be.PST.MSG
He keeps on reading the book.					

– Five-Word VG:-

vəh	kɪtab	pəɽʰ-ta	cəl-a	ja	rəha	tʰa
he	book	read-IMPF.MSG	walk-PFT.MSG	go.VR	live-PFT.MSG	be-PST.MSG

He had gone on reading a book (for a long time).

Our study also shows that a verb group can be broken only by what is called the particle. Particles in Hindi constitute of a few indeclinable words. These words in Hindi are the negative markers (/nəhĩ/, /na/, and /nə/) topicalizers (/hi/"only", /to/"then/so", and /bʰi/"also") question words (e.g. /kya/"what", /kəhã/"where", /kɔn/"who", etc.) and a few other words namely /sa/, /si//se/(all meaning "like" in the sense of its conjunctive or quotative function) and /wala/, /wali/, /wale/. The particles /wala/, /wali/and /wale/ are commonly denoted as the *wala* particle in Hindi. The *wala* particle is multifunctional in Hindi. But when it comes attached with a verb, it has only two functions. It either functions as an agentivizer (example vi) or marks the approximative aspect (example vii).

– Agentivizer use of the *wala* particle

kʰane	wale	ləɽke	ko	bʊlao
eat-INF	AGENT	boy.OBL	ACC.MSG	call.IMP
Call the eating boy!				

– Approximative Aspect Marking by the *wala* particle

ləɽka	kʰane	wala	hɛ
boy	eat-INF	APPROX	be.PRS.MSG

The boy is about to eat.

When the *wala* particle functions as an agentivizer, it may not be considered as part of the verb group because the function it plays together with the verbal word is that of a noun and there is no verbal intent in it. But when functioning as an approximative aspect marker, it must be included as a part of the verb group because it plays a part in denoting the TAM of the verb group. This information is used in defining and identifying the verb group templates and giving a valence to particles inside them.

With the above description we know that a verb group must contain only verbs and if anything else comes in between it must be the particles as described above. While defining the templates, we ignore all the particles except for the *wala* particle functioning as an aspect marker.

5.2   General Verb Group Templates

With the details above, we defined the patterns of Hindi verb groups. We used the morphological information as represented through the PoS annotation of each of the verbs playing a part in the verb groups along with the VM/VAUX dichotomy as specified in the PoS annotation. These templates would have as many variables as the number of verbs playing a role in verb group. Thus, we can have VG templates that would have just one variable to VG templates having up to five variables. A few examples of the VG templates along with their TAM tags are given in Table 4 below.

Table 4. Sample VG templates and TAM Tags

VG template	TAM tag
prs_aux	VG.prs.sim.dcl
VR_impf+prs_aux	VG.prs.impf.dcl
VR_impf+ban_pft+prs_aux	VG.prs.impf.abil
VR_impf+ja+rah_pft+prs_aux	VG.prs.prog_dur.dcl
VR_impf+cal_pft+ja+rah_pft+prs_aux	VG.prs.prog_dur.dcl
VR_pft+ja_pft	VG.pas_pst.sim.dcl
VR_pft+ja_impf+prs_aux	VG.pas_prs.impf.dcl
VR_pft+ja_inf+lag_impf+prs_aux	VG.pas_prs.impf_ince.dcl
VR+dal_fut	VG.cv_fut.sim.dcl
VR+ja_pft	VG.cv_pst.sim.dcl
VR+dal_pft+ja_opt	VG.cv_pas_0.0.opt
VR+de_pft+prs_aux	VG.cv_prs.pft.dcl

We use variables to define the template. These variables are of two kinds- tag variables and the word variables. Tag variables are the variables the values of which are identified through the PoS tags they have in the input. A word variable is identified by the actual word. For example, the variable VR_impf is a tag variable and is identified by the presence of the tag 'impf' in the annotation of the verb. A word variable is identified by the actual value set for that variable. While we have around a dozen of tag variables, we have word variables running in hundreds. A word variable may have more than one value as its variable. The number of word variables is higher because we use a word variable for all the auxiliaries and their various TAM and finiteness marked forms.

Using these variables, we define a total of 177 VG templates that cover all of the verb groups in Hindi except the passive constructions and the VGs having a compound verb.

5.3   Passive Constructions

Passive constructions are rather regular in Hindi. It can be viewed as a transformation of what occurs in the active voice (covered under the general VG templates in preceding section). However, not all the general VG templates have a corresponding passive construction. This is because not all the aspects and moods have a corresponding passive construction. For example the sentences in imperative mood cannot transform into passive voice (it changes into optative mood). Our study shows that out of the total of 177 general VG templates, 67 can transform into passive construction resulting into 67 new VG templates. These templates are marked for their passive marking with the prefix of 'pas' in the TAM tag assigned to them.

5.4   Compound Verb Constructions

The compound verb is a pan-Indian linguistic phenomenon [6] wherein two verbs occur one after the other. In this construction, while the first verb (V1) gives the main meaning to the VG and remains in the root form, the second verb (V2) gets all the inflectional markings and adds a 'shade' into the meaning of V1. These V2s are limited in number though there is no consensus on how many of such V2s should be included in this category. Hook [7] provides a summary of the various lists of V2s of Hindi suggested by several scholars. In our study, we prepared a list of all such words that can possibly appear even once as a V2 inside a VG and made templates for each of them separately, under the compound verb (CV) category. A total of 61 such V2s are included in this list. This is larger than any other such list in Hindi found in the literature. The VGs containing a CV can be identified with the prefix of 'cv' in the TAM tag assigned to them.

Given that a compound verb may also behave more like a main verb where the V2 takes all the TAM markings, it can be proposed that we simply apply the same templates as drawn for general and passive VG constructions to fit into these compound verbs as well. The only change that will take place in the templates will be the addition of the V1 in its stem form at the beginning. For example for the one word VG templates we will have a two word VG templates which will be a compound verb construction.

While the above method of CV template derivation is helpful in deriving the CV templates, it is not true for all the 244 non-CV VG templates (the general and passive VG templates). A subjective study of the possibility of even one CV construction in these templates was done by us. And we found that there are 40 templates out of 244 non-CV VG templates that will not have a corresponding a CV construction.

There are also some semantic restrictions on the combination of V1 and V2 and not all the V2s can form a compound verb with all V1s [8]. Nespital [9] provides a database of Hindi complex predicates including the CV constructions. If one wants to do semantic analysis of the VGs, such a database would be of great help. But we are here concerned merely about the TAM features of the VGs and this we can achieve without such a database.

Based on the description above, we have a total of 204 CV templates which would cover all of the VGs containing a CV. For example for a non-CV template of VR_impf +prs_aux, we can have a corresponding CV template of V1+V2_impf+prs_aux.

However, this is only an abstract drawing. If we leave these templates as they are, they will violate the restrictions on the combination of V1 and V2 and will apply to both of them universally. Although there are some templates in which all the V2s can fit in. We have identified a total of 37 such non-CV templates and call them Universal CV Templates. All the other templates (i.e. 204 − 37 = 167) templates would have only a few V2s forming a CV template.

Thus we have a total of 204 abstract CV templates that can capture all the CV VGs found in Hindi. These abstract templates need to be specified for reasons stated above. That is, the V2s in them must be marked so that they are identified by the word variables and not the tag variables. For example for the abstract CV template of V1+V2_fut, the V2 has to be specified with one of the V2s we have listed. For all the 37 abstract universal CV VG templates, we will have 61 templates for each (the total number templates reaching 61 * 37 = 2257). For the rest of 167 CV templates, we identify the specific V2s that can play a part in them and draw the actual templates accordingly.

6   Verb Group Tags

Tags/Labels are assigned to the verb groups once identified, at the end of their boundary. These tags are meant to identify the TAM of the verb group. Additionally, these tags also identify the voice form of the verb groups and whether it contains a compound verb construction or not. The general construction of the TAM tags is as follows:

VG.Tense.Aspect.Mood

Here the dot '.' functions as the delimiter between two categories. The first label is 'VG' which identifies that the chunk is a verb group. The second label delimited by the '.' indicates tense of the verb group. Similarly, the third and the fourth indicate aspect and mood. The second label of tense can get prefixed by 'pas' or 'cv' or 'cv_pas'. When prefixed with 'pas', the TAM tag indicates that the VG is in passive voice and when prefixed by 'cv', the VG indicates that it contains a compound verb construction. If it is prefixed by 'cv_pas', it indicates that it is in passive voice and also contains a compound verb construction.

7   Evaluation

We developed a tool[1] to implement this mechanism and ran it over the LDC corpus annotated in the IL-PoST framework. The results obtained in the first run over the LDC corpus were not very promising. We had at least one error in a total of 46 % of the sentences. An error analysis showed that these errors were mainly of two types: they

---

[1] The tool can be tested at the following two sites: http://sanskrit.jnu.ac.in/vgt/index.html and http://www.langlex.com/vgt/index.html.

contain a verb group which could not be identified and hence marked as 'Unknown' or there are verb groups consisting of no VM and hence the VAUXes are left orphan.

The number of orphan VAUXes was large. These were basically annotation errors in the input corpus itself. Once we corrected them, the tool identified them correctly.

There can be various reasons for a VG being not recognized. The most incriminating for this test would be the failure of any of the templates to recognize it. Fortunately, that is the case with only a few of the sentences. The most number of unknown occurrences are due to other reasons. The numerous among these is annotation errors. For example there are annotations marked for perfect aspect instead of imperfect and vice versa. Such errors result not only into 'Unknown' marking of the VGs identified but also at times gives incorrect TAM tag. While the VGs marked as 'Unknown' can be identified and the reasons behind this can be ascertained and corrected, the VGs identified incorrectly is hard to find out. We also found a few language specific idiosyncrasies that could not fall into any of the general templates and to capture them we had to prepare a few specific templates just to capture those idiosyncrasies.

We also had to make some modifications in the IL-PoST framework and bring changes accordingly in the LDC corpus for this test. We made changes in three slots of aspect, mood and finiteness of the tags given to a verb.

In the aspect, we removed the progressive aspect marking label of 'prg'. The 'prg' tag in the LDC corpus is given to perfect form of the auxiliary verb 'rəh' because it is this form that indicates the progressive/continuative and durative aspect marking. But because they are marked as 'prg' in the aspect slot, their information about their being in the perfect form is lost. Besides this aspect is marked only periphrastically and should be left to be understood at the local word grouping (LWG) level as we are doing here.

In the modal slot, we removed the marking for habitual mood. Habitual mood marking in Hindi is concurrent with the imperfect marking aspect i.e. both gets realized only if a verb form with the /-tV/ending form of the verb is present in the verb group. Habituality is understood only syntactically. Instead of habitual mood marking, we marked the /-tV/ending verb forms as imperfect 'impf'. Another mood, optative, marked morphologically in Hindi is totally missing from the IL-PoST annotation guidelines[2] for Hindi. So we included this mood with the tag of 'opt' in the tags and marked them wherever required.

Under the finiteness slot, digressing from the current guidelines, we suggest that it is verb roots themselves that should be marked as non-finite 'nfn' and all the '-nV' ending verbs be marked as infinitive with the tag of 'ifn'.

After making these changes in the LDC corpus, we ran the tool again over this corpus and this time 99 % of the sentences did not show up any issues in identification. For the ones that showed up an issue (a total of 45 out of 4832 sentences), a minor change in the code to capture the tags of the auxiliary verbs can fix them. And thus we can achieve a hundred percent accuracy in identifying the verb groups in Hindi and thereby other major Indian languages having similar structures.

---

[2] The details of the guidelines along with the LDC corpus is available at the LDC website: http://www.ldc.upenn.edu/Catalog/CatalogEntry.jsp?catalogId=LDC2010T24.

8 Conclusions

In this paper we have shown that identification of the verb groups in Hindi and their TAM can be achieved through a rule based method. We have also shown that through this method we can ascertain whether the VG is in passive voice and whether it also contains a compound verb construction. At present, wherever this task is required, it is done through statistical methods which require a lot of data input. There is still a dearth of large annotated corpus in Hindi. In this situation, this rule based method can be of great help in various NLP tasks including machine translation and grammar checking.

Given that the major Indian languages (Indo-Aryan and Dravidian) share a great lot of similarity in their verb group structure, this rule based method can be replicated for these languages as well.

References

1. Baskaran, S., Bali, K., Choudhury, M., Bhattacharya, T., Bhattacharyya, P., Jha, G.N., Rajendran, S., Saravanan, K., Sobha, L., Subbarao, K.V.: A common parts-of-speech tagset framework for Indian Languages. In: Calzolari, N. (Conference Chair), Choukri, K., Maegaard, B., Mariani, J., Odjik, J., Piperidis, S., Tapias, D., (eds.) Proceedings of the Sixth International Language Resources and Evaluation (LREC'08), Marrakech, Morocco (2008)
2. Bali, K., Choudhury, M., Biswas, P., Jha, G.N., Choudhary, N., Sharma, M.: Indian Language Part-of-Speech Tagset: Hindi. Linguistic Data Consortium, Philadelphia (2010). ISBN 1-58563-571-5
3. Aikhenvald, A., Dixon, R.M.W. (eds.): Serial Verb Constructions: A Cross-Linguistic Typology. Oxford University Press, Oxford (2006)
4. Kachru, Y.: Hindi. John Benjamins, Amsterdam (2006)
5. Guru, K.: Hindi Vyaakaran. Nagari Pracharini Sabha, Kashi (1978)
6. Abbi, A.: The explicator compound verbs: some definitional issues and criteria for identification. Indian Linguistics **51**(1) (1992)
7. Hook, P.E.: The compound verb in Hindi. The Michigan Series in South and South East Asian Languages and Linguistics: The University of Michigan (1974)
8. Paul, S.: An HPSG account of Bangla compound verbs with LKB implementation. Unpublished Ph.D. thesis submitted to University of Hyderabad (2006)
9. Nespital, H.: Lokabhaaratii: Hindii kriyaa-kosha. Lokbharti Prakashan, Allahabad (1997)

Digging for Names in the Mountains: Combined Person Name Recognition and Reference Resolution for German Alpine Texts

Sarah Ebling[✉], Rico Sennrich, and David Klaper

Institute of Computational Linguistics, University of Zurich,
Binzmuehlestrasse 14, 8050 Zurich, Switzerland
{ebling,sennrich}@ifi.uzh.ch, david.klaper@uzh.ch

Abstract. In this paper, we introduce a module that combines person name recognition and reference resolution for German. Our data consists of a corpus of Alpine texts. This text type poses specific challenges because of a multitude of toponyms, some of which interfere with person names. Our reference resolution algorithm outputs person entities based on their last names and first names along with their associated features (jobs, addresses, academic titles).

Keywords: Named entity recognition · Person name recognition · Reference resolution · German

1   Introduction

Named entity recognition (NER) is a prerequisite for many language technology applications, such as Information Extraction or Question Answering. Commonly it involves identifying people, companies, and locations. The difficulty of NER depends heavily on the language under consideration. For English, it is often sufficient to look for non-sentence-initial capitalized words. In particular, due to the restricted word order of English, a capitalized word preceding a verb of communication has a high likelihood of being a person name or organization name (Rössler, 2004).

For other languages such as German, NER is more challenging. In German, both regular nouns and proper names are capitalized, with only the latter being candidates for named entities (NEs). This means that by itself, capitalization is not a viable indicator of German NEs. Word order is not a stand-alone predictive clue, either, since German allows for multiple positions of the finite verb and the subject.

The task of detecting names of people, known as person name recognition (PNR), is a subtask of NER. In this paper, we describe a combined approach to PNR and reference resolution for German. Our data consists of a corpus of Alpine texts. This text type poses specific challenges because of a multitude of toponyms, some of which interfere with person names. The remainder of this

© Springer International Publishing Switzerland 2014
Z. Vetulani and J. Mariani (Eds.): LTC 2011, LNAI 8387, pp. 189–200, 2014.
DOI: 10.1007/978-3-319-08958-4_16

paper is structured as follows: In Sect. 2, we give an overview of the approaches that have been pursued to tackle PNR for German. In Sect. 3, we describe our approach to this issue and report the results of our experiments. We also outline our take on reference resolution for person entities.

2   Person Name Recognition for German

Volk and Clematide (2001) pursued a "learn—apply—forget" approach to detect person names, geographic names, and company names in a computer magazine corpus. They based their approach on the assumption that last names do not occur unaccompanied when they are introduced but instead appear along with a first name or another predictive marker. The authors used a list of 16,000 first names derived from electronically available telephone directories as well as a handcrafted list of titles and jobs. Their system accepts last names retrieved in this manner in their stand-alone form for a predefined text span (e.g., 15 sentences), after which it "forgets" them. The authors achieved a precision of 92 % when testing their approach on a set of 990 German sentences. Recall was 93 % for full names, and 74 % for stand-alone last names.

Florian et al. (2003) were among the participants of the CoNLL 2003 shared task on "Language-Independent Named Entity Recognition" (Tjong Kim Sang and De Meulder, 2003). This task produced what is to date the only freely available data for German NER, a collection of articles from the newspaper *Frankfurter Rundschau* annotated with four NE categories: person, location, organization, and miscellaneous (Faruqui and Pado, 2010). The training set consists of 220,000 tokens, the development and test set of 55,000 tokens each. Florian et al. combined four classifiers: a robust linear, a maximum entropy, a transformation-based learning, and a hidden Markov model classifier. Among the features they used were words and their lemmas in a 5-word window relative to the word under consideration, part-of-speech tags, typographical cues, and the output of two other NE classifiers. For German, they additionally experimented with lists of first names, last names, place names, and country names. They observed an increase in performance when adding the lists to their classifiers, obtaining results of up to 91.93 % precision, 75.31 % recall, and 82.80 % f-measure.

Rössler (2004) used the same data set as Florian et al. (2003) but focused on the person category exclusively. He applied a linear SVM classifier that relied on context features and word-internal features, e.g., morphological and typographical cues. In addition to this baseline classifier he used a corpus lexicon that recorded the frequency of a word conditioned on its appearance as a person entity. He obtained the lexicon by training a weak SVM classifier on the CoNLL training data and applying it to a 40-million word corpus. The output consisted of 320,000 word forms tagged as potential person names along with a confidence value assigned by the classifier. Rössler observed performance gains when including the corpus lexicon. His approach evaluated to a precision of 89.4 %, a recall of 88.4 %, and an f-measure of 88.9 %.

Faruqui and Pado (2010) applied clustering based on distributional and morphological similarity to unlabeled data in order to obtain classes of words that belonged to the same NE category. They included morphological similarity since distributional similarity by itself leads to unreliable results for infrequent words. By performing morphological analysis, their system was able to recognize infrequent words like *Ostdeutschland* ('East Germany') and *Westdeutschland* ('West Germany') as similar to *Deutschland* ('Germany') and assign them the same NE category tag. The authors experimented with different corpora as their unlabeled data and found that the Huge German Corpus (175M tokens of newspaper text) yielded the best results. They used the Stanford Named Entity Recognizer, which allows for the inclusion of similarity features and, apart from these, considers words, lemmas, and part-of-speech tags. The results for the person category on the CoNLL 2003 shared task test set were 96.2 % (precision), 88.0 % (recall), and 92.0 % (f-measure). Performance dropped by approximately 10 % when the authors applied their system to a set of German sentences from the out-of-domain Europarl corpus.

3   PNR and Reference Resolution

While the above papers offer ample ways to solve the problem of identifying person names in German texts, none of them addresses the issue of reference resolution that needs to succeed PNR. Reference resolution refers to the task of "determining what entities are referred to by which linguistic expressions" (Jurafsky and Martin, 2009). Ideally, annotations below the person name level should be available for this, i.e., at the least, a distinction between first names and last names should exist. This is not the case with the CoNLL 2003 shared task data.

Our motivation to tackle reference resolution for person entities arose from the practical need to provide such output within our *Text+Berg* project (Bubenhofer et al., 2011)[1]. The aim of this project is to compile a multilingual heritage corpus of Alpine texts from different sources that can be used, e.g., as data for domain-specific machine translation (Sennrich, 2011). The corpus consists of the yearbooks of the Swiss Alpine Club from its start in 1864 to today. The yearbooks contain reports on mountain expeditions as well as information about the geology, flora, and fauna of the Swiss mountains. Some of the books are multilingual, with articles written in German, French, Italian, Romansh, and Swiss German; others are available in two monolingual volumes, a German and a French one. In total, they amount to 87,000 pages in 196 volumes. This corresponds to 35.75 million word tokens.

There are several annotation layers to the corpus. One such layer is the recognition of person names in the German part of the corpus. The German part makes up 61 % of the total corpus size. In what follows, we describe our work in this area. We introduce our reference resolution algorithm in Sect. 3.2.

---

[1] http://www.textberg.ch/

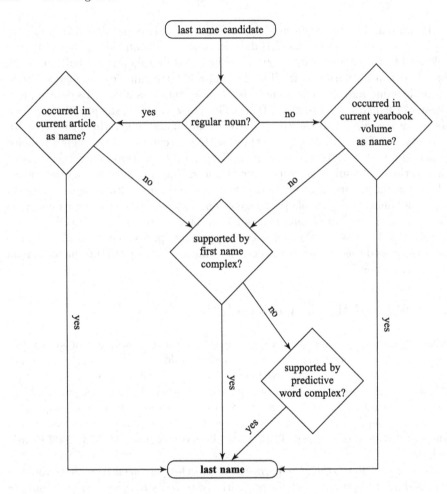

Fig. 1. Deciding whether a candidate is a last name

3.1   Person Name Recognition

Our PNR algorithm is a decision tree with handcrafted rules. It considers stand-alone first names, stand-alone last names, and combinations thereof. Candidates for last names are strings that start with a capitalized letter and are at least three characters long. They may contain hyphens. One or more titles of nobility may immediately precede a core last name so as to capture occurrences like **van der** *Vaart*, **von** *Muralt*, etc. In order to qualify as a last name, a candidate must meet at least one of the following conditions (cf. Fig. 1):[2]

---

[2] The first two restrictions build on the assumption previously made by Volk and Clematide (2001) that last names are generally not introduced in isolated form.

1. **First name complex:** The last name candidate appears after an arbitrary number of full first names (FFN) and/or abbreviated first names (AFN). Optionally, a predictive word complex (cf. 2.) may precede a first name complex.

2. **Predictive word complex:** The last name candidate appears after a predictive word complex, which is made up of a job marker (e.g., *Förster*, 'ranger'), an address marker (e.g., *Herr*, 'Mister'), an academic title marker (e.g., *Dr.*, 'Dr.'), or a combination thereof (e.g., *Herr Förster*, *Herr Dr.*, etc.). Address markers convey gender information that is carried on to the reference resolution step (cf. Sect. 3.2). The order within the predictive word complex is variable, and markers may appear more than once (e.g., *Prof. Dr. Dr.*). First name complexes may not precede predictive word complexes, as a sequence like *Joachim Herr Förster* would not be in accord with the natural naming order.

3. **Recurrence:** A previous occurrence of the last name candidate was marked as a last name in the current yearbook volume. Recall that regular nouns in German start with capital letters; hence, the task of distinguishing a person name from a regular noun is not trivial. If a person name is also a regular noun (which is a common kind of ambiguity in our corpus[3]), the priming span is reduced and the last name candidate is only considered if a previous occurrence was marked as a last name in the current article. We determine whether a candidate is a regular noun by consulting a list of 394,775 regular nouns. A first name complex and/or predictive word complex may optionally precede a recurrent last name.

We prevent a number of last names from being recognized; most of them are toponyms, e.g., *Altmann*, the name of a mountain. In the following two sections, we discuss the first name complex and the predictive word complex in more detail.

First Name Complex. An abbreviated first name (AFN) starts with a capitalized letter and ends with a period mark. Apart from that, it may contain an arbitrary number of lower case letters. Not restricting this number was motivated by the observation that AFN are rather long in our corpus (e.g., *Joach.* is used as an abbreviation for *Joachim*). We blocked a number of abbreviations, such as *Gd.* (for *Gemeinde*,'community') or *Nr.* (for *Nummer*, 'number'). We identified full first names based on a list of 58,969 first names along with their genders obtained from the web. The list does not feature complex first names such as *Jean-Pierre* or *Franz-Sepp*. We split such occurrences and matched their individual parts against the list, assigning the gender of the first part to the entire first name. Both for simple and for complex first names, we only assigned the gender feature if it was not ambiguous (a first name like *Andrea* is ambiguous, as it can be both male and female). We manually removed first names that had

---

[3] Our corpus contains person name instances like *Peter Eimer* ('Peter Bucket'), *Paul König* ('Paul King'), *Herr Sand* ('Mister Sand'), or *M. Held* ('M. Hero').

a high potential of ambiguity—such as *Tod* ('death'), *Lücke* ('gap'), or *Birke* ('birch tree')—from the list.

Predictive Word Complex. Our observation that job markers are an important indicator of person names led us to look for a comprehensive list of jobs. We found the Swiss Standard Classification of Occupations 2000,[4] which is the currently valid classification scheme for demographic surveys. The list comprises 19,000 entries. We performed a number of alterations. In particular, we

- manually removed entries with a high potential of ambiguity, e.g., *Faktor*, which can be a near-synonym of 'criterion' and 'commissioner', with only the second denoting a job title.
- manually marked entries that are well suited to retrieve person names but are not job titles in a strict sense, e.g., *Retter* ('rescuer'), or *Spezialist* ('specialist'). We called them *restricted job markers*.
- automatically extended the list by adding old spelling variants. We applied the following orthographic rules: $t \rightarrow th$, $z \rightarrow c$, $k \rightarrow c$, $ier \rightarrow ir$. They led to additional job hits like *Karthograph* ('cartographer', modern spelling *Kartograph*) or *Diacon* ('deacon', modern spelling *Diakon*).
- automatically extended the list by adding morphological variants

During our preliminary experiments, we observed that two co-occurrence patterns containing job titles produced many errors: Firstly, the pattern *title of nobility+job title* yielded false hits like *Jäger von Pontresina* ('huntsman from Pontresina', where our system correctly identified 'huntsman' as a job title and from there inferred that 'von Pontresina' was a last name containing a title of nobility) or *Führer von Zermatt* ('mountain guide from Zermatt'). Secondly, the co-occurrence of a job title and a last name candidate that was also a regular noun accounted for false last name hits like *Bergsport* in *Sachbearbeiter Bergsport* ('administrative assistant mountaineering'). We therefore decided to drop these two patterns.

3.2   Reference Resolution

Our intended output was a collection of person entities for each yearbook. In practice, this meant that we had to aggregate all features (address, job, academic title) that were available for an entity. We used last names as first-level discriminators and first names (both full first names and abbreviated first names) as second-level discriminators for entities. In other words, we introduced a new entity for each distinct FFN or AFN associated with a particular last name. Where there were only stand-alone occurrences of a last name (i.e., no FFN or AFN), we merged all features and produced one single entity. Where there were

---

[4] http://www.bfs.admin.ch/bfs/portal/en/index/infothek/nomenklaturen/blank/blank/sbn_2000/01.html

stand-alone occurrences as well as one distinct FFN or AFN, we did the same.[5] As an example, assume that a last name *Ferrari* occurred both in its stand-alone form as well as in combination with one first name, *Casimiro*. We aggregated the features of all occurrences and created a single entity *Casimiro Ferrari*.

The procedure is more complex in cases where there were multiple FFN or AFN (or combinations of both) along with stand-alone occurrences of a last name. For example, if a last name *Fischer* appeared by itself as well as in conjunction with the first names *Scott* and *Miriam*, we produced three new entities—*Fischer, Scott Fischer*, and *Miriam Fischer*—, since it was not clear which of the two entities specified with their first names the stand-alone last name referred to. We applied the same strategy on a lower level: If for an AFN there was only one FFN with the same initial letter (e.g., AFN *A.*, FFN *Aegidius*), we considered them as referring to the same entity; otherwise (e.g., AFN *A.*, FFN *Aegidius* and *Arnold*), we refrained from merging. We also merged different AFN, e.g., *Osw.* and *O.*

We allowed for multiple job markers to be output for one entity. This case occurred frequently, with one title often being more specific than the other, e.g., *Bergführer* and *Führer* ('mountaineering guide' and 'guide'). Note that the more general job title (*Führer*) is still more specific than any of the restricted job markers we mentioned in Sect. 3.1.2.; we did not consider restricted job markers in the output.

Below is an example of the output for two entities that belong to the same last name, *Studer*. It summarizes various aspects of our reference resolution algorithm:

- Entities may carry academic title markers (*Prof.*), job markers (*Geologe*, 'geologist'), and address markers (*Herr*, 'Mister')
- AFN and FFN are aggregated (*B.|Bernhard* and *G.|Gottlieb*, respectively)
- Entities receive a gender feature based on gender-annotated first names (*Bernhard*, male) or address markers (*Herr*, male)

```
<person id="83">
  <address></address>
  <titles>Prof.</titles>
  <firstname>B.|Bernhard</firstname>
  <lastname>Studer</lastname>
  <gender>M</gender>
  <profession>Geologe</profession>
  <references>
    <reference>
      <positions>
        <position>32-18-17</position>
        <position>32-18-18</position>
        <position>32-18-19</position>
```

---

[5] Note that both combining multiple stand-alone occurrences into a single entity and merging stand-alone occurrences with distinct FFNs or AFNs is potentially erroneous. We pursued this procedure to obtain a consolidated collection of person entities.

```
        <position>32-18-20</position>
      </positions>
      ...
    </reference>
  </references>
</person>
<person id="84">
  <address>Herr</address>
  <titles></titles>
  <firstname>G.|Gottlieb</firstname>
  <lastname>Studer</lastname>
  <gender>M</gender>
  <profession></profession>
  <references>
    <reference>
      <positions>
        <position>37-54-23</position>
        <position>37-54-24</position>
        <position>37-54-25</position>
      </positions>
      ...
    </reference>
  </references>
</person>
```

3.3 Evaluation

To evaluate our PNR algorithm (Sect. 3.1), we created a gold standard annotation for the German parts of two of our Alpine yearbook volumes, 1901 (development set, 1933 person name tokens) and 1994 (test set, 978 person name tokens). We annotated outer-level entities only, meaning that we did not mark person names within, e.g., toponyms as named entities (cf. Sect. 3.3.2 for examples). We evaluated on two levels: the single-token level and the entity level (cf. Table 1). On the entity level, an entity was a true positive match only if all of its parts were annotated as person name tokens (e.g., for *Horace Benedict de Saussure* to become a true positive entity, all four tokens, including the title of nobility *de*, had to be marked as person names).

Finding the Optimal Configuration. We performed a number of experiments on the development set to determine necessary restrictions to impose on our person name recognition algorithm. Among the configurations we tested were:

1. Permitting a last name recognized via an AFN to be a regular noun, e.g., *Eimer* in *P. Eimer* ('P. Eimer' vs.'P. Bucket')
2. Permitting a title of nobility and a job marker to co-occur, e.g., *Präsident von Planta* (cf. Sect. 3.1.2)

Table 1. Recall (R), precision (P), and f-measure (F) for the different configurations on the development set (in %)

		Single-token level			Entity level		
		P	R	F	P	R	F
1	**yes***	**84.38**	62.34	71.70	**69.07**	54.43	60.88
	no	83.98	61.82	71.22	66.84	53.70	59.55
2	yes	83.29	63.17	71.84	68.06	55.73	61.28
	no*	**84.38**	62.34	71.70	**69.07**	54.43	60.88
3	yes	77.34	64.84	70.54	63.64	56.84	60.05
	no*	**84.38**	62.34	71.70	**69.07**	54.43	60.88
4	yes	82.55	63.34	71.68	67.52	55.80	61.10
	no*	**84.38**	62.34	71.70	**69.07**	54.43	60.88
5	yes	83.57	63.17	71.95	68.39	55.73	61.41
	no*	**84.38**	62.34	71.70	**69.07**	54.43	60.88

3. Permitting AFN from our list of blocked abbreviations, e.g., *St.*, which can be short for both 'Saint' and for the first name 'Stefan' (cf. Sect. 3.1.1)
4. Permitting last names from our list of blocked last names, e.g., *Altmann* (cf. Sect. 3.1
5. Permitting a job marker and a regular noun to co-occur, e.g., in the pattern *Sachbearbeiter Bergsport* (cf. Sect. 3.1.2)

Our initial setting was a combination of the options marked with a star in Table 1, where "yes" means that the features of the respective configuration were considered and "no" means that they were not considered. In other words, in our initial setting, we allowed for a last name recognized via an AFN to be a regular noun (configuration 1), while we did not allow for a title of nobility and a job marker to co-occur (2), we did not permit AFN from our list of blocked abbreviations (3) nor last names from our list of blocked last names (4), and we did not allow for a job marker and a regular noun to co-occur (5).

Table 1 displays the results of our experiments on the development set in terms of recall (R), precision (P), and f-measure (F). We opted for high precision. The better of the two options ("yes" vs. "no") for each of configurations 1 to 5 with respect to precision is printed in bold. We found that the better-performing options were the ones marked with a star; hence, our initial setting (options "yes", "no", "no", "no", "no") performed best. In particular, we gained evidence that blocking the co-occurrence of an AFN and a last name that is a regular noun (option "no" for configuration 1) did not aid precision.

Evaluating on the Test Set. On the test set, we applied the options printed in bold in Table 1. For the single-token level, this yielded a precision of 87.34 %, a recall of 77.61 %, and an f-measure of 82.19 %. For the entity level, the corresponding numbers are 75.47 % (precision), 71.22 % (recall), and 73.28 %

Table 2. Results of fine-grained evaluation

	True pos.	True neg.	False pos.	False neg.	P	R	F
all	759	68566	110	219	0.8734	0.7761	0.8219
LN	298	68566	24	185	0.9255	0.6170	0.7404
FFN	398	68566	124	56	0.7625	0.8767	0.8156
AFN	16	68566	2	14	0.8889	0.5333	0.6667

(f-measure). To get an idea of which of the three person name classes—full first names, abbreviated first names, and last names—was the most difficult to recognize, we performed a more fine-grained evaluation. The results for each class are displayed in Table 2.[6] They show that in terms of precision, last names were the easiest class to recognize, while full first names were the hardest. Paired with the observation that full first names had the highest recall, this suggests that the full first names in our list still have a high potential of ambiguity. At the same time, the low recall score of last names and abbreviated first names indicates that the restrictions we imposed on these two classes, presumably via the lists of blocked last names and blocked abbreviations, were too severe.

When examining the false-positive instances in our overall experiment (row "all" in Table 2), we found one major source of errors: person entities nested within other entities, especially person entities embedded in toponyms. Examples include the first name *Luigi* and the last name *Amadeo* in *Pizzo Luigi Amadeo* ('Luigi Amadeo Peak'). We had refrained from annotating such occurrences since we had only considered outer-level person entities (cf. Sect. 3.3). We found that of 110 false positives, 54 were due to this phenomenon, i.e., were legitimate person name tokens on the inner level.

We also observed that the one-sense-per-document hypothesis did not hold for our corpus: we found instances of (outer-level) person entities whose components later appeared as part of geographic entities. For example, the phrase *Der italienische Alpinist Mannelli* ('The Italian mountaineer Mannelli') preceded appearances of the last name *Mannelli* in the toponyms *Couloir Mannelli* ('Mannelli Channel') and *Capanna Mannelli* ('Mannelli Cabin'). Similarly, the person name *Heinrich Harrer* occurred, and the last name *Harrer* later appeared as part of the toponym *Harrer Lake*. Volk and Clematide (2001) made a similar observation for person names and company names. Upon inspecting the false-negative instances, we found that last names often occurred both in their nominative and in their genitive form (*-s*). For example, our system recognized the person name *John Tyndall* (first name *John*, last name *Tyndall*) but failed to identify the genitive form of the last name, *Tyndalls*, that appeared stand-alone at a later stage.

---

[6] We did not compare our approach with other PNR systems because we aimed for a more fine-grained classification.

4   Conclusion

In this paper, we have reported our work on combined person name recognition and reference resolution for German Alpine texts. Named entity recognition, of which person name recognition forms part, is particularly challenging for German. Our person name recognition algorithm is a decision tree with handcrafted rules. It considers stand-alone first names, stand-alone last names, and combinations thereof. Our starting point was the assumption that last names are not introduced unaccompanied but instead occur in conjunction with either a first name complex or a predictive word complex at their first appearance. Predictive words are job markers, address markers, and academic title markers.

While previous studies offered solutions for the person name recognition problem for German only, this paper has additionally tackled the task of reference resolution. Our output is a collection of person entities for each yearbook. We introduced a new entity for every distinct full or abbreviated first name associated with a particular last name. Where there were only stand-alone occurrences of a last name, we merged all features and produced one single entity.

For the single-token level, we achieved a precision of 87.34 %, a recall of 77.61 %, and an f-measure of 82.19 %; for the entity level, 75.47 % (precision), 71.22 % (recall), and 73.28 % (f-measure). The main source of errors we found upon investigating the false-positive instances were person entities nested within other entities, especially within toponyms. When analyzing the false-negative instances, we found that last names often occurred also in their genitive o form.

5   Post-conference Modifications

Following our experiments, we applied two major changes to our algorithm: Firstly, we implemented an extension that considered genitive forms of last names and mapped them to their base (nominative) forms. Thus, in a phrase like *Wenn sich zwei Führer vom Schlage Alexander Gravens und Alexander Taugwalders zu einer «Sache» zusammentun* ('If two guides of the type of Alexander Graven and Alexander Taugwalder join forces'), the genitive-form last names *Gravens* and *Taugwalders* are recognized and mapped to their nominative forms, *Graven* and *Taugwalder*. The nominative forms need to have been recognized previously for this. This modification improved both components of our system: The recognition component finds stand-alone occurrences of the last name as genitive, and the entity resolution component is able to merge entities in nominative and genitive.

Secondly, we raised the threshold for function words (mostly prepositions) to be recognized as titles of nobility: We caused them to be recognized only when they are preceded by another predictive word or word complex. This was because we observed many false-positive instances of titles of nobility, as in the example of *da dieser Gipfel [...] von Lindt und Dübi in Band XV und XXIII noch berücksichtigt worden ist* ('since this summit has also been considered by Lindt and Dübi in Volume XV and XXIII'), where *von* ('by') was erroneously classified as a title of nobility.

References

1. HLT-NAACL 2003: Proceedings of the Seventh Conference on Computational Natural Language Learning (CoNLL 2003) (2003)
2. Bubenhofer, N., Volk, M., Althaus, A., Jitca, M., Bangerter, M., Sennrich, R.: Text+Berg-Korpus (Release 145). XML-Format (2011), digitale Edition SAC-Jahrbuch 1864–1923 und Die Alpen 1925–2009
3. Faruqui, M., Padó, S.: Training and evaluating a German named entity recognizer with semantic generalization. In: Proceedings of KONVENS 2010, Saarbrücken, Germany (2010)
4. Finkel, J., Manning, C.: Nested named entity recognition. In: Proceedings of EMNLP, Singapore, pp. 141–150 (2009)
5. Florian, R., Ittycheriah, A., Jing, H., Zhang, T.: Named entity recognition through classifier combination. In: HLT-NAACL 2003: Proceedings of the Seventh Conference on Computational Natural Language Learning (CoNLL 2003) [1], pp. 168–171 (2003)
6. Jurafsky, D., Martin, J.H.: Speech and language processing. In: An Introduction to Natural Language Processing, Computational Linguistic and Speech Recognition, 2nd ed. Pearson Education International, Upper Saddle River (2009)
7. Rössler, M.: Corpus-based learning of lexical resources for German named entity recognition. In: LREC-2004: Fourth International Conference on Language Resources and Evaluation, Proceedings, Lisbon, Portugal (2004)
8. Sennrich, R.: Combining multi-engine machine translation and online learning through dynamic phrase tables. In: Proceedings of EAMT 2011, Leuven, Belgium, pp. 89–96 (2011)
9. Tjong Kim Sang, E.F., De Meulder, F.: Introduction to the CoNLL-2003 shared task: language-independent named entity recognition. In: HLT-NAACL 2003: Proceedings of the Seventh Conference on Computational Natural Language Learning (CoNLL 2003) [1], pp. 142–147 (2003)
10. Volk, M., Clematide, S.: Learn - filter - apply - forget. mixed approaches to named entity recognition. In: 6th International Workshop on Applications of Natural Language for Informations Systems, Madrid, Spain (2001)

Enhancing Labeled Data Using Unlabeled Data for Topic Tracking

Fumiyo Fukumoto$^{(\boxtimes)}$, Yoshimi Suzuki, and Takeshi Yamamoto

Interdisciplinary Graduate School of Medicine and Engineering,
University of Yamanashi, Kofu 400-8510, Japan
{fukumoto,ysuzuki,g10mk037}@yamanashi.ac.jp

Abstract. In this paper, we address the problem of dealing with a collection of negative training examples used in the topic tracking task, and propose a method for enhancing positive training examples by using negative training data based on supervised machine learning techniques. We present an algorithm which combines positive example based learning (PEBL) and boosting to learn a set of negative data to train classifiers. The results using Japanese corpus showed that our method attained at 0.161 MIN, and PEBL was 0.332. Similarly, the result using TDT3 showed that the improvement was 0.225 MIN compared to PEBL.

Keywords: Topic tracking · Positive example based learning · Boosting

1 Introduction

As the volume of online documents has drastically increased, it is becoming increasingly difficult to find and organize relevant materials. Topic tracking, i.e., it starts from a few sample stories and finds all subsequent stories that discuss the target topic, is a research to attack the problem [1,2]. Here, a topic is the same as Topic Detection and Tracking (TDT) project: something that occurs at a specific place and time associated with some specific actions. A wide range of statistical and machine learning (ML) techniques have been applied to topic tracking, including k-Nearest Neighbor classification, Decision Tree induction [11,30], relevance feedback method of IR [8,25], unsupervised and supervised clustering [9,13], the latent Dirichlet allocation (LDA) [3], and a variety of Language Modeling [17,18]. The main task of these techniques is to tune the parameters or the threshold for binary decisions to produce optimal results. However, parameter tuning is a difficult issue for tracking because the number of initial positive training stories is very small (from one to four), and topics are localized in space and time. For example, "Iranian National Elections" and "Azerbaijani Presidential Elections" are topics, but "Elections" is not. Therefore, the system must estimate whether the test stories are concerned with the same topic with little information about the topic. Moreover, learning an exact decision surface is much more difficult for event tracking than for the traditional text categorization problems when all the training stories are labelled with a complete category set. Because the majority of training stories consists of negative data.

Z. Vetulani and J. Mariani (Eds.): LTC 2011, LNAI 8387, pp. 201–212, 2014.
DOI: 10.1007/978-3-319-08958-4_17

In this paper, we present a method for enhancing positive training examples by using negative training data based on supervised machine learning techniques. Our method is based on a text classification technique called positive example based learning (PEBL) developed by Yu et al. [31]. The PEBL framework uses a sample of unlabeled data, and learns from additional positive data and the given unlabeled data without requiring labeled data. It consists of two steps: Mapping and Convergence (M-C) that learn from positive and unlabeled data as accurately as a traditional SVM that learns from labeled data. However, once the M-C selects *weak* negative data from unlabeled data, the classification accuracy is decreased. We focused on this problem, and present a topic tracking method which combines PEBL and boosting to learn a set of negative data to train a classifier.

The remainder of the paper is organized as follows: Sect. 2 describes related work. Section 3 reviews PEBL. Section 4 presents our method. Finally, we report experimental results using Japanese and English data and conclude our discussion with some directions for further work.

2   Related Work

There are quite a lot of approaches using a small number of positive examples and unlabeled data. One major approach is called semi-supervised learning which makes use of a large amount of unlabeled data, together with the labeled data, to build better classifiers. The Expectation-Maximization (EM) algorithm is a representative algorithm which can be used for either semi-supervised learning or unsupervised learning. However, the result depends on the critical assumption that the data sets are generated using the same parametric model used in classification. Nigam inserted two parameters into EM, i.e., a parameter for controlling the contributions of labeled data and unlabeled data, and the other parameter for controlling the quantity of mixture components corresponding to one class [23]. Joachims presented a method called transductive SVM, and reported that it is effective, especially on extremely low amount of labeled data while it needs careful parameter settings [15].

Several authors presented a semi-supervised method based on graphs [4,7,14]. Graph-based methods define a graph where the nodes are labeled and unlabeled examples in the dataset, and edges reflect the similarity of examples. These methods usually assume label smoothness over the graph. Graph methods are non-parametric, discriminative, and transductive in nature. They can be viewed as estimating a function f on the graph. One wants f to satisfy two things at the same time: (1) it should be close to the given labels y_L on the labeled nodes, and (2) it should be smooth on the whole graph. This can be expressed in a regularization framework where the first term is a loss function, and the second term is a regularizer.

Other attempts is self-training which is a commonly used technique for semi-supervised learning. In self-training a classifier is first trained with the small amount of labeled data. The classifier is then used to classify the unlabeled data. Typically the most confident unlabeled points, together with their predicted labels, are added to the training set. The classifier is re-trained and the procedure repeated. Maeireizo et al. classified dialogues as "emotional" or "non-emotional" with a procedure involving two classifiers [19]. Blum and Mitchell proposed a method called Co-training which uses a technique of self-training [6]. It assumes that (i) features can be split into two sets; (ii) each sub-feature set is sufficient to train a good classifier, (iii) the two sets are conditionally independent given the class. Initially two separate classifiers are trained with the labeled data, on the two sub-feature sets respectively. Each classifier then classifies the unlabeled data, and "teaches" the other classifier with the few unlabeled examples they feel most confident about classification. Each classifier is retrained with the additional training examples given by the other classifier, and the process repeats. Nigam et al. perform extensive empirical experiments to compare co-training with generative mixture models and EM [24]. They showed that co-training performs well if the conditional independence assumption indeed holds.

Manevitz et al. used one-class SVM which distinguishes one class of data from the rest of the feature space given only positive data set [20]. However, due to lack of the information about negative data distribution, they require much larger amount of positive training data to induce accurate boundary, and their performance is dependent on the user parameters indicating how strictly the boundary should fit around the data. Yu et al. focused on the problem, and presented positive example based learning (PEBL) for Web page classification [31]. The method finds the marginal property of SVM by using positive and unlabeled data. They reported that the results obtained by the PEBL achieved text classification accuracy with positive and unlabeled data as high as that of traditional SVM with positive and negative data. However, if the algorithm produces an error classification of negative or positive training data, the algorithm produces the class boundary that would be far from accurate. In order to solve the problem, we present an algorithm which combines PEBL and boosting to learn a set of negative data to train classifiers, and apply the algorithm to the topic tracking task.

3   PEBL

The PEBL is a SVM based learning method using positive and unlabeled training data. The method finds an accurate class boundary to select strong negative training data repeatedly. It consists of two procedures: mapping and convergence procedures.

3.1   Mapping Procedure

The mapping procedure selects the strongest negative training data from the unlabeled training data U. The strongest negative training data is a data not having any of the positive features/words in the stories. Yu et al. used 1-DNF

(Disjunctive Normal Form) learning [10] to build a disjunction list of positive features. After they constructed the 1-DNF of positive features, they selected the strongest negative training data N_1, each of which did not include any positive features. The remaining data, i.e., $U - N_1$ is set to R.

3.2 Convergence Procedure

The second procedure, convergence procedure trains the SVM repeatedly to aggregate negative training data as close as possible to the unbiased negative training data. The positive training data P and the selected negative training data $N = N_1$ are trained by using SVM. SVM classifier is tested by using the remaining data R. The data which were classified into negative are set to N_2, and N is updated: $N = N_1 + N_2$. The positive training data P and the updated negative training data N are trained by using SVM, and the data $R = U - (N_1 + N_2)$ are tested by using SVM classifier. The data classified into negative are set to N_3, and N is updated: $N = N_1 + N_2 + N_3$.

The procedure is repeated until there are no training stories which are judged to be negative. Finally, the test data is classified by using the final classifier.

4   Enhancing Labeled Data by Boosting

We recall that once the positive training data is incorrectly classified into nega-tive, then the positive training data is included into the negative training data N_i $(1 \leq i \leq n)$, where n is the number of iteration. This causes the result of not only the iteration being not terminated but also the classification accuracy being decreased. We focused on the problem and applied a boosting technique [26] to each iteration of the convergence procedure. Boosting is a general technique for improving the accuracies of machine learning algorithms. The basic idea of boosting is to repeatedly construct "weak learners" by re-weighting training data and form an ensemble of weak learners such that the total performance of the ensemble is "boosted". The flow of the algorithm is shown in Fig. 1. s_i is a story and y_i denotes to a label of classification result. $f_t(s_i)$ refers to each classifier. n is the number of stories and T is the number of boosting iteration. The function I in (b) returns 1 if $y_i = f_t(s_i)$, otherwise returns 0.

We incorporated boosting shown in Fig. 1 into PEBL. In our method, at each round, it increases the weights of positive and negative training stories which are incorrectly classified, and the model created so far. As a result, the learning at the next round will be focused on the creation of a weak hypothesis. Once a hypothesis is built at each round by linearly combining the weak hypotheses constructed so far, the test data is classified by using a vote of each classifier.

5   Experiments

We performed experiments by using two sets of data, namely Japanese and English data to evaluate our method. We used SVM-Light [16] for a machine

(1) Given: $S=\{s_i, y_i\}_{i=1}^m$
    Initialize weighted distribution $D_1(i)$
    $D_1(i) = \frac{1}{n}$ $(i = 1, 2, ..., n)$
(2) For $t = 1, 2, ..., T$
    (a) Train and test SVM classifier by using $D_t(i)$
    (b) Compute accuracy rate r_t
        $r_t = \sum_{i=1}^n D_t(i)I(y_i = f_t(s_i))$
    (c) Compute $\alpha_t = \frac{1}{2} \ln\left(\frac{1+r}{1-r}\right)$
    (d) Update the distribution $D_{t+1}(i)$:
        $D_{t+1} = D_t(i)\exp[-\alpha_t y_i f_t(x_i)]$
        $y_i \in \{-1, 1\}$
    (e) $Z_{t+1} = \sum_{i=1}^n D_{t+1}(i)$,
        $D_{t+1}(i) = D_{t+1}(i)/Z_{t+1}$
(3) Output the final hypothesis:
    $H(s) = \sum_{t=1}^T \alpha_t(i)f_t(s)$

Fig. 1. The flow of boosting

learning technique and linear kernel. Throughout the experiments, we set the maximum number of iterations to 100 times. All Japanese stories were tagged by using a morphological analyzer Chasen [22]. Similarly, English stories were tagged by a part-of-speech tagger [29]. In both data, we selected nouns and verbs. We used them as a feature of a vector used in SVM.

In the mapping procedure, we tested 1-DNF, χ^2 method, mutual information and information gain to select the strongest negative training data [28]. We reported only the result obtained by χ^2 method which is shown in Eq. (1) as it was the best results among them.

$$\chi^2(w, pos) = \frac{n \times (ad - bc)^2}{(a + c) \times (b + d) \times (a + b) \times (c + d)}. \tag{1}$$

Using the two-way contingency table of a term w and positive stories pos, where a is the number of times w occurs within pos, b is the number of times w occurs stories other than pos, c is the number of pos without occurring w, d is the number of times a term other than w occurs stories other than pos, and n is the total number of stories. Throughout the experiments, we selected the topmost 100 words and used them in the mapping procedure.

We set the evaluation measures used in the TDT benchmark evaluations. "Miss" denotes the miss rate, which is the ratio of the stories judged as YES but not evaluated as such for the run in question. "F/A" shows the false alarm rate, which is the ratio of the stories judged as NO, but evaluated as YES. The detection cost function (C_{Det}) is defined by Eq. (2).

$$C_{Det} = (C_{Miss} * P_{Miss} * P_{Target} + C_{Fa} * P_{Fa} * (1 - P_{Target}))$$
$$P_{Miss} = \#ofMisses/\#ofTargets$$
$$P_{Fa} = \#ofFalseAlarms/\#ofNonTargets \tag{2}$$

C_{Miss}, C_{Fa}, and P_{Target} are the costs of a missed detection, false alarm, and priori probability of finding a target, respectively. C_{Miss}, C_{Fa}, and P_{Target} are usually set to 10, 1, and 0.02, respectively. The normalized cost function is defined by Eq. (3), and lower cost stories indicate better performance.

$$(C_{Det})_{Norm} = C_{Det}/MIN(C_{Miss} * P_{Target}, C_{Fa} * (1 - P_{Target})) \qquad (3)$$

5.1 Mainichi Japanese Corpus

We used Mainichi newspaper stories collected from the same period of TDT3, i.e., the corpus covering October 1, to December 31, 1998 consists of 28,778 stories. We recall that TDT3 corpus, developed at LDC, consists of 60 manually identified topics [27]. We then created a Japanese corpus, i.e., we annotated Mainichi newspaper stories against 60 topics. Not all the topics could have seen over the three months Japanese newspaper stories. We used 10 topics which are included in the Japanese newspaper corpus. Table 1 shows the data used in the experiment. "Topic" in Table 1 denotes topic name defined by the TDT3, and "Pos" shows the number of positive data included in the test stories. "Doc" refers to the number of unlabeled training stories and "Test" denotes to the number of test stories.

We set the number of positive training stories to four, i.e., $N_t = 4$. In the TDT condition, the corpus was split at the point right after the N_t-th positive story of that topic; the stories before that split point were allowed to be used for training, and the remaining stories were used for testing. For each topic, we used the stories before the split point as unlabeled data. Table 2 shows a summary result, and Table 3 shows each result consisting of 10 topics. "PEBL+Boosting" refers to the results obtained by our method, and "PEBL" shows the results obtained by PEBL method. "(Iter.)" in Table 2 shows the number of iterations in the convergence procedure. MIN denotes $MIN(C_{Det})_{Norm}$ which is the value of $(C_{Det})_{Norm}$ at the best possible threshold [12].

Table 1. Japanese data used in the TDT

Topic	Pos	Doc	Test
Cambodian government coalition	23	3,572	25,202
Pinochet trial	106	6,124	22,650
NBA labor disputes	17	5,618	23,156
North Korean food shortages	6	19,930	8,844
Shuttle Endeavour mission	38	7,512	21,262
Euro introduced	6	15,368	13,406
Indonesia-East Timor conflict	9	16,620	12,154
IMF bailout of Brazil	12	9,274	19,500
North Korean nuclear facility?	33	13,273	15,501
Clinton's Gaza trip	16	23,440	5,334

Table 2. TDT summary results (Japanese data)

PEBL+Boosting				
Miss(%)	F/A(%)	Prec	F-score (Iter.)	MIN
35.8	0.070	0.618	0.615 (16)	0.161
PEBL				
Miss(%)	F/A(%)	Prec	F-score (Iter.)	MIN
53.0	0.060	0.324	0.478 (17)	0.332

Table 3. Each result (Japanese data)

Topic	PEBL			PEBL+Boosting		
	Miss	F/A	F (Iter.)	Miss	F/A	F (Iter.)
Cambodian government coalition	0.552	0	0.510 (15)	0.422	0	0.612 (13)
Pinochet trial	0.542	0.001	0.537 (18)	0.475	0.001	0.597 (15)
NBA labor disputes	0.606	0	0.500 (17)	0.488	0	0.619 (16)
North Korean food shortages	0.400	0.001	0.475 (23)	0.233	0.001	0.633 (21)
Shuttle Endeavour mission	0.584	0.001	0.464 (14)	0.374	0.001	0.648 (13)
Euro introduced	0.400	0.001	0.400 (17)	0.233	0.001	0.521 (15)
Indonesia-East Timor conflict	0.678	0	0.335 (18)	0.233	0	0.700 (15)
IMF bailout of Brazil	0.567	0	0.464 (12)	0.400	0	0.580 (11)
North Korean nuclear facility?	0.506	0.001	0.526 (14)	0.385	0.001	0.607 (14)
Clinton's Gaza trip	0.462	0.001	0.567 (23)	0.338	0.002	0.629 (22)
Macro Avg.	0.530	0.0006	0.478 (17)	0.358	0.0007	0.615 (16)

As we can see from Tables 2 and 3 that all evaluation measures obtained by boosting outperformed the results by PEBL. Comparing the number of iterations, the result obtained by boosting was slightly better than that with PEBL. These results shows that incorporating boosting into PEBL is effective for the topic tracking task.

5.2 TDT3 English Corpus

We chose the TDT3 English corpus as our gold standard. The stories of TDT3 were collected from 8 sources including APW and CNN Headline News for the period of Oct. through Dec. 1998. It consists of 34,600 stories with 100 manually identified topics (1999 Evaluation Topics and 2000 Evaluation Topics)[1]. We used the number of 30 topics having more than five positive stories. Table 4 shows 30 topics that we used in the experiment. "Pos", "Doc", and "Test" are the same shown in Table 3. Tables 5 and 6 show the results.

---

[1] http://www.itl.nist.gov/iad/mig/tests/tdt/2000/

Table 4. TDT3 English data

Topic	Pos	Doc	Test	Topic	Pos	Doc	Test
Cambodian government coalition	30	5,652	21,077	Gaza international airport opened	29	14,782	11,947
Hurricane Mitch	382	6,201	20,528	PanAm lockerbie bombing trial	104	5,475	21,254
Pinochet trial	308	4,386	22,343	Kurd separatist abdullah ocalan	131	10,097	16,632
Osama bin Laden indictment	84	2,554	24,175	IMF bailout of Brazil	100	900	25,829
NBA labor disputes	217	1,232	25,497	North Korean nuclear facility?	51	11,540	15,189
Congolese rebels vs. pres. Kabila	127	1,305	25,424	U.S. mid-term elections	498	894	11,540
Nov. APEC summit meeting	78	5,981	20,748	Bosnian war crimes tribunal	50	3,436	23,293
Anwar Ibrahim case	101	762	25,967	Olympic Gymnast	21	5,816	20,913
Holbrooke-milosevic meeting	470	983	25,746	Abortion doctor Slepian killed	66	6,397	20,332
Asian games in Thailand	80	11,790	14,939	Yankees vs. Padres	133	3,368	23,361
AOL-Netscape merger	39	14,609	12,120	US federal budget passes	162	236	26,493
Russian financial crisis	316	180	26,549	Yeltsin's illness	134	2,867	23,862
Shuttle endeavour mission	154	17,105	9,624	Microsoft anti-trust case	148	4,449	22,280
Euro introduced	122	3,093	23,636	Joe DiMaggio illness	48	10.007	16,722
Nobel prizes awarded	98	1,945	24,636	American embassy bombing trial	96	1,193	25,536

As shown in Tables 5 and 6, combination of PEBL and boosting outperformed the result by PEBL only. The results obtained by both PEBL and our method were worse than those by using Japanese data, e.g., the Miss rates obtained by both methods were worse than those using Japanese Mainichi corpus. One reason is that the volume of each story of TDT data was smaller than that of Mainichi story. Moreover, TDT corpus consists of a variety of sources including broadcast news. In the broadcast news stories, there are a large number of referring expressions including overt pronouns instead of using the same nouns repeatedly. They sometimes show topics related to a specific time and place, and events referred to notions of who, where, when including what, why and how in a story. The observation indicates that it is necessary to investigate the effect of anaphora resolution [21] in the topic tracking task.

We recall that in mapping procedure, we applied χ^2 statistics to noun and verb words in order to select features. A better set of features, e.g., noun phrases and named entities such as *person, place* and *time* are even more effective at producing high quality results. This is a rich space for further exploration. Moreover, other feature selections such as LDA which is widely used as a topic model is worth trying with our method [3,5].

Table 5. TDT3 English summary results

PEBL+Boosting				
Miss(%)	F/A(%)	Prec	F-score (Iter.)	MIN
22.0	0.200	0.432	0.466 (10)	0.225
PEBL				
Miss(%)	F/A(%)	Prec	F-score (Iter.)	MIN
31.0	0.300	0.391	0.429 (12)	0.470

Table 6. Each result of TDT3 English

ID	PEBL					Boost				
	Miss	F/A	Recall	Precision	F	Miss	F/A	Recall	Precision	F
Cambodian government coalition	0.567	0.001	0.433	0.520	0.473 (12)	0.467	0.001	0.533	0.471	0.500 (10)
Hurricane Mitch	0.704	0.004	0.296	0.604	0.397 (9)	0.678	0.004	0.322	0.612	0.422 (9)
Pinochet trial	0.542	0.005	0.458	0.551	0.500 (14)	0.471	0.006	0.529	0.534	0.532 (11)
Osama bin Laden indictment	0.524	0.001	0.476	0.597	0.530 (9)	0.429	0.001	0.571	0.608	0.589 (8)
NBA labor disputes	0.599	0.004	0.401	0.458	0.428 (8)	0.535	0.006	0.465	0.416	0.439 (8)
Congolese rebels vs. pres. Kabila	0.724	0.001	0.276	0.556	0.368 (10)	0.693	0.001	0.307	0.527	0.388 (9)
Nov. APEC summit meeting	0.564	0.001	0.436	0.630	0.515 (13)	0.500	0.001	0.500	0.639	0.561 (12)
Anwar Ibrahim case	0.644	0.003	0.356	0.293	0.321 (8)	0.574	0.002	0.426	0.478	0.450 (8)
Holbrooke-milosevic meeting	0.598	0.005	0.402	0.610	0.485 (10)	0.568	0.005	0.432	0.597	0.501 (10)
Asian games in Thailand	0.637	0.002	0.362	0.468	0.408 (19)	0.562	0.003	0.438	0.449	0.443 (17)
AOL-Netscape merger	0.692	0.000	0.308	0.750	0.436 (22)	0.538	0.001	0.462	0.692	0.554 (20)
Russian financial crisis	0.636	0.013	0.364	0.256	0.300 (6)	0.500	0.008	0.500	0.416	0.454 (5)
Shuttle endeavour mission	0.552	0.003	0.448	0.676	0.539 (15)	0.494	0.004	0.506	0.655	0.571 (12)
Euro introduced	0.631	0.001	0.369	0.703	0.484 (10)	0.574	0.001	0.426	0.675	0.523 (10)
Nobel prizes awarded	0.643	0.003	0.357	0.337	0.347 (9)	0.582	0.002	0.418	0.471	0.443 (9)
Gaza international airport opened	0.655	0.001	0.345	0.556	0.426 (17)	0.483	0.001	0.517	0.600	0.556 (16)
PanAm lockerbie bombing trial	0.587	0.001	0.413	0.632	0.500 (11)	0.510	0.001	0.490	0.654	0.560 (9)
Kurd separatist abdullah ocalan	0.557	0.002	0.443	0.659	0.530 (13)	0.527	0.002	0.473	0.667	0.554 (10)
IMF bailout of Brazil	0.790	0.001	0.210	0.568	0.307 (8)	0.670	0.001	0.330	0.589	0.423 (7)
North Korean nuclear facility?	0.608	0.001	0.392	0.541	0.455 (24)	0.510	0.001	0.490	0.543	0.515 (20)
U.S. mid-term elections	0.715	0.009	0.285	0.394	0.331 (9)	0.669	0.007	0.331	0.465	0.387 (7)
Bosnian war crimes tribunal	0.580	0.002	0.420	0.313	0.359 (15)	0.480	0.001	0.520	0.433	0.473 (15)
Olympic Gymnast	0.429	0.001	0.571	0.353	0.436 (16)	0.381	0.001	0.619	0.433	0.510 (15)
Abortion doctor Slepian killed	0.636	0.000	0.364	0.706	0.480 (14)	0.576	0.001	0.424	0.622	0.505 (11)
Yankees vs. Padres	0.654	0.002	0.346	0.517	0.414 (10)	0.617	0.002	0.383	0.548	0.451 (9)
US federal budget passes	0.543	0.010	0.457	0.216	0.294 (5)	0.451	0.008	0.549	0.308	0.395 (5)
Yeltsin's illness	0.664	0.003	0.336	0.429	0.377 (11)	0.604	0.003	0.396	0.465	0.427 (11)
Microsoft anti-trust case	0.696	0.000	0.304	0.804	0.441 (10)	0.628	0.001	0.372	0.705	0.487 (9)
Joe DiMaggio illness	0.646	0.001	0.354	0.654	0.459 (16)	0.521	0.001	0.479	0.657	0.554 (13)
American embassy bombing trial	0.583	0.005	0.417	0.244	0.308 (8)	0.531	0.004	0.469	0.294	0.361 (8)
Macro Avg.	0.560	0.003	0.340	0.464	0.376 (11)	0.490	0.002	0.410	0.487	0.436 (10)

6   Conclusion

We presented a method for enhancing positive training examples by using negative training data based on supervised machine learning techniques. The method combines positive example based learning and boosting to learn a set of negative data to train classifiers. The results using Japanese corpus showed that our method attained at 0.161 MIN, while PEBL was 0.332. Similarly, the result using TDT3 showed that the improvement was 0.225 MIN compared to PEBL. Future work will include (i) investigating the effect of anaphora resolution in the topic tracking task, (ii) using other features such as noun phrases and named entities, (iii) applying other feature selection techniques, (iv) comparison to other related work such as EM or co-training techniques, and (v) applying the method to the TDT4 corpus and Web data for quantitative evaluation.

References

1. Allan, J., Carbonell, J., Doddington, G., Yamron, J., Yang, Y.: Topic detection and tracking pilot study final report. In: Proceedings of the DARPA Broadcast News Transcription and Understanding Workshop (1998)
2. Allan, J.: Topic Detection and Tracking. Kluwer Academic Publishers, Boston (2003)
3. AlSumait, L., Barbara, D., Domeniconi, C.: On-line LDA: adaptive topic models for mining text streams with application to topic detection and tracking. In: Proceedings of the 8th IEEE International Conference on Data Mining, pp. 3–12 (2008)
4. Belkin, M., Niyogi, P., Sindhwani, V.: Manifold regularization: a geometric framework for learning from labeled and unlabeled examples. J. Mach. Learn. Res. **7**, 2399–2434 (2006)
5. Blei, D.M., Ng, A.Y., Jordan, M.I.: Latent dirichlet allocation. J. Mach. Learn. Res. **3**, 993–1022 (2003)
6. Blum, A., Mitchell, T.: Combining labeled and unlabeled data with co-training. In: Proceedings of the Workshop on Computational Learning Theory, pp. 92–100 (1998)
7. Blum, A., Lafferty, J., Rwebangira, M., Reddy, R.: Learning from labeled and unlabeled data using graph mincuts. In: Proceedings of the 18th International Conference on Machine Learning (ICML'01), pp. 19–26 (2001)
8. Connell, M., Feng, A., Kumaran, G., Raghavan, H., Shah, C., Allan, J.: UMass at TDT 2004. In: Proceedings of the DARPA Broadcast News Transcription and Understanding Workshop (2004)
9. Cselle, G., Albrecht, K., Wattenhofer, R.: BuzzTrack; topic detection and tracking in email. In: Proceedings of the 12th International Conference on Intelligent User Interfaces, pp. 190–197 (2007)
10. Denis, F.: Pac learning from positive statistical queries. In: Proceedings of the 9th International Conference on Algorithmic Learning Theory (ALT'98), pp. 112–126 (1998)
11. Carbonell, J., Yang, Y., Lafferty, J., Brown, R.D., Pierce, T., Liu, X.: CMU report on TDT-2: segmentation, detection and tracking. In: Proceedings of the DARPA Broadcast News Transcription and Understanding Workshop, pp. 117–120 (1999)

12. Fiscus, J.G., Doddington, G.R.: Topic detection and tracking evaluation overview. In: Allan, J. (ed.) Topic Detection and Tracking, pp. 17–31. Kluwer Academic Publisher, Boston (2002)
13. Franz, M., McCarley, J.S.: Unsupervised and supervised clusteringfor topic tracking. In Proceedings of the 24th Annual International ACM SIGIR Conference on Research and Development in Information Retrieval (SIGIR'01), pp. 310–317 (2001)
14. Getz, G., Shental, N., Domany, E.: Semi-supervised learning - a statistical physics approach. In: Proceedings of the ICML Workshop on Learning with Partially Classified Training Data (2005)
15. Joachims, T.: Transductive inference for text classification using support vector machines. In: Proceedings of the ICML'09, pp. 200–209 (1999)
16. Joachims, T.: SVM Light Support Vector Machine. Dept. of Computer Science Cornell University (1998)
17. Larkey, L.S., Feng, F., Connell, M., Lavrenko, V.: Language-specific model in multilingual topic tracking. In: Proceedings of the 27th Annual International ACM SIGIR Conference on Research and Development in Information Retrieval (SIGIR'04), pp. 402–409 (2004)
18. Lowe, S.A.: The beta-binomial mixture model and its application to TDT tracking and detection. In: Proceedings of the DARPA Broadcast News Transcription and Understanding Workshop, pp. 127–131 (1999)
19. Maeireizo, B., Litman, D., Hwa, R.: Co-training for predicting emotions with spoken dialogue data. The Companion Proceedings of the 42nd Annual Meeting of the Association for Computational Linguistics (ACL'04), pp. 203–206 (2004)
20. Manevitz, L.M., Yousef, M.: One-class SVMs for document classification. J. Mach. Learn. Res. 2, 139–154 (2001)
21. Markert, K., Nissim, M.: Comparing knowledge sources for nonimal anaphora resolution. J. Assoc. Comput. Linguist. 31(3), 367–401 (2005)
22. Matsumoto, Y., Kitauchi, A., Yamashita, T., Hirano, Y., Matsuda, Y., Takaoka, K., Asahara, M.: Japanese morphological analysis system chasen version 2.2.1. In Naist Technical report (2000)
23. Nigam, K.: Text classification from labeled and unlabeled documents using EM. J. Mach. Learn. Res. 32(2), 103–134 (2000)
24. Nigam, K., Ghani, R.: Analyzing the effectiveness and applicability of co-training. In: Proceedings of the 9th International Conference on Information and Knowledge Management (CIKM'00), pp. 86–93 (2000)
25. Oard, D.W.: Topic tracking with the PRISE information retrieval system. In: Proceedings of the DARPA Broadcast News Transcription and Understanding Workshop, pp. 94–101 (1999)
26. Schapire, R.E., Singer, Y.: BoosTexter: a boosting-based system for text categorization. J. Mach. Learn. Res. 39(2), 135–168 (2000)
27. Allan, J.: (2000). http://www.itl.nist.gov/iad/mig/tests/tdt/2000/
28. Yang, Y., Pedersen, J.O.: A comparative study on feature selection in text categorization. In Proceedings of the 6th International Conference on Information and Knowledge Management (ICML'97), pp. 412–230 (1997)
29. Schmid, H.: Improvements in part-of-speech tagging with an application to German. In: Proceedings of the European Chapter of the Association for Computational Linguistics SIGDAT Workshop, pp. 47–50 (1995)

30. Yang, Y., Ault, T., Pierce, T., Lattimer, C.W.: Improving text categorization methods for event tracking. In: Proceedings of the 23rd Annual International ACM SIGIR Conference on Research and Development in Information Retrieval (SIGIR'00), pp. 65–72 (2000)
31. Yu, H., Han, H., Chang, K.C.-C.: PEBL: positive example based learning for web page classification using SVM. In: Proceedings of the ACM Special Interest Group on Knowledge Discovery and Data Mining, pp. 239–248 (2002)

Temporal Expression Recognition Using Dependency Trees

Paweł Mazur[1](✉) and Robert Dale[2]

[1] Institute of Applied Informatics, Wrocław University of Technology,
Wyb. Wyspiańskiego 27, 50-370 Wrocław, Poland
Pawel.Mazur@pwr.wroc.pl
[2] Centre for Language Technology, Macquarie University,
Sydney, NSW 2109, Australia
Robert.Dale@mq.edu.au

Abstract. In this paper we present a previously unexplored approach to recognizing the textual extent of temporal expressions. Based on the observation that temporal expressions are syntactic constituents, we use functional dependency relations between tokens in a sentence to determine which words in addition to a trigger word belong to the extent of the expression. This method is particularly attractive for the recognition of expressions with complex syntactic structure, for which state-of-the-art pattern-based taggers are not effective.

Keywords: Temporal expressions · Event-based expressions · Extent recognition · Dependency parsing

1 Introduction

Temporal expressions (TEs) are linguistic expressions that refer to temporal entities (i.e. points or periods in time). The first step in extraction of TEs from texts is the proper recognition of their occurrence. This is generally divided into two phases: **detection** and **extent recognition**. Detection is concerned with 'spotting' the existence of an expression, i.e. finding at least one of its constituent tokens. The goal of extent recognition is to precisely determine where the expression starts and ends, i.e. to establish exactly which tokens make up the expression.

Very often these two tasks are approached using the idea of a **trigger**. This is a lexical item whose presence is a strong indicator that there may be an instance of a temporal expression; for example, names of months, weekdays and temporal units are triggers. Identification of a trigger which is in fact part of a temporal expression means that we have detected a temporal expression. Recognition then extends the span of the hypothesized temporal expression beyond the trigger word itself. Of course, triggers (here underlined) may constitute complete temporal expressions (here italicised) on their own, as in Example (1), but very often, as in Example (2), they are only parts of longer strings.

© Springer International Publishing Switzerland 2014
Z. Vetulani and J. Mariani (Eds.): LTC 2011, LNAI 8387, pp. 213–225, 2014.
DOI: 10.1007/978-3-319-08958-4_18

(1) I did not go to work on _Monday_.
(2) I spent _three and a half months_ in Spain.

In the majority of systems presented in the literature the remainder of the extent is determined by means of hand-written recognition grammars.[1] Such an approach requires the development of a number of detailed rules centered on a trigger in the context. This is a laborious task requiring the knowledge engineer to foresee what expressions may appear in texts and to control the interaction between the rules; as the grammar grows in size, it becomes increasingly difficult to provide wider coverage while maintaining a high level of precision. What we need is a more general algorithm which, given the trigger as a seed, can grow the extent outwards to find the complete temporal expression. The TIMEX2 guidelines define TEs in syntactic terms [1, pp. 7, 57–58], and so it seems obvious that such an algorithm might be based on the notion of syntactic constituency; but, surprisingly, we can find no reports in the literature of attempts to use a syntactic parser (performing a deeper analysis than chunking) to determine the extent of a TE beyond the trigger.

In this paper we present our experiments with a novel approach that uses functional dependency relations between the tokens in a sentence to determine which words apart from the trigger belong to the extent of the expression. In our model, we assume that the trigger is the head of a dependency tree corresponding to the temporal expression; so, once we have identified a head, we can easily extract the complete temporal expression provided we can correctly determine the dependency structure of the sentence.

2   Related Work

Most existing TE taggers use rule-based grammars which recognize TEs by matching encoded patterns of specific lexical items; some generalisation may be achieved by using POS tags. While it is the case that these taggers achieve high performance, it takes a lot of effort to provide wide coverage without sacrificing precision; this is an issue that becomes increasingly problematic as the coverage of the grammar grows.

To introduce more generalisation to the rules, [2] used shallow (chunk) parsing; this provided them with a sequence of non-overlapping units, which correspond approximately to phrases. Their recognition patterns then looked for chunks headed by trigger words, and combined selected contiguous chunks to form TEs. The results were, however, lower than their corresponding grammar that did not use chunks.

There are also two other approaches to extent recognition that do not involve the identification of a trigger. One, well-known in work on named entity recognition more generally and undertaken in the context of TEs by [3], is to carry out token classification using the B-I-O model: i.e. each token is classified as being

---

[1] Our review of the literature identified 27 temporal expression tagging systems, of which 19 are rule-based.

a Border (the first or last) token of a TE, an Inside token (between two border tokens) or being Outside of the expression. Another approach, proposed by [4], is to use a machine-learning classifier which, for each candidate phrase in a sentence (e.g., each NP or ADVP), decides whether or not it is a TE. Although the two methods scored relatively highly in evaluations, their disadvantage is that they require significant amounts of training data. We attempt to develop a method which does not need to be trained.

3   The Method

Given the observation that temporal expressions are defined as syntactic constituents of sentences, we might attempt to obtain a higher level of generalisation by using syntactic information. Instead of attempting to predict what sequences of individual words around a trigger might constitute TEs, we can develop a conceptually much simpler algorithm that, provided we have a syntactic analysis of a sentence, would choose which parts of a sentence are TEs. This idea bears some similarities to the approach investigated by [4]; however, our task is defined quite differently. Whereas [4] tried to learn a model of what makes a given constituent a TE, we assume we have the head of a TE given, and try to determine the full extent of the expression.

We can distinguish two popular types of syntactic analysis based on the type of information they output; this may be either a phrase structure which defines the syntactic constituents of a sentence, or a set of functional dependencies between the tokens of a sentence. Given TIMEX2's stipulation that the trigger is the syntactic head of a markable expression [1, p. 7], the choice of a dependency-based approach seems most natural; to determine the full extent of a TE, we only have to extract the dependency subtree which has the trigger as root. Consider Example (3):

(3) He returned some gifts *five days after Christmas*.

Here, *days* is the trigger. The analysis of the sentence provides the following dependencies:[2] days:>five, days:>after, and after:>Christmas. Starting from *days* we traverse the tree and get the full extent of *five days after Christmas*. In principle, this approach should also work for more complex cases, where the temporal expression includes a dependent clause, as in the following example:

(4) I recall *the days when he was the best in the team*.

Here, the dependencies found in the subtree headed by the trigger are days:> the, days:>was, was:>he, was:>when, was:>best, best:>the, was:>in, in:>team, and team:>the.

---

[2] We use the notation head:>child to represent a dependency.

4   The Experimental Set-up

4.1   The Parsers and Text Tokenisation

In our experiments, carried out using the GATE framework,[3] we use four off-the-shelf parsers: Minipar,[4] Connexor,[5] the Stanford Parser [5], and the C&C Parser [6]. We do not retrain the parsers because we do not have enough training data; this is a common scenario in real-life applications.

The Stanford Parser uses a very rich set of 48 dependency categories that result in analyses which violate the common assumption that a dependency analysis should be a tree rather than a graph. Based on an analysis of the categories of the Stanford dependencies and parses of a few example sentences from our data, we decided to omit the following link types from our traversal approach: nsubj (nominal subject), cop (copula), cc (coordination), and conj (conjunct) dependencies.

Minipar treats commas as syntactic nodes that are in functional relations with other tokens; accordingly, we implemented a postprocessing step that shortened the extent of a TE if its last token was a comma.

We used the ANNIE sentence splitter from GATE for all parsers, except for Connexor which carries out its own sentence splitting. Only the C&C Parser expects the text to be already tokenized,[6] while all the other parsers do their own tokenization. Note that Connexor can combine several words into a single token: e.g. *25 December 1956* is a single node in a dependency tree.

4.2   The Data

For carrying out the experiment we chose two datasets that are publicly available and which contain temporal expressions annotated in accordance with the TIMEX2 standard; these are the ACE 2005 Training corpus[7] and WikiWars [7]. In Table 1 we compare the sizes of the two datasets in terms of the number of documents, sentences, tokens and temporal expressions they contain.

The ACE corpus contains documents from six different domains: newswire, broadcast news, broadcast and telephone conversations, UseNet discussions, and weblogs. WikiWars contains narratives sourced from Wikipedia; each presents the course of a military conflict.

4.3   The Selection of Triggers

The literature does not provide an agreed-upon or recommended set of temporal expression triggers; even the TIMEX2 annotation guidelines only provide a non-exhaustive list of examples. We therefore needed to derive a trigger list ourselves.

---

[3] See http://gate.ac.uk
[4] See http://webdocs.cs.ualberta.ca/~lindek/minipar.htm
[5] See http://www.connexor.eu/technology/machinese/machinesesyntax
[6] We used the Penn Treebank tokenizer with some minor modifications (e.g. to not break numbers like *3,000* into separate tokens).
[7] See corpus LDC2006T06 in the LDC catalogue.

Table 1. The comparison of the size of the datasets.

	ACE'05 Train	WikiWars
Documents	593	22
Tokens (Alternate Tokeniser)	322k	121k
Sentences (GATE)	18,252	4,869
Sentences (Connexor)	18,843	4,857
TIMEX2	5,428	2,681

```
[Day,]YYYY/MM/DD [HH:MM:SS] [TMZ]
[Day,]DD/MM/YYYY [HH:MM:SS] [TMZ]
HH:MM[:SS] [AMPM] [TMZ]
HH AMPM [TMZ]
HH o'clock [TMZ]
[Day,] YYYY Month DD [HH:MM:SS] [TMZ]
[Day,] DD/Month[/YYYY]
[Day,] Month/DD[/YYYY]
[Day,] [YYYY/]Month/DD
Month/YYYY
```

Fig. 1. Conventionalised patterns in the Trigger Tagger.

We distinguish three types of triggers: word triggers (e.g. month names), four digit numbers (years), and conventionalised alphanumeric patterns (e.g. *17-07-1964*).

We analysed the corpora used in the experiments to check the frequencies of the words that appear in the extents of the gold standard annotations; based on this, we obtained a set of 166 word triggers. Our analysis also showed that four digit numbers commonly appear as denoting both years (e.g. *1997*) and hours (e.g. *0545*, referring to 5:45am). However, we limit the range to 1900–2019 to be consistent with [2] in this regard.[8]

In Fig. 1 we present the conventionalised date and time patterns recognized by rules; elements in square brackets are optional, and the TMZ stands for a time difference or a time-zone code (e.g. *GMT*). We also allow full and abbreviated names of months and weekdays to appear within the patterns (Month and Day, respectively). The implemented grammar is slightly more complex since we allow for some punctuation and ordering variations, and single digit numbers in some positions.

4.4   Evaluation

Performance is measured in terms of **lenient recognition** (detection of the presence of a TE) and **strict recognition** (determination of the full extent of

---

[8] Note that restricting years in this way damages performance on WikiWars, which also contains bare year references to earlier periods.

the TE). The goal of the trigger extraction process here is to detect enough TEs to test our syntactic recognition method. For this experiment, the absolute values of the lenient and strict results do not matter; it is the difference between them that is important. The only caveat is that if the lenient scores are low, then this suggests that we may not have captured the full variety of triggers in the data, or we may be generating too many false-positive (spurious) annotations. We therefore need a reasonably broad sample of triggers, so that we do not accidentally miss expressions that have interesting syntax just because we have omitted the corresponding trigger.

The lenient and strict results determine the lower and upper bounds, respectively, for the approach based on functional dependencies. The strict results for recognizing triggers on their own allows us to measure the improvement obtained by using a syntactic parser; the lenient results, on the other hand, provide the upper limit of what we can expect to achieve in the experiment (i.e. the score obtained if every detected expression was also correctly recognized).

In Table 2 we present the results obtained with a tagger which recognizes only the triggers, which we refer to as the Trigger Tagger. We consider the three classes of triggers identified above individually and together. As anticipated, we get the best performance when all three types of triggers are used; for both corpora we get very good coverage in detection (0.89 and 0.88 lenient recall) without compromising the precision too much (0.89 and 0.92), resulting in high lenient F-measures of 0.89 and 0.90.

The relatively high strict recall (0.49 and 0.54) tells us that about half of the TEs appearing in our corpora do not have very complex structure; they can be correctly recognized just with simple word triggers and a quite limited set of rules. This fact should be kept in mind when evaluating any fully-featured tagger. Matching just trigger words yields 0.29 and 0.13 strict recall on our data; the large difference here shows that differences among datasets may be significant.

Table 2. The results obtained with different sets of triggers by the Trigger Tagger.

| Trigger Set | ACE 2005 Training | | | | | | WikiWars | | | | | |
| | Strict | | | Lenient | | | Strict | | | Lenient | | |
	P	R	F	P	R	F	P	R	F	P	R	F
Words	0.35	0.29	0.32	0.86	0.71	0.78	0.18	0.13	0.15	0.97	0.72	0.83
Dates	0.75	0.16	0.27	0.94	0.20	0.33	0.94	0.29	0.44	1.00	0.31	0.47
Years	0.17	0.04	0.06	0.96	0.21	0.34	0.34	0.12	0.18	1.00	0.35	0.52
Words+Dates	0.48	0.45	0.46	0.90	0.84	0.87	0.55	0.42	0.48	0.97	0.73	0.83
Words+Years	0.31	0.33	0.32	0.82	0.86	0.84	0.23	0.25	0.24	0.80	0.87	0.84
Dates+Years	0.73	0.20	0.31	0.92	0.25	0.40	0.81	0.41	0.54	1.00	0.50	0.67
Words+Dates+Years	0.49	0.49	0.49	0.89	0.89	0.89	0.56	0.54	0.55	0.92	0.88	0.90

Table 3. The results for extent recognition obtained with a dependency-based tagger using the C&C parser.

| Set-up | ACE 2005 Training | | | | | | WikiWars | | | | | |
| | Strict | | | Lenient | | | Strict | | | Lenient | | |
	P	R	F	P	R	F	P	R	F	P	R	F
1 (Words)	0.56	0.46	0.50	0.86	0.71	0.78	0.69	0.51	0.59	0.97	0.72	0.83
2 (Dates)	0.33	0.07	0.12	0.94	0.20	0.33	0.82	0.25	0.38	1.00	0.31	0.47
3 (Years)	0.23	0.05	0.08	0.96	0.21	0.34	0.27	0.09	0.14	1.00	0.34	0.51
4 (Words+Year)+Dates	0.65	0.65	0.65	0.89	0.89	0.89	0.73	0.68	0.71	0.92	0.87	0.89
5 (Words)+Year+Dates	0.65	0.65	0.65	0.89	0.89	0.89	0.75	0.71	0.73	0.92	0.88	0.90

5   Results

On both corpora the best strict results were obtained using the C&C Parser, and the worst using Minipar. The taggers using the Stanford Parser and Connexor fell in the middle, but the differences here were not large; Connexor was slightly more useful on the ACE corpus, but the Stanford Parser yielded slightly better results on WikiWars. Given space limitations, we only report here the results obtained using the C&C Parser; see Table 3.

We first applied our dependency-based approach to each subset of triggers individually; these are the first three set-ups in Table 3. As expected, the lenient results have not changed at all or only insignificantly compared to recognizing just triggers, as these reflect only the performance for the detection task.[9]

With regard to recognition, the strict F-measure got much higher when using word-triggers, much lower when using conventionalised-pattern-based triggers, and slightly better or worse depending on which dataset we consider for four digit numbers (years).

We note that trigger words on their own yield better strict results on ACE than WikiWars, but after applying the syntactic method, the situation changes: the performance is higher on WikiWars. This means that in ACE there are (proportionally) more expressions which are built just with trigger words, but in WikiWars (where the gain obtained with the method is greater), either there are (proportionally) more expressions headed by word triggers, or the parser performs better; the latter in turn may mean that the sentences are more syntactically well-formed and easier to parse.[10]

Two set-ups, #4 and #5, combine all three sets of triggers. In both set-ups the words are used as the syntactic heads of the expressions, but the date-recognition rules are assumed to detect the full extents of the corresponding TEs (i.e. they

---

[9] Growing the extent may impact the scoring of the detection task if the new extents impact the matching of system and gold standard annotations and, in consequence, the number of detected, missing, or spurious expressions.

[10] The ACE corpus contains a number of documents with automatically transcribed speech, weblogs entries and UseNet discussions; these genres are challenging to parse well.

Table 4. The comparison of recognition results of the dependency-based approach with a pattern-based tagger.

| | ACE 2005 Training | | | | | | WikiWars | | | | | |
| | Strict | | | Lenient | | | Strict | | | Lenient | | |
Tagger	Prec.	Recall	F	Prec.	Recall	F	Prec.	Recall	F	Prec.	Recall	F
DepC&C	0.65	0.65	0.65	0.89	0.89	0.89	0.75	0.71	0.73	0.92	0.88	0.90
DANTE	0.75	0.79	0.77	0.88	0.92	0.90	0.93	0.93	0.93	0.98	0.99	0.99

are not further extended by the syntax-driven method). The difference is in the use of four-digit numbers; in set-up #4 we attempt to grow extents containing these, but in set-up #5 we treat the numbers as complete TEs in themselves. The difference in the results for these two set-ups is, however, insignificant.

Just as when we used the individual subsets of triggers, the absolute results for WikiWars are higher than those for ACE: 0.73 vs 0.65 F-measure. However, we are more interested in the gain obtained using the syntactic method as compared to recognizing just the triggers, since this shows just how much the dependency trees are useful for extent recognition.

Set-up #1 provides gains which are quite different for the two corpora: 0.44 for WikiWars and 0.18 for ACE (F-measure). If we compare the results from set-up #5 with those obtained when annotating the three sets of triggers as TEs, the gains are very similar for the two corpora: 0.18 for WikiWars and 0.16 for ACE (F-measure). The gain for WikiWars is now much smaller because many temporal expressions are now matched by the rules that recognize dates and times in conventionalised formats; on the other hand, these rules make little difference when processing ACE documents.

We note, however, that there is still a big gap between the strict and lenient results: 0.24 on ACE and 0.17 on WikiWars (F-measure). Also, the absolute performance is lower than that which we can get with a pattern-based tagger; in Table 4 we compare the best results of the dependency-based approach with the DANTE tagger [8].

The picture is different if we evaluate the method only on what are called **event-based TEs**; we discuss these cases in the following section.

6 Recognition of Event-Based Expressions

Event-based temporal expressions have complex syntactic structures, as their extent typically contains dependent clauses; consider the following example:

(5) During *the three months between the cease-fire and the French referendum on Algeria*, the OAS unleashed a new terrorist campaign.

For such expressions it seems practically impossible to write a recognition grammar based on matching specific lexical items, parts-of-speech or even syntactic

Table 5. The results of recognition of event-based expressions.

Method	TG-Events						WW-Events					
	Strict			Lenient			Strict			Lenient		
	P	R	F	P	R	F	P	R	F	P	R	F
Word-triggers	0.00	0.00	0.00	1.00	0.76	0.86	0.00	0.00	0.00	0.99	0.84	0.91
Word-triggers*	0.00	0.00	0.00	1.00	1.00	1.00	0.00	0.00	0.00	0.99	1.00	1.00
Word-triggers/C&C	0.84	0.64	0.73	1.00	0.76	0.86	0.71	0.59	0.64	0.99	0.83	0.90
Word-triggers*/C&C	0.84	0.84	0.84	1.00	1.00	1.00	0.69	0.69	0.69	0.99	0.99	0.99
DANTE	0.08	0.08	0.08	0.96	1.00	0.98	0.06	0.06	0.06	0.98	0.91	0.94
TERSEO	0.05	0.04	0.04	1.00	0.88	0.94	0.03	0.02	0.03	0.98	0.86	0.92

chunks. It seems that the only reasonable approach is to use a syntactic parser
to find the extent of these temporal expressions.

To test our dependency-based method we created two additional datasets.
The first one, which we call TG-Events, contains 25 event-based expressions
found in Sect. 4.8 of the TIMEX2 guidelines where this type of TEs is discussed.
The second dataset, WW-Events, is sourced from WikiWars and contains 122
event-based expressions.[11]

Because our datasets are quite small we added three more triggers (*time*,
duration and *season*) to ensure maximum detection coverage; the results obtained
with the extended set of triggers are marked in Table 5 with the asterisk (*).

When applying the syntactic method to the word triggers we experimented
with the same four parsers as before. Also this time we obtained the best recognition results with C&C, and because of the space limitations we present only
the results attained with this parser. Strict F-measure was 0.84 and 0.69 for
TG-Events dataset and WW-Events, respectively. Although we can not compare these values to those reported earlier for full ACE and WikiWars corpora,
we note that the absolute values are not higher. However, we draw attention
to the difference between the results for using only the triggers and the results
obtained when using the syntax-based approach. As we now process syntactically complex expressions, the triggers on their own do not constitute any of the
TEs.

In order to make the evaluation more meaningful, we compare the results to
those of the DANTE system, which, as we learnt from the previous experiments,
has quite decent recognition performance and for the whole ACE and WikiWars

---

[11] In the preparation of the WW-Events dataset we did not exactly follow the semantic
properties of the definition of event-based expressions: strictly-speaking these are
only those expressions which in order to be interpreted require the time of the event
which they mention. It really depends on the context whether the eventually of
sightseeing in *four days of sightseeing* is discriminative of the period's temporal
location or not. What we care about in this experiment are the expressions with
syntactically complex extents and to simplify things we will just refer to all of them
as event-based.

corpora performed significantly better than the syntax-based approach. Here, DANTE scored only 0.08 in strict F-measure for TG-Events and 0.06 for the expressions found in WW-Events. This confirms what we hypothesized at the beginning: a rule-based approach is not suited to recognition of event-based expressions. To verify this even further, we also used TERSEO[12] [9], another mature rule-based system, and its performance on these datasets turned out to be very close to the performance of DANTE.

TERSEO recognized only three temporal expressions; they had quite simple structure that can be represented with a single pattern: Det Trigger of (JJ | Det) NN. DANTE recognized seven expressions (however none of those recognized by TERSEO); these were: *the ceasefire period, the monsoon season, the duration of the war* (three occurrences), *the Buddha's birthday*, and *a prolonged period of appeasement*. As we can see, these expressions are also syntactically quite simple. The syntax-based method, on the other hand, successfully recognized the extent of the expression in Example (5) and the extents of the expressions in the following sentences:

(6) a. He argued that with *two months of good weather remaining until the onset of the monsoon*, it would be irresponsible to not take advantage of the situation.
   b. The rate of US combat deaths in Baghdad nearly doubled in *the first seven weeks of the "surge" in security activity*.
   c. The Allies withstood *two full days of Persian attacks, including those by the elite Persian Immortals*.
   d. *The era of Porfirio Daz's government from 1876–1910* has become known as the Porfiriato.

These examples are some of those with the longest and most complex structure we found among the correctly processed in this dataset.

7   Error Analysis

7.1   Sentence Splitting and Tokenisation

We found that in some cases, e.g. an email presenting a trip itinerary where the text was not organized into sentences, sentence splitting negatively impacted extent recognition.

The tokenisation carried out by parsers sometimes resulted in combining two or more tokens into a single syntactic node. This happens, for example, with date ranges like *12–15 September*, where the two hyphen-separated numbers are treated as a single token, resulting in an extent that does not match the gold standard annotations.

---

[12] We used the web demo of the tagger at http://gplsi.dlsi.ua.es/~stela/TERSEO.

7.2 Parsing Errors

A general problem is the attachment of prepositional phrases and dependent clauses, as shown in Example (7); here, the correct extents are marked with italics and the extents found by the tagger are underlined.

(7) The British Army endured *the bloodiest day in its history*, suffering 57,470 casualties including . . .

In other cases the parses are broken and the extents of the temporal expressions include extra tokens from a phrase following the expression:

(8) . . . after stalling for *a day* against the main resistance line to which the enemy had withdrawn.

These problems might be overcome by re-training the parsers on more similar textual data.

7.3 Heads in Dependencies

There is not always a consensus view on what the role of a given token in a dependency relation should be. The differences between parsers in this regard sometime resulted in a different tree than was expected; in particular, the trigger was not always determined to be the head of a relation.

In some cases, for example in the case of conjunctions, a node can occur as a child in two dependencies, with the result that the output is a directed graph rather than a tree. In an expression like *the spring and early summer of 1943*, this has the consequence that both triggers *spring* and *summer* are extended to cover the entire expression.

7.4 Triggers

Recognizing dates and years as 'fully-extended' TEs (i.e. immune from further extension using the dependency-based approach) also contributed to a number of errors, resulting in a failure to recognize references to decades (*the 1950s*) and modified dates (*early 1950*).[13]

7.5 Heads of Temporal Expressions

It turns out that the assumption that the trigger is the syntactic head of the TE that contains it does not always hold. For example, the head of the expression *the middle of August* is *middle* rather than *August*. The source of this problem

---

[13] However, as we discussed earlier, applying the syntax-based method to these triggers did not improve the overall results, because while some expressions obtain the correct extents, other are damaged by including tokens from outside the correct extent because of parsing errors.

lies in an inconsistency in the TIMEX2 guidelines: by their definition of a TE, the expression consists of a trigger and its syntactic pre- and postmodifiers. But in order to capture semantic subtleties (e.g. that only a part of a month is being referred to), the extent is permitted to grow to include additional tokens beyond the syntactic modifiers of the trigger. In WikiWars this affected 14 % of all incorrectly recognized expressions.

A similar issue concerns expressions like *the 28th of that month*, where the head is *28th* rather than *month*; however, we did not use ordinal numbers as triggers, and so expressions with this structure were only partially recognized.

8   Conclusions and Future Work

We have presented a new approach to recognising the extent of temporal expressions in text: given the trigger as a seed, we grow the extent outwards by including all syntactic nodes found in the dependency tree with the trigger as root.

We experimented with four dependency parsers (Minipar, Stanford, C&C and Connexor) using two datasets (the ACE 2005 Training corpus and WikiWars). The best results were achieved using the C&C Parser. The results demonstrate that the method generally works as anticipated. The gap between the performance of the method and the upper bound is, however, significant: 0.24 for the ACE corpus and 0.17 for WikiWars. Our error analysis reveals that in most cases the problem lies in an incorrect syntactic analysis being provided by the parser. We also found that there are TEs where the trigger is not the syntactic head. On WikiWars, this issue is implicated in about 14 % of the incorrectly recognized expressions. The source of this problem lies, however, in an inconsistency in the TIMEX2 guidelines.

The method is most useful for the recognition of event-based TEs; these are expressions with complex syntax which cannot be practically recognized by rule-based grammars using lexical and shallow syntactic information such as POS tags or chunking. On a dataset of 122 event-based TEs drawn from WikiWars, the method achieved a strict F-measure of 0.69, significantly outperforming two rule-based systems which scored 0.03 and 0.06.

References

1. Ferro, L., Gerber, L., Mani, I., Sundheim, B., Wilson, G.: TIDES 2005 Standard for the Annotation of Temporal Expressions. Technical report, MITRE (2005)
2. Ahn, D., Adafre, S.F., de Rijke, M.: Extracting temporal information from open domain text: a comparative exploration. In: Proceedings of the 5th Dutch-Belgian Information Retrieval Workshop, Delft, The Netherlands, March 2005
3. Hacioglu, K., Chen, Y., Douglas, B.: Automatic time expression labeling for English and Chinese text. In: Gelbukh, A. (ed.) CICLing 2005. LNCS, vol. 3406, pp. 548–559. Springer, Heidelberg (2005)
4. Ahn, D., van Rantwijk, J., de Rijke, M.: A cascaded machine learning approach to interpreting temporal expressions. In: Proceedings of HLT: The Annual Conference of the North American Chapter of the ACL, Rochester, NY, USA (2007)

5. de Marneffe, M.C., MacCartney, B., Manning, C.D.: Generating typed dependency parses from phrase structure parses. In: Proceedings of the IEEE/ACL 2006 Workshop on Spoken Language Technology (2006)

6. Clark, S., Curran, J.R.: Wide-coverage efficient statistical parsing with CCG and log-linear models. Comput. Linguist. **33**(4), 493–552 (2007)

7. Mazur, P., Dale, R.: WikiWars: a new corpus for research on temporal expressions. In: Proceedings of the Conference on Empirical Methods in NLP, pp. 913–922 (2010)

8. Mazur, P., Dale, R.: The DANTE temporal expression Tagger. In: Vetulani, Z. (ed.) Proceedings of the 3rd Language and Technology Conference, Poznan, Poland (2007)

9. Saquete, E.: Temporal expression recognition and resolution applied to event ordering. Ph.D. thesis, Departamento de Lenguages y Sistemas Informaticos, Univ. de Alicante (2005)

Pattern Mining for Named Entity Recognition

Damien Nouvel(✉), Jean-Yves Antoine, and Nathalie Friburger

Laboratoire d'Informatique, Université François Rabelais Tours,
3, Place Jean Jaures, 41000 Blois, France
{damien.nouvel,jean-yves.antoine,nathalie.friburger}@univ-tours.fr

Abstract. Many evaluation campaigns have shown that knowledge-based and data-driven approaches remain equally competitive for Named Entity Recognition. Our research team has developed CasEN, a symbolic system based on finite state transducers, which achieved promising results during the Ester2 French-speaking evaluation campaign. Despite these encouraging results, manually extending the coverage of such a hand-crafted system is a difficult task. In this paper, we present a novel approach based on pattern mining for NER and to supplement our system's knowledge base. The system, mXS, exhaustively searches for hierarchical sequential patterns, that aim at detecting Named Entity boundaries. We assess their efficiency by using such patterns in a standalone mode and in combination with our existing system.

1 Introduction

Named Entity Recognition (NER) is an information extraction task that aims at extracting and categorizing specific entities (proper names or dedicated linguistic units as time expressions, amounts, etc.) in texts. These texts can be produced in diverse conditions. In particular, they may correspond to either electronic written documents [1] or more recently speech transcripts provided by a human expert or an automatic speech recognition (ASR) system [2]. The recognized entities may later be used by higher-level tasks for different purposes such as Information Retrieval or Open-Domain Question-Answering [3]. While NER is often considered as quite a simple task, there is still room for improvement when it is confronted to difficult contexts. For instance, NER systems may have to cope with noisy data such as speech recognition errors or speech disfluencies. In addition, NER is no more circumscribed to proper names, but may also involve common nouns (e.g., "the judge") or complex multi-word expressions with embedded NEs (e.g. "the Computer Science Department of the New York University"). These complementary needs for robust and detailed processing explain that knowledge-based and data-driven approaches remain equally competitive on NER tasks as shown by many evaluation campaigns. For instance, the French-speaking Ester2 and Etape evaluation campaigns on radio broadcasts [2] has shown that knowledge-based approaches outperformed data-driven ones on manual transcriptions.

© Springer International Publishing Switzerland 2014
Z. Vetulani and J. Mariani (Eds.): LTC 2011, LNAI 8387, pp. 226–237, 2014.
DOI: 10.1007/978-3-319-08958-4_19

However, despite their advantageous precision, symbolic systems need significant efforts when confronted to new NE types or when the system has to be adapted to diverse modalities (written vs oral transcripts). In this paper, we present an original approach, based on the adaptation of pattern mining techniques as a machine learning process (automatic training on corpora to reach a large coverage), while remaining in the framework of symbolic resources (extraction of intelligible rules of NE recognition). The performances of the resulting system (mXs) on the Etape French-speaking evaluation campaign shows that this novel approach bears comparison with standard machine learning techniques (CRFs). Besides, coupling this system with CasEN [4], our knowledge-based system, provides us with promising results.

In Sect. 2 we present and compare approaches for NER. Sections 3 and 4, we describe how lexico-syntactic patterns may be extracted from annotated corpora and used as a standalone system. Finally, Sects. 5 and 6 reports experimental results on French oral corpora.

2   Related Work

In the 90's and until now, several symbolic systems have been designed that, often, make intensive use of regular expressions formalism to describe NEs. Those systems often combine external and internal evidences [5], as patterns describing contextual clues and lists of proper names by NE categories. Those systems achieve high accuracy, but, as stated by [6], because they depend on the hand-crafted definition of lexical ressources and detection rules, their coverage remains an issue.

Machine learning introduced new approaches to address NER. The problem is then stated as categorizing words that belong to a NE, taking into account various clues (features) in a model that is automatically parametrized by leveraging statistics from a *training corpus*. Among these methods, some only focus on the current word under examination (maximum entropy, SVM) [7], while others also evaluate stochastic dependencies (HMM, CRF) [8]. Most of the time, these approaches output the most probable sequence of labels for a given sentence. This is generally known as the "labeling problem", applied to NER.

Many approaches [9] rely on pre-processing steps that provide additional information about data, often Part-Of-speech (POS) tagging and proper names lists, to determine how to automatically tag a text, resulting in an annotated text. Some make use of data mining techniques [10,11], but we are not aware of work that goes beyond the step of extracting patterns for NER: no model has emerged for using those patterns to recognize NEs.

In this paper, we propose a system that adapts text mining techniques to the NER problem. The benefits of text mining techniques are twofold. On the one hand, pattern mining techniques are data driven and may be combined with standard machine learning approaches. On the other hand, pattern mining allows to extract NER detection rules (e.g. transducers) which are intelligible for a human expert and can be used by a symbolic system. To the best of our knowledge, this way of combining symbolic and machine learning approaches is completely original in the framework of NER.

Besides, our pattern mining system, mXS, focuses on boundaries of NEs, as *beginning or ending markers* that we would like to be inserted at correct positions. To this end, we extract patterns [12,13] that are correlated to those markers. Those patterns, casted as "annotation rules", are not constrained to necessarily recognize both boundaries of NEs. Basically, the system detects each boundary of NEs separately. This strategy is expected to present a more robust behaviour on noisy data such as ASR recognition errors or speech disfluencies. They are evaluated as a standalone system or coupled with our existing knowledge-based system.

3   Mining Hierarchical and Sequential Patterns

3.1   Extracting Patterns

We use data mining techniques to process natural language. In this context, what is detected as a sentence will be considered as a sequence of items, precluding the extraction of patterns across sentences. Two alphabets are defined: $\mathcal{W}$, words from natural language, and $\mathcal{M}$ as *markers*, e.g. the tags delimiting NE categories (e.g. person, location, amount). The annotated corpus $\mathcal{D}$ is a multiset of sequences based on items from $\mathcal{W} \cup \mathcal{M}$. Table 1 exemplifies this with $\mathcal{W} = \{\texttt{The}, \texttt{president}, \texttt{Obama}, \dots\}$ and $\mathcal{M} = \{\texttt{<pers>}, \texttt{</pers>}, \texttt{<loc>}, \texttt{</loc>}, \texttt{<time>}, \dots, \texttt{<org>}, \dots\}$.

Table 1. Sentences from an annotated corpus

$\mathcal{D}$	
Sent.	Patterns from $\mathcal{L}_I$
s_1	The american <pers> president Barack Obama </pers> has arrived in <loc> Moscou </loc>.
s_2	There he has seen the former <pers> chancelor Michelle Bachelet </pers>.
s_3	The <pers> president Dimitri Medvedev </pers> was not present on the beautiful <loc> square Vladimir Lenine </loc>.

Like most systems, the mining process relies as a first step on linguistic analysis of input data. Those preprocessing steps extend the language $\mathcal{W}$ to $\mathcal{W}^*$ by lemmatizing, applying a Part-Of-Speech (POS) tagger and recognizing expressions from lexical resources provided by the ProlexBase [14] database (890 K entries). Those additional elements are inserted as a hierarchical representation of tokens: each may gradually be generalized to its lemma, POS or semantic type. For instance in Table 1, the pattern language contains items

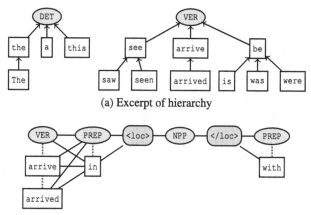

(a) Excerpt of hierarchy

(b) Possible paths to mine patterns for the example sentence
"arrived in <loc> Moscou </loc>"

Fig. 1. POS hierarchy and example of tagged sentence

{arrive, see, VER, JJ, DET, NN, NPP ...}. The POS tagger distinguishes common nouns (NN) from proper names (NPP). Note that we only keep semantic information for proper names, to avoid extracting patterns that would contain instances of proper names. Figure 1 illustrates how POS categories are organized as a hierarchy and what patterns may be mined through an example of a sequence.

We exhaustively extract contiguous patterns over this language. For instance, in Fig. 1, patterns such as 'VER in <loc> NPP' or 'NPP </loc> with' are extracted. The hierarchy and the properties of sequential patterns allow to partially order them. This use of the hierarchy as a modular description of language enables fine-grained generalizations for items inside patterns: extracting accurate patterns relies both on the data that is mined and on specifying a relevant hierarchy for NER.

3.2 Filtering Patterns as Annotation Rules

We mine a large annotated corpus to find generalized patterns that co-occur with NE markers. As usual in data mining, we set thresholds during extraction based on two interestingness measures: support and confidence. The *support* of a pattern P is its number of occurrences in $\mathcal{D}$, denoted by $supp(P, \mathcal{D})$. The greater the support of P, the more general the pattern P. To estimate empirically how much P is accurate to detect markers, we calculate its *confidence*. A function $suppNoMark(P)$ returns the support of P when markers are omitted both in the rule and in the data. Thus, the confidence of P is:

$$conf(P, \mathcal{D}) = \frac{supp(P, \mathcal{D})}{suppNoMark(P, \mathcal{D})} \qquad (1)$$

As we are only interested in patterns correlated with NE markers, we extract patterns containing at least one marker as rules. For instance, consider the rule

$R =$ 'the JJ <pers> NN NPP' in Table 1. Its support is 2 (sentences s_1 and s_2). But its support without considering markers is 3, since sentence s_3 matches the rule when markers (<pers> in rule and <loc> in "the beautiful <loc> square Vladimir") are omitted. Thus the confidence of R is only 2/3.

The collection of transduction rules exceeding minimal support and confidence thresholds is used as a knowledge-base. In practice, the number of discovered rules remains very large (especially when minimal support threshold is low). Thus, we decide to filter-out the redundant rules. We consider two rules to be redundant if they are related by a generalization relation and if they have same support: they cover same sequences in data. Over a set of redundant rules, we only select the most specific ones, that we will actually use for NER. Those are named "Annotation Rules".

4   NER Using Annotation Rules

We now aim at determining when transduction rules should insert markers in texts. Using rules as features, we are able estimate probabilities for marker's presence as a trained model, as we will present in Sect. 4.1. The rules and the model are provided to a simple beam search algorithm described in Sect. 4.2 to actually annotate texts.

4.1   Estimating Likelihood of Annotated Sentences

As previously mentioned, instead of assigning a category to words (or tokens), our annotation rules insert markers at diverse positions in sentences. At a given position of a sentence, a decision should choose between adding any number of beginning or ending markers for NE categories (e.g. <pers>, </pers>, <loc>, etc.) or not to do so, what we denote by inserting a "void marker" ($\emptyset$).

We train as many binary classifiers as distinct markers to estimate local probabilities for each individual markers. The probability of the presence of a single marker $m \in \mathcal{M}$ at a given position i is a random variable conditioned by the set of rules that have been triggered at current position: $P(m \in M_i | R_1, R_2 \cdots R_k)$ that we note $P(m \in M_i)$. Combining those separate probabilities allows a direct computation for the probability of having multiple markers, as a multilabel problem:

$$P(M_i = \{m_1, m_2\}) = \prod_{m \in \{m_1, m_2\}} P(m \in M_i) \prod_{m \in \mathcal{M} - \{m_1, m_2\}} (1 - P(m \in M_i))$$

(2)

Finally, we use those local probabilities of the sequences[1] of markers (including the void marker $\emptyset$) to compute the likelihood of any annotation as n independent

---

[1] Each set of markers is mapped to a predetermined number of corresponding markers sequences, e.g. $P(\{m_1, m_2\}) = P(< m_1, m_2 >) = P(< m_2, m_1 >) = P(< m_1, m_2, m_1 >)$.

decisions over a sentence:

$$P(M_1, M_2 \cdots M_n) = \prod_{i=1 \cdots n} P(M_i) \tag{3}$$

Indeed, what is considered as the most likely annotation within possible ones has to maximize that measure.

4.2 Decoding Step

The probability model may lead to an invalid sequence of markers according to the considered annotation scheme. The decoding algorithm must therefore consider only the valid proposals of the model. Depending on the dataset, we'll expect to be able to generate flat (no embeddings) or structured xml-like (Etape) annotations. Those constraints are implemented into the sequential algorithm, as a simple grammar to be checked while decoding. The latter uses a beam search approach[2], where adding a marker is considered as making a transition: for instance, inserting a <loc> marker at the beginning of a sentence moves from a "not inside any NE" state to a "in loc" state.

The algorithm starts from the beginning of a sequence and, for any position, generates new annotation hypothesis at this point by taking into account probabilities, possible marker sequences and annotation scheme constraints. Annotation hypothesis are then ordered and selected depending on their likelihood. Note that only the best hypothesis is kept for any given state, and that the number of states may be finite (flat annotation schemes) or infinite (when embeddings are allowed without depth restrictions). At the end of the sentence, the resulting annotation is the hypothesis that ends up with a "not inside any NE" state.

5   Ester2 and Etape French Evaluation Campaigns

Our system, mXs, has initially been developed for the Ester2 campaign. Subsections 5.2 and 5.3 present detailed experimental results conducted on this corpus. They give a better insight of the system behaviour and assess the influence of the support and confidence thresholds. Then, Sect. 5.4 presents the official performances during the Etape evaluation campaign, which was a follow up of Ester2.

5.1   Data: French Radio Transcripts

Our system participated to the Ester2 and Etape evaluation campaigns, which involved the French-speaking research community on the problematic of NER on radio transcripts. This task is much more challenging on this kind of noisy data, due to speech disfluencies, speech recognition repairs and absence of sentence boundaries. This accordingly lowers performance of POS tagging and, at a higher level, requires a much more robust approach to find entities.

---

[2] It limits the search space by considering at any position N most probable solutions.

Table 2. Characteristics of Ester2 and Etape corpora

Corpus	Tokens	Sentences	NEs
Ester2-dev	73 386	2 491	5 326
Ester2-held	48 143	1 683	3 074
Ester2-corr	40 167	1 300	2 798
Total	128 477	4 283	8 670
Etape-train	355 975	14 989	46 259
Etape-dev	115 530	5 724	14 112
Etape-test	123 221	6 770	13 055
Total	594 726	27 483	73 426

The French Ester2 and Etape evaluation campaigns included NER on transcribed texts [2]. The competing systems had to recognize persons, locations, organizations, products, amounts, time and positions. Entities were manually annotated for evaluation purposes. As reported by [15], the Ester2 reference corpus contains many annotation inconsistencies. This is why we have decided to re-annotate consistently one half of the corpus. This gold corpus will be named Ester2-corr while the second part was held out (Ester2-held). Such inconsistencies were avoided in the Etape corpus. Its annotation scheme is an extended version of Ester2's: evaluation is fine-grained and substructures of NEs are annotated as "components" [16]. Quantitative characteristics of those corpora are presented in Table 2.

5.2 Annotation Rules Extraction for Ester2

Corpora Ester2-dev and Ester2-held are merged to extract patterns. We used TreeTagger [17] for robustly tokenizing, POS-tagging and lemmatizing words (on French written texts, this tool provides high accuracy, more than 90 % but, as far as we know, no evaluation has been made over oral transcriptions). The mining task requires many optimizations [13] and we used a level-wise algorithm [18] which leverages the generalization over patterns to mine frequent ones. Table 3 reports the number of rules, the number of non-redundant rules and the gain (i.e., the ratio between the number of rules and that of non-redundant ones). This elimination of redundant rules leads to a very significant reduction without loss of information from train corpus, what is very important for using this collection as a knowledge-base.

5.3 mXS Performance for Ester2

To assess efficiency of patterns for NER, we use Ester2-dev and Ester2-held merged to extract patterns and learn model, Ester2-corr to evaluate accuracy of the predicted markers. We train as many binary classifiers as necessary, using

Table 3. Extraction over Ester2 corpus at support and confidence thresholds

Sup.	Conf.	Rules	Rules	Gain
10	.5	207 544	7 172	**29**
5	.5	3 279 248	17 739	**185**
3	.3	85 187 894	46 019	**1851**

extracted rules as features to feed the logistic regression algorithm of SciKit toolkit [19][3]. In order to retrieve a set of rules that covers as much as possible actual markers in texts, we hereby extract rules at low support (3) and confidence (0.3) thresholds. With this exhaustive set of rules, only 52 markers out of 5196 (1 %) are undetectable by the model because no rules are triggered at the considered position.

Table 4 presents global score Slot Error Rate (SER) [20] for diverse support and confidence thresholds. Those are computed by counting typed errors: insertions, deletions, types, extents. Results show that, for any support threshold, the model obtains better results at low confidence: even very generic (and thus less confident) rules are to be included as potentially relevant features. Globaly, using those rules as a standalone system remains unsufficient compared to state-of-the-art, but opens up great possibilities for coupling.

Table 4. Detailed results

Support	Confidence	Insert	Delete	Type	Extent	SER
3	.3	18	**632**	102	287	**38.34**
3	.5	12	751	106	255	40.86
3	.7	13	944	**53**	257	48.60
5	.3	20	641	112	285	39.10
5	.5	10	752	108	271	41.57
5	.7	10	967	60	256	49.06
10	.3	18	693	114	292	40.77
10	.5	12	822	100	263	44.78
10	.7	**9**	1050	55	**238**	52.15

5.4   mXS Performance for Etape

The Etape evaluation campaign extends Ester2 by considering TV broadcasts (including debates) and adding both fine grained and recursivity: NER is more

---

[3] With regularization parameter C = 4.

Table 5. Global performances of participants for Etape

Participant	SER				Prec.	Rec.	F-score
	All	Entities	Comp.	Prim.			
Rules	85.5	80.4	88.2	74.6	36.8	16.5	22.8
Rules	156.0	178.1	143.9	172.3	17.3	28.0	21.4
CRF-bin	36.4	40.4	32.3	39.5	**85.3**	63.2	72.6
Rules	49.9	58.0	43.1	55.0	63.0	64.6	63.8
CRF+PCFG	44.6	39.0	49.3	36.2	66.1	53.6	59.2
CRF+PCFG	37.2	42.3	**32.0**	40.6	78.9	65.5	71.6
CRF	62.4	38.4	78.6	36.4	54.1	34.7	42.3
Rules	39.0	41.8	36.0	37.7	72.0	67.9	69.9
CasEN	**35.2**	**37.6**	34.1	**35.1**	74.2	**73.7**	**73.9**
mXS	37.9	39.2	34.1	36.8	77.6	65.1	70.8
Hybrid	51.3	54.7	45.9	52.7	76.8	49.6	60.3

difficult and requires robust approaches. Besides, the systems are now expected to recognize "components" inside NEs [16], e.g. first names and last names for persons, day, month and year for dates, etc. As reported in Table 5, mXS is ranked 4th after one knowledge-based and two data-driven systems. Results show that the former have better performance for entities, while the latter are more accurate for components. Despite being a data-driven system, mXS exhibits a behaviour similar to knowledge-based ones.

The detailed results by NE types of Table 6 indicates that our system obtains good results for product category, which is the most difficult one. Conversely,

Table 6. f-score of participants per primary NE type

Participant	Loc	Org	Pers	Amo.	Time	Prod	Func
Rules	59.6	29.2	64.4	18.2	17.0	24.3	10.0
Rules	21.4	38.9	51.2	8.8	52.0	39.2	36.9
CRF-bin	73.3	60.1	85.9	**68.7**	63.0	51.5	59.4
Rules	66.7	47.1	69.3	46.7	65.4	50.6	48.3
CRF+PCFG	74.1	61.0	83.3	66.8	64.2	54.3	61.5
CRF+PCFG	78.6	58.5	81.1	49.9	62.7	58.0	62.5
CRF	79.7	54.8	83.4	67.0	70.1	46.3	55.5
Rules	75.7	58.1	82.1	61.5	68.7	**62.5**	63.5
CasEN	**82.0**	**65.6**	**86.5**	44.0	**79.7**	57.0	**70.4**
mXS	81.4	58.4	79.9	60.3	65.1	**62.5**	67.2
Hybrid	71.2	44.1	77.3	51.7	11.6	44.3	52.8

it seems less efficient for recognizing organizations, which are known to be very ambiguous [12]. This points out that pattern mining is accurate for detecting new NE types, but lacks fine-tuning for more traditional ones.

6   Coupling mXS with the CasEN Symbolic System

We aim at improving performances of the existing system, CasEN, with the extracted patterns. Our symbolic system is precise, but lacks coverage because it would have to describe all regular expressions that may constitute a NE. Our idea is that automatically extracted patterns may supplement the symbolic system. We test this coupling by making CasEN's output a feature provided to mXS's input.

Table 7 reports the initial symbolic system's results, the differences of errors by NE categories and the resulting coupled system's performance. The symbolic system alone outperforms our standalone system using rules (28 vs 38 SER). By coupling systems, we observe a significant improvement of the symbolic system's output. The insertion of a small amount (2) of false-positive (Ins. total) is the counterpart for the correction of 26 type errors made by the symbolic system. This mainly concern amounts and the balancing between location and organizations (which are known to be very amibiguous).

Table 7. Error differences on CasEN with extracted rules

	Ins.	Del.	Typ.	Ext.	SER
Symbolic	45	343	165	257	28.7
Amount	−1	+15	−25	−19	37.6
Fonc	+2	+19	−1	−2	41.4
Loc	−9	+8	+73	+22	26.7
Org	+5	−27	−78	+49	41.5
Pers	0	−4	+8	+26	19.4
Prod	0	+2	−2	2	85.2
Time	+5	−11	−1	−74	18.3
Total	+2	+2	−26	0	−1.3
Coupled	47	345	139	257	27.8

We also isolated and manually examined rules that were responsible for the decrease of errors (coverage). Most of these rules are short and generalized rules, and quite frequently inserting only one marker (for instance 'from <pers> NPP NPP' or 'to <loc> NPP'). Interestingly, two time expressions have been found thanks to the separate detection of the beginning and the ending markers using local clues: 'for <time>' and 'years </time>' (recognizing "for a few years" for instance). How those shallow rules may be taken into account by the knowledge base of the symbolic system remains to be investigated.

Due to lack of space, we do not report other configurations and coupling strategies that has been successfully experimented, those are reported in [21]. They achieve performances close to state-of-the-art systems when correctly set up. Our latest experiences that hybridates mXS and CasEN for Etape obtains 32.9 SER (compared with the performance of the best system, CasEN: 35.2). Generally, our experiments suggest that our system is efficient for combining other systems outputs, we plan to conduct more experimentation on this topic in future.

7   Conclusion

In this paper, we reported experimentations on the use of pattern mining techniques to automatically enrich a knowledge-based NER system. We implemented a prototype which extracts patterns correlated to NE markers. The system exhaustively looks for annotation rules from a training corpus and filters out those of interest. During the mining process, the text is represented as a sequence of items, which may be generalized using a hierarchy through POS categories, and where the beginning or ending markers of NEs may be separately mined.

The quality of patterns and their potential to recognize entites has been assessed and allowed us to state which are the most efficient and what markers categories remain to be improved. These experiments also investigated the idea of separately evaluating the probability to begin or end an entity, a beam search being afterwards responsible for finding the most likely and valid annotation. The resulting system was used coupled with a symbolic system, showing significant improvement of the performance. This work provides us with some interesting directions to improve a symbolic NER system, including in its foundations.

References

1. Marsh, E., Perzanowski, D.: Muc-7 evaluation of ie technology: overview of results. In: Proceedings of the 7th Message Understanding Conference (MUC-7) (1998)
2. Galliano, S., Gravier, G., Chaubard, L.: The ester 2 evaluation campaign for the rich transcription of French radio broadcasts. In: 10th Conference of the International Speech Communication Association (INTERSPEECH'2009) (2009)
3. Voorhees, E.M., Harman, D.: International Speech Communication Association (INTERSPEECH'09) (2009)
4. Friburger, N., Maurel, D.: Finite-state transducer cascades to extract named entities in texts. Theor. Comput. Sci. (TCS) **313**, 93–104 (2004)
5. McDonald, D.D.: Internal and external evidence in the identification and semantic categorization of proper names. In: Boguraev, B., Pustejovsky, J. (eds.) Corpus Processing for Lexical Acquisition, pp. 21–39. MIT Press, Cambridge (1996)
6. Mikheev, A., Moens, M., Grover, C.: Named entity recognition without gazetteers. In: 9th Conference of the European Chapter of the Association for Computational Linguistics (EACL'1999) (1999)
7. Borthwick, A., Sterling, J., Agichtein, E., Grishman, R.: Exploiting diverse knowledge sources via maximum entropy in named entity recognition. In: 6th Workshop on Very Large Corpora (WVLC'1998) (1998)

8. McCallum, A., Li, W.: Early results for named entity recognition with conditional random fields, feature induction and web-enhanced lexicons. In: 13th Conference on Computational Natural Language Learning (CONLL'2003) (2003)
9. Nadeau, D., Sekine, S.: A survey of named entity recognition and classification. Linguisticae Investigationes **30**, 3–26 (2007)
10. Freitag, D., Kushmerick, N.: Boosted wrapper induction. In: European Conference on Artificial Intelligence (ECAI'00) - Workshop on Machine Learning for Information Extraction, Berlin, Germany (2000)
11. Etzioni, O., Cafarella, M., Downey, D., Popescu, A.M., Shaked, T., Soderland, S., Weld, D.S., Yates, A.: Unsupervised named-entity extraction from the web: an experimental study. Artif. Intell. **165**, 91–134 (2005)
12. Nouvel, D., Antoine, J.Y., Friburger, N., Soulet, A.: Recognizing named entities using automatically extracted transduction rules. In: Language and Technology Conference (LTC'11) (2011)
13. Nouvel, D.: Reconnaissance des entités nommées par exploration de régles d'annotation. Ph.D. thesis (2012)
14. Bouchou, B., Maurel, D.: Prolexbase et lmf : vers un standard pour les ressources lexicales sur les noms propres. Traitement Automatique des Langues (TAL) **49**, 61–88 (2008)
15. Nouvel, D., Antoine, J.Y., Friburger, N., Maurel, D.: An analysis of the performances of the casen named entities recognition system in the ester2 evaluation campaign. In: 7th International Language Resources and Evaluation (LREC'2010) (2010)
16. Galibert, O., Rosset, S., Grouin, C., Zweigenbaum, P., Quintard, L.: Structured and extended named entity evaluation in automatic speech transcriptions. In: International Joint Conference on Natural Language Processing (IJCNLP'11) (2011)
17. Schmid, H.: Probabilistic part-of-speech tagging using decision trees. In: 2nd International Conference on New Methods in Language Processing (NEMLP'1994) (1994)
18. Mannila, H., Toivonen, H., Verkamo, A.I.: Discovery of frequent episodes in event sequences. In: Data Mining and Knowledge Discovery (DMKD). vol. 1, pp. 259–289 (1997)
19. Pedregosa, F., Varoquaux, G., Gramfort, A., Michel, V., Thirion, B., Grisel, O., Blondel, M., Prettenhofer, P., Weiss, R., Dubourg, V., Vanderplas, J., Passos, A., Cournapeau, D., Brucher, M., Perrot, M., Duchesnay, E.: Scikit-learn machine learning in python. J. Mach. Learn. Res. **12**, 2825–2830 (2011)
20. Makhoul, J., Kubala, F., Schwartz, R., Weischedel, R.: Performance measures for information extraction. In: DARPA Broadcast News Workshop, pp. 249–252 (1994)
21. Nouvel, D., Antoine, J.Y., Friburger, N., Soulet, A.: Coupling knowledge-based and data-driven systems for named entity recognition. In: Innovative Hybrid Approaches to the Processing of Textual Data (HYBRID'12, EACL Workshop) (2012)

Lexical Bundles in Swedish Secondary School Textbooks

Judy Ribeck[✉] and Lars Borin

Språkbanken, Department of Swedish, University of Gothenburg,
Gothenburg, Sweden
{judy.ribeck,lars.borin}@gu.se

Abstract. The present paper describes the process of identifying *lexical bundles*, i.e., frequently recurring word sequences such as *by means of* and *in the end of*, in secondary school history and physics textbooks. In its determination of finding *genuine* lexical bundles, i.e. the word boundaries between lexical bundles and surrounding arbitrary words, it proposes a new approach to come to terms with the problem of extracting overlapping bundles of different lengths. The results of the structural classification indicate that history uses more NP/PP-based and less dependent-clause-based bundles than physics. The comparative analysis manages to restrict this difference to the referential function. History almost only refers to phrases, i.e. within clauses, while physics much more tends to make references across clauses. The article also includes a report on an extension of the study, ongoing work where the automatic identification of multi-word expressions in general is in focus.

Keywords: Lexical bundles · Multi-word expressions · MWE · School language · Textbook language

1 Introduction

This paper describes lexical bundles in Swedish secondary school history and physics textbooks. As far as we know, it is the first time a subject-contrastive perspective has been taken on this problem. It is also the first account of lexical bundles in a Swedish corpus. It should be regarded as an explorative pilot study aiming to find out to what extent lexical bundles are to be found in the texts the students have to read and if there are any structural or functional differences in the way they are used in the natural and social sciences. The incentive for conducting the study is twofold: to evaluate what extraction of lexical bundles can bring into the quest for automatic identification of multi-word expressions at large, as well as the awareness of the great importance language has for learning.

The research reported here was supported in part by the Swedish Research Council (through the project *Swedish FrameNet++*, VR dnr 2010–6013), and by the University of Gothenburg (through its support of the Centre for Language Technology and Språkbanken/the Swedish Language Bank).

© Springer International Publishing Switzerland 2014
Z. Vetulani and J. Mariani (Eds.): LTC 2011, LNAI 8387, pp. 238–249, 2014.
DOI: 10.1007/978-3-319-08958-4_20

1.1 Language and Schooling

The language of schooling can be difficult for students to master, especially for second language learners. Cummins [1] and Macken-Horarik [2] go as far as describing school language as a completely different language from the language used in everyday communication. According to functional linguistic theory, learning a subject means learning its language. Halliday and Martin [3] describe the language of both natural and social sciences as characterised by lots of nominalisations; yet history is said to reason within sentences and natural science between clauses, a claim to which we will return below.

Gardner [4] stresses the importance of teaching language with the most correct notion of what constitutes a word, i.e. the largest possible entities of language correlating to a specific meaning. Many such "words" will in fact be *multi-word expressions*.

1.2 Multi-Word Expressions

The interest in recurrent word sequences goes back to researchers like Palmer and Firth and the mid 1900s. They used the notion of *collocations*, which Halliday some years later defined more precisely, highlighting the propensity of a lexical item to co-occur with one or more other words.

This sort of recurring word patterns have been studied under a number of labels – and with slightly different definitions – over the years, e.g., *conventionalized language forms, speech formulas, ready-made expressions, fixed expressions, pre-fabricated language, multi-word units/expressions* and *lexical bundles* [5,6]. Multi-word expressions (MWEs) of various sorts play a fundamental role in natural languages [7]. Mastering them is crucial for succeeding in any specialised linguistic community, e.g. academic education [4,8].

Many recent studies have focused on the use of different kinds of MWEs in the language of native vs. non-native speakers. Chen and Baker [9] report more NP-based lexical bundles in native academic writing, while non-native writing has a tendency to over-generalise and favour certain idiomatic expressions and connectors. Nekrasova [10] comes across less lexical bundles in the speech of lower-proficiency English learners than in the speech of native students and higher-proficiency learners.

2 Lexical Bundles

The work by Biber and Conrad [11] was the starting point for large-scale corpus linguistic studies of *lexical bundles*, which were defined as "sequences of three or more words that show a statistical tendency to co-occur". Biber and his colleagues have over the years developed a method for identifying, characterising and analysing lexical bundles.

The only criterion used for recognising lexical bundles is frequency. No collocation co-occurrence measures or other means of ranking or filtering the results are used. Instead, fixed-length text word n-grams are sorted according to frequency and the resulting lists manually inspected for interesting results.[1] Thus, Biber and Barbieri [12] ascribe lexical bundles a pre-fabricated or formulaic status, merely due to their high frequency.[2] However, while it has been observed in the NLP literature that frequency certainly is a strong indicator of MWE-hood (termhood, collocational strength), much can actually be done – and has been done – to improve on frequency alone [13,14].

Lexical bundles are said to differ from other kinds of MWE in three major aspects: first, they are extremely frequent; second, they have no idiomatic meaning; and last, they are not perceptually striking in themselves [12]. Another characteristic of lexical bundles is that they often straddle structural boundaries.

Hyland [15] claims that since lexical bundles are transparent in meaning, they are crucial for construing coherence in a discourse. Strunkyte and Jurkanaite [6] add that comprehension of lexical bundles improves the receptive process of reading.

Biber and colleagues [16] treat university textbooks as one register, where they locate relatively few bundles, compared to, e.g., classroom teaching. The textbook bundles found are mostly NP/PP-based ones which are used for referential purposes. There are characteristic sets of lexical bundles with specific discursive functions connected to different registers [12].

Strunkyte and Jurkanaite [6] compare bundles in research articles in humanities and natural science. The language in humanities is found to be more structurally varied, while the language of natural science contains more text-organising bundles.

2.1 Genuineness

A returning question regarding lexical bundles is whether they are pre-fabricated [17], as in forming wholes in our mental lexicons, regarding storage as well as retrieval. Biber and Barbieri [12] hypothesise that high frequency is a reflection of pre-fabricated status.

This approach, of solely taking frequency into account, has been a target of criticism, inter alia by McEnery et al. [18] (see also the preceding section).

There have been few attempts to distinguish between what we will refer to here as *genuine* lexical bundles and non-genuine ones. A genuine lexical bundle would be one that both structurally and functionally forms one piece of language (cf. [4]). To be of true linguistic interest, studies on lexical bundles have to aim for genuine targets.

---

[1] This is a bit like attempting to discover the words in un-word segmented text by looking at the frequency of, e.g., four-character sequences, which seems to be an exercise of doubtful value.

[2] Although it is not very obvious what can be concluded about the language system or the mental lexicon of the language user from the attested high text frequency of a sequence like *in the case of the* cited by Biber and Conrad [11]. See Sect. 2.1.

3   Data and Method

3.1   Text Corpora

For this study, two subcorpora from a Swedish corpus of textbooks – *OrdiL* [19] – were used: one with physics texts and one with history texts. Both subcorpora consisted of two secondary school textbooks each. The physics books contained about 132 kW and the history books about 76 kW. All bundle frequencies given here are relative (occurrences per 300 kW).

To identify the lexical bundles, a search for n-grams of >2 words that were found ≥2 times in both of the subject's textbooks was made using AntConc[3] and an additional script.

3.2   Bundle Selection

Since all bundles containing more than three words inevitably include bundles of shorter word lengths, the initial bundle lists were full of more or less overlapping sequences. In the literature this is solved both by looking at, e.g., only 4-grams [5], or by not attempting to deal with the overlaps at all [15].

The present paper presents a new approach to come to terms with the problem of overlapping sequences. The method is semi-manual. With the intention of removing all overlapping bundles but one, a program was written which identified all overlapping groups and then proposed the one bundle to retain, favoring n-gram length over n-gram frequency.

In the subsequent manual step, it was decided whether to approve of the proposed bundle or choosing another one. At this point, an additional aspect was considered, namely *intuitive genuineness*.

For bundle groups of 3–5 words, exactly one bundle was kept. However exceptions were sometimes made for groups containing sequences of more than 5 words. If the longer sequence consisted of significantly more frequent non-overlapping shorter bundles, the longer sequence would be split, e.g.

32: *vad är det* 'what is it'
 6: *vad är det som gör att* 'what is it that makes'
20: *som gör att* 'that makes'

3.3   Bundle Classification

The structural and functional categories used for classification come from the work of Biber et al. [16]. Structurally the bundles are subdivided into three categories: *NP/PP-based* (P-f), *VP-based* (VP-f) and *dependent clause based fragments* (DC-f). The functional labels are: *stance expressions, referential expressions* and *discourse organizers*.

---

[3] http://www.antlab.sci.waseda.ac.jpl

The structural classification was made manually. The only modification to the adopted classification [16] concerned a subset of *noun phrase with other post-modifier fragment*. To be more precise, bundles containing NP-fragments and relative subordinate clause fragments were labelled as DC-f's, rather than P-f's. This was done in order to better account for phrasal and clausal boundaries.

The functional analysis that required studying the concordances could only be carried out for the 30 highest ranked bundles of each subject. An additional functional category, *lexical n-grams*, was introduced for bundles that could not be accommodated in any of the other three categories.

4   Results

The *bundle density* (BD) of the corpus was defined as the number of occurring bundles divided by the number of words. The higher the bundle density, the more likely it is to find a lexical bundle in a text of a certain word length. The *bundle variation* (BV) is the bundle density divided by the number of bundle types found. This measure is higher the more repetitive the text is regarding bundles. See Table 1.

Table 1. Bundle statistics

Subject	Words	Bundles (types)	Bundles (tokens)	BD	BV
History	75,739	124	3,388	0.045	$3.6 * 10^{-4}$
Physics	131,652	475	10,340	0.079	$1.6 * 10^{-4}$

The left panel of Fig. 1 shows normalised occurrences of structurally classified bundles and their relative frequencies. The most common bundles from each category and subject are shown in the top panel of Fig. 2, where numbers are normalised occurrences. The functional distribution of the 30 most prevalent bundles of the two subjects are presented in the right panel of Fig. 1. The distribution is almost identical across the subjects, with about 70 % being used for referential purposes and the remaining ones for discourse organization.

According to Biber et al. [16], the investigated textbooks contained mostly referential expressions and subsequently discourse organizers and stance expressions to a lower extent. In the present case though, no stance expressions were discovered.

4.1   Comparison Between the Subjects

The left panel of Fig. 3 shows the distributions of structures over functions. The lexical n-grams and the discourse organizers are almost entirely built up by VP-f's and DC-f's. This is in fact the case in both subjects. In other words, the subjects do not differ in structural discourse management. However, when looking at the referential expressions one finds a striking difference between the subjects (see the right panel of Fig. 3).

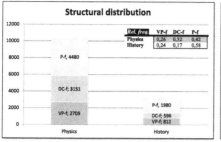
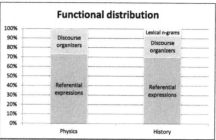

Fig. 1. Structural and functional distribution

History	Physics
NP/PP fragments	
166: *den industriella revolutionen* 'the industrial revolution'	284: *med hjälp av* 'by means of'
134: *en del av* 'a part of'	123: *på grund av* 'because of'
130: *i början av* 'in the beginning of'	113: *en del av* 'a part of'
114: *i slutet av* 'in the end of'	111: *på så sätt* 'in that way'
63: *på så sätt* 'in that way'	82: *på samma sätt* 'in the same way'
VP fragments	
84: *det vill säga* 'that is to say'	83: *men det var* 'but it was'
72: *vad är det* 'what is it'	79: *ta reda på* 'find out'
68: *ta reda på* 'find out'	51: *det var inte* 'it was not'
54: *hur stor är* 'how big is'	31: *men det fanns* 'but there was'
52: *består av en* 'consists of a/one'	31: *ta sig fram* 'advance (v)'
Dependent clause fragments	
91: *det beror på att* 'it is because of'	59: *för att få* 'to get'
86: *det betyder att* 'it means that'	35: *hade rätt att* 'was allowed to'
77: *vad som händer* 'what happens'	35: *ledde till att* 'resulted in'
72: *så att den* 'in order for it to'	31: *det gällde att* 'it was a matter of'
66: *lika stor som* 'as big as'	23: *av dem som* 'of the ones that'

History	Physics
Discourse organisers	
***För att få in** pengarna lade britterna tull och skatt på vissa varor som skulle till Nordamerika*	***Tänk dig ett** järnfilspån som är en tiondels millimeter i diameter*
'**To bring in** the money the Brits added customs and taxes to certain goods destined to North America'	'**Imagine an** iron filing that is a tenth of a millimeter in diameter'
Referential expressions	
***En del av** vägen hade Bartolomeo Diaz redan kartlagt*	***På samma sätt** kan det bildas gnistor när du kammar dig*
'Bartolomeo Diaz had already mapped out **a portion of** the road'	'**In the same way** sparks may form while combing one's hair'

Fig. 2. Structural (top) and functional (bottom) samples

	VP-f	DC-f	P-f
Lexical n-grams	50%	50%	0%
Discourse organizers	47%	40%	13%
Referential expressions	9%	23%	67%

	VP-f	DC-f	P-f
History	10%	5%	86%
Physics	9%	41%	50%

Fig. 3. Structures vs. functions (left) and the structure of referential expressions (right)

5   Discussion

From the numbers in Table 1, we see that physics has a much higher bundle density, while at the same time a more varying language than history. However, a closer investigation reveals that the bundle frequency differs considerably among textbooks within the subjects. One of the physics books stands out by having very many bundles per word, while one of the history books stands out by having very few. Furthermore, it is important to bear in mind that the cut-off frequency applied in the identification process, if normalised with respect to the number of words, becomes much higher in history than in physics.[4] Altogether, this study is not large enough to draw any clear conclusions about the possible differences in bundle density or variation between the two subjects.

The major tendencies seen in Fig. 1 seem to be an equal use of VP-f's, 25 %, across subjects. Both history and physics have mostly P-f's, with history being most extreme with almost 60 % of all the bundles being P-f's. DC-f's are somewhat rare in history, yet more common in physics.

Looking at the bundles presented in Fig. 2 it is obvious that the P-f's are by far most likely to be repeated throughout the texts. The five most common ones are also easily recognised as genuine lexical bundles. They can directly be understood as a whole, both conceptually and functionally. This strongly suggests that they are stored in one piece in our mind. Most of them contain both NP and PP fragments, i.e. nouns and prepositions in a fixed pattern. The prepositions in the bundles are not exchangeable to semantically close ones and the nouns have to be inflected as they appear. Consider, for example, *i början av* 'in the beginning of', which cannot be changed to **på* ('on') *början av*, **i början från* ('from') or *#i starten* ('the start') *av*. Arguably, these all express the same lexical meaning, but would clearly qualify as unidiomatic language by native speakers of Swedish.

When it comes to VP-f's and DC-f's one cannot claim that bundles are genuine to the same extent. Some of them undoubtedly are, namely *ta reda på* 'find out', *ta sig fram* 'advance (v)', *hade rätt att* 'was allowed to' and *det vill säga* 'that is to say'. They are not as fixed as the P-f's though, since the finite verb can be inflected; *tog reda på* 'found out' and *det ville säga* 'that was to say' would also be genuine Swedish bundles.

The remaining bundles among VP-f's and DC-f's are a mixture of sequences containing collocates, e.g. *för att få* 'to get' and *så att den* 'in order for it to',

---

[4] A normalisation gives 30 and 50 times/MW for physics and history respectively.

phrasal verbs, e.g. *ledde till att* 'resulted in' and *består av en* 'consists of a/one' or fixed constructions, e.g. *lika stor som* 'as big as', as well as sequences of frequent words without any added meaning, e.g. *men det var* 'but it was', *av dem som* 'of the ones that' and *hur stor är* 'how big is'.

As for the function of the most frequent bundles (the right panel of Fig. 1), in physics one can discern the subject's need for explaining cause-and-effect connections, e.g. *på grund av* 'because of', *på så sätt* 'in that way', *så att den* 'so that it' and *det beror på att* 'it is because of', and concepts, e.g. *det betyder att* 'it means that' and *det vill säga* 'that is to say'. Moreover, bundles like *vad som händer* 'what happens' and *ta reda på* 'find out' indicate an exploring and analysing discipline. One can also see the necessity to classify and relate terms and notions through *en del av* 'some of', *lika stor som* 'as big as' and *består av en* 'consists of a/one'.

History texts also call for the ability to elucidate ideas, which shows through *på så sätt* 'in that way', *ta reda på* 'find out', *ledde till att* 'resulted in' and *för att få* 'in order to get'. Other more subject-specific recurring sequences point to reasoning, e.g. *men det var* 'but it was' and *det var inte* 'it was not', ordering events chronologically, e.g. *i början av* 'in the beginning of' and *i slutet av* 'in the end of' or defining entities, e.g. *en del av* 'some of' and *av dem som* 'of those that'.

From the left panel of Fig. 3 we see that references in history by means of P-f:s are very much predominant, i.e., references to nominal, prepositional and comparative phrases. References to clauses, by DC-f's, are rarely used in history texts. Conversely, in physics a considerable number of references are made through DC-f's. Physics texts refer to and across clauses almost to the same extent as to phrases. These findings are consistent with the results reported in previous work [3] (see Sect. 1.1 above).

6 Conclusions and Outlook

6.1 Conclusions

The most common bundles in physics have the function of classifying and relating concepts and entities, while history bundles help to discuss events and arrange them in time.

When looking at the relative frequencies of structural distribution across subjects, VP-f's are equally spread, but history has more P-f's and less DC-f's than physics. The difference belongs to the referential function; history refers to phrases, i.e. discusses within the clauses, while physics also tends to make references across clauses. These findings are in accordance with the theoretical claims about the language made by Halliday and Martin [3] of scientific and historical texts respectively.

The most surprising result was the small amount of bundles common to both subjects (i.e. 21 ones). Even though every register previously has been reported to possess its own characteristic set of bundles, the textbook register was assumed to be more homogeneous. In fact, textbooks from different disciplines cannot be generalized with respect to lexical bundles. Instead, more specialised investigations, both across subjects and form levels, are needed to better understand the distribution of lexical bundles across the genre. Extensive usability studies are also called for.

The principal question for the near future to answer is definitely how to improve the identification process in order to find genuine lexical bundles, i.e. the word boundaries between lexical bundles and surrounding arbitrary words.

6.2   Work in Progress: Towards Better MWE Identification

Above (and in [20]) we stress the importance of aiming for identification of *genuine* lexical bundles, i.e., those that both structurally and functionally form one piece of language. To be of true linguistic salience, extraction of lexical bundles must aim for genuine targets, that is trying to find the boundaries between genuine constructions and surrounding arbitrary words. In ongoing work conducted in collaboration with Robert Östling and Mats Wirén at Stockholm University [21], we are now extending the scope of our interest to include the automatic identification of MWEs in general.

MWEs are ubiquitous in language. According to one oft-cited estimate [7], the number of MWEs (in English) is on a par with the number of single words, and others [22] even go as far as to claim that this most likely is an underestimate of the true number. One conclusion to be drawn from this fact – one that many authors in fact do draw [22–24] – is that NLP systems and tools should take MWEs into account at all levels of linguistic processing. This holds true for NLP both in its data-driven and in its knowledge-driven modes.

Thus, in addition to our interest in the language of school textbooks, the background for this ongoing work is also that of a long-term effort to build an integrated richly structured large-scale lexical resource to be used in automatic processing of Swedish text, the *Swedish FrameNet++* [25]. As the name implies, a central component of the resource is a framenet for Swedish, modeled on the English Berkeley FrameNet [26]. However, what we refer to as the "pivot resource" of SweFN++ is SALDO, a large semantic and morphological lexical resource under constant development at Språkbanken (the Swedish Language Bank), University of Gothenburg [27].[5]

Even though SALDO at present contains on the order of 130,000 entries (word and MWE senses), new entries are being added manually and semi-automatically at a pace of a few every day. However, looking at the out-of-vocabulary word lists produced as a result of periodic processing with the morphological component of SALDO of over a billion words of Swedish text [28], it is obvious that there are thousands and thousands of entries missing from SALDO.

SALDO at present has almost 6,400 MWEs, making up about 4.9 % of the entries. However, out of new entries being added to SALDO, the share of MWEs is growing steadily, as indeed is to be expected, given the estimates cited above.

---

[5] http://spraakbanken.gu.se/eng/resource/saldo

We feel that any serious large-scale lexical resource must have a principled and practical way of dealing with MWEs.

In our ongoing work we have endeavoured to go beyond both traditional collocation extraction – which tends to deal with contiguous bigrams [14] – as well as the pure frequency-based methodology adopted for identifying lexical bundles. An important goal is also to be able to automatically identify varying sequences of various kinds, both inflectional variation and non-contiguous sequences.

To this end, we are experimenting with treating the MWE identification problem as analogous to that of *word segmentation* – i.e., the problem of segmenting a continuous sequence of character-level units (typically a phonetic transcription of continuous speech or text in a writing system without word separators) into text words [29] – and to some extent to that of unsupervised morphology learning [30]. We are not the first to make this observation [31], but it seems that the idea has rarely been followed up by actual experiments.

Following up on this idea and inspired by the *hybrid n-grams* introduced in the work on StringNet [32], we have began conducting experiments along these lines, where hybrid n-grams – with text words, lemmas, semantic categories, and parts of speech as possible members – are generated by a segmentation procedure based on *Minimum Description Length* (MDL) [33].

As this work is ongoing, the results are still very preliminary. A manual qualitative evaluation on two data sets, a 1 MW balanced corpus of written Swedish and a corpus of transcribed child-directed speech, shows that the method eliminates 70 % or more of all candidate hybrid n-grams (3 words or longer), on the one hand, and that those remaining include most of the MWE types normally mentioned in the literature [34], on the other. A more formal evaluation is planned for the near future, as well as the inclusion of other kinds of linguistic abstractions, e.g. syntactic dependency relations.

References

1. Cummins, J.: The entry and fallacy in bilingual education. NABE J. **4**(3), 25–29 (1980)
2. Macken-Horarik, M.: Literacy and learning across the curriculum: towards a model of register for secondary school teachers. In: Hasan, R., Williams, G. (eds.) Literacy in Society, pp. 232–279. Longman, London (1996)
3. Halliday, M.A.K., Martin, J.: Writing Science: Literacy and Discursive Power. Falmer Press, London (1993)
4. Gardner, D.: Validating the construct of word in applied corpus-based vocabulary research: a critical survey. Appl. Linguist. **28**(2), 241–265 (2007)
5. Cortes, V.: Lexical bundles in published and student disciplinary writing: examples from history and biology. Engl. Specif. Purp. **23**, 397–423 (2004)
6. Strunkyte, G., Jurkunaite, E.: Written Academic Discourse: Lexical Bundles in Humanities and Natural Sciences. Vilnius University, Vilnius (2008)
7. Jackendoff, R.: The Architecture of the Language Faculty. MIT Press, Cambridge (1997)
8. Atkins, S.B.T., Rundell, M.: Guide to Practical Lexicography. Oxford University Press, London (2008)

9. Chen, Y.H., Baker, P.: Lexical bundles in L1 and L2 writing. Lang. Learn. Technol. **14**(2), 30–49 (2010)
10. Nekrasova, T.M.: English L1 and L2 speakers' knowledge of lexical bundles. Lang. Learn. **59**(3), 647–486 (2009)
11. Biber, D., Conrad, S.: Lexical bundles in conversation and academic prose. In: Hasselgard, H., Oksefjell, S. (eds.) Out of Corpora: Studies in Honor of Stig Johansson, pp. 181–189. Rodopi, Amsterdam (1999)
12. Biber, D., Barbieri, F.: Lexical bundles in university spoken and written registers. Engl. Specif. Purp. **26**, 263–286 (2007)
13. Wermter, J., Hahn, U.: You can't beat frequency (unless you use linguistic knowledge) - a qualitative evaluation of association measures for collocation and term extraction. In: Proceedings of COLING-ACL 2006, Sydney, ACL, pp. 785–792 (2006)
14. Pecina, P.: Lexical association measures and collocation extraction. Lang. Resour. Eva. **44**, 137–158 (2010)
15. Hyland, K.: As can be seen: lexical bundles and disciplinary variation. Engl. Specif. Purp. **27**, 4–21 (2008)
16. Biber, D., Conrad, S., Cortes, V.: If you look at..: lexical bundles in university teaching and textbooks. Appl. Linguist. **25**(3), 371–405 (2004)
17. Wray, A.: Formulaic Language and the Lexicon. Cambridge University Press, Cambridge (2006)
18. McEnery, T., Xiao, R., Tono, Y.: Corpus-Based Language Studies: An Advanced Resource Book. Routledge, London (2006)
19. Lindberg, I., Kokkinakis, S.J.: OrdiL - en korpusbaserad kartläggning av ordförrådet i läromedel för grundskolans senare år. Göteborgs universitet, Göteborg (2007)
20. Ribeck, J.C.: Identifying lexical bundles in secondary school textbooks. In: Vetualani, X. (ed.) Proceedings of the 5th Language and Technology Conference on Human Language Technologies as a Challenge for Computer Science and Linguists, Poznan, Poland, pp. 202–206 (2011)
21. Borin, L., Östling, R., Ribeck, J., Wirén, M.: Towards unsupervised extraction of syntactico-semantic patterns (in progress)
22. Sag, I.A., Baldwin, T., Bond, F., Copestake, A., Flickinger, D.: Multiword expressions: a pain in the neck for NLP. In: Gelbukh, A. (ed.) CICLing 2002. LNCS, vol. 2276, p. 1. Springer, Heidelberg (2002)
23. Villaviciencio, A., Bond, F., Korhonen, A., McCarthy, D.: Introduction to the special issue on multiword expressions: having a crack at a hard nut. Comput. Speech Lang. **19**, 365–377 (2005)
24. Rayson, P., Piao, S., Sharoff, S., Evert, S.: Villada Moirón, B.: Multiword expressions: hard going or plain sailing? Lang. Resour. Eval. **44**, 1–5 (2010)
25. Borin, L., Danélls, D., Forsberg, M., Kokkinakis, D., Gronostaj, M.T.: The past meets the present in Swedish FrameNet++. In: 14th EURALEX International Congress, Leeuwarden, EURALEX, pp. 269–281 (2010)
26. Baker, C.F., Fillmore, C.J., Lowe, J.B.: The Berkeley FrameNet project. In: Proceedings of the Conference on COLING-ACL '98, Montreal, ACL, pp. 86–90 (1998)
27. Borin, L., Forsberg, M., Lönngren, L.: SALDO: a touch of yin to WordNet's yang. Lang. Resour. Eval. (2013). doi:10.1007/s10579-013-9233-4
28. Borin, L., Forsberg, M., Roxendal, J.: Korp - the corpus infrastructure of Språkbanken. In: Proceedings of LREC 2012, Istanbul, ELRA, pp. 474–478 (2012)
29. Hewlett, D., Cohen, P.: Word segmentation as general chunking. In: Proceedings of CoNLL 2011, Portland, Oregon, ACL, pp. 39–47 (2011)

30. Hammarström, H., Borin, L.: Unsupervised learning of morphology. Comput. Linguist. **37**(2), 309–350 (2011)
31. Schone, P., Jurafsky, D.: Is knowledge-free induction of multiword unit dictionary headwords a solved problem? In: Proceedings of EMNLP 2001, Pittsburgh, ACL (2001)
32. Wible, D., Tsao, N.L.: Stringnet as a computational resource for discovering and investigating linguistic constructions. In: Proceedings of the NAACL HLT Workshop on Extracting and Using Constructions in Computational Linguistics, Los Angeles, California, ACL, pp. 25–31 (2010)
33. Rissanen, J.: Modeling by shortest data description. Automatica **14**, 465–471 (1978)
34. Baldwin, T., Kim, S.N.: Multiword expressions. In: Indurkhya, N., Damerau, F.J. (eds.) Handbook of Natural Language Processing, pp. 267–292. CRC Press, Boca Raton (2010)

Text Annotation

Active Learning to Speed-Up the Training Process for Dialogue Act Labelling

Fabrizio Ghigi[1]([✉]), Carlos-D. Martínez-Hinarejos[2], and José-Miguel Benedí[2]

[1] Dpto Electricidad y Electrónica, Facultad de Ciencia y Tecnología,
Universidad Del País Vasco, Sarriena s/n, 48940 Leioa, Spain
fabrizio.ghigi@gmail.com
[2] PRHLT Research Center, Universitat Politècnica de València,
Camino de Vera s/n, 46022 Valencia, Spain
{cmartine,jmbenedi}@prhlt.upv.es

Abstract. The dialogue act labelling task is the process of splitting and annotating a dialogue into dialogue meaningful units; the labelling task can be performed semi-automatically by using statistical models trained from previously annotated dialogues. The appropiate selection of training dialogues can make the process faster, and Active Learning is one suitable strategy for this selection. In this work, Active Learning based on two different criteria (Weighted Number of Hypothesis and Entropy) has been tested for the task of dialogue act labelling by using the N-gram Transducers model. The framework was tested against two heterogeneous corpora, DIHANA and SwitchBoard. The results confirm the goodness of this kind of selection strategy.

Keywords: Dialogue act labelling · Active learning · Data uncertainty

1 Introduction

A spoken dialogue system is a conversational agent able to have a talk with a human, with the perspective to achieve a predetermined goal. While performing the setup process of a dialogue system an indispensable condition for the success of a data-based strategy (Young 2000) is the availability of a big amount of annotated dialogues. Annotating a dialogue corpus in terms of Dialogue Acts (DA) (Bunt 1994) is one of the most expensive, time-consuming and annoying tasks while developing a dialogue system. The common scenario is a situation where an abundant unlabeled data amount is available, and labelling this data is an expensive task in terms of human effort and time. An alternative to this manual annotation is provided by the use of semi-automatic annotation tools which provide a draft annotation that must only be revised by the human annotators. These annotation tools (most of them based on statistical models such as those described in (Stolcke et al. 2000)) can speed-up the annotation process and consequently the construction of a whole dialogue system. To develop an automatic DA labelling system, we need training data, i.e., dialogues

© Springer International Publishing Switzerland 2014
Z. Vetulani and J. Mariani (Eds.): LTC 2011, LNAI 8387, pp. 253–263, 2014.
DOI: 10.1007/978-3-319-08958-4_21

segmented in terms of DAs, that permit to perform the learning process. Usually, the more training data we have, the better performance the system can reach.

In such scenario, it could be desirable to have a criterion that permit us to select just the most informative samples to be manually labeled, reducing the amount of data we need to label in order to reach a good performance for our annotating system. The main idea is to manually label the set of dialogues that will provide a better statistical annotation model, but having a compromise between the amount of human-tagged data and the overall accuracy of an automatic tagging system. Therefore, a criterion must be formulated to obtain the most informative dialogues with respect to a given statistical annotation model. This criterion can be iteratively applied to the remaining unlabeled samples, to select the samples that according to the current model can produce larger improvements in the system performance generating a new model, while a target performance has not been reached.

In general, this problem can be formulated as: having a set of samples we want to use to train a classifier, and consequently need to be manually tagged, how to reduce the cost of the tagging process. Time and human resources needed for the tagging process, as the costs, are proportional to the number of samples we want to tag. The research on a criterion for sample selection is still an open problem, especially in dialogue, and probably task-dependent.

Therefore, we are looking for an effective criterion that permits to select just the most informative and significant samples for the task we are approaching, DA labelling. In such scenario the application of the *Active Learning* technique (Hwa 2000) could be useful in order to reduce the labelling task costs.

In this work we are going to present the results of applying *Active Learning* for the task of DA labelling by using the N-gram Transducers models. Two different uncertainty based criteria, Weighted Number of Hypothesis and Entropy, are tested and compared against a random baseline to check their appropriateness in the Active Learning sample selection. Results are obtained on the transcriptions of two different spoken dialogue corpora, DIHANA (Benedí et al. 2006) (human-computer, semantically restricted) and SwitchBoard (Godfrey et al. 1992) (human-human, semantically not restricted).

2   Dialogue Act Labelling with the NGT Model

DA Labelling is the task of segmenting a dialogue into dialogue meaningful units (segments) and associating to each segment a label (DA) depending on the dialogue-related meaning of that segment.

The DA Labelling problem can be presented as, given a word sequence W that represents a dialogue, obtain the sequence of DA U that maximises the posterior probability $\Pr(U|W)$.

This probability can be modelled by a Hidden Markov Model approach by using the Bayes rule (Stolcke et al. 2000) or by directly modeling the posterior probability $\Pr(U|W)$, for example by using the N-Gram Transducers (NGT) model (Martínez-Hinarejos et al. 2009).

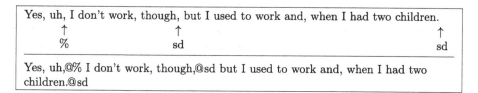

Fig. 1. An alignment between a dialogue turn and its corresponding DA labels (from the SWBD-DAMSL scheme, %: uninterpretable, sd: statement-non-opinion), and the result of the re-labelling process, where @ is the attaching metasymbol.

The NGT model estimates $\Pr(\mathcal{U}|\mathcal{W})$ by means of an n-gram model which acts as a transducer. The definition of this model is based on a Stochastic Finite-State Transducer (SFST) inference technique known as GIATI (Casacuberta et al. 2005). GIATI starts from a corpus of aligned pairs of input-output sequences. These alignments are used in a re-labelling process that produces a corpus of extended words which combine the words in the input and output sentences. The corpus of extended words is used to infer a grammatical model (usually a smoothed n-gram).

When dealing with dialogues, the input and output language are formed by the words and the DA labels of the dialogue, respectively. Each DA label is aligned to the last word of its corresponding segment. Thus, for each turn $w_1 w_2 \ldots w_l$ and its associated DA sequence $u_1 u_2 \ldots u_r$, the re-labelling step attaches the DA label to the last word of the segment using a metasymbol (@). The result of the process is the extended word sequence $e_1 e_2 \ldots e_l$, where: $e_i = w_i$ when w_i is not aligned to any DA, $e_i = w_i @ u_k$ when w_i is aligned to the DA u_k. Figure 1 presents an example of alignment for a dialogue turn and the corresponding extended word sequence.

After the re-labelling process, a grammatical model is inferred (usually, a smoothed n-gram) and converted into a SFST. In the case of dialogues, since alignments between words and DA labels are monotonic (no cross-inverted alignments are possible), no conversion to SFST is necessary to efficiently apply a search algorithm on the n-gram (since for each input word we can decide whether to emit or not a DA label without referring to posterior words). Therefore, this n-gram acts as a transducer and gives the name to the technique.

A Viterbi search decoding is employed on the NGT model to obtain the dialogue annotation. This decoding process builds a search tree, in whose i-th level is represented the i-th input word in the sequence. Each input word is expanded for all the possible outputs it has associated in the alignments in the training corpus, giving as many branches as possible outputs. The probability of each branch is updated according to the corresponding parent node, the n-gram probability of the corresponding extended word sequence and the n-gram probability of the corresponding DA sequence (in case a new DA is produced).

At the end of the search process, a full search tree is produced. In this search tree each leaf node represents a possible solution (an annotation hypothesis) to the annotation problem for the input dialogue. Each leaf node has associated a probability, and the leaf node with highest probability is taken as the optimal solution for the annotation problem. The solution is obtained by going up from the leaf node till the root node of the tree, giving an annotation and a segmentation on the dialogue.

3   Active Learning

Using Machine Learning algorithms we are able to develop systems that can increase their performance by adding more training data. According to this, we can use our system in an active way, choosing the most appropriate actions to improve the model performance in the fastest and cheapest possible way. In case of Active Learning (Riccardi and Tür 2003), we iteratively improve system performance by adding new training data the system can learn from. The system results on unlabelled data can be used to select the samples that would provide a more effective parameter estimation for the model, i.e., suggest which samples must be annotated and added to the training set.

In the description of Active Learning algorithm (Hwa 2000) below, U is a set of unlabeled candidates, L is a small set of labeled training samples, M is the current model, M_{true} is a model that achieves an objective performance in the labelling task, f represents the selection criteria chosen, n the amount of unlabeled samples selected at this iteration, and N the new selected set we are going to label:

```
Initialize
    M ← Train(L)
Repeat
    N ← Select(n, U, M, f)
    U ← U-N
    L ← L ∪ Label(N)
    M ← Train(L)
Until (M=M_true) or (U=∅) or (Human Stops)
```

4   Sample Selection Criteria

The key point in the Active Learning algorithm is the selection criteria. In this section two selection criteria are briefly described: (1) Weighted Number of Hypothesis, and (2) Entropy. The two criteria try to estimate the uncertainty of the sample, i.e., how difficult is for the current model to recognise the sample. In any case, the samples with highest uncertainty will be those to be selected.

4.1 Weighted Number of Hypothesis

This criterion utilizes the set of different hypothesis retrieved by the NGT decoding to compute a score for each dialogue remaining in the unlabeled set. For each dialogue, each hypothesis (leaf node of the search tree) is normalised by the maximum probability among all the hypothesis for the dialogue (the most likely hypothesis). This causes that less probable hypothesis have a lower impact on the final computed score (since hypothesis with small probability do not affect much to uncertainty). The uncertainty is computed using the following expression for each dialogue in the unlabeled set:

$$\sum_i \frac{\Pr_i(x)}{\Pr_{max}(x)} \tag{1}$$

In this equation, $\Pr_i$ represents the probability of i-th hypothesis (a possible decodification of the current dialogue in DA using the current model), and $\Pr_{max}(x)$ is the probability of the most likely hypothesis for this sample x. After calculating this uncertainty for each remaining unlabeled sample, the subset of n dialogues with the highest uncertainty is selected for the next labelling step.

4.2 Entropy

Entropy gives a measure of how difficult finds the system to recognise a specific sample. It is used in several Natural Language Processing tasks to evaluate language models. A lower value of entropy reflects the facility for the system to decode the sample. In our case, the expression that was used to compute the entropy values is the following (Robinson 2008):

$$H_m(s) = -\frac{1}{\Pr_m(s)} \left(\sum_{t \in T} \Pr_m(t) \log \Pr_m(t) \right) + \log \Pr_m(s) \tag{2}$$

with $\Pr_m(s)$ the n-gram probability according to the model M, $\Pr_m(t)$ the NGT decoding probability and T the whole set of hypothesis retrieved by the NGT model. Since this value depends on the length of the dialogue, it is normalised by the length of the current sample. After computing the entropy value for each unlabeled dialogue, those dialogues with highest entropy (uncertainty) values are chosen for the next labelling step.

5 Experiments

Experiments are developed using two corpora, DIHANA (Benedí et al. 2006) and SwitchBoard (Godfrey et al. 1992), that permits us to confirm the goodness of the selection strategy; Active Learning is performed for both criteria, and results (Sect. 5.4) are compared against a random baseline obtained by calculating average and variance of six random experiments with different seeds; the metric chosen to evaluate system performance is SEGDAER, described in Sect. 5.3.

5.1   Corpora

DIHANA Corpus. The DIHANA corpus (Benedí et al. 2006) is a set of spoken dialogues in Spanish language, between a human and a simulated machine, acquired with the Wizard of Oz (WoZ) technique. It is restricted at the semantic level (dialogues are related to the task of obtaining information about train tickets), but natural language is allowed (there are no lexical or syntactical restrictions). The DIHANA corpus is composed of 900 dialogues about a telephone train information system. It was acquired from 225 different speakers (153 male and 72 females), with small dialectal variants. There are 6,280 user turns and 9,133 system turns. The vocabulary size is 823 words. The total amount of speech signal is about five and a half hours. The annotation scheme used in the corpus is based on the Interchange Format (IF) defined in the C-STAR project (Lavie et al. 1997), which was adapted to dialogue annotation. Details on the annotation process are available in (Alcácer et al.2005).

SwitchBoard Corpus. The SwitchBoard corpus (Godfrey et al. 1992) is a set of spoken dialogues in English Language, human-human conversations by telephone not related to a specific task; it includes 1,155 different conversations, performed by 500 different speakers. The number of turns in the dialogues is around 115,000; in average, each turn has 1.8 segments. The vocabulary size is approximately 42,000 words. It was annotated using the 42 different labels present in SWBD-DAMSL set (Jurafsky et al. 1997) a shallow version of the DAMSL (Core and Allen 1997) scheme. These labels represent categories such as statement, backchannel, questions, answers, etc.

5.2   Strategy

For both corpora, DIHANA and SwitchBoard, we have performed Active Learning; for DIHANA we have used 180 dialogues as test and 720 dialogues as training, for SwitchBoard 105 dialogues as test and 1050 for training. The strategy implemented that perform Active Learning (Sect. 3), follows these steps (U is the input set of unlabeled samples, L is the labelled samples set, and M the draft model):

1. Train an initial model M from a small set of tagged samples (set L), picked out by a general criteria (in fact we picked out the two dialogues with more turns).
2. Compute SEGDAER (see Subsect. 5.3) for the NGT model predictions of the system, according to the current model.
3. Apply a function f over the unlabeled set of samples that, according to M and to the selection criteria chosen (Weighted Number of Hypothesis (1) or Entropy (2)), computes a score for each dialogue remaining in the unlabeled set U.
4. Select a subset N of these dialogues with the highest scores.
5. Take out the set N from the unlabeled set U.

6. Manually label the set N (in this case this step is simulated, no human resources were employed, the entire labeled set was available).
7. Add the labeled set N to the labeled set L.
8. Reestimate the model M with the new set L.
9. If sufficient performance is not reached and there are still unlabeled samples and human resources, restart from the first step of the loop.

We have chosen to use an exponential function to determine size of new samples set to select, in fact 2^i, where i is the index of current iteration. This incremental size of selection is desirable because of the asymptotic behaviour of the error rate; thus, with this incremental size approach we can see the improvements with small amounts of training data, checking how fast we can converge to the asymptote, while adding more data to a large training set does not strongly affect the error rate. The Sample Selection Algorithm described in Sect. 3 is used to manage incremental selection of training samples.

5.3   Evaluation Metrics

To evaluate the system performance we use the SEGDAER metric: it is the average edit distance between the reference DA sequences of the turns and the DA sequences assigned by the labelling model; in this case, sequences are a combination of the DA label and its position, which means that it takes into account also the dialogue segmentation, because it is important in DA labelling task not only to predict the correct labels, but also to put them in the correct position in the dialogue.

5.4   Results Analysis

SEGDAER
This section presents the results obtained, using Active Learning for DA Labelling task, against the two corpora considered, DIHANA (Benedí et al. 2006) and SwitchBoard (Godfrey et al. 1992), reporting in each graphic the SEGDAER behaviour obtained with the two criteria described in Sect. 4, compared against the random baseline. Random baseline allows to compare the effect of making an appropriate selection instead of not using any criteria for the selection of samples (an upper bound); lower bound allows to compare the effect of selecting against using (and annotating) all the training data.

As we can clearly see in the results in Fig. 2, the error behaviour is asymptotic, fact confirmed by the small variance of random experiments after 5 iterations. This means that we can reach a good performance in the earlier steps of Active Learning process, and the system performance remains almost unaffected when adding more training data after a small number of iterations of the Active Learning algorithm (Sect. 3). The results shows that Entropy (2) selection criterion works very well in this task, performing better than random baseline in both

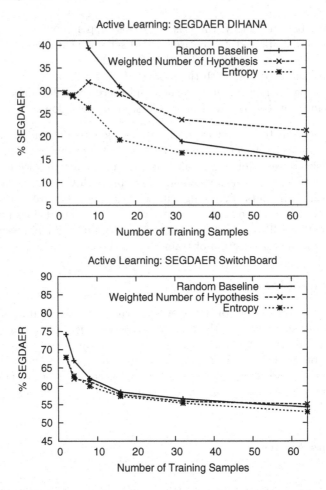

Fig. 2. SEGDAER results while performing Active Learning for DIHANA and Switch-Board. Graphics include results for the two criteria tested, Weighted Number of Hypothesis and Entropy, compared against the random baseline. The lower bound (error rate obtained by training the model with the entire set available) is 12.65 for Dihana and 48.10 for SwitchBoard. The results obtained converge asymptotically to the lower bound, and about 64 and 256 prototypes the results present no significant differences against using all the training data in DIHANA and SwitchBoard corpora, respectively.

corpora tested, while the Weighted Number of Hypothesis (1) criterion had a variable behaviour, retrieving performance similar to Entropy when using the SwitchBoard corpus, and worse than random behaviour when testing with the DIHANA corpus.

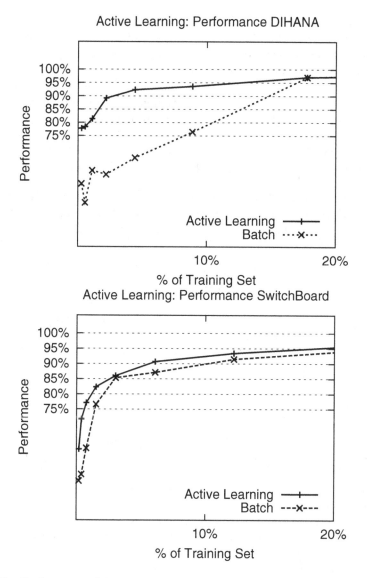

Fig. 3. The Performance of the system, computed at each iteration of the Active Learning algorithm, shows that we can achieve 95 % of the final performance by using just the 20 % of the entire training set available, for both corpora used, DIHANA and Switch-Board. In the figures is represented the performance obtained at each iteration of the Active Learning algorithm implemented with Entropy criterion and the performance obtained with a Batch training process. In this graphic are shown just the results obtained implementing the Active Learning algorithm with Entropy criterion because this is the criterion that has obtained best performance in the experiments, allowing us to better appreciate the improvements achieved with Active Learning technique. Has to be noticed the significant performance improvements obtained in the first iterations implementing Active Learning algorithm with Entropy criterion in the DIHANA corpus.

Performance

With Active Learning we aim to speed up the labelling process, labelling just the most informative samples, but maintaining the system performance; the focus is on saving up money and time in the labelling process, but using just a subset of training sample we do not expect improvements in the error rate, we just expect to achieve a performance as close as possible to the performance obtained training with the entire training set available.

In the graphics in Fig. 3 we present the results obtained in the experiments in another perspective, showing the percentage of training set we need to achieve a given percentage of the final performance obtained training the system with the entire set available.

The "performance" of the system is just the inverse of the SEGDAER, e.g. $100 - SEGDAER$, and then normalized to a percentage, taking the final SEG-DAER obtained training with the entire training set available as the 100 % of the performance as shown in Eq. (3).

$$\frac{(100 - \text{SEGDAER}) * 100}{(100 - \text{FINALSEGDAER})} \tag{3}$$

Has to be noticed that we can achieve 95 % of the performance by using just the 20 % of the training set in both corpora, as shown in Fig. 3, and this performance improvement is very evident in the first iterations of the Active Learning algorithm with the DIHANA corpus.

6   Conclusions

In conclusion we applied Active Learning to DA labelling task, for two very heterogeneous corpora, DIHANA and SwitchBoard, using uncertainty based criteria to perform samples selection at each iteration of the Active Learning algorithm. Results obtained in the two different domains confirm the goodness of the uncertainty based criteria.

For both corpora used the experimental results shows that we can achieve a good perfomance, 95 % of the performance obtained training with the entire set available, labelling just the 20 % of the samples in the unlabeled set. According to these results we can save an important amount of time and money in the labelling task by using Active Learning with uncertainty based criteria to select the most informative samples.

This kind of approach is reusable in other statistical models where we can compute the scores for the two criteria proposed to implement the Active Learning algorithm, the only elements needed to compute these scores are the set of hypotheses with their probabilities, and also an n-gram model in the case of Entropy criterion.

Planned future work includes parallelization of Active Learning algorithm, exploration of other selection criteria, application in an interactive framework, and the analysis of single DA label error rate.

Acknowledgements. Work supported by EC under FP7 project CasMaCat (FP7-28757), and by Spanish MINECO under projects STraDA (TIN2012-37475-C02-01) and Active2Trans (TIN2012-31723), and by Spanish MED/MICINN under the FPI scholarship BES-2009-028965, and by GVA under project AMIIS (ISIC/2012/004).

References

Alcácer, N., Benedí, J.M., Blat, F., Granell, R., Martínez, C.D., Torres, F.: Acquisition and labelling of a spontaneous speech dialogue corpus. In: SPECOM, Greece, pp. 583–586 (2005)

Benedí, J.M., Lleida, E., Varona, A., Castro, M.J., Galiano, I., Justo, R., López, I., Miguel, A.: Design and acquisition of a telephone spontaneous speech dialogue corpus in spanish: DIHANA. In: Fifth LREC, Genova, Italy, pp. 1636–1639 (2006)

Bunt, H.: Context and dialogue control. THINK Q. **3**, 19–31 (1994)

Casacuberta, F., Vidal, E., Picó, D.: Inference of finite-state transducers from regular languages. Pat. Recogn. **38**(9), 1431–1443 (2005)

Core, M.G., Allen, J.F.: Coding dialogues with the DAMSL annotation scheme. In: Traum, D. (ed.) Working Notes: AAAI Fall Symposium on Communicative Action in Humans and Machines, pp. 28–35. AAAI, Menlo Park (1997)

Godfrey, J., Holliman, E., McDaniel, J.: SWITCHBOARD: telephone speech corpus for research and development. In: Proceedings of the ICASSP-92, pp. 517–520 (1992)

Hwa, R.: Sample selection for statistical grammar induction. In: Proceedings of the 2000 Joint SIGDAT, pp. 45–52. Association for Computational Linguistics, Morristown (2000)

Jurafsky, D., Shriberg, E., Biasca, D.: Switchboard SWBD-DAMSL shallow-discourse-function annotation coders manual - draft 13. Technical report 97–01, University of Colorado Institute of Cognitive Science (1997)

Lavie, A., Levin, L., Zhan, P., Taboada, M., Gates, D., Lapata, M.M., Clark, C., Broadhead, M., Waibel, A.: Expanding the domain of a multi-lingual speech-to-speech translation system. In: Proceedings of the Workshop on Spoken Language Translation, ACL/EACL-97, pp. 67–72 (1997)

Martínez-Hinarejos, C.D., Tamarit, V., Benedí, J.M.: Improving unsegmented dialogue turns annotation with N-gram transducers. In: Proceedings of the 23rd Pacific Asia Conference on Language, Information and Computation (PACLIC23), vol. 1, pp. 345–354 (2009)

Riccardi, G., Tür, D.: Active and unsupervised learning for automatic speech recognition. In: INTERSPEECH (2003)

Robinson, D.W.: Entropy and uncertainty. Entropy **10**, 493–506 (2008)

Stolcke, A., Coccaro, N., Bates, R., Taylor, P., van Ess-Dykema, C., Ries, K., Shriberg, E., Jurafsky, D., Martin, R., Meteer, M.: Dialogue act modelling for automatic tagging and recognition of conversational speech. Comput. Linguist. **26**(3), 1–34 (2000)

Young, S.: Probabilistic methods in spoken dialogue systems. Philos. Trans. R. Soc. (Series A) **358**(1769), 1389–1402 (2000)

Direct and Wordgraph-Based Confidence Measures in Dialogue Annotation with N-Gram Transducers

Carlos-D. Martínez-Hinarejos[✉], Vicent Tamarit, and José-Miguel Benedí

PRHLT Research Center, Universitat Politècnica de València,
Camino de Vera s/n, 46022 Valencia, Spain
{cmartine,jbenedi}@dsic.upv.es, tamarit@gmail.com

Abstract. Dialogue annotation is a necessary step for the development of dialogue systems, specially for data-based dialogue strategies. Manual annotation is hard and time-consuming, and automatic techniques can be used to obtain a draft annotation and speed up the process. The presentation of the draft annotation with confidence levels on the correctness of every part of the hypothesis can make even faster the supervision process. In this paper we propose two methods to calculate confidence measures for an automatic dialogue annotation model, and test them for the annotation of a task-oriented human-computer corpus on railway information. The results show that our proposals have a similar behaviour and that they are a good starting point for incorporating confidence measures in the dialogue annotation process.

Keywords: Dialogue annotation · Confidence measures · N-gram transducers

1 Introduction

In the Natural Language Processing field, a dialogue system is defined as a computer system that interacts with a human being by using dialogue [13]. Most dialogue systems employ only speech, and are used in many applications such as information systems that are accessed by telephone [18] (e.g., ticket reservation systems, timetable consultation systems, etc.).

These systems require a model of the dialogue structure in order to mimic this structure in the automatic system. Therefore, a framework for the dialogue structure must be defined. One of the most popular frameworks is that based on the speech act theory [2], that focuses on the communicative acts performed in the dialogue interaction. From this framework, the concept of dialogue act (DA) [4] is derived; a DA is a label which codes the intention of the current interaction, along with its corresponding data related to the task. Since in each interaction several intentions can be distinguished in different subsequences, each of these subsequences (called segments) has an associated DA. In an automatic dialogue system, DA labels can be associated to both computer and human user.

© Springer International Publishing Switzerland 2014
Z. Vetulani and J. Mariani (Eds.): LTC 2011, LNAI 8387, pp. 264–275, 2014.
DOI: 10.1007/978-3-319-08958-4_22

The annotation of a set of dialogues in terms of DA is an important task for the obtainment of data-based automatic dialogue systems, since these systems are based on statistical models which learn the relation between the dialogue state and the DA labels [24]. Many annotation schemes have been proposed in several projects, such as DASML [6] or DATE [22]. In any case, manual annotation of dialogue corpora by human experts is required, but this is a hard and long task. Thus, in the last years some automatic techniques have been proposed to obtain a draft annotation and speed up the annotation process. One of the most promising techniques is based on the N-gram Transducers (NGT) model [20].

However, all these automatic techniques are not error-free, and a human supervision of the annotation must be performed. In this process, it will be very helpful to warn to the human expert about those parts in the proposed hypothesis that, according to the automatic technique, are more error-prone (i.e., the technique has somehow an evidence that its proposal may not be correct). Thus, the reviewer can concentrate on those parts that are probably wrong and avoids to spend time in reviewing parts likely to be correct. The process that decides which part is likely to be correct or not is usually based on confidence measures (CM).

Confidence measures have been very popular in Automatic Speech Recognition (ASR) [12] (where they are applied on recognised words), and in the last few years they have been extended into other NLP fields such as Machine Translation [21] or parsing [17]. In dialogue systems, the use of confidence measures has been mainly directed to the use of ASR confidence measures to improve the reaction of the system on recognition errors and misunderstandings [16], but as far as we know no clear application of confidence measures was proposed for automatic dialogue annotation techniques, and more specifically for NGT.

In this work we propose, implement, and evaluate two different ways of calculating confidence measures for dialogue annotation based on the NGT technique: one of them directly based on the NGT search procedure (direct CM) and the other based on a wordgraph obtained from the NGT search tree (wordgraph-based CM). In Sect. 2, an overview of the NGT model is provided. In Sect. 3, the formulation of the CM is presented. In Sect. 4, the experimental corpus is detailed. In Sect. 5, experiments are described and results are shown and analysed. In Sect. 6, conclusions and future work lines are described.

2   The N-Gram Transducers Model for Dialogue Annotation

The annotation of a dialogue transcription can be formulated as an optimisation problem: given a word sequence $\mathcal{W}$ that represents a dialogue, the aim is to obtain the sequence of DA labels $\mathcal{U}$ that maximises the posterior probability $\Pr(\mathcal{U}|\mathcal{W})$. Since dialogue transcriptions are usually presented in turns, if a dialogue has T turns, we can express the dialogue as the sequence of words of the turns, i.e., $\mathcal{W} = W_1^T = W_1 W_2 \cdots W_T$; the same decomposition can be applied to DA sequences, i.e., $\mathcal{U} = U_1^T = U_1 U_2 \cdots U_T$. In these sequences, W_t and U_t represent the sequence of words and DA labels, respectively, for turn t of the dialogue. W_t^s and U_t^s will represent the sequence of words and DA labels between turns t and s, both included.

As a result, the optimisation problem can be expressed as:

$$\widehat{\mathcal{U}} = \underset{\mathcal{U}}{\operatorname{argmax}} \Pr(\mathcal{U}|\mathcal{W}) = \underset{U_1^T}{\operatorname{argmax}} \Pr(U_1^T|W_1^T) \tag{1}$$

Among several options, this problem can be decomposed using the Bayes' rule (as presented in [14]) or directly solved by other models such as the N-gram Transducers (NGT) model [20]. The NGT model employs a n-gram model that acts as a transducer; the n-gram model is obtained by following the inference process defined by the GIATI[1] Stochastic Finite-State Transducers (SFST) inference technique [5].

GIATI forms, from a corpus of input-output aligned training sentences, an extended training corpus formed by the combination of the input and output words (this process is known as re-labelling); from this extended corpus, a smoothed n-gram model is inferred. This n-gram model can be converted into a SFST by undoing the re-labelling process (see details in [5]), but the NGT technique proposes its direct use as a transducer in its n-gram form. This avoids the difficulties of modelling the smoothing probabilities in a finite-state model, and it is easy to apply when no cross-inverted alignments are present in the original training corpus of aligned sentences.

The search process for NGT is a Viterbi process in which, apart from the NGT model itself, a n-gram model for the output language is included. The search process forms a search tree, where the i-th level is associated to the i-th input word, and each input word is expanded into as many children nodes as different output had associated in the training process. For example, if a word w was associated to outputs o_1 and o_2, apart from the empty output, when $w_i = w$ in the i-th level each node of the tree will produce three children nodes (one for the empty output, another for o_1, and another for o_2).

The probability of each branch in the search process is updated according to the probability of the parent node, the probability of the NGT model and the probability of the output n-gram model. This last probability is taken into account only when the child presents an output. At the end of the search process, the node of the final level with the highest probability is chosen and its associated branch is retrieved, which gives a sequence of extended words that provide both the output symbols and a segmentation of the input sequence.

The NGT model can be applied to dialogue annotation by using as input language the words of the transcribed dialogue, and as output language the corresponding DA labels. Input and output are converted into the extended corpus by attaching the DA label to the last word of the corresponding segment (using a metasymbol such as @). The results obtained by NGT in dialogue annotation are quite better than those obtained with more classical techniques (such as Hidden

---

[1] Grammatical Inference and Alignment for Transducer Infer.

Markov Models [19]). More details on the NGT model and the search process can be consulted in [15, 20].

3 Confidence Measures in Dialogue Annotation

Although the NGT model provides good results in dialogue annotation, for a practical interactive system of dialogue annotation (in which a human annotator provides the final correct annotation) it is important to provide a guide to the user on how confident is the automatic annotation system with respect to its hypothesis. This is similar to what happens in ASR systems which are used in speech transcription, where each word in the decoding result can be signalled to improve the performance of the correctness by the human transcriptor. These guidelines given by the system are based on the so-called confidence measures: a score between 0 and 1 which evaluates how confident is the system in a segment of the decoded hypothesis.

The usual approximation to the obtention of confidence measures for the result of a decoding problem is using what in ASR is called Word Posterior Probabilities [23]. In our case we want to obtain the posterior probability of emitting in position i (which is associated to an input word w_i) a dialogue act label d_i, which can be empty. In general, we can state the problem as knowing the posterior probability of the output sequence $d = d_i d_{i+1} \cdots d_{j-1} d_j = d_i^j$ for an input sequence $w = w_i w_{i+1} \cdots w_{j-1} w_j = w_i^j$. This event of producing d between positions i and j (both included) is denoted as C_{ij}^d. Thus, the posterior probability of this event is $\Pr(C_{ij}^d | w)$. In general, we will be interested in the posterior probability of an individual output, i.e., when $j = i$, and therefore, we reduce the problem to compute the posterior probability $\Pr(C_i^d | w)$.

Now, by using the Bayes' rule, this probability can be calculated as:

$$\Pr(C_i^d | w) = \frac{\Pr(C_i^d, w)}{\Pr(w)} \tag{2}$$

The join probability (numerator of the fraction) can be computed by the classical Forward-Backward process [7] and their associated terms α (for forward) and β (for backward). Thus, the formula in Eq. (2) can be expressed as:

$$\Pr(C_i^d | w) = \frac{\alpha(d_i) f(d_i) \beta(d_i)}{\Pr(w)} \tag{3}$$

Each term in Eq. (3) has the following meaning:

- $\alpha(d_i) = \Pr(w_1, \ldots, w_i, q_i = d_i | \lambda)$; that is, the probability that, given the model λ, the sequence $w_1, \ldots, w_i$ is processed and the state q_i (where d_i may be produced) is reached.
- $f(d_i) = \Pr(d_i | w_i, q_i, \lambda)$; that is, the probability of emitting d_i given the model λ, the input w_i, and the state q_i.

- $\beta(d_i) = \Pr(w_{i+1}, \ldots, w_l | q_i = d_i, \lambda)$; that is, the probability of, given the model λ and that the output d_i is produced in the reached state q_i, the sequence $w_{i+1}, \ldots, w_l$ is processed.
- $\Pr(w) = \Pr(w_1, \ldots, w_l)$; that is, the probability of the input word sequence according to the model.

We call the confidence measure based on Eq. (3) a *Forward-Backward confidence measure* (FBCM), and we propose as well a simplified confidence measure based only on the emission probability:

$$\Pr(C_i^d | w) = \frac{f(d_i)}{\Pr(w)} \tag{4}$$

We will call the confidence measure based on Eq. (4) *Transition confidence measure* (TCM).

The two following subsections describe different approximations to obtain these confidence measures for dialogue annotation. The first proposal, described in Subsect. 3.1, presents confidence measures which are based on the direct NGT decoding process. The second proposal, described in Subsect. 3.2, is based on the use of wordgraphs (WG) and can be applied to any decoding technique that produces WG, although we will present results only on NGT.

3.1 Direct Confidence Measures

A first proposal on confidence measures is based on the result of the Viterbi decoding process for NGT. In the terms of the NGT model, the members of Eq. (3) (FBCM) can be computed as it follows:

- $\alpha(d_i)$ is the sum of all the probabilities of the nodes at level i that may produce output d_i.
- $f(d_i)$ is the sum of all the probabilities of the transitions between all nodes at level i and all nodes at level $i+1$ where the output d_i was produced.
- $\beta(d_i)$ is the sum of all the β computations of the children nodes of all nodes at level $i+1$ that were reached by producing the output d_i.
- $\Pr(w)$ is the sum of the probabilities of all the different solutions that the search process produced for the input sequence w (that is, the sum of the probabilities of all the nodes of the last level).

In the case of TCM (Eq. (4)), only $f(d_i)$ and $\Pr(w)$ must be calculated, but the NGT process does not change.

3.2 Wordgraph-Based Confidence Measures

An alternative approximation is obtaining a wordgraph from the NGT search tree obtained during the NGT decoding process. In this case, each of the terms of Eq. (3) (FBCM) can be calculated according to the wordgraph states, transitions, and associated probabilities as follows:

– $\alpha(d_i)$: probability of the paths in the wordgraph that start in the initial state of the wordgraph and arrive to any state in position i where d_i may be emitted.
– $f(d_i)$: probability of emitting d_i in position i.
– $\beta(d_i)$: probability of the paths that start from any of the states of the wordgraph after position i where d_i is emitted to the final state of the wordgraph.
– $\Pr(w)$: probability of all the paths of the wordgraph (i.e., probability of processing w as input sequence).

Again, in the case of TCM (Eq. (4)), only $f(d_i)$ and $\Pr(w)$ must be calculated, but the use of the wordgraph is the same.

The main advantage of this wordgraph-based approximation is that can be employed in any annotation technique that can produce a wordgraph, not only for NGT.

4   Experimental Data

The calculation of confidence measures for dialogue annotation was performed on the Dihana corpus [3]. Dihana is a dialogue corpus composed of 900 task-oriented human-computer telephone dialogues in Spanish. The corpus is oriented to obtaining information about long-distance railway services in Spain, which covers items such as timetables, fares, and additional services for the trains. This corpus was acquired using the Wizard of Oz (WoZ) technique [9], in which a human expert simulates the behaviour of an automatic system. There were a total of 225 voluntary speakers, which performed the acquisition without restrictions; the only semantic restriction was provided by the scenario they had to accomplish, which varied from acquisition to acquisition.

The acquisition process resulted in 6,280 user turns and 9,133 system turns, with a vocabulary of about 900 words and a total of 5.5 h of speech signal. The dialogues were manually transcribed and annotated with DA at the segment level by using an annotation scheme that is presented in [1]. This scheme defines each DA as a combination of three different levels (speech act, concept and argument, initially defined in [10]). The mean number of segments (label occurrences) per turn is about 1.5, and a total number of 248 labels (153 for user turns and 95 for system turns) were defined. When only the first two levels are considered, the number of labels reduces to 72 labels (45 for user and 27 for system).

5   Experiments and Results

A series of experiments was defined in order to examine the performance of the proposed confidence measures in the annotation by the NGT technique of the Dihana corpus. The direct confidence measures and the wordgraph generation were implemented in the current version of the NGT software[2], and this new software was applied to the Dihana corpus.

---

[2] Available in http://www.dsic.upv.es/~cmartine/research/resources.html

The Dihana corpus was preprocessed to reduce its complexity using a process similar to that reported in previous works [15]: all the words were transcribed to lowercase, a categorisation (which included times, dates, town names, fares, etc.) was performed, the words were speaker-labelled (U for user, S for system), and punctuation marks were separated from words. A cross-validation approach was followed by defining 5 partitions of 180 dialogues each partition. The annotation models that were employed were a 4-gram for the NGT model and a 3-gram of DA as output language model, since the best results reported for Dihana with the NGT model use these models [15]. With respect to the width of the wordgraph, we choose to not limitate the width (i.e., all the possible hypothesis generated during the search process are used to create the wordgraph) in order to keep the experimental conditions similar to those of the direct confidence measures.

Since in the training samples many input words have only associated a possible output (including the empty output), these words must be excluded in the evaluation of the confidence measure (since they always will have a total confidence). For all the other words, the possible outputs depend on the training set, but they are a subset of the extended words that can be formed by the word itself and the word attached to any of the DA labels (248 for the 3-level labelling and 72 for the 2-level labelling).

An initial measure of the quality of the annotation technique can be obtained by computing the Classification Error Rate (CER) measure for the set without single-output words in the baseline experiment (i.e., where no confidence measures are used and every decision is taken as confident enough). In the CER computation the possible events are:

- No output is in the hypothesis:
  - No output is in the reference: correct.
  - Output is in the reference: incorrect.
- An output is in the hypothesis:
  - No output is in the reference: incorrect.
  - Output in the reference, but different: incorrect.
  - Output in the reference, and the same: correct.

Table 1. Dihana CER results (2 and 3-level labels) for NGT model with a 4-gram for NGT and a 3-gram for DA language model.

2 levels	3 levels
3.81	8.48

CER is expressed as the percentage of incorrect events with respect to the total number of events. The corresponding results are presented in Table 1. This CER is quite low, which suggest that even the use of high-quality confidence measures will not produce improvements in this measure. However, the use of CER for the evaluation of confidence measures is unfaithful in many cases, and consequently we will use other wide-accepted evaluation measures that rely on the concepts of correct and incorrect events as well.

The evaluation was performed by using the classical "Receiver Operating Characteristic" (ROC) curves [8] and the "Area under ROC curve" (AROC). A ROC curve is a measure which represents the *true rejection rate* (the proportion of the truly incorrect events considered as incorrect by the confidence measure) against the *false rejection rate* (the proportion of the truly correct events considered as incorrect by the confidence measure) for all possible thresholds between 0 (all events are accepted) and 1 (all events are rejected). All ROC curves are increasing functions that start at (0,0) and finish at (1,1).

In the optimal case, the point (0,1) belongs to the ROC curve (all incorrect events are detected and no correct event was rejected); thus, a ROC curve which is closer to the upper left corner of the graph represents a better confidence measure than a ROC curve which is farther from this point. The AROC measures the normalised area that covers a ROC curve, which provides a single measure of the confidence measure quality that makes results more comparable. AROC is usually normalised between 0 and 100, with 50 the baseline case. The ROC curves for FBCM and TCM (in their direct and wordgraph derived form) for 2 and 3-level labels, are presented in the graphics in Fig. 1. The AROC results are presented in Table 2.

Table 2. AROC measure for the FBCM and TCM confidence measures, for the 2 and 3 levels label set of Dihana. Baseline is 50. The NGT model was a 3-gram and the DA output language model was a 4-gram.

Confidence measure	2 levels		3 levels	
	Direct	Wordgraph	Direct	Wordgraph
FBCM	90.59	90.15	83.91	83.28
TCM	91.16	90.37	83.89	83.28

From these results we can conclude that the proposed confidence measures are good enough for the annotation of dialogues. The measures behave slightly better when applied to a less complex version (with the 2-level labels), which seems reasonable since the number of different events gets reduced and the confusion gets lower. In this case, the TCM behaves slightly better than the FBCM (in both the direct and the word-graph versions), but for 3-level labels differences seem not significant.

Although it seems strange that TCM behaves better than FBCM, the explanation is given by the implementation of the NGT search. Since the search space is very large, the NGT search applies intensive beam search during the process; this makes the α and β computations to be inaccurate, since the beam process affects the computation of the "real" forward and backward measures (specially for β, that can be only computed when the search is finished). Thus, the inclusion of the backward probability may distort the real confidence of the local hypothesis; the forward and transition probability can be computed as the search tree

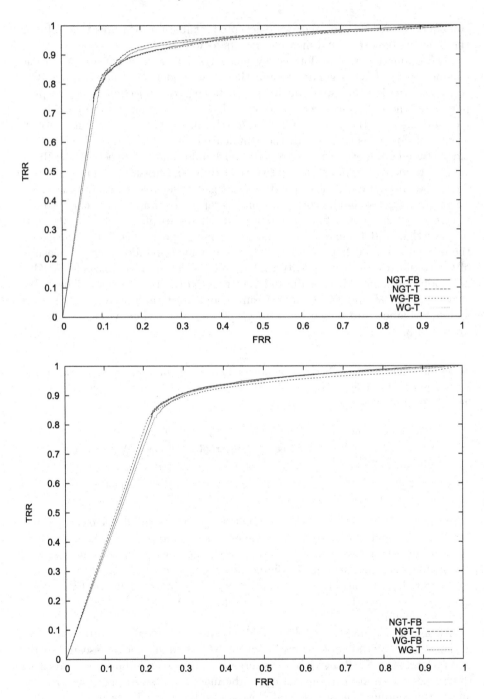

Fig. 1. ROC curves for the direct (NGT-) and wordgraph-based (WG-) FBCM and TCM confidence measures, for the 2 (top) and 3 (bottom) levels label set of Dihana. The NGT model was a 3-gram and the DA output language model was a 4-gram.

is built, but when the beam condition is applied the search starts from a single branch (the current best solution) and they can locally lose precision.

With respect to the direct and wordgraph differences, they are very low, although consintently wordgraph-based confidence measures provide a slightly lower accuracy. This seems reasonable, since a new step (wordgraph derivation) is introduced in the process and new possible errors can be produced in the subsequential steps. Nevertheless, differences seem not significant and both processes can be considered to offer the same quality. However, wordgraph-based confidence measures could be applied with other dialogue annotation models, such as those based on Hidden Markov Models [19], which makes it more versatile than the ad-hoc proposal for NGT.

6   Conclusions and Future Work

In this work we presented a proposal on confidence measures that was adapted and implemented in the NGT technique, as well as a word graph-based proposal that is applied to this technique. We tested the measures on a medium-size task-oriented human-computer dialogue corpus. The results show that our proposals are good enough to provide an appropriate guidance to human correctors that must amend the draft annotation provided by the automatic technique. One of the proposals (TCM) performs slightly better than the other (FBCM), and consequently it seems the most appropriate to be used in a real system. Differences between the direct and the wordgraph-based computation are very low and the two processes could be applied in any case.

Some future work must be completed to confirm the goodness of our proposals. At first term, the use of beam search in the NGT software restricts the computations of the forward and backward probabilities. Thus, the beam factor must be as high as possible to verify the real influence of these probabilities in the computation. However, the use of beam search or limited expansion of the tree is necessary to avoid the excessive spatial cost of the search process. Thus, the combination of confidence measures with a limited expansion (such as that proposed in [20]) is an interesting way to explore. Apart from that, the use of other models (such as Hidden Markov Models with N-grams) in dialogue annotation can provide wordgraphs as well, and the previously defined confidence measures could be applied to verify the performance of the alternative models with respect to the NGT model.

Finally, experiments with more corpora are desirable to confirm the appropriateness of the proposal for data of different nature. The confidence measures can be applied in real annotation tasks and in the selection of the most informative dialogues to be annotated by Active Learning [11], in order to reduce the correction effort.

Acknowledgments. Work supported by EC under FP7 project CasMaCat (FP7-28757), and by Spanish MINECO under projects STraDA (TIN2012-37475-C02-01) and Active2Trans (TIN2012-31723), and by GVA under project AMIIS (ISIC/2012/004).

References

1. Alcácer, N., Benedí, J.M., Blat, F., Granell, R., Martínez, C.D., Torres, F.: Acquisition and labelling of a spontaneous speech dialogue corpus. In: SPECOM, Greece, pp. 583–586 (2005)
2. Austin, J.L.: How to Do Things with Words. Oxford University Press, London (1962)
3. Benedí, J.M., Lleida, E., Varona, A., Castro, M.J., Galiano, I., Justo, R., López, I., Miguel, A.: Design and acquisition of a telephone spontaneous speech dialogue corpus in spanish: DIHANA. In: Fifth LREC, Genova, Italy, pp. 1636–1639 (2006)
4. Bunt, H.: Context and dialogue control. THINK Q. **3**, 19–31 (1994)
5. Casacuberta, F., Vidal, E., Picó, D.: Inference of finite-state transducers from regular languages. Pattern Recogn. **38**(9), 1431–1443 (2005)
6. Core, M.G., Allen, J.F.: Coding dialogues with the DAMSL annotation scheme. In: Traum, D. (ed.) Working Notes: AAAI Fall Symposium on Communicative Action in Humans and Machines, pp. 28–35. AAAI, Menlo Park (1997)
7. Devijver, P.A.: Baum's forward-backward algorithm revisited. Pattern Recogn. Lett. **3**(6), 369–373 (1985)
8. Egan, J.P.: Signal Detection Theory and Roc Analysis. Academic Press, New York (1975)
9. Fraser, M., Gilbert, G.: Simulating speech systems. Comp. Speech Lang. **5**, 81–99 (1991)
10. Fukada, T., Koll, D., Waibel, A., Tanigaki, K.: Probabilistic dialogue act extraction for concept based multilingual translation systems. In: Proceedings of ICSLP, vol. 6, pp. 2771–2774 (1998)
11. Ghigi, F., Tamarit, V., Martínez-Hinarejos, C.-D., Benedí, J.-M.: Active learning for dialogue act labelling. In: Vitrià, J., Sanches, J.M., Hernández, M. (eds.) IbPRIA 2011. LNCS, vol. 6669, pp. 652–659. Springer, Heidelberg (2011)
12. Jiang, H.: Confidence measures for speech recognition: a survey. Speech Comm. **45**(4), 455–470 (2005)
13. Lee, G.G., Mariani, J., Minker, W., Nakamura, S. (eds.): IWSDS 2010. LNCS, vol. 6392. Springer, Heidelberg (2010)
14. Martínez-Hinarejos, C.-D., Benedí, J.M., Granell, R.: Statistical framework for a spanish spoken dialogue corpus. Speech Commun. **50**, 992–1008 (2008)
15. Martínez-Hinarejos, C.-D., Tamarit, V., Benedí, J.M.: Improving unsegmented dialogue turns annotation with N-gram transducers. In: Proceedings of PACLIC23, vol. 1, pp. 345–354. City University of Hong Kong Press, Hong Kong (2009)
16. San-Segundo, R., Pellom, B., Hacioglu, K., Ward, W., Pardo, J.M.: Confidence measures for spoken dialogue systems. In: ICASSP, vol. 1, pp. 393–396. IEEE Computer Society, Los Alamitos (2001)
17. Sánchez-Sáez, R., Sánchez, J.A., Benedí, J.M.: Statistical confidence measures for probabilistic parsing. In: Proceedings of RANLP'09, Borovets, Bulgaria, pp. 388–392, September 2009
18. Seneff, S., Polifroni, J.: Dialogue management in Mercury flight reservation system. In: ANLP-NAACL, pp. 1–6 (2000)
19. Stolcke, A., Coccaro, N., Bates, R., Taylor, P., van Ess-Dykema, C., Ries, K., Shriberg, E., Jurafsky, D., Martin, R., Meteer, M.: Dialogue act modelling for automatic tagging and recognition of conversational speech. Comput. Linguist. **26**(3), 1–34 (2000)

20. Tamarit, V., Martínez-Hinarejos, C.-D., Benedí, J.M.: On the use of N-gram transducers for dialogue annotation. In: Spoken Dialogue Systems Technology and Design, pp. 255–276. Springer, New York (2011)
21. Ueffing, N., Macherey, K., Ney, H.: Confidence measures for statistical machine translation. In: Proceedings of the MT Summit IX, pp. 394–401. Springer (2003)
22. Walker, M., Passonneau, R.: DATE: a dialogue act tagging scheme for evaluation of spoken dialogue systems. In: HLT'01: Proceedings of the 1st International Conference on Human Language Technology, San Diego, pp. 1–8 (2001)
23. Wessel, F., Schlüter, R., Macherey, K., Ney, H.: Confidence measures for large vocabulary continuous speech recognition. IEEE Trans. Speech Audio Process. **9**, 288–298 (2001)
24. Williams, J.D., Young, S.: Partially observable markov decision processes for spoken dialog systems. Comput. Speech Lang. **21**(2), 393–422 (2007)

Orwell's *1984*—From Simple to Multi-word Units

Cvetana Krstev[1(✉)], Duško Vitas[2], and Aleksandra Trtovac[3]

[1] Faculty of Philology, University of Belgrade, Studentski trg 1, Belgrade, Serbia
cvetana@matf.bg.ac.rs
[2] Faculty of Mathematics, University of Belgrade, Studentski trg 16, Belgrade, Serbia
[3] University Library, University of Belgrade,
Bulevar kralja Aleksandra 71, Belgrade, Serbia

Abstract. In this paper we present an alternative version of the morphosyntactically annotated Serbian translation of *1984*. This version follows the basic principles of the MULTEXT-East version, except for one addition—the text will be annotated with multi-word units as well. We will present the resources used for annotation with multi-word units and explain how these resources were enriched with multi-word units extracted from the processed text. Finally, we will present the format of this alternative version and the benefits obtained both from preparing the new resource and from the resource itself.

Keywords: Morphosyntactic annotation · Multi-word units · Finite-state transducers · MULTEXT-East

1 Motivation

The well-known multilingual linguistic resource MULTEXT-East has a long history. Its first version was produced as part of the project that was a spin-off of MULTEXT and ran from '95 to '97. After the project officially ended, the resource was upgraded and enhanced, as part of some other projects, but also independently, as a result of the efforts of different research groups. The core of this resource were in its first, as well as in its subsequent versions: the MULTEXT-East morpho-syntactic specifications of the involved languages, lexica, and aligned and annotated *1984* corpora. The latest version is v4, released in May 2010. The first version covered six languages plus English [1], while the current one contains at least some of the core resources for sixteen languages [2]. Recently, a new modeling of the morphosyntactic annotations of the MULTEXT-East corpora and lexicons was done as an OWL/DL ontology that enables formal specification of the interrelationships between the various features and makes possible logical inferences, based on the relationships between them [3].

The Serbian language was represented in this resource from the very beginning. Although Serbian research groups were not involved in the MULTEXT-East project, they contributed to it by providing a structurally annotated and

© Springer International Publishing Switzerland 2014
Z. Vetulani and J. Mariani (Eds.): LTC 2011, LNAI 8387, pp. 276–287, 2014.
DOI: 10.1007/978-3-319-08958-4_23

aligned version of Orwell's *1984* through the TELRI project [4]. A morphosyntactic description of the linguistically annotated *1984* in Serbian and the basic morphosyntactic lexicon were added in the version 3.0 [5]. In the version 4.0, the Serbian morphosyntactic lexicon was enhanced and it now contains a superset of all lemmas and their forms that appear in *1984*. The morphosyntactic description and annotation of *1984* should have been corrected and improved, but due to the lack of human resources this was not done.

The popularity of this resource is indisputable. According to Google Scholar, only the paper [6] describing its third edition has 177 citations (as of August 2013). The resource itself is still being requested on a weekly basis by members of various research communities. Its popularity can be attributed to the fact that it represents a coherent and comparable resource for many languages. Also, the existence of a comprehensive documentation cannot be overstressed.

The Serbian part of this resource was used for various research purposes for Serbian: for the training of taggers [7–9] and aligners [10], for lemmatization [11], and for a human oriented dictionary web service [12]. Its connection to Serbian morphological e-dictionaries is bidirectional: they were used to semi-automatically produce linguistically annotated *1984*, and were at the same time corrected and improved in the course of this process.

On the other hand, multi-word units (MWUs) have been a topic of great interest in the natural language processing (NLP) field for quite a long time. Much work was devoted to them and they have been analyzed and processed from a variety of different perspectives. In the computational lexicography school led by Maurice Gross in LADL, the interest in MWUs and the production of morphological dictionaries of compounds has been vivid from the very beginning [13]. In recent years, further advances have been achieved enabling effective production of such dictionaries [14]. Also, some work has been done to produce texts annotated with MWUs rather then with simple words. In [15], the authors present an e-version of Verne's novel *Le tour du monde en 80 jours* annotated with multi-word adverbs. The Serbian translation of the same text was used in [16] to show that multi-word tagging can have positive effects on morphosyntactic disambiguation. A corpus annotated with named entities, most of which are MWUs, is presented in [17]. A named entity recognition and tagging system for Serbian is presented in [18].

Having in mind the mutual benefit that Serbian morphological e-dictionaries of simple words and the morphologically annotated Serbian version of *1984* had from each other, our idea was to try to obtain a similar positive result for MWUs. We would like to (a) collect from *1984* new candidates for Serbian morphological e-dictionaries of MWUs, which is still under development, and (b) produce, using these dictionaries, an alternative version of *1984* annotated with MWUs.

In Sect. 2 we will briefly present Serbian morphological e-dictionaries of MWUs, in Sect. 3 we will present our tools for collecting new candidates for these dictionaries from a text, while in Sect. 4 we will give the results obtained for *1984*. In Sect. 5 we will present the format of this alternative version, and finally in Sect. 6 we will give some concluding remarks.

2   Serbian Tools for MWU Processing

By multi-word units we mean contiguous sequences of simple words that have a constant reference which can be treated as a single unit when used in many NLP applications. Two types of such MWUs are of interest. The MWUs with a predictable structure and a potentially infinite number of instances, e.g. date and time expressions, can be described by finite-state automata. The other type of MWUs that are idiosyncratic in nature, have constant reference and show a certain degree of non-compositionality can be listed in a dictionary. The idea and the basic principles of treatment of these two types of MWUs for Serbian were described in [19]. Both types of MWUs are treated in a similar way, as simple word units during text processing: after applying dictionaries and other lexical tools to a text, a lemma and sets of values of grammatical categories are assigned to a recognized MWU. That is, MWUs belong to same Part-of-Speech (POS) as simple words — nouns (N), adjectives (A), adverbs (ADV), interjections (INT), conjunctions (CONJ), prepositions (PREP) — and are, consequently, described by the same morphosyntactic categories. Verb phrases are not contiguous by nature and, therefore, they are not treated in either of these ways.

Finite state transducers that recognize and annotate the following MWUs were developed:

- Numerals, both cardinal and ordinal, written as words, digits (Arabic and Roman) and their combinations (*sto četrdeset i pet miliona* '145 million')[1];
- Inflected and derived forms of numerals written as digits (*30-ak* 'approximately 30') and acronyms (e.g. *SPPT* 'FFCC', *NATO-a* 'NATO (the genitive case)');
- Interjections with a repetition of patterns (*hi-hi-hi-ho-ho-ho*);
- Compounds of consisting of numerals (written as Arabic digits or words) and nouns (*32-godišnjak* '32 years old man') or adjectives (*12-godišnji* '12 years old'), either separated by a hyphen or not. It should be noticed that these occurrences represent simple words written as MWUs;
- Noun phrases expressing measure (*tri stotine metara* '300 meters') and money expressions (*osam funti* 'eight pounds').

The role of these transducers is to assign to a recognized form its lemma and a set of values of grammatical categories, as illustrated by one path in one of these graphs in Fig. 1. The result is the same as if the following line were listed in an e-dictionary (Example 1).

(1)   32-godišnjakom,32-godišnjak.N+Hum+C:ms6v

That is, 32-*godišnjakom* is the singular (s) form of a masculine (m) noun 32-*godišnjak* representing a human (+Hum) in the instrumental case (6).

The other MWUs are actually listed in e-dictionaries. Serbian morphological e-dictionaries are being developed in accordance with the methodology and the

---

[1] All examples in this paper (in English with a Serbian translation) are from the novel *1984*, if such an example occurs in the text.

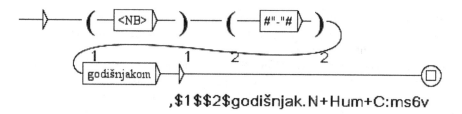

,\$1\$\$2\$godišnjak.N+Hum+C:ms6v

Fig. 1. One path from a transducer that recognizes compound nouns <NB>-*godišnjak*.

format (known as DELAS/DELAF for simple words, and DELAC/DELACF for MWUs) presented for French in [20]. One line from DELACF for the MWU noun *jednakost pred zakonom* 'equality before the law' is:

(2) jednakost(jednakost.N704:fs1q) pred zakonom,NC_N4X1

The paper [19] describes how all inflected forms of a lemma can be generated form such an entry, and highlights the expressiveness and limitations of this approach. As lemma entries are complex in themselves, a tool was developed that produces such entries from a list of MWUs in their normalized (dictionary) form. This tool and its successfulness in producing lemma entries for various types of MWUs (named entities, general lexica, economy domain, etc.) were presented in [21]. We use the Unitex corpus processing system for processing text using finite-state transducers and e-dictionaries.[2]

The code following the lemma in a dictionary entry (e.g. NC_N4X1 in the above example) is at the same time the name of the inflectional transducer that is responsible for the generation of forms and the code that determines the

Table 1. The most frequent structures of Serbian MWU nouns and adjectives

MWU structure	No. of lemmas (in %)	Examples
AXN	67.58	*Veliki Brat* 'Big Brother'
2XN	8.34	*patent-zatvarač* 'zipper'
N2X	7.77	*igra rečima* 'play on words'
N4X	5.68	*ram za slike* 'picture-frame'
		osećanje niže vrednosti 'sense of inferiority'
NXN	3.46	*pištolj-igračka* 'toy pistol'
AXAXN	1.77	*jeftina radna snaga* 'cheap labour'
other	5.42	
2XA	46.95	*vaspitno-popravni* 'correctional'
A4X	20.99	*beo kao kreda* 'white as chalk'
A3XN	16.79	*gladan kao vuk* 'hungry as a wolf'
AXA	9.54	
other	5.73	

---

[2] http://igm.univ-mlv.fr/~unitex/

POS of an MWU lemma (NC — a compound noun) and its structure (N4X1 — it consists of a noun followed by four tokens, including separators, that are re-copied in all inflected forms).

Serbian MWU nouns and adjectives have various structures — some of them are very frequent, while others occur in just a few lemmas. The most frequent structures for lemmas that inflect (MWU nouns and adjectives) are listed in Table 1. The percentages were computed after enlarging the Serbian DELAC with the MWUs retrieved from 1984 (see Sect. 3) at which moment it contained 10,002 lemmas for MWU nouns and adjectives.

In addition to nouns and adjectives, Serbian dictionaries contain MWUs belonging to other POS. These MWUs also have various structures, but their structure cannot be deduced from their POS codes because they do not inflect. However, something can be said about their structure too. The most frequent structure of MWU prepositions is PREP_N — 70 %, MWU conjunctions CONJ_ADV — 32.43 % and CONJ_CONJ — 51.35 %, MWU adverbs PREP_N — 51.59 % and PREP_ADV — 9.63 %. These percentages were computed at the moment when the Serbian DELAC contained 624 MWU lemmas that do not inflect.

The named entity recognition normalization system for Serbian is aimed at the recognition of traditional named entities primarily in newspaper texts: amount and temporal expressions, geopolitical names, personal names and their roles and names of organizations [18]. The that relies on all presented lexical resources for Serbian is developed as a large collection of finite-state transducers organized in a cascade. It aims to solve, to a certain extent, the problems of ambiguity and synonymy of named entities. For this experiment we recognized and tagged amount expressions and multi-word adverbs composed of temporal expressions. Some examples of these expressions retrieved from *1984* are: *dva i po dolara* 'two dollars fifty', *deset-dvadeset metara* 'ten or twenty metres', *dve unce* 'two ounces', *po zavretku prve polovine ovog veka* 'after the middle of the present century', *otprilike do 2050. godine* 'by about the year 2050'.

3   Enhancement of Serbian DELAC Dictionary

The first sources of MWUs to be included in e-dictionaries are traditional dictionaries for general lexica and various gazetteers for proper names such as personal names and geopolitical names. The initial set of MWUs included in the Serbian DELAC dictionary was partly taken from various paper sources and partly from the Serbian Wordnet. However, these sources cannot be the only ones used, because they were produced from a different standpoint compared to that imposed by the NLP applications.

Namely, many compounds that occur in the contemporary texts are not listed in the already used resources either because they are underdeveloped (Wordnet), new or regarded as "uninteresting" from the lexicographic point of view (paper dictionaries). One approach is to (semi-)automatically extract compounds from corpora, which was applied, for instance to Polish, by using both grammatical

A) Recognizes sintagms Noun-Noun in the genitive case that are NOT in the dictionary of MWUs

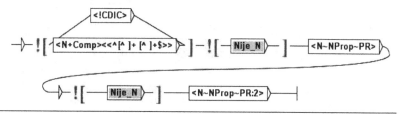

B) if syntagm IS preceded by a preposition which does NOT form with the following noun a MWU preposition or adverb

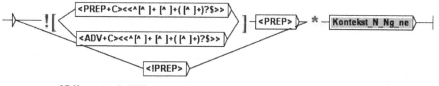

OR if syntagm is NOT preceded by a preposition
NOTE: all prepositions HAVE TO BE unambiguous

Fig. 2. A graph that recognizes syntagms N/N_g that are not in the dictionary of MWUs.

and statistical analysis [22]. We have taken a similar approach by developing a collection of graphs that extract potential MWUs from a chosen text on the basis of their syntactic structure. The aim of these graphs is twofold: (1) to extract with high recall and precision the clauses having a certain syntactic structure; (2) to extract only the clauses that are not already in the DELAC dictionary. We consider an extraction graph to be successful if the extracted clauses have the syntactic structure we are looking for. Whether the extracted clauses are actually MWUs that we wish to include in our e-dictionaries has to be determined manually.

Naturally, we have constructed extraction graphs that cover the most frequent structures presented in the previous sections.

- For nouns, A_N, N_N, N_Ng, N_PREP_N, UNK_N (UNK stands for a MWU component that is not a simple word);
- For adjectives, UNK_A, A_A, A_kao_A;
- For prepositions and adverbs, PREP_N.

One of these graphs is presented in Fig. 2. The recognition of a clause Noun/Noun in the genitive case that is not already in the DELAC is done by the sub-graph KONTEKST_N_NG_NE (the upper graph in Fig. 2). In order to achieve better precision, we reject all noun words that are confusable with other PoS, as well as proper names (the sub-graph NIJE_N which is not presented in Fig. 2). These instances of false recognition are rejected by using positive and negative contexts in the Unitex corpus processing system [23]. Despite all this, the graph

Table 2. New MWUs retrieved from Serbian *1984*

Nouns		325	
	AXN	259	*proleterska revolucija* 'proletarian rebellion'
	N2X	19	*savez omladine* 'the Youth League'
	2XN	7	*šmirgl-papir* 'sandpaper'
	NXN	2	*špijunka amater* 'amateur spy woman'
	N4X	34	*čovek za vezu* 'contacts (man)'
	AXAXN	1	*jeftina radna snaga* 'cheap labor'
	other	1	
Adjectives		7	
	AXA	1	*nijedan drugi* 'no other'
	2XA	3	*mentalno zdrav* 'sane (mentally healthy)'
	A4X	3	*osudjen na smrt* 'condemned to death'
Adverbs		59	*licem u lice* 'face to face'
Prepositions		20	*s tačke gledišta* 'from the point of view'
Interjections		3	*na mestu voljno* 'Stand easy!'
Conjunctions		1	*u nadi da* 'that (he) hoped'

KONTEKST_N_NG_NE leads to many false recognitions, because in Serbian there are some very frequent compound prepositions and adverbs with a simple preposition in the initial position, followed by one or more nouns. In order to achieve better results, the main graph (the lower graph in Fig. 2) accepts only those sequences accepted by KONTEKST_N_NG_NE that are either (i) preceded by a preposition which does not form a MWU preposition or adverb with the nouns that follow it or (ii) are not preceded by a preposition.

By applying these extraction graphs to our text — the Serbian translation of *1984* — and by manually analyzing the obtained concordances, we produced a list of 415 new MWUs that we have further processed to obtain MWU lemmas that we have inflected and the obtained forms were included in our e-dictionaries. The POS and the structure of new lemmas are presented in Table 2. Most of new noun MWUs are common nouns — *1984* is not a kind of text where many named entities or proper names, other then the names of the main characters, are expected. Among the 11 proper names added are *Komunistička internacionala* 'Communist International' and *Deklaracija nezavisnosti* 'Declaration of Independence'.

In addition to these 415 MWUs that were added to our e-dictionaries of general lexica and proper names, we prepared a list of MWUs specific to this particular text. It contains 21 items like *O'Brajenov*, possesive adjective of O'Brien and *Ministarstvo ljubavi* 'the Ministry of Love'. It was not always easy to decide what is specific and what is general enough — we decided that *Veliki brat* 'Big Brother' should become part of general lexica, while *Policija misli* 'the Thought Police' should not be included (yet).

For this type of text, there was no need to develop new or modify any of the existing finite-state transducers already in use for inflection of MWUs in the Serbian texts.

4   Application of MWU Resources

After applying our lexical MWU resources — general e-dictionaries, specific e-dictionaries, and finite-state transducers — to the Serbian translation of *1984*, we obtained the results presented in Table 3. The text itself has approximately 90,000 current simple words.

We wanted to compare our results to the English text processed with English resources. We relied on the resources included in the standard Unitex distribution. They consist of a public e-dictionary developed using the same methodology used for Serbian and its production is described in [24]. It contains a number of MWU forms and lemmas — approximately 70,000 lemmas. For the English text that consists of approximately 105,000 simple word occurrences, this dictionary retrieved 1,172 occurrences of MWUs and 532 different lemmas. Having in mind that finite-state automata for numerals and other expressions — measures, money and temporal expressions — were not supplied in the Unitex distribution for the English language and no specific dictionary was available for *1984*, the results were comparable to those obtained for Serbian. It is not surprising that more MWUs were retrieved in the Serbian text, since our resources were enhanced using this particular text. The comparison of the retrieved MWUs in English and Serbian text is beyond the scope of this paper and asks for a more

Table 3. Application of MWU resources on *1984* — results

		occurrences	lemmas	tokens
FSTs		**395**	**277**	**900**
	Numerals	58	30	132
	Measures	26	21	58
	Money	11	7	24
	Temp.adv.	300	219	686
General dictionaries		**1,781**	**602**	**4,128**
	Nouns	757	415	1,579
	Adjectives	19	11	47
	Adverbs	534	101	1,146
	Prepositions	103	52	244
	Conjunctions	362	19	1,090
	Interjections	6	4	22
Specific dictionaries		**393**	**21**	**798**
	Nouns	369	20	750
	Adjectives	24	1	48
Total		**2,569**	**900**	**5,826**

detailed analysis. All we can say is that among them there is a number of exact equivalents, e.g. *Veliki brat* 'Big Brother', *talasasti lim* 'corrugated iron', *pre ili posle* 'sooner or later'.

Although it was already established that the recognition of MWUs reduces false ambiguities (see, for instance [25]) introduced by high-recall annotation obtained by lexical resources, they cannot be accepted without caution. In our experiment there were few false recognitions, e.g. the sequence *crna kosa* was recognized as the genitive case of a MWU *crni kos* 'blackbird' while in the text it represented a phrase in the nominative case 'black hair'. The instances of ambiguous behavior of frequent MWU prepositions and adverbs were more serious. One such case is *u blizini* - it can be an adverb, like in *On se upita da u blizini ipak nije sakriven kakav mikrofon* 'He wondered whether after all there was a microphone hidden somewhere near' or a preposition, like *Nije bilo pametno čak ni biti vidjen u blizini takvih ljudi* 'It was not wise even to be seen in the neighbourhood of such people'. There are also cases where although a MWU was correctly recognized, annotating text with it could confuse further linguistic analysis. For instance, annotating text with a MWU *pismeni ljudi* 'literate men' in a sequence *jedva pismeni ljudi* 'people who could barely read and write' would mean overlooking the fact that the adverb *jedva* 'barely' modifies the adjective *pismeni*. All such cases have to be manually examined and some of them can be eliminated by disambiguation grammars.

5   An Example from the Alternative Version

We will illustrate the content of the proposed alternative version with one sentence: *Izveštaj o dnevnoj zapovesti Velikog Brata iz Tajmsa od trećeg decembra 1983. krajnje loš.* 'The reporting of Big Brother's Order for the Day in the Times of December 3rd 1983 is extremely unsatisfactory'. It contains three MWUs:

- The noun *dnevnoj zapovesti* 'Order for the Day' in the locative case;
- The noun *Velikom Bratu* 'Big Brother' in the dative case;
- The adverb containing a temporal expressions od *trećeg decembra 1983.* 'of December 3rd 1983'.

```
<s id="Oshs.1.5.18.1.1" >
<w lemma="izvestaj" ana="Ncmsn--n">Izvestaj</w>
<w lemma="o" ana="Sps-">o</w>
<w lemma="dnevna zapovest" ana="Ncfsl--n">dnevnoj zapovesti</w>
<w lemma="Veliki Brat" ana="Ncmsg--y">Velikog Brata</w>
<w lemma="iz" ana="Sps-">iz</w>
<w lemma="Tajms" ana="Ncmsg--n">Tajmsa</w>
<w lemma="od treceg decembra 1983." ana="Rgp">od treceg decembra
    1983.</w>
<w lemma="krajnje" ana="Rgp">krajnje</w>
<w lemma="los" ana="Afpmsnn">los</w>
</s>
```

All recognized MWUs can be described using the MULTEXT-East specification in much the same way as simple words — the MWUs that we recognize at this moment are classified in same POS as simple words. Conjunctions, prepositions and interjections have the attribute 'formation' with values 'simple' and 'compound', while nouns, adjectives, numerals and adverbs do not, so they cannot be described as such. That does not mean that there are no deficiencies in the MULTEXT-East specification (already discussed in [26]), but they did not increase with the use of MWUs. The conversion of grammatical categories and their values used in Serbian morphological dictionaries to the MULTEXT-East attributes and their values, is done using the same procedures that were used for the production of annotated text using simple words [5].

6   Concluding Remarks

With this experiment we have already achieved the following goals:

- We have enlarged our e-dictionaries of MWUs by 415 new entries;
- We have developed a set of finite-state transducers that can extract potential MWUs from processed texts. These transducers were already successfully used on texts from various domains (e.g. in the domain of library and information science);
- We have set the stage for the production of an alternative version of *1984* that will be morphosyntactically annotated with MWUs. This task has not been finalized yet. Before the final production stages can take place we would like to perform some more preparatory work (e.g. annotation of other named entities).

In addition to these, we used the lexical resources for Serbian (presented partially in Sect. 2) and the already developed local grammars to improve the current version of the morphosyntactically annotated Serbian translation of *1984*. We noted that in the case of verbs annotation was not performed consistently although it was restricted to orthographic words. Namely, two attributes — verb form and tense — were not annotated consistently for all analytical tenses:

- Future 1: verb form *streljati* in *opet će te streljati* 'they'll shoot you just the same' is coded with Vmn----an-n---e;
- Future 2: verb form *ispitivao* in *Ako ga ko bude ispitivao* 'If questioned' is coded with Vmps-sman-n---p;
- Past: verb form *bombardovali* in *Bombardovali su je* 'It was bombed' is coded with Vmps-pman-n---e;
- Pluperfect: verb form *popadali* in *Zvončići behu popadali* 'The bluebells had cascaded' is coded with Vmps-pman-n---e;
- Conditional: verb form *mogao* in *Kako bi mogao da umre?* 'How could he die?' is coded with Vmps-sman-n---e.

It can be seen that for all tenses, except Future 1, the main verb was coded as participle in the past tense, whereas for Future 1 the tense was not coded. In the new version we decided to omit the information about tense for analytic tenses. In order to do that we detected the majority of analytical tenses in the text (5,924 occurrences) by applying local grammars [27]. Proper annotation of analytic tenses has been postponed for some new edition of *1984*.

Acknowledgments. This research was supported by the Serbian Ministry of Education and Science (grant NO 178003).

References

1. Dimitrova, L., Ide, N., Petkevic, V., Erjavec, T., Kaalep, H.J., Tufis, D.: Multext-East: parallel and comparable corpora and lexicons for six Central and Eastern european languages. In: Proceedings of the 36th Annual Meeting of the ACL and 17th International Conference on Computational Linguistics, vol. 1, pp. 315–319. ACL, Université de Montréal, Montréal (1998)
2. Erjavec, T.: MULTEXT-East: morphosyntactic resources for central and eastern european languages. Lang. Resour. Eval. **46**(1), 131–142 (2012)
3. Chiarcos, C., Erjavec, T.: OWL/DL formalization of the MULTEXT-East morphosyntactic specifications. In: Proceedings of the 5th Linguistic Annotation Workshop (LAW 2011), Portland, OR, USA. pp. 11–20. ACL (2011)
4. Erjavec, T., Lawson, A., Romary, L. (eds.): East Meets West – A Compendium of Multilingual Resources (CD-ROM). Telri Association e.V, IdS, Mannheim (1998)
5. Krstev, C., Vitas, D., Erjavec, T.: Morpho-syntactic descriptions in MULTEXT-East–the case of Serbian. Informatica **28**, 431–436 (2004)
6. Erjavec, T.: MULTEXT-East version 3: multilingual morphosyntactic specifications, lexicons and corpora. In: Lino, M.T., Xavier, M.F., Ferreira, F., Costa, R., Silva, R. (eds.) Proceedings of the 4th International Conference on Language Resources and Evaluation–LREC, Paris, pp. 1535–1538. ELRA, Paris (2004)
7. Popović, Z.: Taggers applied on texts in Serbian. INFOtheca **11**(2), 21a–38a (2010)
8. Utvić, M.: Annotating corpus of contemporary Serbian. INFOtheca **12**(2), 36a–47a (2011)
9. Delić, V., Sečujski, M., Kupusinac, A.: Transformation-based part-of-speech tagging for serbian language. In: Proceedings CIMMACS'09 of the 8th WSEAS International Conference on Computational Intelligence, Man machine Systems and Cybernetics, pp. 98–103. World Scientific and Engineering Academy and Society, Stevens Point, WI, USA (2009)
10. Božović, M.: Computational linguistics methods of parallel text alignment and their application to the English-Serbian language pair. Master thesis, Faculty of Philology, University of Belgrade, Belgrade (2010)
11. Gesmundo, A., Samardžić, T.: Lemmatisation as a tagging task. In: Proceedings of the 50th Annual Meeting of the Association for Computational Linguistics: Short Papers. ACL '12, vol. 2, pp. 368–372. ACL, Stroudsburg, PA (2012)
12. Ermolaev, N., Tasovac, T.: Building a lexicographic infrastructure for serbian digital libraries. In: Proceedings of the 12th international Conference on Libraries in the Digital Age (LIDA) (2012)

13. Gross, M.: Lexicon-grammar. The representation of compound words. In: Proceedings of Coling 1986, pp. 1–6, Bonn (1986)

14. Savary, A.: Multiflex: a multilingual finite-state tool for multi-word units. In: Maneth, S. (ed.) CIAA 2009. LNCS, vol. 5642, pp. 237–240. Springer, Heidelberg (2009)

15. Laporte, É., Nakamura, T., Voyatzi, S., et al.: A French corpus annotated for multiword nouns. In: Proceedings of the 6th Language Resources and Evaluation Conference. Workshop Towards a Shared Task on Multiword Expressions, Marrakech, Morocco, pp. 27–30. ELRA (2008)

16. Utvić, M., Obradović, I., Krstev, C., Vitas, D.: The effects of multi-word tagging on text disambiguation. In: Proceedings of the 29th International Conference on Lexis and Grammar, Belgrade, Serbia, pp. 333–342. Faculty of Mathematics, University of Belgrade (2010)

17. Savary, A., Waszczuk, J., Przepiórkowski, A.: Towards the annotation of named entities in the National Corpus of Polish. In: Proceedings of the 7th International Conference on Language Resources and Evaluation, Valetta, Malta, pp. 3622–3629. ELRA (2010)

18. Krstev, C., Obradović, I., Utvić, M., Vitas, D.: A system for named entity recognition based on local grammars. J. Logic Comput. **24**, 473–489 (2014)

19. Krstev, C., Vitas, D.: Finite state transducers for recognition and generation of compound words. In: Erjavec, T., Žganec Gros, J. (eds.) Proceedings of IS-LTC 2006, Ljubljana, Slovenia, pp. 192–197. Institut "Jožef Stefan" (2006)

20. Courtois, B., Silberztein, M.: Dictionnaires électroniques du français. Larousse, Paris (1990)

21. Krstev, C., Obradović, I., Stanković, R., Vitas, D.: An approach to efficient processing of multi-word units. In: Przepiórkowski, A., Piasecki, M., Jassem, K., Fuglewicz, P. (eds.) Computational Linguistics. SCI, vol. 458, pp. 109–129. Springer, Heidelberg (2013)

22. Woźniak, M.: Automatic extraction of multiword lexical units from Polish texts. In: Vetulani, Z. (ed.) Proceedings of the 5th Language & Technology Conference on Human Language Technologies as a Challenge for Computer Science and Linguistics, Poznań, Poland, pp. 187–191. Fundacja Uniwersytetu im. A. Mickiewicza (2011)

23. Paumier, S.: Unitex 3.1beta User Manual (2013). http://www-igm.univ-mlv.fr/~unitex/UnitexManual3.1beta.pdf

24. Savary, A.: Recensement et description des mots composés - méthodes et applications. Ph.D. thèse, Université de Marne-la-Vallée (2000)

25. Alegria, I., Ansa, O., Artola, X., Ezeiza, N., Nojenola, K., Urizar, R.: Representation and treatment of multiword expressions in Basque. In: Proceedings of the 2nd ACL Workshop on Multiword Expressions: Integrating Processing, Barcelona, Spain, pp. 48–55 (2004)

26. Przepiórkowski, A., Woliński, M.: The unbearable lightness of tagging: a case study in morphosyntactic tagging of Polish. In: Proceedings of 4th International Workshop on Linguistically Interpreted Corpora (LINC-03), Budapest, Hungary, pp. 13–14 (2003)

27. Đorđević, B.: Automatic recognition of composite verb forms in Serbian. In: Proceedings of the Workshop on Computational Linguistics and Natural Language Processing of Balkan Languages of the 5th Balkan Conference in Informatics, Novi Sad, Serbia, pp. 89–92. Faculty of Sciences, University of Novi Sad (2012)

Application of Audio and Video Processing Methods for Language Research and Documentation: The AVATecH Project

Przemyslaw Lenkiewicz[1]([envelope]), Sebastian Drude[1],
Anna Lenkiewicz[1], Binyam Gebrekidan Gebre[1], Stefano Masneri[3],
Oliver Schreer[3], Jochen Schwenninger[2], and Rolf Bardeli[2]

[1] Max Planck Institute for Psycholinguistics, Wundtlaan 1,
6525 XD Nijmegen, The Netherlands
{Przemyslaw.Lenkiewicz,Sebastian.Drude,
Anna.Lenkiewicz,BinyamGebrekidan.Gebre}@mpi.nl
http://www.mpi.nl/
[2] Fraunhofer Institute for Intelligent Analysis and Information Systems IAIS,
Schloss Birlinghoven, 53757 Sankt Augustin, Germany
{Jochen.Schwenninger,Rolf.Bardeli}@iais.fraunhofer.de
http://www.iais.fraunhofer.de/
[3] Fraunhofer Institute for Telecommunications, Heinrich Hertz Institute,
Einsteinufer 37, 10587 Berlin, Germany
{Stefano.Masneri,Oliver.Schreer}@hhi.fraunhofer.de
http://www.hhi.fraunhofer.de/

Abstract. Evolution and changes of all modern languages is a well-known fact. However, recently it is reaching dynamics never seen before, which results in loss of the vast amount of information encoded in every language. In order to preserve such rich heritage, and to carry out linguistic research, properly annotated recordings of world languages are necessary. Since creating those annotations is a very laborious task, reaching times 100 longer than the length of the annotated media, innovative video processing algorithms are needed, in order to improve the efficiency and quality of annotation process. This is the scope of the AVATecH project presented in this article.

Keywords: Language research · Audio and video processing · Automated annotation

1   Introduction

Languages and cultures have always been evolving due to many well-understood historical factors. However, in recent decades the dynamics of those changes

AVATecH is a joint project of Max Planck and Fraunhofer Institutes, started in 2009 and funded by MPG and FhG. Some of the research leading to these results has received funding from the European Commissions 7th Framework Program under grant agreement n 238405 (CLARA).

© Springer International Publishing Switzerland 2014
Z. Vetulani and J. Mariani (Eds.): LTC 2011, LNAI 8387, pp. 288–299, 2014.
DOI: 10.1007/978-3-319-08958-4_24

got an enormous speedup, partially due to the globalization process. As a consequence UNESCO has reported that currently one of the world's languages becomes extinct every two weeks and even major languages, like English of French, are changing. Similarly to biology, we can see a huge decrease in linguistic diversity [1]. Also the cultures are changing rapidly, identity building for young people becomes very difficult and the stability of societies is affected. We are deemed to loosing part of our cultural heritage since every language can be seen as a unique result of evolution resulting in rather different language systems. We also risk losing much of our knowledge about environment, species etc. since this is to a large extent encoded in the semantics of a given language.

During the last decades we recognize an increasing awareness about these threats resulting in a number of world-wide initiatives to document, archive and revitalize languages (DOBES[1], HRELP[2], PARADISEC[3]). It is well understood now, that we have the obligation to preserve our material and knowledge about languages for future generations, since they may want to understand their roots. Future generations may also want to return to proper linguistic constructions that are currently blurring or which we currently are loosing.

Furthermore, in the last years it has become clear that making recordings alone is not sufficient to guarantee that future generations will indeed be able to access the data. Recordings without appropriate annotations and metadata can be completely useless for anybody that has no knowledge about their creation and purpose. Manual annotation of such recordings is a very laborious task. Therefore the AVATecH project has been started with partners from the HHI and IAIS Fraunhofer Institutes, with the goal to develop automated annotation algorithms [2,3]. Their role is twofold: (1) they would allow a significant decrease of time necessary to perform the annotation task, (2) automation of some parts of the process can greatly increase the uniformity of the annotations created worldwide by different researchers, which would contribute to consistency of the available language data.

In this article we describe in detail the algorithms that operate on video recordings and present some results that we could obtain with them.

2 Audio Analysis Algorithms

Linguistic researchers are interested in annotating many aspects of the audio track. These aspects can vary greatly, and range from word or phonetic transcriptions to prosody and emotional aspects of speech. The diversity of use cases would require numerous dedicated automatic analysis tools. Instead we have decided to focus on smaller annotation building blocks within AVATecH, which accept user feedback and can be combined to speed up complex tasks. Here we present two examples of these blocks.

---

[1] http://www.mpi.nl/dobes
[2] http://www.hrelp.org/
[3] http://www.paradisec.org.au/

2.1 Automatic Detection of Speech

Here, the focus is on detecting the speech portions of the signal, as they are the most interesting parts of the signal with respect to annotation. Data diversity means unprecedented sound environments. To capture this diversity, we use a model-based or data-driven approach for speech detection instead of an approach in terms of heuristics and thresholds. We rely on the algorithm to learn a model of speech and non-speech from examples of corresponding data. Here the assumption is that non-speech sounds display patterns that are very different from speech, and can be effectively represented by a probabilistic model.

User feedback can be used to improve the models. In the user feedback scenario, the user is providing examples of speech or nonspeech segments from the file that is currently being annotated. Non-adapted baseline models can be adapted with a specific file currently annotated, and used for annotation of similar files.

In the first evaluation the models were adapted in a supervised manner, with data known to be either speech or non-speech. In a second experiment the models were used to classify the speech and non-speech segments in a file, and then use these automatic annotations for adaptation. For evaluation we used the metric defined in [4].

2.2 Language-Independent Alignment

The problem of aligning a written transcript to an audio recording of speech, i.e., finding out which of the words in the transcript is spoken at which time, is typically addressed by employing an HMM-based speech recognizer. In a process called forced alignment, the HMMs in the speech recognizer are concatenated in a way determined by the transcript and then a Viterbi decoding step will yield an alignment.

However, when dealing with many different low resource languages, this approach is not viable because it is prohibitive to train speech recognizers for each of these languages. Beyond trying to patch the mainstream approach and reuse speech recognizers for other languages by finding sufficiently good phoneme mappings between the languages, we are looking for a completely language independent approach.

Our approach is divided into two steps. First, we find specific points in the audio — so called anchor points — which are aligned based on structural properties of text and audio. Then, portions of text between those anchor points are aligned based on estimates of the rate of speech and by pause lengths in the audio.

For the first step, we use a mapping between punctuation marks in the text and pauses in the audio as basic anchor points. To this end, punctuation marks are extracted form the text and candidates for speech pauses are extracted from the audio. Based on the type of punctuation mark, the order of punctuation marks and pauses, and the length of the pauses, the algorithm finds a basic mapping between punctuation and pauses. The user can then (but need not) manually correct the punctuation-to-pause alignment by selecting from a list of a fixed number of most probable pauses for each punctuation mark.

In addition to punctuation, we also make use of repetitions in the text. This is enabled by the user marking one occurrence of each repeated word in the audio. Then, our algorithm finds repetitions of these words in the audio and matches them to the text positions. For the alignment of non-anchor words, the rate of speech is estimated based on the length of the transcription of words between two anchors. The length of detected pauses is also incorporated in the rate of speech estimation.

These rather simple cues already give pretty good alignment results with considerably less manual effort than completely manual alignment.

3   Video Analysis Algorithms

The main principle that led the development of video analysis algorithm was to reduce the time needed to perform the annotation process and, when possible, make it completely automatic. The creation of robust and efficient algorithms was mandatory, due to the huge size of the video database of the MPI and the great diversity of the content. These two constraints defined the main guidelines in the creation of new algorithms and in the adaptation of existing ones to this specific problem. All the algorithms are designed to work without user interaction (except for the initial setup of some parameters) to allow batch processing on multiple videos. The implementation is done using a highly modular structure, so that future automatic annotators can be easily integrated in the current framework, using as input the results provided by the previous detectors.

The video analysis framework consists on a set of pre-processing algorithms that provide important information for the core module, the hand and head tracking analysis. In the next subsections, the different modules are described in short.

3.1   Skin Color Estimation

Human body part tracking mainly belongs to skin colour, which is a unique and very relevant feature of human body. Due to the peculiarities of the dataset in the underlying application scenario, there is no unique set of skin color parameters which can achieve good results in the entire dataset and therefore typical approaches that make use of a training set to collect the parameters for skin detection on the entire dataset cannot be applied [5, 6].

Automatic skin colour estimation is performed before any detection and tracking of human body parts will start. It is mainly based on an optimization scheme for a selected range of U and V values in the YUV domain that belongs to human skin colour. Some candidate frames of the video are selected where individual regions are moving assuming that human body parts correlate with moving regions. Based on the selected frames, an optimization scheme is applied that performs a parameter variation in the YUV domain aiming at compact pixel clusters that correlate with the moving region. The resulting parameters define a subset in the YUV color space and all the pixels in the image within this subset are marked as skin.

3.2   Face Detection

In this module, a software library from Fraunhofer IIS is used, the so-called Shore Library[4] [7]. This face detector allows robust frontal and profile face detection and tracking for a large variety of faces. This library is commercially used in many image and video annotation tools as well as in security. Due to a common agreement between Fraunhofer HHI and Fraunhofer IIS, the library can be used within our framework for research purposes. The face detector offers the position and size of any detected face in the image, the left and right eye position, frontal or profile view as well as a rating how likely it is a face. All this information is further exploited for human body part tracking.

3.3   Global Motion Detection and Background Estimation

Accurate motion analysis allows distinguishing between different types of video content and it can be used to segment a video in order to select only the parts which are relevant for the researchers. For example, the presence of zooms and motion inside of a scene are usually the most interesting, while shots containing just panning and a low amount of internal motion are of little interest and can be usually discarded without further analysis. For each frame in the video a motion vector map is computed using the Hybrid Recursive Matching (HRM) algorithm [8]. For each vector both the absolute value (i.e. the speed, calculated as L2 norm) and the phase (i.e. the orientation) are then computed. To detect the direction of global motion an 8-bins histogram of the phase of the motion vectors is also computed. Frames are considered candidates for global motion analysis when a significant amount of motion vectors occurs. Pan, tilt and zoom can be detected as well by exploiting the phase histogram of the motion vectors. The approach used for zoom detection is similar to [9] and is based on the idea that when a zoom happens, the majority of motion vectors point to (or come from) the center of the frame, with phases that range evenly between $[0, 2\pi]$ and absolute values that decrease nearing the center of the image. If no global motion is detected for a particular frame but there is nonetheless a significant amount of motion in the image, the frame is then marked as having motion inside the scene.

The detection and tracking of human body parts can be performed quite robustly if the moving foreground object is detected and tracking is just performed on the skin colour regions of the foreground object. Hence the global motion analysis, i.e. the detection of zoom, pan or tilt, helps to identify when the camera is not moving, in order to start adaptive background estimation. The adaptively estimated background then supports the detection and tracking

---

[4] http://www.iis.fraunhofer.de/bf/bsy/fue/isyst

of human body parts. The detection and tracking framework assumes a static camera and constant lighting; the background subtraction is then performed by subtracting the median image, pre-computed using a set of frames created sampling the input video once a second.

3.4 Hands and Head Tracking

The core algorithm works at first by segmenting the image in skin vs. non-skin pixels, using the information provided by the skin color estimator. The adaptive background estimation module supports the robustness of segmentation as skin colored background does not harm the segmentation and clustering. The subsequent step in the detection process involves the search of seed points where the hands and heads regions most likely occur. Histograms along the horizontal and vertical directions compute the number of pixels with luminance and color values within the desired interval; the pixels where a maximum occur in both the directions are selected as seed points (Fig. 1, left). A region growing algorithm is then applied to the seed points in order to cluster together all the skin pixels in the neighborhood. Each region is approximated by an ellipse (Fig. 1, right). The tracking is performed by analyzing the change in position and orientation of the ellipses along the timeline, assigning labels based on position of the regions in the current and previous frames. The face detection module further supports the robust assignment of the head cluster.

On the frame level we get the following information:

– The x,y-position of each cluster for each person detected in the video;
– The size of the cluster defined by the minor and major axis of the ellipse;
– The orientation of the cluster defined by the orientation of the ellipse;
– The speed of a cluster, i.e. the change in position between succeeding frames.

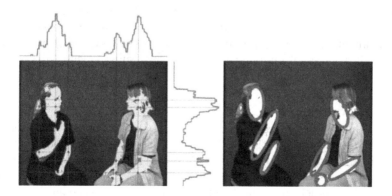

Fig. 1. Histogram of skin color points (left) and examples of ellipses approximating the skin areas in given image (right) (Color figure online)

3.5   Higher Level Analysis and Annotation

The tracking information described in the previous section is then exploited to cluster the frame based information and to achieve a more compact annotation for longer temporal segments. Beside an analysis of the motion of hands, relational and directional information is of interest by researchers in order to detect specific motion patterns and gestures.

Hand Motion Analysis. The hand motion analysis is performed on a temporal segment in which a hand is moving a significant amount. Within the resulting temporal segment, three different properties are calculated. The speed of the hand movement, the area covered by the moving hand in the considered temporal segment and the major orientation of the movement. The threshold defining the start and end of a movement is set by the user amongst three possible values, depending on how much detail the user requires. The lowest threshold allows the detection of the majority of the movements but can also lead to an over-segmentation of the detected movements. Conversely the high threshold may not detect all the occurring movements but avoids the risk of over-segmentation. In order to make it possible for the user to compare movements detected in different videos the values of speed and area covered by the movement are computed as frame and resolution independent values.

On the temporal segment level, we get the following information:

– The movement of a cluster, defined by a threshold for the speed;
– The area covered by the cluster during a motion;
– The orientation of a movement;
– The average speed during a movement.

Directional Analysis of Hand Motion. If the same temporal segment is considered, where a hand is moving, then, a directional analysis of the motion is performed. The analysis of the direction is limited to the four major directions, UP, DOWN. LEFT and RIGHT. Although only temporal segments with a certain amount of motion are considered, several sub-segments may occur, which contain only very small undirected motion. These sub-segments are annotated with the label "SMALL_MOTION".

Relational Analysis of Body Parts. In addition to the motion and direction of the hands, the relative position of body parts is annotated as well. The following relations are investigated, if, and only if, the specific body parts have been labeled: (1) Left hand to head relation; (2) Right hand to head relation; (3) Left hand to right hand relation.

The position of left and right hand is defined relative to the head. Hence the image is divided in a grid and depending on the position of the hand a horizontal and vertical grid coordinate is calculated.

In Fig. 2, an example is given for some sample frames of a testing video. The timeline below shows the different kind of annotations over time. The sample

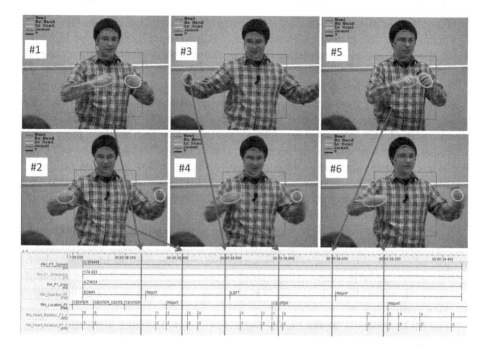

Fig. 2. Example for annotation of human body part movements

frames relate to different time instants. All the annotations relate to the position and movement of the right hand of the person, the orange ellipse (this is the left hand from the observer's view). The first three annotations are single values for the whole motion segment i.e. the speed, the orientation of movement and the area covered by the moving hand. After that, the direction of movement, the location of the right hand in gesture space and the relation between right hand and head in X and Y-direction is shown. It can be seen that the different annotations relate very well to the analysed video.

4 Advanced Machine Learning-Based Annotation Tools

4.1 Media Query Language for Automated Annotation

The process of coding linguistic recordings differs depending on the research question that needs to be answered and the experience and preferences of the annotating person. Even with the support of semi-automated annotation tools more specific annotation still may be required. To influence the unification of codding schema the Media Query Language (MQL) has been designed and partially developed at the Max Planck Institute for Psycholinguistics. The task of this language is to search through the automatically detected annotation segments to find those indicating the desired strategies for multimodal communication, using body movement and addition of a semantics decoded by the researcher.

The MQL implementation and design involves description of rules of syntax in a form of a context-free grammar rules resulting in: a Look-Ahead Left-to-Right (LALR) parser, an implementation of the semantic action to the nodes of the AST of the parser, integration with the AVATecH algorithms.

The design assumes decomposition of the movement according to its kinetic properties followed by assembly of atomic parts of the movement in order to result as kinetically complicated pattern. In the terminology of the MQL the atomic part of the movement is called a pattern. The pattern is a movement primitive associated only to one body part and by design decision is not carrying any semantic meaning. The combination of patterns called an action and it is the part of the MQL where semantics are added. It is created according to the research theory, enabling the possibility of direct comparison with instances of the movement present in the recording.

The relation between MQL elements can be spatial and temporal. Motion can be also described with specific property of the body part relocation over given number of frames. All elements can be saved in user-customizable libraries, which may be exchanged e.g. between colleagues or team members. As the definition of pattern and action depends on user's preferences, the requirements of flexibility for data coding is met.

The MQL typically works on the output of video-analyzing algorithms. The applied pre-processing algorithm increases the feature space R^n in a way that for each detected body part m described with n values calculation is performed changing the dimension of vector describing one frame to $R^{(n-1+l)m+1}$, where l is the number of added features. As the result of pre-processing the vectors describing frames for each body part contain movement classified according to the kinetic properties of the movement with consideration of a threshold determining the movement. The threshold is user-customizable and it is used as the system sensitivity adjustment. Other values present in the frame vector are calculations of total and partial distance and average and local speed. The presided calculations allow user to retrieve the data and formulate theory on a precise information. The principle goal of MQL is to allows research validation and replication of results on different data.

4.2 Speaker Diarization Using Gesturing Activity

Speaker diarization – the task of determining *who spoke when?* in an audio/video recording – has a number of applications in document structuring of multimedia data. Many of these applications come in the form of speaker indexing (used for video navigation and retrieval), speaker model adaptation (used for enhancing speaker recognition) and speaker attributed speech-to-text transcription (used for speech translation or message summarization).

Early research in speaker diarization focused on using audio signals [10] and since recently on audio-video signals [11]. This work performs speaker diarization using only video signals. The basis of our work is the hypothesis that *the gesturer is the speaker*. The hypothesis arose from the observation that although a speaker may not be gesturing for the whole duration of the speech, a gesturer is mostly speaking. Theoretical and empirical evidence for the tight linkage between gesture and speech is also documented in the literature [12].

The synchronization of gesture and speech, which is one of the ways gesture and speech are linked, implies that identifying *who is gesturing* is indicative of *who is speaking*. Based on this idea, we proposed a vision-only diarization algorithm, the details of which are given in [13]. The basic idea is that the algorithm tests for gesture occurrence in regions of the video where there is optical flow. Significant optical flow are associated with particular regions and these regions are generally the same regions occupied by the speakers and not by the listeners.

We evaluated our algorithm on the 13 video recordings of the Augmented Multi-Party Interaction (AMI) meetings[5]. The AMI corpus consists of annotated audio-visual data of four individuals engaged in a meeting. We used a subset of the IDIAP meetings (IN10XX and IS1009x) totaling 8.9 video hours. The best performance obtained, measured in terms of diarization error rate, is 15 %. The result shows that gesture can indeed be used for speaker diarization. Future work will consider combining gesture with audio for more accurate and robust performance.

5   Experiments and Results

For the purpose of analyzing the effectiveness of our solutions we have defined the measure as the difference between the times it takes to create annotation to given media manually and with our algorithms. This value is not easily calculated, as this time depends on factors like: the purpose of the recording and contents of the media; what exactly from the contents needs to be analyzed and annotated; the person performing the annotation process and their expertise.

We have created a scenario in which researchers had to perform annotation tasks to answer different linguistic research questions. The tasks have been chosen to represent a very common set of actions taken by researcher annotating their recordings and they included: (1) labelling the speech segments of all speakers in an audio recording; (2) labeling all gestures of a person in a video recording. For each experiment the tasks have been first performed manually by several researchers and the time necessary to carry them out was measured and averaged. As the next step, the same tasks have been performed with the help of AVATecH recognizers. In each experiment after the automated annotations have been created, a human annotator has verified them in order to perform necessary corrections, as the automated annotations were not flawless. The time to preform these corrections is measured and included in the total time of the automated annotation scenario.

Experiments on labeling speech have been performed using two parts of a field recording, representing typical noise and quality conditions for such recordings. One part was annotated with the help of recognizers, the other one without them.

---

[5] https://www.idiap.ch/dataset/ami/

The two used parts were slightly different in annotation density: the experiment with the manual one resulted with 557 annotation blocks and the recognizers one with 457 blocks. However, the average annotation speed expressed in the number of created annotation blocks per minute is independent of this difference. As it can be seen from table below - the annotation process is almost twice faster for the scenario with recognizers.

	Length	Blocks	Density	Time	Speed
Manual	40.55	557	13.57	1800	0.31
AVATecH	40.07	457	11.405	780	0.58

The column labeled Length shows the length of annotated media, Blocks is the number of annotation blocks created in the final annotation, Density describes the number of annotation blocks per minute of recording to give an idea about the final annotation that was created, Time shows the amount of time necessary to perform the full annotation and Speed describes the speed of the annotation process in number of created annotation blocks per minute.

The experiments on gesture labeling were performed on two videos. The annotations to be created have been first consulted with 2 researchers and then performed by an assistant. Four annotation experiments were performed, 2 for each video with and without the recognizers. As it can be seen in table below the resulting efficiency for gesture segmentation with recognizers has increased by 46 % and 43 % in these two experiments. The length of Video 1 was 1 min and 24 s, the length of Video 2 was 46 s.

	Video 1	Video 2
Manually	30 min 00 s	13 min 10 s
AVATecH	16 min 11 s	7 min 30 s

6   Conclusions and Future Work

The specification and implementation of the above-described video processing recognizers has been performed in a very close contact with linguist researchers and according to the needs they have specified. After testing the relative effectiveness of our methods and witnessing the significant decrease of time necessary for annotations, we can say that our goals have been chosen correctly and our methods have proven very useful.

The successful work started in AVATecH is continued with the extended group of partners in the AUVIS[6] project. As our next steps we are planning to

---

[6] http://tla.mpi.nl/projects_info/auvis

fully develop the possibility of detecting and tracking the hands in the videos and also work together with new partners to develop new recognizers that would create new types of annotations for different research questions.

References

1. Crystal, D.: Language Death. Cambridge University Press, Cambridge (2000)
2. Lenkiewicz, P., Gebre, B.G., Schreer, O., Masneri, S., Schneider, D., Tschöpel, S.: Avatech automated annotation through audio and video analysis. In: Choukri, K., Declerck, T., Doğan, M.U., Maegaard, B., Mariani, J., Odijk, J., Piperidis, S. (eds.) Proceedings of the Eight International Conference on Language Resources and Evaluation (LREC'12) (N. C. C. Chair), Istanbul, Turkey. European Language Resources Association (ELRA), May 2012
3. Lenkiewicz, P., Uytvanck, D.V., Wittenburg, P., Drude, S.: Towards automated annotation of audio and video recordings by application of advanced web-services. In: INTERSPEECH, ISCA (2012)
4. Ajmera, J., Bourlard, H., Lapidot, I., McCowan, I.: Unknown-multiple speaker clustering using hmm. In: INTERSPEECH, Citeseer (2002)
5. Terrillon, J.-C., Shirazi, M., Fukamachi, H., Akamatsu, S.: Comparative performance of different skin chrominance models and chrominance spaces for the automatic detection of human faces in color images. In: Proceedings of the Fourth IEEE International Conference on Automatic Face and Gesture Recognition, pp. 54–61 (2000)
6. Vezhnevets, V., Sazonov, V., Andreeva, A.: A survey on pixel-based skin color detection techniques. In: Proceedings of the GRAPHICON-2003, pp. 85–92 (2003)
7. Kueblbeck, C., Ernst, A.: Face detection and tracking in video sequences using the modified census transformation. J. Image Vis. Comput. 24(6), 564–572 (2006)
8. Atzpadin, N., Kauff, P., Schreer, O.: Stereo analysis by hybrid recursive matching for real-time immersive video conferencing. IEEE Trans. Circuits Syst. Video Technol. 14(3), 321–334 (2004)
9. Dumitras, A., Haskell, B.G.: A look-ahead method for pan and zoom detection in video sequences using block-based motion vectors in polar coordinates. In: Proceedings of the ISCAS, vol. 3, pp. 853–856 (2004)
10. Tranter, S., Reynolds, D.: An overview of automatic speaker diarization systems. IEEE Trans. Audio, Speech, Lang. Process. 14(5), 1557–1565 (2006)
11. Anguera Miro, X., Bozonnet, S., Evans, N., Fredouille, C., Friedland, G., Vinyals, O.: Speaker diarization: a review of recent research. IEEE Trans. Audio, Speech, Lang. Process. 20(2), 356–370 (2012)
12. McNeill, D.: So you think gestures are nonverbal? Psychol. Rev. 92, 350–371 (1985)
13. Gebre, B.G., Wittenburg, P., Heskes, T.: The gesturer is the speaker. In: ICASSP 2013 (2013)

Language Resources: General Issues

Language Resource Gazetteer Issues

Crowdsourcing for Language Resource Development: Criticisms About Amazon Mechanical Turk Overpowering Use

Karën Fort[1]([⊠]), Gilles Adda[2], Benoît Sagot[3], Joseph Mariani[2,4], and Alain Couillault[5]

[1] LORIA & Université de Lorraine, Vandœuvre-lès-Nancy, France
karen.fort@loria.fr
[2] Spoken Language Processing Group, LIMSI-CNRS, Orsay, France
gilles.adda@limsi.fr
[3] Alpage, INRIA Paris–Rocquencourt & Université Paris 7, Rocquencourt, France
benoit.sagot@inria.fr
[4] IMMI-CNRS, Orsay, France
joseph.mariani@limsi.fr
[5] L3i Laboratory, Université de La Rochelle, La Rochelle, France
alain.couillault@univ-lr.fr

Abstract. This article is a position paper about Amazon Mechanical Turk, the use of which has been steadily growing in language processing in the past few years. According to the mainstream opinion expressed in articles of the domain, this type of on-line working platforms allows to develop quickly all sorts of quality language resources, at a very low price, by people doing that as a hobby. We shall demonstrate here that the situation is far from being that ideal. Our goal here is manifold: 1- to inform researchers, so that they can make their own choices, 2- to develop alternatives with the help of funding agencies and scientific associations, 3- to propose practical and organizational solutions in order to improve language resources development, while limiting the risks of ethical and legal issues without letting go price or quality, 4- to introduce an *Ethics and Big Data Charter* for the documentation of language resources

Keywords: Amazon Mechanical Turk · Language resources · Ethics

1 Introduction

Developing annotated corpora, as well as other language resources, involves such high costs that many researchers are looking for alternative, cost-reducing solutions. Among others, crowdsourcing, microworking[1] systems which enable elementary tasks to be performed by a huge number of on-line people, are possible

---

[1] Microworking refers to the fact that tasks are cut into small pieces and their execution is paid for. Crowdsourcing refers to the fact that the job is outsourced via the web and done by many people (paid or not).

© Springer International Publishing Switzerland 2014
Z. Vetulani and J. Mariani (Eds.): LTC 2011, LNAI 8387, pp. 303–314, 2014.
DOI: 10.1007/978-3-319-08958-4_25

alternatives. Nowadays, Amazon Mechanical Turk (MTurk) is the most popular of these systems, especially in the Speech & Language community. Since its introduction in 2005, there has been a steady growth of MTurk use in building or validating language resources [1].

Costs are drastically reduced due to available sparse time of human language experts on-line. But MTurk raises, among others, ethical and quality issues which have been minimized until now, and we will investigate them in this paper. However, because we are aware that the development costs of corpora often stand in the way of language research and technologies, especially for less-resourced languages, we are also sensible of some visible advantages of crowdsourcing. Developing a crowdsourcing system which retains some of the main qualities of MTurk (rapidity, diversity, access to non-expert judgment) while avoiding the ethical and labor laws issues is (theoretically) possible, but this solution will require some delay (in the best case scenario) and the help of our scientific associations (ISCA, ACL, ELRA) and of the national and international funding agencies. Therefore, we will propose existing alternatives aiming at producing high quality resources at a reduced cost, while deliberately keeping ethics above cost savings. In parallel, we created the French *Ethics and Big Data Charter* that will allow funding agencies to select the projects they want to finance according to ethical criteria.

2   MTurk: Legends and Truth

2.1   MTurk, a Hobby for the Turkers?

In order to evaluate the ethics of MTurk, we need to qualify the activity of Turkers while they are participating in MTurk. Is it a voluntary work, as the one in Wikipedia? Looking at the MTurk site or at Turker blogs, where the monetary retribution is a major issue, the answer is clearly no.

Studies in social sciences [2,3], using surveys submitted within MTurk, give some insight[2] into Turkers' socio-economic facts (country, age...) or the way they use MTurk (number of tasks per week, total income in MTurk ...), and how they qualify their activity. 91 % of the Turkers mentioned their desire to make money [5], even if the observed wage is very low;[3] when 60 % of the Turkers think that MTurk is a fairly profitable way of spending free time and getting some cash, only 30 % mentioned their interest for the tasks, and 20 % (5 % of the Indian Turkers) say that they are using MTurk to kill time. Finally, 20 % (30 % of the Indian Turkers) declare that they are using MTurk to make basic ends meet, and about the same proportion that MTurk is their primary source of income.

Looking at the tasks which are performed within MTurk is another way to qualify the Turkers' activity. Innovative kinds of tasks can be found which can be

---

[2] For instance, we learn that Indian Turkers were 5 % in 2008, 36 % in December 2009 [2], 50 % in May 2010 (http://blog.crowdflower.com/2010/05/amazon-mechanical-turk-survey/) and have produced over 60 % of the activity in MTurk [4].

[3] $1.25/hr according to [6] $1.38/hr according to [7].

seen as creative hobby activities. However, many tasks correspond to activities which used to be performed by salaried employees, and therefore are working activities; for these tasks, MTurk could be assimilated to off-shoring on the Web to decrease production costs. For years, speech corpora transcription (and translation) tasks were being performed by employees of agencies like LDC or ELDA: these are jobs. The 20 % of the most active Turkers who spend more than 15 h per week in MTurk [8], and produce 80 % of the activity, can be called laborers when performing these tasks.

It is difficult to be conclusive about the nature of the Turkers' activity. Many different types of tasks are proposed within MTurk and the Turkers' motivations are heterogeneous. Nevertheless, those 20 % of the Turkers for whom MTurk is a primary income, and those Turkers who perform tasks which are actually performed by employees, produce an activity in MTurk corresponding to a real labor.

Qualifying the MTurk activity as labor raises issues about the setup of MTurk. The very low wages (below \$2 an hour [3,6,7]) are a first point. A further point concerns Amazon's choice of hiding any explicit relationship between Turkers and Requesters, even the basic workplace right of unionization is denied and Turkers have no recourse to any channels for redress against employers' wrongdoing, including the fact that they have no official guarantee of payment for properly performed work. Some regulation between Requesters and Turkers exists through Turkers' blogs or forums[4], or the use of Turkopticon[5], a tool designed to help Turkers reporting bad Requesters. However, all these solutions are unofficial and nothing explicitly protects the Turkers, especially the new ones who are mostly unaware of these tools.

2.2 MTurk Drastically Reduces Costs?

Most articles dealing with MTurk and resource production indicate low costs as the primary motivation. Given the observed salaries (for instance \$0.005 to transcribe a 5-second speech segment [9]), the cost may indeed be very low. However, the overall cost is not to be limited to the mere salary: the time needed to develop the interface, and to tackle the spammer problem is not negligible [10]; validation [11] and correction costs [12] to ensure minimal quality are also to be considered. Furthermore, some tasks may become more expensive than expected. This may occur for instance, if the required Turkers' competence is hard to find: to transcribe Korean [9], wages were increased from \$5 to \$35 per hour.

2.3 MTurk Allows for Building Resources of Equivalent Quality?

Many technical papers have reported that at least for translation and transcription, the quality is sufficient to train and evaluate statistical translation

---

[4] For instance http://mechanicalturk.typepad.com or http://turkers.proboards.com.

[5] http://turkopticon.differenceengines.com

or transcription systems [10,13]. However, some of these papers bring to light quality problems.[6]

Limitations Due to the Lack of Expertise. Turkers being non-experts, the requester has to decompose complex tasks into simpler tasks (HITs, Human Intelligence Tasks), to help performing them. By doing so, s/he can be led to make choices that can bias the results. An example of this type of bias is analyzed in [14], where the authors acknowledge the fact that proposing only one sentence per lexical evolution type (amelioration and pejoration) influences the results.

Even more problematic is the fact that the quality produced with MTurk on complex tasks is often not satisfactory. This is for example the case in [15], in which the authors demonstrate that, for their task of word-sense disambiguation, a small number of well-trained annotators produces much better results than a larger group (the number being supposed to counterbalance non-expertise) of Turkers. From this point of view, their results contradict those presented in [16] on a similar, though much simpler, task. The same difficulty arises in [17], in which it is demonstrated that non expert evaluation of summarization systems is "risky", as the Turkers are not able to obtain results comparable to that of experts. More generally, this quality issue can be found in numerous articles in which the authors had to validate Turkers' results using specialists (PhD students in [11]) or use a rather complex post-processing [12]. Finally, the quality of the work from non experts varies considerably [18].

Moreover, there is currently a "snowball" effect going on, that leads to overestimate the resources quality mentioned in articles: some researchers praise MTurk [12], citing research that did use the system, but would not have given usable results without a more or less heavy post-processing [11]. A simplistic conclusion could be that MTurk should only be used for simple tasks, however, besides the fact that MTurk itself induces important limitations (see next section), it is interesting to notice that, for some simple tasks, Natural Language Processing tools already provide better results than the Turkers [19].

Limitations Due to MTurk Itself. In [18], the authors note that the limits of the user interface constitute the "first and most important drawback of MTurk". The authors also regret that it is impossible to be 100 % sure that the Turkers participating in the task are real native English speakers. If pre-tests can be designed to address, at least partly, this issue, they represent an added cost and it will still be very easy to cheat [10]. Of course, one can always organize various protections [10], but here again, this requires time and therefore represents an additional cost that only few requesters are ready to pay for.[7] For example, in [12], the authors identified spammers but did not succeed in eliminating them.

---

[6] Some of the problems reported, such as the interface problems, are not specific to MTurk, but are generic to many crowdsourcing systems.

[7] Interestingly, it seems that MTurk recently decided to no longer accept the non-US Turkers, for quality and fraud reasons: http://turkrequesters.blogspot.fr/2013/01/the-reasons-why-amazon-mechanical-turk.html.

Finally, the impact of task payment should not be neglected, as it induces as logical behavior to place the number of performed tasks above quality, regardless of payment. In [20] the authors thus reached the conclusion that an hourly payment was better (with some verification and time justification procedures).

3   Existing or Suggested Alternatives

MTurk is not the only way to achieve fast development of high quality resources at a low cost. First, and despite the lack of systematic studies, existing automatic tools seem to perform as well as (non-expert) Turkers, if not better, on certain tasks [19]. Second, the cost of tasks like manual annotation can be drastically reduced using the appropriate techniques. Third, exploiting as much as possible existing resources can be an inexpensive alternative to MTurk. Finally, MTurk is not the only crowdsourcing and microworking platform.

3.1   Unsupervised and Semi-supervised Techniques for Low-Cost Language Resource Development

Unsupervised machine learning techniques have been studied in the Speech & Language community for quite a long time, for numerous and sometimes complex tasks, including tokenization, POS tagging [21], parsing [22] or document classification. Although such techniques produce results that are below state-of-the-art supervised or symbolic techniques, which both require resources that are costly to develop, it is unclear whether they produce results that are below what can be expected from MTurk, especially for complex tasks such as parsing. Moreover, unsupervised techniques can be improved at a reasonable cost by optimizing the construction and use of a limited amount of additional information (annotations, external resources). This constitutes the **semi-supervised learning** paradigm [23]. Such approaches for developing language resources rely on two (complementary) principles:

- Training models on a limited amount of annotated data and using the result for producing more annotation. For example, using one model, one can select within the automatically annotated data those that have a high confidence level, and consider that as additional training data (*self-training*, [24]). Using two different models allows to rely on the high-confidence annotations of one model for augmenting the training corpus for the other, thus decreasing systematic biases (*co-training*, [25]). If one accepts to produce a limited amount of manual annotations not only in advance but also while developing the tools, one can request the manual annotation of carefully chosen data, i.e., data for which knowing the expected output of the system improves as much as possible the accuracy of the system (*active learning* [26]).
- Using data containing annotations that are less informative, complete and/or disambiguated than the target annotations, like a morphological lexicon (i.e., an ambiguous POS-annotation) for POS tagging [27], a morphological description for morphological lexicon induction [28] or a partly bracketed corpus for full parsers [29].

3.2 Optimizing the Cost of Manual Annotation: Pre-annotation and Dedicated Interfaces

When using approaches that rely on expert annotation, this annotation can be sped up and sometimes even improved by automatic annotation tools used as **pre-annotators**. For instance, [30] have shown that for POS tagging, a low-quality and non-costly pre-annotation tool can drastically improve manual annotation speed; 50 manually POS-annotated sentences are enough for training a pre-annotation tool that reduces manual work as much as a state-of-the-art POS tagger, allowing to developing a 10,000-sentence standard-size corpus in ~100 h of expert work. On the other hand, on such a task, one could question the ability of anonymous Turkers to correctly follow detailed and complex annotation guidelines.

Obviously, the above-mentioned remarks by [18] about the limitations of MTurk interfaces apply more generally. Past projects aiming at developing syntactically and semantically annotated corpora have shown that both the speed and quality of the annotation is strongly influenced by the annotation interface itself [31]. This provides another source of improvements for annotation efficiency and quality. Put together, it might well be the case that even costly expert work can be used in optimized ways that lead to high-quality resources at a reasonable cost, even compared with that of MTurk.

3.3 Reusing Existing Resources

Even less costly is the **use of existing data** for creating new language resources. An example is the named-entity recognition (NER) task. MTurk has been used for developing NER tools, in particular for specific domains such as medical corpora [32], twitter [33] or e-mails [34]. However, converting Wikipedia into a large-scale named-entity-annotated resource leads to building high-quality NER tools [35], including when evaluated on other types of corpora [36]. Apart from Wikipedia (and the related DBpedia), other wiki projects (e.g., wiktionaries) and freely-available resources (lexicons, corpora) are valuable sources of information.

3.4 Collaborative or Crowdsourced Development Beyond MTurk

All these alternatives require a fair amount of expert work. Other approaches do exist that reduce this requirement to a low level, and in particular collaborative and game-based techniques, as well as crowdsourcing platforms other than MTurk, which try to avoid at least in part its pitfalls.

Collaborative approaches for language resource development rely on the strategy set up by the Wikipedia and other Wikimedia projects, as well as other wikis such as semantic wikis (Freebase, OntoWiki...). Anyone can contribute linguistic information (annotation, lexical data...), but usually contributors are motivated because they are to some extent experts themselves. The quality control is usually done mutually by contributors themselves, sometimes by means of on-line discussions, often leading to high quality results. One of the first collaborative platforms for language resource development was the semantic annotation tool Serengeti [37], currently used within the AnaWiki project.[8]

However, such approaches remain more suitable for developing medium-scale high-quality resources. For the fast development of large-scale resources, another strategy is to attract a large number of non-experts thanks to online games, that fall in the family of so-called **games with a purpose** (GWAP). This idea was initiated by the ESP on-line game [38] for image tagging. Its success led researchers to develop such games for various tasks, including language-related ones. A well-known example is *PhraseDetective* [39] for annotating anaphoric links, a reputedly complex task, which lead the authors to include a training step before allowing players to actually provide new annotations. However, the boundary between GWAPs and crowdsourcing is not clear-cut. It is not the case that MTurk remunerates a work whereas other approaches are purely "for fun". Indeed, even contributing to Wikipedia is a job, though a voluntary unpaid job. GWAP and MTurk cannot be distinguished either by the fact that MTurk gives a remuneration, as some GWAPs do propose non-monetary rewards (e.g., Amazon vouchers for PhraseDetective). Finally, collaborative and GWAP-based techniques are not the only "ethical alternatives", since ethical crowdsourcing platforms do exist.

For gathering language data, in particular for less-resourced languages, **crowdsourcing platforms apart from** MTurk seem to be particularly appropriate, as shown for example by speech corpus acquisition experiments using dedicated applications run on mobile phones [40]. An example of an ethical crowdsourcing platform is Samasource, an NGO that allows really poor people to be properly trained and paid for specific tasks (e.g., translating SMS in Creole after the earthquake in Haiti for helping victims and international rescuers to communicate).[9]

4   Towards Traceability: The *Ethics and Big Data Charter*

To adopt an ethical behavior in developing, funding, using or promoting language resources is first and above all a matter of choice: for the provider, deciding which approach to adopt – crowdsourcing or not –, or which platform to request on, or the level of remuneration of the workers; for the funding agency, choosing which project to fund; for users, choosing which resource to use or acquire. These choices have to be learned ones. We designed the *Ethics and Big Data Charter* [41] in collaboration with representatives of interest groups, private companies and academic organizations, including the French CNRS[10], ATALA[11], AFCP[12]

---

[8] http://www.anawiki.org

[9] http://www.samasource.org/haiti/

[10] Centre National de la Recherche Scientifique/National agency for scientific research.

[11] Association pour le Traitement Automatique des Langues/Natural Language Processing Association http://www.atala.org.

[12] Association Française de Communication Parlée/French spoken communication association, http://www.afcp-parole.org.

and APROGED[13]. The purpose of this charter is to provide resources developers with a framework to document their resources and ensure their traceability and transparency.

4.1 Why Big Data?

In the process of writing the Charter, it soon appeared that the issues raised for language resources apply to a larger range of data sets, which can be described as Big Data. Indeed, Big Data are characterized not only by their volume, but also by the complexity of the data, which is in no doubt the case even for small sets of language resources. Reversely, the reflexions conducted for language resources can be generalized to and benefit to Big Data sets.

4.2 Contents of the Charter

The *Ethics and Big Data Charter* is provided as a form to be filled in by the dataset provider. It is split into three major sections: *traceability, intellectual property* and *specific legislation*, preceded by a short identification section containing the names of the resource, the contact and responsible persons and a short description of the data set.

Traceability. *Traceability* is key to our purpose of putting forward ethical issues. The traceability part of the charter allows to precise the relationship between the resource provider and the workers involved in developing the resource, including legal bounding, workers skills, selection criteria.

Specific focus is put on personal data, i.e., data, like voice or video recording, which can provide a means to identify a person directly or indirectly. The Charter requires to precise if and how the data is de-identified, and if and how the individuals were informed of the purpose of the data collection.

Quality assurance is another major aspect of traceability addressed by the charter, as it requires to document the quality assurance strategy, so that the user of the data set is fully informed on the level of quality s/he can expect: what QA procedure the data were passed through? what portion of the data has been evaluated? What are the actual metrics used and their values?

License and Copyright. Thanks to a great deal of effort accomplished in the definition of – mainly open source – license schemes, it has become common practice to attach a license to a data set. The License and Copyright section of the Charter goes beyond this and puts the focus on questions which may be disregarded, like ensuring that the legal or moral copyrights of the persons who worked on compiling, enriching or transforming the data are respected. As an example, we saw to it that all the writers of the *Ethics and Big Data Charter* are mentioned in the license citation. Also, the Charter reminds data collectors and distributors that they should check whether they comply with any third party data license they may use.

---

[13] Association de la Maîtrise et de la Valorisation des contenus/Association for mastering and empowering content, http://www.aproged.org.

Specific Legal Requirements. A third section of the *Ethics and Big Data Charter* deals with legal requirements that may arise from certain properties of the data set. For example, a country may have issued specifics laws regarding the storing, use and/or dissemination of personal data. The Charter serves as a reminder for checking if such requirements exist.

4.3 Availability

The *Ethics and Big Data Charter* is available on-line.[14] The website is currently in French, and an English translation of the *Ethics and Big Data Charter* is available.[15]

Examples of charters are also provided, including one for a corpus of e-mail messages, and one for a medical dataset. Both corpus raise privacy issues that the *Ethics and Big Data Charter* allows to deal with.

5 Conclusion and Perspectives

We have tried to demonstrate here that MTurk is no panacea and that other solutions exist allowing to reduce the development costs of high-quality language resources, while respecting those working on the resources and their skills.

We would like, as a conclusion, to go beyond the present facts and insist on the longer term consequences of this trend. Under the pressure of this type of low-cost systems, funding agencies could become more reluctant to finance language resources development projects at "normal" costs. The MTurk cost would then become a *de facto* standard and we would have no other choice as for the development method.

We saw, in Sect. 3.3, that a microworking system can generate paid tasks while preserving ethics. This can even represent a chance for people who cannot participate in the usual labor market, due to their remoteness, their handicap, etc., but it requires a strict legal framework to ensure that the system does not violate their rights as workers. This is why we propose that the concerned associations, like the ACL[10] for natural language processing, the ISCA[17] for speech and the ELRA[18] for Language Resources take care of this problem and push to the development and dissemination of the needed tools to better qualify the quality and ethics of the language resources, such as the *Ethics and Big Data Charter*. For that purpose, we already engaged with funding agencies at the French level, some of which have adopted the charter as part of their projects selection process. This effort would need to be extended to international organizations.

---

[14] http://wiki.ethique-big-data.org

[15] http://wiki.ethique-big-data.org/chartes/charteethiqueenV2.pdf

[16] http://www.aclweb.org/

[17] http://www.isca-speech.org/

[18] http://www.elra.info/

Acknowledgments. This work was partly realized as part of the Quæro Programme, funded by OSEO, French State agency for innovation, as well as part of the French ANR project EDylex (ANR-09-CORD-008) and of the Network of Excellence "Multilingual Europe Technology Alliance (META-NET)", co-funded by the 7th Framework Programme of the European Commission through the contract T4ME (grant agreement no.: 249119).

We would like to thank the authors (http://wiki.ethique-big-data.org/index.php? title=Ethique_Big_Data:Accueil#Les_auteurs) of the *Ethics and Big Data Charter* for their dedicated time and effort.

References

1. Fort, K., Adda, G., Cohen, K.B.: Amazon mechanical turk: Gold mine or coal mine? Comput. Linguist. (Editorial) **37**(2), 413–420 (2011)
2. Ross, J., Irani, L., Silberman, M.S., Zaldivar, A., Tomlinson, B.: Who are the crowdworkers?: shifting demographics in mechanical turk. In: Proceedings of the 28th of the International Conference Extended Abstracts on Human Factors in Computing Systems, CHI EA '10. ACM, New York (2010)
3. Ipeirotis, P.: Demographics of mechanical turk. CeDER Working Papers, March 2010. http://hdl.handle.net/2451/29585 (2010). CeDER-10-01
4. Biewald, L.: Better crowdsourcing through automated methods for quality control. In: SIGIR 2010 Workshop on Crowdsourcing for Search Evaluation, January 2010 (2010)
5. Silberman, M.S., Ross, J., Irani, L., Tomlinson, B.: Sellers' problems in human computation markets. In: Proceedings of the ACM SIGKDD Workshop on Human Computation, HCOMP '10, pp. 18–21 (2010)
6. Ross, J., Zaldivar, A., Irani, L., Tomlinson, B.: Who are the turkers? worker demographics in amazon mechanical turk. Social Code Report 2009-01. http://www.ics.uci.edu/jwross/pubs/SocialCode-2009-01.pdf (2009)
7. Chilton, L.B., Horton, J.J., Miller, R.C., Azenkot, S.: Task search in a human computation market. In: Proceedings of the ACM SIGKDD Workshop on Human Computation, HCOMP '10, pp. 1–9 (2010)
8. Adda, G., Mariani, J.: Language resources and amazon mechanical turk: legal, ethical and other issues. In: LISLR 2010, "Legal Issues for Sharing Language Resources workshop", LREC 2010, Valletta, Malta, May 2010 (2010)
9. Novotney, S., Callison-Burch, C.: Cheap, fast and good enough: automatic speech recognition with non-expert transcription. In: Human Language Technologies: The 2010 Annual Conference of the North American Chapter of the Association for Computational Linguistics, HLT '10, Los Angeles, California, USA, pp. 207–215 (2010)
10. Callison-Burch, C., Dredze, M.: Creating speech and language data with amazon's mechanical turk. In: CSLDAMT '10: Proceedings of the NAACL HLT 2010 Workshop on Creating Speech and Language Data with Amazon's Mechanical Turk, Los Angeles, California, USA (2010)
11. Kaisser, M., Lowe, J.B.: Creating a research collection of question answer sentence pairs with amazon's mechanical turk. In: Proceedings of the International Language Resources and Evaluation Conference (LREC), Marrakech, Morocco (2008)

12. Xu, F., Klakow, D.: Paragraph acquisition and selection for list question using amazon's mechanical turk. In: Proceedings of the International Language Resources and Evaluation Conference (LREC), Valletta, Malta, May 2010, pp. 2340–2345 (2010)

13. Marge, M., Banerjee, S., Rudnicky, A.I.: Using the amazon mechanical turk for transcription of spoken language. In: IEEE International Conference on Acoustics Speech and Signal Processing (ICASSP), Dallas, USA, 14–19 March 2010, pp. 5270–5273 (2010)

14. Cook, P., Stevenson, S.: Automatically identifying changes in the semantic orientation of words. In: Proceedings of the International Language Resources and Evaluation Conference (LREC), Valletta, Malta, May 2010 (2010)

15. Bhardwaj, V., Passonneau, R., Salleb-Aouissi, A., Ide, N.: Anveshan: a tool for analysis of multiple annotators' labeling behavior. In: Proceedings of the Fourth Linguistic Annotation Workshop (LAW IV), Uppsala, Sweden (2010)

16. Snow, R., O'Connor, B., Jurafsky, D., Ng., A.Y.: Cheap and fast - but is it good? evaluating non-expert annotations for natural language tasks. In: Proceedings of EMNLP 2008. pp. 254–263 (2008)

17. Gillick, D., Liu, Y.: Non-expert evaluation of summarization systems is risky. In: Proceedings of the NAACL HLT 2010 Workshop on Creating Speech and Language Data with Amazon's Mechanical Turk, CSLDAMT '10, Los Angeles, California, USA (2010)

18. Tratz, S., Hovy, E.: A taxonomy, dataset, and classifier for automatic noun compound interpretation. In: Proceedings of the 48th Annual Meeting of the Association for Computational Linguistics, Uppsala, Sweden, July 2010, pp. 678–687 (2010)

19. Wais, P., Lingamneni, S., Cook, D., Fennell, J., Goldenberg, B., Lubarov, D., Marin, D., Simons, H.: Towards building a high-quality workforce with mechanical turk. In: Proceedings of Computational Social Science and the Wisdom of Crowds (NIPS), December 2010 (2010)

20. Kochhar, S., Mazzocchi, S., Paritosh, P.: The anatomy of a large-scale human computation engine. In: Proceedings of Human Computation Workshop at the 16th ACM SIKDD Conference on Knowledge Discovery and Data Mining, KDD 2010, Washington D.C. (2010)

21. Goldwater, S., Griffiths, T.: A fully bayesian approach to unsupervised part-of-speech tagging. In: Proceedings of ACL, Prague, Czech Republic (2007)

22. Hänig, C.: Improvements in unsupervised co-occurrence based parsing. In: Proceedings of the Fourteenth Conference on Computational Natural Language Learning, CoNLL '10, Uppsala, Sweden, pp. 1–8 (2010)

23. Abney, S.: Semisupervised Learning for Computational Linguistics. 1ère edn. Chapman & Hall/CRC, New York (2007)

24. Yarowsky, D.: Unsupervised word sense disambiguation rivaling supervised methods. In: Proceedings of the 33rd Annual Meeting of the Association for Computational Linguistics, Cambridge, MA, USA, pp. 189–196 (1995)

25. Blum, A., Mitchell, T.: Combining labeled and unlabeled data with co-training. In: COLT: Proceedings of the Workshop on Computational Learning Theory. Morgan Kaufmann Publishers (1998)

26. Cohn, D.A., Ghahramani, Z., Jordan, M.I.: Active learning with statistical models. In: Tesauro, G., Touretzky, D., Leen, T. (eds.) Advances in Neural Information Processing Systems, vol. 7, pp. 705–712. The MIT Press, Cambridge (1995)

27. Smith, N., Eisner, J.: Contrastive estimation: training log-linear models on unlabeled data. In: Proceedings of the 43th Annual Meeting of the Association for Computational Linguistics (ACL'05), Ann Arbor, Michigan, USA, pp. 354–362 (2005)

28. Sagot, B.: Automatic acquisition of a Slovak lexicon from a raw corpus. In: Matoušek, V., Mautner, P., Pavelka, T. (eds.) TSD 2005. LNCS (LNAI), vol. 3658, pp. 156–163. Springer, Heidelberg (2005)

29. Watson, R., Briscoe, T., Carroll, J.: Semi-supervised training of a statistical parser from unlabeled partially-bracketed data. In: Proceedings of the 10th International Conference on Parsing Technologies, IWPT '07, Prague, Czech Republic (2007)

30. Fort, K., Sagot, B.: Influence of Pre-annotation on POS-tagged corpus development. In: Proceedings of the Fourth ACL Linguistic Annotation Workshop, Uppsala, Sweden (2010)

31. Erk, K., Kowalski, A., Pado, S.: The SALSA annotation tool. In: Duchier, D., Kruijff, G.J.M. (eds.) Proceedings of the Workshop on Prospects and Advances in the Syntax/Semantics Interface, Nancy, France (2003)

32. Yetisgen-Yildiz, M., Solti, I., Xia, F., Halgrim, S.R.: Preliminary experience with amazon's mechanical turk for annotating medical named entities. In: Proceedings of the NAACL HLT 2010 Workshop on Creating Speech and Language Data with Amazon's Mechanical Turk, CSLDAMT '10, Los Angeles, California, USA, pp. 180–183 (2010)

33. Finin, T., Murnane, W., Karandikar, A., Keller, N., Martineau, J., Dredze, M.: Annotating named entities in twitter data with crowdsourcing. In: Proceedings of the NAACL HLT 2010 Workshop on Creating Speech and Language Data with Amazon's Mechanical Turk, CSLDAMT '10, Los Angeles, California, USA (2010)

34. Lawson, N., Eustice, K., Perkowitz, M., Yetisgen-Yildiz, M.: Annotating large email datasets for named entity recognition with mechanical turk. In: Proceedings of the NAACL HLT 2010 Workshop on Creating Speech and Language Data with Amazon's Mechanical Turk, CSLDAMT '10, Los Angeles, California, USA, pp. 71–79 (2010)

35. Nothman, J., Curran, J.R., Murphy, T.: Transforming Wikipedia into named entity training data. In: Proceedings of the Australian Language Technology Workshop (2008)

36. Balasuriya, D., Ringland, N., Nothman, J., Murphy, T., Curran, J.R.: Named entity recognition in Wikipedia. In: People's Web '09: Proceedings of the 2009 Workshop on The People's Web Meets NLP, Suntec, Singapore, pp. 10–18 (2009)

37. Stürenberg, M., Goecke, D., Die-wald, N., Cramer, I., Mehler, A.: Web-based annotation of anaphoric relations and lexical chains. In: ACL Workshop on Linguistic Annotation Workshop (LAW), Prague, Czech Republic (2007)

38. von Ahn, L.: Games with a purpose. IEEE Comput. Mag. **39**, 92–94 (2006)

39. Chamberlain, J., Poesio, M., Kruschwitz, U.: Phrase detectives: a web-based collaborative annotation game. In: Proceedings of the International Conference on Semantic Systems (I-Semantics'08), Graz, Austria (2008)

40. Hughes, T., Nakajima, K., Ha, L., Vasu, A., Moreno, P., LeBeau, M.: Building transcribed speech corpora quickly and cheaply for many languages. In: Proceedings of Interspeech, Makuhari, Chiba, Japan, September 2010, pp. 1914–1917 (2010)

41. Couillault, A., Fort, K.: Charte Éthique et Big Data : parce que mon corpus le vaut bien ! In: Linguistique, Langues et Parole : Statuts, Usages et Mésusages, Strasburg, France, July 2013, 4 p (2013)

Extending a Tool Resource Framework with U-Compare

Michael Rosner[1]($\boxtimes$), Andrew Attard[1], Paul Thompson[2], Albert Gatt[1],
and Sophia Ananiadou[2]

[1] Department of ICS, University of Malta, Msida MSD 2080, Malta
{mike.rosner,andrew.attard,albert.gatt}@um.edu.mt
[2] School of Computer Science, University of Manchester, Oxford Road,
Manchester M13 9PL, UK
{paul.thompson,sophia.ananiadou}@manchester.ac.uk

Abstract. This paper deals with the issue of two-way traffic between on the one hand, language resources that have been conceived from a local perspective, i.e. from within a local project or institution, and on the other, a shared framework conceived from a global perspective that supplies such resources for local re-use or enhancement. We believe that a key enabler to such traffic is the choice of an appropriate sharing platform, and here we illustrate the point with respect to a constellation of EU projects that is attempting to enhance the quality and scope of shared resources, and a local project that has some already-developed local functionality. The paper first introduces the underlying projects, then goes on to discuss the proposed platform (U-Compare) whose use is then illustrated for a small module developed for a local project.

Keywords: Language resources · Sharing · Sharing platform

1 Introduction

Access to suitable Language Resources (LRs) is a *sine qua non* for the development of Language Technology. But LRs of the right kind do not always occur naturally and frequently require LTs for their creation. The preparation of an interestingly-large POS-tagged corpus, for example, requires an accurate POS-tagger, unless we happen to have an army of human specialists on tap, which we assume is not the case most of the time. So one cannot consider LRs in isolation from the LTs used to create them. In fact the picture also includes a collection of users from different sectors including academia and industry who may themselves contribute content, as shown in Fig. 1.

This dynamic symbiosis between Resources, Users and Technologies is reflected in the philosophy of the Multilingual Europe Technology Alliance (META), which forms the backdrop to the work described here. In this paper we are focussed on the provision of *tools* as a subclass of LRs spanning a range of functionalities including automatic annotation, parsing, statistical analysis etc. The notion of resources-as-tools is not new, having first been proposed under the name BLARK (Basic Language Resource Kit) by Krauwer [10]. However, it has taken on a renewed importance as efforts towards the development of language technologies become ever more globalised.

© Springer International Publishing Switzerland 2014
Z. Vetulani and J. Mariani (Eds.): LTC 2011, LNAI 8387, pp. 315–326, 2014.
DOI: 10.1007/978-3-319-08958-4_26

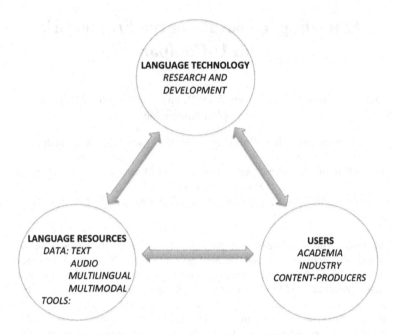

Fig. 1. Resources, users and technologies

One of the main problems when dealing with tool resources is how to guarantee interoperability, both with other tools, and with the data that these tools consume and produce. As we shall explain below, one approach to dealing with this problem is to ensure that all tools operate within a single type system which defines the type of all static data, and the input/output types (or *signatures*) of all the tools.

Such a type system is fine if we are starting from scratch, since everything can be designed to operate within it, but typically this is not the case. A more usual scenario is that we have a mix of tools and data that have been developed at different times, for different projects, in various states of readiness. We might, for example, have a perfectly good parser developed for project A, but in order to use it the grammar data which was developed for project B has to be in a particular format. In short, if we solve the interoperability problem by creating a type-based framework, we are then faced with another problem: how to deal with legacy resources and tools.

This paper concerns just such a problem. Roughly, we have a collection of projects aimed at creating a shared framework for the distribution of language resources in general, and we have an under-funded local project which has been running for some years which has nevertheless developed some tool resources for Maltese. Now the question is how to upgrade those resources and incorporate them into the shared framework.

The structure of the paper is as follows: Sect. 2 describes the background projects from which the work has been conducted. Section 3 mentions MLRS, the local project that has developed its own functionality. Section 4 is devoted to the proposed platform (UIMA and U-Compare), and Sect. 5 shows how the local functionality can be integrated into the platform. The discussion in Sect. 6 assesses the possible impact of proposed framework. Section 7 was added after the conference in order to include consideration of some of the latest developments. Finally Sect. 8 concludes.

2 The Project Constellation

The work reported in this paper takes place within a constellation of EU projects that together are contributing towards the realisation of META. The mission of the Alliance is to further language technologies as a means towards facilitating communication and cooperation across language barriers. The constellation comprises three language-resource-oriented projects: METANET4U, CESAR, META-NORD, and a network of excellence, META-NET, to which they all relate and which to some extent ties them all together.

2.1 META-NET

META-NET is an EU-funded Network of Excellence that supports META through three main objectives aimed at (i) building a community with a shared vision, (ii) building an open resource-sharing framework called META-SHARE, and (iii) building bridges to neighbouring technology fields. The work described here has a direct bearing on the second of these objectives.

2.2 The Language Resource Projects

The three projects are similar in so far as they seek to contribute to META-SHARE by targeting the upgrading, extension, linking, and distribution of language resources. They are also organised along more or less the same lines, as elaborated below. They differ primarily in the language groups handled by each. Broadly, METANORD handles the Nordic Languages and CESAR, the languages of Eastern Europe. METANET4U, with which the present paper is mainly concerned, deals with Spanish, Portuguese, Maltese, English and Romanian.

2.3 METANET4U

The work in METANET4U is split into a number of tasks, each of which is distributed amongst the partner Universities. The main responsibilities include:

(a) Analysis and Selection of Language Resources
(b) Enhancing Language Resources
(c) Cross National Collaboration and Pilot Service
(d) Outreach, Awareness and Sustainability.

In this paper, we are mainly concerned with (ii) and (iii). Although most of the language resources that have been selected for uploading to META-SHARE are useable in some sense, there are various shortcomings that have to be addressed.

For data-oriented resources, these include: cleaning datasets, removal of inconsistencies, particularly where this can be done automatically; ensuring that the data complies with, or can be mapped to, a form that complies with existing standards for character representation, annotation using compliant tagsets etc.; improving descriptive documentation, both informal (text description) and metadata, developed according to a standard developed for META-SHARE. Tool resources present a different set of problems. Obviously, there are operational bugs to be removed, but the most important area of improvement concerns interoperability.

3   Maltese Language Resource Server (MLRS)

The MLRS project [12] was initiated in 1997, with the twin goals of creating a corpus for the Maltese language, together with an associated machine-readable lexicon. The project, which is ongoing, has been intermittently supported by funding from different sources[1]. The current version of the system, which was released online[2] (Gatt and Borg [4]) in May 2011, is centred around a text corpus of about 100 million words, represented in a standard format and implemented using the IMS Open Corpus Workbench (Hardie [6]). This provides for the definition of certain corpus-related services which target Maltese linguistic research in the first instance, and includes certain preprocessing steps, which facilitate the translation of different input formats into the standard representation, word frequency calculations, and concordancing. POS tagging is currently under development. The medium term aim here is to gradually ascend the "semantic food chain" and to include chunking, named-entity recognition, text classification etc.

Presently, MLRS can be regarded as a tool with a fairly high level of "macro" functionality that presents itself to the user as a query engine over corpora that can be used mainly for linguistic research. However, this macrofunctionality is constructed from a number of "microfunctionalities" - components that implement, for example, tokenisation, sentence and paragraph splitting, source document format translation, stop word removal, POS tagging (eventually). The main problem, from the perspective of META-SHARE, is that the interface does not expose these microfunctionalities and so they are not accessible individually.

The challenge we address is how to remedy this situation - i.e. to retain the macro functionality whilst in addition allowing the micro functionalities to be exposed and reused within META-SHARE.

4   UIMA and U-COMPARE

Architecturally, the solution to this problem is a framework that enables microfunctionalities to be composed systematically.

---

[1] University of Malta and Malta Council for Science and Technology.

[2] http://mlrs.research.um.edu.mt/

In effect, such a framework has already been developed for building powerful analysis techniques such as information retrieval, information extraction, textual inference, automated reasoning for "unstructured information", i.e. data lacking an accepted data model which does not obviously fit into relational tables. Unstructured Information Management Architecture[3] (UIMA) is an architecture and software framework which facilitates the integration of arbitrary components to work in collaboration within the same application. This section gives an overview of the UIMA framework, and following that an overview of U-Compare.

4.1 UIMA

UIMA makes it possible to put together a workflow of different components, each of which would be responsible for carrying out a specific type of analysis over a document (text file, audio or video). Such components are referred to as *Analysis Engines* (AEs). AEs can be either primitive or aggregate. In the former case, the AE would be hosting one annotator, whereas aggregate AEs are defined to contain other AEs within themselves.

The annotator itself is the constituent inside the AE which contains the analysis algorithm. The annotator's role is to annotate regions within the document and to create *annotation objects* of a particular type. For example, a commonly used pre-defined UIMA type is Annotation. This type is used to label regions within the document, specifying the beginning and end position of the region. These offsets are stored in the type's features. Features can be seen as properties associated with a particular type. Thus, in the case of the annotation type, two of its features are *begin* and *end* offsets. UIMA has a set of such pre-defined basic types, and gives the developer the possibility to extend these for a richer Type System. Hence, AEs search within the document for the types of objects defined by the respective assigned type system. An important feature within the UIMA architecture is the Common Analysis Structure (CAS). Throughout the execution of the workflow, all the generated annotations are recorded and shared amongst the other AEs through the use of the CAS. So when we talk about searching the document, we actually mean searching within the CAS for objects that collectively hold all information about the document in the form of annotations.

It is easy to see how tools can be made to work together given such a setup. In order to create a workflow in which, for example, two tools are chained together so that the output of one is compatible with the input of the other. This is achieved by ensuring that input and output expectations of the tools are observed with respect to the CAS.

---

[3] Apache UIMA is an Apache-licensed open source implementation of the UIMA specification, which is being developed concurrently by a technical committee within OASIS (http://www. oasis-open.org/committees/uima/).

4.2   U-COMPARE

UIMA is a domain-independent framework. In order to apply it to a specific domain, users need to create a type system defining the data types used by tool resources. Based on the UIMA framework, U-Compare[4] defines just such type system that is specifically oriented towards the domain of text mining. A U-Compare compatible component is a UIMA component which makes use of the U-Compare type system, or extends its types, in order to read objects from the CAS and to record and share results.

U-Compare provides an integrated platform, currently containing an extensive repository of ready-to-use natural language processing components, all of which operate within its compatible type system. Furthermore, through an intuitive graphical user interface, the user is able to construct, edit and compare the performance of different workflows (Kano et al. [7, 8]) - as suggested by its name.

Because U-Compare includes a considerable level of language-handling functionality (and in fact currently holds the largest single repository of type-compatible UIMA components), it has been proposed by METANET4U as a promising starting point for the creation and distribution of LT tools within the META-SHARE framework (Ananiadou et al. [1]). The proposal is not without challenges, however. The U-Compare type system has been designed for the text mining domain. However, the demands of META-SHARE are considerably more general, since the set of resource types includes not just written resources, but also audio, video and multi-modal modalities as well as more structured resources like lexicons and grammars.

Therefore, a major issue for investigation is the extent to which the existing type system is the U-Compare type system adequate. In this paper we report on a first experiment that incorporates a small piece of the micro-functionality of MLRS as a test case.

5   Integration

5.1   Converting Modules to UIMA Components

MLRS, mentioned in Sect. 3, hosts an evolving set of textual resources and natural language processing services for Maltese. As an example, it currently includes a tokeniser which has been specifically designed to handle the peculiarities of Maltese tokenisation. Amongst these we count, for example, the use of the hyphen, apostrophe, clitic pronouns etc.

If METANET4U is to export a Maltese tokeniser to META-SHARE, there would be considerable advantages in making it U-Compare compliant in order to exploit the advantages such as incorporation into workflows, generation of statistics, comparison of performance etc.

---

[4] U-Compare is a joint project between the University of Tokyo, the Center for Computational Pharmacology (CCP) at the University of Colorado Health Science Center, and the National Centre for Text Mining (NaCTem) at the University of Manchester.

In order to make the tokeniser compliant with U-Compare, one can consider two options: either re-implement the components or create a UIMA wrapper, i.e. write code to map the U-Compare types to the local types used by MLRS for input, and then vice versa for outputting tokenisation results. In this case and in general, reimplementation is undesirable, so we need to look at the UIMA wrapper solution. This is depicted in Fig. 2.

Fig. 2. UIMA wrapper

The MLRS tokeniser being considered makes use of a sentence splitter for Maltese and then tokenises each sentence. The existing tokeniser reads the data to be tokenised from a file, executes the tokenisation task, and writes the result to an XML file.

The new component (the outer box in Fig. 2) will need to be modified with regard to its input and output requirements; but the main computation of the component will remain the same. Hence, instead of reading the input from a file, the component will now retrieve it from the CAS, and instead of writing the results to a file, the component will now write the results to the CAS again. This will enable the components executing later in the workflow to use these results by reading them from the CAS.

As explained in *The Apache UIMA Development Community* (2010) the steps which need to be completed are:

1. Define the CAS types the annotator will use
2. Generate the Java classes for these types
3. Write the actual annotator code
4. Create the AE descriptor.

Since our component needs to be U-Compare compatible, steps 1 and 2 are already done. The annotator will be making use of the U-Compare type system, and the corresponding Java classes are already implemented.

Step 3 is where the type conversion comes in. Assuming that a tokeniser instance would take as input a string containing the whole document, this method would (i) retrieve the document from the CAS, and store it in a string variable, (ii) create an instance of the tokeniser and (iii) pass the string as argument.

Since the document object obtained from the CAS is now converted to a string – the type which the tokeniser was already using for computation – now the execution could take place normally. Upon completion of the tokenisation, for each token identified: (i) a U-Compare token object is instantiated (ii) *begin* and *end* offsets of the token are set, corresponding to its position in the document and (iii) the token object is added to the CAS.

Step 4 involves writing the AE descriptor. This is an XML file which specifies the component's properties and requirements, and which could be easily completed using UIMA pluggable tools for Eclipse[5].

Here we specify (i) that the AE is subscribed to the U-Compare Type System, (ii) the location of the tokeniser (iii) its input and output capabilities, i.e. the input would be left empty, since the component would retrieve the whole document, rather than some specific types and the output would correspond to U-Compare token object, hence it would be of type *Token*.

We have carried out these steps successfully for the MLRS tokeniser, which means that, in principle, we have shown how the MLRS tokeniser can be made available within U-Compare without any change to the U-Compare type system. Furthermore, if the UIMA framework is accepted within META-SHARE, we have also demonstrated a basis for extending the functionality of the latter.

6 Discussion

In order to assess where we go from here, we need to take a step back. We have to bear in mind that MLRS has been conceived locally, and that local functionality has been developed, as exemplified by the tokeniser. This functionality is now in principle available to META-SHARE i.e. to anybody wishing to tokenise documents written in Maltese.

We envisage two-way traffic between modules developed locally and those available through META-SHARE. Hence, where appropriate, not only should the results of local developments be made available to META-SHARE, as we have seen with the tokeniser, but also, where appropriate, components available through META-SHARE should be freely available for the development of local functionality.

MLRS currently includes a POS tagger, but there are two major shortcomings: (i) it is not very accurate and (ii) the architecture is monolithic. We envisage that the first problem will be solved by providing better training data, and an effort to address this is currently under way. We are proposing to address the second problem using the U-Compare framework involving a UIMA workflow.

Figure 3 shows a possible UIMA workflow, consisting of four components, for implementing such a POS tagger. The labels on the arrows name the corresponding U-Compare types. Source Document Information (the first input) is the document which is given as input to be analysed. The components' outputs are all U-Compare types.

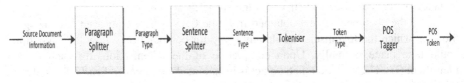

Fig. 3. POS-Tagger workflow

---

[5] A Java Integrated Development Environment (http://www.eclipse.org/).

The advantage of such an arrangement is that the each individual component is reusable and exportable. The realisation of such a workflow could be achieved in a number of different ways.

- The individual modules could be fashioned from already existing MLRS components. For instance, the underlying functionality of the box marked POS tagger already exists. However, it needs to be wrapped in the manner described in Fig. 2.
- The individual modules could be imported from META-SHARE. In this case the drag and drop interface available within U-Compare can be used to insert the respective processing element into the workflow.

Alternatively some mixture of these two approaches might be used to develop a new, U-Compare-compatible processing element involving an interaction between existing processing elements that cannot be easily constructed in terms of a workflow.

An example of this might be a Named Entity Tagger for Maltese (which in fact we are planning to develop in future). One could imagine that the construction of such a tagger might not involve just a pipeline of existing processes - but more complex interactions between, say, an (existing) POS tagger, a locally produced gazetteer linking names and to entities, and a (shared) semantic classifier for distinguishing between locations and organisations using sentence context. In such a case, it could prove most efficient to simply program the interaction in terms of the underlying platform and create a new module for subsequent export to META-SHARE.

Before concluding, as already pointed out, ongoing work is currently focusing at increasing the number of Maltese tool resources. Since the study carried out in this paper revolves around *available* resources, this conversion procedure was necessarily carried out on a fairly simple component. However, other more sophisticated components have been successfully wrapped up to be U-Compare compliant, including corpus readers, as well as semantic and syntactic tools[6], and we propose to adopt this methodology to other components for Maltese as and when they are developed.

7 Post Conference Section

This section of the paper was added in 2013 to reflect the results of developments that have been carried out since the Poznan LTC conference. The section is divided into three subsections that reflect the parties responsible for the work reported.

7.1 U-COMPARE

One branch of development directly impacts the question mentioned at the end of Sect. 4 whether the existing U-Compare type system is adequate to support the inherently multilingual and multimodal demands of META-NET. This has to some extent been demonstrated through the creation of 46 new components, all compliant

---

[6] Navigate to http://u-compare.org/components/index.html for the full list of U-Compare components.

with the single type system, that support 15 different languages. Extensions have also been made to the U-Compare interface to support the handling of multiple subjects of analysis (Sofas) that are useful for handling multi-lingual workflows, where each Sofa can represent a different language (e.g. source and target) and have different annotations associated with it. The sofa mechanism can also be useful for automatic summarisation, where the summary is stored in a different sofa. The new U-Compare interface allows 2 sofas to be viewed side by side. Another U-Compare extension allows speech-based output to be played and 'visualised' as a waveform. All of these are further described in Kononatsios et al. [9]. Some extensions to the type system have also been made to allow a wider range of components to be integrated into U-Compare, e.g. discourse-related components. For further details, see Mihăilă et al. [11].

7.2   MLRS

Various other developments concern different aspects of MLRS. The first involves the corpus contents, addressing the lack of representativeness caused by the initially opportunistic methods used to collect materials. This has resulted in a corpus where journalistic texts are over-represented whilst other types of text, especially works of literature, are under-represented. The corpus is now being expanded to incorporate more texts from under-represented categories. One million words of literary texts have already been added. In addition, more attention is being paid to the inclusion of resources reflecting the bilingual nature of Maltese society and how this affects representativeness and balance. For example, due to the influence of English, there is a comparatively low proportion of texts in some subject areas such as economics or mathematics as compared to other languages of similar size and status. Further details are available in Gatt and Céplö [5].

From the perspective of services, a POS-tagger, under development at the time of the conference, is now fully operational with an accuracy above 95 %. There is also ongoing work on rationalising the POS tagset and improving tagger performance (currently better than 95 % accuracy), The availability of a POS-tagger has opened the way to further resources and tools. A grammatical collocations database is under construction in collaboration with Lexical Computing Ltd.[7] A prototype chunker has been written and is now available as a web service.

The inclusion of Maltese in the Grammatical Framework (GF) project (Dannélls and Camilleri [3]) has given rise to another strand of computational linguistic research culminating in an MSc Thesis (Camilleri [2]) whose contributions include a first computational grammar of Maltese covering both syntax and morphology, a new language implementation for the GF Resource Grammar Library, and an online collection of digital lexical resources for Maltese which is searchable in a unified way. The morphological part of the grammar includes a set of smart paradigms that has been used to automatically produce some 4 million inflection forms thus extending the collection into a full-form computational lexicon that can be used for morphological lookup and spell-checking.

---

[7] See http://mlrs.research.um.edu.mt/index.php?page=6 for the latest updates.

7.3   METANET4U

Although METANET4U ended in February 2013, the resources developed within the project are still in place thanks to the network of local repositories that continue to be maintained under the META-NET umbrella. Further resources continue to be added and maintained thanks to the largely volunteer efforts of so many members of that project along with other projects in the cluster. The contents of this section testifies to the steady progress that is being made with respect to resources and tools for Maltese. The biggest challenge is to maintain a coherent organization for web services given the large number of players actively involved in their development from rather different perspectives. We still believe that U-Compare provides an excellent framework within which to build such coherence, and we look forward to future developments that will strive to integrate the diversity of contributions into a globally accessible collection of resources.

8   Conclusion

We have presented a project cluster which aims to improve LT across a wide range of languages by developing, amongst other things, a framework for sharing language resources and LT tools. We have illustrated how U-Compare can be used to elevate the status of an existing module from something strictly internal to something that can be shared by the community at large. Conversely, we have suggested that in future, the adoption of a framework like U-Compare can be used to facilitate the creation of new functionality by adopting a mix and match approach which freely draws from shared and locally produced modules, thus contributing to the shareable resources.

The post-conference section assesses the latest contributions from the perspectives of U-Compare, MLRS, and METANET4U. We hope to address the issue of integrating these contributions coherently though U-Compare in future projects.

Acknowledgment. The work described above has been carried out under the auspices of the METANET4U project jointly funded by the EU (grant number 270893) and the Universities of Malta and Manchester.

References

1. Ananiadou, S., Thompson, P., Kano, Y., McNaught, J., Attwood, T.K., Day, P.J.R., Keane, J., Jackson, D., Pettifer, S.: Towards interoperability of European language resources. Ariadne **67** (2011)
2. Camilleri, J.J.: A computational grammar and lexicon for Maltese. M.Sc. thesis, Department of Computer Science and Engineering, Chalmers University of Technology and University of Gothenburg (2013)
3. Dannélls, D., Camilleri, J.J.: Verb morphology of Hebrew and Maltese - towards an open source type theoretical resource grammar in GF. In: Proceedings of the Workshop on Language Resources (LRs) and Human Language Technologies (HLT) for Semitic Languages: Status, Updates, and Prospects, LREC 2010, Malta, April 2010

4. Gatt, A., Borg, C.: Using the MLRS interface. Institute of Linguistics, University of Malta (2011). http://mlrs.research.um.edu.mt/corpusquery/cwb/doc/mlrs_userdoc.pdf

5. Gatt, A., Céplö, S.: Digital corpora and other electronic resources for Maltese. In: Proceedings of Corpus Linguistics Conference, University of Lancaster, July 2013

6. Hardie, A.: CQPweb - combining power, flexibility and usability in a corpus analysis tool. http://www.lancs.ac.uk/staff/hardiea/cqpweb-paper.pdf (draft) (forthcoming)

7. Kano, Y., McCrohon, L., Ananiadou, S., Tsujii, J.: Integrated NLP evaluation system for pluggable evaluation with extensive interoperable toolkit. In: Proceedings of the NAACL HLT Workshop on Software Engineering, Testing, and Quality Assurance for Natural Language Processing, Boulder, Colorado, Association for Computational Linguistics, pp. 22–30. Association for Computational Linguistics, Boulder (2009)

8. Kano, Y., Baumgartner Jr., W.A., McCrohon, L., Ananiadou, S., Bretonnel Cohen, K., Hunter, L., Tsujii, J.: U-Compare: share and compare text mining tools with UIMA. Bioinformatics 25(15), 1997–1998 (2009)

9. Kontonatsios, G., Thompson, P., Batista-Navarro, R.T., Mihăilă, C., Korkontzelos, I., Ananiadou, S.: Extending an interoperable platform to facilitate the creation of multilingual and multimodal NLP applications. In: Proceedings of the 51st Annual Meeting of the Association for Computational Linguistics, Sofia, Bulgaria, 4–9 August 2013, pp. 43–48 (2013)

10. Krauwer, S.: The basic language resource kit as the first milestone for the language resources roadmap. Survey Lecture delivered at SPECOM, Moscow, October 2003. http://www.elsnet.org

11. Mihăilă, C., Kontonatsios, G., Batista-Navarro, R.T., Thompson, P., Korkontzelos, I., Ananiadou, S.: Towards a better understanding of discourse: integrating multiple discourse annotation perspectives using UIMA. In: Proceedings of the 7th Linguistic Annotation Workshop & Interoperability with Discourse, Sofia, Bulgaria, pp. 79–88, 8–9 August 2013 (2013)

12. Rosner, M., Caruana, J., Fabri, R.: Maltilex: a computational lexicon for Maltese. In: Rosner, M. (ed.) Computational Approaches to Semitic Languages: Proceedings of the Workshop COLING-ACL98, Université de Montréal, Canada, pp. 97–105 (1998)

Language Resources:
Ontologies and Wordnets

Aligning GermaNet Senses with Wiktionary Sense Definitions

Verena Henrich[(✉)], Erhard Hinrichs, and Tatiana Vodolazova

Department of General and Computational Linguistics,
Wilhelmstr. 19, 72074 Tübingen, Germany
{verena.henrich,erhard.hinrichs,tatiana.vodolazova}@uni-tuebingen.de
http://www.sfs.uni-tuebingen.de

Abstract. Sense definitions are a crucial component for wordnets and enhance the usability of wordnets for a wide variety of NLP applications. Many wordnets for languages other than English – including the German wordnet GermaNet – lack comprehensive coverage of such definitions. The purpose of this paper is to automatically align sense descriptions from the web-based dictionary Wiktionary to lexical units in GermaNet in order to extend GermaNet with sense descriptions. An alignment algorithm based on word overlaps is developed and different setups of the algorithm are compared. This algorithm yields as the best result an accuracy of 93.8 % and an F1-score of 84.3, which confirms the viability of the proposed method for automatically enriching GermaNet. This best result crucially involves the use of coordinated relations as a novel concept for calculating sense alignment.

Keywords: Word sense alignment · Mapping lexical resources · Germa-Net · German wordnet · Wiktionary · Sense definitions

1 Introduction

Sense definitions in a wordnet serve a number of important functions: (i) They help to distinguish different senses of a word both for humans and computers. (ii) They enhance the usability of wordnets for a wide variety of NLP applications, including word sense disambiguation, machine translation, information retrieval, and semantic similarity measures. (iii) They facilitate the sense alignment of wordnets with other lexical resources.

The Princeton WordNet [3] for English provides sense definitions for most of its synsets. However, many wordnets for languages other than English – including GermaNet [6,7] – lack comprehensive coverage of such definitions.[1] Rather,

---

The present paper substantially extends the research described earlier in [9] and presents the results of a detailed evaluation of the automatic GermaNet-Wiktionary alignment.

[1] The reason for this lack of sense definitions is entirely pragmatic: the inclusion of descriptions requires considerable human resources, which are often not available.

© Springer International Publishing Switzerland 2014
Z. Vetulani and J. Mariani (Eds.): LTC 2011, LNAI 8387, pp. 329–342, 2014.
DOI: 10.1007/978-3-319-08958-4_27

these wordnets rely on the implicit mutual disambiguation of word senses by the members of a synset. This type of implicit disambiguation has its limits for those words where the individual senses are synsets with only one member.

GermaNet's coverage of definitions is far from complete. Prior to the research reported here[2], only 10 % of all synsets in GermaNet were accompanied by definitions. Given the broad coverage of GermaNet, adding descriptions to the missing 62 582 synsets by purely manual, lexicographic work would be an arduous task. Therefore, the possibility of employing automatic or semi-automatic methods for adding sense descriptions would be extremely valuable. The purpose of this paper is to explore this possibility on the basis of Wiktionary, a freely available, web-based dictionary containing sense definitions. The idea is to automatically harvest Wiktionary's definitions by mapping[3] word senses in GermaNet to the corresponding entries in Wiktionary. Such a sense mapping relies heavily on word sense disambiguation, i.e., the task of identifying the correct sense of a word in one resource that matches the corresponding sense of the word in a second resource requires the disambiguation of the matching word senses.

Section 2 briefly introduces GermaNet and Wiktionary and motivates why Wiktionary has been used for the automatic harvesting of sense definitions. A word sense alignment algorithm is developed in Sects. 3 and 4. Different setups of the algorithm are evaluated and discussed in Sect. 5. Section 6 reports on related work before the paper ends with concluding remarks in Sect. 7.

2   Resources

GermaNet [6, 7] is a lexical semantic network that is modeled after the Princeton WordNet for English [3]. It partitions adjectives, nouns, and verbs into a set of concepts (called *synsets*) that are interlinked by semantic relations. A synset is a set of words (referred to as *lexical units*) where all the words are taken to be (near) synonyms. There are two types of semantic relations in GermaNet. *Conceptual relations* hold between two semantic concepts, i.e. synsets. They include relations such as hypernymy, part-whole relations, entailment, or causation. *Lexical relations* hold between two individual lexical units. The current version of GermaNet (version 6.0 of April 2011) covers 93 407 lexical units, which are grouped into 69 594 synsets.

Wiktionary[4] is a web-based dictionary that is available for many languages, including German. It is written collaboratively by volunteers and provides information such as part-of-speech, hyphenation, possible translations, inflection, etc. It covers, among others, the word classes of adjectives, nouns, and verbs that are also available in GermaNet. Wiktionary provides relations to other words, e.g., in the form of synonyms, antonyms, hypernyms, hyponyms, holonyms,

---

[2] That is, for GermaNet release 6.0, April 2011.

[3] Note that the terms *mapping* and *alignment* are used interchangeably throughout this paper.

[4] See http://www.wiktionary.org.

and meronyms. In contrast to GermaNet, the relations are (mostly) not disambiguated. For the present project, a downloaded copy of the German Wiktionary as of February 2, 2011 is utilized, consisting of 46 457 German words comprising 70 339 word senses. The reason why Wiktionary has been chosen to harvest sense definitions for GermaNet is threefold: (i) Wiktionary is freely available and its license allows the redistribution of harvested materials. (ii) There is a freely available Java-based library JWKTL[5] that allows to access all Wiktionary data programmatically. (iii) The overlap of terms that are in both resources is large enough, as reported by a survey of the overlaps of GermaNet and Wiktionary which shows that, disregarding word sense disambiguation, about 30,488 terms (45.23 %) in GermaNet are also present in the German Wiktionary [21].

3   The Idea of the Alignment Algorithm

In the current scenario of Wiktionary and GermaNet, the aim is to correctly map a GermaNet lexical unit to a Wiktionary sense definition in order to harvest sense definitions from Wikionary. This task includes word sense disambiguation, i.e., given a sense from one resource it has to identify (disambiguate) the correct matching sense from the other resource. For each lemma (also referred to as the *target word*, i.e., the word under consideration) contained in GermaNet, it takes all lexical units representing that lemma and tries to disambiguate which of Wiktionary's senses for that lemma is the correct match.

There can be more than one occurrence of a target word in GermaNet, thus a target word can correspond to a number of lexical units, each belonging to a distinct semantic concept, i.e., synset. The mapping of each sense definition in Wiktionary needs to consider all synsets containing the target word in GermaNet. Further, due to different sense granularities and distinct coverages of Wiktionary and GermaNet, some senses in GermaNet may correspond to more than one, exactly one, or even no senses in Wiktionary. In the other direction, some Wiktionary senses correspond to more than one sense in GermaNet. Even if there is exactly one sense in both resources, this does not necessarily mean that they match. For example, there is exactly one sense for *Angeln* 'fishing' in GermaNet and exactly one sense for *Angeln* in Wiktionary described as *Landschaft im Nordosten Schleswig-Holsteins* 'region in the north-east of Schleswig-Holstein'; but these two senses are clearly distinct.

The other challenge for the mapping is the absence of sense definitions in GermaNet, which prohibits, e.g., simply applying a word overlap disambiguation (such as the Lesk algorithm [12]) out-of-the-box. We hence develop a word sense alignment algorithm, which accommodates auxiliary information from GermaNet and Wiktionary to enable a word overlap approach.

Lexical fields: Therefore, we introduce the notion of *lexical fields*, which substitute sense descriptions in GermaNet by encapsulating relations and semantic

---

[5] http://www.ukp.tu-darmstadt.de/software/jwktl

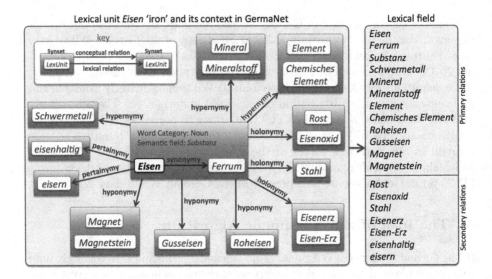

Fig. 1. Lexical field example using *Eisen* 'iron'

field information.[6] That is, lexical fields are a bag of words that represent the lexical unit in question. Figure 1 visualizes the extraction of the lexical field information for one sense of the word *Eisen* 'iron' in GermaNet. All lexical units (the items in the boxes with a white background in Fig. 1) related to the target word are extracted. For example, the synonym *Ferrum* 'ferrum', the hypernyms *Schwermetall* 'heavy metal', *Mineralstoff* 'mineral', etc., the holonyms *Eisenerz* 'iron ore', *Stahl* 'steel', etc., the hyponyms *Magnet* 'magnet', *Gusseisen* 'cast iron', etc. – to name only a few. In addition to the terms obtained via lexical and conceptual relations, the lexical fields are further enriched by the semantic field (semantic fields are closely related to major nodes in the semantic network – in WordNet terminology also called *unique beginners*) that the target word belongs to. The word *Eisen*, for example, belongs to the semantic field *Substanz* 'substance'. This is why the term *Substanz* is added to the lexical field. All words that have been added to the lexical field in the example are listed on the right in Fig. 1.

Given a target word, the alignment algorithm counts the overlaps between each of Wiktionary's sense definitions and each of the lexical fields representing lexical units in GermaNet. For example, the lexical field of *Eisen* 'iron' in GermaNet contains the hypernym *Chemisches Element* (see the box on the right in Fig. 1), which appears in the first sense definition of *Eisen* in Wiktionary described as *Chemie, ohne Plural: chemisches Element, silberweißes, bei Feuchtigkeit leicht oxidierendes Metall* 'Chemistry, without plural: chemical element, silver-white, on dampness easily rusting metal'.

---

[6] A similar kind of technique using all related words for constructing *pseudo glosses* has been used by Gurevych [5] for the purpose of computing semantic relatedness for any two words in GermaNet.

Coordinated relations: Besides the application of lexical fields for counting word overlaps, the alignment algorithm utilizes the occurrence of the same relations in GermaNet and Wiktionary – which we call *coordinated relations*. As mentioned in the introductory sections on Wiktionary and GermaNet, the two resources have several relations in common, for example the hypernymy and the hyponymy relations. Thus, if a lexical unit in GermaNet and a sense in Wiktionary both show the same hypernyms, this is a strong indicator for their equality. For example, *Eisen* in the sense of 'iron' in GermaNet and the first sense of *Eisen* in Wiktionary both show, among others, the same hypernym *Schwermetall* and the same two hyponyms *Roheisen* and *Gusseisen*, which are a good indicator that these two entries express the same semantic concept.

Utilizing the overlap information of lexical fields and coordinated relations is the underlying idea of the developed alignment algorithm.

4   Implementation of the Alignment Algorithm

Preprocessing: Wiktionary sense descriptions are tokenized and stopwords, such as determiners, are withdrawn. All words can also be normalized using either stemming or lemmatization.[7] As compounding is a highly productive word formation process in German [2], it is necessary to split compounds occurring in the sense descriptions in Wiktionary and in the lexical fields in GermaNet to achieve a higher overlap rate. After splitting the compound *Wasserwelle* 'water-wave' into its two components *Wasser* 'water' and *Welle* 'wave', an overlap (of *Wasser*) with the first sense definition in Wiktionary, i.e. *Physik: Erhebung von Wasser* 'physics: elevation of water', can be captured. Duplicates, which arise due to compound splitting, are eliminated to avoid multiple overlap counts for the same word. For example, one sense of the word *Welle* has the compound *Wasserwelle* as a synonym and therefore the compound appears in the lexical field of *Welle*. Compound splitting would therefore result in two occurrences of *Welle* in the same lexical field.

Different versions: Basically, two versions of the alignment algorithm are implemented, which can be run separately or in combination. The first variant utilizes the lexical fields in GermaNet as described above. All words are included into the lexical field that are directly connected[8] to the target word. For experimenting with different sets of words, two types of relations are distinguished: *Primary relations*, such as synonymy, hypernymy, and hyponymy, constituting the fundamental structure of a wordnet; and *secondary relations*, such as association, causation, entailment, holonymy, meronymy, and pertainymy with a subordinated importance. In the previous example of *Eisen* 'iron', all words that are

---

[7] Experiments with stemming and lemmatization yielded better results with stemming. Thus, all below described experiments use stemming (Snowball stemmer [19]) as a preprocessing step.

[8] Here, *directly connected* means that the path length between two words is exactly one – disregarding the type of relation (lexical or conceptual).

connected by a primary relation are listed above the line in the box on the right in Fig. 1, and all words connected by a secondary relation are listed below the line. An overlap of single words is calculated between a tokenized Wiktionary sense description and a lexical field belonging to a target lexical unit in GermaNet.

The second variant of the alignment algorithm counts the overlaps of coordinated relations between GermaNet and Wiktionary (as explained in Sect. 3). Therefore, all relations that occur in both resources, such as synonymy, antonymy, hypernymy, hyponymy, meronymy, and holonymy, are considered.

Overlap count: More precisely, each of the target lexical units in GermaNet is represented by a lexical field (as described in Sect. 3). An overlap is calculated between a lexical field in GermaNet and a sense description in Wiktionary. The overlap is a mere count of the number of words x_i for $x_i \in X$, where X is a set of words representing the lexical field of a target lexical unit in GermaNet found in the set of words of a Wiktionary sense description – optionally augmented by the coordinated relations overlap. Further, in case that there is exactly one sense in both resources for a given word, an initial count of 1 is given to the overall count of overlaps.[9]

The alignment algorithm maps the Wiktionary sense definitions with the highest overlap counts to a given lexical unit in GermaNet and disregards all other overlap counts (even if those are above zero). Notice that the overlap calculation can result in the same overlap score for several senses in Wiktionary. In these cases, more than one Wiktionary sense definition is mapped onto the lexical unit in question and is taken to mean that the lexical unit in GermaNet is jointly described by the Wiktionary sense descriptions in question.

Algorithm setups: As the lexical fields do not consist of continuous word sequences but rather of single words, it is not possible to give more weight to longer sequences of word matches as it is done by Banerjee and Pedersen [1]. In order to be able to fine-tune the most reliable set of relations, the algorithm includes the possibility of specifying individual weights for different relations.

A set of alignment experiments were conducted that differ from each other in the weight assigned to the terms that make up the lexical field of a given GermaNet lexical unit (see Table 1). For setups A – C, only the terms contributed by a single primary relation are considered (given a non-zero weight). Setup D considers only all secondary relations and setup E only all coordinated relations. In setup F, all terms obtained by the primary, secondary, and coordinated relations are given equal weight. In addition, a set of experiments has been conducted where the terms obtained by the different relations were given different weights. Setup G shows the weight assignments that produced optimal results for a precision and recall evaluation (see Sect. 5 below).

---

[9] Needless to say, assigning an arbitrary count of at least 1 to the overlap score between words occurring exactly once in both resources will result in a positive mapping of these two senses which, in turn, will result in a prediction of false positives for all cases, where those senses do not match (see the example of *Angeln* in Sect. 3 above). However, such cases are rare and therefore the heuristic in question works well in practice (see the evaluation section below).

Table 1. Different algorithm setups (numbers indicate weights)

Setup	Lexical field overlap				Coordinated relation
	Primary relations			2nd-ary relations	
	Hyper.	Hypo.	Syno.		
A	1	0	0	0	0
B	0	1	0	0	0
C	0	0	1	0	0
D	0	0	0	1	0
E	0	0	0	0	1
F	1	1	1	1	1
G	2	0.5	3	0.5	3

5   Evaluation and Results

In order to be able to evaluate the automatic alignment of lexical units in GermaNet with senses in Wiktionary, the mappings produced by the developed disambiguation algorithm were manually checked by two experienced lexicographers. In order to ensure a comprehensive evaluation of lexical items with different degrees of polysemy, the evaluation reports results for five different polysemy classes: words having (i) one sense in GermaNet, (ii) two senses in GermaNet, (iii) three or four senses, (iv) five to ten senses, and (v) more than ten senses in GermaNet. Table 2 shows the total number of words in each polysemy class for the three word classes contained in GermaNet that were available for the evaluation. Altogether, 20 997 distinct words[10] with an average of 1.3 senses (i.e., 27 309 lexical units of which 3 241 adjectives, 19 423 nouns, and 4 645 verbs) were manually checked by the lexicographers.

Table 2. Evaluated words and their sense distributions

No. of senses	Adjectives	Nouns	Verbs
1	2 328	13 391	1 393
2	319	1 872	510
3 – 4	71	557	320
5 – 10	8	91	135
> 10	0	1	23
Total	2 726	15 912	2 381

---

[10] The numbers from Table 2 do not exactly add up to 20 997 because some words have more than one part-of-speech.

Since the number of senses assigned to a word in GermaNet and Wiktionary may differ and since the lexical coverage of the two resources only partially coincides, a given word sense in GermaNet may have no counterpart in Wiktionary at all, or it may correspond to exactly one or more than one senses in Wiktionary. The same holds true in the inverse direction.

A truly meaningful evaluation has to reflect the nature of the task at hand: the semi-automatic enrichment of lexical units in GermaNet with appropriate sense descriptions from Wiktionary. A very crude approach would simply map all word senses recorded in GermaNet for a given word with all corresponding sense descriptions documented in Wiktionary. Such an approach would require a lot of human post-editing to eliminate all inappropriate mappings. Since the unwanted mappings far outnumber the number of correct mappings, this approach would be clearly inappropriate. In fact, the motivation behind the developed alignment algorithm is precisely to map only plausible candidates for correct mappings in terms of word overlap between lexical fields in GermaNet and sense descriptions in Wiktionary. These considerations clearly show that the task at hand requires maximizing accuracy in order to minimize the amount of human post-processing required. Accuracy, precision, and recall are computed per word by their standard formulas. The overall accuracy, precision, and recall values are then computed as the average of all word values.

Table 3 shows the results for the described task separately for the previously defined polysemy classes (columns). The rightmost column depicts the overall results without classifying words with respect to their number of different senses. The rows show the different algorithm setups A – E (described in Sect. 4) separately for each of the three word classes of adjectives, nouns, and verbs (column *POS*, i.e., parts of speech). Rows marked with *All POS* denote results for all word classes.

To begin with, the average scores for all three word classes in all setups A – G are above 90 % accuracy. This suggests that human correction is needed for only one out of 10 mappings between GermaNet and Wiktionary suggested by the algorithm.[11] This underscores the overall feasibility of the approach.

As setups A – E each take into account only one property (see Table 1), a comparison of the results directly reflects the suitability of the different relation types when applied independently of each other. One of the most striking findings among the results of this evaluation is that the use of hypernyms (setup A) and synonyms (setup C) outperforms the use of hyponyms (setup B) and secondary relations (setup D). The fact that hypernyms and synonyms outperform the other relations is not surprising since sense definitions often refer to a hypernym or synonym term which is then described in more detail to fit the specific properties of the entity being described. For example, the English Word-Net defines the noun *convertible* as 'a car [hypernym] that has a top that can be folded or removed'.

---

[11] To be even more precise, the accuracies for setups A to E are actually above 93 % and thus human correction is needed only for one out of 14 mappings.

Table 3. Accuracy of the alignment

Setup	POS	Number of senses in GermaNet					
		1	2	3 – 4	5 – 10	> 10	All
A	Adj.	94.7 %	83.2 %	93.6 %	99.0 %	N/A	93.3 %
	Nouns	94.3 %	89.0 %	92.9 %	90.0 %	100 %	93.6 %
	Verbs	92.3 %	87.0 %	92.2 %	93.6 %	85.8 %	91.2 %
	All POS	94.2 %	88.0 %	92.7 %	92.4 %	86.4 %	93.3 %
B	Adj.	94.4 %	79.3 %	91.9 %	99.1 %	N/A	92.6 %
	Nouns	94.2 %	88.4 %	89.9 %	87.0 %	0 %	93.3 %
	Verbs	92.3 %	88.5 %	94.6 %	92.9 %	85.4 %	91.8 %
	All POS	94.1 %	87.3 %	91.7 %	90.8 %	81.9 %	93.1 %
C	Adj.	95.0 %	81.9 %	93.9 %	97.9 %	N/A	**93.4 %**
	Nouns	94.6 %	90.2 %	93.6 %	92.3 %	0 %	**94.0 %**
	Verbs	92.3 %	89.7 %	96.9 %	97.3 %	97.8 %	92.7 %
	All POS	94.5 %	89.1 %	94.8 %	95.4 %	93.7 %	**93.8 %**
D	Adj.	93.1 %	81.1 %	93.6 %	99.4 %	N/A	91.7 %
	Nouns	94.2 %	89.4 %	94.5 %	91.0 %	0 %	93.6 %
	Verbs	92.4 %	87.7 %	96.8 %	94.7 %	92.4 %	92.1 %
	All POS	93.9 %	88.1 %	95.2 %	93.5 %	88.5 %	93.2 %
E	Adj.	94.1 %	85.3 %	91.8 %	97.3 %	N/A%	93.0 %
	Nouns	94.4 %	87.2 %	88.1 %	85.6 %	100 %	93.3 %
	Verbs	92.6 %	90.5 %	97.3 %	95.6 %	97.1 %	**93.0 %**
	All POS	94.2 %	87.6 %	91.5 %	91.8 %	97.3 %	93.2 %

The single application of coordinated relations (setup E), in turn, is better than all previous setups (for verbs) or among the best (for adjectives). Again, this result is hardly surprising since coordinated relations are present when the same two terms are connected by the same lexical relations in both resources (see Sect. 3 for a more detailed discussion on coordinated relations). Such a scenario is highly predictive for a correct mapping between corresponding senses in the two resources. In contrast, the results for nouns on setup E do not outperform the other setups. One explanation for this lower performance[12] is the preference of related terms (setups A – D) being often referred to in definitions of nouns with which the occurrence of coordinated relations cannot compete.

A comparison of the results for the three different word classes yields the following tendencies: The results for nouns are slightly higher for all of the different lexical relations (93.3 % to 93.6 %) than the results for the other two word classes

---

[12] Denoting the performance as *lower* is meant in a relative sense, i.e., compared to the results for the other setups for nouns. Note that setup E for nouns does not perform lower than setup E for adjectives and verbs.

(91.7 % to 93.4 % for adjectives and 91.2 % to 93.0 % for verbs). One explanation for this higher performance must be, that related terms are often referred to in order to describe nominal concepts. For verbs, the hypernymy relation (setup A) seems to perform particularly poorly. The explanation for this low performance is probably, that definitions of verb senses rarely use hypernyms, which supports the outcome that verbs are usually defined differently than adjectives and nouns. For words with one sense or with five to ten senses adjectives almost always outperform the other two word classes, whereas for words with two senses adjectives show lowest performance compared to nouns and verbs.

Perhaps the three most remarkable observations when comparing the results for the different polysemy classes in Table 3 are: (i) The drop in performance for all three word classes for words with exactly two senses. Compared to the performances for words having one sense there is a drop of between 2.0 % to 15.1 % for words having two senses for all algorithm setups. (ii) The increase in performance for all three word classes for words with 3–4 senses compared to words with 2 senses in GermaNet. (iii) There is no regularity in performance for words with more than 4 senses in GermaNet.

At first glance, one would suspect that the performance of the algorithm would decrease as the number of senses increases. In other words, the difficulty of the task of aligning sense definitions with lexical units should increase with the number of senses available. This expectation holds true for the comparison of words with one and two senses (see (i) above) but is not empirically confirmed for words with more than two senses (see (ii) and (iii) above). The real explanation for what looks like contradictory findings has to do with the ratio of true positives and true negatives. For the task at hand of aligning sense definitions with word senses in GermaNet, the true negatives outnumber the true positives, and the ratio between the two becomes more and more skewed as the number of word senses and the number of corresponding sense descriptions increases. The fact that the alignment algorithm shows no attested degradation in performance for highly polysemous words attests to the suitability of the algorithm for the task at hand.

What still remains to be explained is why words with exactly one sense do not necessarily show best performance. This is due to the heuristic that adds a count of one to the count of overlaps in cases where there is exactly one sense in both resources.

The extreme scores of 0 % and 100 % for the nouns having more than ten senses in GermaNet also require some explanation. The explanation is simple: There is only one noun with more than ten senses. It is the word *Dollar*, which has a total of 15 different senses denoting national currencies such as *US-Dollar, Canadian Dollar, Hongkong-Dollar*, etc. with one common hypernym *Währungseinheit* 'currency unit'. In Wiktionary, there is one sense definition for *Dollar* with the wording *Währungseinheit in verschiedenen Staaten, z.B. den USA und Kanada* 'currency unit in different countries, e.g., in the USA and Canada'. Since the hypernym *Währungseinheit* matches the Wiktionary sense description, the alignment algorithm detects an overlap for each sense resulting

Table 4. Accuracy, precision, recall, and F1-measure

Setup	Accuracy (%)	Recall (%)	Precision (%)	F1
A	93.3	72.1	71.3	71.7
B	93.1	61.2	60.8	61.0
C	93.8	63.8	63.4	63.6
D	93.2	61.3	60.8	61.0
E	93.2	73.6	73.5	73.5
F	92.3	83.8	82.8	83.3
G	91.9	84.6	84.1	84.3
Baseline	53.7	50.7	44.2	47.2

in a 100 % score for setup A which considers only the hypernymy relation. The same holds true for setup E (coordinated relations) since the GermaNet sense of *Dollar* and the Wiktionary sense description of *Dollar* have the same hypernym *Währungseinheit*. For the other relations (setups B, C, and D) the score is 0 % because there is simply no lexical overlap for any of them.

As mentioned above, for the task at hand, the true negatives outnumber the true positives by a wide margin, and this distribution becomes more and more skewed as the number of senses for a word increases. For this very reason, an accuracy-based evaluation is particularly important since it takes false positives into account. However, apart from the accuracy of the mappings proposed by the algorithm, the recall behaviour of the alignment algorithm is also relevant. Poor recall would mean that many empirically correct mappings go undetected by the algorithm and therefore have to be manually added. We therefore also computed recall for different setups of the algorithm (see Table 4). Recall of the single application of hypernyms (setup A) and coordinated relations (setup E) proves better than all other setups of single relations (setups B, C, and D). Again, this result is hardly surprising since coordinated relations are present when the same two terms are connected by the same lexical relations in both resources.

The best recall values are obtained by those settings where all relations are taken into account for the construction of the lexical field (setups F and G). Notice also that, compared to accuracy, there is a much wider spread in the results for recall, ranging from 61.2 % (setup B) to 84.6 % (setup G). This is hardly surprising since recall is bound to improve with the number of terms included in the lexical field as candidate for overlap.

For completeness, Table 4 also contains the scores for precision and F1. The fact that precision does not rise much above 84 % means that there still is an error rate of 16 %, i.e., 16 % of the proposed links are wrong. The baseline of randomly mapping Wiktionary senses to lexical units in GermaNet (see row *Baseline* in Table 4) demonstrates that the mapping task as such is far from trivial. All setups A to G significantly outperform the baseline. This constitutes strong evidence of the feasibility of the approach.

6   Related Work on Aligning Wordnets

Most of the work on the alignment of lexical resources has focused on English resources – investigating the alignment of the Princeton WordNet with other lexical resources. Early studies reported on mapping WordNet to the Longman Dictionary of Contemporary English and with Roget's thesaurus [11], to the Hector lexicon [13], or to the Suggested Upper Merged Ontology [17] – to name only a few. More recently, several studies investigated the alignment of WordNet or GermaNet with Wikipedia (including [4,8,16,18,20]).

The study that is closest in spirit to the approach presented here is the one by Meyer and Gurevych [15], which maps WordNet to the English Wiktionary. It was developed in parallel to ours (first published in 2011 [9]). Their alignment has very much followed the approach by Niemann and Gurevych [16] who aligned WordNet with Wikipedia – especially in the conception of their alignment algorithm, i.e., the application of similarity measures and the use of a threshold. In a recent study, Matuschek and Gurevych [14] developed a graph-based algorithm for automatically aligning several datasets available for German and English including GermaNet and Wiktionary. The GermaNet-Wiktionary mapping described in the present paper was used as a gold standard in their evaluation. What distinguishes our work from earlier studies is the fact that all automatically aligned data were manually checked and post-corrected if necessary.

7   Conclusion

Sense definitions are a crucial component for wordnets. However, as GermaNet rarely contained sense definitions, comprehensive sense definitions were badly needed in order to enhance its usability for a wide variety of NLP applications. The present paper has described a method for semi-automatically enriching lexical units in GermaNet with appropriate sense descriptions from Wiktionary. It has resulted in harvested definitions for about 30 % of all GermaNet senses, which have already been included into GermaNet (since release 7.0) and which also have been made freely available online[13]. An accuracy of more than 90 % suggests that human correction is needed on average only for one out of 10 mappings suggested by the algorithm. Moreover, the estimations of recall and precision result in 84.6 % and 84.1 %, respectively. These numbers underscore the overall feasibility of the approach and verify its usability for the task at hand. This suggests the applicability of the approach to other resources.

A natural next step would be to implement more elaborate alignment algorithms such as Personalized PageRank, cosine similarity on word vectors, or graph-based Dijkstra that have been used in other approaches (see Sect. 6). Though, a comparison with related work shows that the resulting improvement

---

[13] http://www.sfs.uni-tuebingen.de/GermaNet/wiktionary.shtml

is likely to be modest.[14] Of course, a better automatic alignment would make the manual post-correction easier for human annotators and thus it would definitely be worth experimenting with more elaborated alignment algorithms, if the mapping between Wiktionary and GermaNet had not yet been completely manually post-corrected and the goal of harvesting definitions from Wiktionary not yet been achieved. Apart from that, as our sense alignment dataset is freely available, we highly encourage others to use it as a gold standard in their experiments with more elaborated alignment algorithms – as it has already been done by Matuschek and Gurevych [14].

In ongoing work, the sense-alignment between GermaNet and Wiktionary has been used as a basis to automatically create a German sense-annotated corpus [10]. The construction of this corpus relies on the mapping between GermaNet and Wiktionary (described in the present paper) to harvest sense-specific example sentences from Wiktionary itself and additional textual materials from other web-based textual sources such as Wikipedia and online newspaper materials.

Acknowledgments. The research reported in this paper was jointly funded by the SFB 833 grant of the DFG and by the CLARIN-D grant of the BMBF. We would like to thank Reinhild Barkey, Sarah Schulz, and Johannes Wahle for their help with the evaluation reported in Sect. 5.

References

1. Banerjee, S., Pedersen, T.: Extended gloss overlaps as a measure of semantic relatedness. In: Proceedings of the 18th International Joint Conference on Artificial Intelligence, IJCAI'03, pp. 805–810. Morgan Kaufmann Publishers Inc., San Francisco (2003)
2. Eisenberg, P.: Das Wort - Grundriss der Deutschen Grammatik, 3rd edn. Verlag J. B. Melzer, Stuttgart/Weimar, Germany (2006)
3. Fellbaum, C. (ed.): WordNet: An Electronic Lexical Database. MIT Press, Cambridge (1998)
4. Fernando, S., Stevenson, M.: Mapping WordNet synsets to Wikipedia articles. In: Proceedings of the Eight International Conference on Language Resources and Evaluation, LREC'12, Istanbul, Turkey, pp. 590–596 (2012)
5. Gurevych, I.: Using the structure of a conceptual network in computing semantic relatedness. In: Dale, R., Wong, K.-F., Su, J., Kwong, O.Y. (eds.) IJCNLP 2005. LNCS (LNAI), vol. 3651, pp. 767–778. Springer, Heidelberg (2005)
6. Hamp, B., Feldweg, H.: GermaNet - a lexical-semantic net for German. In: Proceedings of ACL Workshop Automatic Information Extraction and Building of Lexical Semantic Resources for NLP Applications, Madrid (1997)

---

[14] The only comparable work on the same language and resource pair is the one by Matuschek and Gurevych [14]. They have reported results that are 4.2 % (for recall), 9.9 % (for precision), and 2.7 (for F1-score) higher and 8.8 % (for accuracy) lower than ours (for this comparison, always the setup that reports highest numbers is taken). The reason why our accuracy is higher than theirs whereas our precision is lower than theirs lies in the differing focus of parameter adjudication; we aimed at high accuracy.

7. Henrich, V., Hinrichs, E.: GernEdiT – the GermaNet editing tool. In: Proceedings of the 7th International Conference on Language Resources and Evaluation, LREC'10, Valletta, Malta, pp. 2228–2235 (2010)

8. Henrich, V., Hinrichs, E., Suttner, K.: Automatically linking GermaNet to Wikipedia for harvesting Corpus examples for GermaNet senses. J. Lang. Technol. Comput. Linguist. (JLCL) **27**(1), 1–19 (2012)

9. Henrich, V., Hinrichs, E., Vodolazova, T.: Semi-Automatic extension of GermaNet with sense definitions from Wiktionary. In: Proceedings of the 5th Language and Technology Conference, LTC'11, Poznań, Poland, pp. 126–130 (2011)

10. Henrich, V., Hinrichs, E., Vodolazova, T.: WebCAGe – a web-harvested corpus annotated with GermaNet senses. In: Proceedings of the 13th Conference of the European Chapter of the Association for Computational Linguistics, EACL '12, pp. 387–396, Avignon, France (2012)

11. Kwong, O.Y.: Aligning wordnet with additional lexical resources. In: Proceedings of the COLING-ACL'98 Workshop on 'Usage of WordNet in Natural Language Processing Systems', Montreal, QC, Canada, pp. 73–79 (1998)

12. Lesk, M.: Automatic sense disambiguation using machine readable dictionaries: how to tell a pine cone from an ice cream cone. In: Proceedings of the 5th Annual International Conference on Systems Documentation, SIGDOC '86, pp. 24–26. ACM, New York (1986)

13. Litkowski, K.C.: Towards a meaning-full comparison of lexical resources. In: Proceedings of the ACL Special Interest Group on the Lexicon Workshop on Standardizing Lexical Resources, College Park, MD, USA, pp. 30–37 (1999)

14. Matuschek, M., Gurevych, I.: Dijkstra-wsa: a graph-based approach to word sense alignment. Trans. Assoc. Comput. Linguist. (TACL) **1**, 151–164 (2013)

15. Meyer, C.M., Gurevych, I.: What psycholinguists know about chemistry: aligning wiktionary and wordnet for increased domain coverage. In: Proceedings of the 5th International Joint Conference on Natural Language Processing, IJCNLP '11, pp. 883–892 (2011)

16. Niemann, E., Gurevych, I.: The people's web meets linguistic knowledge: automatic sense alignment of Wikipedia and WordNet. In: Proceedings of the 9th International Conference on Computational Semantics, IWCS '11, pp. 205–214, Association for Computational Linguistics, Stroudsburg (2011)

17. Niles, I., Pease, A.: Linking Lexicons and ontologies: mapping WordNet to the suggested upper merged ontology. In: Proceedings of the IEEE International Conference on Information and Knowledge Engineering, IKE'03, pp. 412–416, Las Vegas, Nevada (2003)

18. Ponzetto, S.P., Navigli, R.: Knowledge-rich word sense disambiguation rivaling supervised systems. In: Proceedings of the 48th Annual Meeting of the Association for Computational Linguistics, ACL '10, pp. 1522–1531. Association for Computational Linguistics, Stroudsburg (2010)

19. Porter, M.: An algorithm for suffix stripping. Program **14**(3), 130–137 (1980)

20. Ruiz-Casado, M., Alfonseca, E., Castells, P.: Automatic assignment of wikipedia encyclopedic entries to wordnet synsets. In: Szczepaniak, P.S., Kacprzyk, J., Niewiadomski, A. (eds.) AWIC 2005. LNCS (LNAI), vol. 3528, pp. 380–386. Springer, Heidelberg (2005)

21. Zesch, T.: What's the difference? - comparing expert-built and collaboratively-built lexical semantic resources. In: FLaReNet Forum 2010, Barcelona, Spain (2010)

A Tool for Transforming WordNet-Like Databases

Marek Kubis[✉]

Department of Computer Linguistics and Artificial Intelligence,
Faculty of Mathematics and Computer Science, Adam Mickiewicz University,
Ul. Umultowska 87, 61-614 Poznań, Poland
mkubis@amu.edu.pl

Abstract. The paper presents WUpdate – a data manipulation language designed for WordNet-like lexical databases. The language can be used to perform modifications of a wordnet, such as adding word senses, removing words, interlinking synsets, etc. The focus of the paper is on solving wordnet-specific problems that are not addressed by other data manipulation languages. In particular, the paper addresses the problem of preserving the properties of semantic hierarchies while they are being transformed and the problem of changing the granularity of a WordNet-like database. The paper outlines the syntax and semantics of the WUpdate language and describes the underlying data model. Alternative approaches that may be undertaken to modify a WordNet-like database are discussed.

Keywords: WordNet · Data manipulation language · Query language

1 Introduction

WordNet [4] and other lexical databases that store data in a structure built upon interlinked sets of synonymous words[1] (synsets) are exploited in a vast number of projects that involve natural language processing. As the majority of wordnets are general purpose databases that represent concepts from various domains of knowledge and store them at different levels of granularity, a problem arises of adjusting the structure and content of a wordnet to a particular task. Such an adjustment may involve the removal and creation of synsets and word senses, changing semantic and lexical relations, establishing a new definition of synonymy, augmenting synsets with additional data, etc. The paper presents WUpdate – a tool designed to perform such transformations while preserving invariants imposed by the structure of a WordNet-like database. WUpdate is a data manipulation language that, with respect to wordnets, plays a similar role as SQL [1] with respect to relational databases, or Lorel [2] to semi-structural ones. WUpdate is based on WQuery [9] – a query language operating on wordnet-specific data types that has been previously used as a module of

---

[1] We call such lexical databases wordnets or WordNet-like databases in the paper.

© Springer International Publishing Switzerland 2014
Z. Vetulani and J. Mariani (Eds.): LTC 2011, LNAI 8387, pp. 343–355, 2014.
DOI: 10.1007/978-3-319-08958-4_28

an NLP/AI system supporting information management of mass events [8,20]. WUpdate extends WQuery syntax with constructs responsible for modifying a WordNet-like database and ensures that the proper structure of a wordnet is preserved while transformations are applied at the semantic level. Emphasis is placed on solving wordnet-specific problems that are not considered in other data manipulation languages. In particular, the WUpdate language provides:

1. Proper handling of semantic hierarchies built with such relations as *hypernymy* and *meronymy*.
2. Special operators for managing granularity of a WordNet-like database.

The WUpdate interpreter is available for download as a part of the WQuery system distribution.[2] WUpdate inherits from WQuery the ability to import wordnets stored in the Global Wordnet Grid [5] and Wordnet-LMF [17] documents.

2   Related Work

The problem of transforming and enriching WordNet-like databases is addressed in many papers (e.g. [11,12,15]), but most of them do not describe the tools used for the task. Princeton WordNet website [13] enlists a wide variety of application programming interfaces designed for general purpose programming languages that could be used for the task, but these are mostly low level interfaces that provide only basic operations such as finding a synset by a sense or accessing related synsets. Hence, elaborate updates such as those described in Sect. 8 require considerable programming effort. In fact, most of the APIs do not provide any commands that would be responsible for modifying a wordnet. Thus, in such cases a transformation of the wordnet must involve the generation of an entirely new database.

Another possible approach to the problem is to use a data manipulation language designed for other data models such as SQL [1] or Lorel [2]. However, these languages do not incorporate wordnet-specific data types and do not provide operators responsible for adjusting the granularity of a wordnet that is analogous to those described in Sect. 7. Furthermore, preservation of the *Transitive* property as defined in Sect. 6 requires additional programming work to be performed in these tools. The same difficulties arise if one tries to use an XML [17] or RDF [6] representation of a WordNet-like database and generate a new wordnet directly using query languages such as XQuery [3] or SPARQL [14].

Finally, wordnet editors such as DEBVisDic [7] may be used to modify a database. These editors are easier to use than our tool for local modifications, such as editing a gloss or adding a semantic link between two synsets, but they do not provide any mechanisms that would allow to apply modifications to multiple objects at once, as can be done by the WUpdate expressions shown in Sect. 8. If a wordnet editor is built on the client-server architecture (e.g. DEBVisDic), such

---

[2] See http://www.wquery.org for details.

serial modifications can be done via the server API. However, if the API does not incorporate a versatile query language then the custom scripts in a general-purpose programming language have to be built on the client side in order to perform complex modifications which are directly representable in WUpdate.

3   Data Model

WUpdate adopts the WQuery data model as presented in Fig. 1. A WordNet-like lexical database is represented in this model by a set of domain-specific and general purpose data types (called, jointly, *basic data types*) interlinked via relations. The values of the domain-specific data types are stored in unary relations called domain sets. In Fig. 1 the names of the domain sets are enclosed in parentheses and placed below the names of their corresponding data types. The basic structure of a wordnet is determined by the binary relations *synset, word, sensenum* and *pos*, which are represented in Fig. 1 by edges with boldfaced labels. These relations connect a word sense to its synset, word, sense number and part of speech (POS) symbol, respectively. Additional relations may be introduced to represent data that vary among wordnets, such as the attributes of synsets (e.g. *gloss* and *nl* in Fig. 1) or particular semantic and lexical relations (e.g. *meronym* and *antonym*). Although all of the relations presented in Fig. 1 are either unary or binary, it should be noted that the model permits relations of arbitrary arity. Every argument of a relation in the data model has an assigned position, name and data types that it can take. For instance, the first argument of the relation *pos* as shown in Fig. 1 has the name *src* and it has to take synsets

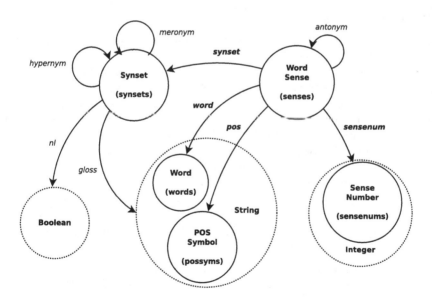

Fig. 1. Basic data types (as nodes of the graph) and the relations among them (as edges) in an instance of the WQuery data model.

(i.e. values of the *Synset* data type), and the second one is named *dst* and has to take part of speech symbols.

The data stored in an instance of the WQuery data model are described by a distinguished set of relations called the *metamodel*. The names of the relations stored in an instance of the model are gathered in the relation *relations*. The assignments of data types, positions and names to the arguments of relations are kept in the relation *arguments*. Both relations are directly accessible for the query language.

4   WQuery Language

We use the WQuery language in our tool to identify objects that have to be transformed and to define the results of a transformation. The WQuery construct we use most extensively is a path expression. It is an expression that describes a multiset of paths in an instance of the data model presented in Sect. 3. For the purpose of path expressions, the instance is treated as a directed graph. This graph's set of nodes consists of values of the basic data types that belong to the active domain[3] of the instance. The set of edges is given by pairs of values that belong to tuples of relations gathered in the instance. A path expression begins with a *generator*, i.e. an expression that identifies a subset of values of one of the data types represented by the nodes of the graph. The generator is followed by zero or more regular expressions formulated over the names of relations stored in the instance of the WQuery data model. A regular expression specifies which edges have to be traversed in order to extend the paths retrieved by the preceding expression. For example, the query[4]

`{auto:1:n}.hypernym+`

consists of a generator `{auto:1:n}` which retrieves the synset that contains the first noun sense of the word *auto* (Eng. *a car*) followed by a regular expression `hypernym+` which traverses one or more times through the edges that link hyponyms (the values of the first argument of the `hypernym` relation) to their hypernyms (the values of the second argument). Thus, the result of the query consists of paths that link `{auto:1:n}` with its transitive hypernyms through zero or more intermediate nodes. Figure 2 presents some paths retrieved by the query as formulated above.

In order to retrieve paths that link synsets to their transitive hyponyms by using the `hypernym` relation, one has to traverse the edges that link the values of the second argument of this relation to the values of the first argument.[5] The backward edges are accessed by prepending the `^` sign to the relation name. Hence, the paths that link `{auto:1:n}` with its transitive hyponyms are given by the following query

---

[3] I.e. the set of values referenced by at least one relation of the instance.

[4] Unless stated otherwise, the queries in the paper are invoked against PolNet [18, 19] – a WordNet-like database developed for the Polish language.

[5] In the paper we skip the methods of accessing the arbitrary arguments of non-binary relations. The details can be found in [10].

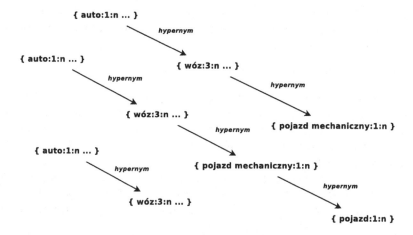

Fig. 2. Sample paths returned by the query {auto:1:n}.hypernym+.

{auto:1:n}.^hypernym+

One can place a variable after a specific step[6] of a path expression in order to reference the values reached by the step. For example, the expression

{auto:1:n}$a.hypernym+$b

attaches bindings to every retrieved path that associate the variable $a with the first node on the path and the variable $b with the last node.

Variable bindings may be referenced in filters, i.e. bracketed conditional expressions that may be placed after the step of a path expression to eliminate undesirable paths from the query result. For instance, the following query returns paths that begin with a synset that contains the word *auto* and ends with its meronym that contains at least two word senses.

{auto}.meronym$a[count($a.^synset) >= 2]

One may use the **from** expression in order to iterate through all the bindings of a path expression. For example, one may formulate the expression

from {auto:1:n}.hypernym+$a
    emit $a

to pass to the output (i.e. emit) only values that are bound to the variable $a.

5   WUpdate Language

A WUpdate expression consists of two WQuery expressions interleaved by a relation name and a transformation operator. The tuples of the specified relation

---

[6] By a step we mean the generator or any of the regular expressions of a path expression that follow.

which are determined by the left-hand expression are updated using the values determined by the right-hand expression with regard to the transformation operator.[7] For instance, the expression

```
{autobus:1:n} hypernym += {auto:1:n}
```

connects the synset { *autobus:1:n* } (Eng. *a bus*) to the synset { *auto:1:n* } via the relation **hypernym**. Besides the **+=** operator, which adds tuples to a relation, one can also use **-=** to remove them and **:=** to replace the tuples conforming to the objects determined by the left-hand expression with new tuples that end in the right-hand objects.

Values of wordnet-specific data types, shown in Fig. 1 as nodes, may be added or removed from the database by modifying relations that correspond to their data type names. For example, to add the second noun sense of the word *auto* one may execute the following expression

```
senses += auto:2:n
```

In order to change the set of relations that are stored in an instance of the WQuery data model one has to modify the relations of the metamodel. For example, to create the relation **usage** that connects synsets to the sentences that are examples of their usage, one may execute the following commands

```
relations += 'usage'
'usage' arguments += 'src','synset',1
'usage' arguments += 'dst','string',2
```

The first expression adds the relation named **usage** to the instance. The second one specifies that the first argument of **usage** is named **src** and takes synsets as its values. The last one states that the second argument of **usage** is named **dst** and is restricted to string values. The comma (,) operator in the expressions above represents the concatenation of the paths. By default the elements of paths returned by the arguments of an update operator have to correspond to the consecutive arguments of the modified relation. Thus, in the expression

```
'usage' arguments += 'dst','string',2
```

the string **usage** is assigned to the first argument of the relation **arguments**, the string **dst** to the second one, etc. One can reference the arguments of a relation by name with ^ signs placed in between in order to assign values to them in an arbitrary order. Hence, the tuple added by the expression above may also be created by the command

```
'usage' relation^arguments^position^name^type += 2,'dst','string'
```

---

[7] The left-hand expression is optional. If it is not specified, all the tuples of the relation are considered as shown in the examples later in this section.

6   Preserving Relation Properties

Modifying the content of a wordnet may corrupt its structure. For example, if we add a new connection through the **hypernym** relation, we may accidentally create a cycle in the hypernymy hierarchy which by definition is acyclic. In order,to prevent such situations we have extended the WQuery data model by introducing properties that may be associated with arguments of relations in order to preserve the valid structure of a wordnet while its content is being modified. We present the available properties in Table 1. The $Required(\alpha)$, $Functional(\alpha)$, $Symmetric(\alpha, \beta)$ and $Antisymmetric(\alpha, \beta)$ properties are simple constraints that have natural counterparts in other database systems. The $Transitive(\alpha, \beta)$ property has been introduced to ease maintenance of semantic hierarchies built using such relations as hypernymy or meronymy. It may become compromised if a tuple is removed from R or if for some tuple $t \in R$ the value $t(\alpha)$ or $t(\beta)$ is removed from a domain set. In the first case the default action is to permit such an operation assuming that the change has been introduced intentionally. In the second case the tuples that contain the removed value on the β position have to be joined with the tuples that contain it on the α position, as is shown in the example in Fig. 3. Hence, the removal of intermediate objects from a transitive relation preserves the reachability of values as defined in Table 1. It should be noted that in the case of non-binary relations the join operation will succeed only if the tuples being joined are equal except for the values of α and β, otherwise an error will be reported.

By default WUpdate reports an error if $Required(\alpha)$, $Functional(\alpha)$ or $Antisymmetric(\alpha, \beta)$ becomes compromised by a command submitted to the interpreter. The default action undertaken in the case of the $Symmetric(\alpha, \beta)$ property is to restore the symmetry. Thus, if a new tuple is added to a symmetric relation then the backward tuple is also created, and if a tuple is removed the backward one is removed also. If the default action associated with a property is not adequate, it may be replaced by an alternative from Table 2.

Descriptions of properties are stored in two new relations added to the meta-model:

1. *properties(relation, argument, property, action)* that collects properties (arg. *property*) assigned to the arguments (arg. *argument*) of relations (arg. *relation*) and the actions bound to them (arg. *action*)
2. *pair_properties(relation, source, destination, property, action)* that collects properties (arg. *property*) of pairs of arguments (arg. *source* and *destination*) of relations (arg. *relation*) and the actions bound to them (arg. *action*).

These relations have to be modified in order to add or remove the properties of relation arguments. For instance, to make the **hypernym** relation antisymmetric, one can invoke the following command

```
'hypernym', 'src', 'dst'
    pair_properties := 'antisymmetric', 'preserve'
```

Table 1. Properties of relation arguments. α, β – arguments of the relation R, $dt(x)$ data type of the argument x

Name	Definition	Example
$Required(\alpha)$	If v is a value of of the type $dt(\alpha)$ then there exists a tuple $t \in R$ such that $t(\alpha) = v$	`pos(src)`
$Functional(\alpha)$	If v is a value of of the type $dt(\alpha)$ then there exists at most one tuple $t \in R$ such that $t(\alpha) = v$	`gloss(src)`
$Symmetric(\alpha, \beta)$	if there exists a tuple $t \in R$ such that $t(\alpha) = v$ and $t(\beta) = w$ then there exists a tuple $s \in R$ such that $s(\alpha) = w$ and $s(\beta) = v$	`antonym(src,dst)`
$Antisymmetric(\alpha, \beta)$	if there exists a tuple $t \in R$ such that $t(\alpha) = v$ and $t(\beta) = w$ then there is no tuple $s \in R$ such that $s(\alpha) = w$ and $s(\beta) = v$	`meronym(src,dst)`
$Transitive(\alpha, \beta)$	if w is reachable from v through R (i.e. there exist tuples $t_1, t_2, \ldots, t_k \in R$ such that $t_1(\alpha) = v$, $t_k(\beta) = w$, $t_i(\beta) = t_{i+1}(\alpha)$ for $i < k$) before transformation and the transformation does not remove either w or v then w is reachable from v after the transformation is performed	`hypernym(src,dst)`

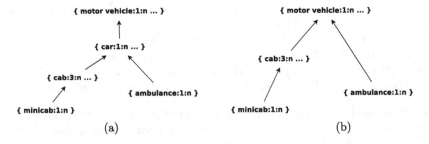

Fig. 3. The `hypernym` relation before (a) and after (b) the removal of the synset { *car:1:n* } from the Princeton WordNet

Table 2. Alternative actions that may be undertaken if a property is compromised

Property	Cause	Alternative Actions
$Required(\alpha)$	A tuple t has been removed	Remove the value $t(\alpha)$
$Functional(\alpha)$	A tuple t has been added	Remove the tuple s such that $t(\alpha) = s(\alpha)$
$Symmetric(\alpha, \beta)$	A tuple has been added or removed	Report an error
$Antisymmetric(\alpha, \beta)$	A tuple t has been added such that for some tuple s holds $t(\alpha) = s(\beta)$ and $t(\beta) = s(\alpha)$	Remove the tuple s
$Transitive(\alpha, \beta)$	$t(\alpha)$ or $t(\beta)$ has been removed for some tuple $t \in R$	Report an error

7   Managing Granularity of a Wordnet

Since the problem of adjusting the granularity of a wordnet to a target application has been discussed in several papers (e.g. [11,12,15], in the context of word sense disambiguation), we decided to introduce the `split` and `merge` operators that simplify adjustment of the partition of senses into synsets.

The `split` operator takes as an argument a set of synsets and creates separate synsets for all of their senses. For example, to split the synset { *auto:1:n samochód osobowy:1:n bryka:2:n samochodzik:2:n* } into the synsets { *auto:1:n* }, { *samochód osobowy:1:n* }, { *bryka:2:n* }, { *samochodzik:2:n* } one may formulate the following expression

```
split {auto:1:n}
```

The `merge` operator takes as an argument a set of synsets and/or word senses and relocates senses to the new synset. For instance, to create a new synset from all synsets that contain the word *pojazd* (Eng. *a vehicle*), one may execute the following command.

```
merge {pojazd}
```

The main problem that arises while relocating senses is how to deal with the connections of their synsets. By default new synsets inherit all connections after the merged/split ones, and in the case of the `merge` operator edges that point from the new synset to the same object are joined together. Since the `split` and `merge` operators preserve relation properties as defined in Sect. 6, they may report an error if such an action is associated with a property. For instance, if one merges synsets that belong to different levels of the hierarchy determined by a transitive antisymmetric relation (e.g. hypernymy), one may encounter the error as shown in the example below.

```
merge {pojazd:1:n} union {auto:1:n}
```

```
ERROR: Update breaks property 'transitive antisymmetry'
of relation 'hypernym'
```

In order to avoid errors one has to prepend and/or append additional expressions that will guarantee that the properties of the relations will not become compromised. Due to the limited space we skip the details, which can be found in [10].

8   Examples of Complex Transformations

In order to show how the WUpdate language may be used to perform complex database transformations in this section we consider problems that require more elaborate changes to be performed on a wordnet. We have chosen problems that do not depend on the existence of particular synsets, word senses or words in the database, but which rely only on the structural properties of a wordnet, such as existence of hypernymy and meronymy relations. Thus, the WUpdate expressions presented in this section may be invoked against different WordNet-like databases without introducing adjustments.

8.1   Removing Redundant Connections

Hypernymy is a transitive relation. Hence, if two synsets are reachable via hypernymy through one or more intermediate synsets then maintaining a direct hypernymy link between them is redundant. Such links may be removed with the following expression[8]

```
from {}$a.hypernym.hypernym+$b[$b in $a.hypernym]
  $a hypernym -= $b.
```

A similar problem arises if we assume that hyponyms inherit meronyms from their hypernyms. In this case we can remove the meronymy links from the hyponyms.

```
from {}$a.meronym$b[$b in $a.hypernym+.meronym]
  $a meronym -= $b
```

---

[8] The {} generator represents all synsets in the database.

8.2   Separating Senses by Parts of Speech

WUpdate does not enforce synsets to be composed only from senses that belong to the same part of speech. If such a separation is necessary for a given task, it can be introduced by iterating through synsets and merging senses that belong to the same part of speech.

```
from {}$a
  from possyms$b
    merge $a.^synset[$a.pos = $b]
```

The cross-part-of-speech hypernymy links (if any exist) can be removed with the following expression

```
from {}$a.hypernym$b[$a.pos != $b.pos]
  $a hypernym -= $b
```

9   Conclusion

The paper describes a tool designed to perform transformations of WordNet-like lexical databases. WUpdate incorporates several features that have been designed to simplify manipulation of wordnet data that are not found in other wordnet-oriented and general purpose data management tools. First, it is built upon a query language that incorporates wordnet-specific data types. Second, it adopts a data model that preserves the properties of semantic relations while the content of a wordnet is being transformed. Third, it provides a set of operators for managing the granularity of a WordNet-like database. We have shown how these features, when combined together, can be exploited to perform complex wordnet transformations.

In the future we would like to extend the language with constructs responsible for processing multiple WordNet-like databases at once. As WUpdate performance is coupled to the performance of the WQuery engine, we also plan to investigate query optimization methods that exploit the structure of a wordnet.

Acknowledgments. This research was supported by a scholarship within the project "Scholarship support for Ph.D. students specializing in majors strategic for Wielkopolska's development", Sub-measure 8.2.2 Human Capital Operational Programme, co-financed by European Union under the European Social Fund.

References

1. Abiteboul, S., Hull, R., Vianu, V.: Foundations of Databases. Addison-Wesley, Boston (1995)
2. Abiteboul, S., Quass, D., McHugh, J., Widom, J., Wiener, J.L.: The Lorel query language for semistructured data. Int. J. Digit. Libr. **1**(1), 68–88 (1997)

3. Boag, S., Chamberlin, D.D., Fernández, M.F., Florescu, D., Robie, J., Siméon, J.: XQuery 1.0: an XML query language (2nd Edition). W3C recommendation, W3C (December 2010). http://www.w3.org/TR/2010/REC-xquery-20101214/
4. Fellbaum, C. (ed.): WordNet: An Electronic Lexical Database. MIT Press, Cambridge (1998)
5. Global Wordnet Association: Global Wordnet Grid DTD. http://globalwordnet. org/gwa/grid/bwn2.dtd (2010). Accessed 23 Sep 2010
6. Graves, A., Gutierrez, C.: Data representations for WordNet: a case for RDF. In: Sojka et al. [16], pp. 165–169
7. Horak, A., Pala, K., Rambousek, A., Povolny, M.: DEBVisDic - First version of new client-server wordnet browsing and editing tool. In: Sojka et al. [16], pp. 325–328
8. Kubis, M.: An access layer to PolNet – polish WordNet. In: Vetulani, Z. (ed.) LTC 2009. LNCS (LNAI), vol. 6562, pp. 444–455. Springer, Heidelberg (2011)
9. Kubis, M.: A query language for WordNet-like lexical databases. In: Pan, J.-S., Chen, S.-M., Nguyen, N.T. (eds.) ACIIDS 2012, Part III. LNCS, vol. 7198, pp. 436–445. Springer, Heidelberg (2012)
10. Kubis, M.: WQuery User Guide (2013). http://wquery.org/user-guide.pdf
11. Mihalcea, R., Moldovan, D.I.: EZ.WordNet: principles for automatic generation of a coarse grained WordNet. In: Russell, I., Kolen, J.F. (eds.) Proceedings of the Fourteenth International Florida Artificial Intelligence Research Society Conference, 21–23 May, Key West, Florida, USA, pp. 454–458. AAAI Press (2001)
12. Navigli, R.: Meaningful clustering of senses helps boost word sense disambiguation performance. In: Proceedings of the 21st International Conference on Computational Linguistics and the 44th Annual Meeting of the Association for Computational Linguistics, pp. 105–112. ACL-44. Association for Computational Linguistics, Stroudsburg (2006)
13. Princeton University: WordNet - Related Projects (2011). http://wordnet. princeton.edu/wordnet/related-projects/, Accessed 28 April 2011
14. Prud'hommeaux, E., Seaborne, A.: SPARQL query language for RDF. W3C recommendation, W3C (January 2008). http://www.w3.org/TR/2008/ REC-rdf-sparql-query-20080115/
15. Snow, R., Prakash, S., Jurafsky, D., Ng, A.Y.: Learning to merge word senses. In: Proceedings of the Joint Meeting of the Conference on Empirical Methods on Natural Language Processing and the Conference on Natural Language Learning, pp. 1005–1014 (2007)
16. Sojka, P., Choi, K.S., Fellbaum, C., Vossen, P. (eds.): Proceedings of the Third International WordNet Conference - GWC 2006. Masaryk University, Brno, Czech Republic (2005)
17. Soria, C., Monachini, M., Vossen, P.: Wordnet-LMF: Fleshing out a standardized format for wordnet interoperability. In: Proceeding of the 2009 International Workshop on Intercultural Collaboration, pp. 139–146. ACM, New York (2009)
18. Vetulani, Z.: Wordnet based lexicon grammar for polish. In: Calzolari, N., et al. (eds.) Proceedings of the Eight International Conference on Language Resources and Evaluation (LREC'12). European Language Resources Association (ELRA), Istanbul, Turkey (2012)

19. Vetulani, Z., Kubis, M., Obrebski, T.: PolNet - Polish WordNet: Data and Tools. In: Calzolari, N., et al. (eds.) Proceedings of the 7th International Conference on Language Resources and Evaluation (LREC'10), pp. 3793–3797. European Language Resources Association (ELRA), Valletta, Malta (2010)
20. Vetulani, Z., Marciniak, J.: Natural language based communication between human users and the emergency center: POLINT-112-SMS. In: Vetulani, Z. (ed.) LTC 2009. LNCS (LNAI), vol. 6562, pp. 303–314. Springer, Heidelberg (2011)

KABA Subject Heading Language as the Main Resource Subject Organization Tool in a Semantic Knowledge Base

Cezary Mazurek, Krzysztof Sielski[✉], Justyna Walkowska,
and Marcin Werla

Poznań Supercomputing and Networking Center, ul. Noskowskiego 12/14,
61-704 Poznań, Poland
{mazurek, sielski, ynka, mwerla}@man.poznan.pl

Abstract. KABA is a subject heading language used in Polish library catalogues to describe document subjects. An attempt has been made to convert KABA into a thesaurus compliant with the CIDOC CRM ontology to embed it in a semantic knowledge base comprising the foundation of the Integrated Knowledge System created in the SYNAT Project. Information objects (e.g. books) in the knowledge base are described with KABA headings, which increases the search engine recall based on the information about relations between the subjects. This paper presents the process of transforming KABA into a fully machine-readable thesaurus form and the challenges that must be overcome in order for this process to succeed.

Keywords: Authority file · CIDOC CRM · Digital libraries · KABA · Semantic web · Subject headings

1 Introduction

SYNAT is a national research project aimed at the creation of universal open repository platform for hosting and communication of networked resources of knowledge for science, education, and open society of knowledge. It is funded by the Polish National Center for Research and Development (grant no SP/I/1/77065/10) and is coordinated by University of Warsaw - ICM.

Poznań Supercomputing and Networking Center (PSNC) is one of the key SYNAT partners, responsible, among other things, for the creation of a prototype of the Integrated Knowledge System (IKS). The system will integrate knowledge from distributed heterogeneous sources such as digital libraries, digital museums, scientific and technical information systems. The system will process the data and present it to its users, but it will also allow for further automatic processing of the data on the Semantic Web.

A significant portion of data in the Integrated Knowledge System comes from Polish digital libraries, participating in the Digital Libraries Federation [1]. Some of the libraries use descriptions from the NUKAT catalogue, effectively introducing KABA subjects to the digital libraries world. There is also a number of subjects constructed using the KABA grammar, but from lexical units that are not found in the

© Springer International Publishing Switzerland 2014
Z. Vetulani and J. Mariani (Eds.): LTC 2011, LNAI 8387 pp. 356–366, 2014.
DOI: 10.1007/978-3-319-08958-4_29

KABA dictionary. It is possible to relate some of such subjects to existing, valid KABA subjects. These are the main reasons of choosing KABA to represent subjects in the IKS.

The remaining part of this paper describes the process of mapping KABA Subject Headings from its native MARC 21 format to the OWL-encoded CIDOC CRM ontology which is used in IKS. A short description of these formats is given in the paper. The paper also mentions problems encountered during automatic KABA processing and summarizes the obtained results.

2 KABA Subject Headings

KABA is a subject heading language used to describe publication subjects by a number of Polish libraries cooperating within the NUKAT National Union Catalog. KABA stands for Katalogi Automatyczne Bibliotek Akademickich (Academic Libraries Automatic Catalogues).

2.1 KABA History

The creation of KABA started in 1991 at the University of Warsaw Library. It is coordinated by the NUKAT centre [2, 3]. KABA is compatible with (and was modeled on) three earlier subject heading languages: French RAMEAU (*Répertoire d'Autorité-Matière Encyclopédique et Alphabétique Unfié*) [4], American LCSH (*Library of Congress Subject Headings*), and Canadian RVM (*Répertoire de vedettes-matière*). The initial KABA creation process was reminiscent of the so-called expand model [5] of building semantic networks. The expand model, as opposed to the merge model, implies the translation of concepts and then developing them in detail. The merge model implies independent development and linking to other languages at a later stage. This means that a number of records and relations between the records were translated from other languages (mostly French), possibly bringing a slightly different conceptualization.

2.2 NUKAT Cataloguing Model

The NUKAT catalogue is created by means of shared cataloguing. There are over 1100 librarians from 81 libraries contributing to NUKAT. If a library (*bibliographic*) record or a subject headings (*authority*) record does not exist, a librarian creates it and waits for the NUKAT Centre's acceptance. The accepted record may then be used by any cataloguer. The structure of a KABA record is described in the following section.

2.3 KABA Record Structure

KABA records are stored in the MARC 21 format. Each record is described by of a group of control fields (containing metadata about the record, such as last modification date) and datafields containing information about the subject. The meaning of each datafield is determined by the value of its tag property. For example, a datafield with the 100 tag is used with subjects representing personal names. The contents of datafields are divided into atomic pieces of information stored in subfields. This way, the person subject "Pentzikis, Nikos-Gabriel (1908–1993)" is described in detail as consisting of a surname ("Pentzikis"), first names ("Nikos-Gabriel") and biographical dates ("1908–1993"). A record is constructed from a main subject and zero or more subdivisions (determiners) which bring more detail to the subject.

This format is expressive enough to represent all relevant information about subject headings. The most important elements of a subject heading definition from the Integrated Knowledge System's semantic data base's point of view are:

- the type of the subject (personal name, corporate name, genre/form term etc.) – this information is encoded in the two last numbers of datafield tag, i.e. "XX" in datafield 1XX),
- the authorized form of the subject heading (the contents of datafield 1XX),
- unauthorized forms of subject heading (datafield 4XX),
- relations with other records: broader terms, narrower terms, earlier and later forms of heading (datafield 5XX).

2.4   Subject Hierarchies Alternative to KABA

Apart from subject headings, a number of libraries also use classifications, such as Dewey Decimal Classification [6] or Library of Congress Classification [7]. Others use structured subject indices. Classifications are usually more general than subject headings. Also, the "broader term" (or "is a") relation can be treated more strictly within classifications. Ideally, resources should be described both by means of a classification (which is smaller, and thus easier to browse) and with a subject headings hierarchy.

3   Problems with Automatic Processing

KABA was designed to be browsed manually by people looking for a particular subject to use in the cataloguing process or to find publications on the subject. Although KABA records are now stored in computer databases, some of their features do not suit automatic processing well. Subjects defined in KABA are often closely related to each other, but automatic discovery of all such relationships is a difficult task. A particular challenge is the processing of fields 260 and 360 of record definition which describe complex subject references using natural language. For example, field 360 of heading "Handel międzynarodowy" ("International trade") states that the record is related to all headings containing subdivision "-- handel zagraniczny" ("-- foreign trade") after geographical name combined, if necessary, with geographical subdivision expressed by the name of country, city etc. with which the trade exchange is conducted. The language used in those fields is formalized to a large extent and a few common templates of the content can be distinguished, but still the semantics are very complicated for automatic processing and finding the enumeration of referenced records is difficult.

Most of the relations between records indicate the referenced subject directly, in which case the problems mentioned before do not occur. Based on such relations, we transformed KABA to a thesaurus with *has broader term* as the main relation (corresponding to the *is a* hierarchical relation). The results were surprising.

Performing only the *has narrower term* reasoning we learned that (see Fig. 1):

(a) "death is a life", and
(b) "a lighthouse is a life".

The former sentence can be justified: life always ends up with death so death as a subtopic of life is reasonable according to some cataloguers. It is not precise though and regarding the *has broader term* relation as transitive results in the latter sentence which is apparently wrong. A part of the obtained subject hierarchy is shown in Fig. 1. A similar experiment based on LCSH also led to wrong conclusions such as "a doorbell is a mammal" [8].

An apparent proof of mistakes in hierarchical relations are structural inconsistencies, especially cycles (Fig. 2). The thesaurus obtained from KABA records has

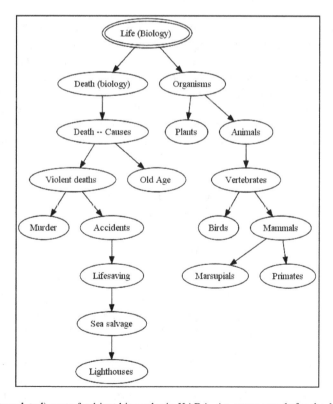

Fig. 1. A (translated) part of subject hierarchy in KABA. An arrow stands for the *has narrower term* relation

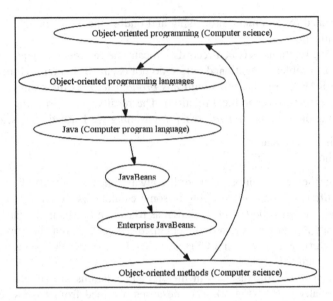

Fig. 2. A (translated) cycle in KABA. An arrow stands for the *has narrower term* relation

been examined with the Tarjan algorithm [9], which revealed some 270 cycles. An example of such cycle is shown in Fig. 2. The majority of cycles consist of just two elements. In some cases a record is defined to be a broader term of itself.

Another challenge in the automatic processing of KABA is the fact that KABA does not explicitly define all relations between records. The missing relations are usually easy to deduce when browsing manually through the catalogue for a particular subject, because they result from the grammar of the subject headings language. A NUKAT webpage full-text search for "Malarstwo" ("Painting") will return, among others:

- "Malarstwo",
- "Malarstwo -- techniki" ("Painting -- techniques"),
- "Malarstwo -- Japonia" ("Painting -- Japan"),
- "Malarstwo -- 20 w." ("Painting -- 20th century").

All those subjects are indeed very closely related, but their definitions do not contain references to each other, which is crucial for automatic thesaurus construction. An attempt to discover those implicit relations was made by [10] and is based on observations of common practices, but has not been confirmed by official rules of creating KABA records stated by the NUKAT and can also introduce mistakes.

Another problem that arises from the human-centric nature of KABA Subject Headings are mistakes in record definitions which can be easily discovered automatically, but not all of them are easy to correct. The errors include typographical errors, duplicates, and specification incompatibilities. The format specification [11] describes a list of fields that may be a part of record definition and of subfields that may occur in each of those fields. We found 77 records that violate this specification and define subfield incompatible with the particular field. As a result, their semantics is undocumented and unknown. This issue arose mainly from translating RAMEAU records and incorporating them into KABA, whereas those two subject heading systems are not fully compatible.

Still, the advantages of using KABA to describe digital library resources outweigh the problems described above (see Sects. 5 and 6 for discussion). The following section describes in detail how KABA is represented in the CIDOC-CRM-compliant semantic Knowledge Base.

4 Semantic Knowledge Base: KABA and CIDOC CRM

KABA is used in the Integrated Knowledge System to organize publications' subjects in the semantic database. This section describes the ontology used to represent resources in the semantic Knowledge Base and the way KABA is automatically transformed to match the ontology.

4.1 CIDOC CRM

CIDOC Conceptual Reference Model (CRM) is a formal ontology intended to facilitate the integration, mediation and interchange of heterogeneous cultural heritage information [12]. Work on this standard began in 1996. The project was led by International Committee for Documentation of the International Council of Museums (ICOM-CI-DOC). The development of the CRM was later delegated to the CRM Special Interest Group, collaborating with the ISO working group ISO/TC46/SC4/WG9.

CIDOC CRM was chosen for the SYNAT project as it is a mature and expressive ontology allowing to describe cultural heritage objects. It is tailored to describe mostly museum collections, but a dedicated application profile has been developed in the project for use with digital libraries. The ontology data and the Knowledge Base (i.e. the instances of ontology classes generated by mapping the heterogeneous sources' metadata to the Erlangen CRM CIDOC implementation in OWL [13]) are stored in an RDF repository capable of OWL-DL reasoning.

4.2 Mapping Process

The process of mapping KABA Subject Headings into the Knowledge Base conformant with the CIDOC CRM ontology starts with parsing a file in MARC 21 XML format. An intermediate structure is created to represent KABA records in a relational database. It is validated against the MARC 21 specification. Some transformations must be made because records do not reference related subjects with their id but with the authorized form of their heading – this structure must be converted into a relational one. At this stage, references pointing to non-existing subjects are removed.

All 4 rules of creating implicit relations proposed in [10] are included in this process. These rules are heuristic, so it cannot be guaranteed that the resulting relation set is entirely correct, but the set is too numerous for manual verification. The most important rule says that a broader term can be built from a subject heading containing subdivisions by removing some of them (see the "painting" search example in the previous section). This rule has produced over 200,000 new relations in the Knowledge Base, almost doubling the number of relations.

In the final step, the mapping of KABA records into a set of RDF triples is performed. Each subject is mapped into an instance of the E55g_Subject_Hierarchy class which is a subclass of E55_Type. The E55_Type class plays a special role in the CIDOC ontology. It has been designed as an interface to domain specific ontologies and thesauri. A new ontology, thesaurus, or classification is connected with the ontology and semantic base by creating a new subclass of the E55_Type class. The instances of such a subclass represent concepts from the external classification.

It may seem unnatural that instances of a class represent concepts, but it makes perfect sense when taken into consideration that the KABA hierarchy of subjects consists of almost 900,000 records – were they represented by classes, the original CIDOC ontology would be completely invisible among them.

The authorized form of each subject heading is connected to E55g_Subject_Hierarchy instance with the P1_is_identified_by property, and the unauthorized forms are connected by means of the P139_has_alternative_form property. Relations to other records are mapped based on the similarTo property borrowed from the OpenVocab (http://open.vocab.org/) namespace. We also introduced subproperties of this property to represent each relation type:

- P214_see_also_broader_term,
- P214i_see_also_narrower_term,
- P213_see_also_earlier_form,
- P213i_see_also_later_form.

Although CIDOC defines two properties to represent hierarchical relations (P127_has_broader_term and P127i_has_narrower_term), finally a decision was made not to use them. Their semantics is equal to that of the relations enumerated above, but the original P127 relations are transitive. Relations defined in KABA records are often imprecise and long transitive chains of *has broader term* relation often resulted in deducing incorrect relations, as shown above in the "life" example.

We also decided not to adopt SKOS vocabulary [14], which was designed to represent controlled vocabularies (such as subject heading systems) and defines separate predicates for transitive (skos:broaderTransitive) and non-transitive relation (skos:broader). However, since skos:broader is a subproperty of skos:broaderTransitive, an inference engine with implicit statement materialization (such as is used in our system) would add a full transitive closure of skos:broaderTransitive relation for every triple with skos:broader predicate. This would introduce a lot of triples and cause unnecessary storage and performance overhead: a transitive closure of a chain of n transitive relations would generate $O(n^2)$ implicit triples.

5   Knowledge Base Content Analysis

The Integrated Knowledge System's semantic database at the early stage of development was described in [15, 16]. At that time (the middle of 2011), it contained information about 500,000 publications from the Digital Libraries Federation (DLF) and consisted of about 23M explicit RDF triples (this number includes about 6M triples representing mapped KABA records). Additional several millions of triples were introduced by the inference engine with our custom rule set, which is a subset of OWL 2 RL/RDF entailment rules [17]. At the beginning of 2013, the number of explicit RDF triples in the Knowledge Base increased ten times and came to 235M. Apart from metadata about 1,100,000 publications that were aggregated in DLF at that time, new data sources had been attached and mapped to the Knowledge Base: NUKAT library catalogue (some 2,000,000 publications), museum catalogues from The National Museum in Warsaw and The National Museum in Krakow (some 16,000 items altogether). Furthermore, some auxiliary Linked Open Data sources, such as VIAF (The Virtual International Authority File), Geonames or Lexvo, were included in the Knowledge Base to represent information about authorities (people and legal bodies), places and languages respectively.

Publications' subjects can be of distinct classes: places, persons, legal bodies, meetings or general term (represented in KABA or not). Places are recognized in the metadata text based on information from the Geonames.org service and on TERYT, the publicly available national administrative register of populated places maintained by Polish Central Statistical Office. Persons and legal bodies are recognized based on the VIAF database. A number of subjects was successfully mapped to KABA. When a subject was not recognized in any of mentioned auxiliary data source, an instance of a user subject was created.

Table 1 shows information about subjects of different classes in the Knowledge Base. There are 6,287,293 relations connecting publications to their subjects (publications can have any number of subjects) and almost exactly half of them (3,184,396) are KABA subjects. This makes KABA the main subject organization tool in the current version of Knowledge Base. Within all *is about* relations, 1,153,583 unique subjects are present, and almost exactly half of them are unique KABA subject instances: 551,075. This means that on average each subject is reused in 5.45 publications (this ratio is only slightly larger when considering only KABA: 5.78).

Table 1. Publications' subjects distribution

Subject type	*is about* relations	Unique subjects	Subject reuse ratio
KABA subject	3,184,396	551,075	5.78
Place	676,746	20,419	33.14
Other (person, legal body, meeting name)	688,209	262,095	2.63
Unrecognized (user subject)	1,737,942	319,994	5.43
Any (sum of above)	6,287,293	1,153,583	5.45

Table 2. Publications' from Digital Libraries Federation subjects distribution

Subject type	*is about* relations	Unique subjects	Subject reuse ratio
KABA subject	610,967	23,550	25.94
Place	668,270	15,272	43.76
Other (person, legal body, meeting name)	140,530	140,530	1.00
Unrecognized (user subject)	1,592,461	196,523	8.10
Any (sum of above)	3,012,228	375,875	8.01

The statistics from the previous paragraph might be biased since the largest portion of the data comes from the NUKAT library catalogue, which directly references KABA subject headings. In order to assess the impact of usage KABA subject headings in organizing subjects, Table 2 provides statistics restricted to records from DLF. In this subset of the Knowledge Base, 3,012,228 *is about* relations exist, from which 610,967 (about 20 %) have KABA subjects. The interesting thing is that only 23,550 unique KABA subject instances are used, which means that on average each KABA subject is reused in 26 publications. This is good news for knowledge base constructors, as it facilitates the clustering of search results. However, it is important to note here that in data from this source subsequent issues of old regional newspapers and magazines substitute a significant part of the data (around 70 %), which bias the results (different issues of the same periodical have almost identical metadata).

It is worth noticing that places are more often reused than KABA subjects – on average 33.14 publications concern the same place (43.76 when restricted only to the DLF data). On the other hand, subjects recognized as persons or legal bodies were rarely reused: only 2.63 publication per subject instance (moreover, in the DLF data they were never reused).

6   Conclusions

KABA is widely used, interconnected, exhaustive, extensible, understandable for both humans and computers. Incorporating this subject headings system into the Knowledge Base helps organize information objects by their topics and estimate the similarity among them. It increases the recall of the Integrated Knowledge System because a user query for a particular subject can return resources on closely related subjects as well. The Knowledge Base contents analysis proves the value of using an organized subject headings hierarchy.

Some problems were discovered when converting KABA into a machine-readable thesaurus, most of which result from the fact that KABA was intended to be used by people in libraries and not for automatic processing. Certain design decisions, such as handling the *has broader term* relation as intransitive, have been made to avoid wrong statements in the Knowledge Base. The mentioned problems decrease the quality of obtained thesaurus but are outweighed with the benefits of using KABA.

References

1. Lewandowska, A., Mazurek, C., Werla, M.: Enrichment of European digital resources by federating regional digital libraries in Poland. In: Christensen-Dalsgaard, B., Castelli, D., Ammitzbøll Jurik, B., Lippincott, J. (eds.) ECDL 2008. LNCS, vol. 5173, pp. 256–259. Springer, Heidelberg (2008)
2. Nasiłowska, M.: Opis przedmiotowy w katalogu NUKAT – rola i miejsce jhp KABA (subject indexing in NUKAT union catalog – the role and place of KABA subject Heading). In: Rola katalogu centralnego NUKAT w kształtowaniu społeczeństwa wiedzy w Polsce, pp. 73–80 (2010)
3. NUKAT webpage. http://www.nukat.edu.pl. Accessed 27 Oct 2011
4. Kotalska, B.: The RAMEAU/KABA network: an example of multi-lingual cooperation. Slav. East Eur. Inf. Res. 3(2–3), 149–156 (2002)
5. Vossen, P.: Euro WordNet General Document. University of Amsterdam (2002). http://www.vossen.info/docs/2002/EWNGeneral.pdf. Accessed 27 Oct 2011
6. Dewey, M.: A Classification and Subject Index for Cataloguing and Arranging the Books and Pamphlets of a Library. Amherst, Mass (1876)
7. Library of Congress Classification Outline. http://www.loc.gov/catdir/cpso/lcco. Accessed 27 Oct 2011
8. Spero, S.: LCSH is to thesaurus as doorbell is to mammal: visualizing structural problems in the library of congress subject headings. In: Proceedings of the 2008 International Conference on Dublin Core and Metadata Applications (DCMI'08). Dublin Core Metadata Initiative, pp. 203–203 (2008)
9. Tarjan, R.E.: Depth-first search and linear graph algorithms. SIAM J. Comput. 1, 146–160 (1972)
10. Daćko, D., Józefowska, J., Ławrynowicz, A.: An ontology based semantic library catalogue. In: Proceedings of 3rd Language and Technology Conference, Poznań, Poland, 3–7 October 2007, pp. 109–113 (2007)
11. Paluszkiewicz, A.: Format MARC 21 rekordu kartoteki haseł wzorcowych: zastosowanie w Centralnej Kartotece Haseł Wzorcowych NUKAT. In: Formaty, Kartoteki, Volume 17. SBP, Warszawa (2009)
12. Crofts, N., Doerr, M., Gill, T., Stead, S., Stiff, M.: Definition of the CIDOC Conceptual Reference Model, 5.0.2 edn., January 2010. http://www.cidoc-crm.org/docs/cidoc_crm_version_5.0.2.pdf. Accessed 27 Oct 2011
13. Görz, G., Oischinger, M., Schiemann, B.: An implementation of the CIDOC conceptual reference model (4.2.4) in OWL-DL. In: Proceedings of CIDOC 2008 – The Digital Curation of Cultural Heritage. ICOM CIDOC, Athens (2008)
14. SKOS Simple Knowledge Organization System Reference. W3C Recommendation 18 August 2009. http://www.w3.org/TR/skos-reference/
15. Mazurek, C., Sielski, K., Stroiński, M., Walkowska, J., Werla, M., Węglarz, J.: Transforming a flat metadata schema to a semantic web ontology: the polish digital libraries federation and CIDOC CRM case study. In: Bembenik, R., Skonieczny, L., Rybiński, H., Niezgodka, M. (eds.) Intelligent Tools for Building a Scient. Info. Plat. SCI, vol. 390, pp. 153–177. Springer, Heidelberg (2012)

16. Mazurek, C., Sielski, K., Walkowska, J., Werla, M.: KABA subject heading language as the main resource subject organization tool in a semantic knowledge base. In: Vetulani, Z. (ed.) Human Language Technologies as a Challenge for Computer Science and Linguistics. Proceedings of the 5th Language and Technology Conference (LTC 2011), Poznań, Poland, 25–27 November 2011
17. Reasoning in OWL 2 RL and RDF Graphs using Rules. OWL 2 Web Ontology Language Profiles. http://www.w3.org/TR/owl2-profiles/#Reasoning_in_OWL_2_RL_and_RDF_Graphs_using_Rules

Enhancing Tagging Systems by Wordnet Based Ontologies

Jacek Marciniak[✉]

Faculty of Mathematics and Computer Science,
Adam Mickiewicz University, ul. Umultowska 87, 61-614 Poznań, Poland
jacekmar@amu.edu.pl

Abstract. This article deals with ways of enhancing the functionality of tagging systems, by introducing wordnet based ontologies. Tagging systems are a very popular way of describing resource contents, by using words or expressions (this is especially true for the Internet). Introducing wordnet based ontologies enables broadening or narrowing down the search, by referring to other concepts from the same semantic field. This approach significantly improves searching resources gathered in any computer system. The article presents a model, in which the wordnet-like ontology structure is broadened by specific domain relations. This model also assumes that the ontology will be transformed into the so-called normalized form with all the necessary relations for the needs of the enhanced tagging system. This method was implemented in the Wilanów Palace Museum vortal, where the available system of a couple of thousand tags, from the field of Polish history and culture, was used to build an enhanced tagging system.

Keywords: Tagging systems · Wordnet based ontologies · Intelligent user interfaces

1   Introduction

IT systems directed at a wide audience which facilitate storing and sharing information and knowledge need to have well-developed tag-searching mechanisms in order to raise their effectiveness. Tagging is a process that enables users with access to certain resources (web pages, video files, documents etc.), to assign words or expressions (tags) acting as keywords describing the subject matter. The tagging system is understood to be the computer system itself, users who use it, the resources and tags it contains and the types of interactions it supports [4]. It is especially popular in Internet services, especially those that realize the demand for Web 2.0 (blogs, forums etc.).

In order to effectively look through the resources by using tags it is necessary for the users to know the vocabulary (set of tags) of the tagging system in question. This can prove to be a serious drawback in looking through resources in topics foreign to the user, or ones tagged in a way diverging from his/her linguistic competence. This means that a user who does not know the tags used in the repository will not be able to gain access to the required information. Moreover, looking through tags is problematic due to the way in which the vocabulary of the tagging system was constructed.

© Springer International Publishing Switzerland 2014
Z. Vetulani and J. Mariani (Eds.): LTC 2011, LNAI 8387, pp. 367–378, 2014.
DOI: 10.1007/978-3-319-08958-4_30

The vocabulary used to describe resources is often created spontaneously by many users (which is common). It is hence possible that within the vocabulary system there will be many synonymous tags i.e. tags describing the same concept, or the same tag will be used to describe various concepts. This means that resources similar in character can be described using different tags or the same tag can describe resources with various contents. The user looking through the repository data is therefore not certain if he will find the information that he is searching for[1].

One of the possible approaches when enhancing tagging systems is to introduce solutions which help the user find the needed information and to aid users in the process of tagging resources in choosing tags for which the search will be conducted. The expected solution is one in which the user does not have to know the entire vocabulary to conduct a search. This means that entering a certain word into the system will enable specification or broadening the request by proposing similar tags, i.e. tags from the same semantic field. Similarly, whilst tagging (after choosing the most appropriate tag for the given resource-type), the user should be provided by the computer system with a set of tags from the semantic field of the entered word which can either replace or complement it.

The article introduces a solution, which enhances tagging systems by integrating wordnet based ontology. Once the solution is used, after entering a certain word into the enhanced tagging system, it suggests other words from the same semantic field and provides a range of information useful in searching and tagging. This approach uses ontology which is generated from wordnet based ontology considered as canonical form in the so-called normalized form. Canonical form is nothing less than wordnet expanded with domain and expert knowledge. This form of ontology is created in order to express all the indispensable relations. The normalized form of ontology contains relations between words which are deemed to come as coming from a certain semantic field. Moreover the information about the semantic distance between two related words is given, which is what distinguishes normalized form from wordnets. Ontology thus formed is directly adjusted to suit the needs of enhanced tagging systems. The normalized form of ontology is generated by using heuristic rules responsible for listing words that are in the same semantic fields and by determining the semantic distance between two words.

2   The Needs of Enhanced Tagging Systems Users

In order to effectively look through the repositories and tag resources after entering one word or expression (tag) users of enhanced tagging systems should after entering one word or expression (tag) gain access to information such as:

- Synonyms,
- Other words from the semantic field in question,
- Categories to which the tag belongs.

---

[1] It is outside of the scope of this article to discuss if whilst tagging the user chose the best concept to describe the resources.

Providing the user with synonyms will ease the search when the user does not know the specialist vocabulary needed (he/she will be able to find the wanted information after entering a commonly used word instead of the specialist one) or e.g. when whilst tagging archaic vocabulary was used. After gaining access to other words from the semantic field in question the user will be able to refine or reformulate the query to the repository. This is based on the assumption that the user will gain access to words, which are easily associated with the entered word, e.g. for king these would be terms such as crown or sovereign.

An interesting type of cases while proposing other relevant vocabulary from within the same semantic field are the ones related to events (e.g. historical), with dates, places and people associated with them. For example, for the battle of Vienna we would like to obtain the year in which it took place (1683), the place where it was fought (Vienna) and the name of its main actor (Jan III Sobieski). Similarly, after e.g. entering the year 1683, we would like to obtain the word/expression from the same field: battle of Vienna (since obviously when entering a certain date, we are interested in the events that took place then). In the above example, these relationships run along the lines of individual entities expressed by proper names (e.g. Vienna, Jan III Sobieski), not by classes, which are described by common names (e.g. field, soldier).

The information about which category the given word was classified as, will allow the user to be aware of the subject area that it belongs to. Moreover, thanks to categories it is possible to improve searching through resources as long as the enhanced tagging system makes available the functionality of indicating all words tied to the category in question. Thanks to such functionality, the user will have the possibility to specify or broaden the search by choosing other words from the same (sub)domain. The mechanism of tying words together by domain categories will also enable building common indexes (known especially in paper publications) be they of persons, objects or geographical. Indexes are a reliable mechanism for searching through resources. Constructing them in a similar way as categories will allow building hierarchical indexes, i.e. a certain index will include (sub)indexes, just as each category allows access to subcategories. It is important to mention that the way in which tags will be tied to categories and which categories will be created will always depend on the domain conceptualization of the field in question.

The needs of users responsible for tagging (indexing) resources (editors) are analogical to those, of users searching through the repository. The editor should choose tags/words in a way that suits the subject matter the best. The information made available through the enhanced tagging system for the entered tag will allow substituting a certain tag with another one if the editor feels that amongst the ones proposed there is one better describing the resource.

The information about categories to which the word belongs allows the editor to indirectly (through the tag, not directly by ascribing the resource to the category) tie the resource with the category. Category based taxonomic systems are a popular way of describing resources, in which each resource is (mostly) ascribed to one category [4]. In the case of tagging, it is widely accepted that direct ascription of categories to resources should not take place (instead of classifying the resource by using a category, one can tie it to multiple tags). Indirect (through tags) tying of categories and resources, as it is proposed in this paper, is in accordance with category based taxonomic systems, which further defines the field that the resource is from.

3 Wordnet and the Needs of Enhanced Tagging Systems

The above discussion leads to the conclusion that the natural candidate for a word (but also expressions) database, is a lexical database i.e. wordnet. Wordnet is a lexical database which contains information about nouns, verbs, adjectives and adverbs and is organized around the notion of synset [5].

Because of its structure, wordnet can be treated as a dictionary, but also as an ontological system. Wordnet consists of:

- Synsets, i.e. the possibility of connecting synonymous words,
- Relations between synsets,
- Linking synsets with Top Concept Ontology,
- The possibility of connecting synsets with Domain Ontology.

Synset is a set of words with the same-part-of-speech which can be used inter-changeably in a certain context. The level of granularity of word-meaning, being part of the synset depends on the approach taken when constructing it. If the words are not connected by the synset they can be tied by a near synonym relation.

Between words and concepts in wordnet you can find relations basing on similarity and contrast [2]. These relations are to define the meanings of words that wordnet encompasses. Amongst the basic relations there are hyponymy, antonymy, holonymy (e.g. king and sovereign, which exist in a hyponymy relation). Relations express the ties between classes of entities. In wordnet there also exists a relation that is to describe the ties between individual entities (instances) and classes – belongs to class [5].

Top Concept Ontology is a hierarchy of language-independent concepts, reflecting important semantic distinctions, e.g. Object and Substance, Location, Dynamic and Static [5]. Connecting synsets to top concepts allows determining the character of a concrete synset in isolation from its specific field conditions. Domain Ontology is used to group meanings by taking into consideration the taxonomies adopted in the given field.

4 Limitations of Wordnet Use

Wordnet in the form in which it was constructed can be problematic in use as a part of enhanced tagging systems as mentioned above. The first limitation is the fact that wordnet does not include information about the semantic distance between words. The relations in wordnet are defined between those two words (synsets) for which one of given relation (i.e. holonymy) can be determined (one-edge distance, if we were to interpret the wordnet as a graph). The relations between any words can of course be calculated. Nevertheless wordnet does not give any information about the ways in which such calculations could be undertaken, i.e. when it is possible to see if such words could be defined as ones coming from the same semantic field or not. The absence of the distance between words requires constructing mechanisms (rules) which would allow calculating them. Only then will it be possible to provide other words from the given semantic field.

Moreover wordnet contains no relations that indicate the word's shared membership in a given topic of discourse [2]. This means that wordnet does not have direct relations linking words which in a certain context are naturally connected (e.g. king and crown). This limitation is known as the tennis problem (there is a lack of relations linking the racquet, ball, net and court game) [2].

Apart from the limitations mentioned above there exist ones technical in nature. These are connected with the effectiveness of using wordnet in enhanced tagging systems in the form that it is in. Amongst them it is important to mention efficiency and maintenance problems.

Efficiency problems are all caused by the need to define the ways in which it is most appropriate to generate words from the same semantic field, that is how to create relations between words if they are not directly provided by wordnet. Two approaches are possible here:

- Relations are calculated "on the fly" according to needs by using wordnet based on the reasoning system [3] (larger time complexity),
- Relations (those found relevant) are calculated before placing the vocabulary in the system (larger space complexity).

Maintenance problems are connected to the need of constantly updating the ontology and the rules calculating relations. The changeability of these rules is caused by the fact that mainly being heuristic they have to be optimized for the processed ontology (its content), field conditions and expectations of system users (e.g. users do not want given words to appear within a concrete semantic field, calculated by a certain rule). If the system was built in a way that calculated relations according to needs (first approach) then maintaining the system would be very difficult because of mounting errors in a couple of consequent levels. Erroneous relations between words (interpreted by the user as a system error) can result from:

- Wrongly transcribed relations in wordnet, due to a false conceptualization of the given semantic domain,
- Wrongly transcribed relations in wordnet due to errors made whilst building it,
- Incorrect algorithms of heuristic rules,
- Incorrect choice of heuristic rules,
- Incorrect upload of ontology to the computer system in which it is processed,
- Incorrect implementation of system rules.

It is clear that from a software engineering point of view, building systems in which errors can appear as a result of at least six different reasons is very difficult (if at all possible).

5   Two-Level Model for the Creation of Ontology for Enhanced Tagging System

In order to avoid the above limitations when building vocabulary systems for enhanced tagging systems, a two-level model for the creation of ontology was introduced. The model determines the way in which target resources will be constructed. This is made up of two levels:

- Canonical form,
- Normalized form.

The canonical form is wordnet adapted to the needs of the created application. This type of ontology is called wordnet based ontology. Tags in canonical form are organized as follows:

- Words are clearly connected into synsets[2],
- For synsets, their relations with other synsets are known (relations given by wordnets can be used as well as domain relations between synsets),
- Synsets can be connected to Top Concept Ontology,
- Synscts can be connected to Domain Ontology.

New type of relations i.e. domain relations between synsets that indicate the word's shared membership in a given topic of discourse have been added to the canonical form. The number of words in the ontology in the canonical form, depends on the needs of the created system – it may be the subset of wordnet if the field is limited. Whether the synsets within the wordnet will be connected to Top Concept Ontology, or Domain Ontology depends on the heuristic rules responsible for creating the normalized form.

The normalized form is ontology generated from canonical form, but with a different structure and different organization of words (tags). Tags in normalized form are organized as follows:

- Words clearly connected into synsets,
- For synsets, the relations with all other synsets which were calculated by the heuristic rules as belonging to the same semantic fields (not only those determined directly in wordnet); for relations the distance (weight) between synsets is determined,
- Synsets can be connected to Domain Ontology.

In the normalized form, synsets are not connected to Top Concept Ontology. If such a connection was given in the canonical form, then it was possible to use it due to heuristic rules in order to introduce new relations between synsets in normalized form.

6   Wordnet Extensions

As it was already mentioned wordnet does not include relations that indicate the word's shared membership in a given topic of discourse, i.e. it is not possible to

---

[2] Meanings are given to words.

directly determine the relation between words such as king and crown. In certain situations it would be possible to try to calculate such relations using ones available between synsets in wordnet (by looking through paths of the graph). Nevertheless, an easier solution is to introduce relations which determine relationships between words, specific in character, i.e. they are a result of specific field needs and context. This type of relations is called domain relations between synsets.

The form which these relations will take depends on the character of the field. These relations could expose different relationships between words. For example, between words such as soldier and sword, one could place a relation equipped with. For the words battle of Vienna and 1683, one could introduce a relation took place. Despite this however for the purposes of the enhanced tagging system discussed in this paper i.e. enhanced tagging system in the Wilanów Palace Museum vortal, two general relations have been adopted in the wordnet based ontology created:

- Attribute,
- Link.

The relation of the attribute shows a strong relationship between two words within the framework of the same field. For the ontology Old Polish History and Culture, the relation of the attribute was used to expose events (e.g. battles), dates, places and people connected to them. Similarly for places (e.g. Wilanów), their relation with people was presented (e.g. Jan III Sobieski). At the same time there seem to be no contradictions to use this relation for other synset connections.

Links are relations between two concepts in a certain field but considered weaker than attributes. By using them a field-expert can tie together any two words without the need to clarify the character of their relationship. This relation was used for connections such as those between king and crown.

The relations of attribute and link detailed above are of associative character. The necessity to introduce this type of relations has been indicated e.g. in standard ISO 25964, which regulates establishment and development of thesauri [1]. The fact that in the presented solution two associative relations have been singled out means that semantic similarity expressed by them is disparate. To generalize, one has to assume that in the process of creating a wordnet based ontology its creator must decide whether such distinction is necessary or not. Thus, it is possible not to include such distinction at all, then associative relation will not distinguish semantic similarity between words synsets. Additionally, a situation may occur in which a larger number (more than two) of types of associative relations will be introduced. In this case, relations may be derived from wordnet based lexicon grammar [6, 7].

7 Heuristic Rules Used in the Creation of the Normalized Form of Ontology

The normalized form is built in accordance with rules which for each synset form its semantic field, i.e. the relations with other synsets and the distance (weight) between them. The weight determines how semantically close the two synsets are (i.e. the words they encompass).

Rules make use of relations contained in canonical form (i.e. relations know from wordnets) including domain relations such as attributes and links. Rules differ in character that is they look through the graph (wordnet) in different depth. The basic rules directly use the relations between synsets contained in canonical form; they search through the graph in a one-edge distance. Other rules look through the graph from a multiple-edge distance. Relations can be transitive or not.

Exemplary rules are:

1. Rule: If between two synsets there is a hyponymy relation, then in the normalized form introduce a relation with the distance between them being 1; e.g. *king* and *sovereign*
2. Rule: If two synsets have the same hyperonym then introduce a relation with the distance between them being 1; e.g. *king* has_hyperonym *sovereign* and *sultan* has_hyperonym *sovereign* hence there is a relation between *king* and *sultan*
3. Rule: If synset X has synset Y as its hyperonym, while synset Y has synset Z as its hyperonym, then between synset X and synset Z there is a relation with the distance between them being 2; e.g. *king* has_hyperonym *sovereign* and *sovereign* has_hyperonym *ruler* hence between *king* and *ruler* there is a relation with the distance between them being 2.

Figure 1 presents a normalized form generated from ontology in canonical form shown in Fig. 2. The example demonstrates relations generated by using rules 1–3 above.

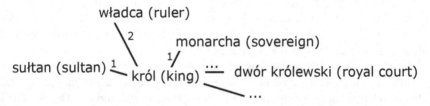

Fig. 1. Example of normalized form of wordnet based ontology

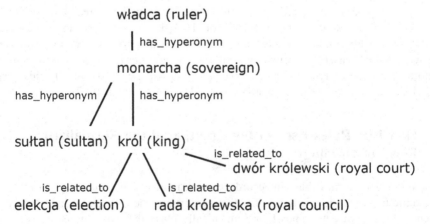

Fig. 2. Example of wordnet based ontology (canonical form)

8   Enhanced Tagging System in the Wilanów Palace Museum Vortal

The method of enhancing the tagging system presented above was used in the Wilanów Palace Museum vortal. It helped in creating an effective indexing and searching mechanism for resources collected on the vortal. In this case, the enhanced tagging system is composed of:

- Wordnet based ontology Old Polish History and Culture,
- Functionalities made available to the users searching the vortal resources,
- Functionalities made available to the editors indexing vortal resources.

8.1   Wordnet Based Ontology – Old Polish History and Culture

The Old Polish History and Culture is a wordnet based ontology (canonical form) used to generate ontology in a normalized form. The ontology was built basing on 5434 tags which were created and used on the Wilanów Palace Museum vortal for a period of a couple of years to tag resources (around 2000 articles from the field of Polish history and culture). The tagging (indexing) was designed in a way which allowed assigning a desired number of tags to each article. Before introducing enhanced tagging systems the tags were classified into four flat indexes (alphabetical, chronological, geographical, and personal). Amongst these tags there were also common names and proper names. Its components were words and expressions.

While working on the ontology the initial set of tags was widened by around 1300 new words and expressions. New elements were introduced to the ontology because of the adopted algorithm which assumed a bottom-up approach, i.e. to the primary set of tags new ones were added with a broader meaning. The enhanced algorithm based on approach presented in [8] was used for building the ontology. Tags are organized into synsets. In the ontology apart from relations given by wordnet (hyponymy, meronymy, antology, belongs to class etc.), also associative relations of two types (attribute and link) were used. They describe relations between expressions shown by the domain experts as important in the context of the resources gathered on the vortal.

The domain experts also created also a set of hierarchical categories which functioned as the domain ontology. There are 378 categories and subcategories in total. Each synset (and hence tag) in the ontology is tied to one or more (sub)categories. Categories and the tags tied to them form five hierarchical indexes: subject, people, important places, geographical and chronological.

The normalized form of the ontology is generated using 20 heuristic rules. These rules were chosen during initial phase of the project after verification of given results (i.e. relations between synsets in ontology in the normalized form) by the domain experts. This was dependent on the acceptance of results given by the different set of heuristic rules as ones coming from the given semantic field.

8.2 Functionalities in Searching for Tags

The web surfer using the Museum vortal has access to mechanisms of the enhanced tagging system while searching the resources gathered there. Thanks to the introduced mechanisms the user can search through the resources by tags in a way which guarantees a very precise manner of asking questions, thanks to the possibility of broadening or narrowing the search[3]. This mechanism of looking through tags is a competitive way of searching for information to searching engines that look for words in the resources.

Thanks to the introduced functionalities the user gains access to other tags (i.e. vortal is proposing them) from the given semantic field after entering a tag. Synonyms, attributes and links are shown among them. Those tags are considered as best candidates for further searching because either they refer to the same meaning, or they introduce concepts directly connected in a given domain Other tags proposed by the system are considered as good candidates for searching. For a given tag system is proposing tags connected by relations having different weights. So, semantic 'closeness' between them could be different. All tags proposed by the system were determined for a given tag by heuristic rules during generation of normalized form of ontology.

For each tag the category (or categories) that it belongs to is/are given. The user can hence look through the vortal resources by using other tags from a certain field having access to expert conceptualization of this domain. It can be done by choosing a category and finding other tags related by the domain expert with this category.

Figure 3 shows the vortal proposition after entering king ("król") tag; between them court ("dwór królewski"), royal town ("miasto królewskie"), sovereign ("monarcha"), sultan ("sułtan") and governor ("namiestnik") are proposed as tags for further search. Choosing any of these tags would launch the search for resources tagged by it. King is assigned to kings and sovereigns ("królowie i władcy") category, so user can access other tags from this category just by choosing it.

8.3 Functionalities in the Tagging of Resources

Similar mechanisms have also been made available to editors of the vortal, responsible for tagging (indexing) its resources. The editor, after entering a tag gains access to its synonyms, attributes, linked tags and tags in relations with different weights. Thanks to this he or she can describe the meaning of the resource content more precisely.

---

[3] The quality of the search depends on the fact if the tags from a certain resource describe its contents in a clear and accurate manner. In the case of the Wilanów Palace Museum vortal, tagging of resources was undertaken by the domain experts with great care.

Fig. 3. Vortal proposition for *king* (*"król"*) tag

9 Conclusions

The presented method of enhanced tagging systems guarantees a new quality of using tagging mechanisms in any computer system. The application of this method to the Wilanów Palace Museum vortal shows that the domain relations between concepts are very important for the effectiveness of the search results. The mechanisms of attributes, links and hierarchical categories proved to have answered that need. The challenge for the future is to introduce more detailed domain relations between synsets than the two relations proposed in this article. The application of the system also shows that heuristic relations, despite their general and intuitive character, which will be used to define the semantic fields for tags will be different depending on the domain and users needs. This is because domain experts responsible for the resources define what level of 'closeness' of concepts is acceptable in a given domain. Further research assumes carrying out experiments using testing groups to find out if the proposed search-outcomes are accurate.

References

1. Clarke, S.G.D., Zeng, M.L.: From ISO 2788 to ISO 25964: the evolution of thesaurus standards towards interoperability and data modeling. ISO Inf. Stand. Q. **24**, 20–26 (2012). (Winter 2012)
2. Fellbaum, C. (ed.): WordNet: An Electronic Lexical Database. MIT Press, Cambridge (1998)
3. Kubis, M.: An access layer to PolNet – Polish WordNet. In: Vetulani, Z. (ed.) LTC 2009. LNCS, vol. 6562, pp. 444–455. Springer, Heidelberg (2011)
4. Smith, G.: Tagging: People-Powered Metadata for the Social Web. New Riders, Thousand Oaks (2008)
5. Vossen, P. (ed.): Euro WordNet General Document, Version 3, University of Amsterdam (2002)
6. Vetulani, Z.: Wordnet based lexicon grammar for Polish. In: Proceedings of the Eight International Conference on Language Resources and Evaluation (LREC 2012), Istanbul, Turkey, 23–25 May 2012, pp. 1645–1649. ELRA, Paris (2012)
7. Vetulani, Z., Vetulani, G.: Through Wordnet to lexicon grammar. In: Kakoyianni Doa, F. (Ed.). Penser le lexique-grammaire : perspectives actuelles, Editions Honoré Champion, Paris, France, pp. 531–545 (2013)
8. Vetulani, Z., Walkowska, J., Obrębski, T., Marciniak, J., Konieczka, P., Rzepecki, P.: An algorithm for building lexical semantic network and its application to PolNet - Polish WordNet project. In: Vetulani, Z., Uszkoreit, H. (eds.) LTC 2007. LNCS, vol. 5603, pp. 369–381. Springer, Heidelberg (2009)

Natural Language Ontology of Action: A Gap with Huge Consequences for Natural Language Understanding and Machine Translation

Massimo Moneglia[✉]

University of Florence, 1 Piazza Savonarola, Florence, Italy
moneglia@unifi.it

Abstract. Action verbs are the less predictable linguistic type for bilingual dictionaries and they cause major problems for MT technologies that are immediately evident to the user. This is not only because of language specific phraseology, but is rather a consequence of the peculiar way each natural language categorizes events i.e. it is a consequence of semantic factors. In ordinary languages the most frequent Action verbs are "general", since they extend productively to actions belonging to different ontological types. Moreover, each language categorizes action in its own way and therefore the cross-linguistic reference to everyday activities is puzzling. But the actual variation of verbs across action types is largely unknown. This paper sketches the problem constituted by the Ontology of Action when disambiguation and cross-linguistic reference to action is concerned and presents the IMAGACT Ontology Infrastructure, which aims at filling this gap by exploiting multilingual spoken corpora.

1 The Semantic Variation of Action Verbs Within and Across Languages

In all language modalities Action verbs bear the basic information that should be processed in order to make sense of a sentence. Especially in speech, they are the more frequent structuring elements (Moneglia and Panunzi, 2007), but no one to one correspondence can be established between action predicates in different languages, since the action types they refer to vary within and across languages (Majid et al. 2008; Kopecka and Narasimhan 2012). For instance, the English instruction *to take* can lead to qualitatively different actions, some of which are identified in Fig. 1.

In model 1 the actor assumes the control of an object and changes its location; in 4 the actor obtains the object; in 5 the actor receives the object away from somebody else, and so on. In short, in the above circumstances more than one single action type occurs.

This judgment is confirmed by the productivity of each type; i.e. types are Action concepts since they are productive. For instance, despite the fact that the predicate is applied to different objects, humans are able to judge that the same type of action is performed in all examples reported in each cell of Fig. 1.

© Springer International Publishing Switzerland 2014
Z. Vetulani and J. Mariani (Eds.): LTC 2011, LNAI 8387, pp. 379–395, 2014.
DOI: 10.1007/978-3-319-08958-4_31

	English	Italian	French	Spanish
1.	- *take* the glass - *take* the dishes - *take* the candle - *take* the coat	- *prendere* il bicchiere - *prendere* i piatti - *prendere* la candela - *prendere* il cappotto	- *prendre* le verre - *prendre* les plats - prendre la bougie - prendre le manteau	- *coger* el vaso - *coger* los platos - *coger* el candil - *coger* el abrigo
2.	- *take* the umbrella and leave - *take* the money and leave - *take* the foodstuffs for the journey - *take* the horse outside	- *prendere* l'ombrello per uscire - *prendere* gli spiccioli - *prendere* delle cose da mangiare per il viaggio - *prendere* il cavallo per partire	- *prendre* le parapluie pour sortir - *prendre* l'argent - *prendre* des choses à manger pour le voyage	- *coger* el paraguas al salir - *coger* el dinero - *coger* comida para el viaje - *ccoger* el caballo para salir
3.	- *take* the laptop out of the bag - *take* the liquid out of the bottle - *take* out the milk from the freezer to give to the mikman	- *prendere* il portatile dalla borsa - *prendere* il liquido dalla provetta - *prendere* il latte dal freezer per consegnarlo al lattaio	- *prendre* l'ordinateur portable du sac - *prendre* le liquide de l'éprouvette - *prendre* le lait du réfrigérateur pour le consigner	- *coger* (*sacar*) el portatil de la funda - *coger* (*sacar*) el liquido de proveta - *coger* la leche del congelador para darsela al lechero
4.	- *take* the book from the assistant	- *prendere* il libro dall'assistente	- *prendre* (*recevoir*) le livre à l'assistant	- *coger* el libro del asistente
5.	- *take* the money from the girl - *take* the hat off the lady - *take* the food from the people	- *prendere* il portafogli alla ragazza - *prendere* il capello alla signora - *prendere* i prodotti della terra alla gente del posto	- *prendre* le portefeuille à la fille - *prendre* le chapeau à la fille - *prendre* les produits de la terre aux paysans	- *coger* (*quitar*) el monedero a la chica - *coger* (*quitar*) el sombrero a la senora - *coger* (*tomar*) los productos de la tierra a los lugareños

Fig. 1. Parallel cross-linguistic variation of action verbs

Moreover, *to take* applies in its own meaning when it extends to the action types in the gallery, and none of these types can be considered more appropriate than the others in characterizing the meaning of the verb. In other words, each one could be a prototypic instance of the verb (Givon, 1986).

We call "General" all natural language verbs that share this property. Therefore, in the case of general verbs, ordinary language does not mirror the ontology of action, causing a huge problem for all natural language understanding tasks. As a matter of fact, the language label does not specify the referred ontological entity.

This problem becomes even more sensible when cross-language communication is concerned. The variation in Fig. 1 is also shared by the verbs roughly translating *to take* in Italian, Spanish and French. However, the translation relation does not hold if the full range of the possible actions in the extension of these verbs is considered, as in the models of Fig. 2.

For instance only *to take* can be extended to models 6 and 7 while each romance language requires another verb (*portare, llevar, amener*). On the contrary only Italian can refer to 13 with the same verb (*prendere*), and only Italian and Spanish to 12 (*prendere* and *coger*). French and English cannot be applied in 12 and 13. These languages respectively require *attrapper* and *to catch* in 12 and *toucher* and *to hit* in 13. In summary, no one to one translation relation between these action predicates in the four languages holds, since they are not equivalent for what regards the range of their possible extensions (hence not equivalent in intension).

This paper sketches in 2 the problem constituted by general verbs for MT and the need for a language independent Action Ontology, for grounding MT

	English	Italian	French	Spanish
6.	- *take* the book to the professor	- *portare* il libro alla professoressa	- *amener* le livre à le professeur	- *llevar* el livro a la profesora
7.	- *take* the dog to the beach	- *portare* il cane in spiaggia	- *amener* le chien à la plage	- *llevar* el perro a la playa
8.	- *take* the hammer to Gina - *take* the groceries to grandmother - *take* the suitcases for the customer - *take* the tea box for someone	- *prendere* il martello a Gina - *prendere* la spesa alla nonna - *prendere* le valigie per il cliente - *prendere* la scatola del tè per qualcuno	- *apporter* le marteau à Gina - *apporter* les corse à grand-mère - *apporter* les valises au client - *apporter* la boîte à thè à quelqu'un	- *coger* el martillo a Gina - *coger* la compra a la abuela - *coger* las maletas para el cliente - *coger* la caja del te para alguien
9.	- *get* the water from the fosset	- *prendere* l'acqua dal rubinetto	- *prendre* l'eau du robinet	- *coger* el agua del grifo
10.	- *hold* the ice with the tongs - *hold* the material to take the hem	- *prendere* il ghiaccio con le pinze - *prendere* il bordo della stoffa per fare l'orlo	- *prendre* le morceau de glace avec des pinces - *prendre* le bord du tissu pour faire l'ourlet	- *coger* el hielo con las pinzas - *coger* el borde de la tela para coserlo
11.	- *pick* the flower in the garden - *pick* the tomatoes in the garden - *pick* the blackberries off the plant	- *prendere* il fiore dal giardino - *prendere* i pomodori nell'orto - *prendere* le more	- *cueillir* des fleurs du jardin - *cueillir* (*prendre*) les tomates dans le potager - *cueillir* des mûres	- *coger* la flor del jardín - *coger* los tomates del huerto - *coger* moras
12.	- *catch* the theif that is fleeing - the dog *catches* the thrown biscuit - *catch* the snake in the river	- *prendere* il ladro che scappa - il cane *prende* il biscotto lanciato dal padrone - *prendere* la biscia nell'acqua	- *attraper* le voleur qui s'enfui - le chien *attrape* le biscuit lancé par le maître - *attraper* le serpent dans l'eau	- *coger* (*atrapar*) al ladron que escapa - el perro *coge* la galleta lanzada por el dueno - *coger* la serpiente del agua
13.	- *hit* the bottle with the ball - *hit* (*catch*) the fish with the spear - *hit* the enemy in the leg - *hit* the guard rail with the wheel	- *prendere* la bottiglia con la pallina - *prendere* il pesce con la fiocina - *prendere* il nemico alla gamba - *prendere* lo spartitraffico con la ruota	- *toucher* la bouteille avec la boule de papier - *toucher* le poisson avec le harpon - *toucher* l'ennemi à la jambe - *toucher* la barrière avec la roue	- *golpear* la botella con la bola - *golpear* el pez con el tridente - *golpear* al enemigo en la pierna - *golpear* el vaden con la rueda

Fig. 2. Cross-linguistic variation of action verbs

on a solid semantic basis. In 3 the IMAGACT ontology is briefly presented. In 3 the methodology and the annotation infrastructure used to bootstrap action concepts from English and Italian spontaneous speech resources are outlined, starting from scratch. In 4 we present the interface accomplished in IMAGACT for implementing languages and concepts, therefore providing a method for filling language resource gaps in this crucial area of the lexicon.

2 Action Ontology and Translation

More generally, no translation relation can be established between action predicates in different languages, as far as the ontological entity referred by action verbs is not identified and there is no guarantee that two predicates in a bilingual dictionary pick up the same entity. For this reason Action verbs are puzzling for MT, which may fail the lexical choice even for simple sentences.

For instance, according to pragmatic circumstances, the Italian sentence in (1) can be interpreted as an instance of models 1, 7, or 10 and can be translated into English respectively with *to take* / *to hold* / *to catch*, but this information can be foreseen only if action types are identified cross-linguistically:

(1)   Mario prende il gatto
(1′)   Mario takes the cat
(1″)   Mario holds the cat
(1‴)   Mario catches the cat

This problem is evident when the translation of such simple sentences is required from a system. Asking Google to translate to take and prendere from English to Italian, and vice versa, we get results which are not consistent with the actual sentence interpretation. For instance, the system selects the standard option in (2), despite the fact that *to take* under-extends with respect to *prendere* in type 12 of Fig. 2:

(2) Mario prende il gatto per la coda
is translated as Mario takes the cat by the tail
instead of Mario catches the cat by the tail

The other way around is also the case when to take over-extends with respect to *prendere* (type 6 of Fig. 2):

(3) Mario takes the book to the professor downstairs
is translated as Mario prende il libro al professore di sotto
instead of Mario porta il libro al professore di sotto

As a whole, the verb chosen by the system does not fit what is needed in all cases of systematic mismatch.

The failure of automatic translation systems to ensure a proper translation of simple sentences is one of the main reasons that these technologies are not presently considered robust enough by users. This problem is sensible in practice since action verbs are high frequency both in speech and in all basic translation tasks, but the existence of the above semantic relations cannot be predicted, since they require general ontological knowledge which is not available to present systems.

Nevertheless, the application of general verbs to the action types in their extension is productive in the above cases and should, in principle, be predictable. Once one action type is identified, then we can foresee that the translation relation among predicates referring to that type in different languages holds in all instances of the type. For instance we should not expect that the translation relation holding between *prendere* and *to catch* in 12 might hold of *thief* but not of *cats*.

The Sapir-Whorf hypothesis notwithstanding, the productivity of translation through the instances of a type is proof that humans categorize those actions in the same way, despite the fact that the verbs referring to those actions in the various languages are not equivalent in intension. Therefore, Action types can be considered an ontological level that is independent from the language.

2.1   Action Ontology and Lexical Databases

Existing verb typologies have gone a long way in systematically categorizing verbs into classes, be it on the basis of syntactic grounds, semantic grounds, or a combination of both, by capturing the relationship between lexical properties, semantic roles and syntactic behavior.

There is a range of lexical resources and ontologies which provide information on verb meaning variation and a number of initiatives which extend the information provided according to each frame to many languages.

Verbs are an important part of WordNet (Fellbaum, 1998). Roughly 11,000 verbs are present, divided into 24,632 senses in the original English database, which has been extended to many other languages.

The Berkeley FrameNet project (Baker et al. 1998) is an English resource based on Frame Semantics (Fillmore and Atkins, 1992). More recently, similar resources have been developed for several languages (German, Spanish, Chinese, Japanese, Swedish, Brazilian Portuguese). In this model, each sense of a polysemous word belongs to a different semantic frame, identified through a script-like conceptual structure that describes a situation, object or event along with its participants and their roles. Currently, FrameNet defines about 3040 verbs attached to 320 different frames.

VerbNet and PropBank exploit Levin's classification of verbs, in which syntactic frames are assumed to be a direct reflection of the underlying semantics. (Levin, 1993).

The VerbNet database (Kipper-Schuler, 2005) is a broad coverage English verb lexicon organized into semantic classes (more than 5000 verb senses, corresponding to approximately 3700 lemmas divided in 274 classes). Each verb class is constituted by a set of verbs sharing syntactic frames, thematic roles and selection restrictions.

PropBank (Palmer et al. 2005) focuses on the argument structure of verbs, providing a complete corpus annotated with semantic roles specifying verb alternation behaviour in Levin's sense. The lexicon contains about 3600 verbs, with quantitative data regarding their alternation patterns.

"Cross linguistic mapping" should be one of the main requirements for lexical ontologies. Since resources like VerbNet and PropBank are strongly based on the syntactic behaviour of verbs, they cannot be applied to different languages, which of course show completely different syntactic projection. More generally, the variation in thematic structures of a general verb do not define the set of action types in its extension and cannot give an account of its variation. For instance, the sentence in (1) can be interpreted according to models 1, 7 and 10, but the verb still assigns the same theta roles (Agent and Theme) in all interpretations.

The problems encountered by present ontologies in dealing with the categorization of action at a cross-linguistic level can be made explicit by looking to Wordnet. For instance Wordnet identifies 42 *synsets* for the verb *to take*. Let's focus on just three of these entries:

(a) S: (v) **take**, get hold of (get into one's hands, take physically) *"Take a cookie!"*; *"Can you take this bag, please"*
(b) S: (v) lead, **take**, direct, conduct, guide (take somebody somewhere) *"We lead him to our chief"*; *"can you take me to the main entrance?"*; *"He conducted us to the palace"*
(c) S: (v) assume, acquire, adopt, take on, **take** (take on a certain form, attribute, or aspect) *"His voice took on a sad tone"*; *"The story took a new turn"*; *"he adopted an air of superiority"*; *"She assumed strange manners"*; *"The gods assume human or animal form in these fables"*

Despite its richness, this information is hard to use for disambiguation and translation tasks not only because it originates from English, but also for theoretical reasons. The first one is that the identification of the actual use of a verb among all its *synsets* is hard for humans. Descriptions given of each *synset* are too vague and difficult to be used for disambiguation tasks even by expert annotators (Ng et al. 1999).

A second crucial reason is that the productivity of verb application cannot be guaranteed by all *synsets* in the same manner. More specifically Wordnet does not distinguish the *synsets* instantiating the proper application of the verb (for instance *a* and *b*, correspond to models 1 and 7) from those which instantiate phraseological or metaphorical usages (for instance *c*).

Verbs have a lot of applications which depart from their actual meaning, but those usages do not constitute any productive action type. It is reasonable to foresee that the Italian verb *prendere* can be applied to all instances of *a* and in no instances of *b*:

(4) he takes / a cookie / a glass / a bag
(4') lui prende un biscotto / un bicchiere / la borsa
(5) he takes the car / the dog / his friend there
(5')* lui prende la macchina / il cane / il suo amico là

On the contrary this is not the case in c, which is a metaphorical usage of the verb. We cannot foresee any regularity in the application of the Italian verb *prendere* to the possible instances of *c*.

(6) he took an air of superiority
(6') ha preso un'aria di superiorità
(7) he took on strange manners
(7')* ha preso strane maniere

In summary, despite the high number of usages registered in Wordnet, there is no possibility of identifying those types that constitute the basis for a productive cross-linguistic relation. This is crucial since Wordnet interlingual indices (ILI) are viable only for *synsets* regarding productive types.

3   The IMAGACT Resource

The IMAGACT project, which has been funded in Italy within the PAR/FAS program (undertaken by the University of Florence, ILC-CNR, Pisa, and the

University of Siena) uses both corpus-based and competence-based methodologies for simultaneous bootstrapping of a language independent action ontology from spontaneous speech resources of different languages.

IMAGACT faces key issues in Ontology Building. It grounds a productive translation relation since it distinguishes the proper usage of verbs from their metaphorical or phraseological extensions; it allows easy identification of types in the variation, it is cross-linguistic in nature, it derives from the actual use of language but it can be freely extended to other languages through competence-based judgements and it is therefore suitable for filling gaps in lexical resources.

IMAGACT has now delivered a corpus-based language infrastructure covering the set of actions most frequently referred to in everyday language. Using English and Italian spoken corpora, we have identified 1010 distinct action concepts and visually represented them with prototypical scenes (Moneglia et al. 2012b), either animated or filmed.

Around 1,200 high frequency action verbs of English and Italian corpora (600 verbs per language) have been processed, and the reference to physical action in their corpus occurrences (100,000) have been identified and distinguished from metaphors and phraseology.

The result is a database of action concepts represented through scenes in which the set of physical activities referred in everyday speech is linked to English, Italian, Spanish and Chinese verbs. Each verb can express one or more concepts, while each concept can refer to one or more verbs (within and across languages). This ontology gives a picture of the variety of activities that are prominent in our everyday life and specifies the lemma used to express each one in ordinary communication in English, Italian, Spanish and Chinese.

3.1   The Exploitation of Spontaneous Speech Repositories

The first idea developed in IMAGACT is to strictly define the relevant domain of language usage from which data about linguistic reference to actions can be derived. Actions specified by those verbs that are most frequently used in ordinary communication are also the actions which are more relevant and constitute the universe of reference for the language. The actual use of Action oriented verbs in linguistic performance can therefore be appreciated by observing their occurrence in spontaneous speech resources in which reference to action performance is primary.

Spontaneous Speech Corpora have been published in the last decade and are exploited in IMAGACT to extract this information. The IMAGACT database focuses on high frequency verbs, which can provide sufficient variation in spoken corpora i.e. roughly 600 verbs referring to actions which represent the full basic action oriented verbal lexicon. IMAGACT identifies the variation of this set in the BNC spoken text and in parallel will exploit the Italian Spoken corpora in order to get a higher probability of occurrence of relevant action types. The project foresees the annotation of verb occurrences in each language corpus (around 50,000 occurrences for each).

3.2   The IMAGACT Annotation Infrastructure

The corpus-based strategy relies on the identification of productive types through manual annotation. IMAGACT has developed a robust technical infrastructure for deriving action types from corpus occurrences. The annotation procedure is accomplished through a web based annotation interface (Moneglia et al. 2012a, 2012b). The annotation is structured in two shots leading from the occurrences of each verb in a language corpus to the identification of the action types extended therein.

The first shot foresees the standardization of corpus occurrences and then gathering of proper occurrences into types. The task is achieved in four steps:

1. Generation of a simple sentence in third person representing the meaning of the instance in the corpus in a clear manner;
2. Negative selection of occurrences which do not instantiate the verb in its own meaning (metaphors or idioms);
3. Grouping of standardized proper occurrences into classes according to the equivalent verbs fitting with the group;
4. Selection of one "best examples" representing the class for all possible argument structures.

The annotator derives from the vague content provided by the oral context of verb occurrences a simple sentence that well represents the action. On the basis of this representation the annotator judges whether or not the occurrence is a proper instance of the verb. In other words he splits the metaphorical and phraseological usages which do not instantiate the actual meaning of the verbs from productive occurrences and then classifies only the latter into types.

The decision concerning the status of the occurrence makes use of an operational test roughly derived from Wittgenstein (1953). The occurrence is judged PRIMARY if it is possible to say to somebody who does not know the meaning of the verb V that "the referred action and similar event are what we intend with V", otherwise the occurrence is MARKED.

In accordance with this criterion, occurrences in (2), (3), (4) and (5) will be judged as PRIMARY, while those in (6) and (7) will be judged MARKED. Only Primary occurrences are classified into types, since they are in principle productive. Figure 3 shows how one corpus occurrence (highlighted in dark) is standardized and assigned to PRIMARY or MARKED variation fields (on bottom).

Once all instances are in standard form, the annotator identifies the action types instantiated by the verb in the corpus. The annotation infrastructure is designed to allow the annotator to create types ensuring both cognitive similarity among instances end pragmatic differences between types.

The overall criterion for type creation is to keep granularity to its minimal level, assigning instances to the same type as long as they fit with one "best example". Clustered sentences should be similar as regards:

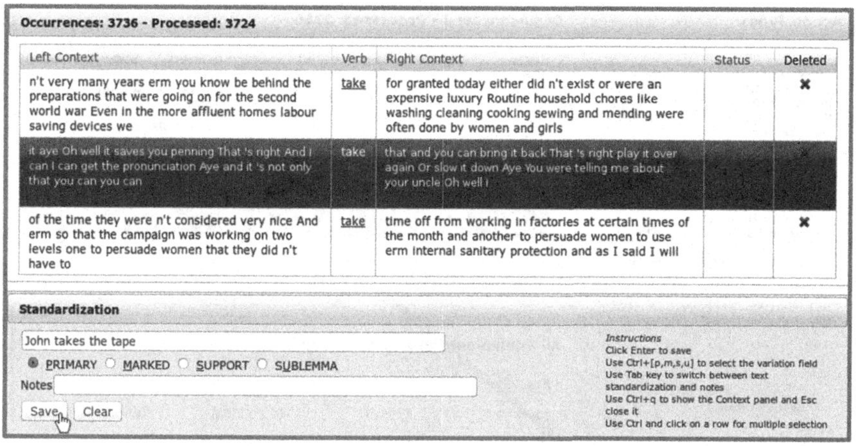

Occurrences: 3736 - Processed: 3724				
Left Context	Verb	Right Context	Status	Deleted
n't very many years erm you know be behind the preparations that were going on for the second world war Even in the more affluent homes labour saving devices we	take	for granted today either did n't exist or were an expensive luxury Routine household chores like washing cleaning cooking sewing and mending were often done by women and girls		✗
it aye Oh well it saves you penning That 's right And I can I can get the pronunciation Aye and it 's not only that you can you can	take	that and you can bring it back That 's right play it over again Or slow it down Aye You were telling me about your uncle Oh well I		
of the time they were n't considered very nice And erm so that the campaign was working on two levels one to persuade women that they did n't have to	take	time off from working in factories at certain times of the month and another to persuade women to use erm internal sanitary protection and as I said I will		✗

Standardization

```
John takes the tape
● PRIMARY  ○ MARKED  ○ SUPPORT  ○ SUBLEMMA
Notes
 Save   Clear
```

Instructions
Click Enter to save
Use Ctrl+[p,m,s,u] to select the variation field
Use Tab key to switch between text
standardization and notes
Use Ctrl+q to show the Context panel and Esc
close it
Use Ctrl and click on a row for multiple selection

Fig. 3. Standardization of a corpus occurrence and assignment to a variation class

- The possibility to extend the occurrence by way of similarity with the virtual image provided by the best example (Cognitive Constraint);
- "Equivalent verbs applied in their proper meaning" i.e. the synset (Fellbaum, 1998) (Linguistic Constraints).

Among the occurrences the annotator chooses the most representative as *best examples* of the recorded variation, creates types headed by one (or more) *best example(s)*, and assigns each individual standardization to a type by dragging and dropping.

Figure 4 shows on the left side the set of types (here a subset for space reasons), created by the annotator, headed by one or more best examples; in the centre the set of standardized occurrences to be classified, and at bottom the set of equivalent verbs alternatively used to identify each type.

The Figure shows how the infrastructure allows for identifying types and drag and drop standardized occurrences within them. For instance, the annotator distinguished "John takes the rubbish to the collection centre" (Type 1), in which *take* is equivalent to *bring*, from "John takes the phone" (Type 6) where the equivalence is rather with *grasp* and *hold*. He will select a type and will gather together all occurrences which share its properties by dragging and dropping them (as "John takes the iron" in Type 6). He will create new types when needed.

The choice of a best example heading the type and the identification of equivalent verbs which characterize the type is crucial to test the consistency of the typology derived from corpus data. This is the main task achieved in the second shot, which is devoted to the "Validation and Annotation of types". The second shot is achieved in four steps:

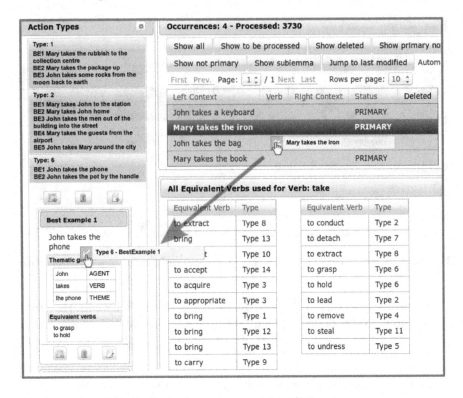

Fig. 4. Gathering occurrences into Action types

1. Comparison of the types to ensure that two claimed types do not refer to the same action (cutting granularity);
2. Assignment of thematic roles and aspectual class to the best example(s);
3. Assessment that each instance of a type corresponds to the best example and alignment of occurrences to the thematic structure of the best examples;
4. Scripting of the type.

Figure 5 shows how this work is accomplished with respect to sentences gathered into Type 14 (at the bottom, left side). In this type, *take* is equivalent to *accept* and *receive*, and the best example "John takes a present from a stranger" represents it. To the best example is assigned a thematic structure (Agent / Verb / Theme / Source) (on top) and an aspectual class (*event*, in this case). When the type is selected, all sentences gathered therein are presented to the annotator (at the bottom). He verifies the consistency of this assignment in of the face to the best example. In so doing he will align each sentence to the thematic structure of the best example. All instances of the type will then inherit the properties of the best example.

The annotation of verb occurrences in a language corpus ends with the scripting of each type for the production of a scene representing its best examples.

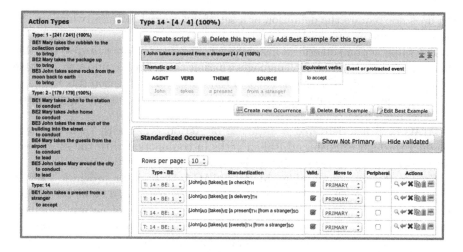

Fig. 5. Types validation and annotation

3.3 The Cross-Linguistic Definition of the Ontology of Action in a Wittgenstein-Like Scenario

A cross-linguistic set of action types achieved through definitions agreed by linguists working on different language corpora could be considered hopeless. The experience in ontology building has shown that the level of consensus that can be reached in defining entities which are objective of language reference is very low, since the identification of such entities relies on a definition. Definitions are highly underdetermined, since they depend on the granularity of feature retrieval (Brown et al. 2010).

The traditional methodology will require reconciling in a unique definition all definitions given by linguists to classify the actions occurring in each language corpus. Definitively unrealistic.

The key innovation of IMAGACT is to provide a methodology which exploits the language independent capacity to appreciate similarities among scenes, distinguishing the *Identification* of action types from their *Definition*. Only the identification is required to set up the cross-linguistic relations. In Wittgenstein's terms, how can you explain to somebody what a *game* is? Just point out a game and say "this and similar things are games" (Wittgenstein, 1953).

In IMAGACT the ontology building makes use of the universal language of images which allows reconciling in a unique ontology the descriptions derived from the annotation of corpora belonging to different languages. For instance, the distinction between type 1 in Fig. 1 and type 8 in Fig. 2 is relevant in foreseeing cross linguistic variation. More specifically the same general verbs apply to both types in Italian (*prendere*) and Spanish (*coger*), while both a general verb and a more specific verb are required in French (*prendre - cueillir*) and in English (*to take - to pick*). The difference between 1 and 8 is easily recognized by humans and does not require the definition of a set of differential features, which on the contrary is radically underdetermined.

The same action sometimes has different meanings across cultures, but this restriction is not an issue for languages sharing the reference universe as those considered in IMAGACT at this stage of the work. For this reason this Wittgenstein like scenario will be exploited to identify action types at a cross-linguistic level avoiding direct comparison.

IMAGACT has delivered a database of Action types with their language encoding through English and Italian verbs in conjunction with the set of sentences (derived from corpora) instantiating each type.

Scenes are not computable objects. IMAGACT however provides a set of information that may ground new generation computational tools for disambiguation and MT. Crucially it will target disambiguation of natural language action verbs with respect to a closed list of productive types and will establish automatic cross-linguistic correspondences for each type. Moreover it provides the linguistic correlations of each type in the implemented languages (argument structures, thematic structures, aspectual type, preferential arguments).

More specifically IMAGACT will provide the explicit comparison of the set of actions that can be extended by verbs of different languages. For instance, comparing the English verb *take* and the Italian verb *prendere*, the system will show the set of actions in which both can be extended and their differential. Figure 6 shows in the middle the range of actions which can be equivalently described by both verbs (i.e. when the translation relation holds) , *to take*, but not *prendere*, extends to actions that are equivalently described as *lead*, *bring* and *remove*, while *prendere*, but not *take*, extends to actions which are equivalently described by *catch*, *strike* and *hit*.

4   Competence-Based Extension to Languages and Ontology Implementation

Because IMAGACT's direct representation of actions through scenes can be interpreted independently of language, the infrastructure allows the mapping of lexicons from different languages onto the same cross-linguistic ontology. On this basis, it is possible to ask mother-tongue informants what verb(s) in his language should be applied to each scene, implementing whatever language within this ontology.

IMAGACT has delivered an infrastructure that allows collaborative work and supervision for: (a) mapping the verbal lexicon of any language onto the ontology through competence-based judgments; and (b) implementing the number of represented concepts in the ontology itself. These objectives can be achieved at two independent levels of complexity.

In the first simplified interface (*CBE light*) the work is direct. An informant can receive the set of action types as input. Figure 7 shows the interface the

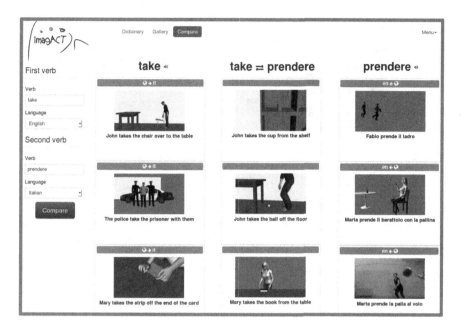

Fig. 6. Comparison *take / prendere*

informant would use for one action type. It presents to the informant the scene prototype and the English and Italian verbs derived from corpus analysis that match it.

The informant assigns one or more verbs from his language that satisfy the scene. Figure 7 shows how this has been done in the case of Spanish and Chinese with respect to one prototypic instance in the set of action types of the verbs *take / prendere*.

The Chinese mother tongue annotator assigned the verb *ná*, while the Spanish one assigned the verbs *tomar*, *agarrar* and *coger*. In so doing they have been provided with suggestions, i.e., the English and Italian verbs originally assigned to the type during corpus annotation.

The figure also shows that the work can be supervised. For instance, in this case, the supervisor rejected two supplementary Italian verbs that have been assigned to the scene beyond those found in the corpus. Through this method, it is possible to find the appropriate categorization of the concepts settled in the ontology in any language.

This work generates an enormous amount of new knowledge for Lexicography, Language typology and Translation theory.

In IMAGACT the action ontology provides equivalences for languages with high global impact but with strong diversity in cultural tradition and linguistic tendencies (Spanish and Mandarin Chinese).

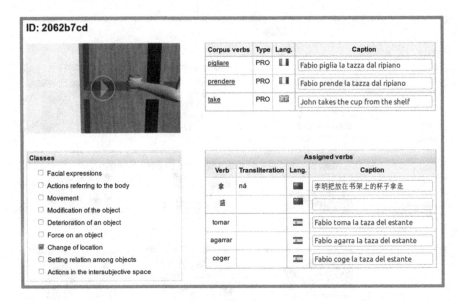

Fig. 7. Scene metadata assignment for competence-based extension (CBE light)

Competence-based extensions are also foreseen in the future for many other languages (for instance, beyond EU languages, Hindi-Urdu, Arab, Japanese, Korean, Russian).

A further implementation of IMAGACT can be achieved using the corpus data stored in the database. The corpus data from which the ontology originates are exploited in a *heavy CBE interface*, which can be used to validate the cross-linguistic productivity of the IMAGACT prototypes. The lexical competence of a mother-tongue informant will be more deeply challenged in this effort.

Crucially, the informant will verify whether or not the verb choice chosen for the prototypic scene is correct for all arguments retrieved from the original corpora and assigned to that type. The translation relation between the lexical entries in whatever language and the validated set of equivalences in IMAGACT will follow from this work.

Figure 8 shows how the annotation infrastructure presented data to the Chinese annotator in the same type of Fig. 7. The infrastructure shows the set of sentences from the corpus which have been assigned to that scene and asks what verb(s) can be applied to all sentences in the set.

In this case, the Chinese informant verified that the scene requires two verbs which were appropriate for all occurrences. The concept is therefore productive in Chinese.

This work is conceived in a way that exploits linguistic diversity to implement the action typology. If some instance requires a different categorization, a new verb is added and the language-specific categorization can be introduced in IMAGACT. This leads to the implementation of the number of action concepts

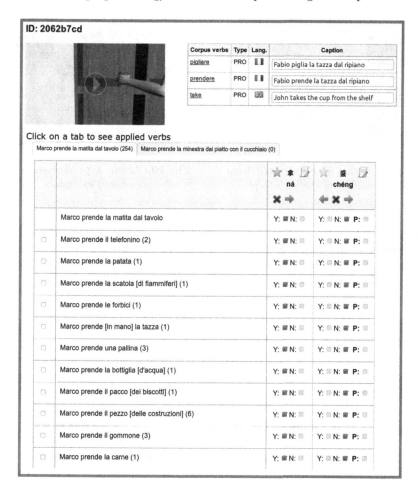

Fig. 8. Heavy CBE interface

in the ontology according to the language-specific categorization of actions that different languages convey.

For instance, contrary to English and Italian which record a lot of General Verbs, Danish has a very specific verbal lexicon which crucially categorizes *Manner* (Korzen, 2005). Therefore, we expect that action types which are relevant for Danish are not identified working on other languages. For instance the type in Fig. 9 will record a lot of occurrences of the verb *to put* instantiating the type:

(7) John put the glass on the table
(8) The wife put the pot on the stove
(9) John put his dresses on the bed

Many languages will go in parallel with English, however this will not be the case when a Danish mother tongue informant will go through the same instances

Fig. 9. Action type extracted from corpus, analyzing the verb to put

Fig. 10. Action type derived from competence-based extension

of the type. The informant will apply *at sætte* looking to the scene in Fig. 9 and will verify the consistency of this verb through the occurrences of the type. The translation will run in parallel with the same general verb *at sætte* in (7) and (8), but not in (9):

(7′) Marco har sat [stillet] glasset på bordet
(8′) Konen har sat [stillet] gryden over ilden
(9′) Moderen har lagt tøjet på sengen

In (9) a different verb is strictly required. Danish, which is a language encoding *mood* in its action verbs (Talmy, 1985), applies *at lægge* in all cases where the object lies on its destination, like in Fig. 10. Therefore, a new type will arise in the database as a function of this language-specific categorization. The new prototypic scene in Fig. 10 will be generated.

We expect a huge amount of data from this task, which will ground in a core part of the lexicon the traditional concept of "Language specific categorization". The IMAGACT infrastructure will grow freely as a function of its competence-based implementation in an open set of languages.

References

Baker, C.F., Fillmore, C.J., Lowe, J.B.: The Berkeley FrameNet project. In: Proceedings of the 36th Annual Meeting of the Association for Computational Linguistics and 17th International Conference on Computational Linguistics (COLING-ACL 1998). Montreal, Canada (1998)

Brown, S.W., Rood, T., Palmer, M.: Number or nuance: which factors restrict reliable word sense annotation? In: Calzolari, N. (ed.) Proceedings of the 7th International Conference on Language resources and Evaluation, pp. 3237–3243. ELRA, Paris (2010)

Fellbaum, Ch. (ed.): WordNet: An Electronic Lexical Database. MIT Press, Cambridge (1998)

Fillmore, ChJ, Atkins, B.T.S.: Towards a frame-based organization of the lexicon: the semantics of RISK and its neighbors. In: Lehrer, A., Kittay, E.F. (eds.) Frames, Fields, and Contrasts. Lawrence Erlbaum Associates, New Jersey (1992)

Givon, T.: Prototypes: between Plato and Wittgenstein. In: Craig, C. (ed.) Noun Classes and Categorization, pp. 77–102. Beniamin, Amsterdam (1986)

Kipper-Schuler, K.: VerbNet: a broad-coverage, comprehensive verb lexicon. Ph.D. thesis. Computer and Information Science Department, University of Pennsylvania, Philadelphia (2005)

Kopecka, A., Narasimhan, B.: Events of Putting and Taking, A Cross-Linguistic Perspective. Benjamins, Amsterdam (2012)

Korzen, I.: Endocentric and esocentric languages in translation. Perspect. Stud. Translatol. **13**(1), 21–37 (2005)

Levin, B.: English Verb Classes and Alternations: A Preliminary Investigation. University of Chicago Press, Chicago (1993)

Majid, A., Boster, J.S., Bowerman, M.: The cross-linguistic categorization of everyday events: a study of cutting and breaking. Cognition **109**, 235–250 (2008)

Moneglia, M., Panunzi, A.: Action predicates and the ontology of action across spoken language corpora. The basic issue of the SEMACT project. In: Alcántara, M., Declerck, T. (eds.) Proceeding of the International Workshop on the Semantic Representation of Spoken Language (SRSL7), pp. 51–58. Universidad de Salamanca, Salamanca (2007)

Moneglia, M., Monachini, M., Calabrese, O., Panunzi, A., Frontini, F., Gagliardi, G., Russo, I.: The IMAGACT cross-linguistic ontology of action. A new infrastructure for natural language disambiguation. In: Calzolari, N., Choukri, K., Declerck, T., Doğan, M.U., Maegaard, B., Mariani, J., Odijk, J., Piperidis, S. (eds.) Proceedings of the 8th International Conference on Language Resources and Evaluation (LREC'12), 2606–2613. ELRA, Paris (2012a)

Moneglia, M., Gagliardi, G., Panunzi, A., Frontini, F., Russo, I., Monachini, M.: IMAGACT: deriving an action ontology from spoken corpora. Paper Presented at the 8th Joint ACL - ISO Workshop on Interoperable Semantic Annotation (ISA-8), Pisa, 3–5 October 2012 (2012b)

Ng, H.T., Lim, C.Y., Foo, S.K: A case study on inter-annotator agreement for word sense disambiguation. In: Proceedings of the ACL SIGLEX Workshop on Standardizing Lexical Resources (SIGLEX99), College Park, MD, pp. 9–13 (1999)

Palmer, M., Gildea, D., Kingsbury, P.: The proposition bank: an annotated corpus of semantic roles. Comput. Linguist. **31**(1), 71–106 (2005)

Talmy, L.: Lexicalization patterns: semantic structure in lexical form. In: Shopen, T. (ed.) Language Typology and Syntactic Description, Vol. III: Grammatical categories and the lexicon. Cambridge University Press, Cambridge (1985)

Wittgenstein, L.: Philosophical Investigations. Blackwell, Oxford (1953)

IMAGACT.: (2013). http://www.imagact.it

Classification-Based Extension of Wordnets from Heterogeneous Resources

Benoît Sagot[1]([✉]) and Darja Fišer[2]

[1] Alpage, INRIA and Université Paris-Diderot, rue Albert Einstein,
75013 Paris, France
benoit.sagot@inria.fr
[2] Department of Translation, University of Ljubljana, Aškerčeva 2,
SI – 1000 Ljubljana, Slovenia
darja.fiser@ff.uni-lj.si

Abstract. This paper presents an automatic and language-independent approach for word net extension by reusing existing freely available bilingual resources, such as machine-readable dictionaries and on-line encyclopaedias. The approach is applied to Slovene and French. The words from the bilingual resources are assigned one or several synset ids based on a classifier that relies on a set of features, the most important one of which is distributional similarity. Automatic, manual and task-based evaluations show good results in terms of both coverage and quality.

1 Introduction

Lexical knowledge is important in a number of natural language processing tasks, which is why several frameworks for organizing and representing it have been proposed: ACQUILEX, MindNet, ConceptNet or Cyc. One of the best-known and most widely used lexico-semantic resources is Princeton WordNet [8] and its sister wordnets for languages other than English, such as EuroWordnet [24] and BalkaNet [23].

Manual construction of such resources is too time-consuming and expensive to be feasible for most research scenarios, which is most teams resort to semi- or fully automatic approaches that exploit existing resources for the development of a new wordnet. However, this is accompanied by a common problem; the trade-off between coverage and accuracy, both of which are needed for the resource to be useful in a practical application. In this paper we present an approach for extending existing wordnets by extracting lexico-semantic information from the available bilingual language resources and then training a maximum entropy classifier on the existing core wordnet in order to assign the new vocabulary to the appropriate synsets. Our approach, applied on the French wordnet WOLF and the Slovene wordnet sloWNet, handles monosemous and polysemous words from all parts of speech.

This paper is structured as follows: Sect. 2 gives an overview of related work. Section 3 introduces WOLF and sloWNet. Section 4 gives a detailed account

© Springer International Publishing Switzerland 2014
Z. Vetulani and J. Mariani (Eds.): LTC 2011, LNAI 8387, pp. 396–407, 2014.
DOI: 10.1007/978-3-319-08958-4_32

of the extraction process of lexico-semantic information from bilingual lexical resources. Section 5 presents the wordnet enrichment experiment that uses a maximum entropy classifier which helped us determine whether a translation extracted from the existing resources is appropriate for a given synset. Section 6 is dedicated to the evaluation of the extended resources: we performed manual and automatic evaluations of both extended wordnets, and a task-based evaluation of the extended sloWNet in a machine translation setting.

2   Related Work

Most automatic wordnet creation approaches take Princeton wordnet as a backbone and extend it with the vocabulary of the target language. Machine-readable bilingual dictionaries are the most straightforward resources of the required lexicon-semantic information. Entries from the dictionary are linked to PWN synsets under the assumption that their counterparts in the target language correspond to the same synset [16]. Since bilingual dictionaries are generally not concept-based but follow traditional lexicographic principles, the biggest obstacle is the disambiguation of dictionary entries. This problem is addressed by a different set of approaches that take parallel corpora as a starting point and extract bi- and multilingual lexicons from them [12]. The main assumption in these approaches is that senses of ambiguous words in one language are often translated into distinct words in another language [6,15]. Furthermore, if two or more words are translated into the same word in another language, then they often share some element of meaning. This results in sense distinctions of a polysemous source word or yields synonym sets.

The most recent set of approaches are those that use Wikipedia to induce a wordnet by using structural information to assign Wikipedia categories to WordNet [20] or by extracting keywords from Wikipedia articles [21]. Vector-space models to map Wikipedia pages to Wordnet have been developed (e.g., by Ruiz-Casado and colleagues [22]) and the most advanced approaches use Wikipedia and related projects, such as Wiktionary, to bootstrap wordnets for multiple languages [5,19].

3   Wordnets for French and Slovene

Previous work on the development of sloWNet and WOLF [7,10] has focused on benefitting from available resources of three different types: general and domain-specific bilingual dictionaries, parallel corpora and Wiki resources (Wikipedia and Wiktionaries).

More precisely, the development of the initial versions of WOLF and sloWNet was achieved in a three-step process. First, baseline versions of these wordnets were created [10] by using only (literal, synset) pairs obtained from a word-aligned multilingual parallel corpus, which could be disambiguated based on all languages but French and Slovene, as well as pairs extracted from lexical resources (dictionaries, lexica and Wikipedia) via monosemous English literals:

such pairs required no disambiguation. The resulting wordnets were relatively reliable but did not use full potential of the available lexical resources.

This is why we describe here a large-scale extension process, aiming at taking full advantage of these lexical resources for improving the coverage of both wordnets without lowering their accuracy. In the next section, we describe the lexical resources we used and how we extracted (literal, synset) candidates from them. In Sect. 5 we introduce the maximum entropy classifier we used for filtering these pairs and extending both wordnets, which are then evaluated in Sect. 6.

4   Bilingual Lexicon Extraction

In this section we describe the extraction of translation pairs from two types of resources: structured (general and domain-specific dictionaries and lexica), and semi-structured (Wikipedia articles). In the extraction process, our task is to extract as many translation variants for each word as possible in order to capture as many senses of that word as possible, in order to create wordnet candidates from the extracted translation pairs in the form of (literal, synset) pairs, i.e. translation of a source word with an assigned synset id from wordnet. We used English, French and Slovene Wiktionary and extracted translation pairs for all parts-of-speech from these three resources on the basis of translation sections within the articles. The number of pairs extracted from each resource is given in Table 1 (upper part). In order to extract the general vocabulary that was available in Wiktionary for French but not for Slovene we used a traditional English-Slovene [14] and a Slovene- English dictionary [13].

For domain-specific vocabulary we used Wikispecies, a taxonomy of living species that includes both Latin standard names and vernacular terms. We also obtained translation pairs from the domain-specific thesaurus Eurovoc, an on-line dictionary of informatics islovar and a military glossary [17] that will at least partially make up for the difference in the sizes of French and Slovene Wikispecies (cf. Table 1, upper part).

The result of our extraction process is two large bilingual lexicons containing all English-French and English-Slovene translation pairs with the name of the resources they originate from. The figures for both extracted bilingual lexicons are summarized in the upper part of Table 1.

Less structured than dictionaries but still with a much more predefined structure than free text is the on-line multilingual collaborative encyclopaedia Wikipedia. We used English, French and Slovene Wikipedia for extracting bilingual lexicons by following inter-language links that relate two articles on the same topic in the two corresponding wikipedias. We enhanced the extraction process with a simple analysis of article bodies with which we resolved ambiguities arising from to the capitalization of article titles (e.g., *Grass-author, Grass-plant*). With the analysis we also identified synonyms for the key terms (e.g., *Cannabis, also known as marijuana*), their definitions (e.g., *Hockey is a family of sports in which two teams play against each other by trying to manoeuvre a ball or a puck into the opponent's goal using a hockey stick.*) and usage examples. The number of translation pairs extracted is shown at the bottom of Table 1.

Table 1. Bilingual lexicon extracted from structured resources and from Wikipedia

Input Resource	En-Fr unique pairs	En-Sl unique pairs
English wiktionary	39,286	6,052
French / Slovene wiktionary	59,659	7,029
Wikispecies	48,046	2,360
Slovene-English dictionary	—	72,954
English-Slovene dictionary	—	207,972
Eurovoc + specialized voc.	—	31,702
Wikipedia	286,818	32,161
Total (duplicates removed)	*130,601*	*282,789*

The bilingual entries we extracted from lexical resources are numerous. However, they suffer from an important drawback: they do not necessarily contain any additional information that can help to map them to PWN, neither do they contain contextual information from specific corpus occurrences. For example, an English-French entry we extracted from Wiktionary (*dog, chien*) does not contain any information that would make it possible for us to determine which of the 8 synsets containing *dog* as a literal in PWN would be appropriate to be translated with *chien* in WOLF. In Wiktionary articles, translations of a given word are sometimes organized by senses that are associated with short glosses. These have been compared to PWN glosses in order to map Wiktionary senses to PWN synsets [3]. The first sentence of a Wikipedia article can be used in a similar way [22]. However, this is not the case for all Wiktionary entries or for other resources. Therefore, at this point, we assign to each translation pair all possible synset ids.

5   Automatic Wordnet Extension

5.1   Baseline Wordnets

The first step in the development of sloWNet and WOLF was achieved in 2008, when the first versions were created [10]. Then, all PWN literals were used for adding target language literals in the synsets found by the alignment-based approach, but only candidates generated from lexical resources via monosemous PWN literals were used.

After the restricted versions of wordnets were produced, they underwent some improvement steps that were performed independently, according to the specific needs of the two research teams. Quantitative information about the first two versions of WOLF are given in the second column in Table 2, which is compared to PWN 2.0, to the result of the work presented here (WOLF 0.2), as well as wordnets for French that were developed by other researchers (French EuroWordNet [24] and JAWS [18]). Parallel figures for sloWNet are shown as well. Table 2 uses the three Base Concept Sets (BCS) for assessing the coverage

Table 2. Quantitative data about the different versions of WOLF and sloWNet, and comparison with the PWN 2.0, the French wordnet from the EuroWordNet project (FWN) and the JAWS nominal wordnet for French

	PWN 2.0	WOLF 0.1.4	WOLF 0.1.6	WOLF 0.2	FWN	JAWS
All	115,424	32,351	32,550	46,449	22,121	34,367
BCS1	1,218	869	870	1,067	1,211	760
BCS2	3,471	1,665	1,668	2,519	3,022	1,729
BCS3	3,827	1,796	1,801	2,585	2,304	1,706
Non-BCS	106,908	27,492	28,211	40,278	15,584	30,172
N	79,689	28,187	28,559	36,933	17,381	34,367
V	13,508	1,546	1,554	4,105	4,740	0
Adj	18,563	1,422	1,562	4,282	0	0
Adv	3,664	667	871	1,125	0	0

	PWN 2.0	sloWNet 2.0	sloWNet 2.2	sloWNet 3.0
All	115,424	29,108	17,817	42,919
BCS1	1,218	714	1,203	1,208
BCS2	3,471	1,361	2,192	3,111
BCS3	3,827	1,611	1,232	2,698
Non-BCS	106,908	25,422	13,190	35,902
N	79,689	22,927	16,234	30,911
V	13,508	1,547	1,097	5,337
Adj	18,563	4,376	429	6,218
Adv	3,664	258	57	453

of the most basic word senses. BCS were introduced in the BalkaNet project and cover the 8,516 most basic synsets in wordnet.

5.2   Large-Scale Wordnet Extension

Restricting the use of bilingual lexicon to monosemous English literals is a safe but limited approach that does not exploit the available resources to their full potential. However, using lexicon-based candidates generated from polysemous English literals is only possible if we can establish the likelihood with which a word should be added to a particular synset, i.e. can compute the semantic distance between a given French or Slovene literal and synset id. We designed such a technique based on already-existing French and Slovene wordnets, which we introduce in this Section.

Our technique relies on a probabilistic classifier that uses various features associated with each (literal, synset) candidate. The underlying idea is as follows: we start from baseline wordnets and a large set of lexicon-based candidates to be evaluated. We extract all (literal, synset) pairs that are already in the baseline wordnets and consider these candidates as valid ones (score 1) while all other candidates are considered invalid (score 0), thus creating a "copper standard," i.e., a reasonable although noisy training set for a probabilistic model. It is noisy for two reasons: first, our baseline wordnets do contain noise, as not all synsets were manually validated; second, and more importantly, many of our new candidates are valid even though they are not in the baseline wordnets. In fact, such candidates are exactly those we are looking for. In order to use the copper standard as training set for a classifier and then to assign scores to all candidates, we have to extract from them suitable features.

The most important feature that we use models the semantic proximity between a literal and a synset. Let us illustrate it on our running example (*dog, chien*). In PWN, 8 synsets contain the literal *dog*, which is why we generated 8 different (literal, synset) candidates from this bilingual entry. We now need to know which of them are valid, i.e., to which of the 8 corresponding synsets the French literal *chien* should be added in WOLF. We therefore compute the semantic similarity of the literal *chien* w.r.t. each of these 8 synsets. For doing this, we first represent each WOLF synset by a bag of words obtained by extracting all literals from this synset and all the synsets up to 2 nodes apart in WOLF. For example, the synset {*andiron, firedog, dog, dog-iron*} in PWN, which is empty in WOLF 0.1.4, is represented by the bag of words {*appareil, mécanisme, barre, rayon, support, balustre, dispositif...*} (∼*device, mechanism, bar, shelve, baluster, device...*). Next, we use a distributional semantic model for evaluating the semantic similarity of *chien* w.r.t. this bag of words. We use the freely available SemanticVectors package [25]. The documents we used for building our distributional semantic models are 65,000 lemmatised webpages from the web-based frWaC corpus [9] for French (390,000 distinct lemmas) and 334,000 lemmatised paragraphs from the reference FIDA-Plus corpus [2] for Slovene (180,000 distinct lemmas). On our example, the semantic similarity between *chien* and the synset {*andiron, firedog, dog, dog-iron*} is only 0.035, while the similarity between *chien* and one of its valid synsets, {*dog, domestic dog, Canis familiaris*} is as high as 0.331.

Apart from that semantic similarity measure, we used several other features. Let us consider a candidate (T, S) that has been generated because our bilingual resources provided us with entries of the form $(E_1, T) \ldots (E_n, T)$, where all PWN literals E_i's are among S's literals. The number of such PWN literals is one of the features. Each possible source (e.g., the English Wiktionary) corresponds to one feature, which receives the value 1 if and only if at least one of the (E_i, T) entries was extracted from this source. Moreover we extract the lowest polysemy index among all E_i's: if one of the E_i's is monosemous, this feature receives the value 1; if the least polysemous E_i is in two PWN synsets, this features receives the value 2. The idea is that if the candidate is generated from at least one monosemous PWN literal, then it is very likely to be correct, whereas if it was generated from only highly polysemous PWN literals, it is much more questionable. Finally, the number of tokens in T is used as a feature (literals with many tokens are usually not translations of PWN literals but rather glosses, and are therefore incorrect).

Based on these features, we trained one classifier per language using the Maximum-Entropy package *megam* [4]. A look at the resulting models (not shown here for space restrictions) shows that the semantic similarity we computed is relevant as it is the feature with the highest weight. As expected, the lowest polysemy index among English literals also contributes positively, as does the number of different English literals yielding the generation of the candidate, and the number of sources involved. On the other hand, also as expected, the number of tokens in the target language literal negatively contributes to the certainty score.

The result of our classifiers on a given (literal, synset) candidate is a score between 0 (bad candidate) and 1 (good candidate). We empirically set the threshold at 0.1 (see Sect. 6.1) for further addition in the corresponding wordnet. This resulted in retaining 55,159 French candidates (out of 177,980) and 68,070 Slovene candidates (out of 685,633). Among the 55,159 French candidates, 15,313 (28 %) correspond to (literal, synset) pairs already present in WOLF 0.1.6, which means that 39,823 (72 %) new ones were added. As a consequence, 13,899 synsets that were empty in WOLF 0.1.6 now have at least one French literal. Among the 68,070 Slovene candidates, 5,056 (7 %) correspond to (literal, synset) pairs already present in sloWNet, which means that 63,010 (63 %) new ones were added; as a consequence, 25,102 synsets that were empty in sloWNet have now at least one Slovene literal.

Quantitative information on the resulting wordnets (WOLF 0.2 and sloWNet 3.0) is provided in Table 2. In short, WOLF 0.2.0 has 43 % more non-empty synsets than before the extension, and sloWNet 3.0 as much as 141 % more. For (literal, synset) pairs, the increase is even higher: the extension of WOLF has increased the number of such pairs from 46,411 to 76,436 (+65 %), and the extension of sloWNet has increased this number from 24,081 to 82,721 (+244 %).

6   Evaluation

Before assessing the accuracy of the wordnets extended using the above-described approach, we begin with a manual evaluation of the extension step per se. We evaluate the accuracy of the candidates we obtained as well as the accuracy of the candidates we discarded. Next, we perform an automatic evaluation of the extended wordnets against a gold standard or a comparable resource developed by other authors. Finally, we describe a task-based evaluation, solely on the extended sloWNet.

6.1   Manual Evaluation

For measuring the accuracy of our extension approach (see Sect. 5.2), we randomly selected 400 (literal, synset) candidates for each language and evaluated them manually, using only two tags: "OK" if it would be correct to add that literal to the synset, and "NO" if it would be wrong, regardless of the cause of

Table 3. Manual evaluation of (literal, synset) candidates generated for extending WOLF and sloWNet

LANGUAGE	FRENCH	SLOVENE
No. of candidates evaluated manually	400	400
... among which are added to the wordnet (score ≥ 0.1)	110 (27%)	36 (9%)
Accuracy over all candidates	52%	25%
Accuracy of candidates added to the wordnet (score ≥ 0.1)	81%	64%
Accuracy of discarded candidates (score < 0.1)	40%	21%
Accuracy in the upper (4th) quartile	83%	44%
Accuracy in the third quartile	63%	32%
Accuracy in the second quartile	41%	13%
Accuracy in the lower (1st) quartile	20%	10%

the error and how semantically close it was to the synset. The accuracy of a set of candidates is the proportion of candidates tagged "OK." Moreover, in order to assess the quality of our scoring technique, we compared the accuracy of the candidates per quartile w.r.t. their certainty scores. The results (see Table 3) show a strong correlation between the certainty score and the accuracy of the candidates, leading us to set the threshold value at 0.1. Other threshold values could have been used: higher values would have provided candidates with even a higher accuracy but the scale of the wordnet extension would have been lower; on the other hand, lower threshold values would have extended our wordnets even more, but would have introduced much more noise. The 0.1 value, which corresponds approximately to the upper quartile for French and to the upper decile for Slovene, seemed to provide a good balance — even if the candidates retained exhibit a higher precision in French (83%) than in Slovene (64%), because of many rare and archaic words coming from the English-Slovene dictionary that have often been evaluated as incorrect —, and lead us to retain similar numbers of candidates in both languages (55,159 for French and 68,070 for Slovene), even though many more Slovene candidates (685,633) were generated in comparison to French candidates (177,980).

6.2 Automatic Evaluation

In this section we report the results of automatic evaluation of the generated wordnets, which are compared to other wordnets that exist for the two target languages. However, such an evaluation is only partial, because the detected discrepancies between the two resources are not only errors in our automatically created wordnets but can also stem from a missing literal in the resource it is compared to. Automatic evaluation was performed on non-empty synsets, which means that adjectival and adverbial synsets in WOLF could not be evaluated this way at all because other existing French wordnets do not cover them.

The results of automatic evaluation of WOLF w.r.t. the FWN are not given here in full details due to space restrictions. However, let us consider first non-empty synsets in FWN. Any (literal, synset) pair that is common to both resources is considered correct. There also exist WOLF pairs that are not present in FWN although their synsets are not empty in FWN. Some of these are correct (i.e. even non-empty FWN synsets are incomplete), others not (i.e. these are errors in WOLF). For an estimate of the precision of such pairs, we manually evaluated 100 randomly selected such nominal and 100 verbal pairs. This allowed us to estimate the number of correct vs. incorrect (literal, synset) pairs among those present in WOLF but not in FWN. And last but not least, many synsets are empty in FWN. We manually validated 100 randomly chosen pairs for such synsets and obtained an accuracy as high as 92 %. In fact, empty synsets in FWN are rare or specific concepts whose literals are often monosemous and therefore easy to translate. Adding up the (exact or estimated) number of valid (literal, synset) pairs of all types, we reach a total of ∼65,690 valid pairs out of 76,436, hence a ∼86 % accuracy.

The reference we used for evaluating sloWNet is a manually built gold standard (SWN) that was built by validating the results of the preliminary Slovene wordnet construction experiments based on the Serbian wordnet (Fišer, 2008). The result is approximately the same: we get a ∼85 % accuracy.

6.3   Task-Based Evaluation

In this section we present the results of a task-based evaluation of the extended sloWNet, which we used to improve machine translation at lexical level [11]. Mistranslations often arise due to inadequate word-sense disambiguation of polysemous words and detection of multi-word expressions, and parallel wordnets can help with both problems. First, we created a small parallel corpus of 500 EU news that contained about 120,000 Slovene and 140,000 English tokens. We lemmatized, PoS-tagged and sentence-aligned the corpus and then disambiguated all content words in the corpus with the freely-available graph-based UKB tool [1]. Next, we machine-translated both parts of the corpus with two MT systems; the rule-based Presis[1] and the statistical GoogleTranslate,[2] and compared machine-translated solutions with human translations, which we treated as a gold standard, and translation equivalents obtained via synset ids from the two wordnets.

A comparison of MT-output, WN-equivalents and the human translations show that there were 1,558 tokens for which Slo→Eng Presis and 867 Google translations did not match translations in the gold standard and could therefore be improved with wordnets. This is illustrated in Fig. 1 where the word *koza* was incorrectly translated by Presis as *smallpox*, while *goat*, the correct translation, was suggested by sloWNet. When translating in the opposite direction, the discrepancy was even larger: 3,730 tokens were mistranslated according to the gold standard by Presis, and 901 by Google. In a random sample of 200 sentence pairs that were manually checked, there were also 166 multi-word expressions

---

sloWNet→PWN	081114: {koza} → {goat, caprine animal}
Presis:	Almost 360 million of pigs, sheep, a **smallpox** and cattle and more billion of poultry execute every year in European Union because of meat.
Human:	Every year nearly 360 million pigs, sheep, **goats** and cattle and several billion poultry are killed for their meat in the EU.

Fig. 1. An example of an improved lexical translation in MT with sloWNet

which were not identified as such by the machine-translation system and therefore uncorrectly translated, but were found in wordnet, e.g., *biotska raznovrstnost* 'biotic diversity' instead of *biodiversity; vezani les* 'tied wood' instead of *plywood*.

This analysis shows that the extended sloWNet, when used in parallel with PWN, can be a very useful resource in MT systems, especially with polysemous words and multi-word expressions that are a major source of errors by MT systems, rule-based and statistical alike. The reason why GoogleTranslate performed better than Presis overall is that Google's MT is using parallel texts found on the web, which was also the source of our parallel corpus and had probably already been detected by Google.

7   Conclusion

We have presented the resources and techniques used to automatically extend wordnets for French and Slovene. By training a simple classifier that relies on various features including distributional similarity, we were able to reuse automatically extracted bilingual lexicons for translating and disambiguating polysemous literals. The extended semantic lexicons, which are now large and accurate enough for real NLP applications, are freely available.

The extended wordnets were evaluated in terms of accuracy which is estimated at 86 % for WOLF 0.2 and 85 % for sloWNet 3.0 for (literal, synset) pairs. In terms of quantity, they have a much higher coverage than the baseline wordnets but they also outperform the French EuroWordNet as well as JAWS. A direct comparison with other related resources developed by Navigli and Ponzetto [19] and de Melo and Weikum [5] is not straightforward because even though the resources we used overlap to a great extent, their aim was to create a multilingual network while we focused only on the two target languages. Also, while Navigli and Ponzetto machine-translated the missing translations, we only use resources that were created by humans, which is why we expect to have more accurate translations but would have to carry out a detailed comparison to be certain. While de Melo and Weikum's wordnet for French has a slightly higher accuracy, it is smaller than ours. Together with the results of our task-based evaluation of the extended sloWNet, this shows that the approach we used, namely trying to benefit as much as possible from the resources we have at our disposal by only using basic NLP tools, is extremely efficient and versatile for building reliable and usable wordnets on a large scale.

References

1. Agirre, E., Soroa, A.: Personalizing pagerank for word sense disambiguation. In: Proceedings of the 12th Conference of the European Chapter of the Association for Computational Linguistics (EACL'09). pp. 33–41. Athens, Greece (2009).
2. Arhar, Š., Gorjanc, V.: Korpus fidaplus: nova generacija slovenskega referenčnega korpusa. Jezik in slovstvo **52**(2), 95–110 (2008)
3. Bernhard, D., Gurevych, I.: Combining lexical semantic resources with question and answer archives for translation-based answer finding. In: Proceedings of the Joint Conference of the 47th Annual Meeting of the ACL and the 4th International Joint Conference on Natural Language Processing of the AFNLP: Volume 2, Vol. 2. pp. 728–736. ACL '09, Association for Computational Linguistics, Stroudsburg, PA, USA (2009). http://dl.acm.org/citation.cfm?id=1690219.1690248
4. Daumé III, H.: Notes on CG and LM-BFGS optimization of logistic regression (August 2004), paper. http://pub.hal3.name#daume04cg-bfgs, implementation. http://hal3.name/megam/
5. De Melo, G., Weikum, G.: Towards a universal wordnet by learning from combined evidence. In: Proceedings of the 18th ACM Conference on Information and Knowledge Management, pp. 513–522. ACM (2009)
6. Dyvik, H.: Translations as semantic mirrors: from parallel corpus to wordnet. Lang. Comput. **49**(1), 311–326 (2004)
7. Erjavec, T., Fišer, D.: Building the slovene wordnet: first steps, first problems. In: Proceedings of the 3rd International WordNet Conference (GWC'06). vol. 2006 (2006)
8. Fellbaum, C. (ed.): WordNet: An Electronic Lexical Database. MIT Press, Cambridge (1998)
9. Ferraresi, A., Bernardini, S., Picci, G., Baroni, M.: Web corpora for bilingual lexicography: a pilot study of english/french collocation extraction and translation. In: Using Corpora in Contrastive and Translation Studies. Cambridge Scholars Publishing, Newcastle (2010)
10. Fišer, D., Sagot, B.: Combining multiple resources to build reliable wordnets. In: Sojka, P., Horák, A., Kopeček, I., Pala, K. (eds.) TSD 2008. LNCS (LNAI), vol. 5246, pp. 61–68. Springer, Heidelberg (2008)
11. Fišer, D., Špela Vintar: Uporaba wordneta za boljše razdvoumljanje pri strojnem prevajanju. In: Proceedings of the 13th International Multiconference Information Society (IS'10). Ljubljana, Slovenia (2010)
12. Fung, P.: A pattern matching method for finding noun and proper noun translations from noisy parallel corpora. In: Proceedings of the 33rd Annual Meeting on Association for Computational Linguistics, pp. 236–243. Association for Computational Linguistics (1995)
13. Grad, A., Leeming, H. (eds.): Slovensko-Angleški Slovar. DZS, Ljubljana (1998)
14. Grad, A., Škerlj, R., Vitorovič, N. (eds.): Angleški-Slovenski Slovar. DZS, Ljubljana (1999)
15. Ide, N., Erjavec, T., Tufis, D.: Sense discrimination with parallel corpora. In: Proceedings of ACL'02 Workshop on Word Sense Disambiguation: Recent Successes and Future Directions, pp. 54–60. Philadelphia (2002)
16. Knight, K., Luk, S.K.: Building a large-scale knowledge base for machine translation. AAAI **94**, 773–778 (1994)
17. Korošec, T., Fekonja, M., Jehart, A., Pečelin, F., Ulčar, M., Žabkar, A., Dernovšek, Z.: Vojaški slovar. Ministrstvo za obrambo (2002)

18. Mouton, C., de Chalendar, G.: Jaws: Just another wordnet subset. Actes de TALN (2010)
19. Navigli, R., Ponzetto, S.P.: BabelNet: Building a very large multilingual semantic network. In: Proceedings of the 48th Annual Meeting of the Association for Computational Linguistics, pp. 216–225. Uppsala, Sweden (2010)
20. Ponzetto, S.P., Navigli, R.: Large-scale taxonomy mapping for restructuring and integrating wikipedia. In: IJCAI, vol. 9, pp. 2083–2088 (2009)
21. Reiter, N., Hartung, M., Frank, A.: A Resource-poor approach for linking ontology classes to wikipedia articles. In: Bos, J., Delmonte, R. (eds.) Semantics in Text Processing. STEP 2008 Conference Proceedings, Research in Computational Semantics, vol. 1, pp. 381–387. College Publications (2008)
22. Ruiz-Casado, M., Alfonseca, E., Castells, P.: Automatic assignment of wikipedia encyclopedic entries to wordnet synsets. In: Szczepaniak, P.S., Kacprzyk, J., Niewiadomski, A. (eds.) AWIC 2005. LNCS (LNAI), vol. 3528, pp. 380–386. Springer, Heidelberg (2005)
23. Tufis, D.: Balkanet design and development of a multilingual balkan wordnet. Rom. J. Inf. Sci. Technol. **7**(1–2), 107–124 (2000)
24. Vossen, P. (ed.): EuroWordNet : A Multilingual Database with Lexical Semantic Networks for European Languages. Kluwer, Dordrecht (1999)
25. Widdows, D., Ferraro, K.: Semantic vectors: a scalable open source package and online technology management application. In: LREC (2008)

PolNet – Polish WordNet

Zygmunt Vetulani[✉]

Department of Computer Linguistics and Artificial Intelligence,
Adam Mickiewicz University, Poznań, Poland
vetulani@amu.edu.pl

Abstract. We present a long term project aiming at the construction of a lexical database and ontology for Polish. The specific objective of the PolNet project is to provide a human-and-computer friendly description of the Polish language for direct application in language processing software.

Keywords: WordNet · FrameNet · VerbNet · PolNet · Wordnets · Linguistically motivated ontology · Collocations

1 Introduction

The "PolNet-Polish Wordnet" project started in 2006 within the grant of the Polish Platform for Homeland Security "Language Resources and text processing technologies oriented to public security applications". The project, inspired by the Princeton WordNet, intended to serve two main objectives: first to provide a reference semantic lexicon for the core of the Polish language, second to serve as a linguistically motivated ontology to support reasoning in the AI systems with natural language competence. The research was anticipated by our earlier studies on linguistically motivated ontologies (cf. Vetulani 2003, 2004). As is the case for practically all wordnet development projects, PolNet is a time-unlimited project run by an interdisciplinary team of experts involving linguists, language engineers and computer scientists[1]. Since the beginning, the project has evolved from a network of noun-based synsets[2] organized in a hyponymy/hyperonymy hierarchy towards a lexicon grammar containing a verbnet part as backbone.

2 Methodology

The initial PolNet was built as a wordnet for nouns organized into synsets interrelated first of all by relations corresponding to traditional hyponymy/hyperonymy. Keeping

---

[1] Since very beginning PolNet has been realized as a team project involving many people, each contributing with experience and enthusiasm. In this group were: Agnieszka Kaliska, Bartłomiej Kochanowski, Paweł Konieczka, Marek Kubis, Jacek Marciniak, Beata Nadzieja, Tomasz Obrębski, Paweł Rzepecki, Grzegorz Taberski, Agnieszka Vetulani, Grażyna Vetulani, Zygmunt Vetulani, Justyna Walkowska, Marta Witkowska, Weronika Wojciechowska. Several are still active in the project.

[2] By *synset* we mean a class of synonyms.

© Springer International Publishing Switzerland 2014
Z. Vetulani and J. Mariani (Eds.): LTC 2011, LNAI 8387, pp. 408–416, 2014.
DOI: 10.1007/978-3-319-08958-4_33

in mind that a correctly constructed wordnet should render the conceptualization of the real word (reflected in the language), we decided to apply the so called "merge development model" where the lexical network is built from scratch, in opposition to the so called "expand method" consisting in "translating" a wordnet built for some other language (typically English). Application of the merge model is expensive and time consuming, as it requires essential involvement of well trained staff, mainly lexicographers. Building a wordnet from scratch, we followed the methodology elaborated within the Princeton WordNet and EuroWordNet projects so that we could reuse the existing linguistic knowledge accumulated in traditional written grammatical resources, mainly dictionaries and grammars.

In order to limit methodological arbitrariness, we deliberately decided to avoid statistic and AI-based methods (like genetic algorithms, machine learning, etc.) at this stage.[3] The PolNet development algorithm (Vetulani et al. 2007) makes essential use of traditional Polish dictionaries and the DEBVisDic platform (Pala et al. 2007) as a wordnet development tool. The work was organized in an incremental way, starting with general and frequently used vocabulary extracted from a corpus (IPI PAN corpus; Przepiórkowski 2004). The one important exception to this rule was caused by the need to have the system tested in a real application at a possibly early stage of development. This is why we introduced, since the beginning, some basic domain terminology from the area of homeland security. (From 2009 to 2010 PolNet was tested as ontology in the application POLINT-112-SMS (Vetulani et al. 2009, 2010a, b)).

With inclusion of the verb category we brought ideas inspired by the FrameNet (Fillmore et al. 2002) and VerbNet (Palmer 2009) projects to PolNet. The verbal part became the backbone of the whole network. Its organizing part was the system of semantic roles.

Semantic roles, as relations connecting noun synsets to verb synsets, describe the semantic requirements of the predicate. This permits us to consider the verb-extended PolNet as a situational semantics network of concepts where verb synsets represent situations (events, states), whereas semantic roles (Agent, Patient, Beneficent,…) provide information on the ontological nature of the actors involved in the situation. The abstract roles (Manner, Time,…) describe the situation (event, state) with respect to time, space and possibly also to some abstract, qualitative landmarks. Formally, the semantic roles are functions (in a mathematical sense) associated to the argument positions in the syntactic patterns corresponding to synsets. Values of these functions are ontological concepts represented by synsets[4]. For example, for many verbs, the semantic role BENEFICENT takes as value the concept of *humans*. The set of semantic roles we used is adapted from (Palmer 2009).

---

[3] PolNet should not be confused with another wordnet project for Polish, i.e. "plWordnet" (Piasecki team, Wrocław) which uses intensively such methods in order to automatize (and speed-up) the synsets production process. Within the PolNet project, application of AI and statistical methods to accelerate the wordnet development will be considered at future stages, after having completed the hard core of the wordnet which will be used as the training resource for the sophisticated AI methods.

[4] We use PolNet synsets as role values, but it is possible to use concepts from some general ontology, as e.g. Sumo, cf. Pease (2011).

Example 1: entry for "school":

```
<SYNSET>
<ID>POL-2141601597</ID>
<POS>n</POS>
<DEF>Pies o umaszczeniu czarnym, podpalanym bądź brunatnym.</DEF
<SYNONYM>
<WORD>wilk</WORD>
<WORD>owczarek</WORD>
<WORD>niemiecki</WORD>
<WORD>owczarek</WORD>
<WORD>alzacki</WORD>
<WORD>wilczur</WORD>
<LITERAL lnote="U2a" sense="2">wilk</LITERAL>
<WORD>wilk</WORD>
<LITERAL lnote="U1" sense="1">owczarek niemiecki</LITERAL>
<WORD>owczarek</WORD>
<WORD>niemiecki</WORD>
<LITERAL lnote="U1" sense="1">owczarek alzacki</LITERAL>
<WORD>owczarek</WORD>
<WORD>alzacki</WORD>
<LITERAL lnote="U1" sense="1">wilczur</LITERAL>
<WORD>wilczur</WORD>
</SYNONYM>
<ILR type="hypernym" link="POL-2141701478">owczarek:1</ILR>
<BCS/>
<NL>false</NL>
<STAMP>krzyzang 2007-07-15 12:52:15</STAMP>
<CREATED>krzyzang 2007-07-15 12:52:15</CREATED>
</SYNSET>

<ILR type="hypernym" link="POL-2141701478">owczarek:1</ILR>
<BCS/>
<NL>false</NL>
<STAMP>krzyzang 2007-07-15 12:52:15</STAMP>
<CREATED>krzyzang 2007-07-15 12:52:15</CREATED>
</SYNSET>
```

3 Development Phases

The PolNet project was supported by several research programs and grants. After the initial phase of the noun-based lexical ontology development (to be used in the public security application), PolNet continued with the support of the City of Poznań[5], then within a resources-oriented project of the National Program for Humanities (NPRH)[6], and finally as a part of research program of the Faculty of Mathematics and Computer Science AMU. At the end of the first phase (March 2010) PolNet was built of env. 10600 synsets, 18800 word senses for 10900 nouns. At that time preparative works for inclusion of the verb component were already advanced. For this resource we did mapping experiments between PolNet and the so called Global Wordnet Grid (for 1200 noun synsets), as well between PolNet and Princeton Wordnet (for env. 2400 synsets). Intensive works within the CITTA-Ontology project resulted in the first public PolNet distribution at the Language and Technology Conference 2011 (November) in Poznań, Poland and the Global Wordnet Conference 2012 (January) in Matsue, Japan.

This first release was freely distributed as PolNet 1.0 under a CC (Creative Commons) license. The released resource amounted – for nouns – to approximately 11,700 synsets for over 20,300 word-senses (and 12,000 nouns). The verb part of PolNet was composed of more than 1,500 synsets corresponding to some 2,900 word + meaning pairs for 900 of the most important Polish simple verbs. We refer to this release as to PolNet 1.0.

4 From PolNet 1.0 to PolNet 2.0

The present development is being operated within the NPRH project "Development of Digital Resources of Polish in the Area of Valency Dictionaries Towards the Lexicon Grammar Oriented to Computer Applications in the Humanities"/11H11 010080/. It focuses on development of the verbnet part of PolNet. Although verb synsets may be related to other verb synsets through the hyponymy/hyperonymy relation, the main interest is in relating verb synsets (representing predicative concepts) to noun synsets (representing general concepts) in order to show the semantic connectivity constraints that correspond to the particular argument positions opened by verbs. Inclusion of the predicative information, combined with morphosyntactic constraints, gives PolNet the status (and strength) of a lexicon grammar. Our attempts to transform PolNet into a Lexicon Grammar of Polish were inspired by two historical reference projects of the 1970s: Lexicon-Grammar (Gross 1994) and Syntactic-Generative Dictionary of Polish Verbs (Polański 1992).

---

[5] "CITTA-ontology" to develop resources for tourism-oriented applications.

[6] "Development of digital resources of Polish in the area of valency dictionaries towards the lexicon grammar oriented to computer applications in the humanities" (Grant of the Polish Ministry of Research and Higher Education/11H11 010080).

At the present stage we focus our efforts on inserting verb-noun collocations into PolNet. Collocations assume predicative functions in a similar way to simple verbs. Verb-noun collocations often do not have one-word synonyms and, therefore, must be considered an essential part of the Polish predication system.

Example 2. A fragment of the entry describing the predicative noun "pomoc" (compiled from a traditional dictionary):

pomoc, f/ [help]
udzielać(Gen)/N1(Dat), "udzielać komuś pomocy" [to help](imperfective)
udzielić(Gen)/N1(Dat), "udzielić komuś pomocy" [to help](perfective)
pospieszyć na(Acc)/N1(Dat), "pospieszyć komuś na pomoc"
pospieszyć z(Instr)/N1(Dat), "pospieszyć z pomocą ofierze" [to help a victim]
przyjść z(Instr)/N1(Dat), "przyjść z pomocą choremu" [to help sb who is ill]
przyjść na(Acc)/N1(Dat) "przyjść na pomoc oblężonemu miastu" [to bring help to a surrounded town]
 (N1(Dat) – complement in the dative case)

Our present work benefits from the recent advances of descriptive research on collocations. We directly use the "Dictionary of Polish Verb-Noun Collocations" (Vetulani, G. 2000, 2012) as basic resource. This resource is still in development and we may expect its essential expansion in the future. The most challenging and time consuming part of our work consists in adding semantic information missing in the G. Vetulani's verb-noun collocations dictionary (cf. Example 1 above for the form of dictionary entries). This part of work may hardly be done automatically without uncontrolled quality loss.

The intended release of PolNet 2.0 (planned for 2014)/2015 will contain new synsets corresponding to some 3600 collocations.

Example 3. DEBVisDic presentation of a PolNet synset containing both simple verbs and collocations(simplified):

POS: v ID: 3441
Synonyms: {pomóc:1, pomagać:1, **udzielić pomocy**:1, **udzielać pomocy**:1} (*to help*)
Definition: "wziąć (brać) udział w pracy jakiejś osoby (zwykle razem z nią), aby ułatwić jej tę pracę"(*"to participate in sb's work in order to help him/her"*)
VALENCY:
Agent(N)_Benef(D)
Agent(N)_Benef(D) Action('w'+NA(L))
Agent(N)_Benef(D) Manner
Agent(N)_Benef(D) Action('w'+NA(L)) Manner
Usage: Agent(N)_Benef(D); "Pomogłam jej." (I helped her)

Usage: Agent(N)_Benef(D) Action('w'+NA(L)); "Pomogłam jej w robieniu lekcji."
(*I helped her in doing homework*)
Usage: Agent(N)_Benef(D) Manner Action('w'+NA(L)); "Chętnie udzieliłąm jej pomocy w lekcjach." (*I helped her willingly doing her homework*)
Usage: Agent(N)_Benef(D) Manner; "Chętnie jej pomagałam." (*I used to help her willingly*)
Semantic_role: [Agent] {człek:1, człowiek:1, homo sapiens:1, istota ludzka:1, zwierzę:2, jednostka:1, łepek:3, łebek:3, łeb:5, głowa:8, osoba:1, twarz:2, umysł:2, dusza:3} (*{man:1,...,animal:2,...}*)
Semantic_role: [Benef] {człek:1, człowiek:1, homo sapiens:1, istota ludzka:1, zwierzę:2, jednostka:1, łepek:3, łebek:3, łeb:5, głowa:8, osoba:1, twarz:2, umysł:2, dusza:3} (*{man:1,...,animal:2,...}*)
Semantic_role: [Action] {czynność:1} (*{activity:1}*)
Semantic_role: [Manner] {CECHA_ADVERB_JAKOŚĆ:1} (*qualitative adverbial*)

5 Future Research

The "PolNet - Polish WordNet" project is in progress, and will be continued in the foreseeable future. Our short term priority is to complete first of all the verbnet part of the project. This means inclusion of both simple verbs and collocations. In parallel, we plan to continue our work, already started for PolNet 1.0, on the alignment of synsets to the upper ontology SUMO (Pease 2011). The long term goal doesn't change: it is to transform PolNet into a complete lexicon grammar of Polish integrating all grammatical information necessary (and sufficient) for advanced AI and Language Engineering (LE) applications.

Acknowledgements. This work was done within several research frameworks: a grant of Polish Platform for Homeland Security (2006–2010, MNiSW, Nr R0002802), National Program for Humanities (grant 0022/FNiTP/H11/80/2011), projects CITTA (2009) and CITTA Ontology (2010) of the City of Poznań and within the long term research program of the Department of Computer Linguistics and Artificial Intelligence.

Bibliography and References

PolNet Bibliography

Vetulani, Z., Walkowska, J., Obrębski, T., Konieczka, P., Rzepecki, P., Marciniak, J.: PolNet - Polish WordNet project algorithm. In: Vetulani, Z. (ed.) Proceedings of the 3rd Language and Technology Conference: Human Language Technologies as a Challenge for Computer Science and Linguistics, 5–7 October 2007, Poznań, Poland, pp. 172–176. Wyd. Poznańskie, Poznań (2007)

Pala, K., Horák, A., Rambousek, A., Vetulani, Z., Konieczka, P., Marciniak, J., Obrębski, T., Rzepecki, P., Walkowska, J.: DEB Platform tools for effective development of WordNets in application to PolNet. In: Vetulani, Z. (ed.) Proceedings of the 3rd Language and Technology Conference: Human Language Technologies as a Challenge for Computer Science and Linguistics, 5–7 October 2007, Poznań, Poland, pp. 514–518. Wyd. Poznańskie, Poznań (2007)

Vetulani, G., Vetulani, Z., Obrębski, T.: Verb-noun collocation SyntLex dictionary - corpus-based approach. In: Proceedings of 6th International Conference on Language Resources and Evaluation, 26 May–1 June 2008, Marrakech, Morocco (Proceedings). ELRA, Paris (2008)

Vetulani, Z., Walkowska, J., Obrębski, T., Marciniak, J., Konieczka, P., Rzepecki, P.: An algorithm for building lexical semantic network and its application to PolNet - Polish WordNet project. In: Vetulani, Z., Uszkoreit, H. (eds.) LTC 2007. LNCS (LNAI), vol. 5603, pp. 369–381. Springer, Heidelberg (2009)

Vetulani, Z.: Natural language based communication between human users and emergency center in critical situations. A short-text-message based decision assisting system POLINT-112-SMS. In: Vetulani, Z. (ed.) Proceedings of the 4th Language and Technology Conference: Human Language Technologies as a Challenge for Computer Science and Linguistics, 6–8 November 2009, Poznań, Poland, pp. 79–84. Wyd. Poznańskie, Poznań (2009)

Vetulani, Z., Obrębski, T.: Resources for extending the PolNet-Polish WordNet with a verbal component. In: Bhattacharyya, P., Fellbaum, C., Vossen, P. (eds.) Principles, Construction and Application of Multilingual Wordnets. Proceedings of the 5th Global Wordnet Conference, pp. 325–330. Narosa Publishing House, New Delhi (2010)

Vetulani, Z., Kubis, M., Obrębski, T.: PolNet – Polish WordNet: data and tools. In: Calzolari, N. (ed.) Proceedings of the Seventh International Conference on Language Resources and Evaluation (LREC 2010), 19–21 May 2010, Valletta, Malta, (Proceedings), pp. 3793–3797. ELRA, Paris (2010a)

Vetulani, Z., Marcinak, J., Obrębski, J., Vetulani, G., Dabrowski, A., Kubis, M., Osiński, J., Walkowska, J., Kubacki, P., Witalewski, K.: Zasoby językowe i technologie przetwarzania tekstu. POLINT-112-SMS jako przykład aplikacji z zakresu bezpieczeństwa publicznego (in Polish) (Language resources and text processing technologies. POLINT-112-SMS as example of homeland security oriented application). Adam Mickiewicz University Press, Poznań (2010b). ISBN 978-83-232-2155-5

Kubis, M.: An access layer to PolNet – Polish WordNet. In: Vetulani, Z. (ed.) LTC 2009. LNCS, vol. 6562, pp. 444–455. Springer, Heidelberg (2011) (This is a revised version of the paper "An access layer to PolNet in POLINT-112-SMS" published in Proceedings of the 4th Language and Technology Conference, 6–8 November 2009, Poznan, Poland, pp. 437–441. Wydawnictwo Poznańskie, Poznań)

Vetulani, Z., Vetulani, G.: Through Wordnet to lexicon grammar (Abstract). In: Proceedings of the 5th Language and Technology Conference: Human Language Technologies as a Challenge for Computer Science and Linguistics, 25–27 November 2011, Poznań, Poland, p. 258. Wyd. Fundacja UAM, Poznań (2011)

Vetulani, Z., Marciniak, J.: Natural language based communication between human users and the emergency center: POLINT-112-SMS. In: Vetulani, Z. (ed.) LTC 2009. LNCS (LNAI), vol. 6562, pp. 303–314. Springer, Heidelberg (2011)

Vetulani, Z.: Wordnet based lexicon grammar for Polish. Proceedings of the Eight International Conference on Language Resources and Evaluation (LREC 2012), 23–25 May 2012, Istanbul, Turkey (Proceedings), pp. 1645–1649. ELRA, Paris (2012). ISBN 978-2-9517408-7-7. http://www.lrec-conf.org/proceedings/lrec2012/index.html

Vetulani, Z.: Language resources in a public security application with text understanding competence. A case study: POLINT-112-SMS. Proceedings of the LRPS Workshop at LREC 2012, 27 May 2012, Istanbul, Turkey. ELRA, Paris (2012). ISBN 978-2-9517408-7-7

Walkowska, J.: Modelowanie kompetencji dialogowej człowieka na potrzeby jej emulacji w zarządzających wiedzą systemach informatycznych współpracujących z wieloma użytkownikami (in Polish). Ph.D. thesis, IPI PAN, Luty 2012, Warszawa (2012)

Kubis, M.: A tool for transforming WordNet-like databases. In: Vetulani, Z., Mariani, J. (eds.) Human Language Technology Challenges for Computer Science and Linguistics, LTC 2011. Lecture Notes in Computer Science (Lecture Notes in Artificial Intelligence), LNCS (LNAI), vol. 8387, pp. xx–yy. Springer, Heidelberg (2014)

Vetulani, Z., Kochanowski, B.: "PolNet - Polish WordNet" project: PolNet 2.0 - a short description of the release. In: Orav, H., Fellbaum, C., Vossen, P. (eds.) Proceedings of the Global Wordnet Conference, 2014, Tartu, Estonia, pp. 400–404. Ed. by Global Wordnet Association, Amsterdam (2014). ISBN 978-9-9493249-2-7

Vetulani, Z.: PolNet – Polish WordNet. In: Vetulani, Z., Mariani, J. (eds.) Human Language Technology Challenges for Computer Science and Linguistics, LTC 2011. Lecture Notes in Computer Science (Lecture Notes in Artificial Intelligence), LNCS (LNAI), vol. 8387, pp. xx–yy. Springer, Heidelberg (2014)

Vetulani, Z., Vetulani, G.: Through Wordnet to lexicon grammar (Full text). In: Kakoyianni Doa, F. (ed.) Penser le lexique-grammaire: perspectives actuelles, pp. 531–545. Editions Honoré Champion, Paris (2014)

Other Publications

Vetulani, Z.: Linguistically motivated ontological systems. In: Callaos, N., Lesso, W., Schewe, K.-D., Atlam, E. (eds.) Proceedings of the 7th World Multiconference on Systemics, Cybernetics and Informatics, 27–30 July 2003, Orlando, FL, USA, vol. XII (Information Systems, Technologies and Applications: II), pp. 395–400. Int. Inst. of Informatics and Systemics (2003)

Gross, M.: Constructing lexicon-grammars. In: Sue Atkins, B.T., Zampolli, A. (eds.) Computational Approaches to the Lexicon, pp. 213–263. Oxford University Press, Oxford (1994)

Fillmore, C.J., Baker, C.F., Sato, H.: The FrameNet database and software tools. In: Proceedings of the Third International Conference on Language Resources and Evaluation, vol. IV. LREC, Las Palmas (2002)

Palmer, M.: Semlink: linking PropBank, VerbNet and FrameNet. In: Proceedings of the Generative Lexicon Conference, September 2009. GenLex, Pisa, Italy (2009)

Pease, A.: Ontology: A Practical Guide. Articulate Software Press, Angwin (2011)

Polański, K. (ed.): Słownik syntaktyczno - generatywny czasowników Polskich, vol. I–IV, Ossolineum, Wrocław, 1980–1990, vol. V. Instytut Języka Polskiego PAN, Kraków (1992)

Przepiórkowski, A.: Korpus IPI PAN. Wersja wstępna (The IPI PAN CORPUS: Preliminary version). IPI PAN, Warszawa (2004)

Vetulani, G.: Rzeczowniki predykatywne języka polskiego. W kierunku syntaktycznego słownika rzeczowników predykatywnych (In Polish). Wyd. Nauk. UAM, Poznań, Poland (2000)

Vetulani, G.: Kolokacje werbo-nominalne jako samodzielne jednostki języka. Syntaktyczny słownik kolokacji werbo-nominalnych języka polskiego na potrzeby zastosowań informatycznych. Część I (In Polish). Wyd. Nauk. UAM, Poznań, Poland (2012)

Vetulani, Z.: Towards a linguistically motivated ontology of motion: situation based synsets of motion verbs. In: Barr, V., Markov, Z. (eds.) Proceedings of the Seventheens International Florida Artificial Intelligence Research Society Conference (FLAIRS-04), pp. 813–817. AAAI Press, Menlo Park (2004)

Machine Translation

Improving the Distribution of N-Grams in Phrase Tables Obtained by the Sampling-Based Method

Juan Luo[1]([✉]), Adrien Lardilleux[2], and Yves Lepage[1]

[1] IPS, Waseda University, 2-7 Hibikino, Wakamatsu-ku,
Kitakyushu-shi, Fukuoka 808-0135, Japan
juan.luo@suou.waseda.jp, yves.lepage@waseda.jp
[2] Affinity Engine, 4 Rue Doaren Molac, 56610 Arradon, France
adrien.lardilleux@affinity-engine.fr

Abstract. We describe an approach to improve the performance of sampling-based sub-sentential alignment method on translation tasks by investigating the distribution of n-grams in the phrase tables. This approach consists in enforcing the alignment of n-grams. We compare the quality of phrase translation tables output by this approach and that of the state-of-the-art estimation approach in statistical machine translation tasks. We report significant improvements for this approach and show that merging phrase tables outperforms the state-of-the-art techniques.

Keywords: Sub-sentential alignment · Statistical machine translation

1 Introduction

Phrase tables play an important role in the process of building statistical machine translation systems. Their quality is crucial for the quality of translation outputs. The most widely used state-of-the-art tool to generate phrase tables is MGIZA++ [1], which trains the IBM models [2] and the HMM introduced in [3] in combination with the Moses toolkit [4]. Phrase tables are also used in other domains, e.g., bilingual terminology extraction [5], creation of lexicon entries [6].

A phrase table is a list of phrase pairs that are translations of each other with feature scores (see Table 1). It is normally constructed in two steps by using MGIZA++ and Moses toolkit. The first step consists of the using alignment tool MGIZA++ to generate source-to-target and target-to-source word alignments between two languages. The second step uses Moses to extract bilingual phrase pairs from alignments through heuristic combination of both directions and compute feature scores.

A. Lardilleux – The work was done while the author was at TLP Group, LIMSI-CNRS, France.

© Springer International Publishing Switzerland 2014
Z. Vetulani and J. Mariani (Eds.): LTC 2011, LNAI 8387, pp. 419–431, 2014.
DOI: 10.1007/978-3-319-08958-4_34

Table 1. Example of a phrase table.

Source language	Target language	Feature scores			
French	English	$\phi(f\|e)$	$lex(f\|e)$	$\phi(e\|f)$	$lex(e\|f)$
rapport	report	0.921	0.924	0.917	0.841
parlement européen	european parliament	0.811	0.187	0.897	0.773
mais	, but	0.087	0.719	0.044	0.190
activités et	activities and	0.615	0.502	0.889	0.613
le président,	president,	0.953	0.889	0.870	0.965
monsieur le président	mr president	0.918	0.979	0.947	0.874
l' union européenne	european union	0.836	0.661	0.851	0.886
la commission européenne	european commission	0.836	0.852	0.968	0.987

In this article, we investigate a different approach to the production of phrase tables: the sampling-based approach [7], available as a free open-source tool called Anymalign.[1] Being in line with the association alignment approach (see e.g. [8–10]), it is much simpler than the models implemented in MGIZA++, which are in line with the estimation approach (e.g. [11–14]).

In sampling-based alignment, only those sequences of words that appear exactly in the same sentences of the corpus are considered for alignment. The key idea is to produce more candidate words by artificially reducing the size of the input corpus, i.e., many subcorpora of small sizes are obtained by sampling and processed one after another. Indeed, the smaller a subcorpus, the less frequent its words, and the more likely they are to share the same distribution.

The subcorpus selection process is guided by a probability distribution that ensures a proper coverage of the input parallel corpus:

$$p(k) = \frac{-1}{k \, \log(1 - k/n)} \quad \text{(to be normalized)}$$

where k denotes the size (number of sentences) of a subcorpus and n the size of the complete input corpus. This function is very close to $1/k^2$ and gives more credit to small subcorpora, which happen to be the most productive [7]. Once the size of a subcorpus has been chosen according to this distribution, its sentences are randomly selected from the complete input corpus according to a uniform distribution. Then, from each subcorpus, sequences of words that share the same distribution are extracted to constitute alignments along with the number of times they were aligned.[2]

Eventually, the list of alignments is turned into a full-fledged phrase table by calculating various features for each alignment. In the following, we use two translation probabilities and two lexical weights as proposed by [15], as well as the commonly used phrase penalty, for a total of five features.

---

[1] http://anymalign.limsi.fr/

[2] Contrary to the widely used terminology where it denotes a set of links between the source and target words of a sentence pair, we call "alignment" a (source, target) phrase pair, i.e., it corresponds to an entry in the so-called [phrase] translation tables.

One important feature of the sampling-based alignment method is that it is *anytime* in essence: the number of random subcorpora to be processed is not set in advance, so the alignment process can be interrupted at any moment. Contrary to many approaches, *quality* is not a matter of time, however *quantity* is: the longer the aligner runs (i.e. the more subcorpora processed), the more alignments produced, and the more reliable their associated translation probabilities.

Intuitively, since the sampling-based alignment process can be interrupted without sacrificing the quality of alignments, it should be possible to allot more processing time for n-grams of similar lengths in both languages and less time to very different lengths. For instance, a source bigram is much less likely to be aligned with a target 9-gram than with a bigram or a trigram. The experiments reported in this paper make use of the anytime feature of Anymalign and of the possibility of allotting time freely.

This article is organized as follows: Sect. 2 defines the problem. Section 3 proposes a variant in order to improve the translation performance. Section 4 describes the merge of two aligners' phrase tables. Section 5 provides the conclusion.

2   Description of the Problem

In order to measure the performance of the sampling-based alignment app-roach implemented in Anymalign in statistical machine translation tasks, we conducted a preliminary experiment and compared with the standard alignment setting: symmetric alignments obtained from MGIZA++. Although Anymalign and MGIZA++ are both capable of parallel processing, for fair comparison in time, we run them as single processes in all our experiments.

2.1   Experimental Setup

A sample of the French-English parts of the Europarl parallel corpus was used for training, tuning and testing. A detailed description of the data used in the experiments is given in Table 2. To perform the experiments, a standard statis-tical machine translation system was built for each different alignment setting, using the Moses decoder [4] MERT (Minimum Error Rate Training) [16] and the SRILM toolkit [17]. As for the evaluation of translations, the BLEU metric [18] was used.

2.2   Problem Definition

In a first setting, we evaluated the quality of translations output by the Moses decoder using the phrase table obtained by making MGIZA++'s alignments symmetric. In a second setting, this phrase table was simply replaced by that produced by Anymalign. Since Anymalign can be stopped at any time, for a fair comparison it was run for the same amount of time as MGIZA++: seven hours in total. The experimental results are shown in Table 3. In order to investigate

Table 2. Statistics on the French-English parallel corpus used for the training, development, and test sets.

		French	English
Train	Sentences	100,000	
	Word tokens	3,986,438	2,824,579
	Word types	42,919	32,588
Dev	Sentences	500	
	Word tokens	18,120	13,261
	Word types	2,300	1,941
Test	Sentences	1,000	
	Word tokens	38,936	27,965
	Word types	3,885	3,236

Table 3. Evaluation results on a statistical machine translation task using phrase tables obtained from MGIZA++ and Anymalign (baseline).

	BLEU
MGIZA++	27.42
Anymalign (baseline)	22.85

the differences between MGIZA++ and Anymalign phrase tables, we analyzed the distribution of n-grams of both aligners, The distributions are shown in Table 4 and Table 5.

In Anymalign's phrase table, the number of alignments is 8 times that of 1×1 n-grams in MGIZA++ phrase table, or twice the number of 1×2 n-grams or 2×1 n-grams in MGIZA++ phrase table. Along the diagonal (m × m n-grams) for $m > 2$, the number of alignments in Anymalign table is approximately hundred

Table 4. Distribution of phrase pairs in phrase tables (MGIZA++).

		Target							
		unigrams	bigrams	trigrams	4-grams	5-grams	6-grams	7-grams	total
	unigrams	**89,788**	44,941	10,700	2,388	486	133	52	148,488
	bigrams	61,007	**288,394**	86,978	20,372	5,142	1,163	344	463,400
	trigrams	19,235	149,971	**373,991**	105,449	27,534	7,414	1,857	685,451
Source	4-grams	5,070	47,848	193,677	**335,837**	106,467	31,011	9,261	729,171
	5-grams	1,209	13,984	73,068	193,260	**270,615**	98,895	32,349	683,380
	6-grams	332	3,856	24,333	87,244	177,554	**214,189**	88,700	596,208
	7-grams	113	1,103	7,768	33,278	91,355	157,653	**171,049**	462,319
	total	176,754	550,097	770,515	777,828	679,153	510,458	303,612	3,768,417

Table 5. Distribution of phrase pairs in phrase tables (Anymalign).

		Target								
		unigrams	bigrams	trigrams	4-grams	5-grams	6-grams	7-grams	···	total
Source	unigrams	**791,099**	105,961	9,139	1,125	233	72	37	···	1,012,473
	bigrams	104,633	**21,602**	4,035	919	290	100	44	···	226,176
	trigrams	10,665	4,361	**2,570**	1,163	553	240	96	···	92,268
	4-grams	1,698	1,309	1,492	**1,782**	1,158	573	267	···	61,562
	5-grams	378	526	905	1,476	**1,732**	1,206	642	···	47,139
	6-grams	110	226	467	958	1,559	**1,694**	1,245	···	40,174
	7-grams	40	86	238	536	1,054	1,588	**1,666**	···	35,753
	...	...	...	...	...	...	...	...	...	...
	total	1,022,594	230,400	86,830	55,534	42,891	37,246	34,531	···	1,371,865

times less than in MGIZA++ table. This confirms the results given in [19] that the sampling-based approach excels in aligning unigrams, which makes it better at multilingual lexicon induction than, e.g., MGIZA++. However, its phrase tables do not reach the performance of symmetric alignments from MGIZA++ on translation tasks. This basically comes from the fact that Anymalign does not align enough long n-grams.

3 Anymalign1-N

3.1 Phrase Subtables

To solve the above-mentioned problem, we propose a method to force the sampling-based approach to align more n-grams.

Consider that we have a parallel input corpus, i.e., a list of (source, target) sentence pairs, for instance, in French and English. Groups of characters that are separated by spaces in these sentences are considered as words. Single words are referred to as unigrams, and sequences of two and three words are called bigrams and trigrams, respectively.

Theoretically, since the sampling-based alignment method excels at aligning unigrams, we could improve it by making it align bigrams, trigrams, or even longer n-grams as if they were unigrams. We do this by replacing spaces between words by underscore symbols and reduplicating words as many times as needed, which allows to make bigrams, trigrams, and longer n-grams appear as unigrams. Table 6 depicts the way of forcing n-grams into unigrams. The same trick was used in a work by [20].

It is thus possible to use various parallel corpora, with different segmentation schemes in the source and target parts. We refer to a parallel corpus where source n-grams and target m-grams are assimilated to unigrams as a *unigramized n-m corpus*. These corpora are then used as input to Anymalign to produce phrase subtables, as shown in Table 7. Practically, we call Anymalign1-N the process of running Anymalign with all possible unigramized *n-m* corpora, with *n* and

Table 6. Transforming n-grams into unigrams by inserting underscores and reduplicating words for both the French part and English part of the input parallel corpus.

n	French	English
1	le debat est clos .	the debate is closed .
2	le_debat debat_est est_clos clos_.	the_debate debate_is is_closed closed_.
3	le_debat_est debat_est_clos est_clos_.	the_debate_is debate_is_closed is_closed_.
4	le_debat_est_clos debat_est_clos_.	the_debate_is_closed debate_is_closed_.
5	le_debat_est_clos_.	the_debate_is_closed_.

Table 7. List of n-gram phrase subtables (TT) generated from the training corpus. These subtables will then be merged together into a single phrase table.

		Target					
		unigrams	bigrams	trigrams	4-grams	⋯	N-grams
Source	unigrams	TT1 × 1	TT1 × 2	TT1 × 3	TT1 × 4	⋯	TT1 × N
	bigrams	TT2 × 1	TT2 × 2	TT2 × 3	TT2 × 4	⋯	TT2 × N
	trigrams	TT3 × 1	TT3 × 2	TT3 × 3	TT3 × 4	⋯	TT3 × N
	4-grams	TT4 × 1	TT4 × 2	TT4 × 3	TT4 × 4	⋯	TT4 × N
	⋯	⋯	⋯	⋯	⋯	⋯	⋯
	N-grams	TTN × 1	TTN × 2	TTN × 3	TTN × 4	⋯	TTN × N

m both ranging from 1 to a given N. In total, this corresponds to N × N runs of Anymalign. All phrase translation subtables are finally merged together into one large phrase table, where translation probabilities are re-estimated given the complete set of alignments.

Although Anymalign is capable of directly producing alignments of sequences of words, we use it with a simple filter[3] so that it only produces (typographic) unigrams in output, i.e., n-grams and m-grams assimilated to unigrams in the input corpus. This choice was made because it is useless to produce alignments of sequences of words, since we are only interested in *phrases* in the subsequent machine translation tasks. Those phrases are already contained in our (typographic) unigrams: all we need to do to get the original segmentation is to remove underscores from the alignments.

3.2 Equal Time Configuration

The same experimental process (i.e., replacing the phrase table) as in the preliminary experiment was carried out on Anymalign1-N with equal time distribution, i.e., uniformly distributed time among subtables. For a fair comparison, the same amount of time was given: seven hours in total. The results are given in

---

[3] Option -N 1 in the program.

Table 8. Anymalign1-4 with equal time for each $n \times m$ n-grams alignments.

		Target							
		unigrams	bigrams	trigrams	4-grams	5-grams	6-grams	7-grams	total
	unigrams	**171,077**	118,848	39,253	13,327	0	0	0	342,505
	bigrams	119,953	**142,721**	67,872	24,908	0	0	0	355,454
Source	trigrams	45,154	75,607	**86,181**	42,748	0	0	0	249,690
	4-grams	15,514	30,146	54,017	**60,101**	0	0	0	159,778
	5-grams	0	0	0	0	0	0	0	0
	6-grams	0	0	0	0	0	0	0	0
	7-grams	0	0	0	0	0	0	0	0
	total	351,698	367,322	247,323	141,084	0	0	0	1,107,427

Table 12. On the whole, MGIZA++ significantly outperforms Anymalign1-N, by more than 4 BLEU points. However, the proposed approach, Anymalign1-N, produces better results than Anymalign in its basic version, with the best increase with Anymalign1-4 (+1.4 BP).

The comparison of Table 8 and 4 shows that Anymalign1-N delivers too many alignments outside of the diagonal ($m \times m$ n-grams) and still not enough along the diagonal. Consequently, this number of alignments should be lowered. A way of doing so is by giving less time for alignments outside of the diagonal.

3.3   Time Distribution among Subtables

To this end, we distribute the total alignment time among phrase subtables according to the standard normal distribution:

$$\phi(n, m) = \frac{1}{\sqrt{2\pi}} e^{-\frac{1}{2}(n-m)^2}$$

The alignment time allotted to the subtable between source n-grams and target m-grams will thus be proportional to $\phi(n, m)$.

In a third evaluation, we compare this new setting (with a total amount of processing time of 7 h) with MGIZA++, Anymalign in its standard use, and Anymalign1-N with equal time distribution (Table 12). There is an increase in BLEU scores for almost all Anymalign1-N, from Anymalign1-3 to Anymalign1-10, when compared with equal time distribution. The greatest increase in BLEU is obtained for Anymalign1-10 (almost +2 BP). Anymalign1-4 shows the best translation quality among all other settings, but gets a less significant improvement (+0.2 BP).

Again, we investigated the number of entries in Anymalign1-N run with this normal time distribution. We compare the number of entries in Anymalign1-4 with equal time distribution (Table 8) and standard normal time distribution (Table 9). The number of phrase pairs on the diagonal roughly doubled when using standard normal time distribution. We can see a significant increase in the number of phrase pairs of similar lengths, while the number of phrase pairs with

Table 9. Anymalign1-4 with standard normal time distribution.

	Target							total
	unigrams	bigrams	trigrams	4-grams	5-grams	6-grams	7-grams	
unigrams	**255,443**	132,779	13,803	469	0	0	0	402,494
bigrams	134,458	**217,500**	75,441	8,612	0	0	0	436,011
trigrams	15,025	86,973	**142,091**	48,568	0	0	0	292,657
4-grams	635	10,516	61,741	**98,961**	0	0	0	171,853
5-grams	0	0	0	0	0	0	0	0
6-grams	0	0	0	0	0	0	0	0
7-grams	0	0	0	0	0	0	0	0
total	405,561	447,768	293,076	156,610	0	0	0	1,303,015

(Source labels along left: unigrams, bigrams, trigrams, 4-grams, 5-grams, 6-grams, 7-grams, total — under "Source")

different lengths tends to decrease slightly. This means that the standard normal time distribution allowed us to produce much more numerous useful alignments (a priori, phrase pairs with similar lengths), while maintaining the noise (phrase pairs with different lengths) to a low level, which is a neat advantage over the original method.

3.4   Pruning Phrase Tables

Inspired by the work of Johnson et al. [21], we applied the technique of pruning on phrase tables of Anymalign (standard normal time distribution).

In [21], Fishers exact significance test is used to eliminate a substantial number of phrase pairs. The significance of the association between a (source, target) phrase pair is evaluated and their probability of co-occurrence in the corpus is calculated. A two by two contingency table for the phrase pair $(\tilde{s}, \tilde{t})$ is shown in Table 10.

The hypergeometric distribution is used to compute the observed probability of joint occurrence $C(\tilde{s}, \tilde{t})$, with $\tilde{s}$ a source phrase and $\tilde{t}$ a target phrase:

$$p_h(C(\tilde{s}, \tilde{t})) = \frac{\binom{C(\tilde{s})}{C(\tilde{s},\tilde{t})} \binom{N-C(\tilde{s})}{C(\tilde{t})-C(\tilde{s},\tilde{t})}}{\binom{N}{C(\tilde{t})}} \tag{1}$$

Table 10. 2×2 contingency table for $\tilde{s}$ and $\tilde{t}$

$C(\tilde{s}, \tilde{t})$	$C(\tilde{s}) - C(\tilde{s}, \tilde{t})$	$C(\tilde{s})$
$C(\tilde{t}) - C(\tilde{s}, \tilde{t})$	$N - C(\tilde{s}) - C(\tilde{t}) + C(\tilde{s}, \tilde{t})$	$N - C(\tilde{s})$
$C(\tilde{t})$	$N - C(\tilde{t})$	N

Here, N is the number of sentences in the input parallel corpus. The p-value is calculated as:

$$\text{p-value}(C(\tilde{s}, \tilde{t})) = \sum_{k=C(\tilde{s}, \tilde{t})}^{\infty} p_h(k) \tag{2}$$

Any phrase pair with a p-value greater than a given threshold will be filtered out.

In a fourth evaluation, we compare with the previous settings. We used $\alpha + \varepsilon$ and $\alpha - \varepsilon$ filters. The proportion of phrase pairs filtered out from the phrase tables is shown in Fig. 1. In both cases, the number of phrase pairs discarded from phrase tables varies according to N: it amounts to around 87 % for Anymalign1-1, but only to about half of the phrase pairs for Anymalign1-3 to Anymalign 1-10.

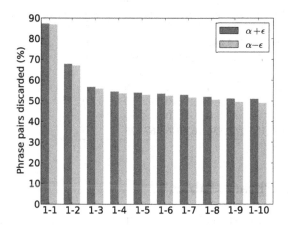

Fig. 1. Proportion of entries discarded in phrase tables of Anymalign1-N.

Evaluation results are given in Table 12. The phrase table size reduction results in slight but consistent improvements in translation quality. Among all Anymalign1-N, Anymalign1-4 once again gets the highest BLEU score of 25.11 ($\alpha + \varepsilon$ filter) and 25.14 ($\alpha - \varepsilon$ filter). This allowed us to achieve a slight improvement ($+0.7$ BLEU points) over Anymalign1-4 with standard normal time distribution and a significant improvement ($+2.2$ BLEU points) over Anymalign baseline.

The distribution of phrase pairs in pruned phrase tables are shown in Table 11(a) with $\alpha + \varepsilon$ filter and Table 11(b) with $\alpha - \varepsilon$ filter. The largest difference when compared with the non-pruned phrase table of Anymalign 1-4 with standard normal time distribution (Table 9) is visible in the cell corresponding to 1-to-1 entries. As a consequence, the largest number of entries are now 2-to-2 phrase pairs, which account for around 19 % of the total number of phrase pairs in both cases.

Table 11. Anymalign1-4 with standard normal time distribution (after pruning).

(a) $\alpha + \varepsilon$

	Target							
	1-grams	2-grams	3-grams	4-grams	5-grams	6-grams	7-grams	total
1-grams	**60,297**	59,099	8,819	328	0	0	0	128,543
2-grams	58,232	**110,415**	51,557	6,954	0	0	0	227,158
3-grams	9,777	58,604	**69,431**	28,046	0	0	0	165,858
4-grams	474	8,586	31,209	**31,666**	0	0	0	71,935
5-grams	0	0	0	0	0	0	0	0
6-grams	0	0	0	0	0	0	0	0
7-grams	0	0	0	0	0	0	0	0
total	128,780	236,704	161,016	66,994	0	0	0	593,494

(b) $\alpha - \varepsilon$

	Target							
	1-grams	2-grams	3-grams	4-grams	5-grams	6-grams	7-grams	total
1-grams	**63,252**	59,621	8,844	332	0	0	0	132,049
2-grams	58,595	**115,664**	52,062	7,006	0	0	0	233,327
3-grams	9,801	58,850	**69,749**	28,287	0	0	0	166,687
4-grams	477	8,701	31,391	**31,848**	0	0	0	72,417
5-grams	0	0	0	0	0	0	0	0
6-grams	0	0	0	0	0	0	0	0
7-grams	0	0	0	0	0	0	0	0
total	132,125	242,836	162,046	67,473	0	0	0	604,480

(Source labels along the left side of both tables.)

4   Merging Phrase Tables

In order to check exactly how different the phrase table of MGIZA++ and that of Anymalign are, we performed an additional set of experiments in which MGIZA++'s phrase table is merged with that of Anymalign baseline. As for the feature scores in the phrase tables for the intersection part of both aligners, we adopted parameters either from MGIZA++ or from Anymalign for evaluation.

Evaluation results on machine translation tasks with merged phrasse tables are given in Table 12. This setting outperforms MGIZA++ on BLEU scores.

Table 12. Evaluation results.

MGIZA++	**27.42**									
Anymaslign (baseline)	**22.85**									
	1-1	1-2	1-3	1-4	1-5	1-6	1-7	1-8	1-9	1-10
Anymalign1-N (equal time)	19.84	24.06	24.03	**24.23**	23.76	23.49	23.71	22.53	22.96	21.82
Anymalign1-N (std.norm.)	19.84	24.04	24.41	**24.42**	24.36	24.03	24.05	23.66	24.02	23.61
Anymalign1-N (std.n., $\alpha + \varepsilon$)	19.53	24.25	24.13	**25.11**	24.57	24.59	24.19	24.46	24.61	24.59
Anymalign1-N (std.n., $\alpha - \varepsilon$)	19.76	24.10	24.70	**25.14**	24.57	24.47	24.16	24.18	24.58	24.40
Merge (MGIZA++ para.)	**27.54**									
Merge (Anymalign para.)	**27.47**									

The phrase table with Anymalign parameters for the intersection part is slightly behind the phrase table with MGIZA++ parameters. This may indicate that the feature scores in Anymalign phrase table need to be revised.

5   Conclusions and Future Work

In this article, we proposed a method to improve the performance of the sampling-based sub-sentential alignment method on statistical machine translation tasks.

We analyzed the strengths and weaknesses of this method according to the distribution of phrase pairs in phrase tables, and pointed to directions for proposed work building on its strengths. By introducing a method to enforce the alignment of n-grams, called Anymalign1-N, we increased the phrase coverage. A gain of 1.3 BLEU point over Anymalign baseline was observed. In order to balance the distribution of n-grams in phrase tables, a standard normal time distribution has been introduced. Within the same amount of processing time, the number of n-m phrase pairs of similar lengths increased substantially, which led to additional improvements in translation quality with Anymalign1-N ($+0.2$ BLEU point). The translation quality was further improved by pruning phrase tables. In total, the experiments proposed in this article allowed us to achieve a significant improvement of more than 2.2 BLEU point over Anymalign baseline. Finally, merging Anymalign's phrase table with that of MGIZA++ allowed to outperform MGIZA++ alone.

In the future, we intend to modify the feature scores computed by Anymalign in order to make it better suited to statistical machine translation tasks.

Acknowledgments. Part of the research presented in this paper has been done under a Japanese grant-in-aid (Kakenhi C, 23500187: Improvement of alignments and release of multilingual syntactic patterns for statistical and example-based machine translation).

References

1. Gao, Q., Vogel, S.: Parallel implementations of word alignment tool. In: Software Engineering. Testing, and Quality Assurance for Natural Language Processing, Columbus, Ohio, pp. 49–57 (2008)
2. Brown, P., Pietra, S.D., Pietra, V.D., Mercer, R.: The mathematics of statistical machine translation: parameter estimation. Comput. Linguist. **19**(2), 263–311 (1993)
3. Vogel, S., Ney, H., Tillman, C.: HMM-based word alignment in statistical translation. In: Proceedings of the 16th International Conference on Computational Linguistics, Copenhagen, Denmark, pp. 836–841 (1996)
4. Koehn, P., Hoang, H., Birch, A., Callison-Burch, C., Federico, M., Bertoldi, N., Cowan, B., Shen, W., Moran, C., Zens, R., Dyer, C., Bojar, O., Constantin, A., Herbst, E.: Moses: open source toolkit for statistical machine translation. In: Proceedings of the 45th Annual Meeting of the Association for Computational Linguistics, Prague, Czech Republic, pp. 177–180 (2007)

5. Ideue, M., Yamamoto, K., Utiyama, M., Sumita, E.: A comparison of unsupervised bilingual term extraction methods using phrase-tables. In: Proceedings of MT Summit XIII, Xiamen, China, pp. 346–351 (2011)
6. Thurmair, G., Aleksic, V.: Creating term and lexicon entries from phrase tables. In: Proceedings of the 16th Annual Conference of the European Association for Machine Translation, Trento, Italy, pp. 253–260 (2012)
7. Lardilleux, A., Lepage, Y.: Sampling-based multilingual alignment. In: Proceedings of International Conference on Recent Advances in Natural Language Processing, Borovets, Bulgaria, pp. 214–218 (2009)
8. Gale, W., Church, K.: Identifying word correspondences in parallel texts. In: Proceedings of the 4th DARPA Workshop on Speech and Natural Language, California, pp. 152–157 (1991)
9. Melamed, D.: Models of translational equivalence among words. Comput. Linguist. **26**(2), 221–249 (2000)
10. Moore, R.: Association-based bilingual word alignment. In: Proceedings of the ACL Workshop on Building and Using Parallel Text, Ann Arbor, pp. 1–8 (2005)
11. Brown, P., Lai, J., Mercer, R.: Aligning sentences in parallel corpora. In: Proceedings of the 29th Annual Meeting of the Association for Computational Linguistics, California, pp. 169–176 (1991)
12. Och, F.J., Ney, H.: A systematic comparison of various statistical alignment models. Comput. Linguist. **29**(1), 19–51 (2003)
13. Liang, P., Taskar, B., Klein, D.: Alignment by agreement. In: Proceedings of the Human Language Technology Conference of the North American Chapter of the Association of Computational Linguistics, New York, pp. 104–111 (2006)
14. Dyer, C., Chahuneau V., Smith, N. A.: A simple, fast, and effective reparameterization of IBM model 2. In: Proceedings of the Conference of the North American Chapter of the Association for Computational Linguistics: Human Language Technologies, Atlanta, pp. 644–648 (2013)
15. Koehn, P., Och, F.J., Marcu, D.: Statistical phrase-based translation. In: Proceedings of the Human Language Technology Conference of the North American Chapter of the Association of Computational Linguistics, Edmonton, pp. 48–54 (2003)
16. Och, F.J.: Minimum error rate training in statistical machine translation. In: Proceedings of the 41st Annual Meeting on Association for Computational Linguistics, Sapporo, Japan, pp. 160–167 (2003)
17. Stolcke, A.: SRILM-an extensible language modeling toolkit. In: Proceedings of the 7th International Conference on Spoken Language Processing, vol. II, pp. 901–904 (2002)
18. Papineni, K., Roukos, S., Ward, T., Zhu, W.-J.: BLEU: a method for automatic evaluation of machine translation. In: Proceedings of the 40th Annual Meeting of the Association for Computational Linguistics, Philadelphia, pp. 311–318 (2002)
19. Lardilleux, A., Chevelu, J., Lepage, Y., Putois, G., Gosme, J.: Lexicons or phrase tables? an investigation in sampling-based multilingual alignment. In: Proceedings of the 3rd Workshop on Example-based Machine Translation, Dublin, Ireland, pp. 45–52 (2009)

20. Henríquez Q, A.C., Costa-jussà, R.M., Daudaravicius, V., Banchs, E. R., Mariño, B. J.: Using collocation segmentation to augment the phrase table. In: Proceedings of the Joint Fifth Workshop on Statistical Machine Translation and MetricsMATR, Uppsala, Sweden, pp. 98–102 (2010)
21. Johnson, J.H., Martin, J., Foster, G., Kuhn, R.: Improving translation quality by discarding most of the phrasetable. In: Proceedings of the Joint Conference on Empirical Methods in Natural Language Processing and Computational Natural Language Learning, Prague, Czech Republic, pp. 967–975 (2007)

Marker-Based Chunking in Eleven European Languages for Analogy-Based Translation

Kota Takeya and Yves Lepage[✉]

IPS, Waseda University, Hibikino 2-7, Kitakyushu, Fukuoka 808-0135, Japan
kota-takeya@toki.waseda.jp, yves.lepage@waseda.jp

Abstract. An example-based machine translation (EBMT) system based on proportional analogies requires numerous proportional analogies between linguistic units to work properly. Consequently, long sentences cannot be handled directly in such a framework. Cutting sentences into chunks would be a solution. Using different markers, we count the number of proportional analogies between chunks in 11 European languages. As expected, the number of proportional analogies between chunks found is very high. These results, and preliminary experiments in translation, are promising for the EBMT system that we intend to build.

1 Introduction

The work reported in this paper is part of the aim at building an EBMT system based on proportional analogies similar to the one described in [1]. For such an EBMT system to work well, the more numerous the proportional analogies, the better the translation outputs are expected to be. The translation method which we introduce in Sect. 2 can work on small sentences, but cannot handle long sentences, like the ones in the Europarl corpus. For long sentences, translating chunk by chunk could be a solution. As the number of analogies is the crucial point, this paper inspects ways of cutting sentences into chunks using different markers and examines the number of proportional analogies between them in 11 European languages.

The paper is organized as follows. Section 2 explains the notion of proportional analogy and shows how to translate using proportional analogy. Section 3 describes the basic notion of marker-based chunking used in the reported experiments. Section 4 presents the data for the experiments and the experimental protocol. Section 5 gives the results of the experiments. A conclusion summarizes this work in Sect. 6.

2 Proportional Analogy

2.1 Examples and Formalization

Proportional analogy is a general relationship between four objects, A, B, C and D, that states that 'A is to B as C is to D'. Its standard notation is $A : B :: C : D$.

This paper is part of the outcome of research performed under a Waseda University Grant for Special Research Project (project number: 2010A-906).

© Springer International Publishing Switzerland 2014
Z. Vetulani and J. Mariani (Eds.): LTC 2011, LNAI 8387, pp. 432–444, 2014.
DOI: 10.1007/978-3-319-08958-4_35

The following are proportional analogies between words (1), chunks (2) and sentences (3):

$$\text{relate : unrelated :: modulate : unmodulated} \tag{1}$$

$$\text{a key : the key :: a first visit : the first visit} \tag{2}$$

I like music. : Do you go to lives? : I like jazz music. : Do you go to jazz lives?

$$\tag{3}$$

A formalization has been proposed in [2]. This formalization reduces to counting number of occurrences of symbols and computating edit distances. Precisely:

$$A : B :: C : D \Rightarrow \begin{cases} |A|_a - |B|_a = |C|_a - |D|_a, \ \forall a \\ \delta(A, B) = \delta(C, D) \\ \delta(A, C) = \delta(B, D) \end{cases}$$

where $|A|_a$ stands for the number of occurrences of character a in string A and $\delta(A, B)$ stands for the edit distance between strings A and B with only insertion and deletion as edit operations.

2.2 Translation by Proportional Analogy

A translation method based on proportional analogies has been proposed by Lepage and Denoual [1]. The following procedure gives the basic outline of the method to perform the translation of an input chunk. Let us suppose that we have a corpus of aligned chunks in two languages. Let $D =$ "ein großes programm und" be a source chunk to be translated into one or more target chunks $\widehat{D}$. Let the bilingual corpus consists of four chunks with their translations:

ernste programme	↔	programmes sérieux
ein ernstes programm	↔	un programme sérieux
große programme und	↔	gros programmes et
das ernste programm	↔	le programme sérieux

The proposed method forms all possible analogical equations in C with all possible pairs of chunks from the parallel corpus. Among them:

ernste programme : ein ernstes programm :: C : ein großes programm und

The solution of this analogical equation is $x =$ "große programme und". As the pair of chunks "große programme und" ↔ "gros programmes et" is already part of the parallel aligned corpus, an analogical equation can be formed in the target language:

programmes sérieux : un programme sérieux :: gros programmes et : $\widehat{D}$

Its solution is a candidate translation of the source chunk: $\widehat{D} =$ "un gros programme et".

3   Marker-Based Chunking

In order to be able to apply the previous proposed method to various languages, we want to segment in a fully automatic and universal way sentences in different languages into sub-sentential units like chunks.

3.1   The Marker Hypothesis

We use the marker hypothesis for this. This hypothesis was first laid by Green [3].

> The marker hypothesis states that all natural languages contain a small number of elements that signal the presence of particular syntactic constructions.

We perform chunking based on this notion and use a method called marker-based chunking [4–6]. We define a chunk as a sequence of words delimited by markers. Markers should be words such as determiners (the), conjunctions (and, but, or), prepositions (in, from, to), possessive and personal pronouns (mine, you). A chunk can be created at each occurrence of a marker word. In addition, a further constraint requires that each chunk contains at least one non-marker word. Without non-marker words, a chunk would become meaningless as it would not contain any meaningful word.

As result examples, the following English, French and German sentences were processed by marker-based chunking using 50 markers. The underlined words are markers.

- [it _is_] [impossible _to_] [see why] [_the_ resale right should] [_be_ imposed _on_] [artists against their will] [_as_ a form _of_] [copyright _._]
- [on ne voit pas pourquoi] [_le_ droit _de_] [suite doit être imposé comme une forme _du_] [droit _d'_] [auteur aux artistes , _et_] [ce contre leur volonté _._]
- [es _ist_] [nicht einzusehen _,_] [warum] [_das_ folgerecht als ausformung des urheberrechts] [_den_ künstlern gegen ihren willen aufgezwungen werden soll _._]

3.2   Determining Markers by Informativity

Gough and Way [4] use marker-based chunking as a preprocessing step in SMT to improve the quality of translation tables and get improved results when combining their chunks with GIZA++/Moses translation table. They define a list of markers by hand and always cut left for European languages.

In contrast with their approach, we choose to automatically compute the list of markers. Frequency cannot do it: in the Europarl corpus "European" is a frequent word, but cannot be considered as a marker. We rely on some results from information theory and from our experimental results. In addition, to decide whether to cut to the left or the right of a marker, we compare the values of its branching entropy on both of its sides.

To determine which words are markers, we proceed as follows. If a language would be a perfect code, the length of each word would be a function of its number of occurrences, because, according to information theory, its emission length would be proportional to its self-information. The self-information of a word that appears $C(w)$ times in a corpus of N words is: $-\log(C(w)/N)$. In an ideal code, thus: $l(w) = -\log(C(w)/N)$ with $l(w)$ the length of the word, $C(w)$ its number of occurrences and N the total number of words in the text. Consequently, a word in a corpus of N words can be said to be informative if its length is much greater than its self-information in this text: $l(w) > -\log(C(w)/N)$. Consequently again, words with the smallest values for the following function can be said to be informative.

$$-\log \frac{C(w)}{N} \ / \ l(w) \tag{4}$$

Conversely, markers, that is words that are not informative, should be the words with the largest values for the previous function. However, our experiments with this formula were deceptive. Rather, considering the absolute number of occurrences instead of the frequency delivers words that meet more the human intuition about linguistic markers. To summarize, the list of markers we use is the list of words with the smallest values for the following function:

$$-\log C(w) \ / \ l(w) \tag{5}$$

Table 1 shows markers obtained in accordance with the two proposed formulae. Those obtained with (5) are true markers, on the contrary to those obtained with (4). Figure 1(a) and (b) visualize the better efficiency of (5) over (4) to isolate words that correspond to the intuitive notion of a marker.

Table 1. Words ranked according to two different formulae. Formula (4) on the left, (5) on the right. For (5), the place where to cut is also given.

Rank	$-\log \frac{C(w)}{N} / l(w)$		$-\log C(w) / l(w)$		
	Word	Value	Word	Value	Cut
1	z	21.81	,	-19.00	right
2	/	21.08	.	-18.57	right
3	\$	20.08	a	-17.37	left
4	q	19.94	i	-16.84	left
5	x	19.70	-	-15.15	left
6	l	19.40	s	-15.01	right
7	u	19.40	)	-14.37	right
8	w	19.15	(	-14.36	left
9	r	19.15	:	-13.74	right
10	&	19.15	'	-13.10	left
⋮	⋮	⋮	⋮	⋮	⋮

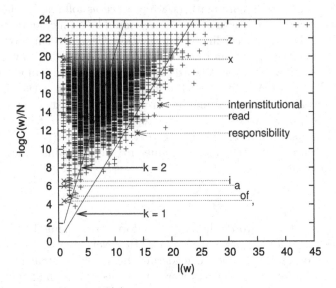

(a) Formula (4): $-\log \frac{C(w)}{N}$ against $l(w)$ for all words w. The lines stand for different values of $-\log \frac{C(w)}{N} / l(w)$. Words that correspond to the intuitive notion of a marker cannot be separated from other words using these lines.

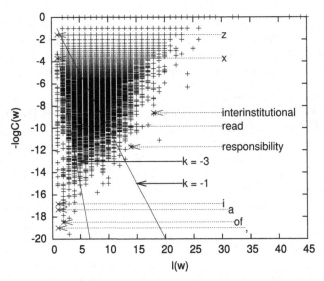

(b) Formula (5): $-\log C(w)$ against $l(w)$ for all words w. Words that correspond to the intuitive notion of a marker are clustered at the bottom left part of the triangle of dots and can thus be easily isolated using lines that stand for different values of $-\log C(w) / l(w)$.

Fig. 1. Distribution of words using two different formulae.

3.3 Left or Right Cutting

Following the famous intuition by Harris [7] about branching entropy, Tanaka-Ishii [8], Jin and Tanaka-Ishii [9] or Magistry and Sagot [10] have shown how Japanese and Chinese can be segmented into words by formalizing the uncertainty at every position in a text using branching entropy.

The entropy of a random variable X with m outcomes x_i is defined as its mathematical expectation and is a measure of its overall uncertainty:

$$H(X) = -\sum_{i=1}^{m} p(x_i) \log p(x_i)$$

with $p(x_i)$ the probability of the outcome x_i.

The branching entropy at every position in a text is the entropy of the right context knowing the left context. Tanaka-Ishii [8] computes it as the entropy of the characters that may follow a given left context of n characters.

$$H(X|X_n = x_n) = -\sum_{x} p(x|x_n) \log p(x|x_n)$$

with x being all the different characters that follow the string x_n in a given text.

For each marker in a text, we determine on which side of the marker to cut, left or right, by comparing the branching entropy on its left and the branching entropy on its right. In opposition to Tanaka-Ishii [8], we compute branching entropies not in characters but in words. If the branching entropy on the left is greater than the one on the right, it means that there is more uncertainty on the left context of the marker, i.e., the connection of the marker to its left context is weaker. In other words, the marker is more tightly connected to its right context so that it should be grouped as a chunk with its right context, rather than its left context.

The rightmost column of Table 1 shows examples of which side to cut for different markers. In English, "(" is separated on the left while ")" is separated on the right, which is a felicitous results. On the whole, except for few mismatches, the segmentation that we obtained seems roughly acceptable.

4 Experimental Setting

We present similar experiments as the ones reported for Japanese in [11], but on 11 European languages. Here, we examine several sampling sizes and different numbers of markers. Our sampling sizes range from 10 to 100,000 sentences, and the number of markers ranges from 10 to 300 markers.

The data that we use in our experiments is the Europarl corpus [12] because our ultimate goal is to apply the analogy-based EBMT method to this kind of data. The Europarl corpus is a collection of proceedings of the European Parliament. The corpus comprises of about 10 million words for each of 11 official languages of the European Union: Danish (da), German (de), Greek (el), English

Table 2. Statistics on the Europarl corpus of 11 parallel European languages. The number of sentences is the same in all languages.

	da	de	el	en	es	fi	fr	it	nl	pt	sv
Sentences					384,237						
Words (million words)	10.4	10.5	10.0	10.9	11.5	7.9	12.1	10.9	11.0	11.3	9.9
Voc. (thousand words)	162.2	177.1	156.3	70.9	104.9	315.9	90.4	103.8	132.2	107.5	165.8

(en), Spanish (es), Finnish (fi), French (fr), Italian (it), Dutch (nl), Portuguese (pt) and Swedish (sv). Since the corpus is not exactly aligned, we aligned nearly 400,000 sentences across 11 languages properly. This gives about 13,000 words in each of the 11 languages for more than 380,000 utterances. Precise statistics are given in Table 2.

5   Experimental Results

5.1   Number of Different Chunks Obtained from Different Markers

By varying the number of markers, we measure how different markers affect the number of different chunks obtained. By doing so, it is possible to determine which markers are the most productive ones. Increasing the number of markers should increase the number of different chunks generated.

Figure 2(a) shows the number of different chunks obtained using different numbers of markers on 1,000 sentences in each different language. This graph shows that when the number of markers increases, the number of chunks may first increase and then decreases after some value.

Figure 2(b) shows the number of different chunks obtained using different numbers of markers on 100,000 sentences. After 20 markers, the increase slows down for every language except for Finnish. The low number of different chunks for Finnish may be explained by the morphological richness of this language, and its relative lack in prepositions.

5.2   Number of Analogies Between Sentences and Chunks

Figure 3(a) plots the number of proportional analogies between sentences for different numbers of sentences. Until 25,000 sentences, no analogies are found. After 50,000 sentences, the increase looks at least polynomial. The minimal number of proportional analogies is 159 for Greek for 100,000 sentences and the maximal number of proportional analogies is 698 for Danish. These absolute numbers show clearly that an EBMT system using proportional analogies between sentences will not be able to translate any sentence.

In comparison with Fig. 3(a) and (b) plots the number of proportional analogies between chunks extracted from 10 to 2,500 sentences using 100 markers.

In Fig. 3(b), chunks obtained from 100 sentences form very few analogies. After some 2,500 sentences, the number of proportional analogies found increases

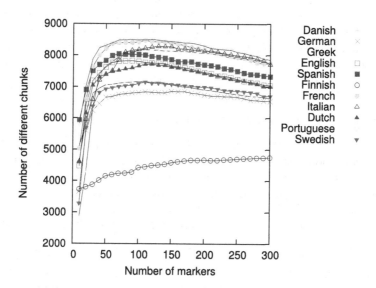

(a) Number of different chunks against number of markers used for 1,000 sentences in 11 different languages. On the contrary to Fig. 2(b), except for Finnish, the number of different chunks obtained does not always increase.

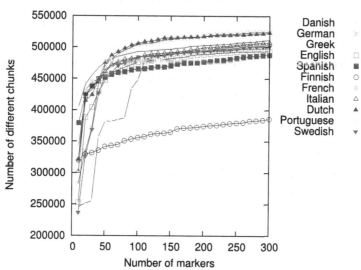

(b) Number of different chunks against number of markers used for 100,000 sentences in 11 different languages. As expected, the more the markers, the more the number of different chunks obtained.

Fig. 2. Number of different chunks against number of markers used.

to more than 5,000 to 550,000 analogies with much variation. The minimal number of proportional analogies is 4,777 for Finnish. The maximum number is 548,928 for Spanish. It is important to note that in contrast to Fig. 3(a), not only the abscissae scale is different, but also the ordinates scale, different by two orders of magnitude in both graphs. The curve on Fig. 3(b) grows in fact ten thousand times faster than the one on Fig. 3(a).

5.3   Translation of Chunks by Analogy

In this section, we perform an experiment in translation using an analogy-based machine translation system similar to the one reported in [1], and in conformity to the description given in Sect. 2. The experiment reported here is between French and English. For each language, we perform marker-based chunking with different numbers of markers. We determine the number of necessary markers in each language so as to obtain various average numbers of chunks per sentence, from three to nine.

In a first step, we perform word-to-word alignment between English and French on a training part of the Europarl corpus using the sampling-based subsentential alignment tool Anymalign [13]. In a second step, we compute a chunk-to-chunk translation table for each possible value of number of chunks per sentence, with lexical weights [14] and translation probabilities in both directions, by maximizing the lexical weights between chunks computed on the basis of the word-for-word alignments. As a final translation table, we use the merge of the two translation tables: word-to-word and chunk-to-chunk.

We translate each chunk of a test set using the analogy-based translation system fed with the previous translation tables. As we are dealing with chunks, which are shallow syntactic units, in this experiment, we do not use the recursion normally allowed in the analogy-based framework. For each chunk in the test set, there are three cases:

- the chunk cannot be translated;
- the chunk can be translated, but none of the translation hypotheses obtained correspond to a translation in the references;
- the chunk can be translated, and at least one of the translation hypotheses matches exactly one of the references.

Tables 3(a) and (b) give the percentages corresponding to the two last cases in different configurations that correspond to each different average number of chunks per sentence. As this number increases, the number of chunks that can be translated increases strongly, from 60 % to 80 % in English to French and from 56 % to 76 % in French to English. As for the number of chunks that could be translated and that have at least one perfect match in the references, this number is just below half of the chunks, varying from 40 % to 45 % in English to French and from 41 % to 46 % in French to English.

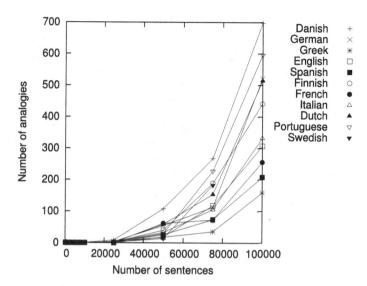

(a) Number of proportional analogies between sentences obtained with an increasing number of sentences.

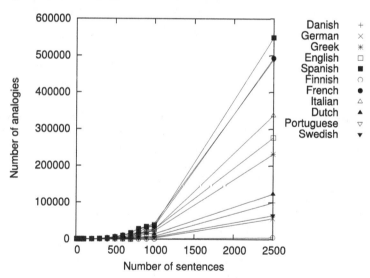

(b) Number of proportional analogies between chunks extracted from an increasing number of sentences using 100 markers. The horizontal axis extends from 0 to 2,500, i.e., forty times less than in Fig. 3(a). The vertical axis reaches 600,000, i.e., almost thousand times more than in Fig. 3(a).

Fig. 3. Number of proportional analogies between sentences and chunks.

Table 3. Translation of chunks by analogy.

(a) English to French.

Average number of chunks per sentence	Number of chunks in test set	Number of translated chunks	Number of translated chunks with an exact match in the references
3	919	541 (58.86%)	369 (40.15%)
4	1,633	1,076 (65.89%)	660 (40.41%)
5	2,054	1,447 (70.44%)	836 (40.70%)
6	2,739	2,065 (75.39%)	1,131 (41.29%)
7	3,922	3,035 (77.38%)	1,663 (42.40%)
8	5,624	4,464 (79.37%)	2,511 (44.64%)
9	7,387	5,932 (80.30%)	3,291 (44.55%)

(b) French to English.

Average number of chunks per sentence	Number of chunks in test set	Number of translated chunks	Number of translated chunks with an exact match in the references
3	924	513 (55.51%)	380 (41.12%)
4	1,678	1,095 (65.25%)	717 (42.72%)
5	2,017	1,376 (68.22%)	856 (42.43%)
6	2,659	1,929 (72.54%)	1,162 (43.70%)
7	4,015	2,994 (74.57%)	1,771 (44.10%)
8	5,699	4,309 (75.60%)	2,675 (46.93%)
9	7,192	5,451 (75.79%)	3,337 (46.39%)

6 Conclusion

It was understood from previous work [1] that analogies between reasonably long sentences are too scarce to help in translating longer sentences using an analogy-based machine translation system. In a series of previous experiments [11,15,16], it has been shown, on a small number of languages, that the number of analogies between chunks is quite high, so that segmentation into chunks could contribute to translation of longer sentences by analogy.

The contribution of this paper was to show that it is possible to segment into chunks in a completely automatic way while keeping a high number of analogies between chunks. We tested our proposal on a reasonable number of languages: 11 European languages. We obtained more than several tens of thousands of analogies between chunks extracted from only 2,500 sentences in each language in average, a number by far much higher than between sentences.

The completely automatic segmentation into chunks that we proposed in this paper relied on insights from information theory. First, we relied on the marker hypothesis and gave an automatic way of determining markers, that differs from the usual approach with stop words. Our method consists in extracting the words with a length closest to an ideal length in an ideal code. Second, we rely on the change of entropy at the boundary between markers to determine whether markers start or end a chunk.

We also briefly reported a preliminary experiment in translation of chunks by analogy on the French-English language pair. Alignment of chunks was performed based on word-for-word alignment and maximization of lexical weights. Almost three quarters of the chunks in our test set could be translated. 40 % of the chunks had an exact match in the target part of the translation tables, showing that a direct application of analogy can predict between a third and a half of unknown chunks.

References

1. Lepage, Y., Denoual, E.: Purest ever example-based machine translation: detailed presentation and assessment. Mach. Transl. **19**(3), 251–282 (2005)
2. Lepage, Y.: Analogy and formal languages. Electron. Notes Theoret. Comput. Sci. **53**, 180–191 (2004)
3. Green, T.: The necessity of syntax markers: two experiments with artificial languages. J. Verbal Learn. Verbal Behav. **18**(4), 481–496 (1979)
4. Gough, N., Way, A.: Robust large-scale EBMT with marker-based segmentation. In: Proceedings of TMI-04, pp. 95–104 (2004)
5. Stroppa, N., Way, A.: MaTrEx: the DCU machine translation system for IWSLT 2006. In: Proceedings of the International Workshop on Spoken Language Translation, pp. 31–36 (2006)
6. Van Den Bosch, A., Stroppa, N., Way, A.: A memory-based classification approach to marker-based EBMT. In: Proceedings of the METIS-II Workshop on New Approaches to Machine Translation, Leuven, Belgium, pp. 63–72 (2007)
7. Harris, Z.: From phoneme to morpheme. Language **31**(2), 190–222 (1955)
8. Tanaka-Ishii, K.: Entropy as an indicator of context boundaries: an experiment using a web search engine. In: Dale, R., Wong, K.-F., Su, J., Kwong, O. (eds.) IJCNLP 2005. LNCS (LNAI), vol. 3651, pp. 93–105. Springer, Heidelberg (2005)
9. Jin, Z., Tanaka-Ishii, K.: Unsupervised segmentation of Chinese text by use of branching entropy. In: Proceedings of the COLING/ACL on Main Conference Poster Sessions, pp. 428–435. Association for Computational Linguistics (2006)
10. Magistry, P., Sagot, B.: Unsupervized word oogmentation: the case for Mandarin chinese. In: Annual Meeting of the Association for Computational Linguistics (ACL 2012), Jeju, Korea, ACL, July 2012 (2012)
11. Lepage, Y., Migeot, J., Guillerm, E.: A measure of the number of true analogies between Chunks in Japanese. In: Vetulani, Z., Uszkoreit, H. (eds.) LTC 2007. LNCS, vol. 5603, pp. 154–164. Springer, Heidelberg (2009)
12. Koehn, P.: Europarl: A parallel corpus for statistical machine translation. In: Proceedings of MT Summit X, Phuket, Thailand, pp. 79–86 (2005)
13. Lardilleux, A., Lepage, Y.: A truly multilingual, high coverage, accurate, yet simple, subsentential alignment method. In: Proceedings of the Xth conference of the Association for Machine Translation in the Americas, Waikiki, Hawai'i, October 2008, pp. 125–132 (2008)
14. Koehn, P., Och, F., Marcu, D.: Statistical phrase-based translation. In: Proceedings of the Human Language Technology and North American Association for Computational Linguistics Conference (HLT/NAACL), Edmonton, Alberta, pp. 127–133 (2003)

15. Lepage, Y., Migeot, J., Guillerm, E.: Analogies of form between chunks in Japanese are massive and far from being misleading. In: Proceedings of the 3rd Language and Technology Conference (LTC 2007), Poznań, Poland, October 2007, pp. 503–507 (2007)

16. Lepage, Y., Migeot, J., Guillerm, E.: A corpus study on the number of true proportional analogies between chunks in two typologically different languages. In: Proceedings of the seventh international Symposium on Natural Language Processing (SNLP 2007), Kasetsart University, Pattaya, Thailand, December 2007, pp. 117–122 (2007). ISBN:978-974-623-062-9

Comparing CBMT Approaches
for German-Romanian

Monica Gavrila and Natalia Elita[✉]

University of Hamburg, School of Mathematics, Informatics and Natural Sciences,
30 Vogt-Koelln Str, 22527 Hamburg, Germany
{gavrila,elita}@informatik.uni-hamburg.de
http://www.informatik.uni-hamburg.de

Abstract. There is no doubt that in the last couple of years corpus-based machine translation (CBMT) approaches have been in focus. Each of the CBMT approaches (statistical MT and example-based MT) has its advantages and disadvantages. Therefore, hybrid approaches have been developed. This paper presents a comparative study of CBMT approaches, using three types of systems: a statistical MT (SMT) system, an example-based MT (EBMT) system and a hybrid (EBMT-SMT) system. For our experiments we considered German-Romanian as language-pair, in this direction of translation, and a domain-restricted corpus, manually created and aligned (RoGER). The translation results have been both automatically and manually evaluated. For both evaluation types, the SMT system is ranked best in our experiments.

Keywords: Moses · OpenMaTrEx · Lin-EBMT^{REC+} · SMT, EBMT · hybrid MT

1 Introduction

There is no doubt that in the last couple of years corpus-based machine translation (CBMT) approaches have been in focus. Among them, the statistical MT (SMT) approach has been by far more dominant. However, the example-based machine translation (EBMT) Workshop at the end of 2009[1] and the new open-source systems (e.g. OpenMaTrEx) showed a revived interest in EBMT and hybrid MT approaches.

The unclear definitions and the mixture of ideas make the difference between EBMT and SMT difficult to distinguish. One of the main characteristics of an EBMT system, as presented in [16], is, in contrast to SMT, the run-time use of the examples. In order to show the advantages of one or another method, comparisons between SMT and EBMT (or hybrid) systems have been presented in the literature. Moreover, to take advantage of the positive sides of both CBMT approaches, hybrid systems have been developed. The results, depending on the data type and the MT systems considered, seem to be positive for various

---

[1] http://computing.dcu.ie/~mforcada/ebmt3/

© Springer International Publishing Switzerland 2014
Z. Vetulani and J. Mariani (Eds.): LTC 2011, LNAI 8387, pp. 445–455, 2014.
DOI: 10.1007/978-3-319-08958-4_36

approaches. The marker-based EBMT system described in [20] outperformed the SMT system presented in the same paper. In [17] the hybrid EBMT-SMT system is outperformed by a Moses-based SMT system. In both papers the language pair under consideration is English - French.

In this paper we compare several CBMT approaches, using three MT systems: an SMT system (Mb_SMT), an EBMT system (Lin-EBMT^{REC+}) and a hybrid (EBMT-SMT) system (OpenMaTrEx). MT experiments are run for German - Romanian, in this direction of translation. In contrast to other authors, for example [17], we use a small-size domain-restricted corpus for training. While it is usually stated that SMT needs a large amount of training data, EBMT is believed to be better suited when only a small training corpus is available.

The use of small-size corpora for SMT has been tried out before in [15]. The authors present results for Serbian-English and a training data size of approx. 2.6 K sentences. However, to our knowledge, no comparisons among various CBMT systems using small-size data have been published. Moreover, for the language pairs employed in this paper, publications which describe comparisons between any CBMT approaches have not been found. SMT experiments for German-Romanian using the JRC-Acquis[2] corpus have been described in [9], where the BLEU score reported is 0.2373.

Our paper is organized in four sections. The following section presents the MT systems employed. In Sect. 3 we describe the data used and analyze the translation results. Moreover, a manual analysis of the results in terms of adequacy, fluency and system ranking is presented. The paper ends with conclusions.

2   System Description

In this section we present the three CBMT systems we used in our tests: an SMT system (Mb_SMT), an EBMT system (Lin-EBMT^{REC+}) and a hybrid (EBMT-SMT) system (OpenMaTrEx).

2.1   The SMT System: Mb_SMT (A)

The pure SMT system (Mb_SMT) follows the description of the baseline architecture given for the EMNLP 2011 Sixth Workshop on SMT[3]. Mb_SMT uses Moses[4], an SMT system that allows the user to train translation models automatically for the language pair needed, considering that the user has the necessary parallel aligned corpus. More details about Moses can be found in [10].

While running Moses, we used SRILM - [18] - for building the language model (LM) and GIZA++ - [13] - for obtaining word alignment information. We made two changes to the specifications given at the Workshop on SMT: we left out the tuning step and we changed the LM-order from 5 to 3. Leaving out the tuning step has been motivated by the results we obtained in experiments

---

[2] http://optima.jrc.it/Acquis/index_2.2.html

[3] http://www.statmt.org/wmt11/baseline.html

[4] http://www.statmt.org/moses/

which are not the topic of this paper, when comparing different settings for the SMT system. Not all tests for the system configuration which included tuning showed improvement in the evaluation scores. Changing the LM order has been motivated by the results reported in the literature[5], in which it was concluded that 3-gram configurations provide best translation results.

2.2   The EBMT System: Lin-EBMT^{REC+} (B)

Lin-EBMT^{REC+} is an EBMT system developed at the University of Hamburg [7], which combines the linear EBMT approach with the template-based one [see [12] for the classification of EBMT approaches and the definition of a template].

Before starting the translation, training and test data are pre-processed as in the Moses-based SMT system: the data is tokenized and lowercased. The algorithm for translation consists of the three steps presented in [16]: matching, alignment and recombination.

The matching procedure of this EBMT system is an approach based on surface-forms, focusing in finding recursively the longest common substrings. We use a word-index in order to reduce the search space in the matching process. In case the test sentence is found in the training corpus during the matching procedure, its translation represents the output. Otherwise, the alignment and recombination steps are performed. The word-alignment information is extracted from the same GIZA++ output of the SMT system described previously. To reduce the appearance of boundary friction problems, the longest target language (TL) aligned subsequences are used in the recombination step. In Lin-EBMT^{REC+} ideas from the template-based EBMT approach are incorporated in the recombination step, by extracting and imposing three types of word-order constraints, which are extracted from templates built at run-time. The recombination step is based on 2-gram information, word-order constraints and a recombination matrix defined as follows:

Definition: Given the outcome of the alignment - n word-sequences $sequence_1$, $sequence_2$, ..., $sequence_n$ that form the output and which are not necessarily different, with $sequence_i = w_{i1}w_{i2}...w_{ilast}$ - and a set of constraints $C - \{(w_{iq}, w_{ir})\}$, with $1 \le iq, ir \le n$, then $A = (a_{i,j})$, $1 \le i, j \le n$ is a square matrix of order n that is defined as in 1.

$$A_{n,n} = (a_{i,j})_{1 \le i,j \le n} = \begin{cases} -3, & \text{if } i = j; \\ -1, & \text{if } i \neq j, \ count(w_{i_{last}}w_{j_1}) = 0; \\ -2, & \text{if } i \neq j, \ (w_{i_{last}}w_{j_1}) \in C; \\ \frac{2*count(w_{i_{last}}w_{j_1})}{count(w_{i_{last}})+count(w_{j_1})}, & \text{if } i \neq j, \ count(w_{i_{last}}w_{j_1}) > 0, \\ & (w_{i_{last}}w_{j_1}) \notin C. \end{cases}$$

$$(1)$$

where $count(s)$ represents the number of appearances of a token s in the corpus.

---

[5] Results reported in the SMART project (an EU project).

We make a distinction between the case when there is no entry in the language model $(count(w_{i_{last}}w_{j_1}) = 0, i \neq j)$ and the case when constraints are set $((w_{i_{last}}w_{j_1}) \in C, i \neq j)$. For the case when no language model (**LM**) entry is found we set the value higher than the value for the case when a constraint is set. Finding no entry in the LM does not necessarily mean that the words are not allowed to appear in this order: it could just mean that the data is sparse. Setting a constraint on two words means that the words are not allowed to appear in that specific order. This is why the value in the matrix is lower than in the previous case.

The recombination algorithm is based on finding the maximum value $a_{i,j}$, 'combining' $sequence_i$ and $sequence_j$, and deleting all the values from the matrix corresponding to $sequence_j$ (line and column j). When $sequence_i$ and $sequence_j$ are combined, they are concatenated and the matrix values for the new element $sequence_i sequence_j$ are the ones which previously corresponded to $sequence_j$. Given a certain corpus, the maximum value for $a_{i,j}$ means that the probability that $sequence_j$ follows $sequence_i$ is the highest.

The whole recombination process starts with the first maximum value found in the initial matrix and it continues until the order of the matrix becomes one and the output is obtained. More information about the system, templates and how combinations of constraints influence the evaluation results is presented in [6,7].

2.3 The Hybrid System: OpenMaTrEx (C)

OpenMaTrEx[6] is a free (open-source) MT system based on the marker hypothesis - see [4] - developed at the Dublin City University.

The marker hypothesis (see [8]) is a universal psycholinguistic constraint which states that natural languages are marked for complex syntactic structure at surface form by a closed set of specific lexemes and morphemes. That is, a basic phrase-level segmentation of an input sentence can be achieved by exploiting a closed list of known marker words to signalize the start and end of each segment.

OpenMaTrEx consists of a marker-driven chunker, several chunk aligners and two engines: one is based on the simple proof-of-concept monotone recombinator (called Marclator[7]) and the other uses a Moses-based decoder (called MaTrEx).

The system uses GIZA++ for word alignments and IRSTLM[8] to obtain the language model. The complete architecture of OpenMaTrEx is described in [4,19]. OpenMaTrEx can be run in two modes: Marclator and MaTrEx. In the MaTrEx mode it wraps around the Moses statistical decoder, using a hybrid translation table containing marker-based chunks as well as statistically extracted phrase pairs.

For our experiments we followed the training and translation steps as described in [4]. Only the results of the run in MaTrEx mode (the hybrid MT architecture) are shown in the current article.

---

[6] http://www.openmatrex.org/

[7] http://www.openmatrex.org/marclator/

[8] http://hlt.fbk.eu/en/irstlm

Marker Words Files. In this subsection we present the marker words files for Romanian developed during this research. The markers for German were already contained in OpenMaTrEx and have been extracted from the "Ding" dictionary by Sarah Ebling[9].

We extracted the markers for Romanian during the experiments presented in this paper by considering the morpho-syntactic specifications from MULTEXT-East[10] and Wikipedia[11]. The set of markers for Romanian consists of the chunking and non-chunking punctuation that has been acquired from the English marker words file[12]. The other word categories included in the file are: determiners, pronouns (personal, demonstrative, possessive, interrogative, relative), prepositions, conjunctions (coordinative and subordinative), (cardinal) numerals, adverbs and auxiliary verbs.

Definite articles and weak forms of the personal pronouns are two examples of clitic forms in Romanian. Therefore, we have not considered them as markers in these experiments. The definite articles appear within the word as endings (e.g. ro: dosareLE - en: THE files). Some weak forms of the personal pronoun are separated from other words (such as verbs) by a hyphen: e.g. ro: LE-am citit - en: I read THEM. Part of the determiners are ambiguous, as they can also be pronouns or numerals (e.g. ro. O fată - en: A girl; ro: ia-O - en: take IT; ro: O pară si doua mere - en: A pear and two apples). Only given the context it can be determined whether the word is a determiner, a numeral or a pronoun. In order to avoid ambiguity, indefinite articles were introduced as determiners in the set of markers and the category determiner pronoun was included only once under the category of pronouns. There are currently 366 Romanian and 656 German markers. As the corpus is ignoring diacritics, we have also eliminated diacritics in both of the marker files.

3   Evaluation

In this section, before the evaluation results are presented, we describe the training and test data used in the experiments.

3.1   Data Description

We used a small-size corpus developed during the research: RoGER[13] for the evaluation. It is a domain-restricted parallel corpus (a manual of an electronic device), which includes four languages (Romanian, German, English and Russian). It is manually aligned at sentence level. Moreover, the text is manually corrected and

---

[9] http://www-user.tu-chemnitz.de/~fri/ding/

[10] http://nl.ijs.si/ME/V4/msd/html/msd-ro.html

[11] http://ro.wikipedia.org/wiki/ - Search: Parti de vorbire.

[12] The markers for English have been provided by OpenMaTrEX.

[13] For research purposes, the RoGER corpus can be obtained from the authors of this paper.

Table 1. Statistics on the data (SL = source language, voc. = vocabulary, sent. = sentence, token = word, number or punctuation sign)

Data SL	No. of tokens	Voc.	Average sent. length
Training	28,361	3,230	12.89
Test	1,657	604	12.46

preprocessed, by replacing concepts such as numbers and web pages, with 'meta-notions' – for example numbers with NUM. It contains no diacritics. More information about RoGER can be found in [5].

Its small size (2333 sentences) is compensated by the correctness of the translations and sentence alignments.

We randomly extracted 133 sentences, which we used as test data for all three MT systems. The rest of 2200 sentences represent the training data. Statistical information about RoGER is shown in Table 1. It has not been verified if test sentences already are included in the training data, as we wanted to keep the experimental settings as realistic as possible (- when translating a text, no one verifies first if sentences have already been translated).

The languages considered in this paper present characteristics which can make the process of automatic translation even more challenging. Romanian is a less resourced language with a highly infected morphology and high demand for translation after joining the European Union in 2007. It is a Romance language, with influences from Slavic languages especially in vocabulary and phonetics. Features, such as its inflectional system or the three genders, make difficult the adaptation of language technology systems for other family-related languages.

German is a Germanic language, which is also inflected and presents a 3-gender system and well defined inflection classes. Two special features are represented by the verbs with particles (the separation of the particle from the verb inside the sentence and the challenge that the particle can be ambiguous) and the compounds. Compounds in German are normally written as single words, without spaces or other word boundaries[14].

3.2   Automatic Evaluation Results

We evaluated the obtained translations automatically using the BLEU (bilingual evaluation understudy) score. BLEU measures the number of n-grams, of different lengths, of the system output that appear in a set of references. More information on BLEU can be found in [14]. We considered the twelfth version of

---

[14] The longest German word verified to be actually in (albeit very limited) use is Rindfleischetikettierungsüberwachungsaufgabenübertragungsgesetz, which, literally translated, is "beef labelling supervision duty assignment law" [from Rind (cattle), Fleisch (meat), Etikettierung(s) (labelling), Überwachung(s) (supervision), Aufgaben (duties), Übertragung(s) (assignment), Gesetz (law)].

the BLEU implementation from the National Institute of Standards and Technology (NIST)[15]: mteval_v12.

Although usually criticized, the choice of the BLEU score is motivated by the available resources (software, linguistic resources, etc.) and, for comparison reasons, by previous results reported in the literature. Due to lack of data and further translation possibilities, the comparison with only one reference translation is considered.

The obtained results are 0.3240 for Mb_SMT, 0.2646 for the EBMT system (Lin-EBMT^{REC+}) and 0.2564 for OpenMaTrEx.

In order to be able to analyze the results better, we examined the test data set from two points of view: the number of out-of-vocabulary words (OOV-words) and the number of test sentences already found in the training data. Both aspects have a direct influence on the translation quality and evaluation results. By comparing the vocabulary files of the training and test data we could find 101 OOV-words in the test data. This represents 16.72 % of the whole vocabulary size. Thirty-one test sentences (approx. 23.3 %) have been already included in the training data. For this test and training data and language combination the best corpus-based maschine translation (CBMT) system is the Moses-based pure SMT system. The hybrid system is the last, although its evaluation score is quite close to the EBMT one.

3.3 Manual Evaluation

To be able to better understand the BLEU scores, we manually evaluated the obtained translations manually by means of adequacy and fluency and ranked the MT systems. Two human evaluators (1 and 2), who speak German and have Romanian as mother-tongue, performed the evaluation.

Adequacy refers to the degree to which information in the original sentence is also communicated in the translation. Fluency refers to the degree to which the target sentence is well-formed according to the rules of the target language. The evaluation scale for adequacy and fluency is the one described in the Linguistic Data Consortium specification[16]:

– Adequacy: 1 = None, 2 = Little, 3 = Much, 4 = Most, 5 = All.
– Fluency: 1 = Incomprehensible, 2 = Disfluent, 3 = Non-native, 4 = Good, 5 = Flawless.

The ranking of the MT systems is done following the instruction found in [3], i.e. "Rank translations from Best to Worse relative to the other choices (ties are allowed)." (1 = Best, 3 = Worst). Being ranked first does not mean that the system has a perfect translation; it only means that it provides the best translation, compared to the other two systems.

---

[15] http://www.itl.nist.gov/iad/mig/tests/mt/2008/scoring.html
[16] http://projects.ldc.upenn.edu/TIDES/Translation/TransAssess04.pdf

Table 2. Average results for the manual analysis (1 and 2 = first and second human evaluator, respectively)

MT System	Adequacy		Fluency		Rank	
	1	2	1	2	1	2
Mb_SMT	**3.41**	**3.33**	**3.20**	**3.42**	**1.15**	**1.24**
Lin-EBMT^{REC+}	3.11	3.00	2.93	3.02	1.54	1.62
OpenMaTrEx	3.13	3.05	2.95	3.12	1.48	1.48

Table 3. Inter-annotator agreement: Kappa coefficient

MT System	Adequacy	Fluency	Rank
Mb_SMT	**0.43**	**0.52**	**0.76**
Lin-EBMT^{REC+}	0.41	0.50	0.48
OpenMaTrEx	0.37	0.44	0.50
All three	0.41	0.48	0.58

We evaluated the inter-annotator agreement as in [2], using the Kappa coefficient [1]:

$$KAPPA = \frac{P(a) - P(e)}{1 - P(e)},$$

where $P(a)$ is the proportion of times that the annotators agree and $P(e)$ is the proportion of time that they would agree by chance. For adequacy and fluency $P(e) = 1/5 = 0.2$ (there are 5 possibilities) and for the ranking $P(e) = 1/3$ (there are 3 possibilities: $a > b$, $a = b$, $a < b$). Depending on the Kappa coefficient, the inter-annotator agreement can be slight (0–.2), fair (0.21–.4), moderate (0.41–.6), substantial (.61–.8) or almost perfect (.81–1) - see [11]. The results in [2] for adequacy and fluency for the Kappa coefficient were fair and for ranking moderate. Our results are shown in Tables 2 and 3.

Each of the CBMT systems has its advantages and each provided best translations for various test sentences (the best results in the examples below are boldface):

Examples:
1.
Input: Empfangen einer Visitenkarte (English: Receiving a business card)
Reference: Receptionarea unei carti de vizita
Mb_SMT: Receptionarea unei carti de vizita
Lin-EBMT^{REC+}: Puteti primi expedia cartea de vizita
OpenMaTrEx: primirea unei carti de vizita

2.
Input: Druecken Sie Menue, waehlen Sie Verzeichnis und anschliessend Dienstnummern. (English: Press Menu, and select Contacts and Services.)

Reference: Apasati Meniu, si selectati Agenda telefon si Numere servicii.
Mb_SMT: Apasati Meniu si selectati Agenda telefon si apoi numere de servicii.
Lin-EBMT^{REC+}: Apasati Meniu si selectati Agenda telefon si Numere servicii
OpenMaTrEx: Apasati Meniu, si selectati Agenda telefon si apoi selectati perioada de servicii.

3.

Input: Anklopfen (English: Call waiting)
Reference: Serviciu de apel in asteptare
Mb_SMT: Apel in asteptare
Lin-EBMT^{REC+}: Apel in asteptare
OpenMaTrEx: Serviciu de apel in asteptare

Overall, Mb_SMT provided perfect translations (similar to the references) in 37 cases, Lin-EBMT^{REC+} in 33 cases and OpenMaTrEx in 31 cases.

In the Tables 2 and 3 the boldface numbers represent best results.

Analyzing the results in Table 3, it can be concluded that the Kappa coefficient usually shows a moderate inter-annotator agreement. Two exceptions appear: the adequacy for OpenMaTrEX (System C) is fair and the ranking for the SMT system (System A) is substantial. The inter-annotator agreement in general is the best for ranking. Overall, our inter-annotator agreement is better than the one in [2].

4   Conclusions and Further Work

In this paper three corpus-based MT systems have been compared using the same test and training data. MT experiments were made for German-Romanian (this direction of translation) using a small-size domain-restricted corpus. Such a framework is thought to be better suited for the EBMT approach. As the BLEU score has been criticized in the last couple of years, in order to establish which system is really the best, a manual analysis of the results has been made. The SMT system outperformed the other two approaches (the EBMT and the hybrid approaches), for both automatic and manual evaluation. Further work will include testing how the systems react to different, larger corpora and to various language pairs. Other interesting aspects connected with OpenMaTrEx are represented by running the experiments using the Marclator mode and testing how changing (e.g. increasing) the list of markers influences the translation results.

References

1. Carletta, J.: Assessing agreement on classification tasks: the Kappa statistic. Comp. Ling. **22**(2), 249–254 (1996)
2. Callison-Burch, C., Fordyce, C., Koehn, P., Monz, C., Schroeder, J.: (Meta-) evaluation of machine translation. In: Proceedings of ACL-2007 Workshop on Statistical Machine Translation, StatMT '07, pp. 136–158. Association for Computational Linguistics, Stroudsburg (2007)

3. Callison-Burch, C., Koehn, P., Monz, C., and Schroeder, J., Findings of the 2009 workshop on statistical machine translation. In Proceedings of the 4th EACL Workshop on Statistical Machine Translation, Athens, Greece, pp. 1–28, 30–31 March 2009

4. Dandapat, S., Forcada, M.L., Groves, D., Penkale, S., Tinsley, J., Way, A.: OPEN-MATREX: a free/open-source marker-driven example-based machine translation system. In: Loftsson, H., Rögnvaldsson, E., Helgadóttir, S. (eds.) IceTAL 2010. LNCS, vol. 6233, pp. 121–126. Springer, Heidelberg (2010)

5. Gavrila, M., Elita, N.: Roger - un corpus paralel aliniat. In: Proceedings of the Resurse Lingvistice si Instrumente pentru Prelucrarea Limbii Romane Workshop, Workshop held in November 2006, pp. 63–67. Univ. Alexandru Ioan Cuza, December 2006. ISBN: 978- 973-703-208-9

6. Gavrila, M.: Constrained recombination in an example-based machine translation system. In: Proceedings of the EAMT-2011: the 15th Annual Conference of the European Association for Machine Translation, Leuven, Belgium, pp. 193–200, May 2011. ISBN 9789081486118

7. Gavrila, M.: Improving Recombination in a Linear EBMT System by Use of Constraints, Ph.D. Thesis, University of Hamburg (2012)

8. Green, T.R.G.: The necessity of syntax markers: two experiments with artificial languages. J. Verbal Learn. Verbal Behav. 18(4), 481–496 (1979)

9. Ignat, C.: Improving Statistical Alignment and Translation Using Highly Multilingual Corpora. Ph.D. thesis, INSA - LGeco- LICIA, Strasbourg, France, 16 June 2009

10. Koehn, P., Hoang, H., Birch, A., Callison-Burch, C., Federico, M., Bertoldi, N., Cowan, B., Shen, W., Moran, C., Zens, R., Dyer, C., Bojar, O., Constantin, A., Herbst, E.: Moses: open source toolkit for statistical machine translation. In: Proceedings of the Annual Meeting of the Association for Computational Linguistics (ACL), Demonstration Session, Prague, Czech Republic, June 2007

11. Landis, J.R., Koch, G.G.: Biometrics the measurement of observer agreement for categorical data. Biometrics 33, 159–174 (1977)

12. McTait, K.: Translation Pattern Extraction and Recombination for Example-Based Machine Translation. Ph.D. thesis, Centre for Computational Linguistics, Department of Language Engineering, UMIST (2001)

13. Och, F.J., Ney, H.: A systematic comparison of various statistical alignment models. Comput. Linguist. 29(1), 19–51 (2003)

14. Papineni, K., Roukos, S., Ward, T., Zhu, W.-J.: Bleu: a method for automatic evaluation of machine translation. In: Proceedings of the 40th Annual Meeting on Association for Computational Linguistics, Session: Machine Translation and Evaluation, pp. 311–318, Philadelphia, Pennsylvania. Association for Computational Linguistics, Morristown (2002)

15. Popovic, M., Ney, H.: Statistical machine translation with a small amount of bilingual training data. In: LREC-2006: Fifth International Conference on Language Resources and Evaluation. 5th SALTMIL Workshop on Minority Languages: Strategies for developing machine translation for minority Languages, pp. 25–29. Genoa, Italy, May 2006

16. Somers, H.: An Overview of EBMT. In: Carl, M., Way, A. (eds.) Recent Advances in Example-based Machine Translation, vol. 21, pp. 3–57. Kluwer Acad. Publ, Dordrecht (2003)

17. Smith, J., Clark, S.: EBMT for SMT: a new SBMT-SMT hybrid. In: Forcada, M.L., Way, A. (eds.) Proceedings of the 3rd International Workshop on Example-Based Machine Translation, pp. 3–10, Dublin, Ireland, 12–13 November (2009)

18. Stolcke, A.: Srilm - an extensible language modeling toolkit. In Proceedings of the International Conference Spoken Language Processing, pp. 901–904, Denver, Colorado, September 2002
19. Stroppa, N., Groves, D., Way, A., Sarasola, K.: Example-based machine translation of the basque language. In: Proceedings of AMTA 2006–7th Conference of the Association for Machine Translation in the Americas, Cambridge, MA, USA, pp. 232–241, August 2006
20. Way, A., Gough, N.: Comparing example-based and statistical machine translation. Nat. Lang. Eng. **11**, 295–309 (2005)

Text Genre – An Unexplored Parameter in Statistical Machine Translation

Monica Gavrila and Cristina Vertan[(⊠)]

University of Hamburg, 30 Vogt-Koelln Str, 22527 Hamburg, Germany
gavrila@informatik.uni-hamburg.de,
cristina.vertan@uni-hamburg.de
http://www.informatik.uni-hamburg.de

Abstract. It is generally accepted that the performance of a statistical machine translation (SMT) system depends significantly on the concordance between the domain of training and test data. During the last years several methods have been proposed in order to deal with out-of-domain words. Less to no attention has been paid however to text genre within the same domain. In this paper we demonstrate that the style of the training corpus may influence the quality of the translation output even when the domain of the training and test data remains al- most unchanged, but the text genre changes. We use as training data the JRC-Acquis and as test data the Europarl corpus. We include also experiments with an out-of-domain test data, as comparison for the variation of performance of the SMT system.

Keywords: Statistical machine translation · Text genre · Europarl · JRC-Acquis · RoGER · SMT evaluation

1 Introduction

It is generally accepted that statistical machine translation (SMT) provides sufficiently good translation results with in-domain test data and "enough" training data. Results are rapidly decreasing for out-of-domain test data. Therefore, lot of research has been directed in the last years towards domain adaptation of SMT systems - e.g. [10]. Especially for European languages, current state-of-the-art SMT-engines are trained on one of the two large corpora available: JRC-Acquis[1] or Europarl[2]. Special techniques are applied in a second phase in order to ensure lexical domain adaptation. Less attention is paid to the fact that, even inside one domain, corpora belong to different text genres or, at least, have different discourse structures and, therefore, other types of syntactic structures or semantic frames. These differences may have a bigger influence on the quality of an SMT-system than assumed until now.

1.1 The Context for the Experiments

This aspect is of particular importance in scenarios where a machine translation engine is part of a complex architecture exposed to textual input from heterogeneous

---

[1] http://ipsc.jrc.ec.europa.eu/index.php?id=198
[2] http://www.statmt.org/europarl/

© Springer International Publishing Switzerland 2014
Z. Vetulani and J. Mariani (Eds.): LTC 2011, LNAI 8387, pp. 456–467, 2014.
DOI: 10.1007/978-3-319-08958-4_37

domains or text genres. This is the case of a Web- Content-Management System (WCMS) as the ATLAS System[3].

In this system several web-services based on advanced language technology components are built for seven European languages. Among the key technologies which are incorporated, a central role is played by machine translation. Due to lack of enough training data for all possible domains, the data-driven translation engine is trained mostly on the JRC-Acquis corpus and afterwards domain adaptation is performed. For domains for which no training model is available, the user is informed that the translation quality can lack accuracy.

As the acceptance of such system depends extensively from the user acceptance we decided to investigate also to which extent the text genre of the input can influence the translation quality.

This paper shows several SMT experiments with different test data (in- domain vs. out-of-domain vs. 'similar' data) using the JRC-Acquis corpus for training. The language-pair considered is English-Romanian. The originality of the work is not in the MT approach involved, but in the way of choosing the test data. SMT experiments using JRC-Acquis and Romanian-English as language pair have been presented in [2, 6] and [9]. The results are presented in a tabular form in Table 1.

Table 1. Previous reported results

Direction of translation	Paper	BLEU score
English-Romanian	[2]	0.5464
	[6]	0.3208
	[9]	0.4900
Romanian-English	[2]	0.4604
	[6]	0.3840
	[9]	0.6080

SMT experiments have been usually performed and presented with in-domain data, for example see the experiments from [9] or [6].

An overview of how (rule-based) machine translation (MT) reacts to various text genres is shown in [1], where the MT system used is SYSTRAN[4]. The study analyzed machine translated extracts from four text genres with respect to different linguistic errors. Best results were obtained for technical sets of instructions.

Our paper is organized in seven sections. After this short introduction we will present the environmentof the MT-Engine in Sect. 2, while in Sect. 3 we describe our experimental settings: the MT system and the training and test data.

In Sect. 4 we show the evaluation results, followed in Sect. 5 by presenting factors which influence the results. The paper presents the conclusions and further work in Sect. 6. The last part of the paper shows our acknowledgments.

---

[3] http://www.atlasproject.eu

[4] http://www.systranet.com/

2   The ATLAS Content Management System

The core online service of the ATLAS platform is i-Publisher, a powerful Web-based instrument for creating, running and managing content-driven Web sites. It integrates the language-based technology to improve content navigation e.g. by interlinking documents based on extracted phrases, words and names, providing short summaries and suggested categorization concepts. Currently two different thematic content-driven Web sites, i-Librarian and EUDocLib, are being built on top of ATLAS platform, using i-Publisher as content management layer. i-Librarian is intended to be a user-oriented web site which allows visitors to maintain a personal workspace for storing, sharing and publishing various types of documents and have them automatically categorized into appropriate subject categories, summarized and annotated with important words, phrases and names. EUDocLib is planned as a publicly accessible repository of EU legal documents from the EUR-LEX collection with enhanced navigation and multilingual access.

The i-Publisher service:

- is mainly targeted at small enterprises and non-profit organizations,
- gives the ability to build via point-and-click user interface content-driven Web sites, which provide a wide set of pre-defined functionalities and the textual content of which is automatically processed, i.e. categorized, summarized, annotated, etc.,
- enables publishers, information designers and graphic designers to easily collaborate,
- aims at saving authors, editors and other contributors valuable time by automatically processing textual data and allows them to work together to produce high quality content. The last evaluation round of the service indicates that users do really see the benefit of LT-Technologies embedded into the system

The i-Librarian service:

- addresses the needs of authors, students, young researchers and readers,
- gives the ability to easily create, organize and publish various types of documents,
- allows users to find similar documents in different languages, to share personal works with other people, and to locate the most relevant texts from large collections of unfamiliar documents.

The EUDocLib service is a particular refinement of i-Librarian targeted to the management of documents from the European Commission.

The facilities described above are supported through intelligent language technology components like automatic classification, named entity recognition and information extraction, automatic text summarization, machine translation and cross-lingual retrieval. These components are integrated into the system in brick-like architecture, which means that each component is building on top of the other. The baseline brick is the language processing chains component which ensure a heterogonous linguistic processing of all documents independent of their language. A processing chain for a given language includes a number of existing tools, adjusted and/or fine-tuned to ensure their interoperability. In most respects a language processing chain does not require development of new software modules but rather combining existing tools. The basic ATLAS software[5] is distributed as a software package under GPL license. LT-plug-ins like e.g. the language processing chains or the MT-engine follow a commercial licensing. The iLibrarian is available as web-service and it has unrestricted access.

2.1   Machine Translation in ATLAS System

Machine Translation is a key component of the ATLAS system. The development of the engine is particular challenging as the translation should be used in different domains. Additionally, the considered language-pairs belong to less resourced group[6], for which bilingual training and test material is available in limited amount.

The machine translation engine is integrated in 2 distinct ways into the ATLAS platform:

- for i-Publisher Service (generic platform for generating websites) the MT is serving as a translation aid tool for publishing multilingual content. Text is submitted to the translation engine and the result is subject to the human post processing
- for i-Librarian and EuDocLib (dedicated web services for collecting documents) the MT-engine provides a translation for assimilation, which means that the user retrieving documents in different languages will use the engine in order to get a clue about the documents, and decide if he will store them. If the translation is considered as acceptable it will be stored into a database.

The integration of a machine translation engine into a web based content management system in general and the ATLAS system in particular, presents from the user point of view several challenges among which we mention two, which ATLAS-System dealt with

1. The user may retrieve documents from different domains. Domain adaptation is a major issue in machine translation, and in particular in corpus–based methods. Poor lexical coverage and false disambiguation are the main issues when translating documents out of the training domain
2. The user may retrieve documents from various time periods. As language changes over time, language technology tools developed for the modern languages do not work equally well on diachronic documents.

With the current available technology it is not possible to provide a translation system which is domain and language variation independent and works for a couple of heterogeneous language pairs. Therefore our approach envisages a system of user guidance, so that the availability and the foreseen system-performance are transparent at any time.

---

[5] http://atlasproject.eu

[6] see http://www.meta-net.eu/whitepapers

For the MT-Engine of the ATLAS system we decided on a hybrid architecture combining EBMT [4] and SMT [8] at word-based level (no syntactic trees will be used). An original approach of our system is the interaction of the MT-engine with other modules of the system:

- The document categorization module assigns to each document one or more domains. For each domain the system administrator has the possibility to store information regarding the availability of a correspondent specific training corpus. If no specific trained model for the respective domain exists, the user is provided with a warning, telling that the translation may be inadequate with respect to the lexical coverage.
- The output of the summarization module is processed in such a way that ellipses and anaphora are omitted, and lexical material is adapted to the training corpus.

The information extraction module is providing information about metadata of the document including publication age. For documents previous to 1900 we will not provide translation, explaining the user that in absence of a training corpus the translation may be misleading.

The domain and dating restrictions can be changed at any time by the system administrator when an adequate training model is provided. The described architecture is presented in Fig. 1.

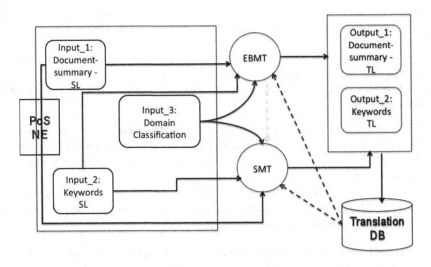

Fig. 1. System architecture for ATLAS-Engine

3   Experiments

In this section we present the SMT system and the training and test data used in the experiments.

3.1   The SMT System

The SMT system follows the description of the baseline architecture given for the EMNLP 2011 Sixth Workshop on SMT[7]. The system uses Moses[8], an SMT system that allows the user to automatically train translation models for the language pair needed, considering that the user has the necessary parallel aligned corpus. More details about Moses can be found in [8].

While running Moses, we used SRILM - [16] - for building the language model (LM) and GIZA++ - [11] - for obtaining word alignment information. We made two changes to the specifications given at the Workshop on SMT: we left out the tuning step and we changed the order of the language model (LM) from 5 to 3.

Leaving out the tuning step has been motivated by results we obtained in experiments which are not the topic of this paper, when comparing different settings for SMT: not all tests for the system configuration which included tunning showed improvement in the evaluation scores. Changing the LM order has been motivated by results reported in the SMART project, in which it has been concluded that 3-gram configurations provide best results – see [13].

3.2   Training Data

The training data is part of the JRC-Acquis corpus for English-Romanian. JRC-Acquis is a freely available parallel corpus in 22 languages, which consists of European Union (EU) documents of a legal nature. It is based on the Acquis Communautaire (AC), the total body of European Union (EU) law applicable in the EU Member States. This collection of legislative text changes continuously and currently comprises selected texts written between the 1950s and today.

From the two types of sentence alignments available (Vanilla and HunAlign), we used the Vanilla alignments. The same alignments have been also used in [6]. The sentence alignment is done at paragraph level[9], where a paragraph can be a simple or complex sentence, a sub-sentential phrase (e.g. noun phrase) or even more sentences. In order to reduce possible errors, only one-to-one alignments have been considered for the experiments presented in this paper. More details on the JRC-Acquis corpus can be found in [15].

The corpus has not been (manually) corrected. Therefore, translation, alignment or spelling errors can have an influence on the output quality.

For the SMT experiments, from 391324 links in 6557 documents, only 336509 links (the one-to-one alignments) have been considered. Due to the cleaning step of the SMT system[10], the number of one-to-one alignment links used for the LM was reduced to 240219 links for the Translation Model (TM). This represents 61.38 % of the initial corpus. The average sentence length is around 14.5 tokens. (In this paper token means a word, a number or a punctuation sign.)

---

[7] www.statmt.org/wmt11/baseline.html

[8] www.statmt.org/moses/

[9] The tag $< p >$ from the initial HTML files.

[10] In the Moses description, all sentences longer than forty tokens are excluded.

3.3   Test Data

We used test data from three different corpora:

- JRC-Acquis itself (Case A) in-domain data;
- Europarl (Case B) 'similar' data (in-domain, different genre out-of-genre data);
- RoGER (Case C) out-of-domain data.

The first two corpora could be considered in the same domain, as both refer to EU matters, but they are of a different genre: JRC-Acquis contains EU regulations; Europarl is extracted from the literal reports of the debates in the European Parliament. RoGER represents a totally different domain, as it contains text from a manual of an electronic device. The separation of these texts has been done by inspection and intuition.

A: JRC-Acquis The tests were run on parts of the JRC-Acquis, which were not used for training. 897 sentences (three sets of 299 sentences A: Test 1, A: Test 2, A: Test 3) were removed before the training step from the initial corpus, in order to be used as test data. Sentences were removed from different parts of the corpus to ensure a relevant lexical, syntactic and semantic coverage. A: Test 1+2+3 data set contains all the sentences.

The test data has not been cleaned, this means that no length restriction is considered and sentences might be repeated. For example, the paragraph "Article NUMBER" repeats itself 53, 44 and 11 times in A: Test 1, A: Test 2 and A: Test 3, respectively. The data is in-domain data. The average sentence length is around 21 tokens.

B: Europarl The Europarl parallel corpus [7] is extracted from the proceedings of the European Parliament (the literal reports of the debates) dating back to 1996 and contains in its last version twenty-one languages.

We extracted from version 6 of the corpus[11] three different test data sets, each of 299 sentences from the English-Romanian data. As for JRC-Acquis, we extracted the data from different parts of the corpus: from the beginning, middle and the end of the corpus. Small corrections have been done, as sometimes also sentences in other languages have been encountered.

The test data sets from this corpus are: B: Test 1, B: Test 2, B: Test 3 and B: Test 1+2+3. The average sentence length is around 13 tokens. However, for B: Test 1 and B: Test 2 it is around 7.5 and for B: Test 3 it is 24.5. The data is in-domain, but it has a different genre when compared with the training data: the structure and discourse of the text are totally different than the ones of the JRC-Acquis. The text refers to similar matters as the training data: European regulations. We consider these test data sets as 'similar' test data.

C: RoGER In order to analyze the performance of SMT systems to a total different type of text input, we used the RoGER corpus.

RoGER is a parallel corpus, aligned at sentence level. It is domain-restricted, as the texts are from a users' manual of an electronic device. The languages included in

---

[11] Status: February 2011; http://www.statmt.org/europarl/

the development of this corpus are Romanian, English, German and Russian. The corpus was manually compiled and verified: the translations and the (sentence) alignments were manually corrected. It is not annotated and diacritics are ignored. More about the RoGER corpus can be found in [5].

From the 2333 sentences, we extracted 300 sentences from the middle of the corpus and used them as test data (C: Test). The average sentence length is around 15 tokens. The data is entirely out-of-domain.

4 Evaluation Results

We evaluated our translations using three automatic evaluation metrics: BLEU, NIST and TER. The choice of the metrics is motivated by the (linguistic) resources we had available and the results reported in the literature. Due to lack of data and further translation possibilities, the comparison with only one reference translation is considered in these experiments.

Although criticized, BLEU (bilingual evaluation understudy) is the score mostly used in the last years for MT evaluation. It measures the number of n- grams, of different lengths, of the system output that appear in a set of reference translations. More details about BLEU can be found in [12].

The NIST Score, described in [3], is similar to the BLEU score in that it also uses n-gram co-occurrence precision. If BLEU considers a geometric mean of the n-gram precision, NIST calculates the arithmetic mean. Another difference is that n-gram precisions are weighted by the n-gram frequencies.

TER calculates the minimum number of edits needed to get from obtained translations to the reference translations, normalized by the average length of the references. It considers insertions, deletions, substitutions of single words and an edit-operation which moves sequences of words. More information about TER can be found in [14].

The obtained evaluation results are presented in Tables 2 and 3. The BLEUresults are graphically presented in Fig. 2.

The results for in-domain data are similar to other BLEU scores published in the literature (with the exception of the test data set A: Test 1 for Romanian- English)[12]. The out-of-domain data provides quite low results. The results for 'similar' data, somehow surprisingly, are closer to the ones of the out-of-domain data.

A direct comparison with the results in [1] is not possible as there are several important differences, such as the MT approach and the evaluation methodology.

5 Analyzing the Results – Factors of Influence

Several aspects connected with the type of test data can influence the translation results. We will analyze in this paper the number of out-of-vocabulary words

---

[12] A one-to-one comparison is not possible, as the training and test data are not the same.

Table 2. Evaluation results (Romanian-English)

Test data	BLEU	NIST	TER
A: Test 1	0.2545	3.8325	0.5020
A: Test 2	0.5628	7.6956	0.3756
A: Test 3	0.4271	6.8134	0.4684
A: Test 1+2+3	0.4255	6.9261	0.4457
B: Test 1	0.1372	2.9406	0.9723
B: Test 2	0.1228	3.9758	0.7751
B: Test 3	0.1582	3.6708	0.7562
B: Test 1+2+3	0.1324	4.0559	0.8044
C: Test	0.0621	2.7640	0.7623

Table 3. Evaluation results (English-Romanian)

Test data	BLEU	NIST	TER
A: Test 1	0.3997	6.6279	0.5007
A: Test 2	0.4179	6.8431	0.4898
A: Test 3	0.3797	6.3857	0.5208
A: Test 1+2+3	0.4015	7.4039	0.502
B: Test 1	0.1114	2.7237	0.8315
B: Test 2	0.1057	3.6875	0.7844
B: Test 3	0.1403	3.4697	0.7043
B: Test 1+2+3	0.1128	3.8770	0.7781
C: Test	0.0623	2.7285	0.7340

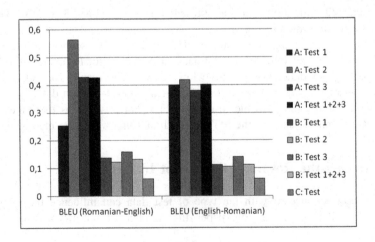

Fig. 2. BLEU results

Table 4. Data description (Romanian-English)

Test data	OOV-words	Sentences in the corpus
A: Test 1	51 (4.10 %)	69 (23.07 %)
A: Test 2	7 (0.76 %)	117 (39.13 %)
A: Test 3	111	81 (27.09 %)
A: Test 1+2+3	169	267 (29.76 %)
B: Test 1	59	0 (0 %)
B: Test 2	697	0 (0 %)
B: Test 3	94	2 (0.66 %)
B: Test 1+2+3	837	2 (0.22 %)
C: Test	330	0 (0 %)

Table 5. Data description (English-Romanian)

Test data	OOV-words	Sentences in the corpus
A: Test 1	33 (3.15 %)	69 (23.07 %)
A: Test 2	2 (0.27 %)	134 (44.81 %)
A: Test 3	96 (8.64 %)	85 (28.42 %)
A: Test 1+2+3	131 (5.59 %)	288 (21.10 %)
B: Test 1	30 (7.5 %)	21 (7.02 %)
B: Test 2	288 (18.68 %)	3 (1 %)
B: Test 3	60 (11.62 %)	22 (7.35 %)
B: Test 1+2+3	366 (17.99 %)	46 (5.12 %)
C: Test	93 (14.65 %)	0 (0 %)

(OOV-words) and test sentences already encountered in the training data. The tests have been run in a realistic scenario, with no human interference (choosing specific sentence average lengths, testing the inclusion in the training data, etc.) on the test data.

The overview of the OOV-words and test sentences already encountered in the training data is presented in Tables 4 and 5. The OOV-words are extracted analyzing only the surface forms. This means that a word can be in the training data as lemma, but a specific word-form[13] might be missing.

Comparing the OOV-words for Test 1+2+3 for Europarl and Test 1+2+3 for JRC-Acquis, we could conclude that these two sets of OOV-words are (al- most) totally different: only three words for English-Romanian and two for Romanian-English are in common in these two sets of OOV-words.

As expected, for the translation direction Romanian-English, the highest number of OOV-words appear in data C (RoGER; out-of-domain data) data (37.67 %). However, for English-Romanian, Test 2 from Europarl (data B; 'similar' data)

---

[13] Word-form = Declination form, conjugation form, etc.

contains the highest numer of OOV-words: 18.68 %. The out-of-domain data (data C) has only 14.65 % of OOV-words.

A better analysis of the OOV-words in different test data-sets should be made to have a more realistic overview. For example, it could be possible that in data B, due to the text genre, more declination or conjugation forms have been used, when compared with data A. Therefore, the use of a lemmatizer in the translation process could improve the translation results. Concerning the number of test sentences already found in the training data, excluding in-domain data, more sentences have been found for English-Romanian and 'similar' data. For Romanian-English the results for this aspect is similar for both out-of-domain and 'similar' data: under 1 %.

6 Conclusions

In this paper we showed several SMT experiments with different test data (in- domain vs. out-of-domain vs. 'similar' data) using the JRC-Acquis (English- Romanian) corpus for training. The results for in-domain and out-of-domain data are as expected. Somehow surprisingly, the results for 'similar' data are closer to the results for out-of-domain data. The differences in discourse and vocabulary lowered the translation scores for the Europarl tests, although we find ourselves in the same European framework as in the training data. This shows that having only 'similar' data for a specific domain, we cannot always expect good translation results. We can consider the conclusion of this paper limited to the data we used and only as a starting point for further analyses. A manual analysis of the translations should bring a better overview on the automatic scores and the sources of errors. Further experiments with various corpora and language pairs are needed before drawing a final (more general) conclusion

Acknowledgments. Part of the work in this paper was part of the EU-Project ATLAS, supported through the ICT-PSP-Programme of the EU-Commission (Topic "Multilingual Web") and the PhD research conducted by Monica Gavrila at the University of Hamburg (see [4]).

References

1. Calude, A.: Machine translation of various text genres. Presented at 7th Language and Society Conference of the New Zealand Linguistic Society. Hamilton, New Zealand, 12 p., November 2002. (unpublished) (http://www.mt-archive.info/Calude-2003.pdf)
2. Cristea, D.: Romanian language technology and resources go to Europe. Presentation held at the FP7 Language Technology Informative Days, January, 20–11 (2009)
3. Doddington, G.: Automatic evaluation of machine translation quality using n-gram co-occurrence statistics. In: Proceedings of the Second International Conference on Human Language Technology Research, pp. 138–145. Morgan Kaufmann Publishers Inc., San Francisco (2002)
4. Gavrila, M.: improving recombination in a linear EBMT system by use of constraints, Ph.D. thesis, University of Hamburg (2012)

5. Gavrila, M., Elita, N.: Roger - un corpus paralel aliniat. In: Resurse Lingvistice si Instrumente pentru Prelucrarea Limbii Romane Workshop Proceedings, pp. 63–67, Ed. Univ. Alexandru Ioan Cuza, December 2006. Workshop held in November 2006. ISBN: 978-973-703-208-9

6. Ignat, C.: Improving Statistical Alignment and Translation Using Highly Multilin- gual Corpora. Ph.D. thesis, INSA - LGeco- LICIA, Strasbourg, France, 16 June 2009

7. Koehn, P., Europarl: A Parallel Corpus for Statistical Machine Translation, MT Summit (2005)

8. Koehn, P., Hoang, H., Birch, A., Callison-Burch, C., Federico, M., Bertoldi, N., Cowan, B., Shen, W., Moran, C., Zens, R., Dyer, C., Bojar, O., Constantin, A., Herbst, E.: Moses: open source toolkit for statistical machine translation. In: Proceedings of the Annual Meeting of the Association for Computational Linguistics (ACL), demonstration session, pp. 177–180, Prague, Czech Republic, June 2007

9. Koehn, P., Birch, A., Steinberger, R.: 462 Machine Translation Systems forEurope, MT Summit (2009)

10. Niehues, J., Waibel, A.: Domain adaptation in statistical machine translation using factored translation models. In: Proceedings of EAMT, Saint-Raphael (2010)

11. Och, F.J., Ney, H.: A systematic comparison of various statistical alignment models. Comput. Linguistl. **29**(1), 19–51 (2003)

12. Papineni, K., Roukos, S., Ward, T., Zhu, W-J.: Bleu: a method for automatic evaluation of machine translation. In: Proceedings of the 40th Annual Meeting on Association for Computational Linguistics, Session: Machine Translation and Evaluation, pp. 311–318. Association for Computational Linguistics Morristown, Philadelphia (2002)

13. Rousu, J., SMART Project: Workpackage 3 advanced language models. Report of the EU project: SMART (2008)

14. Snover, M., Dorr, B., Schwartz, R., Micciulla, L., Makhoul. J.: A study of translation edit rate with targeted human annotation. In: Proceedings of Association for Machine Translation in the Americas, pp. 223 231, August 2006

15. Steinberger, R., Pouliquen, B., Widiger, A., Ignat, C., Erjavec, T., Tufis, D., Varga, D.: The JRC-Acquis: A multilingual aligned parallel corpus with 20+ languages. In: Proceedings of the 5th International Conference on Language Resources and Evaluation (LREC'2006), pp. 2142–2147, May, Genoa, Italy (2006)

16. Stolcke, A.: SRILM - An extensible language modeling toolkit. In: Proceedings of the International Conference on Spoken Language (2002)

Problems Concerning Less
Resourced Languages

Detecting Gaps in Language Resources and Tools in the Project CESAR

Marko Tadić[1]([✉]), Tamás Váradi [2], Radovan Garabík[3], Svetla Koeva[4],
Maciej Ogrodniczuk[5], and Duško Vitas[6]

[1] Faculty of Humanities and Social Sciences, University of Zagreb, Zagreb, Croatia
marko.tadic@ffzg.hr
[2] Research Institute for Linguistics,
Hungarian Academy of Sciences, Budapest, Hungary
[3] L'udovít Štúr Institute of Linguistics,
Slovak Academy of Sciences, Bratislava, Slovakia
[4] Institute for Bulgarian Language Prof Lyubomir Andreychin,
Bulgarian Academy of Sciences, Sofia, Bulgaria
[5] Institute of Computer Science of the Polish Academy of Sciences, Warsaw, Poland
[6] Faculty of Mathematics, University of Belgrade, Belgrade, Serbia

Abstract. In this paper the first preliminary results of the analysis
of marks collected within the tables of META-NET series of Language
White Papers of CESAR project languages are demonstrated. Although
they are preliminary results, we can consider them useful for showing us
where real gaps in language resources and tools can be detected.

1 Introduction

This paper presents the first preliminary analysis of marks collected within the
META-NET series of the Language White Papers (LWP) concerning the languages involved in the CESAR project [1]. The CESAR project is part of the
META-NET Network of Excellence and its purpose is to provide the necessary input regarding the language resources and language tools and/or services
for languages included in the project, namely, Bulgarian, Croatian, Hungarian,
Polish, Serbian and Slovak. Instead of producing another "vertical" survey of
existing language resources and tools for each language separately, we wanted
to turn our viewpoint into a "horizontal" direction that would give us the view
on the situation within each category for all CESAR languages, thus pointing us to the area in which the project has to put more effort. The paper is
organised as follows: in the Sect. 2 we discuss the data source, in Sect. 3 the
results for languages resources are given and discussed, in Sect. 4 we present
the results for language tools and discuss them, while the Sect. 5 gives the
conclusion.

© Springer International Publishing Switzerland 2014
Z. Vetulani and J. Mariani (Eds.): LTC 2011, LNAI 8387, pp. 471–478, 2014.
DOI: 10.1007/978-3-319-08958-4_38

2   Collecting Data

The first source of data for our analysis are the tables for individual languages produced by the subjective marks given for each of predefined categories. Within the META-NET campaign for producing Language White Papers for 30 European languages in Spring 2011, a collection of marks given by selected national experts from the LRT field was prepared in the form of tables. One can argue that this procedure is highly dependent on the subjectivity of persons giving the marks, as well as on the availability and reliability of the information for different resources, but the META-NET collecting procedure requested that marks should be given by several experts and then averaged. We can not investigate whether this procedure was respected completely - this was left to the national representatives within the CESAR project and META-NET as a whole to check - so we have taken over the collected marks and did the analysis for the CESAR languages. Also, a list of categories could be speculated upon, but at this moment we have accepted them as they are and we shall see whether this list will be submitted to any reshaping.[1] We have taken the marks from the tables of first, unpublished versions of the respective Language White Papers [2–7] and processed them in a manner that for each given LRT category we calculated an average of all marks.[2]

All averages were then mapped to a single space where marks for each category were joined with the language identifier. The same procedure was applied for another type of calculation that included the overall sum of all marks in an individual category instead of their average. As comparison of data produced by these two methods yielded no significant differences between the general shape of results in these two calculations, we selected only one of them - the average of marks. In the rest of the paper all marks regarding individual languages are averaged in the way described above. Having marks spread in this way we could immediately spot the categories in which most of the CESAR languages had very low marks.

3   Results for Language Resources

The results for language resources were produced separately from the language tools/technologies/applications not just because they describe different phenomena or because they have been represented by two different tables in Language White Papers, but also because in this way comparison of results between these

---

[1] In the final version of all META-NET Language White Papers, the overall methodology of collecting and merging marks was changed. It was decided that the peer-evaluation of the original fine-grained categories would not be practical and feasible to carry out at the META-NET community level. Therefore the categories were merged and the further process of evaluation and the final decisions at the META-NET meeting in Berlin in 2011 were based on the summary categories.

[2] Each LRT category was originally marked (on a scale of 0 to 6) for quantity, availability, quality, coverage, maturity, sustainability and adaptability. See the respective tables in Sect. 4.6 of the individual LWP volumes.

Table 1. Average marks for CESAR language resources

	Bulgarian	Croatian	Hungarian	Polish	Serbian	Slovak	average
1. Reference Corpora	4.71	3.29	5.71	3.71	3.43	3.86	4.12
2. Syntax-Corpora (treebanks, dependency banks)	2.14	2.00	4.86	2.86	0.00	2.43	2.38
3. Semantics-Corpora	3.43	0.00	4.14	1.86	0.00	0.00	1.57
4. Discourse-Corpora	1.43	0.00	0.00	1.14	0.00	1.86	0.74
5. Parallel Corpora, Translation Memories	2.43	2.43	5.71	3.86	2.57	2.29	3.21
6. Speech-Corpora (raw speech data, labelled/annotated speech data speech dialogue data)	2.29	3.00	2.57	1.86	2.86	2.86	2.57
7. Multimedia and multimodal data (text data combined with audio/video)	1.00	2.57	0.57	0.71	1.57	2.14	1.43
8. Language Models	1.57	0.00	4.71	1.29	2.29	2.71	2.10
9. Lexicons, Terminologies	3.57	3.29	4.00	3.29	3.14	3.14	3.40
10. Grammars	2.57	0.00	4.29	2.86	0.71	2.00	2.07
11. Thesauri, WordNets	4.00	2.71	3.43	3.71	3.00	2.86	3.29
12. Ontological Resources for World Knowledge (e.g. upper models, Linked Data)	2.00	0.00	2.43	1.86	0.71	0.00	1.17

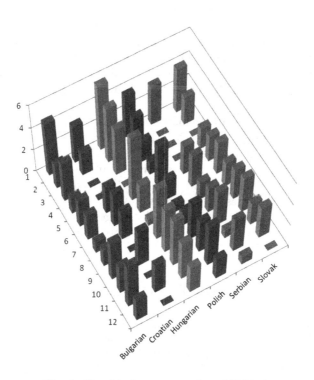

Fig. 1. Graphical representation of Table 1

two types of LT products can be performed. The results for language resources can be seen at Table 1 and Fig. 1. The numbers of categories from the Table 1 are equal to the numbers on the left side of the graphical representation of the table in Fig 1.

From the Table 1 and also from Fig 1 it is clearly observable which category of LR are deficient. The lowest overall average (0.74) is in Category 4 Discourse Corpora, but also below average mark 2.00 are Category 3 Semantics-Corpora (1.57), Category 7 Multimedia and multimodal data (1.43) and Category 12 Ontological Resources for World Knowledge (1.17).

What is worth noting is the fact that in half of the categories at least one language has mark 0.00 and there are two categories where three languages have mark 0.00: Category 3 Semantics-Corpora and Category 4 Discourse-Corpora.

Also, a considerable discrepancy between individual languages can be noticed in certain categories, e.g. in Category 3 Semantics-Corpora Bulgarian, Hungarian and Polish have 3.43, 4.14, and 1.86 respectively while Croatian, Serbian and Slovak have 0.00.

If we look at the contents of these categories then some very low marks (e.g. Categories 3 and 4) are explainable by the status of under-resourced languages as more languages exhibit 0.00 there. The opposite case, when only one language had mark 0.00 (e.g. Serbian in Category 2 Syntax Corpora, or Croatian in Category 8 Language Models), can be interpreted as significant deficiency in this type of resource for this particular language. The reasons for this deficiency could be different, starting from researchers' preferences in research priorities, up to insufficient national funding for these resources. However, it is a very good indicator that this type of resources should be developed in the near future for a particular language. Such figures could be helpful in argumentation for future funding applications.

Consistent results over all languages are visible in Categories 1 Reference corpora, 5 Parallel corpora, 6 Speech corpora, 9 Lexicon, Terminologies, and 11 Thesauri, WordNets. This leads to the conclusion that for these types of resources there are good representatives in respective languages and that they reached certain level of maturity. One could argue that this result is to be expected since these are basic language resources and usually development of LT for a certain language starts with them. Also, in some languages the LR&T community goes back to several decades and in spite of usually poor funding from industry, they managed to build basic resources funded from other directions.

4   Results for Language Tools

The results for language tools were produced separately from the language resources following the same procedure of averaging. The results are given in Table 2 and Fig. 2. The numbers of categories from the Table 2 are equal to the numbers on the left side of the graphical representation of the table in Fig. 2.

The top view over the Table 2 and Fig. 2 can lead us to the general observation that the number of lower grades is higher in the case of language tools compared

Table 2. Average marks for CESAR language technology (Tools, Technologies, Applications)

	Bulgarian	Croatian	Hungarian	Polish	Serbian	Slovak	average
1. Tokenization, Morphology (tokenization, POS tagging, morphological analysis/generation)	4.00	3.57	4.00	4.57	4.29	3.00	3.90
2. Parsing (shallow or deep syntactic analysis)	3.00	1.57	3.57	3.57	2.43	0.00	2.36
3. Sentence Semantics (WSD, argument structur, semantic roles)	2.43	1.14	1.57	2.14	0.00	0.00	1.21
4. Text Semantics (coreference resolution, context, pragmatics inference)	1.43	0.00	1.29	1.00	0.00	0.00	0.62
5. Advanced Discourse Processing (text structure, coherence, rhetorical structure/RST, argumentative zoning, argumentation, text patterns, text types etc.)	0.00	0.00	0.00	0.57	0.00	0.00	0.10
6. Information Retrieval (text indexing, multimedia IR, crosslingual IR)	2.00	2.29	0.86	3.29	2.43	2.29	2.19
7. Information Extraction (named entity recognition, event/relation extraction, opinion/sentiment recognition, text mining/analytics)	2.29	2.43	5.57	2.57	2.14	1.71	2.79
8. Language Generation (sentence generation, report generation, text generation)	1.43	1.29	0.00	1.14	0.00	0.00	0.64
9. Summarization, Question Answering, advanced Information Access Technologies	1.86	0.29	0.00	1.29	0.71	1.71	0.98
10. Machine Translation	2.29	0.71	4.86	3.29	0.71	1.86	2.29
11. Speech Recognition	2.00	2.57	2.71	2.71	1.14	2.29	2.24
12. Speech Synthesis	2.00	3.57	3.71	4.14	3.29	3.00	3.29
13. Dialogue Management (dialogue capabilities and user modelling)	0.00	1.29	0.00	1.00	0.00	0.00	0.38

to language resources for CESAR languages. It is particularly noticeable by the number of marks 0.00, where there are 17 cells (21.79 %) with that mark for language tools, while in language resources there were only 11 cells (15.28 %).

For particular categories the lowest overall average (0.1) is in Category 5 Advanced Discourse Processing, but also below average mark 1.00 are Category 4 Text Semantics (0.62), Category 8 Language Generation (0.64), Category 9 Summarization. Question Answering, advanced Information Access Technologies (0.98) and Category 13 Dialogue Management (0.38). These numbers tell us that 38.46 % of all categories have mark below 1.00 on the scale from 0 to 6 and this is very low.

Also in seven categories (53.85 %) at least one language has mark 0.00 and there are categories where four or five languages have mark 0.000.

A considerable discrepancy between individual languages can be noticed only in the Category 2 Parsing where Slovak has 0.00, while all other languages have above 1.50, with the average of 2.36 for the whole category. In other cases there are marks zero for more than one language or the overall average mark is below 1.00. This means that more languages have low marks for many language tools

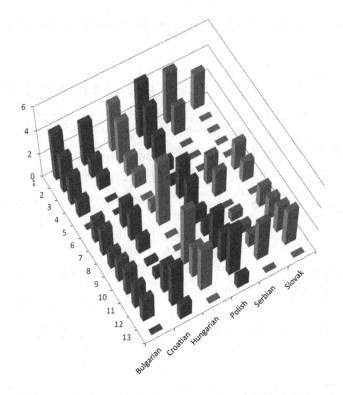

Fig. 2. Graphical representation of Table 2

and this clearly defines the under-resourced status of CESAR languages regarding the necessary language tools.

Consistent results over all languages are visible only in Categories 1 Tokenization. Morphology, 7 Information Extraction, and 12 Speech synthesis. Knowing that most of the languages in the CESAR project do have rather complex inflectional and derivational morphology (e.g. noun inflection complexity starts from Bulgarian where there are no cases, just singular and plural wordforms, to other Slavic CESAR languages, having, usually seven cases in singular and plural, up to the extremely complex Hungarian with about twenty cases in both numbers), it is no surprise that the majority of efforts of development of LT were concentrated previously in Category 1. Also, Category 7 Information Extraction is the next expected field where the fundamental findings from Category 1 can find their application, particularly with the NERC systems that could more easily find their market niche than other types of tools. Speech synthesis is also expected in this bunch since it is easier to start with synthesis than speech analysis and thus it is the usual direction of development in speech processing for a given language.

Like in the case of language resources, the detected gaps are very good indicators that this type of tools/services should be developed in the near future for a particular language. The above findings could be used as very strong arguments in requests for additional funding at the national level.

5   Conclusion and Future Directions

We have just presented the first preliminary results of the analysis of marks collected within the tables of META-NET series of Language White Papers for the languages of the CESAR project. Although they are preliminary results, we can consider them useful for showing us where real gaps in language resources and tools can be detected. Since we were aware that the CESAR languages are under-resourced compared to e.g. English or German, we were prepared for some low grades, but some categories had marks below any expectation.

The standard preprocessing steps (tokenization, morphology, shallow parsing etc.) are more-or-less completed, but the more difficult semantics and discourse analysis need further research. The higher the linguistic processing level the lower the scores are, as can be seen in the first five rows of Table 2 (Tokenization. Morphology: 3.91, Parsing: 2.36, Sentence Semantics: 1.21, Text Semantics: 0.62, Advanced Discourse Processing: 0.10). This is justified by the fact that syntax and semantics are more difficult to process than morphology. The more semantics a tool takes into account, the more difficult it is to find the right data and more efforts for supporting deep processing are needed. Semantic tools and resources are scored very low. Thus, programs and initiatives are needed to substantially boost this area both with regard to basic research and the development of annotated corpora.

One of the future directions could involve studying the discrepancy between the existing tool and the non-existing resource for a combined set of categories that depend on each other, e.g., in language resources Category 2 Syntax corpora and in language tools Category 2 Parsing.

Since this first analysis was not done using any elaborated statistical instruments, but simply by comparison of averages of marks, it might happen that the results obtained by a proper statistical treatment (median, standard deviation, hypothesis testing, etc.) will be somewhat different, at least the possible bias in giving marks for certain categories and/or languages could be avoided.

Also, a set of categories can be statistically verified for their significance and this may lead to joining or disjoining of some categories making the grid for marking more dense or coarse.

It should be noted that, for reasons mentioned in Sect. 2, the categories in the tables presented here and the categories in the tables in the final version of Language White Papers are not mutually comparable. However, we have shown that the more dense grid presented here allowed the precise detection of the weak spots in the development of LRT for each of CESAR languages.

References

1. Váradi, T.: Veni, Vidi, Vici: the language technology infrastructure landscape after CESAR. In: Gajdošová, K., Žáková, A. (eds.) Natural Language Processing, Corpus Linguistics, E-Learning, Bratislava, pp. 261–278. RAM-Verlag (2013)
2. Blagoeva, D., Koeva, S., Murdarov, V.: Българският език в дигиталната епоха_ The Bulgarian Language in the Digital Age. META-NET White Paper Series. Springer (2012). http://www.meta-net.eu/whitepapers, Rehm, G., Uszkoreit, H. (Series eds.)
3. Tadić, M., Brozović-Rončević, D., Kapetanović, A.: Hrvatski Jezik u Digitalnom Dobu - The Croatian Language in the Digital Age. META-NET White Paper Series. Springer (2012), http://www.meta-net.eu/whitepapers, Rehm, G., Uszkoreit, H. (Series eds.)
4. Simon, E., Lendvai, P., Németh, G., Olaszy, G., Vicsi, K.: A magyar nyelv a digitális korban - The Hungarian Language in the Digital Age. META-NET White Paper Series. Springer (2012). http://www.meta-net.eu/whitepapers, Rehm, G., Uszkoreit, H. (Series eds.)
5. Miłkowski, M.: Język polski w erze cyfrowej - The Polish Language in the Digital Age. META-NET White Paper Series. Springer (2012). http://www.meta-net.eu/whitepapers, Rehm, G., Uszkoreit, H. (Series eds.)
6. Vitas, D., Popović, L., Krstev, C., Obradović, I., Pavlović-Lažetić, G., Stanojević, M.: Српски језик у дигиталном добу_ The Serbian Language in the Digital Age. META-NET White Paper Series. Springer (2012). http://www.meta-net.eu/whitepapers, Rehm, G., Uszkoreit, H. (Series eds.)
7. Šimková, M., Garabík, R., Gajdošová, K., Laclavík, M., Ondrejović, S., Juhár, J., Genči, J., Furdík, K., Ivoríková, H., Ivanecký, J.: Slovenský jazyk v digitálnom veku - The Slovak Language in the Digital Age. META-NET White Paper Series. Springer (2012). http://www.meta-net.eu/whitepapers, Rehm, G., Uszkoreit, H. (Series eds.)

A First LVCSR System for Luxembourgish, a Low-Resourced European Language

Martine Adda-Decker[1,2], Lori Lamel[2], Gilles Adda[2(✉)],
and Thomas Lavergne[3]

[1] Laboratory of Phonetics and Phonology,
CNRS-Paris 3/Sorbonne Nouvelle, Paris, France
[2] Spoken Language Processing Group LIMSI-CNRS, Orsay, France
[3] ILES Group LIMSI-CNRS, Orsay, France
martine.adda-decker@univ-paris3.fr,
{lori.lamel,gilles.adda,thomas.lavergne}@limsi.fr

Abstract. Luxembourgish is embedded in a multilingual context on
the divide between Romance and Germanic cultures and remains one
of Europe's low-resourced languages. We describe our efforts in building
a large vocabulary ASR system for such a "minority" language without
resorting to any prior transcribed audio training data. Instead, acoustic
models are derived from major European languages. Furthermore, most
Luxembourgish written sources include significant parts in other languages. This poses specific challenges to Language Model estimation.
Some scientific and technological issues addressed include: (i) how to
build acoustic models if no labeled acoustic training data are available
for the under-resourced target language? (ii) how to make use of the
new system to accelerate resource production for the target language?
(iii) how to build a vocabulary and a language model with multilingual
written texts? (iv) how to determine the "best" phonemic inventory for
ASR? First ASR results illustrate the accuracy of the various sets of
monolingual and multilingual acoustic models and what these suggest
concerning language typology issues.

Keywords: Forced alignment · Acoustic modeling · Multilingual models · Luxembourgish · Germanic languages · Romance languages

1 Introduction

Luxembourg, a small country of less than 500,000 inhabitants in the center of
Western Europe, is composed of about 65 % of native inhabitants and 35 % of
immigrants. The national language, Luxembourgish ("Lëtzebuergesch"), has only
been considered as an official language since 1984 and is spoken by natives [1].
The population (both natives or residents) generally speak one of Luxembourg's
other official languages: French or German. Recently, English has joined the set
of languages of communication, mainly in professional environments.

© Springer International Publishing Switzerland 2014
Z. Vetulani and J. Mariani (Eds.): LTC 2011, LNAI 8387, pp. 479–490, 2014.
DOI: 10.1007/978-3-319-08958-4_39

As pointed out by [2,3], Luxembourgish should be considered as a partially under-resourced language, due to the fact that the written production remains relatively low, and linguistic knowledge and resources, such as lexica and pronunciation dictionaries, are sparse. Written Luxembourgish is not systematically taught to children in primary school: German is usually the first written language learnt, followed by French.

This paper presents the development of a first Luxembourgish large vocabulary continuous speech recognition (LVCSR) system. To the best of our knowledge, there has never been an LVCSR system for this European language. Efforts were put on gathering all required resources and developing missing blocks: written data for word list and language model development, orthographically transcribed speech data to serve as a reference for system evaluation, a phonemic inventory and a pronunciation dictionary for acoustic phone and word models. The proposed system makes use of acoustic models stemming from different major European languages, without making use of Luxembourgish language specific acoustic training data. The written data gathered for this first system is very limited; we present a new approach to build word lists and language models from multilingual heterogeneous written sources. This first system will serve as a baseline for further improvements, and will allow us to address some technical linguistical questions. (i) how to build acoustic models if no labeled acoustic training data are available for the under-resourced target language? If multiple monolingual acoustic models from different languages are available for transcribing Luxembourgish audio data, is there a clear preference for one of these languages? (ii) how to make use of the new system to accelerate resource production for the target language? (iii) how to build a vocabulary and a language model with multilingual written texts? These issues may have important implications for acoustic model development for other under-resourced languages.

The next section introduces the phonemic inventory of Luxembourgish and its correspondence with one of the three languages (German, French, and English) used as source languages for acoustic model seeds. Written and spoken corpora are introduced in Sect. 3. Section 4 presents the development of acoustic models as well as of Luxembourgish language models. Results are given in Sect. 5 for different sets of acoustic models using either one single or several source languages. Section 6 presents an automatic language identification system to filter Luxembourgish texts from heterogeneous multilingual texts from the web, in order to build improved pronunciation dictionaries and language models. Finally, Sect. 7 provides a summary of the results and discusses some future challenges for speech technology and linguistic studies of Luxembourgish.

2   Phonemic Inventory of Luxembourgish

The phonemic inventory plays a crucial role at the interface of pronunciations and acoustic-phonetic modeling. The phonemic symbols are the basic units to express pronunciation details in the dictionary. The phonemic units also determine the acoustic modeling units. The acoustic unit represented by phonemic symbol will

Table 1. Sample cross-lingual phoneme associations: Lux. target phonemes associated to identical or similar (in grey) symbols in 3 source languages (Fre, Ger, Eng).

Carrier word (Eng)	Lux	Fre	Ger	Eng
ORAL VOWELS				
liicht (light)	i	i	i	i
schützen (shelter)	Y	y	Y	I
fäeg (able)	ɛ:	ɛ	ɛ:	ɛ
DIPHTHONGS				
léien (to tell lies)	eɪ̯	e	e	e
lounen (to hire)	ɔʊ̯	o	o	o

Table 2. "Lëtzebuergesch" text sources (in number of words) for training and development of word lists and language models estimation.

Source	CHAMBER www.chd.lu 2002–2008		RTL www.rtl.lu 2007–2008	
	train	dev	train	dev
Volume	10.10 M	104 k	0.67 M	14 k

be modeled by a set of 3-state HMMs, thus entailing a minimum duration per symbol. The adopted Luxembourgish phonemic inventory includes a total of 60 phonemic symbols including 3 extra-phonemic symbols (for silence, breath and hesitations). Table 1 presents a selection of the phonemic inventory together with illustrating examples (see [4] for more information on the phonemic inventory of Luxembourgish). Luxembourgish is characterized by a particularly high number of diphthongs. To minimize the phonemic inventory size, we could have chosen to code diphthongs using two consecutive symbols, one for the nucleus and one for the off-glide (e.g. the sequence /a/ and /j/ for diphthong aɪ). For acoustic-phonetic reasons however, we preferred the option of coding diphthongs and affricates using specific unique symbols. Given the importance of French imports, nasal vowels were included in the inventory, although they are not required for typical Luxembourgish words. Furthermore, native Luxembourgish makes use of a relatively complex set of voiced/unvoiced fricatives.

3   Text and Speech Corpora

Text sources consist in the CHAMBER (House of Parliament) debate reports and to some extend in news channels, such as delivered by the Luxembourgish radio and television broadcast company RTL. These texts have been filtered according to the criterion described in [2] in order eliminate sentences which are not in Luxembourgish, because of a frequent switch to French especially in the Chamber debates). Table 2 gives a summary of the different training and development texts

Table 3. Phoneme and training volume information for native and pseudo-Lux. acoustic models in English, French, German.

Language	#native phon.	#train. #(h)	#Lux. phon.
English	48	150	60
French	37	150	60
German	49	40	60
Superset(E,F,G)	-	340	3×60

used for the study (note that the text used for the development of the word list and language models is different from the set used for the ASR experiments).

Beyond large amounts of not yet transcribed audio data, we have 80 min of manually transcribed speech from the CHAMBER debates (70') and from news (10') broadcast by RTL [2]. The manual transcripts include all audible speech events, including disfluencies and speech errors.

4 Acoustic and Language Models

4.1 Acoustic Models

The need to develop acoustic seed models for low-resourced languages has already been addressed in previous research [5]. In the current study, three sets of context-independent acoustic models were built, from each of the well-resourced seed languages (i.e., English, French, German). These models were trained on manually transcribed audio data (between 40 and 150 h) from a variety of speech material, using language-specific phone sets. The amount of data used to train the native acoustic models and the number of phonemes per language are given in Table 3 (left). Each phone model is a tied-state left-to-right, 3-state CDHMM with Gaussian mixture observation densities (typically containing 64 components). Figure 1 (left) illustrates the development of three sets of pseudo-Luxembourgish acoustic models, for a 60 phonemes inventory, starting from the English, French and German seed models and mapping the Luxembourgish phonemes to a close equivalent in each of the source model sets (IPA(i,n) in Fig. 1). Table 1 shows a sample of the adopted cross-lingual associations that were used to initialize seed models for Luxembourgish. Some symbols of the source language are used several times for different Luxembourgish target phonemes. For the diphthongs that are missing in French, phonemes corresponding to the nucleus vowel were chosen. A fourth model set (called super-set) was then formed by concatenating the first three model sets, allowing the decoder to choose among the three languages (see Table 3). Finally a set of multilingual acoustic models were trained (see Fig. 1, right part) using the pooled English, French and German audio data that were labeled using their respective IPA(i,n) correspondences.

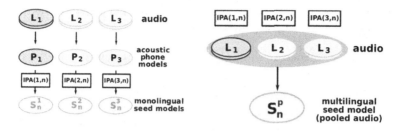

Fig. 1. Acoustic seed models for a target language n (Luxembg.) given audio corpora of source language L_i ($i = 1, 2, 3$: English, French, German) phone models P_i and IPA symbol correspondences between language i and n IPA(i,n). Left: monolingual S_n^i models. Right: pooled multilingual S_n^p model.

As a perspective, we plan to use the huge amount of non transcribed Luxembourgish speech data (over 1000 h) to develop low supervised Luxembourgish acoustic models using these seed models and Luxembourgish language models.

4.2 Word List and Language Models

Given the relatively low amount of available written data, we decided to limit our word list size to 65 k entries, although a larger vocabulary would certainly be more appropriate for a poorly normalizing and generously word-compounding language such as Luxembourgish.

A 65 word list was defined from the two training source texts so as to minimize the OOV (out of vocabulary) rate on the CHAMBER dev text according to the method described in [6]. To this end, two unigram language models were first estimated using the CHAMBER and RTL training data respectively. Using the CHAMBER development text, the LM perplexity was then minimized by optimizing the interpolation between the two unigram LMs. As a result, the 65 k most probable words according to the optimal interpolated unigram LM are kept for the final word list. The OOV rate of this 65 k word list is 2.4 % on the CHAMBER dev text, and 6.4 % on the RTL dev text (see Table 4).

A similar LM interpolation procedure is used to establish the 2, 3 and 4-grams language models. For each order, a back-off LM was built using modified Kneser-Ney smoothing [7,8], for both CHAMBER and RTL text source, and linearly interpolate them so as to minimize the perplexity on the CHAMBER dev text. Figures describing the LMs are summarized in Table 4.

We can see from the figures in Table 4, that the RTL source is poorly modeled by both the word list and the LMs, with OOV rate and perplexities being three times higher than the ones obtained on the CHAMBER data. Due to the differences in training volumes (15 times more words in CHAMBER than in RTL), an optimization on the RTL text gives no improvement on OOV rates and only a slight improvement on perplexity (355 instead of 406 for a 3-g). Beyond the limited volume of RTL texts, these data also include more writing variants which entail poorer lexical coverage and contribute to higher LM perplexities.

Table 4. OOV rates of the 65 k word list and 2, 3, 4-grams LM perplexities as measured on the CHAMBER and RTL development texts.

Source	CHAMBER dev	RTL dev
OOV (%)	2.4	6.4
2-gram (pp)	162.4	460.3
3-gram (pp)	117.0	406.8
4-gram (pp)	110.7	400.3

Table 5. Sample pronunciation dictionary.

LEXICAL ENTRY	PRONUNCIATION
huet (has)	huət
lafen (to run)	lafən
héieren (to hear)	heɪərən
dausend (thousand)	dɛwzənt

We describe in Sect. 6 an improvement of word list and language models by the use of larger noisy texts, filtered using an automatic language identification system.

4.3   Pronunciation Dictionary

A grapheme-to-phoneme tool has been developed as a PERL script and pronunciation dictionaries have been produced [2]. Table 5 shows a small excerpt of the pronunciation dictionary. Pronunciation development is complex as Luxembourgish spelling rules are permissive and words from different origins follow different pronunciation rules.

Spelling. Lëtzebuergesch spelling standards aim at minimizing pronunciation ambiguities which is in favor of easy pronunciation rules. However, depending on a Germanic or Romance origin, a given writing may result in different pronunciation. Concerning Romance or Germanic origins of "Lëtzebuergesch" lexical entries, writing standards may stay more or less close to the language of origin. As an example, qu letter sequence of Germanic items such as quälen, quëtschen, Quetschen calls for a /kw/ pronunciation, whereas French rules generally advocate a simple /k/ pronunciation (enquêtéieren, Qualitéit, Parquet).

Multilingual Entries. Lexical entries can be shared by multiple languages as far as they rely on similar alphabets. For short words, combinatorics are reduced and hence many forms can be shared without any etymological link: ville means "city" /vɪl/ in French, and "many" /fɪlə/ in Luxembourgish, net means "clear, tidy" /nɛt/ in French, and stands for the negation "not" /nœt/ in Luxembourgish. Among the longer words, shared entries generally imply shared origins and semantics. Here one typically finds French or German imports and proper names Stagiaire, Quartier, Porto, Dubrovnik, Notre-Dame....

Pronunciation Variants. Variants concerning the "Lëtzebuergesch" specific phonological process of mobile-n deletion [3] have been introduced and studied [9]. French imports may be pronounced according to French standards, or adapted to Luxembourgish, potentially entailing various spellings. Typically the nasal vowel /ã/ changes to /aŋ/, (**Jean**, /ʒã/ becomes **Jang** /ʒaŋ/) and for /õ/ the vowel may become diphthongized with a nasal coda as /ɔun/ in -tion words, such as **Abstention, Abstraction, Fonction, Situation**.... A large amount of such imports can be found both in the CHAMBER and in the RTL corpora. Not only the spelling of the vowel can be adapted, but also the French c-letter may be changed to the German k- or z-counterparts **Abstention, Abstentioun; Abstraction, Abstractioun, Abstraktioun; Akzeptabel** (acceptable).

German imports may be pronounced according to German standards, or adapted to Luxembourgish. Spelling and pronunciation variation here corresponds to items including -ung, which may be written and pronounced either with "u" or with "o" (**Stëmmung, Stëmmong** (eng. mood); **Meenung, Meenong** (eng. opinion)).

Similar to German, the Luxembourgish language is very creative with respect to produce compounds, especially noun-noun compounds. Compounding items merging different origins, such as **Beispillfonctioun, Bensinsstatiounen, Wunnengsagglomeratiounen**, are commonly observed in the collected corpora.

5 Results

First recognition experiments were run on our set of manually transcribed data (70 min from CHAMBER and 10 min from RTL). Different sets of acoustic models stemming from one single source (En, Fr, Ge) or from pooled audio data were used. Results are reported in Table 6 in terms of %correct, %substituted, %deleted and %inserted words. The last column gives the word error rate (which includes substitution, deletion and insertion errors). ASR output words which achieved low acoustic likelihood scores were rejected, resulting in relatively high deletion rates (24.2–30.4 %). These rates give an indication of the match/mismatch between the test data and the system's speech models.

We can see that the best results are achieved for the acoustic models stemming from the German audio. German ranks best (54.5 % WER, 256 Gaussians) before the pooled models (56.6 %). English (62.6 %) and French (71.5 %) produce significantly higher error rates. It is interesting to note that French acoustic models give the lowest performance although the Luxembourgish-French language contact is rather high in both the Luxembourgish vocabulary and in people's every day life practice.

6 Automatic Language Identification for Heterogeneous Multilingual Text Filtering

In the previous sections, the textual data used to build the lexicon and language model have been filtered through a rule-based process. This process and the

Table 6. Recognition results using context-independent (CI) acoustic phone models from German, English, French and Pooled speech data (labeled using the Luxembourgish phonemes) on both Chamber and RTL evaluation datasets. Two sets of models include respectively 64 and 256 Gaussians per state.

CI models		ASR RESULTS (%)				
source	#Gaussians	correct	substitution	deletion	insertion	WER
German	64	46.3	29.5	24.2	2.1	55.8
English	64	37.0	32.5	30.4	1.7	64.6
French	64	28.0	34.7	37.3	1.2	73.2
Pooled	64	44.6	27.5	28.0	1.3	56.8
German	256	47.4	28.0	24.7	1.8	**54.5**
English	256	39.1	30.5	30.4	1.7	62.6
French	256	29.8	32.6	37.6	1.2	71.5
Pooled	256	45.0	26.6	28.4	1.6	56.6

Fig. 2. A typical multilingual web page from a Luxembourgish news magazine. Source: weekly issue **woxx** http://www.woxx.lu/

corresponding results are described in details in [2]. This process is language and source dependent, and becomes less efficient in case of heterogeneous multilingual texts such as the ones typically harvested we find on the web (see for instance Fig. 2 a typical web page from a news magazine). We saw in Sect. 4.2 that the lexicon and the language model present a performance drop on RTL data, while, which could be recovered using data available on the web. To solve this problem, we decided to use a stochastic language identification system to efficiently filter Luxembourgish from German, French and English languages [13].

6.1 Melis: Language Detection with Discriminative Models

An automatic language identification module based on a log-linear maximum entropy approach [11] has been used to decide of the language identity on a

Table 7. (left) language identification errors as a function of training size (in sentences) and number of languages to identify; (right) detection of one language (with 100 % precision) among the other languages.

#train	Fre,Eng	+Ger	+Spa	+Cze
10k	3.3‰	7.5‰	21.1‰	21.2‰
50k	0.8‰	2.4‰	9.8‰	9.8‰
100k	0.3‰	1.6‰	3.7‰	4.2‰

	Fre	Eng	Ger	Spa	Cze
recall	0.3‰	0.5‰	0.1‰	0.3‰	0.0‰

sentence by sentence basis. As an example, a plurilingual sentence such as `Dat hu mier par main levée ofgestëmmt` (This has been voted by a show of hands) – a typical sentence in Luxembourgish Chamber debates – may be identified as Luxembourgish or rejected as French.

The formulation of the problem can be expressed as follows:

$$p(l \mid x) = \frac{\exp\left(\sum_k \theta_k f_k(x, l)\right)}{Z_\theta(x)}$$

where, l is the language identity, x is the written segment (here a sentence), f_k are the features describing the input x, and θ_k the weights. This model is simple and efficient to train, and we can use various interdependent features. The features used in the present experiments are limited to simple n-grams of characters (sequences of n chars), with $n \in [1, 4]$. In the future, we plan to add some lexical features as well as some context information. The system was evaluated on a multilingual corpus of news texts, with 5 different languages (French, English, German, Spanish and Czech). The results (expressed in ‰) summarized in Table 7, exhibit excellent identification and detection results.

The impact of training data size is illustrated by varying the training volume from 10 k to 100 k sentences. In the most difficult case with 5 different languages (Table 7 (left) last column on the right) identification errors rates drop from 2.12 % to 0.42 %.

6.2   Filtering Heterogeneous Multilingual Data

Besides the sources described in Sect. 3, other data including Luxembourgish texts, have been collected from the web. The texts belong to 3 domains:

1. **'New/information' related written sources**:
   - RTL2008: old RTL data (2008 and earlier) manually filtered.
   - RTL2012: Web sites affiliated to RTL (collected in 2012).
   - WIKIPEDIA: Luxembourgish Wikipedia.
   - MISC: miscellaneous reports, books, reviews . . . collected on the web.
2. **Oral transcriptions**:
   - CHAMBER: *bona fide* transcriptions [12] of the Luxembourgish Parliament debates.

Table 8. Text sizes (in thousands of words). (left) Raw texts per data source (7 sources, totaling 51Mwords) (right) Luxembourgish labeled text sizes and percentages of rejected texts.

source	type	size
RTL2008	written	611
RTL2012	written	10,307
WIKIPEDIA	written	3603
MISC	written	1677
CHAMBER	transcript	22,110
BLOGS	social	10,243
BLOGS_COMMENTS	social	3106
total		51,657

source	type	size	% filtered
RTL2008	written	607	<1
WIKIPEDIA	written	3483	3
RTL2012	written	7948	23
BLOGS_COMMENTS	social	2386	23
CHAMBER	transcript	16,108	27
MISC	written	855	49
BLOGS	social	3265	68
total		34,653	33

3. **Social media:**
 - BLOGS: 90 blogs (out of 400 preselected Luxembourgish blogs).
 - BLOGS_COMMENT: user comments from the selected blogs.

The volume of raw texts and of filtered texts are summarized in Table 8. The amount of rejected data (average 33 %) strongly depends on the source as expected: for WIKIPEDIA only 3 % of the data were rejected[1], while 68 % of the Luxembourgish BLOGS were not written in Luxembourgish, according to the automatic identification system, even though only the blogs (90 out of 400) with a significant part of written Luxembourgish were kept. 27 % of the CHAMBER texts have been rejected: beyond transcripts in French language due to occasional switches to French language in oral debates, this rather high rejection rate is due to the presence of reports written in French. After filtering, the amount of Luxembourgish-labeled data sums to above 34 Mwords, with an average rejection rate of 33 % of the raw texts.

6.3   Effect of Filtering on Word List and Language Model

Raw and filtered texts were used to build and compare word lists and language models, using the methods described in [2] and in Sect. 4.2. The 200 k most probable words were selected from the 7 Web data sources, so as to minimize the perplexity of unigrams (see Sect. 4.2 for more details). An OOV (Out of Vocabulary) rate of 2.35 % was achieved with the filtered sources, to be compared to an OOV rate of 3.23 % with the raw texts (28 % of relative improvement). With respect to the language model, the best interpolated 3-gram model exhibits a perplexity of 369.35 with the filtered sources (387.20 without filtering, +5 %). Due to filtering, the OOV rate exhibits a large improvement, while the gains remain limited on language models; this is generally observed when the amount of texts is insufficient: filtering improves the precision of the word list, however

---

[1] some residual non-Luxembourgish languages such as ancient Greek was rejected because of its special coding alphabet.

the negative impact on perplexity of filtering out few correct Luxembourgish n-grams counterbalance the positive impact of improving the precision. We need to evaluate the real impact on the ASR Word Error Rate.

7 Summary and Prospects

The present work focused on the development of a first LVCSR recognition system in Luxembourgish. Luxembourgish language models and a 65 k pronunciation dictionary were produced. The issue of producing acoustic seed models for Luxembourgish, a language with strong Germanic and Romance influences was addressed by relying on to related languages' acoustic models. A phonemic inventory was defined for Luxembourgish and linked to inventories from major neighboring languages (German, French and English), using the IPA symbol set. For each of these languages, acoustic seed models were built using either monolingual German, French, English data or multilingual pooled audio.

Our approach to build acoustic models via IPA associations between the Luxembourgish phonemic inventory and those of other languages for which acoustic models are available gives encouraging results. The source language identity of the acoustic models reveals to have a strong influence on the system performance (17 % difference between best and worst results). The Luxembourgish speech data are best processed using the German models. English models appear to perform better than the French ones. These first ASR results are in line with earlier automatic speech alignment results, where a free choice between German, English and French acoustic models showed a clear preference for the Germanic models over the French models [10]. An improvement of the word list and language models, using 34M words of filtered web data has been presented.

The present system, although perfectible along many dimensions, is already useful for further resource development. A major bottleneck today is the lack of acoustic training data. Manual transcription can be envisioned. However, orthographic standards are only poorly applied by native speakers and manual transcriptions tend to include many writing variants and writing errors. Automatic transcription may be used first to select speech subsets which are relatively easy to transcribe. Second, a speech recognizer produces a normalized transcript, even though it may be more or less correct. An ASR system for Luxembourgish will contribute to produce new resources for this tiny European language, to enable numerous corpus-based studies of spoken and written Luxembourgish and promote Luxembourgish as an e-language. Finally the system may serve to study pronunciations and acoustic properties of the Luxembourgish sound set.

Acknowledgments. This work has been partially financed by OSEO under the QUAERO program, and supported by LABEX EFL (ANR/CGI).

References

1. Schanen, F.: Parlons Luxembourgeois. L'Harmattan, Paris (2004)
2. Adda-Decker, M., Pellegrini, T., Bilinski, E., Adda, G.: Developments of Lëtze-buergesch resources for automatic speech processing and linguistic studies. In: Proceedings of the International Language Resources and Evaluation Conference LREC (2008)
3. Krummes, C.: Sinn si or si si? mobile-n deletion in Luxembourgish. Papers in Linguistics from the University of Manchester: Proceedings of the 15th Postgraduate Conference in Linguistics, Manchester (2006)
4. Snoeren, N.D., Adda-Decker, M., Adda, G.: The study of writing variants in an under-resourced language: some evidence from mobile N-deletion in Luxembourgish. In: Proceedings of the Seventh Conference on International Language Resources and Evaluation (LREC'10), 19–21 May, Valletta, Malta (2010)
5. Schultz, T., Waibel, A.: Experiments on cross-language acoustic modeling. In: Proceedings of Eurospeech, Aalborg (2001)
6. Allauzen, A., Gauvain, J.-L.: Construction automatique du vocabulaire d'un système de transcription. Journées d'Etude sur la Parole 2004, Fès (2004)
7. Chen, S.F., Goodman, J.: An empirical study of smoothing techniques for language modeling. Technical Report TR-10-98, Center for Research in Computing Technology (Harvard University), August 1998
8. Kneser, R., Ney, H.: Improved backing-off for m-gram language modeling. In: Proceedings of the IEEE International Conference on Acoustics, Speech, and Signal Processing, vol. 1, pp. 181–184 (1995)
9. Snoeren, N.D., Adda-Decker, M.: Pronunciation and writing variants in Luxembourgish: the case of mobile N-deletion in large corpora. In: Proceedings of 4th Language&Technology Conference, 6–8 November, Poznan, Poland, pp. 119–123 (2009)
10. Adda-Decker, M., Lamel, L., Snoeren, N.D.: Studying Luxembourgish phonetics via multilingual forced alignments. In: Proceedings of the 17th International Congress of Phonetic Sciences (ICPhS XVII), 17–21 August, Hong Kong (2011)
11. Lavergne, T.: Wapiti - a simple and fast discriminative sequence labelling toolkit. http://wapiti.limsi.fr/
12. Adda-Decker, M., Barras, C., Adda, G., Paroubek, P., Boula De Mareüil, P., Habert, B.: Annotation and analysis of overlapping speech in political interviews. In: Proceedings of the International Language Resources and Evaluation Conference LREC (2008)
13. Adda-Decker, M., Adda, G., Lavergne, T.: Luxembourgish: towards a linguistic description based on large corpora and automatic speech processing. In: Proceedings of PPLC 13 'Phonetics, Phonology and Language Contact' Workshop, 21–23 August, Paris (2013)

Developing LRs for Non-scheduled Indian Languages

A Case of Magahi

Ritesh Kumar[1,2(✉)], Bornini Lahiri[1], and Deepak Alok[1]

[1] Centre for Linguistics, Jawaharlal Nehru University, New Delhi, India
{riteshkrjnu,lahiri.bornini,deepak06alok}@gmail.com
[2] Department of Linguistics, K.M.I., Dr. B.R. Ambedkar University, Agra, India

Abstract. Magahi is an Indo-Aryan Language, spoken mainly in the Eastern parts of India. Despite having a significant number of speakers, there has been virtually no language resource (LR) or language technology (LT) developed for the language, mainly because of its status as a non-scheduled language. The present paper describes an attempt to develop an annotated corpus of Magahi. The data is mainly taken from a couple of blogs in Magahi, some collection of stories in Magahi and the recordings of conversation in Magahi and it is annotated at the POS level using BIS tagset.

Keywords: LRL · Magahi · Magahi corpus · Magahi annotation · Non-scheduled languages · Annotated corpora · Language resources · ILCIANN

1 Introduction

Grierson (1903) has classified Magahi under Eastern group of Outer sub-branch of Indo-Aryan languages. Scholars like Turner have clubbed the 'Bihari' languages with Eastern and Western Hindi (Masica 1991). Chatterji (1926) has given an entirely different classification where Western Hindi is almost an isolated group while Eastern Hindi, Bihari and other languages of Eastern group are clubbed together. But the classification by Grierson (1903) is most widely accepted one. Jeffers (1976) have given a similar classification.

Magahi is spoken mainly in Eastern states of India including Bihar and Jharkhand, along with some parts of West Bengal and Orissa. The variety of Magahi spoken in and around Gaya, Jehanabad and Patna is generally considered standard.

1.1 Linguistic Features of Magahi

There have been very few linguistic studies on Magahi. However a basic (although not completely accurate) description of Magahi is given by Verma (2003). A basic description of the linguistic features is given here.

An initial analysis of the Magahi sound system shows that it has 35 phonemic sounds – 27 consonants and 8 vowels. Some of the major phonological features, which

Z. Vetulani and J. Mariani (Eds.): LTC 2011, LNAI 8387, pp. 491–501, 2014.
DOI: 10.1007/978-3-319-08958-4_40

distinguish Magahi from Hindi, include absence of word-initial consonant cluster, absence of word-initial glides and absence of word-medial and word-final dental laterals.

Like other Eastern Indo-Aryan and unlike other Indo-Aryan languages, including Hindi, it does not have number and gender agreement. It has only person and honorificity agreement with the verb (Verma 1991). It is a nominative-accusative, highly inflected language with almost free order of constituents within phrases and sentences. Both adjectives and nouns in Magahi have two basic forms, which may be loosely termed as form 1 and form 2. For example, g^hora 'horse', $sona$ 'gold', $ujar$ 'white', etc. are the form 1 while g^hor-ba, son-ma, $ujar$-ka are their respective form 2. The suffixes attached to these words may be considered some kind of affix particles with different kinds of linguistic functions such as specificity/definiteness/focus etc. (Alok 2010). Magahi also has some mensural classifiers – go/t^ho, $məni$, sun (Alok 2012). Among these while go/t^ho measures nouns in terms of length or discrete quantity, $məni$ and sun are used for measuring nouns in terms of amount (and so are used with the mass nouns) (Alok 2012). It is to be noted that broadly these are numeral classifiers since they are always attached with the numeral and quantifiers in a noun phrase and never with the noun itself. Two of the most unique features of Magahi are simultaneous agreement of verb with subject as well as direct object and also agreement of verb with the addressee, who is not mentioned in the sentence (Verma 1991, 2003).

1.2   Indian Linguistic Scenario and Socio-Political Situation of Magahi

Census of India (2001) gives the following details about the linguistic scenario of India

- A total of 6661 raw number of languages were returned by the people.
- These were processed to come at a total of 3592 rationalised mother tongues, out of which 1635 are classified Mother Tongues (MT) while 1957 are unclassified MT.
- The classified MTs are further processed to yield 234 identifiable MTs which are spoken by more than 10,000 speakers.
- Out of these 234 MTs, 93 MTs are clubbed under 22 scheduled languages while 141 are clubbed under 100 non-scheduled languages.

Constitution of India contains Eighth Schedule which has 22 major languages listed in it and are considered scheduled/official languages of the country. Along with these 100 more languages are officially considered to be spoken in India which may be termed non-scheduled languages. However this does not include the languages, which are spoken, by less than 10,000 speakers as well as several languages which are wrongly labeled as 'dialects' or 'mother tongues' under these 122 officially recognised languages. Taking all these into account the scientific community puts the estimated number of languages spoken in the country to be over 1600. However even if we go by the political estimates of 234 languages being spoken in the country, managing such a huge number of languages are quite a challenge and a nightmare for developing language technologies for them.

While it is the responsibility of the Govt. of India to provide safeguard to the Scheduled languages and develop resources and technologies for them, the rest of the languages do not enjoy such patronage. Furthermore the interest and development of these languages are further marred by their non-recognition as even languages in the non-linguistic academic circles.

Like most of these non-scheduled languages, although linguistically it is not even part of the same sub-family as Hindi (as is clear from the Grierson's classification) and they have very different grammars, politically as well as socially Magahi is labeled as a 'dialect' of Hindi (so always clubbed with Hindi in any kind of Government schemes or funding for the languages). Constitutionally also being a non-scheduled language, Magahi (along with several other languages of India) is a completely ignored language. It is not the official medium of instruction in any school and neither the language itself nor its literature studied anywhere in the formal education system. This has further resulted in the depletion of the use of language for literary and other such purposes which involve writing. However, at present, Magahi has more than a few volumes of written literature. Along with this a couple of quarterly journals are published in Magahi. Besides this some books on Magahi literature and grammar and linguistic studies on Magahi written in Hindi or English are available.

However despite this attitude of the Indian government and a comparatively scant availability of written materials, a large population (counting up to 13.978,565 according to Census of India, 2001) residing in the villages and small towns still speak and use the language as their medium of communication and information-sharing. Consequently it becomes very necessary that the language resources (LRs) and language technologies (LTs) be developed for Magahi also (separately from the dominant language, Hindi), which is expected to have an impact at two different levels – one, it may affect the overall attitude towards the language and inculcate more positive attitude towards it, two, it will open a whole new world of information and knowledge (which could be disseminated with the help of the technology) to millions of people in a language in which they are most comfortable and familiar with.

As of now very little has been done towards the development of language technology for Magahi. The only notable exception, to the best of our knowledge is the 'Magahi Verbs Project' done by Ritesh Kumar, under the supervision of Dr. Girish Nath Jha (hosted at http://sanskrit.jnu.ac.in/student_projects/magahi-search.jsp). It is a very rudimentary tool which gives the analysis of a Magahi verb form and also generates the rest of the forms of that verb.

In this paper we present the first steps in an attempt to develop a deeply annotated corpus of Magahi, which could prove to be very useful for the development of other resources like lexical databases, dictionaries, etc. and also more sophisticated language technologies for Magahi. It is also expected to serve as a model and inspiration for the development of LR and LT for other non-scheduled and smaller languages of India.

2   Compiling the Corpus

2.1   Data Sources

Considering the fact that Magahi does not have a vast collection of written literature, getting data for the corpus was a big challenge. The major part of the corpus, till now, is taken from the following sources -

- The two blogs (http://magahi-sahitya.blogspot.com/ and http://hindiloghindiprem. blogspot.com/). These are the only blogs which we could find in Magahi. So in order to have a representation of the kind of language used on the Internet, the data from these two blogs were included. Out of these two, one consists of the texts taken from different sources like collection of stories and texts on Magahi grammar, while the other one contains the original jottings of the writer.
- Some volumes of two Magahi magazines – Magadhbhumi and Alkaa Maagadhi.
- A Collection of Magahi folktales.
- Transcript of the recordings of the spontaneous conversation in Magahi. The recordings have been carried out both in private, home domain as well as in the public domain. The recordings mainly includes from the speakers of the Central Magahi variety.

As of now, altogether a corpus of around 1 million words has been prepared.

2.2   Structure of the Corpus

The corpus is divided into three subcorpora -

corpora of indirect written communication
corpora of direct written communication
corpora of spoken communication

Corpora of Indirect Written Communication

It basically includes the data taken from the literary texts and other written texts. They are not meant to communicate anything *directly* to the readers in the same way as conversation; while in conversation a reciprocal is expected and considered appropriate, in these written texts, it is generally a one-way communication with very little answer expected from the readers. This subcorpora is further divided into two subcorpora -

- Data from the Magahi magazines
- Data from Magahi books

Both of these are further divided into four different classes -

1. Data from the prosaic literary texts (includes short stories and novels)
2. Data from dramatic literary texts (includes full length plays and one-act plays)
3. Data from the poetic literary texts
4. Data from the non-fictional texts

Corpora of Direct Written Communication

It includes the data taken from the computer-mediated communication as well as in some other forms of written conversation. It is further divided into two subcorpora –

CMC Corpora
Data from Magahi used in Computer-mediated communication (CMC), which is again divided into two classes –

– Synchronous CMC
– Asynchronous CMC

Non-CMC Corpora
Non-CMC Magahi Data – It includes data chiefly from the letters and is divided into two domains -

– Personal Domain – Letters shared among family members, relatives, etc.
– Public Domain – Letters written to the newspapers, magazines, etc.

Corpora of Spoken Communication

It includes the transcripts of the recordings made in two domains -

Personal Domain
Conversation among family members in the home domain.

Public Domain
Conversation among neighbours and fellow-villagers outside the home domain.

At present the data is arranged in several excel files; each file containing data from one source (for example, one story or one blog entry, etc.). Each sentence in the corpus is given a unique ID assigned to it. However it will be later exported to the standard XML database for an easier and more efficient use in NLP.

2.3   Preparing the Metadata

Preparation of metadata is one of the most significant steps in the creation of any corpus since it, on one hand, helps in arranging the data in a proper format, and on the other hand, it helps other people in making an optimum, informed and clear use of the corpus.

In the present corpus three separate metadata files are maintained for each sub-corpora. One file contains the *cataloguing* and *administrative* metadata (as named by Austin 2006) grouped together as Type 1 metadata. The other file contains the other kinds of metadata including the *descriptive*, *structural* and *technical* metadata (as described by Austin 2006) grouped together as Type 2 metadata.

Type 1 Metadata

Indirect Written Corpora
For the indirect written communication, the information like title of the chapter/story from which the data is taken, the name of its author, the name of the book/magazine, the date of publication, the page numbers from which the sentences are taken, the date on which the entry has been made in the corpus and the name of the person who has made the entry in corpus are included in the metadata. This information, along with the ID of the sentences related to this information, is maintained for each file in the corpus.

Asynchronous CMC Corpora
For the asynchronous CMC in direct written communication, the information like the name of the blog/web portal, the name of the writer, the date on which the entry was

put up on the web, the date on which it was included in the corpus and the web link from which the entry was retrieved are included in the metadata. For synchronous CMC and non-CMC, only the date and the details about the participants are included in the metadata file.

Spoken Corpora

For the transcripts of spoken communication, a detailed information regarding the recordings from which the data is taken (which includes the information regarding date, time and place of recordings, the person who has recorded the data, the original format and encoding details of recording, the format and encoding details of the recordings in the current state, the machine on which recordings were made, a small description of the context in which recording was made, the total duration of the recorded file from which the data is taken, the name of the software used, if any, for exporting data from the recorder to the computer, the people involved in the conversation and others present on the spot) is maintained.

Type 2 Metadata

The other metadata file contains a short summary of the kind of data found in the subcorpora, the theme of each file (descriptive metadata), a specification of the way data is arranged in the corpora (structural metadata) and also a description of the softwares that could be used to access the files (technical).

Type 3 Metadata

Besides these a general metadata file will be created for the whole corpora which could also be used to access the corpora. This will contain the information about location of different kinds of files, the subcorpora to which they belong, the statistical information (like the number of words and the sentences) and the hyperlinks leading to those files/folders.

3   Annotating the Corpus

It is very necessary to annotate the data to make it useful for NLP research. Considering the fact that it consists of both written and spoken data and it will also be used for the development of several applications for Magahi, it needs to be annotated at several different levels including POS, syntactic, semantic, discourse level, etc. in order to make its complete and efficient use. The POS annotation of the corpus has started and we also plan to annotate it at deeper levels.

POS annotation of the corpus is being carried out using the tagset derived out of the standard POS tagset for Indian Languages, designed, developed and recognised by the Bureau of Indian Standards (BIS). This tagset has been released in the year 2010 and then subsequently modified in 2011 and is now supposed to be followed as a national standard for the POS annotation of any data or corpus in any of the Indian languages. It is a hierarchical tagset prepared with inputs from two of the most popular tagsets for Indian languages - Microsoft Research India's Indian Languages Part of Speech Tagset (ILPOST) and the tagset of Indian Languages Machine Translation (ILMT) project. The general annotation scheme consists of two levels of categories. Top-level consists of 11 categories and includes nouns, verb, demonstrative, pronoun, etc. This category has a sub-category at the second level like proper noun, common noun, etc. for the top-level category 'noun'. A tag has been assigned to categories at both the levels. While the tag of the lower level has to be assigned manually, the tag of the upper level is assigned automatically.

3.1   Preparing the Magahi Tagset

The Magahi tagset is derived and prepared out of this super-tagset approved by BIS tagset. The tagset is listed in Table 1 below. This tagset is a little different from the Hindi tagset (even though Magahi is considered a dialect of Hindi). Hindi, does not have classifiers, Magahi has a couple of them; so it is added in the Magahi tagset.

This tagset is used to tag the corpora with POS information. Till now around 10,000 words in the corpus have been annotated with POS information.

3.2   The Annotation Tool: ILCIANN

ILCIANN (Indian Languages Corpora Initiative Annotation Tool) is an online annotation tool developed as part of Indian Language Corpora Initiative (ILCI Project) (Jha 2010) for annotating the ILCI corpora. This tool is being used to annotate this corpus also. Some of the advantages of using such a tool include –

- No need of setting up any extra software or resources for tagging.
- The tool automatically tags a lot of words (based on an autotag list), thereby, saving lots of effort and time
- The annotated files are saved in a uniform and clean format (with no noise whatsoever) since it is saved by the tool itself in the required format, thereby, saving efforts and time on post-processing and data clean-up. A snapshot of the tool is given in Fig. 1 below.

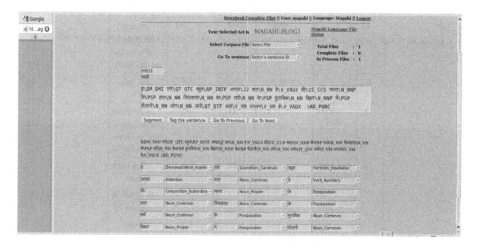

Fig. 1. A snapshot of the ILCIANN tool used for annotating the corpus data

Table 1. The Magahi POS tagset

Sl. No	Category		Label	Annotation Convention	Examples (in IPA)
	Top level	Subtype (level 1)			
1	**Noun**		N	N	cʰɔːʈɑ (boy)
1.1		Common	NN	N__NN	cəcəriː (a small bridge-like st.) ləŋgte (naked)
1.2		Proper	NNP	N__NNP	pʰuləva
1.3		Nloc	NST	N__NST	əgaɽiː, picʰaɽiː
2	**Pro-**		**PR**	**PR**	
	noun				
2.1		Personal	PRP	PR__PRP	həm, həməniː
2.2		Reflexive	PRF	PR__PRF	əpəne
2.3		Relative	PRL	PR__PRL	ɟe, ɟekər
2.4		Reciprocal	PRC	PR__PRC	əpəne
2.5		Wh-word	PRQ	PR__PRQ	kɑ, ke
2.6		Indefinite	PRI	PR__PRI	koi, kekrɑ
3	**Demon-strative**		**DM**	**DM**	
3.1		Deictic	DMD	DM__DMD	īhā, ūhā
3.2		Relative	DMR	DM__DMR	ɟe, ɟəun
3.3		Wh-word	DMQ	DM__DMQ	kekrɑ, kəun
3.4		Indefinite	DMI	DM__DMI	i, ʊ
4	**Verb**		**V**	**V**	ləukna (to see)
4.1		Main	VM	V__VM	pʰīcna (to wash clothes) əɟʰurana (to get entangled)
4.2		Auxiliary	VAUX	V__VAUX	həi, həliː, həʈʰiː
5	**Adjec-tive**		**JJ**	**JJ**	cəkəitʰ (short and well-built) bəʈpʰəros (use-lessly talkative)
6	**Adverb**		**RB**	**RB**	cəbʰɑk (with splash) cəbʰər-cəbʰr (a manner of eating)

Table 1. *(Continued)*

Sl. No	Category		Label	Annotation Convention	Examples (in IPA)
	Top level	Subtype (level 1)			
7	Postpo-sition		**PSP**	PSP	ke, me, pər, ɟore
8	Con-junction		**CC**	CC	
8.1		Co-ordinator	CCD	CC_CCD	aʊ, bakiː, bəluk
8.2		Subordinator	CCS	CC_CCS	kɑheki, ʈə, ki
9	Parti-cles		**RP**	RP	
9.1		Default	RPD	RP_RPD	ʈə, bʰiː
9.2		Classifier	CL	RP_CL	ɡo, tʰo
9.3		Interjection	INJ	RP_INJ	əre, he, cʰiː, bɑpre
9.4		Intensifier	INTF	RP_INTF	təhtəh, tuh-tuh, bʰək-bʰək
9.5		Negation	NEG	RP_NEG	nə, məʈ, binɑ
10	Quanti-fiers		**QT**	QT	ek, pəhilɑ, kucʰ
10.1		General	QTF	QT_QTF	təniːsun, dʰer-məniː
10.2		Cardinals	QTC	QT_QTC	ek, du, igɑrəh
10.3		Ordinals	QTO	QT_QTO	pohilɑ, dʊsrɑ
11	Residu-als		**RD**	RD	
11.1		Foreign word	RDF	RD_RDF	A word in foreign script.
11.2		Symbol	SYM	RD_SYM	For symbols such as $, & etc
11.3		Punctuation	PUNC	RD_PUNC	Only for punctuations
11.4		Unknown	UNK	RD_UNK	
11.5		Echowords	ECH	RD_ECH	(pɑni:-) uni: (kʰɑnɑ-) unɑ

4 Further Developments: POS Tagger for Magahi

Our recent developments include the extension of the POS annotated corpus of Magahi, which now contains around 70,000 annotated words. We have used this corpus to develop a POS tagger for Magahi (Kumar et al. (2012). It is based on TnT and in its current form it gives an accuracy of slightly below 90 %.

5 The Way Ahead

POS annotation is the most basic level of annotation in order to make the corpus useful for NLP. However in order to make the corpus more powerful and capable of being used for more complex tasks, it is very necessary to annotate it with lot more information. Moreover, along with this, the development of some basic technologies like morphological analysers and parsers are required so that higher-level applications could be developed for the language. We are currently working on improving the performance of the POS tagger using different features as well by preparing more manually annotated data. After the POS tagging, the data will be further annotated with detailed morpho-syntactic and semantic information (using 'construction-labelling' method, suggested by Hellan et al. (2009) for LRLs) as well as for the discourse-level information (by adapting DIT++ dialog act annotation scheme[1] for the present purposes).

References

Alok, D.: Magahi noun-particles: a semantic and pragmatic study. Paper presented in Fourth Students' Conference of Linguistics in India (SCONLI 4), Mumbai, India, February 2010

Alok, D.: A language without articles: the case of Magahi. Unpublished M.Phil. dissertation, Jawaharlal Nehru University, New Delhi (2012)

Chatterji, S.K.: The Origin and Development of the Bengali Language, 3 vols. George Allen and Unwin, London (1926) (Reprint 1970)

Grierson, G.A.: Linguistic Survey of India, Vol. V: Indo-Aryan Family, Eastern Group, Pt. II: Specimens of the Bihari and Oriya Languages. Motilal Banarsidass, Delhi (1903) (Reprint 1967)

Hellan, L., Mary E.K.D.: A methodology for enhancing argument structure specification. In: Proceedings of the 4th Language and Technology Conference: Human Language Technologies as a Challenge for Computer Science and Linguistics, LTC 2009, Poznan, Poland, 6–8 November 2009

Jeffers, R.J.: The position of the Bihari dialects in Indo-Aryan. Indo-Iran. J. **18**, 215–225 (1976)

Jha, G.N.: The TDIL program and the Indian Language Corpora Initiative (ILCI). In: Proceedings of the Seventh International conference on Language Resources and Evaluation, LREC'10, pp. 982–985 (2010)

---

[1] http://dit.uvt.nl/

Kumar, R., Lahiri, B., Alok, D.: Developing a POS tagger for Magahi: a comparative study. In: Proceedings of the 10th Workshop on Asian Language Resources, 24th International Conference on Computational Linguistics (COLING-24), IIT-Bombay, Mumbai, India (2012)

Masica, C.P.: The Indo-Aryan Languages. Cambridge University Press, Cambridge (1991)

Verma, M.K.: Exploring the parameters of agreement: the case of Magahi. Lang. Sci. **13**(2), 125–143 (1991)

Verma, S.: Magahi. In: Cardona, G., Jain, D. (eds.) The Indo-Aryan Languages, pp. 498–514. Routledge, London (2003)

Quizzes on Tap: Exporting a Test Generation System from One Less-Resourced Language to Another

Montse Maritxalar[1], Elaine Uí Donnchadha[2(✉)], Jennifer Foster[3], and Monica Ward[3]

[1] University of the Basque Country, Leioa, Spain
montse.maritxalar@ehu.es
[2] Trinity College, Dublin, Ireland
uidhonne@tcd.ie
[3] Dublin City University, Dublin, Ireland
{jfoster,mward}@computing.dcu.ie

Abstract. It is difficult to develop and deploy Language Technology and applications for minority languages for many reasons. These include the lack of Natural Language Processing resources for the language, a scarcity of NLP researchers who speak the language and the communication gap between teachers in the classroom and researchers working in universities and other centres of research. One approach to overcoming these obstacles is for researchers interested in Less-Resourced Languages to work together in reusing and adapting existing resources where possible. This article outlines how a multiple-choice quiz generator for Basque was adapted for Irish. The Quizzes on Tap system uses Latent Semantic Analysis to automatically generate multiple choice test items. Adapting the Basque application to work for Irish involved the sourcing of suitable Irish corpora and a morphological engine for Irish, as well as the compilation of a development set. Various integration issues arising from differences between Basque and Irish needed to be dealt with. The QOT system provides a useful resource that enables Irish teachers to produce both domain-specific and general-knowledge quizzes in a timely manner, for children with varying levels of exposure to the language.

Keywords: Less-resourced languages · Irish · Morphological analysis · Multiple choice test item generation · Educational applications

1 Introduction

Like many Less Resourced Languages (LRLs), there are few Natural Language Processing (NLP) resources available for the Irish language, and in common with many LRLs, this is due to the limited number of researchers working in the language and the difficulty of finding the multi-skilled experts required to develop these resources. What few resources are available can be difficult to integrate into an existing application for the same reasons.

One approach to overcoming these obstacles is to adapt an existing NLP application that has been developed for another language. This involves integrating

Z. Vetulani and J. Mariani (Eds.): LTC 2011, LNAI 8387, pp. 502–514, 2014.
DOI: 10.1007/978-3-319-08958-4_41

language-specific modules into the application, and is made easier if the original application has been designed in a modular fashion. This article reports on a project to adapt a Multiple-Choice Quiz (MCQ) generation system, originally developed for Basque and subsequently adapted to English, to the Irish language, in order to be able to generate both domain-specific and general-knowledge multiple-choice quizzes for use in an Irish classroom environment.

The article is organised as follows. In Sect. 2, we introduce the topic of automatic MCQ generation and describe related work in this area. In Sect. 3, we turn our attention to the Irish language, giving a brief overview of its grammatical properties, surveying recent work in Irish NLP and describing the current situation with regards to how Irish is taught in schools. In Sect. 4, we describe how the Quizzes on Tap system uses latent semantic analysis and morphological analysis in order to generate MCQ items. In Sect. 5, we provide a preliminary evaluation of the Quizzes on Tap system including pointers to how it could be improved. Finally, in Sect. 6 we summarise our contribution and conclude.

2 Background

Multiple-choice items consist of a *stem* and a set of options. The stem is the part of the item that presents the item as a problem to be solved, that is, a question or an incomplete statement. The options are the possible answers that the students can choose from. In our work, we focus on fill-in-the-blank questions: the question is an incomplete statement and only one of the options is the correct answer, i.e. the *key*. The other options of the MCQ are those that are incorrect in the given context, i.e. the *distractors*.

The automatic generation of MCQ questions has been an active area of research in the use of NLP in computer-aided learning. Previous works differ with respect to the language, the subject being tested, the type of MCQ generated and the part of the generation task that is emphasised. Hoshino and Nakagawa (2005) automatically generate fill-in-the-blank questions which test English grammar and vocabulary, focusing on the use of machine learning to decide on the position of the blank (key). Sumita et al. (2005) generate distractors for MCQ fill-in-the-blank questions using a thesaurus and verify them using web lookup. Lee and Seneff (2007) concentrate on a common grammatical error made by learners of English, namely preposition errors, and develop a system for automatically generating preposition distractors, which employs a corpus of non-native English. Aldabe et al. (2006) - whose work we build on - and Smith et al. (2009) both use distributional semantics to automatically choose suitable distractors but differ with respect to when in the process the distractors are generated: Smith et al. (2009) generate the distractors before selecting the sentences, whereas for Aldabe et al. (2006), the sentence-selection task precedes the distractor-generation task.

The MCQ generation system on which are work is based, termed *Arikiturri*, was developed for the Basque language (Aldabe et al. 2006; Aldabe 2011). The Basque term "ArikIturri" is a portmanteau of "Ariketen Iturria" where Iturria means "fountain" and Ariketen means "of exercises". Therefore, the name refers to a system which is able to automatically generate tests from texts, to be included in testing tasks. In order to generate good quality items, ArikIturri makes use of two kinds of language resources: off-the-shelf Natural Language Processing (NLP) tools and linguistic information. It is a system with an open architecture that facilitates the integration of new tools and resources. In fact, the two main characteristics of the system are multilingualism and modularity. ArikIturri has been used to generate Basque MCQs (Aldabe et al. 2006) embedded in a whole text and isolated English MCQs (Aldabe et al. 2009).

Almost all research on the automatic generation of MCQs based on NLP methods has focused on English. In this article we present a system, Quizzes on Tap (QOT), which builds on the work carried out in developing the ArikIturri system in order to automatically generate isolated MCQs for the Irish language.

3   The Irish Language

We begin with a brief overview of Irish grammar, followed by a description of existing resources for Irish and a discussion of the teaching of Irish.

3.1   Grammatical Properties of Irish

Irish is a member of the Celtic branch of the Indo-European family of languages. It is an inflectional language with a gender system, and it is a VSO word order language. Verbs can be inflected for tense, mood, number and person. Nouns have either masculine or feminine gender and can be inflected for case, number, definiteness and emphasis/contrast. Adjectives agree with the nouns they modify in terms of gender, case and number. The definite article also agrees with the noun in terms of gender, case and number. There is no indefinite article. Prepositions can stand alone or combine with a pronoun (these forms are known as prepositional pronouns), therefore prepositions display the full paradigm of number and person.

The verbal system is quite regular, apart from eleven commonly used irregular verbs. The subject can either be a noun phrase/pronoun or the verb can be inflected for person and number (a synthetic verb form). However, it is ungrammatical to have both at the same time (1)d.

(1)   a *Chuala Máire* 'Máire heard' (analytic form)
      b *Chualamar* 'We heard' (synthetic form)
      c *Chuala muid* 'We heard' (analytic form)
      d **Chualamar muid* 'We we heard' (ungrammatical)

The nominal inflectional system is more varied and irregular than the verbal inflectional system. There are a variety of ways in which the plural can be formed, and in general this is not predictable for the stem. Although a standard form will be listed in the dictionary, in practice there may be dialectal variant plurals (2).

(2) *an capall* 'the horse'
     na capaill 'the horses' (official standard)
     na caiple 'the horses' (dialectal variant)

Morphosyntax: Inflectional forms usually require a suffix to the stem, and they frequently require modification of the stem. The modifications are of two distinct categories - initial mutations (lenition, eclipsis, prefixing of vowel-initial and s-initial words), which affect the initial sound/letter of the word, and final mutations (slenderisation, broadening, syncopation, syllable replacement), which affect the final syllable.

Irish morphology and syntax are closely inter-related. Initial mutations to a word are dependent on its syntactic relationship with a preceding word.

Many functional words (determiners, prepositions, particles etc.) trigger initial mutations in the following word-form. Examples (3) to (5) show how the definite article, possessive determiners, numerals and simple prepositions all trigger various initial mutations in nouns. These initial mutations vary depending on the noun's initial consonant or vowel and on its gender.

(3) *cos* (fem.) 'foot'
     *an **chos*** 'the foot'
     *mo **chos*** 'my foot'
     *ar a **cos*** 'on her foot'
     *ar a **chos*** 'on his foot'
     *seacht **gcos*** 'seven feet'
     *faoin **chos*** 'under the foot'
(4) ***arán*** (masc.) 'bread'
     *an **t-arán*** 'the bread'
(5) ***aerlíne*** (fem.) 'airline'
     *an **aerlíne*** 'the airline'

Genitive case is used in several constructions including possessive modifiers (6) and (7)(6)(7), after some prepositions (8)(8), and after verbal noun constructions (9)(9).

(6) ***an fear*** (masc.) 'the man';
     *hata **an fhir*** (masc.), the man's hat
(7) ***an fhuiseog*** (fem.), lark
     *sciathán **na fuiseoige*** 'the lark's wing'
(8) ***an tír*** (fem.)'the country'
     *timpeall **na tíre*** 'around the country'
(9) ***obair (fem.)*** 'work'
     *ag déanamh **oibre*** 'working'

This means that creating MCQs is not only a matter of finding a word with the relevant part of speech and semantic properties, one must also consider the local morphosyntactic environment.

3.2 Language Technology and Irish

The development of Language Technology for Irish is quite limited. There are some basic resources such as online dictionaries, a part-of-speech tagged corpus (Uí Dhonnchadha and van Genabith 2006), and a small treebank of syntactically-annotated sentences (Lynn et al. 2012). A new English-Irish Dictionary is under development which will replace the current English-Irish Dictionary (Ó Dónaill 1978). As regards NLP tools there is a spelling/grammar checker (Scannell 2008), a text-to-speech synthesizer (Ní Chasaide et al. 2011), a finite-state morphology part-of-speech tagger (Uí Dhonnchadha and van Genabith 2006) (following Beesley and Karttunen 2003), a partial dependency parser and chunker (Uí Dhonnchadha and van Genabith 2010; Uí Dhonnchadha 2010), as well as MaltParser (Nivre et al. 2006) and Mate (Bohnet 2010) dependency parsing models (Lynn et al. 2013).

There are very few commercial products for Irish since it is a lesser-used language with little commercial potential for private developers. In order to ensure up-to-date technology for the language it would be necessary to have a government backed strategic plan for Irish language technology and regular funding. However such a plan is not in place and funding is sporadic.

3.3 Irish in the Classroom

Irish is one of the two official languages of Ireland, along with English, but only a small percentage (1.7 %) of the population speak it as their first language on a daily basis (CSO 2011). Irish is a compulsory subject in both primary and secondary schools, but after 13 years the level of attainment is low. There are socio-cultural, pedagogical and linguistic issues behind this discrepancy. People hold negative attitudes towards the language e.g. perceiving it as useless, spoken only by rural communities (similar to attitudes to other languages in a similar position), and forced upon them by the cultural-elite. Attitudes towards the language are usually passed down from generation to generation to the present day, where some, but not all, parents question the need or usefulness of studying the language. Paradoxically, many Irish adults support the preservation of Irish for heritage and cultural reasons (Mac Gréil and Rhatigan 2009) and would like their children to grow up learning the language (Ó'Riagáin 2007), but this does not always translate itself into actual support for the language in school.

There are several pedagogical issues to consider with how Irish is taught is schools. Lack of modern pedagogical techniques (Irish is taught differently from other languages) and an emphasis on grammar and literature which most students do not understand make it hard for the students. However, there have been some recent changes, including an increased emphasis on oral language, with the oral exam marks comprising 40 % of the total marks in the state exams, up from 25 % (SEC 2010). This is to encourage students to speak the language, rather than focus on the written form.

Furthermore, Irish is linguistically challenging for the majority of Irish school students (mainly native English speakers), especially as it is usually their first exposure to another language. Morphological issues (see Sect. 3.1 above), VSO word order and the orthographical issues with the language (Hickey and Stenson 2011) make it difficult for the students to be comfortable with learning the language, let alone becoming proficient in it.

With regards to Irish schools, there are three types of schools: English-medium (the vast majority), Irish-medium in a Gaeltacht[1] area (very few) and Irish-medium outside a Gaeltacht area (very few, but increasing in number). Around 3 % of secondary school students attend an Irish-medium post-primary school. As in most modern schools, there is a need for up-to-date pedagogical resources and a place for Computer-Aided Learning (CAL) resources. Outside of Irish language resources for the study of the language itself, there are few Irish-medium resources available for other subjects (e.g. biology), apart from textbooks and related materials – and even these are very limited in number. This is understandable given the market size, lack of NLP resources and the difficulty in developing the resources (i.e. the need for a multi-disciplinary team and the difficulties e.g. financial and logistical, in assembling such a team).

However, these difficulties do not negate the need for modern Irish language technology applications in the classroom. Some schools are piloting the use of i-pads (rather than textbooks) and smartphone language apps, although a complementary approach is probably best. While not a panacea, Language Technology applications could make a contribution to schools in Ireland e.g. computer-based materials for Irish or any other subject. Applications such as Quizzes on Tap could potentially be of benefit to both teachers and students in every classroom in the country.

4   Quizzes on Tap

We begin this section with a general description of the procedure for generating MCQ. This is followed by a brief description of the method that is used to find distractors. The section ends with a discussion of the difficulties that arise due to morphosyntactic properties of Irish.

4.1   General Procedure

We apply a corpus-based approach for the generation of the MCQ items. The automatisation of this process is limited to the generation of the distractors of the MCQs, and the generated items are limited to Irish nouns and verbs since this is the one of the type of tests teachers conduct in class. The process of generating and analysing the Irish MCQs consists of the following steps:

1. **Selection of the texts:** experts on the generation of didactic resources select the texts, taking into account the level of the learners.
2. **Marking the blanks:** the terms to be considered as keys have to be relevant to the learning process of the students. The marking is carried out manually.

---

[1] A Gaeltacht is a region designated as an Irish-speaking part of the country, where the majority of the population use Irish as the language of communication.

3. **Generation of distractors:** for each stem and key selected in the previous step, distractors are automatically generated.
4. **Discarding incorrect distractors:** experts eliminate any automatically generated distractors that cannot fit the blank.
5. **Evaluating the distractors:** experts evaluate the quality of the remaining generated distractors.

4.2 Generating Distractors Using LSA

Distributional similarity measures are based on the idea that the similarity of two words depends on the commonality of their contexts. Thus, two words are similar if they occur in similar contexts. In our experiments, we use Latent Semantic Analysis (LSA) (Deerwester et al. 1990) to automatically generate suitable distractors given a stem, key and corpus of suitable documents. LSA has achieved good results in a number of NLP tasks such as Information Retrieval (Deerwester et al. 1990), Machine Translation (Banches and Costa-jussa 2011) and Computer-Aided Learning (Landauer et al. 2007). In automatic test generation it has been used in the evaluation of synonym test questions (Turney 2001), and in the generation of MCQ questions (Aldabe and Maritxalar 2010).

In order to carry out latent semantic analysis, our Quizzes on Tap system makes use of the Infomap software (Dorow and Widdows 2003). Words are represented as vectors in a low-dimensional space and these vectors are then compared using the cosine similarity metric. The assumption here is that the closer two word vectors are according to this metric, the closer the two words are in meaning. The vectors are computed by indexing the documents in a large corpus. Thus, given an input corpus, Infomap can be used to retrieve the words that best match the key: these words are potential distractors.

4.3 Generating Distractors Using LSA and Morphological Analysis

In order to avoid the possibility of students guessing the correct choice by simply discarding options with the wrong morphological characteristics, the QOT system offers as candidate distractors the first words of the InfoMap output which match the part-of-speech of the key. This means that a morphological analyser and generator are needed.

Before creating the LSA models used to generate the distractors, a morphological analyser is applied to the input corpus in order to extract the lemmas and parts-of-speech of the corpus words.[2] The same morphological analyser is applied to the selected key. The QOT system provides InfoMap with the lemma of the selected key, and InfoMap returns a list of candidate distractor lemmas. The morphological analyzer attaches the morphological information of the key to the potential distractor lemmas

---

[2] In addition some pre- and post-processing to handle, for example, accented Irish characters, is carried out.

given by Infomap. The morphological generator will produce the distractors, i.e. the inflected wordforms.

In the case of Irish, the inflected wordform differs depending on the gender, therefore, the morphological information associated with the key is sometimes not enough to generate the distractors corresponding to the lemma provided by Infomap. For example, in the case of the word *próitéin* (feminine) one of the lemmas given by Infomap is *núicléas* (masculine). In this case the morphological generator is not able to produce the distractor because the gender of both lemmas does not match.

(10)   key: *phrotéin* 'protein'
       features: próitéin+Noun+Fem+Com+Sg+Len

In order to generate an inflected form of a noun in Irish using the finite-state morphology transducer, its gender (masc/fem), type (common/proper/ substantive/ verbal) and number (sing./pl.) features need to be supplied. Only the number feature can be taken from the key as the other two features (gender and type) are specific to the distractor lemma. In order to overcome this problem we would need to look up the gender and noun type of distractor lemmas (e.g. in the morphological analyser) before generating the required inflected forms. As we can see from the examples, a feminine noun (10) is lenited (+Len) whereas a masculine noun (11) is not.

(11)   key: *núicléas* 'nucleus'
       features: núicléas +Noun+Masc+Com+Sg

Currently we use only distractors with the same gender and type as the key, which obviously limits our choice of distractor. In addition, if the key noun is in the genitive case, the preceding definite article will vary to agree with the gender of the noun. Ideally we should mark both the article and the noun and supply both article and noun when generating distractors in the genitive case.

(12)   méid *na protéine* (fem) 'amount of the protein'
(13)   méid *an núicléas* (masc) 'size of the nucleus'

We encounter similar challenges in relation to verb features. The features tense, mood, person and number apply to all verbs, however transitivity is specific to the lemma and therefore the transitivity of the key lemma will need to be reflected in the distractor lemma.

(14)   key: *braitheann* 'depends'
       features: braith+Verb+VTI+PresInd

The key verb form *braitheann* 'depends' has the features Verb and PresInd (tense: present indicative) which are necessary for the generation of the distractor verb forms. The transitivity feature VTI (i.e. verb can be both transitive and intransitive) is specific to the key lemma. However, it makes sense to limit our distractor verbs to those with the same transitivity feature as the key, in order to fit in with the syntactic structure of the sentence.

5 Preliminary Evaluation

In order to carry out a proof-of-concept evaluation of the QOT system, we created two LSA models using a general Irish language corpus of 12 million words and a smaller scientific corpus of almost 300,000 words. The smaller scientific corpus was used as a development corpus during the initial system development. The larger corpus was used to create the LSA model used in our evaluation. Nouns, adjectives, verbs and adverbs were used to create the models.

Our test set consists of 21 MCQ stem/key pairs. 10 of these are on the topic of biology and are suitable for teenagers attending an Irish-speaking secondary school. The remaining 11 are general-knowledge items, aimed at teenagers attending both Irish-speaking and English-speaking secondary schools. We examine the distractors produced by the QOT system for each of these 21 items.

The QOT system produced distractors for 15 of the 21 input items. 7 of these 15 required no editing whatsoever, i.e. all of the generated distractors were suitable. An example is the following (the key is underlined and the distractors are listed below):

(A) Bíonn <u>teocht</u> áirithe agus pH áirithe ag teastáil le go n-oibreodh na heinsímí ar fad i gceart.

'For the enzymes to work properly particular <u>temperature</u> and pH levels are required'.

(1) frasaíocht 'precipitation'
(2) ocsaíd 'oxide'
(3) radaíocht 'radiation'
(4) báisteach 'rainfall'
(5) ocsaigin 'oxygen'
(6) aeráid 'climate'
(7) nítrigin 'nitrogen'

The remaining 8 items were associated with distractors of varying quality. The unsuitable distractors fell into two categories:

A distractor that is semantically too similar to the key.

An example is the following:

(B) Is deacair sútha talún na hÉireann a fháil i gcaitheamh an <u>gheimhridh</u>.

'Irish strawberries are hard to find in <u>winter</u>'.

(1) shamhraidh 'summer'
*(2) **shneachta** 'snow'*
*(3) **sheaca** 'frost'*
(4) earraigh 'spring'
(5) ghriain 'sun'
(6) theasa 'heat'

Here, distractors (2) and (3) (*snow* and *frost*) are unsuitable as distractors because they make sense in the context of the stem. In order to overcome this problem, a post-Infomap filtering process would have to be implemented so that words that are too closely related to the key, e.g. synonyms, hypernyms or hyponyms, are not selected.

A distractor that is grammatically incorrect.
An example is the following:

(C) Chuir a mháthair pláta bia ar an mbord.
'His mother put a plate of <u>food</u> on the table'.

(1) glasra 'vegetable'
(2) ithe 'eat'
(3) arán 'bread'
(4) béile 'meal'
(5) ocras 'hunger'
(6) bainne 'milk'
(7) éasc 'a flaw in timber'
(8) tobac 'tobacco'

In this example, distractors (1) and (3) (*vegetable* and *bread*) are unsuitable not only because they are too similar in meaning to the key (as in the previous example) but also because they are not correctly inflected for the genitive case. This difficulty arises due to morphological ambiguity in sentence (C) where both *pláta* (plate) and *bia* (food) have the same form in the nominative and genitive case. Therefore, the POS tagger cannot identify the boundaries of the subject and object constituents, which in a VSO language are adjacent. In this case the tagger cannot tell whether *pláta* is in genitive relation to *máthair* as in *(a)*, or *bia* is in genitive relation to *pláta* as in *(b)*.

(a) **Chuir [a mháthair pláta] [bia] ar an mbord.*
     *Put [his mother plate][food] on the table
(b) *Chuir [a mháthair][pláta bia] ar an mbord.*
     Put [his mother][a plate of food] on the table

To tag this sentence correctly, the POS tagger would need to know that 'plate' and 'food' arc more likely to form a noun phrase than 'mother' and 'plate'. In addition, the noun *bia* (food) is a mass noun and therefore has no plural form, but distractors such as glasra (vegetable) which are count nouns should be in the plural form, i.e. a plate of vegetables. Therefore we cannot simply apply the number feature taken from the key form; we must also check whether the distractor lemmas are mass or count nouns and generate the appropriate inflected form. The finite-state lexicon does not have this information currently encoded.

Distractor (7) *éasc* is an interesting candidate since it is similar in spelling to the Irish word for *fish (éisc, genitive case of iasc),* but semantically quite unrelated. As such, it makes a good distractor.

The first problematic case illustrates the difficult nature of the task itself – it is a non-trivial problem to generate good distractors that can be reliably used to test a person's knowledge of a particular subject area. The second problematic case is related to the integration of the Irish morphological analyser/generator into the system – there remains quite a bit of work to be done here to guarantee morphologically well-formed distractors. The generation of ill-formed distractors does however have the potential to be of use in applications that aim to test grammatical knowledge.

In general, the distractors produced for the scientific sentences were of higher quality than those produced for the general sentences.

6 Conclusion

We have described the process of adapting a multiple-choice-question generation system, developed initially for Basque, to the Irish language. Although the underlying system is, in theory, language-independent, in practice, much work still needs to be done to port it from one language to another. The resulting system, Quizzes on Tap, relies on a morphological analyser/generator for Irish, and aims to take into account the complexities of Irish morphosyntax. Although the system development is still in its early stages, the results of our initial evaluation are encouraging enough to suggest that the system has the potential to be useful to teachers.

References

Aldabe, I., de Lacalle, M.L., Maritxalar, M., Martinez, E., Uria, L.: AriklIturri: an automatic question generator based on corpora and NLP techniques. In: Ikeda, M., Ashley, K.D., Chan, T.-W. (eds.) ITS 2006. LNCS, vol. 4053, pp. 584–594. Springer, Heidelberg (2006)

Aldabe, I., Maritxalar, M., Mitkov, R.: A study on the automatic selection of candidate sentences and distractors. In: Dimitrova, V., Mizoguchi, R., Boulay, B., Graesser, A. (eds.) Artificial Intelligence in Education. Building Learning Systems that Care: From Knowledge Representation to Affective Modelling. Frontiers in Artificial Intelligence and Applications, vol. 200, pp. 656–658. IOS press, Amsterdam (2009)

Aldabe, I., Maritxalar, M.: Automatic distractor generation for domain specific texts. In: Loftsson, H., Rögnvaldsson, E., Helgadóttir, S. (eds.) IceTAL 2010. LNCS, vol. 6233, pp. 27–38. Springer, Heidelberg (2010)

Aldabe, I.: Automatic exercise generation based on corpora and natural language processing techniques. Ph.D. thesis, University of the Basque Country (2011)

Banchs, R.E, Costa-jussa, M: A semantic feature for statistical machine translation. In: Proceedings of the Fifth Workshop on Syntax, Semantics and Structure in Statistical Translation, Portland, Oregon, pp. 126–134 (2011)

Bohnet, B.: Top accuracy and fast dependency parsing is not a contradiction. In: Proceedings of COLING (2010)

Chao-Lin, L., Chun-Hung, W., Zhao-Ming, G., Shang-Ming, H.: Applications of lexical information for algorithmically composing multiple choice cloze items. In: Proceedings of the 2nd Workshop on Innovative Uses of NLP for Building Educational Applications, Ann Arbor, pp. 1–8 (2005)

CSO: Irish Language Statistics. Central Statistics Office (2011). http://www.cso.ie/px/pxeirestat/Statire/SelectVarVal/Define.asp?maintable=CD936&PLanguage=0. Accessed 23 July 2013

Deerwester, S., Dumais, S., Furnas, G., Landauer, T., Harshman, R.: Indexing by latent semantic analysis. J. Am. Soc. Inf. Sci. **41**(6), 391–407 (1990)

Dorow, B., Widdows, D.: Discovering corpus-specific word senses. In: Proceedings of EACL (2003)

Hickey, T., Stenson, N.: Irish orthography: what teachers and learners need to know about it, any why? Lang. Learn. Technol. **24**(1), 2011 (2011)

Hoshino, A., Nakagawa, H.: A real-time multiple-choice question generation for language testing. In: Proceedings of the 2nd Workshop on Innovative Uses of NLP for Building Educational Applications, Ann Arbor, pp. 17–20 (2005)

Landauer, T.K., McNamara, D.S., Dennis, S., Kintsch, W.: Handbook of Latent Semantic Analysis. Lawrence Erlbaum Associates, Mahwah (2007)

Lee, J., Seneff, S.: Automatic generation of cloze items for prepositions. In: Proceedings of Interspeech (2007)

Lynn, T., Cetinoglu, O., Foster, J., Uí Dhonnchadha, E., Dras, M., van Genabith, J.: Irish treebanking and parsing: a preliminary evaluation. In: Proceedings of the International Conference on Linguistic Resource and Evaluation (LREC), Istanbul, Turkey (2012)

Lynn, T., Foster, J., Dras, M., van Genabith, J.: Working with a small dataset: semi-supervised dependency parsing for Irish. In: Proceedings of the 4th Workshop on Statistical Parsing of Morphologically Rich Languages (SPMRL), Seattle, WA (2013)

Mac Gréil, M., Rhatigan, F.: The Irish language and the Irish people. National University of Ireland Maynooth: Survey and Research Unit, Department of Sociology (2009)

Ní Chasaide, A., Ní Chiaráin, N., Wendler, C., Berthelsen, H., Kelly, A., Gilmartin, E., Uí Dhonnchadha, E., Gobl, C.: Towards personalised synthesis-based content in Irish (Gaelic) language education. In: Proceedings of Speech and Language Technology in Education (SlaTE), Venice (2011)

Nivre, J., Hall, J., Nilsson, J.: MaltParser: a data-driven parser-generator for dependency parsing. In: Proceedings of the Fifth International Conference on Language Resources and Evaluation (LREC), Malta (2006)

Ó Dónaill, N.: Foclóir Gaeilge-Béarla, Dublin, An Gúm (1978)

Ó' Riagáin, P.: Relationships between attitudes to Irish social class, religion and national identity in the republic of Ireland and northern Ireland. Int. J. Biling. Educ. Biling. **10**(4), 369–393 (2007)

Scannell, K.: An Gramadóir: a grammar-checking framework for the Celtic languages and its applications. In: Proceedings of 14th Annual NAACLT Conference, Madog Center for Welsh Studies, University of Rio Grande (2008)

SEC: The Irish examination in the leaving certificate for 2012 onwards. State Examinations Commission (2010). http://www.examinations.ie/schools/S_90_10_The_irish Examination_in_the_Leaving_Certificate_for_2012_onwards.pdf. Accessed 23 July 2013

Smith, S., Kilgarriff, A., Sommers, S., Wen-liang, G., Guang-zhong, W: Automatic cloze generation for English proficiency testing. In: Proceedings of the LTTC Conference (2009)

Sumita, E., Sugaya, F., Yamamota, S.: Measuring non-native speakers' proficiency of English by using a test with automatically-generated fill-in-the blank questions. In: Proceedings of the 2nd Workshop on Innovative Uses of NLP for Building Educational Applications, Ann Arbor, ACL, pp. 61–68 (2005)

Turney, P.: Mining the web for synonyms: PMI-IR versus LSA on TOEFL. In: Proceedings of the Twelfth European Conference on Machine Learning, pp. 491–502 (2001)

Uí Dhonnchadha, E.: Natural Language Processing Tools: Developing a Part-of-Speech Tagger and Partial Dependency Parser for Irish. LAP LAMBERT Academic Publishing, Saarbrücken (2010)

Uí Dhonnchadha, E., Van Genabith, J.: Scaling an Irish FST morphology engine for use on unrestricted text. In: Yli-Jyrä, A., Karttunen, L., Karhumäki, J. (eds.) FSMNLP 2005. LNCS (LNAI), vol. 4002, pp. 247–258. Springer, Heidelberg (2006)

Uí Dhonnchadha, E., Van Genabith, J.: Partial dependency parsing for Irish. In: Proceedings of the International Conference on Language Resources and Evaluation Conference, Malta (2010)

A Multilingual Text Normalization Approach

Brigitte Bigi[(⊠)]

Laboratoire Parole et Langage, CNRS, Aix-Marseille Université,
5 avenue Pasteur, BP 80975, 13604 Aix-en-Provence, France
brigitte.bigi@lpl-aix.fr

Abstract. The creation of text corpora requires a sequence of processing steps in order to constitute, normalize, and then to directly exploit it by a given application. This paper presents a generic approach for text normalization and concentrates on the aspects of methodology and linguistic engineering, which serve to develop a multi-purpose multilingual text corpus. This approach was applied on written texts of French, English, Spanish, Vietnamese, Khmer and Chinese and on speech transcriptions of French, English, Italian, Chinese and Taiwanese. It consists in splitting the text normalization problem in a set of minor sub-problems as language-independent as possible. A set of text corpus normalization tools with linked resources and a document structuring method are proposed and distributed under the terms of the GPL license.

1 Introduction

There are more than 6000 languages in the world but only a small number possess the resources required for implementation of Human Language Technologies (HLT). Thus, HLT are mostly concerned by languages which have large resources available or which suddenly became of interest because of the economic or political scene. On the contrary, languages from developing countries or minorities were less treated in the past years. Among HLT, this paper focuses on text normalization which is a well known problem in Natural Language Processing (NLP). The first task faced by any NLP system is the conversion of input text into a linguistic representation. Digital written texts contain a variety of "non-standard" token types such as digit sequences, acronyms and letter sequences in all capitals, mixed case words, abbreviations, roman numerals, URL's and e-mail addresses... Speech transcriptions also contain truncated words, orthography reductions, etc. Normalizing or rewriting such texts using ordinary words is an important issue for various applications.

Text normalization is commonly considered as language-dependent and/or task-dependent. In the Machine Translation community, we can cite [7]. In the ASR community for English, the Linguistic Data Consortium tools [12] are widely used for the text normalization task. The LDC tools perform text normalization using a set of ad hoc rules, converting numerals to words and expanding abbreviations listed in a table. The Johns Hopkins University Summer Workshop research project [19] made a systematic effort to build a general solution to the text normalization problem for English. The text normalization process involves first splitting complex tokens using a simple set of rules, and then classifying all tokens as one of their 23 categories using a decision

© Springer International Publishing Switzerland 2014
Z. Vetulani and J. Mariani (Eds.): LTC 2011, LNAI 8387, pp. 515–526, 2014.
DOI: 10.1007/978-3-319-08958-4_42

tree. JTok is a configurable tokenizer for German, developed at DFKI by Joerg Steffen. It is part of "Heart of Gold", a XML-based middleware for integrating shallow and deep NLP components. It is a package comprising 4 tokenizers: White Space, Regex, Break Iterator and Sentence Tokenizer. Papageorgiou et al. in [15] discuss a regex-based tokenizer and sentence splitter that contains a list of abbreviations for Greek texts. Martínez et al. in [13] have developed the IULA Processing Tool, a system for sentence splitting, tokenization and named-entity recognition of Spanish. The tool is based on rules which depend on a series of resources to improve obtained results: a grammatical phrase list, a foreign expression list, a follow-up abbreviation list, a word-form lexical database and a stop-list to increase lexical-lookup efficiency. Less-resourced languages are also investigated, as Hindi in [14].

There is a greater need for work on text normalization, as it forms an important component of all areas of language and speech technology. The text normalization development can be carried out specifically for each language and/or task but this work is laborious and time consuming. However, for many languages there has not been any concerted effort on text normalization. In the context of genericity, producing reusable components for language-and-task-specific development is an important goal. The aim of this study was to create tools that would represent the common text normalization for many languages including less-resourced languages.

The primary goal of this paper is to present techniques and methods that can be used to efficiently develop text normalization resources and tools for new languages based on existing ones. This study develops a text normalization method as language-and-task-independent as possible. This lets the possibility to add new languages with a significant time-reduction compared to the entire development of such tools. Current development involves: French, English, Spanish, Italian, Vietnamese, Khmer, Chinese and Taiwanese. The method is implemented as a set of tools that are applied sequentially to the text corpora. The advantage of this modular approach is that we can develop easily and rapidly. Moreover, it is also possible to add some new tools, even modify and remove existent tools from the toolkit. The portability to a new language consists of heritage of all language independent tools and rapid adaptation of other language dependent tools. In the same way, for a new task, we can inherit from general processing tools, and adapt rapidly to create specific other tools. A specific XML scheme was designed for this purpose.

Next section describes the proposed text normalization workflow and implemented modules, Sect. 3 describes the XML format used to work with these tools. Section 4 is dedicated to the resource description and examples for written texts and Sect. 5 for speech transcriptions.

2   Text Normalization

2.1   Overview

For normalization, rule- and regular expression-based systems are the norm, including the tokenizers in the RASP system [5], the LT-TTT tools [8], the FreeLing tools [1], and the Stanford tokenizer, which is based on Penn Treebank tokenization (included as part of the Stanford parser [9]).

The proposed text normalization solution undergoes a set of levels: these was divided in a set of modules which can be shared by various languages. Of course, in some cases a language implies to develop a specific module. In this case, this module is inserted in the generic process. First thing that should be made was to determine modules which are shared modules (the modules which do not depend on the language) and variable modules (the modules which depend on each language). This splitting and determination work is really important. For a new language modelling, we will inherit the shared modules and fast adapt the variable modules to that language. It will economize the time consuming to build a complete corpus normalization. The key idea is to concentrate the language knowledge in a set of dictionaries and to develop modules which implement rules to deal with these knowledges.

Figure 1 summarizes the entire text normalization workflow. Gray boxes represent tools and White boxes represent resources. Normal fonts are used to mention shared modules or resourced while italic font is dedicated to language-specific entities.

2.2   A Set of Shared Modules

Utterance Segmentation. The first module implements an algorithm to split the text in utterances. It is a rule-based algorithm using punctuations and/or white space. The major part of rules are shared by many languages, and some specific rules are added for some languages. For example, the Chinese punctuation 。 is a non-ambiguous utterance segmentation mark. This module is only applied on written texts, not on transcribed speech.

Basic Unit Splitting. This module consists in a basic tokenization. White space is used for some languages as French, Spanish or English. Like English and some South Asian languages, Vietnamese also uses white space to tokenize a string of characters into a separate syllable. Then, for Vietnamese, this module splits into syllables which is the minimal unit. It is also the case for pinyin texts (Taiwanese or Chinese in our case). Character-based languages, as Chinese in our case, are splitting into characters which is the minimal unit for this language. However, this basic segmentation is not adapted to the Khmer language (as described in Sect. 2.3).

Replacement. This module implements a dictionary look-up algorithm to replace a string by an other one. This module can be optionally used during the text normalization process. It can be used to replace some specific characters as for example:

- ° is replaced by degrees (English), degrés (French), grados (Spanish), gradi (Italian), mức độ (Vietnamese), ឌីក្រេ (Khmer), 度 (Chinese), du (Chinese pinyin and Taiwanese).
- ² is replaced by square (English), carré (French), quadrados (Spanish), quadrato (Italian), bình phương (Vietnamese), កាម (Khmer), 平方 (Chinese), ping fang (Chinese pinyin)

depending on the input language dictionary.

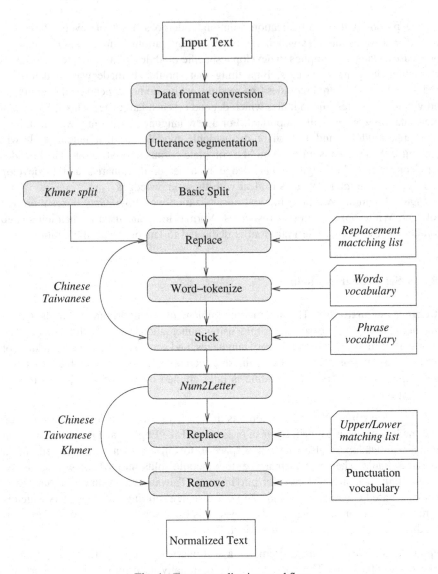

Fig. 1. Text normalization workflow

This module can also be used to convert the character case when the 'upper/lower' function of the toolbox does not support the character encoding of the language. Here are examples of the Vietnamese dictionary used to lower characters: Ơ ơ, Ờ ờ, Ớ ớ.

Obviously this upper/lower conversion is not relevant for Chinese. It is also not possible to apply this conversion if the upper (or lower) font or encoding does not exists for the given language.

Word-Tokenization. This module fixes a set of rules to segment strings including punctuation marks. The algorithm split strings into words on the basis of a dictionary and a set of rules which was established manually. For example, in French "trompe-l'oeil" (*sham*) is an entry in the vocabulary and it will not be segmented. On the other way, an entry like "l'oeil" (*the eye*) have to be segmented in 2 words. This module is language-independent. Obviously, it is not relevant to apply it for Chinese (with characters or pinyin) and Taiwanese.

Sticking. This module implements an algorithm to concatenate strings into words based on a dictionary with an optimization criteria: *longest matching*. This module can be applied only if a phrase vocabulary is created for the target language. Here is a set of words which are stuck with the character '_' by this algorithm:

- English: once_upon_a_time, game_over, white_space
- French: au_fur_et_à_mesure, prix_nobel,
- Vietnamese: tính_nhẩm, câu_lạc_bộ

Chinese characters are grouped without adding a character to stick them:

- Chinese: 登记簿.
  Khmer character clusters are grouped using the '-' character:
- Khmer: សិ-ទ្ធិ-ក្រា-ណា.

Unlike the character to stick, this algorithm is completely language-independent.

Removing. This module can be applied to remove strings of a text. The list of strings to remove is fixed in a vocabulary file. This module is relevant for example to remove punctuation marks. The punctuation list is only encoding-dependent (UTF8, iso-8859-1, etc.) but not language-dependent.

Other Tools. Text normalization is also a technical problem. Then, some other language-independent tools are necessary to format data depending on the input format: html, ASCII or some other specific input format and encoding.

2.3 Language-Specific Modules

As mentioned previously, the basic splitting is not relevant to the Khmer language: there are no white space or other segmentation marks and characters are a too small unit. The character-cluster is a good basic unit as its segmentation is trivial because of its non-ambiguities atomic structure. Then for this language, a character cluster (CC) segmentation is applied using rules created with linguistic knowledge, as illustrated in Fig. 2. Word segmentation is then obtained by using the language-independent longest matching algorithm to stick character clusters.

The number to letter module is also an optional language-specific module. For example, the number "123" is normalized as:

- French: cent vingt trois.
- English: one hundred twenty-three.
- Spanish: ciento veintitres.

Sentence	ព្រះពុទ្ធជាព្រះបរមគ្រូនៃយើង						
Word	ព្រះពុទ្ធ	ជា	ព្រះបរម	គ្រូ	នៃ	យើង	
CC	ព្រះ	ព	ុ	ទ្ធ	ជា	ព្រះ	ប	រ	ម	គ្រូ	នៃ	យើ	ង
Translation	Buddha is our supreme teacher						

Fig. 2. Khmer segmentation example (from [17])

- Italian: centoventitré.
- Vietnamese: một trăm hai mươi ba.
- Khmer: មួយ រយ ម្ភ ៃ បី.
- Chinese: 一百二十三.

Consequently, it is necessary to implement this module for each new language. However, algorithms to perform the transformation are close and a new implementation can be very fast with the help of already done languages.

3 Data Format

To deal with written texts, the data format is based on the XML standard as it is currently a common practice. Among others we can cite that of LDC: the "LCTL Tokenized Text XML Files"[1]. An important feature in our XML format development was genericity: the proposed XML format can be used in various applications like: language modelling, statistical linguistics, information retrieval, machine translation... for any language. Then, for example, the LCTL proposes to fix the language name and the corresponding encoding as attributes of the entire text corpus. In our case, they are attributes of each sentence, which allows code-switching:

```
<sent num="4">
   <orig> and voilà! </orig>
   <elts id="word" length="1" lang="EN">
      <wd num="1"><str> and </str></wd>
   </elts>
   <elts id="word" length="1" lang="FR">
      <wd num="1"><str> voilà </str></wd>
   </elts>
</sent>
```

It is also possible to add alignments between the series of elements, with an alignment score, to deal with the machine translation application, for example:

---

[1] http://www.ldc.upenn.edu/Creating/creating_annotated.shtml#DTDs

```
<sent num="1">
  <orig> mot </orig>
  <elts id="target" length="1" lang="ZH">
    <wd num="1"> <str> 文字</str> </wd>
  </elts>
  <elts id="source" length="1" lang="FR">
    <wd num="1"><str> mot </str></wd>
  </elts>
  <align idtgt="target" idsrc="source">
    <a numsrc="1" numtgt="1" score="0.235" />
  </align>
</sent>
```

To facilitate the technical tool development and also to facilitate queries on the corpus, we concentrated linguistic informations in elements and attributes are often used only to define properties like id. numbers, types, etc.

4   Implementation and Results: Written Texts

4.1   Language Resources

This approach implies to develop the following resources for each language:

1. a list of words: the vocabulary, used by the tool to tokenize;
2. optionally a list of phrases, used by the tool to stick;
3. optionally a list of character to be replaced, used by the tool to replace;
4. optionally an upper-lower mapping dictionary, used by the tool to lower.

All created resources described in this section was collected from free data on the web or free tools, and are distributed under the terms of the GNU Public License.

French. The vocabulary is made of 785 k words (with upper and lower cases). The phrases vocabulary is made of 32 k phrases created from frequent entries, and words containing spaces like "pomme de terre" (*potato*) and "petit à petit" (*gradually*) or city names like "New Orleans", "New York"...

English. Text normalization resources are frequent, then, we did not focused on this language. The English vocabulary is made of 87 k entries plus 500 phrases.

Spanish. The vocabulary is made of 370 k words with only lower cases. The phrase vocabulary should be done in future work.

Vietnamese. The vocabulary was collected and created from broadcast news on the web [11]. It is made of about 13000 syllables (with upper and lower cases) and 600 words with several syllables separated with a '-' like "ca-vát" (*tie*). We also created a vocabulary made of 68 k words. It includes words corresponding to several sticked syllables like "Áo tưởng" (*illusion*).

Khmer. The vocabulary we collected is made of 20,000 words [17]. 16,000 was obtained from a numerical version of the official Khmer dictionary "Chhoun Nat". We also added 4000 words extracted from the manual segmentation of 1000 Khmer sentences. Similar to Chinese and Thai, Khmer is written without spaces between words. A sentence in Khmer ក ណ ឲ ស ម ដ ច ឲ ឌ could be segmented into ក ណ ឲ ស ឲ ម ដ ច ឲ (*color | white | why | say | black*) or ក ណ ឲ ស ម ដ ច ឲ ឌ ឲ ឌ (*color | king | say | black*). A correct segmentation of a sentence into words requires the full knowledge of the vocabulary and of the semantics of the sentence. We estimated that the segmentation based on this vocabulary gives 95 % of correct word segmentation.

Chinese. The character-based vocabulary is made of only 88 k words. The pinyin is only made of 355 syllables without tones, and will have to be improved in the future.

Italian. The vocabulary was constructed during the Evalita evaluation campaign. Evalita is an initiative devoted to the evaluation of Natural Language Processing and Speech tools for Italian. In Evalita 2011 the "Forced Alignment on Spontaneous Speech" task was added. Training data is about 15 map task dialogues recorded by couples of speakers exhibiting a wide variety of Italian variants. Systems were required to align the audio sequences of spoken dialogues to the provided relative transcription. The Italian dictionary of [2] was downloaded from the Festival synthesizer tool[2]. This dictionary was enriched by words and their pronunciations observed in the Evalita training corpus. The resulting dictionary is made of 389 k words.

Taiwanese. The dictionary was constructed from the data described in [18], a Taiwan Southern Min spontaneous speech corpus primarily constructed and annotated for studying discourse prosody.

4.2   XML Output Examples

The output of this work, when applied on written texts, is an xml file with a text in a normalized form. First example of this paper is a French text with a tokenized utterance. We also included POS-tags to show that the xml format can easily be extended.

```
<?xml version="1.0" encoding="iso-8859-1"?>
<!DOCTYPE corpus SYSTEM "corpus.dtd">
<corpus>
  <doc num="1">
    <descr>
      <creator>Robert Bouvier</creator>
      <title>Le parler marseillais</title>
      <date d="07" m="01" y="1999"/>
    </descr>
    <text>
      <par>
        <sent num="1">
```

---

[2] The Centre for Speech Technology Research: The festival speech synthesis system.

```
<orig>La langue d'un peuple est inscrite dans sa
culture ; elle en est le véhicule naturel, en
même temps que le support de sa pensée et de sa
sensibilité. </orig>
<elts>
   <wd>
      <str> la </str>
      <pos> DETFS </pos>
      <lem> le </lem>
   </wd>
   <wd>
      <str> langue </str>
      <pos> NFS </pos>
      <lem> langue </lem>
   </wd>

      ...
   </elts>
  </sent>
 </par>
</text>
</doc>
...
</corpus>
```

As a word tokenization can be ambiguous the data format proposed in this paper lets the possibility to keep all possible tokenizations, and eventually to provide some kind of alignments between tokenization variants. Here is an example with a Vietnamese word made of 2 syllables which can be grouped into one word:

```
<sent num="4">
   <orig> Việt Nam </orig>
   <elts id="syll" length="2">
      <wd num="2"><str> Việt </str></wd>
      <wd num="3"><str> Nam </str></wd>
   </elts>
   <elts id="word" length="1">
      <wd num="1"><str> Việt_Nam </str></wd>
   </elts>
   <align idtgt="syll" idsrc="word">
      <a numsrc="1" numtgt="1" />
      <a numsrc="1" numtgt="2" />
   </align>
</sent>
```

4.3   Toolkit Distribution and Applications

The system (tools and resources) is available on the web [4] as open source under the terms of the GNU GPL license. The tool was designed for research purposes so it is presented as a set of scripts using the *gawk* language.

The major benefit of such a tool is that it allows to rapidly process a very large text corpus with several millions of documents from different sources. For example, one year of the French newspaper "Le Monde" (20 million words) was normalized in 2 h 30 min with a 2009-Desktop PC: Intel Xeon 2.6 Ghz with hard drive SATA 7200 RPM.

This toolkit was successfully applied for statistical language modelling in Automatic Speech Recognition systems: in French [4], in Vietnamese [11] and in Khmer [17]. It was also used for the creation of a French-Vietnamese translation system [6].

5 Implementation and Results: Speech Transcription

The last ten years or so have witnessed an explosion in the quantity of linguistic data which have become available as evidence for the nature of linguistic representations of *speech*. When a speech corpus is transcribed into a written text, the transcriber is immediately confronted with the following question: how to reflect the reality of oral speech in a corpus? Conventions are then designed to provide a set of rules for writing speech corpora. These conventions establish which phenomena have to be annotated and also how to annotate them. For example, the speech signal can include specific productions like reductions (*je suis* pronounced as /SHi/instead of the standard pronunciation /ZsHi/). The spelling can then be deliberately modified. Moreover, transcribers can provide an enriched orthographic transcription (EOT), which include short pauses, noises, laughter, filled pauses, truncated words, repeats.

In the context of the development of a tool named SPPAS [3], we recently introduced the text normalization approach proposed in this paper. SPPAS is a tool to produce automatic annotations which include utterance, word, syllabic and phonemic segmentations from a recorded speech sound and its transcription. The whole procedure is a succession of 4 automatic steps: Text normalization, Phonetization, Alignment, Syllabification, and resulting alignments are a set of TextGrid files (see Fig. 3). TextGrid is the native file format of the Praat software which became one of the most common tool for phoneticians [16].

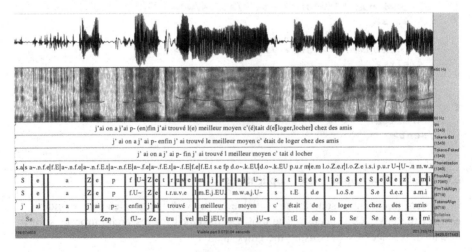

Fig. 3. SPPAS output example

SPPAS, version 1.5, is designed for French, English, Italian, Chinese (characters or pinyin) and Taiwanese (pinyin). Additionally, the tokenization module includes Spanish and Vietnamese. SPPAS is implemented using the programming language *Python*. Thanks to being scripting language with module architecture, syntax simplicity and rich text processing tools, Python is object-oriented programming.

The modules described in Sect. 2 (except utterance segmentation) were re-implemented in Python. A specific module has been implemented to deal with enriched orthographic transcriptions. Thereby, from the manual EOT, two derived transcriptions are generated automatically by the tokenizer: the "standard" transcription (the list of orthographic tokens); the "faked spelling" that is a specific transcription from which the obtained phonetic tokens are used by the phonetization system.

The following illustrates an utterance text normalization in French:

Transcription: j'ai on a j'ai p- (en)fin j'ai trouvé l(e) meilleur moyen c'était d(e) [loger,locher] chez des amis (*I've we've I've - well I found the best way was to live in friends' apartment*').

Standard tokens: j' ai on a j' ai p- enfin j' ai trouvé le meilleur moyen c'était de loger chez des amis.

Faked tokens: j' ai on a j' ai p- fin j' ai trouvé l meilleur moyen c'était d loche chez des amis.

The speech tokenizer is integrated in SPPAS, and it can also be used as a command-line, at the level of the shell. We tested the tokenizer on 16 transcribed files with EOT, each one representing the transcription of 1 hour speech in the context of dialogues, with a 2009-Desktop PC (the same as Sect. 4). The process was accomplished in 2 min 25 s. The result is a set of 16 TextGrid files containing the normalized text (a total of 120,000 tokens) including standard spelling and faked spelling.

6   Conclusion

In principle, any system that deals with unrestricted text need the text to be normalized. Text normalization is a very important issue for Natural Language Processing applications. This paper presented a text normalization system entirely designed to handle multiple languages and/or tasks with the same algorithms and the same tools. Hence, we hope this work will be helpful in the future to open to new practices in the methodology and tool developments: thinking problems with a generic multilingual aspect.

Acknowledgements. This research was partially supported by the Ortolang project: http://www. ortolang.fr. The support is gratefully acknowledged.

We address special thanks to Tatsuya Watanabe for the help in the python development.

References

1. Atserias, J., Casas, B., Comelles, E., González, M., Padró, L., Padró, M.: FreeLing 1.3: Syntactic and semantic services in an open-source NLP library. In: The Proceedings of Language Resources and Evaluation Conference, Genoa, Italy (2006)
2. Bigi, B.: The SPPAS participation to the forced-alignment task of Evalita 2011. In: Sprugnoli, R. (ed.) EVALITA 2012. LNCS, vol. 7689, pp. 312–321. Springer, Heidelberg (2012)
3. Bigi, B.: SPPAS: a tool for the phonetic segmentations of speech. In: The Proceedings of Language Resources and Evaluation Conference, Istanbul, Turkey, pp. 1748–1755, (2012) ISBN 978-2-9517408-7-7
4. Bigi, B. (2013). http://www.lpl-aix.fr/~bigi
5. Briscoe, T., Carroll J., Watson, R.: The second release of the RASP system. In: Proceedings of the COLING/ACL Interactive Presentation Sessions, Sydney, Australia (2006)
6. Do, T.-N.-D., Le, V.-B., Bigi, B., Besacier, L., Castelli, E.: Mining a comparable text corpus for a Vietnamese-French machine translation system. In: Fourth Workshop on Statistical Machine Translation, Athens, Greece, pp. 165–172 (2009)
7. Graliński, F., Jassem, K., Wagner, A., Wypych, M.: Text normalization as a special case of machine translation. In: The Proceedings of the International Multiconference on Computer Science and Information Technology, Wisła, Poland, pp. 51–56 (2006)
8. Grover, C., Matheson, C., Mikheev, A., Moens, M.: LT TTT - a flexible tokenisation tool. In: The Proceedings of Language Resources and Evaluation Conference, Athens, Greece (2000)
9. Klein, D., Manning, C.D.: Accurate unlexicalized parsing. In: The Proceedings of annual meeting of the Association for Computational Linguistics, pp. 423–430 (2003)
10. Lamy, R., Moraru, D., Bigi, B., Besacier, L.: Premiers pas du CLIPS sur les données d'évaluation ESTER. XXV-èmes Journées d'Études sur la Parole, Fès, Morocco (2004)
11. Le, V.-B., Besacier, L., Seng, S., Bigi, B., Do, T.-N.-D.: Recent advances in Automatic Speech Recognition for Vietnamese. In: International Workshop on Spoken Languages Technologies for Under-resourced languages, Hanoi, Vietnam (2008)
12. Linguistic Data Consortium (1998). http://ldc.upenn.edu
13. Martínez, H., Vivaldi, J., Villegas, M.: Text handling as a Web Service for the IULA processing pipeline. In: The Proceedings of Language Resources and Evaluation Conference, La Valetta, Malta, pp. 22–29 (2010)
14. Panchapagesan, K., Talukdar, P.P., Krishna, N.S., Bali, K., Ramakrishnan, A.G.: Hindi text normalization. In: The Proceedings of 5th International Conference on Knowledge Based Computer Systems, Hyderabad, India (2004)
15. Papageorgiou, H., Prokopidis, P., Giouli, V., Piperidis, S.A.: Unified tagging architecture and its application to Greek. In: The Proceedings of the 2nd Language Resources and Evaluation Conference, Athens, Greece (2000)
16. Praat (2013). http://www.fon.hum.uva.nl/praat/
17. Seng, S., Sam, S., Le, V.-B., Bigi, B., Besacier, L.: Which unit for acoustic and language modeling for Khmer Automatic Speech Recognition. In: International Workshop on Spoken Languages Technologies for Under-resourced languages, Hanoi, Vietnam (2008)
18. Wang, S.-F., Fon, J.: A Taiwan Southern Min spontaneous speech corpus for discourse prosody. In: The Proceedings of Tools and Resources for the Analysis of Speech Prosody, Aix-en-Provence, France, pp. 20–23 (2013)
19. Sproat, R., Black, A., Chen, S., Kumar, S., Ostendorf, M., Richards, C.: Normalization of non-standard words. Comput. Speech Lang. 15(3), 287–333 (2001)

Creating Multilingual Parallel Corpora in Indian Languages

Narayan Choudhary[✉] and Girish Nath Jha

Jawaharlal Nehru University, New Delhi, India
{choudharynarayan,girishjha}@gmail.com

Abstract. This paper presents a description of the parallel corpora being created simultaneously in 12 major Indian languages including English under a nationally funded project named Indian Languages Corpora Initiative (ILCI) run through a consortium of institutions across India. The project runs in two phases. The first phase of the project has two distinct goals - creating parallel sentence aligned corpus and parts of speech (POS) annotation of the corpora as per recently evolved national standard under Bureau of Indian Standard (BIS). This phase of the project is finishing in April 2012 and the next phase with newer domains and more national languages is likely to take off in May 2012. The goal of the current phase is to create parallel aligned POS tagged corpora in 12 major Indian languages (including English) with Hindi as the source language in health and tourism domains. Additional languages and domains will be added in the next phase. With the goal of 25 thousand sentences in each domain, we find that the total number of words in each of the domains has reached up to 400 thousands, the largest in size for a parallel corpus in any pair of Indian languages. A careful attempt has been made to capture various types of texts. With an analysis of the domains, we divided the two domains into sub-domains and then looked for the source text in those particular sub-domains to be included in the source text. With a preferable structure of the corpora in mind, we present our experiences also in selecting the text as the source and recount the problems like that of a judgment on the sub-domain text representation in the corpora. The POS annotation framework used for this corpora creation has also seen new changes in the POS tagsets. We also give a brief on the POS annotation framework being applied in this endeavor.

Keywords: Corpora creation · Source text for multilingual parallel corpus · Parallel corpus in Indian languages · Tourism and health corpus in Indian languages · Parts of speech annotation · Annotated corpora · LRL

1 Introduction

Parallel corpora are of great importance in various natural language processing (NLP) and non-NLP tasks. Starting from a comparative and contrastive linguistic analysis for various linguistic features of the languages concerned to machine translation, there are various use for such a corpus in any given language pair.

© Springer International Publishing Switzerland 2014
Z. Vetulani and J. Mariani (Eds.): LTC 2011, LNAI 8387, pp. 527–537, 2014.
DOI: 10.1007/978-3-319-08958-4_43

India is nation with great linguistic diversity with over 452 individual languages listed by Ethnologue[1]. Out of these, 22 languages are listed as 'scheduled' (also sometimes called 'national') languages comprising a total of 96.56 % of the national population[2] accessed 4th September, 2011. Hindi is the largest spoken language across India (sharing above 41 % of the national population) and also the official language of the Indian state (along with English).

Electronic content came rather late into Indian languages. The importance of corpus studies itself came into fore with the prevalence of e-text. In such a scenario, the corpus study in Indian languages was negligible prior to this century. With the advent of common use of computers, the Indian languages also got some share and e-content gradually started growing in Indian languages. Though Unicode standards in Indian languages has helped grow the content, there is not enough content available that can be used to create parallel corpus in Indian languages.

There have been attempts to develop parallel corpora in Indian languages earlier as well. But none of such corpora have been developed from the scratch and is mostly not publically available for the research community. Barring one exception of the EMILLE parallel corpus (Baker et al., 2004) of 200 thousand words in three languages in general domain, there is no other parallel corpus made in Indian languages. For the annotated parallel corpus, there are none available in Indian languages. To fill this gap, the Department of Information Technology (DIT), Govt. of India sanctioned a project run through a consortium involving 11 institutions across India (Jha 2010). This paper presents a summary of the work carried out under this project. This is an attempt to build a representative and comprehensive corpus of two domains in 12 major scheduled Indian languages. The structure of consortium has been given in the following table with the names of the principle investigator, language(s) and the name of the host institute (Table 1).

Table 1. Summary of the Consortium Structure

Principle investigator	Language(s)	Host institute
Girish N. Jha	Hindi, English, Oriya[a]	JNU, New Delhi
S. Virk	Punjabi	Punjabi Uni., Patiala
M.M. Hussain	Urdu	JNU, New Delhi
Niladri S. Dash	Bangla	ISI, Kolkata
M. A. Kulkarni	Marathi	IITB, Mumbai
Kirtida S. Shah	Gujarati	Guj. Uni., Ahm'bad
Jyoti D. Pawar	Konkani	Goa Uni., Goa
S. Arulmozhi	Telugu	Drav. Uni., Kuppam,
S. Rajendran	Tamil	Tamil Uni.,Thanjavur
Elizabeth Sherly	Malayalam	IIITM-K, Trivandrum

[a] Oriya was earlier assigned to Utkal University, Bhubaneswar but now it has been transferred to the consortium head institute of JNU, New Delhi.

---

[1] http://www.ethnologue.com/show_country.asp?name=inaccessed:4September,2011

[2] as per Census of India, 2001 http://censusindia.gov.in/Census_Data_2001/Census_Data_Online/Language/Statement5.html

These languages represent both the two major language families present in India, namely Indo-Aryan and Dravidian. Being the Associate Official Language (AOL) of India, English, a Germanic language, is also included.

The corpora creation has two principal tasks: creation of the raw parallel aligned text and POS annotation. The translation is done manually by especially trained native speakers of the language in their regions. Annotation is also done manually with no use of available automatic taggers.

For translation there are minimal guidelines with respect to format and structure of the target sentences. The source text is formatted to be one sentence per line and each sentence is given a unique identification (ID) number. The translated text in the target languages are also formatted accordingly i.e. they are one sentence per line and correspond to the sentence ID number of the source text. This ensures that we have the source and the target text aligned as we progress. We do not use any alignment tool for this purpose.

Creating the source text is equivalent to corpus creation. As the source text corpus is domain specific and has limitations with regard to the size each of these domains can grow, a careful selection of the text had to be followed. The two domains of health and tourism are not very prolific ones in Hindi. Most of the works done in these two domains are in English. Therefore finding original text in Hindi in these two domains has been a difficult task. The average of words per sentence (out of a total of 25000 sentences per domain) comes out to be 16. Thus we get a corpus consisting of a total of about 400,000 words in each domain.

2   Creating the Source Text

While it is possible to collect the source text online, it is advisable that one should do this with extra caution when creating an ambitious corpus as presented here, particularly for less resourced languages like the Indian languages. Besides, most of the text over the internet would need editing and proofing (Choudhary, 2010). For the source text or the base corpus, we first tried selecting text online. But then we realized that most of the text that was available in Hindi over the internet was translated from English or other languages. Besides, our choice necessarily had to be very eclectic as we were specific about the domain and ensure that proper representation was given to the various sub-domains and genres within the domains. So, we went on to collect text from various other sources e.g. promotional materials published and distributed by government and/or private institutions/agencies. We also selected extracts from books, articles and stories from magazines and newspaper.

2.1   Domain Analysis

To ensure that the diversity of the corpus with regard to various types of genres available in the domain is maintained and gets reflected in the corpus, we did a domain analysis before embarking on the text selection. Both the health and tourism domains are vast topics and collecting text within a specific size in the domain necessitated eclecticism. So, we divided both the domains into several sub-domains and gave a priority to the texts that are more common in use. Therefore some sub-domains have greater representation in the corpus than others. These sub-domains were further divided into other categories of text so that a cap is maintained for each variety of text and an even representation of the domain as a whole gets reflected through the corpus.

2.2   Health Domain

Health domain was divided into a total of 16 sub-domains. These sub-domains were made mainly to capture the different disciplines within the medical arena. No sub-domain was allotted to different genres of medical practice like allopath, ayurveda, acupressure, acupuncture etc. However, these were included in the corpus in a certain proportion with the total of the text. For example a disease, its description and symptoms are given only once as these are common in each of the medical practices. It is the diagnosis and treatment where the difference would be reflected.

As summarized in Table 2, the health domain has a total of 419420 words, with the total number of words per sentence being 16.77. The total number of unique words in this domain comes out to be 21446.

Table 2. Summary of the Health Domain Corpus

Major domains	Domain code	No. of sentences	Percentage
Blood, Heart and Circulation	H1	2192	8.76
Bones, Joints and Muscles	H2	1022	4.09
Brain and Nerves	H3	1792	7.17
Digestive System	H4	2175	8.70
Ear, Nose and Throat	H5	620	2.48
Endocrine System	H6	111	0.44
Eyes and Vision	H7	824	3.30
Immune System	H8	634	2.54
Kidneys and Urinary System	H9	575	2.30
Lungs and Breathing	H10	573	2.29
Oral and Dental	H11	610	2.44
Skin, Hair and Nails	H12	2104	8.42
Female Reproductive System	H13	2099	8.40
Male Reproductive System	H14	325	1.30
Life style	H15	4591	18.37
Miscellaneous	H16	3431	13.73
Pediatrics	H17	1321	5.28
Total		25000	100.00

2.3   Tourism Domain

Tourism domain was divided into a total of 17 major sub-domains. These were further divided into categories as per the requirement. For example, pilgrimage was divided into two categories of Indian and extra-Indian, ecotourism was divided into wildlife, hill stations, desert and others. There were also sub-domains that did not have any categories like leisure tourism, medical tourism etc. Table 3 gives a summary of the tourism corpus. The tourism corpus has a total of 396204 words with a per sentence word average of 15.8. Total number of unique words in the tourism corpus is 28542.

Table 3. Summary of the Tourism Domain Corpus

Major domains	Domain code	No. of sentences	Percentage
Pilgrimage	T1	3401	13.60
Ecotourism	T2	6803	27.21
Heritage Tourism	T3	4012	16.05
Adventure Tourism	T4	1843	7.37
Mass Travel and Tour	T5	1576	6.30
Leisure Tour	T6	50	0.20
Medical Tourism	T7	16	0.06
Nautical Tourism	T8	605	2.42
Culinary Tourism	T9	144	0.58
Disaster Tourism	T10	171	0.68
Dark Tourism	T11	16	0.06
Space Tourism	T12	0	0.00
War Tourism	T13	9	0.04
Shopping Tourism	T14	202	0.81
Others	T15	2037	8.15
General Description	T16	4115	16.46
Total		25000	100.00

3   Data Storage, Maintenance and Dissemination

The Hindi source data collected manually with careful selection criteria in mind was mostly typed out by language editors. Out of the 25 thousand sentences in each of the domains only a meager 1500 sentences or 6 % were taken from the internet. The whole of the corpus was first typed into spread sheets on normal PCs by the language editors of the source text. It was further validated by the present authors. Each sentence in the corpus has a unique ID which gets carried forward to each of the translated languages. Thus the alignment is done simultaneously as the translation in each of the languages progresses.

All the data collected and incorporated in the source text are stored with their metadata information which includes various information e.g. the source, number of words selected from the source, names of the authors/copyright holders and their sub-domain details. For the archiving purposes, all the source text is hyperlinked with a scanned image file of the source document from where the text was taken.

The source text is encoded in Unicode. All the translated texts in other languages are also in Unicode. As for the quality of the source or the translated text, we believe this to be the best possible. We say the source text to be the best possible for a corpus because of the following reasons:

a. it is typed by the trained language editors
b. it has been internally and externally validated by language experts

For the translated text, usually we seek only one translation. However, wherever possible, if two or more options are available for a sentence, we encourage the translators to provide those translations as optional ones. Once the text was translated, we evaluated the translation through external evaluators of each of the language pairs and the suggestions/corrections recommended by them have been incorporated in the target text. The whole of the corpus creation process has been supervised and the corpus principally has 0 % 'noise' in terms of spelling mistakes, wrong character encodings, incorrect translations etc.

Govt. of India has started a data centre (http://tdil-dc.in). The ILCI corpora is in the process of being uploaded to this data centre and will be available for free download as per the Govt. of India guidelines.

4   Parallel Corpus Creation and Alignment

As noted above, the parallel corpora are created simultaneously, in each of the language pairs as the translation progresses. As the source text is created it is electronically sent to the other members of the consortium where the respective translators translate the source text in the respective target languages and send back to us. We achieved the raw parallel sentence-wise aligned corpus in a period of about one and a half years.

5   POS Annotation

We are now in the middle of the second principal task - doing POS annotation of the parallel corpora in each language. The annotations are done manually for each of the languages. Although there are some POS taggers available for some of the Indian languages, their efficacy and standard input/output has been doubtful. Moreover, Indian did not have a common standard till very recently when it got its first national standard in POS annotation through the efforts of BIS and ILCI. There are some POS taggers developed with various accuracies for the languages like Hindi (Shrivastava and Bhattacharya 2008), Telugu (Avinesh and Karthick, 2007), Bengali (Dandpat et al., 2007) etc. (for a survey report see Kumar and Josan, 2010). The Indian Languages Machine Translation (ILMT) project funded by DIT (Govt. of India) claims to have developed several POS taggers, but they are yet to find users in the corpora community.

5.1 POS Tagset

Until recently, there have been two major types of tagsets used for POS annotation of texts in Indian languages. These two include a tagset developed by IIIT Hyderabad (Bharti et al., 2006) and another one developed under the leadership of Microsoft Research, India (MSRI), known as IL-POST (Baskaran et al., 2008). The IIIT tagset is a flat tagset based on the Penn tagset (Santorini 1990) with some modifications to suit major Indian languages. The IL-POST tagset is a rather new annotation framework put to use in Indian languages. The IL-POST framework provides for a hierarchical, multi-layered tagset where much of the linguistic information is captured through explicit tags, including the ones that can be possibly identified through a morphological ana-lyzer. Advocates of the IIIT tagset emphasizes that the information that can be extracted through the use of a language specific morphological analyzer should not be marked manually because it would only increase the amount of human labor put to use.

There is no sizeable POS annotated corpus available in any of the Indian languages at present. As POS annotation is a part of this project, the tagset to be used for the corpora of these 12 languages became an issue. Several meetings were held under the aegis of BIS to come to a conclusion. Finally, a POS tagset was agreed upon by the stake-holders. This tagset has come to be known as the BIS parts-of-speech annotation tagset[3].

The BIS Tagset contains the features of the hierarchical tagset. However, it has tags for only first two tiers of linguistic information (POS and their subtypes) and excludes information from tier three onwards as these can be provided by morph analyzers and parsers. Morphological analyzers are available for some of the languages in the group and many more are in the process of being developed. For Hindi, morphological analyzers have been reported from various quarters e.g. (Goyal and Singh Lehal, 2008; Bögel, et al., 2007; etc.).

5.1.1 Principles for Designing Linguistic Standards for Corpora Annotation

The BIS standard has set the following principles for designing linguistic standards for corpora annotation.

1. Generic Tag Sets.
2. Layered approach.

   - Layer I: Morphology.
   - Layer II: POS <morphosyntactic>.
   - Layer III: LWG.
   - Layer IV: Chunks.
   - Layer V: Syntactic Analysis.
   - Layer VI: Thematic roles/Predicate Argument structure.
   - Layer VII: Semantic properties of the lexical items.
   - Layers VIII, IX... Word sense, Pronoun referents (Anaphora), etc.,.

---

[3] No standard published reference can be given for this tagset as yet. We refer to the document circulated in the consortia meetings. This document was referred as "Linguistic Resource Standards: Standards for POS Tagsets for Indian Languages", ver. 005, August, 2010.

3. Hierarchy within each layer.
4. Extensibility (including the language specific requirements and additional languages).
5. If a tag is redundant for a language, it should be deprecated.
6. ISO 639:3[4] Language code should be used <in metadata>.
7. Follow global guidelines such as EAGLES (Leech and Wilson 1999) where available.
8. Standards should be mappable to/compatible with existing schemes to and from.
9. Standard is designed to handle wide range of applications and also should support all types of NLP Research efforts independent of a particular technology development approach.
10. The scheme should be Annotator friendly.

5.1.2 Super Set of POS Tags

Guided by the principles above, a super set of POS tags for Indian languages has been developed (Appendix I). Tagsets for different Indian languages have been drawn from this super tagset. As can be seen in Appendix I below, there are 11 top level categories. These are further classified into types and subtypes. There are a total of 45 tags in this set. If a language demands further sub-types, the principles above allow that. However, top level categories cannot be changed or new top level categories are not recommended to be added. No individual language has used all of these categories. The tagsets for all the 12 languages have been drawn from this super tagset.

5.2 Manual POS Annotation

The annotation is being done manually by the language experts/native linguists following the annotation guideline prepared for respective languages. There are some languages in the group that are morphologically agglutinating. For such languages direct annotation is not possible and morphological segmentation is required before POS annotation can begin. For such languages e.g. Tamil, Telugu and Malayalam, segmentation is recommended as a pre-processing task before the POS annotation. Additionally, a server-based, access-anywhere, annotation tool is put in place where the annotators can annotate the text in their respective language over the internet. The tool can be accessed here:

http://sanskrit.jnu.ac.in/ilciann/index.jsp

6 Conclusion

In this paper we have presented a description of processes involved in creating the parallel corpora in two specified domains of health and tourism for 12 major Indian languages. We have shown how the source text was created and how the raw corpora in target languages have been created/translated.

---

[4] http://www.sil.org/iso639-3/default.asp

We have shown the representation given to different genres of writing within these two domains and tried to show that the source corpus created represents the domains under study in their totality. As the source text is created specifically for parallel corpora development, we have also shown that the process of its creation gives us an aligned corpus by default. Qualitatively, the corpus created is richer than other corpora in terms of lack of noise and integrity. This can be corroborated with the fact the corpus does not have any spelling mistakes, errors of character encoding (as is common in Indian languages written in their native scripts), and that the translations have been verified through external evaluators.

For POS annotation, we are following the latest annotation framework approved by the BIS and the annotated corpora generated through this task will prove to be a great resource in the NLP and related areas of Indian languages in particular and other languages in general.

The process of corpora creation has been though labor intensive, the result so far is worthwhile. Additional Indian languages will be added following the same process. That is the source Hindi text can be translated into any language and then POS tagged. This will give newer pairs of parallel corpora in 12 languages simultaneously.

The chosen two domains are of great importance in itself as both the health and tourism are the focus areas of any government in general and the Indian government in particular. Both the raw corpus and the annotated corpus can be used for various purposes of language engineering and linguistic analysis.

By the end of the project, we expect to achieve one million tagged words in each of the 12 languages because there is some additional data collection in the process of selecting 50 thousand words in each language.

Appendix I: Super Set of POS Tags for Indian Languages

Sl. No.	Category (Category. Type. Subtype)	Label	Annotation convention
1	1 Noun	N	N
2	1.1 Common	NN	N_NN
3	1.2 Proper	NNP	N_NNP
4	1.3 Verbal	NNV	N_NNV
5	1.4 Nloc	NST	N_NST
6	2 Pronoun	PR	PR
7	2.1 Personal	PRP	PR_PRP
8	2.2 Reflexive	PRF	PR_PRF
9	2.3 Relative	PRL	PR_PRL
10	2.4 Reciprocal	PRC	PR_PRC
11	2.5 Wh-word	PRQ	PR_PRQ

(Continued)

12	3 Demonstrative	DM	DM
13	3.1 Deictic	DMD	DM_DMD
14	3.2 Relative	DMR	DM_DMR
15	3.3 Wh-word	DMQ	DM_DMQ
16	Verb	V	V
17	4.1 Main	VM	V_VM
18	4.1.1 Finite	VF	V_VM_VF
19	4.1.2 Non-finite	VNF	V_VM_VNF
20	4.1.3 Infinitive	VINF	V_VM_VINF
21	4.1.4 Gerund	VNG	V_VM_VNG
22	4.2 Auxiliary	VAUX	V_VAUX
23	5 Adjective	JJ	
24	6 Adverb	RB	
25	7 Postposition	PSP	
26	8 Conjunction	CC	CC
27	8.1 Co-ordinator	CCD	CC_CCD
28	8.2 Subordinator	CCS	CC_CCS
29	8.2.1 Quotative	UT	CC_CCS_UT
30	9 Particles	RP	RP
31	9.1 Default	RPD	RP_RPD
32	9.2 Classifier	CL	RP_CL
33	9.3 Interjection	INJ	RP_INJ
34	9.4 Intensifier	INTF	RP_INTF
35	9.5 Negation	NEG	RP_NEG
36	10 Quantifiers	QT	QT
37	10.1 General	QTF	QT_QTF
38	10.2 Cardinals	QTC	QT_QTC
39	10.3 Ordinals	QTO	QT_QTO
40	11 Residuals	RD	RD
41	11.1 Foreign word	RDF	RD_RDF
42	11.2 Symbol	SYM	RD_SYM
43	11.3 Punctuation	PUNC	RD_PUNC
44	11.4 Unknown	UNK	RD_UNK
45	11.5 Echo-words	ECH	RD_ECH

References

Baker, P., Hardie, A., McEnery, T., Xiao, R., Bontcheva, K., Cunningham, H., Gaizauskas, R., Hamza, O., Maynard, D., Tablan, V., Ursu, C., Jayaram, B.D., Leisher, M.: Corpus linguistics and South Asian languages: corpus creation and tool development. Literary Linguist. Comput. **19**, 509–524 (2004)

Jha, G.N.: The TDIL program and the Indian language corpora initiative (ILCI). In: Calzolari, N., et al. (ed.) Proceedings of the 7th Conference on International Language Resources and Evaluation (LREC'10). European Language Resources Association (ELRA) (2010)

Choudhary, N.: Web-drawn Corpus for Indian languages: a case of Hindi. In: Singh, C., Singh Lehal, G., Sengupta, J., Sharma, D.V., Goyal, V. (eds.) ICISIL 2011. CCIS, vol. 139, pp. 218–223. Springer, Heidelberg (2011)

Shrivastava, M., Bhattacharyya, P.: Hindi POS tagger using naive stemming: harnessing morphological information without extensive Linguistic knowledge. In: Proceedings of the International Conference on NLP (ICON08), Pune, India (2008)

Avinesh, P.V.S., Karthik, G.: Part-of-speech tagging and chunking using conditional random fields and transformation-based learning. In: Proceedings of the IJCAI and the Workshop On Shallow Parsing for South Asian Languages (SPSAL), pp. 21–24 (2007)

Dandapat, S., Sarkar, S., Basu, A.: Automatic part-of-speech tagging for Bengali: an approach for morphologically rich languages in a poor resource scenario. In: Proceedings of the Association for Computational Linguistic, pp 221–224 (2007)

Kumar, D., Josan, G.S.: Part of speech taggers for morpho-logically rich Indian languages: a survey. Int. J. Comput. Appl. **6**(5), 1–9 (2010). Foundation of Computer Science

Bharati, A., Sharma, D.M., Bai, L., Sangal, R.: Anncorra: Annotating Corpora. LTRC, IIIT, Hyderabad (2006)

Baskaran, S., Bali, K., Choudhury, M., Bhattacharya, T., Bhattacharyya, P., Jha, G.N., Rajendran, S., Saravanan, K., Sobha, L., Subbarao., K.V.: A Common parts-of-speech tag set framework for indian languages. In: Nicoletta Calzolari (Conference Chair), Choukri, K., Maegaard, B., Mariani, J., Odjik, J., Piperidis, S., Tapias, D. (eds.) Proceedings of the 6th International Language Resources and Evaluation (LREC'08), Marrakech, Morocco (2008)

Santorini, B.: Part-of-speech Tagging Guidelines for the Penn Treebank Project. Technical report MS-CIS-90-47, Department of Computer and Information Science, University of Pennsylvania (1990)

Goyal, V., Lehal, G.S.: Hindi morphological analyzer and generator. In: Proceedings of the 1st International Conference on Emerging Trends in Engineering and Technology (2008)

Bögel, T., Butt, M., Hautli, A., Sulger, S.: Developing a finite-state morphological analyzer for Urdu and Hindi. In: Proceedings of the 6th International Workshop on Finite-State Methods and Natural Language Processing, Potsdam (2007)

Leech, G., Wilson, A.: Standards for tagsets. In: van Halteren, H. (ed.) EAGLES Recommendations for the Morphosyntactic Annotation of Corpora, (1999). http://www.ilc.cnr.it/EAGLES96/browse.html

Inducing Grammars from IGT

Lars Hellan[(⊠)] and Dorothee Beermann

Norwegian University of Science and Technology, 7491 Trondheim, Norway
{lars.hellan,dorothee.beermann}@ntnu.no

Abstract. We suggest a strategy for incremental construction of deep parsing grammars from Interlinear Glossed Text (IGT). Essential to the approach is that both the IGT and the grammar deploy a rich inventory of linguistic types and categories in their respective domains, with a view to be able to directly accommodate strings and constructions from ideally any type of language. This involves a heavy load of linguistically-based encoding in the initial phase, but on the other hand a simple technology residing basically in XML export from one application to the other, and the possibility for linguists working on specific languages to present data to the system in a form which does not go beyond common linguistic technique, and is useful for general linguistic purposes as well. The tool hosting the IGT is *TypeCraft*, and the system hosting the grammars is the *LKB* system, generally employed for implementing HPSG grammars. The strategy is illustrated with induction of a grammar fragment from a small set of IGTs from the Kwa language Ga.

Keywords: IGT · Deep parsing grammar · Grammar induction · Cross-linguistic categories · Ga · Construction enumeration · Valence types · Construction labeling · Typecraft · HPSG · Typegram

1 Introduction

We describe a strategy for incremental construction of 'deep' computational parsing grammars (henceforth 'DG') from a repository of Interlinear Glossed Text (henceforth 'IGT'), the latter containing both standard morphological annotation, parts-of-speech information and valence- and construction type information. The IGT is hosted in *TypeCraft* (cf. (Beermann and Mihaylov 2014), (Beermann forthcoming))[1]. The deep grammars are built with the *LKB* system (Copestake 2002), used for implementation of the HPSG grammar framework (cf. (Pollard and Sag 1994)), and instantiated for the present application in the grammar system *TypeGram*. The IGT is exported from TypeCraft in XML format to pertinent modules of TypeGram. As an intermediate point in this process, we define a level of 'meta-grammar', where the objects treated by the parser are strings of analytic symbols rather than expressions of the language itself.

The methodology of valence- and construction specification derives from early attempts to compactly enumerate valence and argument frames for Germanic languages,[2]

---

[1] http://typecraft.org
[2] See (Hellan et al. 1989).

© Springer International Publishing Switzerland 2014
Z. Vetulani and J. Mariani (Eds.): LTC 2011, LNAI 8387, pp. 538–547, 2014.
DOI: 10.1007/978-3-319-08958-4_44

and has more recently been applied to a Kwa and an Ethio-Semitic language, respectively Ga (ISO_639-3 gaa; cf. (Hellan and Dakubu 2010), (Dakubu 2008), and Kistaninya (ISO 639-3 gru; cf. (Wakjira 2010)); in the descriptions below we will focus on Ga.

Essential to the approach is that both the IGT and the grammar deploy a rich inventory of linguistic types and categories in their respective domains, with a view to be able to directly accommodate strings and constructions from ideally any type of language. This involves a heavy load of linguistically-based encoding in the initial phase, but on the other hand a simple technology residing basically in XML export from one application to the other, and the possibility for linguists working on specific languages to present data to the system in a form which does not go beyond common linguistic technique, and is useful for general linguistic purposes as well. The IGT glossing system is thus an extension of the Leipzig Glossing Convention (cf. (Bickel et al. 2008)), securing both typological representativeness and cross-framework consensus, and the grammar system likewise reflects agreed-on terminologies.

Another current approach involving interaction between IGT and DG is described in (Bender et al. 2013), using as DG reference system the HPSG Grammar Matrix, cf. Section 3 below. Compared to the above, this approach so far has more weight on the development of usable IGT resources (e.g., from sources like the Odin corpus[3]) than on the deployment of existing ones, and while its predefined stock of linguistic concepts plays less of a role than the corresponding stock of concepts in the Type-Craft-TypeGram interaction, its ultimate aim of facilitating induction and construction of deep grammars is close to that of the present approach.

Section 2 in the following gives a brief characterization of TypeCraft (henceforth TC), and Sect. 3 gives a description of TypeGram and the method for importing POS, morphological, and lexical information from TC into TypeGram. The valence- and construction encoding system is explained in Sect. 4, and Sect. 5 shows how the 'metagrammatical' specification is created in TypeGram. Section 6 describes a few scenarios of deployment of the system for a small corpus of Ga, and Sect. 7 gives an assessment of the results and the design.

2   TypeCraft

TypeCraft (TC) is specialised on manual morpheme-to morpheme annotation of natural language texts. This makes it an interesting tool for linguists working with less-described and endangered languages. The user imports raw texts in order to create Interlinear Glossed Texts (IGT). The activities supported by the system are creation, storage and retrieval of user data. Figure 1 illustrates how an IGT is seen from inside the TypeCraft editor. The editor allows linguistic annotations on 8 tiers. An additional annotation window can be opened for sentence level annotations, where construction specification can be made.

TC data is structured throughout, which makes it possible to search on all levels (text, phrase, word and morpheme). The system allows for incomplete annotations,

---

[3] Cf. (Lewis 2006), (Lewis and Xia 2010). A similar design is defined in (Beermann 2010).

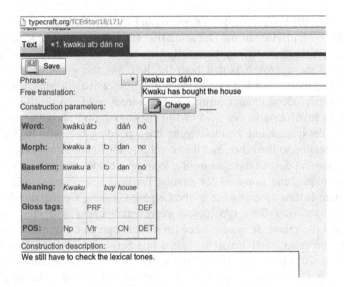

Fig. 1. Interlinear Glossed Text seen from within the TypeCraft linguistic editor

and the storage of extensive comments together with the data. Both features are crucial for an exploratory, collaborative annotation procedure.

Next to export to the main editors, TypeCraft supports XML export which allows the exchange of data with other applications.

Annotations made by linguists working on their own research reflect differences in interest and linguistic expertise. TypeCraft uses closed tag-sets, yet there is no restriction on how many items in a token sentence need to be annotated, or procedures that need to be followed to ensure that the annotations are linguistically sound. The approach thus presents a range of challenges having to do with inter- and intra-annotator consistency.

3   TypeGram

A well-known tool for multilingual grammar engineering based on the LKB platform is the 'HPSG Grammr Matrix *Matrix* ('Matrix') (Bender et al. 2002, Bender et. al 2010). It functions essentially as a 'grammar intersection' – a set of types and rules assumed to be common to languages, and useful as a first step in the construction of a fuller grammar. The opposite perspective is that of a 'grammar union' – a set of types and rules formed by the *union* of the set of types and rules of individual grammars. This is the strategy pursued in TypeGram[4], and we may refer to such a system as a *pan-grammar*[5]. The feature geometry of TypeGram is comparable to that of

---

[4] TypeGram is as yet unpublished; see http://typecraft.org/tc2wiki/TypeGram.

[5] The notion 'meta-grammar' might suggest itself for this kind of approach. However, apart from the use of that term which was just introduced, we prefer using it in the way of Clement and Kinyon 2003, as a formalism distinct from that used in the 'actual' grammar(s) in question.

Sag et al. 2003., and can have the semantic representation system MRS (Minimal Recursion Semantics; cf. Copestake et al. 2005) added to it. At the level of sentential constructions it currently defines 19 types of serial verb constructions, and 36 further types of multi-verb constructions; relative to derivational verb morphology it defines 85 types of processes like causativization, applicative formation and the like in different valence frames and for different arguments, and 41 types of combinations of such processes. Among valence frames it defines 51 types of possible secondary predicate constructions, alongside the expected array of single-predicate constructions across languages including case combinations and the ergativity parameters, altogether reaching 5–600 valence types. This spans an over-all range of construction types well beyond that described in Kroeger 2004, with detail especially based on studies of representatives of language families such as Germanic, Kwa, Bantu, Ethio-semitic and Indo-Iranyan.

The pan-grammar is technically divided into three core types-files (a general one and two more specific ones – see below), a file for lexical rules, and a file for phrasal combination rules. Unlike the grammar of a single language, it does not have a lexicon, and not a file for inflectional rules. The formation of a single-language grammar *XGram* for a language *X* is done through the following steps:

(i)   A copy of the most general pan-grammar types-file is inserted in the XGram catalogue, named *XGram-types*.

(ii) A file *XGram-rules* is created consisting of a small subset of the phrasal rule types of the rules-file of the pan-grammar (general rules for head-complement, head-subject, head-modifier, reflecting inventories as often used in text books) (see Sect. 6).

(iii) An empty file *XGram-lexicon* is created, to be filled through automatic import of lexical items of X, being assigned lexical types suited to those defined in *XGram-types*.

(iv) A empty file *XGram-infl* is created, to be filled through automatic import of inflectional rules from some source.

In the present setting, imports under (iii) and (iv) come from the TypeCraft IGTs through XML export of these IGTs. To illustrate, the Ga perfective verb form *etee* with an annotation as indicated in the TC annotation snippet in the uppermost part of (2) below is assigned a snippet of an XML such as (1),

(1)
```
<word id="30409" text="etee" citation="etee">
      <pos>V</pos>
      <morpheme id="46593" text="eɪ□">
            <gloss>PERF</gloss>
      </morpheme>
      <morpheme id="46594" text="tee" meaning="go"/>
</word>
```

from which a lexicon entry and an inflection rule are defined, as indicated in the lower part of (2) (in the grammar-internal code '*' represents the stem to which the prefix is attached).

(2)

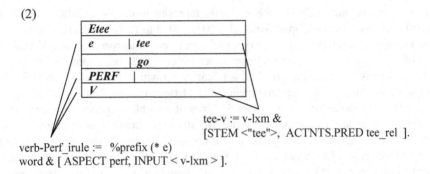

tee-v := v-lxm &
[STEM <"tee">, ACTNTS.PRED tee_rel].

verb-Perf_irule := %prefix (* e)
word & [ASPECT perf, INPUT < v-lxm >].

Attributes such as 'STEM', 'ASPECT' and 'INPUT', and value categories such as *v-lxm, perf* and *word*, are all defined in the pan-grammar and *Xgram-types*, and inherited by the actual grammar being derived.

On imports under (i) and (ii), see below.

4   Valence and Construction Encoding

The 'Construction Labeling' system (CL) is a notation system for verb constructions and verb valence, proposed in (Hellan and Dakubu 2009, 2010); (Dakubu 2008); (Hellan 2008, 2010). The system has been used in establishing fairly large-scale construction inventories for a few languages from Germanic, Niger-Congo and Ethio-Semitic. Essential in its code is a cross-linguistically grounded repertoire of properties of linguistic constructions, such as 'has Valence Frame X', 'has Aspect Y', 'has a Subject with properties Z', 'expresses situation type S', etc. Each such property is packaged in the code as an atomic *element*, and construction types and lists of construction types are represented in a perspicuous manner through combinations of such elements. The array of construction types so represented corresponds roughly to the inventory of construction types for which TypeGram is defined. The way this definition is done is that each *element* has an independent definition in TypeGram, and a combination of elements is technically interpreted as the unification of the specifications of the elements, just as the construction represented is conceptually interpreted as having the sum of properties represented by each element. It follows that what TypeGram independently defines is not a large number of construction types one by one, but a limited number of building blocks of construction type specifications – the elements -, leaving for the unification operation to reflect all the types actually described by linguists.

We give two examples of the code applied to Ga constructions, (3a) being a ditransitive construction and (3b) a serial verb construction; in the latter case both verbs occur with an expressed object; their subjects are identical, and likewise their aspects, expressed in the code element *svSuAspIDALL*.

(3)

a. ```
    v-ditr-suAg_iobTrgt_obThmover-COMMUNICATION
    ```
    | **E-fɔ** | **mi** | **nīne** |
    |----------|--------|---------|
    | 3S.AOR-throw | 1S | hand |
    | V | Pron | N |

    'She waved to me; invited me'

b.  ```
    svSuAspIDALL-v1tr-v2tr
    ```
Á-gbele	**gbɛ**	**á-ha**	**bo**
3.PRF-open	road	3.PRF-give	2S
V	N	V	Pron

    'You have been granted permission'

When the IGT of these sentences is expanded with the CL specifications shown, the grammar induced receives two types of information. For (3a), the impact will be in the lexicon, the lexical type of the verb being not just *v-lxm* as in (2), but the string *v-ditr-suAg_iobTrgt_obThmover-COMMUNICATION* which serves as a detailed valence constraint; this type is correspondingly defined in the types file. For (3b), *GaGram-rules* will have added a rule of type *svSuAspIDALL-v1tr-v2tr*, enforcing precisely the properties of the combination of the two VPs in question. This exemplifies the types of information that the parser under construction receives when the sentence-level code – CL – is added to the input data.[6]

5 From TypeGram to Meta-Grammars

We now illustrate how single-language meta-grammars may be constructed from IGT annotation sets. A sentence like the one in (3a), instead of a constituent analysis like (4),

(4)

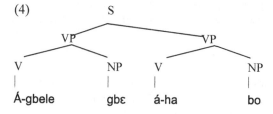

can be given an analysis tree such as (5),

(5)

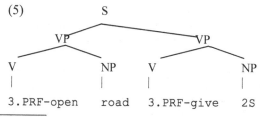

---

[6] As a supplement to the machine-readable code of CL just illustrated, TypeCraft provides a 'global' annotation level where from 8 parameters (cf. Section 2) of construction specification, the annotator can select one specification for each, such as 'transitive', 'passive+causative', 'svc', etc.

where words and morphemes of the actual language are replaced by analytic symbols used in the IGT annotation of the string in question, and English glosses - what we may call a 'meta-string'; cf. (Bruland 2011). This can serve as an intermediate stage in the grammar construction in question, and also as a window into syntactic variation parameters between grammars and languages, abstracting away from morpho-phonology and lexical items.[7]

6   Exemplifying the Methodology

To illustrate the methodology, we describe three scenarios making use of the strategy now described, for inducing a grammar of Ga, based on the meta-strings of a set of 170 IGTs.[8] The scenarios vary according to whether CL annotation is part of the IGT or not, and to whether the word items of the IGT are the sole occupants of the lexicon, or additional lexical resources are used. The scenarios have in common using just the inflectional information induced from the IGTs:

a. Annotation is restricted to the morphological part of the IGTs, and lexicon is restricted to the words in the IGTs.
The 170 IGTs are parsed with only minimal valence specification of the verbs, based on the POS value in the IGTs. All sentences parse, the mean number of parses per sentence being 14, with the 28 multi-verb sentences among the 170 sentences having an average of 30 parses. None of the multiverb construction-parses show argument identities in their semantic specification, since the rules in use are underspecified for such properties.

b. Annotation also includes CL code, lexicon is only words from the IGTs.
The import into the grammar from IGT now takes into account the CL specifications: in cases where the code starts with 'v-', the formula is entered as the lexical type of the *head* verb ('head' being marked in the TC gloss). When the formula starts with 'sv' or 'ev', it is entered in the file *GaGram-rules* (see Sect. 4, 'Ga' here for 'X'), meaning that for the sentence in question, the rule so labeled is available as a candidate among the rules used for parsing. These CL specifications are loaded into their respective grammar files as a batch, thus being available for all the sentences.

When the number of phrasal rules is kept as in scenario a, the mean number of parses per sentence is about 4. For single-verb constructions the number of parses is reduced significantly from the previous scenario, since each verb now has a very concise valence requirement; moreover, the preciseness of these parses exceeds that of the 'best parses' of the previous approach, since argument identities and other semantic factors are built into the valence specifications.

---

[7] This use of English meta-strings partly resembles a strategy described in (Bender et al. 2013) based on work by Xia and Lewis, where English glosses for strings in an arbitrary language L are parsed by a grammar of English; however, the point of the present approach is that the syntactic rules are those of L, thus, in casu, the rules of Ga.

[8] The tests described were run in January 2013.

When *phrasal* rules reflecting CL code are added, the over-all mean number of parses increases to 14. This is because, for multi-verb constructions, there is now a new set of rules, added to those operative from before. In return, for each construction, the addition of tailor-made rules of the CL code ensures that each of these constructions now has at least one semantically correct parse.

c. Annotation is with CL code, lexicon is enriched by Toolbox import:
From a Toolbox lexicon underlying Dakubu 2009, we import 8000 lexical entries into the lexicon file of the grammar;[9] of these, nearly 2000 are verb entries, classified with CL specifications matching those used in the IGT of the 170 sentences. Despite a large parse forest due to multiple (in terms of valence type) entries for each given verb, one parse for each sentence is guaranteed to induce a correct analysis. The same degree of parse precision is therefore obtained here as in scenario b, meaning that the gain in added lexical coverage does not compromise the precision obtained with CL-code in the characterization of verb types.

The linguistic effort invested in this action resides, first, in the compiling of an enumeration of the valence and construction types of Ga, as described in Dakubu (2008) and Hellan and Dakubu (2010), and second, in the design of a testsuite reflecting this enumeration, which is exactly the content of the 170 IGTs. By itself, a 'corpus' of 170 sentences is hardly mention-worthy, but once it reflects a careful selection of construction types, it represents an organization of information which in a way approaches a grammar. Ga being morphologically rather simple, this range of IGTs also covers the main inflection possibilities (apart from tonal representation), and has thus grammar-like representativeness also in that respect. A successful replication of this experiment for another language, with similarly few IGTs, will depend on an equally well-composed CL inventory and morphological IGT to start with.

What the example also illustrates is that the assembly CL-IGT-TypeGram is not a closed circle, but can be supplemented by lexical resources such as a Toolbox lexicon.

7 Assessment

The linguistic resources going into the present methodology are independently created, for typological and other research. They are highly analysis-intensive – that goes both for compiling a construction enumeration, for conducting a morphological annotation, and for creating a lexicon – and are thus contributions which essentially only professional linguists can make.

In evaluating the methodology, at least the following questions can be asked: (i) How far does it bring one towards significantly-sized grammars of the languages in question? (ii) How much effort does one have to invest in code-writing and minute specifications to make the IGT from TypeCraft, the CL specifications, and TypeGram fit together?

---

[9] The conversion of Toolbox lexicons into LKB lexicons was pioneered by Hirzel (2006, 2012); a slightly different procedure, designed by Tore Bruland, is used in this project. Specific to this Toolbox file is the use of CL code, encoded in the fields '\sl1', '\sl2', etc. ('sl' for 'slot'), otherwise the field names are standard. For a similar use of a Toolbox project, see (Bender et al. 2012).

To the latter question, once done in general for the construction *elements*, as described in Sect. 4, and for the individual TypeCraft tags, the main bulk of specification is done. Of course, for any language, additional specifications may well be needed.

Just as for the 'matrix' strategy (cf. Sect. 3), the methodology takes the grammar to a certain point, from which an individual developer must take over, and just as Matrix grammars vary widely as to how far they get developed, no expectations can so far be stated relating to question (i) for the present methodology either.[10]

Acknowledgments. The Ga data and material employed have been all contributed by Prof. Mary Esther Kropp Dakubu, University of Ghana. Tore Bruland, NTNU, has designed the conversion from TypeCraft XML to grammar and lexicon specifications in TypeGram, as well as the conversion from the Ga ToolBox lexicon to the LKB grammar; we are grateful to both. This paper is an updated version of (Hellan and Beermann 2011).

References

Beermann, D.: Endowment. Project proposal submitted to The Norwegian Research Council (2010)

Beermann, D.: Data management and analysis for less documented languages. In: Jones, M. (ed.) Language Documentation and New Technology. Cambridge University Press, Cambridge (forthcoming)

Beermann, D., Mihaylov, P.: Collaborative databasing and resource sharing for linguists. Lang. Resour. Eval. **48**(2), 203–225 (2014)

Bender, E.M., Flickinger, D., Oepen, S.: The grammar matrix: an open-source starter kit for the rapid development of cross-linguistically consistent broad-coverage precision grammars. In: Proceedings of the Workshop on Grammar Engineering and Evaluation, Coling 2002, Taipei (2002)

Bender, E.M., Drellishak, S., Fokkens, A., Poulson, L., Saleem, S.: Grammar customization. Res. Lang. Comput. **8**(1), 23–72 (2010)

Bender, E., Schikowski, R., Bickel, B.: Deriving a lexicon for a precision grammar from language documentation resources: a case study of Chintang. In: Proceedings of COLING 2012, pp. 247–262 (2012)

Bender, E., Goodman, M.W., Crowgey, J., Xia, F.: Towards creating precision grammars from interlinear glossed text: inferring large-scale typological properties. In: Proceedings of the 7th Workshop on Language Technology for Cultural Heritage, Social Sciences, and Humanities, pp. 74–83, Sofia (2013)

Bickel, B., Comrie, B., Haspelmath, M.: The Leipzig Glossing Rules: Conventions for Interlinear Morpheme-by-Morpheme Glosses. Max Planck Institute for Evolutionary Anthropology, Department of Linguistics, University of Leipzig, Leipzig (2008)

Bruland, T.: Creating TypeGram data from TypeCraft. In: Presentation at India 2011, NTNU (2011)

---

[10] For instance, we have not been in a position to experiment with a grammar development spurred by the methodology presented, compared with a 'standard' development of a large grammar. We will be able to do this at least for Norwegian, relative to the grammar Norsource (http://www. typecraft.org/tc2wiki/Norwegian_HPSG_grammar_NorSource).

Clément, L., Kinyon, A.: Generating parallel multilingual LFG-TAG grammars from a MetaGrammar. In: ACL '03 Proceedings of the 41st Annual Meeting on Association for Computational Linguistics,vol. 1 (2003)

Copestake, A.: Implementing Typed Feature Structure Grammars. CSLI Publications, Stanford (2002)

Copestake, A., Flickinger, D., Pollard, C., Sag, I.: Minimal recursion semantics. J. Lang. Comput. 3(2–3), 281–332 (2005)

Dakubu, M.E.K.: The Construction label project: a tool for typological study. In: Presented at West African Languages Congress (WALC), Winneba (2008)

Dakubu, M.E.K.: Ga-English Dictionary. Accra (2009)

Hellan, L., Johnsen, L., Pitz, A.: TROLL. Ms, NTNU (1989)

Hellan, L.: Enumerating verb constructions cross-linguistically. In: Proceedings from COLING Workshop on Grammar Engineering Across Frameworks. Manchester (2008). http://www.aclweb.org/anthology-new/W/W08/#1700

Hellan, L.: From descriptive annotation to grammar specification. In: Proceedings of the 4th Linguistic Annotation Workshop (LAW4), 2010, ACL, pp. 172–176, (2010). http://www.aclweb.org/anthology/W10-1826

Hellan, L., Dakubu, M.E.K.: A methodology for enhancing argument structure specification. In: Proceedings from the 4th Language Technology Conference (LTC 2009), Poznan (2009)

Hellan, L., Dakubu, M.E.K.: Identifying verb constructions cross-linguistically. In: SLAVOB series 6.3, University of Ghana (2010)

Hellan, L. Beermann, D.: Inducing grammar from IGT. In: Proceedings from the 5th Language Technology Conference (LTC 2011), Poznan (2011)

Hirzel, H.: Deriving LKB lexicons from Toolbox. In: Talk Given at Workshop on Grammar Engineering, NTNU, June (2006)

Hirzel, H.: Converting a Toolbox lexical database to LKB format. (2012). http://typecraft.org/tc2wiki/Converting_a_Toolbox_lexical_database_to_LKB_format

Kroeger, P. (2004). Analyzing Syntax. Cambridge University Press

Lewis, W.: ODIN: a model for adapting and enriching legacy infrastructure. In: e-science, Second IEEE International Conference on e-Science and Grid Computing (e-Science '06), pp. 137 (2006)

Lewis, W., Xia, F.: Developing ODIN: a multilingual repository of annotated language data for hundreds of the world's languages. Literary Linguist. Comput. 25(3), 303–319 (2010)

Pollard, C., Sag, I.: Head-Driven Phrase Structure Grammar. Chicago University Press, Chicago (1994)

Wakjira, B.: Kistaninya Verb Morphology and Verb Constructions. Ph.D. Dissertation, NTNU (2010)

Author Index

Printed in the United States
By Bookmasters